BUILDING WEB SITES WITH MACROMEDIA® STUDIO MX

BY
Tom Green
Chris S. Flick
Jordan L. Chilcott

New Riders

201 West 103rd Street, Indianapolis, Indiana 46290

An Imprint of Pearson Education

Boston • Indianapolis • London • Munich • New York • San Francisco

Building Web Sites with Macromedia® Studio MX

International Standard Book Number: 0735712727

Library of Congress Catalog Card Number: 2002100384

Printed in the United States of America

First edition: November 2002

06 05 04 03 02   7 6 5 4 3 2 1

Interpretation of the printing code: The rightmost double-digit number is the year of the book's printing; the rightmost single-digit number is the number of the book's printing. For example, the printing code 02-1 shows that the first printing of the book occurred in 2002.

Trademarks

Warning and Disclaimer

Publisher
David Dwyer

Associate Publisher
Stephanie Wall

Senior Acquisitions Editor
Linda Anne Bump

Acquisitions Editor
Kate Small

Senior Marketing Manager
Tammy Detrich

Publicity Manager
Susan Nixon

Development Editor
Susan Hobbs

Indexer
Larry Sweazy

Composition
Amy Parker

Manufacturing Coordinator
Jim Conway

Book Designer
Louisa Adair

Cover Designer
Aren Howell

To James Wallace Green, my father.

~

Tom Green

Table of Contents

About the Authors

Tom Green

Self-employed in the digital media field since 1986, Tom Green has lived and worked through the rise of desktop publishing, multimedia, and the popularity of the web. Tom is currently the Interactive Multimedia Program Coordinator for Humber College's School of Media Studies, in Toronto, Ontario. He developed the first process-based prepress curriculum in Canada for the Canadian Prepress Institute, and was intrumental in creating a fully interactive online Photoshop course for Humber College. Tom works closely with secondary and post-secondary educators across Canada to improve the level of digital media education delivery. He also lectures on the digital media industry to students, teachers, and community groups.

Tom and Keltie, his wife of 25 years, live in Oakville, Ontario with their two children, Lindsay and Robert, a cat, a dog, a turtle, and three fish.

Jordan L. Chilcott

Born and raised in Toronto and now a resident of Guelph, Ontario, Canada, Jordan Chilcott graduated from Radio College of Canada's Electronic Engineering Technology program in 1983 only to discover that he had a passion for computer programming. Spending his days working as a service technician, Jordan invested many sleepless nights learning Assembly Language at his computer. He published his first program in 1985, and started learning higher-level languages, such as C and C++. Jordan co-founded The Computer Software Specialists, now Interactivity Unlimited, but eventually left the hardware industry to focus on support and programming. Today, Jordan does application programming for both desktops (loves Mac OS X's Cocoa framework) and the Internet—in various languages from Actionscript to ColdFusion to C/C++/Objective-C. When not programming or administering the Dreamweaver-Talk list, he spends time with his wife, Joelle, and five children (Margot, Dina, Henry, Jack, and Joshua), composes and records music—including Flash soundtracks, and studies martial arts.

Chris S. Flick

Chris graduated from Radford University (Radford, Virginia) in 1991 with a Bachelor of Science degree in graphic arts. At Radford, he had the unique opportunity of being a university mascot for a year and a half.

Always looking for ways to combine his illustration and graphic design skills, he has worked in a multitude of fields, gaining skills as diverse as a T-shirt silk-screener to an ad agency graphic designer. As an ad agency graphic designer, Chris ultimately discovered his love for the web over the print design world. Currently, Chris is working at a prominent consulting firm in McLean, Virginia where he has been an art director and webmaster for the last three years, and uses all the major programs from Macromedia.

When he isn't spending precious time with his wife and two kids, Chris enjoys pursuing his other great passion…playing amateur baseball in Northern Virginia.

About the Technical Reviewers

These reviewers contributed their considerable hands-on expertise to the entire development process for *Building Web Sites with Macromedia Studio MX*. As the book was being written, these dedicated professionals reviewed all the material for technical content, organization, and flow. Their feedback was critical to ensuring that *Building Web Sites with Macromedia Studio MX* fits our reader's need for the highest-quality technical information.

Dorian Nisinson

Born and raised in New York City, Dorian is an artist, graphic designer, illustrator, and muralist who discovered Flash back when Macromedia first acquired it. Needless to say, code was not a feature that was dealt with much in art school, but with the development of Flash through its versions, Actionscript has come to be an obsession.

She was one of the founding members of FlashCentral.com and FlashBible.com, which were two of the first web sites dedicated to Flash. She designed the graphics for the Widgets Sample file that shipped with Flash 4, and has contributed articles to several Flash books, and is currently involved in a project exploring the uses of Flash as a tool for the creation of interactive art. Her web site, nisinson.com, has also been featured in a number of Flash books.

Matthew Manuel

Matthew graduated with a Bachelor of Applied Science from University of Waterloo in Systems Design Engineering. He worked as a software engineer and producer with fledgling multimedia company Sanctuary Woods, most notably on the acclaimed adventure game, "The Riddle of Master Lu." After the studio was acquired by Disney Interactive, he developed numerous children's edutainment products. After Disney, Matthew moved to Creative Capers Entertainment where he produced "Adam Blaster—Atomic Enforcer," a science fiction bounty hunter game. In 2002 Matthew started a game development studio in the Los Angeles area called TriStrip Inc.

Acknowledgments

A Word from Tom Green

Writing a book of this size and scope couldn't be completed without the help of a number of people.

I would first like to acknowledge William Hanna, Dean of the School of Media Studies at Humber College. William is one of the very few educators I have met who really does get "New Media," understands my vision, and makes it fit in with his even grander vision of a Media School—unafraid to embrace, explore, adopt, and even abandon technologies in a time of profound change. I would also like to acknowledge my wife, life partner, and best friend, Keltie. She put up with my moods, lost weekends where I holed up in a cabin to pull this book together, and generally managed the family to allow me to concentrate on this book.

I would also like to acknowledge my co-authors, Jordan and Chris. When I first breezed the idea of our working together on this book, their reactions ranged from shock— "Jeeze, I have never written a book before."—to panic—"Holy smokes. Did you see those deadlines?" Their agreements to work on this project were eerily similar—"Why not. It might be fun." It was. Along the way we learned a lot about each other and gained a deeper insight into the tools in our toolbox than we had ever thought imaginable. I am deeply honored and grateful to have had the opportunity to work with these gentlemen and learn from them.

Thomas J. Green

Toronto (Summer, 2002)

A Word from Chris Flick

This is my chance, my moment, to thank all the wonderful people who have meant so much to me through the years, such as my childhood (and still) best friend, Jeff Lacquement who has never stopped promoting me or my art. Of course, my most ardent fan continues to be, without a doubt, my lovely and most-cherished wife, Judi, for whom my input on this book would not have been possible without her unyielding faith in me. Thanks also must go out to my two children, Danielle and Tyler, who have become my daily inspiration.

Lastly, I'd like to thank my grandmother, Jeannie ("Gee") Wallace, who was wise enough—and brave enough—to put a crayon into a little boy's hand and let him use up all of her expensive typing paper while he tried valiantly to copy the cartoon characters that lived on her drinking glasses oh so long ago.

Chris Flick

Woodbridge, Virginia (Summer, 2002)

A Word from Jordan Chilcott

If someone told me when I got my first computer 20 years ago that I would be writing a book one day, I would have split my sides laughing. After all, this was the guy who was barely getting by in English classes. Funny enough, when Tom approached us and said, "Let's write a book…" my instincts kept telling me that the ideas presented in this book are extremely solid for today's web designers. It was time to share the craft I call web design and help provide information that budding web designers can grasp.

I owe a lot to my late father, Henry Chilcott, for somehow passing his passion for technology on to me even long after he passed away. He also gave me a determination to the point of stubbornness. I also owe a lot to my mother in that she helped bring out the creativity inside—mostly in the form of music. I can't forget about my recently departed sister, Karen, as well. She started me playing guitar and that is something that travels with me throughout my lifetime. More important was that learning to play gave me the passion to accomplish things like this in life.

My biggest fans are my family who are always by my side. My wife, Joelle, is my biggest support and has been a lifelong friend and partner. My children, Margot, Dina, Henry, Jack, and Joshua inspire me as they all help me to realize more about the things in life that are found within. They also give me the passion to push ahead in life.

I also want to thank the list members on the Dreamweaver Talk list. They are an inspiration. I learn a lot from them. I also enjoy the pleasure of sharing what I know with them. Kudos to you guys, you are what makes the web so enjoyable.

Lastly, I owe it all to God. In my years growing up looking for Him, I had discovered that He found me long before. Without God, I am nothing. With God, there's nothing I cannot do, for nothing is impossible to Him.

Jordan Chilcott

Guelph, Ontario (Summer, 2002)

Thanks to the New Riders Team

This book started over a year ago when Tom happened to bump into Jeff Schultz at Macromedia's UCON. Over the next couple of months, a lively and pointed conversation occurred between Jeff and Tom, and concluded in New York with the toss of a Canadian dollar called a Loonie. At that point, this book became reality.

Jeff introduced us to Kate Small, our Acquisitions Editor. We can't thank Kate enough for her patience—and the odd kick in the pants as we got halfway through the book and ran right into the introduction of Studio MX and Macromedia's reinvention of itself. Kate helped us through redoing the outline and then proceeded to make sure we produced the best book we could by enforcing her unique brand of "tough love."

Our Development Editor, Susan Hobbs, is a unique individual. Passionate about her craft, she instilled that passion into us as she patiently helped us discover our voice. Our Technical Editor, Dorian Nissinson, also can't go unacknowledged. When you work with an acknowledged expert you are forced to meet that individual's standards. Along the way, we benefited from her wisdom, knowledge, and experience, and passed that on to the readers. Ditto for Matt Manuel who came late to the party, but was the last to go home.

Thanks, guys. It has been quite the trip.

Last but Not Least...

A very special thanks goes to Steve Minton, a friend and colleague on the Dreamweaver Talk list, for coming to our rescue when Murphy's laws started testing our optimistic theories on our Sitespring server (everything from power failures to the NIMDA virus). Without Steve's assistance in allowing us to use his server, this book may have been that much more of a challenge. Chapter 3 is dedicated to you, Steve. Thanks, buddy.

Tell Us What You Think

As the reader of this book, you are the most important critic and commentator. We value your opinion and want to know what we're doing right, what we could do better, what areas you'd like to see us publish in, and any other words of wisdom you're willing to pass our way.

As the editor on this book, I welcome your comments. You can fax, email, or write me directly to let me know what you did or didn't like about this book—as well as what we can do to make our books stronger. When you write, please be sure to include this book's title, ISBN, and author, as well as your name and phone or fax number. I will carefully review your comments and share them with the author and editors who worked on the book.

Please note that I cannot help you with technical problems related to the topic of this book, and that due to the high volume of email I receive, I might not be able to reply to every message.

Fax: 317-581-4663

Email: Linda.Bump@newriders.com

Mail: Linda Bump
        Senior Acquisitions Editor
        New Riders Publishing
        201 West 103rd Street
        Indianapolis, IN 46290 USA

Introduction

The Long, Strange Trip to This Page

Your journey to this book, in part, is a result of the dot.com meltdown of the past couple of years. Although we will leave the definitive story to those whose profession it is to sift through recent history, we couldn't help but have a sense of Yogi Berra's "déjà vu all over again."

Between 1989 and 1991 a similar meltdown swept through another new industry—desktop publishing. Lots of technology was being pushed at clients, as well as at the industry. Due to its sheer novelty, both groups bought in. At the same time, the software, hardware, and operating system suppliers sparked off a standards war that saw the rise of .tiff, .eps, PageMaker, QuarkXPress, Illustrator, FreeHand, and Photoshop—to name a few. It also saw the death of formats such as .RIFF and applications such as Ready,Set, Go. We won't deny it wasn't fun and hugely entertaining. Whenever the industry folks gathered, we would swap stories where we sold the client on a technique or effect, took the retainer check to the computer store, bought the application that was best suited for what we had promised, and spent two weeks trying to figure out how we could deliver what we promised.

That all changed when a client, somewhere, looked at the ideas and asked a simple question, "Why?". That one word changed everything because clients were now asking for us to justify why the technique was being used. The poor desktop publisher to whom the client posed the question didn't have the answer. The client found someone else who could not only answer the question, but also could do it cheaper and faster. Suddenly a lot of used computer equipment and software started appearing at Fire Sale prices.

When the web took hold around 1995, lots of technology was pushed at clients and web designers. Clients bought in. Standards? What standards? We think you can see where this going.

Two similar meltdowns—desktop publishing and web development—and the client emerges as the inevitable winner. One other winner also appeared in both situations: the company that developed the tools that became the standards—allowing us to get into the game. For desktop publishing, it was Adobe. For the web, it is Macromedia.

Macromedia is an amazing company that rose from relative obscurity to completely dominate an industry. It did it, so it seemed, almost overnight by supplying some pretty awesome tools to the market. One day web designers were using text editors to build web pages. The next day they were using Dreamweaver. We saved our images and line art on Monday evening, and the next morning we were using Fireworks. On Friday we were building GIF animations and on Monday morning we were Flash animators. It gets better.

Macromedia spends an inordinate amount of its time listening to the people who actually use its products. You will always find one overt or covert Macromedian at any web gathering, whether it is a conference or an online web list. They never dominate, pontificate, or control the discussion. Instead, they listen quietly. If they detect a feature idea that is both cool and makes sense from a business and production point of view, you can bet it will appear in the next release of the product. Which brings the long, strange trip to New York City on April 10, 2001.

It is 9:00 a.m., and the clan has gathered at Macromedia's biennial user conference named UCON. A serious number of the meltdown survivors are in the audience. You can tell who they are because they have a 10,000-yard stare that seems to say, "Dude, you don't want to even know what I have been through." They are here. They are pumped. They are ready for some good news. Surely, Macromedia's CEO, Rob Burgess, has the answers.

The lights go down. Burgess emerges from the wings and strides purposefully across the stage to the podium where he is to give the keynote address. He shuffles his notes, looks out at the audience, leans into the microphone, and the first words out of his mouth are, "Good morning, everyone. Welcome to the new, new, new economy." Those simple words signaled a fundamental shift in the company's focus and, at the time, hardly anyone got it.

What they didn't get was that the market had changed, and Macromedia was changing with it. Macromedia was now in the business of providing the tools that could solve customer needs rather than a ton of cool software. The entire tone of the conference focused on making the web usable for our clients and that Macromedia was, for better or worse, in it for the duration.

Fast forward three months later. Another conference, FlashForward 2001. Same city. Same group looking for salvation, or at least some direction to the path out of this mess. It wasn't provided. Presenter after mystified presenter showed amazing Flash work that "the client turned down." Even Kevin Lynch, Macromedia's product guru, had no pearls of wisdom. He wanted to talk usability. Usability? That's business stuff. Where's the cool Flash stuff? Kevin wanted to talk project management. In fact, he demonstrated a new product—Sitespring—that was currently in beta. That's client stuff. Where's the cool stuff? You just saw it—Sitespring. Suddenly it occurred to the audience that maybe, just maybe, the long, strange trip of the early web was over and, to paraphrase a session at FlashForward, that "maybe we are no longer in Kansas, Toto."

Clients were asking, "What's in it for me?". Macromedia was going to supply the tools to help us answer that question. The company's answer is the Macromedia MX Studio.

What's In It for You

This book is for those of you who get it. You understand that web development is now a delicate minuet between you and the client. It is a market where cool loses to Return On Investment. It is now a business where efficiency and the *brand* far outweigh cutting-edge design and spinning globes.

This is not a how-to manual that teaches you to survive the new, new, new economy. That book has yet to be written. This is not a book that will show you all the cool stuff you can do in Flash, Fireworks, and Dreamweaver. This is not a book that focuses on the production aspects of web site development. Those books have been written with more to come.

We have written this book to show you how six of Macromedia's products in the MX Studio combine to provide you, the web developer, with the opportunity to become more creative and efficient. Along the way we hope you will pick up some tips, tricks, and techniques that provide an answer to that question posed by the client: Why?

We have made a few assumptions. The first is that you are already familiar with the basics of each of the applications presented. The second assumption is that you are in the industry either on a full-time or part-time basis as a professional or a hobbyist. The final assumption is that you are wondering if there has to be a better way of dealing with clients and streamlining the approval process.

There are many books out there that focus on a specific Macromedia product. Very few show you how Flash MX, Fireworks MX, and Dreamweaver MX can actually make you more productive. Toss Sitespring, ColdFusion, and FreeHand into the mix, and you can add *more efficient* to the equation as the opportunity and implications of more efficient communication between you and clients becomes more and more important in today's web-development industry.

The rebranding and repositioning of Macromedia to the MX product range also adds to the importance of this book. Macromedia, too, sees how its tools can make you more productive, and the MX Studio stresses the fact that the tools are all linked to each other. The capability to move between the applications, which at times seems like the click of a mouse, is a fundamental change and reinforces the fact that the tools are no longer seen by Macromedia as individual applications.

How This Book Works

This book follows typical web workflow from concept to final posting of the site to a web server. Obviously, dealing with six Macromedia applications can be a bit confusing; thus, we have broken the book into five sections that mirror typical web-development workflow.

To accomplish this, you follow the development of a site for a mythical company—JCT—that runs a series of mall-based clothing stores aimed at the high-school crowd. Rather than present a full ecommerce solution, which would be out of the scope of this book, we build a site that incorporates all the techniques laid out in the book. In this way, the book has a focal point and allows you to work through the development process.

We also present a series of typographic, imaging, navigation, and animation techniques that will not necessarily wind up in the JCT site. These techniques present basic or alternative ways of doing things, and are used by web designers on a regular basis. We do this because when it comes to web development, there are at least a dozen ways of doing the same task. The client doesn't care how it was done—they just care that you did it.

The first section, "Managing a Web Project," starts where all sites begin—with a blank piece of paper—and finishes with building a project site. Along the way, you learn how Sitespring can help you to communicate your concepts to your client, and how your client can communicate their reactions—positive or negative—to you. Naturally, we don't overlook the fact that web development is a team-based process and discuss building a team and the roles of each team member. But we also show how the Macromedia Studio provides the team with a host of effective communications and project-management tools.

Web development is a complex process, and managing content is critical in today's hyper-fast development environment. This first section also discusses how to manage content, and how the Macromedia tools have management features built into them. Naturally, the client figures into this process, so how to build a client site using the Studio and Sitespring is covered.

The second section of the book, "Developing the Site Concept," outlines how ideas developed on paper carefully evolve into a functioning prototype submitted for client approval. You are shown how to develop site and page views, create wireframe and navigation models of the site, and how to involve the client in each step of the process.

The third section of the book, "Developing the Content," outlines many of the creative decisions that will have to be made. This section covers how to rough out the content, and how to build and submit a prototype to the client for approval. Along the way, typography, color choices, models, and the development of rough content for placement into a prototype submitted for client approval are all discussed.

In this section, you also learn how to create images, develop line art, create special effects, build animations, and create a variety of navigation elements. This section shows how the various elements of the JCT site were created and incorporated into the building of the site in Dreamweaver.

The last section of the book, "Testing and Delivering the Final Product," deals with what has to happen after the site is built. For instance, you can't work on the web without encountering coding issues. This section shows how to optimize the HTML and JavaScript written by the applications. This is the code that developers refer to as *ugly code*. Although Dreamweaver will write the HTML code for you as the page is built, you learn how to optimize that code. The result is a more efficient site. This section also examines code optimization in Flash, as well as several image-optimization techniques.

The process doesn't stop there. After the site is created, it has to be tested. This identifies potential user problems, and is the final opportunity to make sure everything does what it is supposed to do. This is also the client's last chance to make changes.

This last section deals with the steps involved before the site goes live. Join any web-development list and the most common source of frustration is posting the site to a server and making sure it works. In this section, you learn the process from FTP upload to flipping the switch, and you'll learn many of the common problems and solutions to this often-overlooked part of the process.

The days of cool are over. The craft of web development has moved from its novelty and experimental phase to one driven by management and creative processes with clients who are involved from beginning to end. No longer are projects taken from concept to upload by one person. As said earlier, it is now a delicate minuet of hard-nosed business decisions and the desire to expand the creative possibilities of this medium. *Building Web Sites with Macromedia Studio MX* exposes you to those decisions and possibilities.

How to Use This Book

The applications presented in this book are cross-platform. In fact, many of the figures show a Mac or a PC screen. The great thing about cross-platform applications is that the interfaces are identical, except for the OS differences. To cater to both groups, we clearly show the differences between the two operating systems when we use the keyboard commands. For example, here's how you learn to open a new Fireworks document:

To open a new Fireworks document, select File, New, or use the following keyboard combination: Control-N (PC) or Command-N (Mac).

Menu commands are presented as Menu, Submenu, Submenu. In this example, you would select New from the File menu.

Keyboard commands are presented as keystroke-keystroke followed by the platform in brackets. The previous example tells you to press the Control and N keys if you use a PC or the Command and N keys if you use a Macintosh to open a new Fireworks MX document.

In certain instances, we ask you to use the mouse for particular tasks. When you are asked to select an item, you click the item. When asked to drag an item from one part of the screen to another, you click once and then move the mouse.

You can't avoid code when you are working on the web. This book is not going to teach you how to code, but it is going to show you how to optimize the code, or ask you to enter a particular code snippet.

You are able to quickly see what is code and what is text because of the use of a special typeface. For example:

```
<HTML>
<Head>
<Title> Hello World ! </title>
</head>
</HTML>
```

When code needs to be changed, we indicate the change by first indicating the section that is to be changed in this manner:

```
<HTML>
<Head>
<Title> Hello World ! </title>
</head>
</HTML>
```

By showing the new code in bold type, you quickly identify what needs to be changed and to select the code. The change is indicated using bold italic type:

```
<HTML>
<Head>
</head>
</HTML>
```

To avoid a 500-page typing lesson, we explain why the change has been made. In this instance, we explain the change immediately after the requested change. For example:

```
<HTML>
<Head>
<Title> A big shout out to Jord and Chris! </title>
```

Simply changing the text between the tags allows you to change the head.

```
</head>
</HTML>
```

You can clearly differentiate between text and code. As well, you can read why the change is being made.

This book follows a few typographical conventions:

- A new term is set in *italics* the first time it is introduced.

- Program text, functions, variables, and other "computer language" are set in a fixed-pitch font—for example, `insert example from book here`.

- Code lines that do not fit within the margins of the printed page are continued on the next line and are preceded by a code continuation character ➥.

Moving On

Where do you go after finishing this book? The simple answer is: You go to work.

We present a ton of techniques, and it is up to you to use them, modify your way of developing content or managing projects, or simply say, "That isn't the way I would do it," and then find a better way of doing what needs to be done. That's the web development process.

We are not so arrogant as to assume we provide the definitive word on the use of the Macromedia MX Studio of web tools. We recognize the fact that the day of the guru who knows it all is over because the business of web development became very complex very quickly. We are in the age of specialization where teams are formed from in-house resources or independent contractors. These teams bring their varied talents to bear on a project and then disband upon the project's completion.

Yet, as you will discover, much of what we present can benefit your workflow in ways you may not have considered. If we can do that, we have met our objective.

The process doesn't stop with this book. There are any number of sites and tutorials out there designed to answer those "How do I?" questions that crop up. We have included a number of our favorites—the web equivalent of well-thumbed "How To" books —on the book web site.

You might also want to consider participating in your local MMUG—Macromedia User Group. These are invaluable opportunities for you to meet with your fellow developers to swap techniques, share ideas, and simply network. In Toronto, for example, the local group meets monthly and details can be found at `http://www.FlashinTO.com`, or you can visit `http://www.macromedia.com/v1/usergroups/` to see if there is a group near you. If there isn't, Macromedia will help you start one.

Online discussion forums are a source of invaluable information, tips, and techniques freely shared by some of the top minds in the business. In some cases, these lists function as a level one trauma center when you are facing a deadline, your client is breathing smoke and fire down your neck, and something just isn't working. They provide you with the opportunity to outline your problem, post a link, and ask for immediate help. The advice may be direct and pointed, but it is also a life saver. Also, don't be terribly surprised if someone from Macromedia jumps in to help. These forums can also be used as alpha and beta testers. In this case, prepare yourself for some rather pointed questions and comments regarding your site. A list of some of the more popular groups is included on the book web site.

Let's go to work.

Part I

Managing a
Web Project

Chapter 1

MX

fireworks flash freehand coldfusion dreamweaver fireworks
reamweaver fireworks flash freehand coldfusion dreamweav
coldfusion dreamweaver fireworks flash freehand coldfusi
reehand coldfusion dreamweaver fireworks flash freehan
orks flash freehand coldfusion dreamweaver firework
eaver fireworks flash freehand coldfusion dreamweav

Planning the Site

To those of us who were there, the early
days of web site development are wistfully
referred to as the time of the "Wild, Wild
Web." There were no standards. There were
no graphical editors. We learned what-
worked and what didn't—and our clients
funded our learning curve. Those days are
over.

The web has established itself as a fundamental media, and with it has come a high degree of seriousness and planning that is proportionate to the size of the budgets clients have for their web sites. Over the past couple of years, the word *branding* has driven our efforts as clients expect their sites to mirror the *corporate* look of everything they present to their markets. Clients are demanding involvement in the development process every step of the way. It is no longer acceptable to breeze a couple of ideas by the client and then go to work. It is also no longer acceptable to purchase a computer and a couple of applications, and hang out a "Web Developer" shingle. The reason is because the web site development business got very complex, very fast. In short, web development became a profession, and the meticulous planning and execution of the web development process started to appear.

Even more profound was the rise of the work group. When life was simpler and graphical web browsers were just starting to establish themselves—the one-man or two-man full-service web shop was the norm. With the rise of ecommerce and the establishment of the web as a major marketing vehicle, the technical and creative demands placed on web developers started to increase. Along with this came the growing realization that one person simply couldn't do it all. In today's fast-paced development environment with strict budgetary constraints, deadline pressures are such that projects can only be completed by a team of specialists working toward the benchmarks laid out in a carefully crafted development schedule.

The ability to manage the workflow and communications process in today's creative environment is an art. The days of sitting down with a client, getting a rough idea of what they want, and then flaming up the software to first work out the ideas and concepts and secondly to produce the pages, is a thing of the past. The new workflow never starts with software. It starts with a simple, blank piece of paper.

That piece of paper can be used to map out the steps of the production process from concept to upload (the site map, initial sketches of the concepts for each page), and to present the creative brief to the team—or to present the client with a document that can be signed and dated.

Defining the Site

Before the team goes to work, the Account Manager, using his trusty note pad, has spent what seems like an inordinate amount of time with the client gathering a lot of information ranging from the broad issues of the audience to be reached to the specific issues around technology. This information is carefully analyzed both with the client and in-house developers to clearly understand and identify the planning, management, and communications needs for the project as well as the scope of the project. The team is then presented with a creative brief, content is planned, and a schedule developed. All of this and not one creative pixel has been illuminated.

The Soft Skills of Site Development

The site development process inevitably involves a number of skilled people bringing their expertise to bear upon a project. In an ideal world, they would simply undertake their tasks in isolation and then submit a finished product that fits, seamlessly, with the work of all the other team members. Unfortunately, the complexity of the site development process has moved that concept into the realm of Utopian ideal.

The skills of the team—coding, design, imaging, writing, usability, and so on—can be regarded as *hard skills*. Those are the skills that actually produce a tangible product. Managing this team requires another set of skills that are rarely acknowledged. They include the ability to pull the team together, motivate each team member to achieve their deadlines, clearly communicate the goals of the project to the team members, and keep the team on task to ensure they are meeting the client's needs and expectations. These are the *soft skills* of web development. They come into play after the scope of the project has been determined, and are equally important as the skills necessary to master the tools of the trade. These soft skills can be broken down into three broad areas: project planning, project management, and communication.

What makes these three areas so interesting though is they are inevitably the responsibility of the individual charged with the execution and delivery of the final product; they are also the responsibility of each member of the team.

Project Scope

Before the creative team presses the power buttons on their computers, each member has to know the parameters of the project. This includes budget, deadlines, a creative brief, and the technical needs of the site. This is referred to as the project scope, and defines the purpose of the project as well as what will be produced.

To use a house building analogy, each item in the building process will ultimately contribute to the size of the foundation. That foundation, in certain respects, determines the dimensions and layout of each room in the house. Start adding different materials or moving items in the room to different locations, and the price goes up. This can occur through the purchaser requesting the changes, or the builder recommending modifications with the purchaser's approval. In either case, the final product will not resemble the original, and will cost considerably more than originally presented.

There is a dangerous temptation in today's production environment to go for cool and add spinning globes and rollovers and pop-down menus that don't support the original plan. Web design is often associated with a coolness factor in which designers and clients would rather do something that looks really cool in their eyes, but is far from useable. The pressure to go for cool comes to bear on two fronts—from the client or from within the team. Instead of the JavaScript buttons originally planned for, why not do them in Flash using stills from a series of video clips? Suddenly, a job that was budgeted for one hour involves three hours of work and might even require the retaining of yet another team member to accomplish the task. In the general scheme of things, this might appear to be an insignificant change. In actual fact, it adds to the number of items originally planned for and increases the budget. This is called *scope creep*.

Scope creep is a lot like the infamous Chinese Water Torture. Looked at rationally, one drop of water on the forehead will not drive you crazy. It's the collection of drops that accomplish the task. Scope creep will affect every project with which you are involved. The problem is those small changes occur subtly, but they do add up. Plan for scope creep, and ensure each member of your team as well as the client clearly understand the financial and deadline implications of subtle changes to the project. The greatest danger of scope creep, though, is the volume of little changes and additions can take you off track and actually dilute the impact of the site.

So, how do you avoid scope creep? Create a specific and detailed document regarding what is to be produced; then have the client sign and date it. Some agencies have a standard document called a *General Working Agreement*. This agreement, which accompanies an estimate of all costs and is signed by both the client and the agency, lays out the working relationship between the client and the agency. One of the major topics covered is scope creep. The General Working Agreement ensures that the client clearly understands that items requested outside of the scope will incur extra charges. Just because the job is being done on a computer is no reason to assume a change will take no time at all. Some agencies will actually produce a separate printed estimate for the change. You would be amazed at how quickly the client changes their mind when confronted with the cost.

Always make sure that the client understands they will be charged for any extra time resulting from deletions from the scope. There is a tendency for clients who are late getting content to you to simply remove the section of the site. These events ripple through the process and take time to accommodate. If you are part way through the section and the client kills it, the client should be made aware that they are still liable for the work to date.

Planning Web Site Production

There is an old management adage that states, "Plan your work and then work your plan." Many times, developing a solid production plan is not a creative undertaking because it requires the skills of a manger or administrator. Though many creative types profess to abhor structure, ignore this part of the process at your peril.

Planning swings out of the client's acceptance of the Account Team's proposals. Usually involving a sales person and a member of the agency's management group, the Account Team, led by an Account Manager, will have spent quite a bit of time with the client in an effort to determine the client's needs and expectations. At this stage, the project moves from nebulous concepts and ideas to a concrete form that usually results in the creation of a formal project plan document. It is then inevitably submitted to the client for approval and sign off.

After that signature is obtained, the first step is to set the budget, because it literally defines the contents of each room of the house and who will be doing the building. Budgets are usually based on what the client is willing to spend on the project. Not quite. You will quickly discover that clients rarely know how much a site costs to produce, and their idea of the cost is significantly lower than your practical experience. Though developing a budget can be complex, it is a simple concept: The costs are based on actual production hours. If it takes one hour to create a Flash button, and the contractor or employee bills $50.00 per hour, the math is really simple.

The plan should also include a method of tracking time because, in the process of web development, time is money. Any number of software solutions are available, ranging from spreadsheets to specialized software. If a team member has a specific task, ensure that they know how much time has been allotted to the task, and make sure they agree to do it. In the case of contractors or subcontractors, this is especially critical—and if their estimate looks too good to be true, it probably is. Don't be afraid to hold them to their estimate.

> **Note**
>
> In the print world, graphic artists and printers are used to the docket system. Under this system, each hour is traditionally broken into six-minute segments, called *units*.
>
> The job moves from person to person in the form of a big envelope, containing all the documents and files, with a sheet of paper attached to it that contains the units. If a person spends 30 minutes on a particular task, they note what was done and how many units were used—in this case five—to accomplish the task. When the project is completed, the units are totaled up and an invoice issued.

After the budget is set, the manager determines who does what by when creating the production schedule. This should include the client and will, most likely, necessitate the creation of a staging area for client approvals and the creation of a project plan document to be submitted to the client for approval.

The project plan document should include a budget, the schedules, a creative brief (discussed later in this chapter), and any other documents or tasks, such as the General Working Agreement, that define the scope of the project.

Managing the Web Site Creative Process

Though a bit of an anathema to the freewheeling web development community, a solid management structure with clear lines of responsibility is critical in today's production environment. The ability to manage a team of creative individuals and motivate them to achieve specific goals within very short timeframes is a black art that requires the skills of a hard-nosed businessman along the lines of Neutron Jack Welch of GE and the diplomatic skills of a Metternich.

Though management structures vary from shop to shop, there has to be clear lines of responsibility and accountability with one person at the top of the pyramid. If there are specific teams developed for the project, one person will have to be assigned responsibility and accountability for the accomplishment of the tasks laid out, for each team, in the plan.

As well, web site development is a business and standard management tools—such as financial and accounting controls, Human Resource considerations, division of labor, and so on—have to be a part of the mix.

The Project Communication Process

When you strip out all the hype and hyperbole from the web, you are left with the fact that it is a communications vehicle. Many teams accept this and use the web as the core of the project communication process. This communication process can be client-team communications or inter-team communications, but the bottom line is that everybody is getting the same message through a common communications vehicle.

It is critical that clear lines of communication be established at the outset. This includes exactly who is allowed to talk to the client and who isn't. It also wouldn't hurt to set up the same parameters with the client.

In the course of everyday workflow, the parameters for intra- and inter-team communications have to be established. This can take the form of an email protocol, the use of the Notes features in Dreamweaver and Fireworks (covered in Chapter 2, "Content Management"), or the use of a virtual docket.

Many projects involve the use of a client site (discussed in Chapter 3, "Communicating Through Sitespring or a Client Site"), referred to as an extranet, for the exchange of information between the client and the team or between members of the team. The beauty of an extranet is it saves a huge amount of time in communicating ideas and concepts among the team and between the team and the client. Macromedia's SiteSpring is a good example of this and one of its major features is that, as you will see in Chapter 3, it lays down the critical paper trail for those inevitable disputes and differences of opinion that arise over the course of a project.

Management, communication, and planning aren't necessarily appealing, but if they are not in place, the project will degrade into a state of chaos. Though some creative people tend not to favor a structured workflow, the successful teams are those managed by individuals who use plain, common sense as well as excellent judgment to motivate what at times seems like a group of cowboys. The Project Manager makes sure that the team completes a project on time and on budget in a production environment based on collaboration rather than the traditional hierarchical division of labor.

The Creative Brief

The team essentially receives its marching orders from the *creative brief.* This document is a written summary of the objectives and goals of the project and the site. For the creative team, a thorough brief gets the creative juices flowing because they now see the overall direction for the project. It lays down the parameters for the conceptual framework of the site by outlining the audience, what they expect from the site, and what the site will communicate to that audience.

The creative brief springs out of those careful fact-finding sessions between the developer and the client. Along with setting the creative parameters of the project, it also clearly restates the client's goals for the project. In many respects, this document will be the bridge between the client's expectations, which can be unrealistic, and the pragmatism of the creative team developed through years of experience. It also gives both groups the opportunity to clearly understand each other and to align behind a common set of objectives. Figure 1.1 shows a sample creative brief.

JCT Clothing Store Website Design

Creative Brief 1/29/02

PROJECT SUMMARY

JCT Clothing store is a popular clothing store franchise catering to the "Gen-X," MTV, hip-hop crowd. The JCT stores are typically located in upscale malls. Although a franchise, each store is known for creating its own unique style. Typically, that means catering greatly to the "urban hip." Loud music and graffiti/air brush artwork decorate the store's wild interiors. The stores are known to have "personality." The goal for the JCT website is to give JCT an equal personality on the web while also offering the wide assortment of clothing that JCT is known for.

TARGET AUDIENCE

The typical JCT shopper ranges from late teens to early 20s with a large percentage being of the male persuasion-although JCT does carry a wide selection of female attire, as well. Because JCT caters to such a young audience, the typical JCT web surfer lives at home. In-store surveys reveal the following statistics:

- 97% of JCT shoppers who surf the web have either a 56k or cable modem.
- 62% of them surf the web on a Mac; 22% on a APC; 10% use a laptop; the rest use "other."
- The web browser of choice is mixed-everything from Netscape to IE to Opera.

  96% of those surveyed said they enjoy Flash content, and often frequent Flash-related sites.

TONE/GUIDANCE

The goal is to match the "uniqueness" of the JCT stores and to give the JCT web site a "personality." The goals in mind are:

- Energy, lots and lots of energy.
- Fun and entertainment.
- A tight cross-promotion between the JCT cyber-store and their brick and mortar counterparts.

  Eye candy. Eye candy. Eye candy.

COMMUNICATION STRATEGY

The goal for the JCT web site is to concentrate on the four clothing categories that sell the best inside of the JCT stores. They are: shoes, hats, T-shirts, and jeans. Another underlining goal of the JCT web site is to promote and encourage people to visit the JCT stores...to come see what all of the excitement is about. The underlining theme throughout the site should be: If you're cool and hip, you need to be shopping at JCT!

COMPETITIVE POSITIONING

Because JCT caters to such a focused group of individuals, there are very few stores out there that are able to offer the wide-range of "unique, one of a kind" clothing that JCT is famous for. Most clothing retail chains carry a wide assortment of, typically, boring or mundane outfits. The goal of JCT is to shock and energize the Gen-X crown because they are typically more willing to be more rebellious in their clothing choices. JCT is all about promotion, promotion, and promotion. We're attention getters and seek to turn people's heads. That should be the goal of the web site as well. We're different. We're loud. We like to have fun!

SINGLE-MINDED MESSAGE

Hip. Classy. Brash

Figure 1.1   *The JCT creative brief will drive all our efforts from concepts to upload.*

The great thing about the brief is its brevity. At one or two pages, it is one of those documents the team will actually read. Also by keeping it text based, you are not interfering with the conceptualization process. Nothing could be worse than including a couple of sketches in the brief because the team will be tempted to use them as their creative foundation.

Depending upon the nature of the project, the brief can take the form of an email or a printed document. In certain instances, the client may supply the brief. If this happens to you, don't regard the client's document as being The Bible. It does not replace the brief you should produce. Regardless of the form, it is a document that has to be signed and dated by the client.

The form the brief takes is not standard, so each one is unique to the company producing it. Try to incorporate how the site will work. Give the reader, usually a creative individual, a sense of the experience the site visitor should have. Make sure every individual reading the brief gets a sense of the purpose of the project and, in certain instances, the broad marketing, advertising, and public relations goals behind the project.

Planning Content

There was a children's CD called *Nicolai's Train* developed by Hoffman and Associates a few years ago. There is a game on the CD where Nicolai is in a forest, and the user has to find certain objects by clicking onscreen to help Nicolai out of the forest. One of the objects is a bird's nest. Click the nest and a baby bird pops up, screaming, over and over, "I'm hungry." He only settles down when the mother flies to the nest and feeds him a worm. After a couple of seconds, he starts the yelling cycle all over again.

The web is a lot like that little bird. It needs to be fed a constant supply of well-considered and executed content. Your efforts will be driven by your content needs, and the site will actually develop around the content for each page and collection of pages. Essentially, this means that the content will drive structure, and one can't have one without the other.

There are those who would disagree with this statement. They would claim it is the developer's job to help the client discover what is to be conveyed and to draw from our professional expertise and experience to guide them in the proper direction. This is essentially true. The developer would never have been retained were they not a professional. In certain cases, the client will make extensive use of the developer's expertise. In other instances, it might be the client's marketing department driving the process as well as the developer's efforts. In either case, the decisions being made around content are always subjective and rarely objective.

At this phase of the process, the content needs to be devised conceptually—"What do we need?"—and practically—"What do we have?" When you are planning content, never for a moment lose sight of that invisible person driving your efforts: the user.

Put yourself in the user's shoes and ask if the content is being organized in a rational manner. Look at how easy it is to access the content, and look at the grouping of the content. In the early days of the web, users were resigned to drilling for information. It was not unheard of to spend 20 minutes or more searching a site for a precise bit of information. Today's user is much more sophisticated. Asking a user to drill for information is no longer an option. If the user can't find information quickly and easily, the user will look elsewhere on the web.

Identifying the Current Content Assets

More often than not, there is a great temptation to use the existing content on a site simply because it is there and accessible. Don't fall into this trap. There obviously was a problem with the existing content and structure, or you wouldn't have been retained.

To deal with this situation, be dispassionate and conduct a content audit, which is simply a listing of all the content, already existing as well as needed to be prepared for the site. This includes copy, diagrams, images, animations, video, and anything else that would appear on a page. Your list will quickly identify the content that should be discarded, that which should be retained, and new content that needs to be created.

Identifying the Content to Be Created

When you have that list, review each piece of that content carefully and ask yourself if it is really needed and does it *further* the action? Does the asset reinforce the client's branding message, and does it benefit the project? There are a lot of Flash sites out there that have been developed simply because the developer wanted to do something cool. In this case, the client is funding the efforts of a developer to show his or her peers, "Aren't I clever?"

Going for cool might work in certain instances, but always discern if that cool piece of content meets the needs of the client's intended audience.

Is there a more efficient way of presenting the content? It might just be more efficient to prepare the interface as an image map in Fireworks that loads quickly rather than a Flash-based site requiring a 20 second preload. Then again, a series of buttons currently designed as JavaScript rollovers might be done more effectively in Flash.

After the client agrees to the content audit, you can then develop a content delivery plan that answers a simple question—"How long will each element take to create?"

Deadlines for Content

At this stage, you should be looking at rough deadlines for the creation of the content. In this case you would determine how long it might take to create the various elements contained in the content audit.

We use the words *rough* and *roughly* because nothing ever arrives exactly according to plan. Build in a buffer, if at all possible. If an item requires 72 hours to create, add a couple of hours to the total to accommodate the unexpected, such as computer crashes, interruption of Internet services, and so on. Having this extra padding of time can allow you to develop a realistic production schedule that can be presented to the client for signature.

After determining how long it is going to take to create the content, you also might consider a second question—"What tools will be used to create the content?"

Web Content Creation Tools

When it comes to web development, a guaranteed recipe for failure is to focus on the technology and not the process. The MX Studio is all about process. Macromedia regards Fireworks MX, Flash MX, Dreamweaver MX, and Freehand as tools for content creation and web page design. For example, all these applications will enable you to create buttons for your pages. It is up to you to decide what tool is the most efficient one for the task at hand. It is up to you to decide whether to incorporate Flash buttons created in Dreamweaver over those created in Flash. The decision should be from the perspective of the user because they couldn't care less whether the button was created in Flash or Dreamweaver. They just want it to do what it is supposed to do.

With the content audit in place and an idea of what tools will be used, you can start to consider who will do what.

Defining the Project Team

The day of the One Man, Do-It-All web shop is over. The business of creating web sites is complex, detailed, and, depending upon the scope of the project, requires a variety of skills from project management to database programming. The rise of the team-based production environment, therefore, grew from a very real need to segment the production process into a series of manageable job functions.

After the scope of the task is determined, it is the Project Manager's job to identify specific functions and fill them. The individuals charged with the tasks are either internal staff or freelancers with whom the company has developed a working relationship through collaboration in past projects. Naturally, the individuals who work in the web site development environment don't exactly fit the traditional corporate mold. Many of them are multitalented, and the best teams are those whose skill sets compliment and overlap each other. That might sound a bit contradictory but it is a fact of web life.

One of the authors of this book was involved in a web development project as a Flash developer. The team was small, the deadlines tight, and the technical requirements were quite complex. About two days before a critical client presentation, the individual responsible for editing some digital video and preparing it to stream was stricken with the flu. This could have been a huge problem except for the fact the author stepped in and prepared the video for the presentation. Two completely separate skill sets, but an overlap in video kept the project moving forward.

The team structure is rarely formalized. Teams are formed based upon project complexity, and the skills brought to bear on a particular aspect of a project could be done by one individual, or spread among several individuals.

Team Members

The following is a breakdown of the members of a team and their respective roles. Not every team will be this large, but their duties should be covered in any project.

- **Project Manager**. This individual is the liaison between the client and the team. They could have that particular corporate title, or be one of the principals of the firm. Regardless of internal role, this individual is charged with managing the team and the client through the creative process from concept to upload.

  There could also be a Project Manager on the client side. In this case, they are responsible for the approvals, delivering content when needed, and generally ensuring that the client's needs and expectations are being met.

- **Information Architect**. This is a relatively new role and one that is becoming increasingly critical in the development process. This individual works with the Creative Director, the Technical Director, and the client to develop the framework for the content. They determine how the information in the site is structured; how the information flows through the site, and works on the development of the technological infrastructure. Never, for an instant, forget the purpose of a site is to provide access to information. It is the Information Architect's job to ensure that information is both accessible and understandable. Jakob Nielson, Jeffrey Veen, and Steve Krug have all written excellent books on this subject, and at least two of those books should be in every agency or web development shop.

- **Creative Director**. The Creative Director (or Art Director, as they're sometimes called) sets the parameters for what the user sees, hears, and experiences through interactivity throughout the site.

  The Creative Director also serves as the creative team's manager, and is charged with setting the vision, building and motivating the team, and articulating the vision to ensure each member of the team clearly understands the look and feel of the site. This individual develops the creative strategy and storyboards, and then works with the entire team to develop the project. In some shops this individual is involved with the audio and visual design, as well.

- **Content Manager**. Large and technologically complex projects might require the services of this individual. They are responsible for gathering the site content. This might involve marshalling in-house resources in the areas of copy, images, illustration, video, audio, animation, or any other element that will appear on a page. If the resources are unavailable in-house, this individual will sub-contract to obtain the content required.

- **Technology Director**. Though affectionately regarded by many as the "Lead Geek," don't fall into the trap of accepting stereotypes. This individual's role is to assume responsibility for how the site functions.

  They might write the document that outlines the site's technical and functional specifications. As well, this individual might handle the forms, shopping carts, databases, content management systems (CMS), and a host of greater or lesser coding tasks.

- **Web Designer**. Reporting to the Creative Director, this individual works on the site's appearance. Other tasks could include motion graphics design, imaging, and light coding using Fireworks, Dreamweaver, or Flash. Though sometimes referred to as the "Pixel Monkey," this role is more important than simply shoving pixels around on the screen. In many ways, this job is comparable to that of the Assembly Artist in traditional graphics workflow.

- **Flash Developer**. Reporting to the Creative Director, this individual is responsible for creating the Flash animations or ensuring the designs from Freehand are converted to Flash content. They are also responsible for organizing the content and optimizing it for web playback.

- **Actionscript Programmer**. Three years ago, this position did not exist. The addition of Actionscript—Flash's programming language—to version 4 of the application spawned this career. This individual is responsible for the site's interactivity through the user interface, and for the management of dynamic content.

- **Database Designer**. If ecommerce is involved, you need this person. The Database Designer is responsible for developing the database that drives an ecommerce site as well as the relationships between the various bits of information in the database.

- **Web Programmer**. Reporting to the Technology Director and working with the Database Programmer, this individual is responsible for many of the coding tasks—XML, HTML, DHTML, JavaScript—that integrate the look of the site with the back-end programming functions that make the site work.

- **Quality Assurance Tester**. This is one of the more thankless, yet critical jobs, in the entire process. This individual simply assures everything does what it is supposed to do. They test each element of every page and report any problems back to the Creative Director and Technology Director. In many cases, they also function as proofreaders—paying close attention to spelling, grammar, and facts on each page.

Though these are the key roles, the nature of the business is the structure derived from the project scope; thus, there is no one particular way of developing a team. In certain instances the team might be extremely large with clear lines of responsibility and duties. In other circumstances the team might be extremely small with the tasks shared by all members of the team.

Developing the Project Schedule

The astute Project Manager realizes the key to successful project completion is a schedule, and that the team has to buy into the deadlines. A properly developed schedule is a straight line from lighting up that first pixel to posting the site to a server and, in many respects, is the single most important element in the communications process.

The web development process is complex, and the best way of dealing with complexity is from a position of simplicity. Scheduling, if properly done, segments the process into a series of compartmentalized tasks, each with its own due date. In this manner, everyone involved in the process, from the Project Manager who determines the deadlines, to the Web Programmer who clearly understands what they have to do by when.

If the content audit has been thorough, the time necessary to create the web site and post it is a simple matter of totaling the time allotted to each element. Don't fall into that trap. Instead, have the team managers meet with their team members to carefully review the allotted times. In many cases, your idea of how long it will take to create an image map might differ from that of the person responsible for creating that map. Prepare to negotiate a schedule that is agreeable to all concerned. It will then allow the Project Manager to assign realistic deadlines.

Project Deadlines

Inevitably two schedules that clearly present the deadlines are developed. The first is an overview, or Key Event Schedule, that lays out the broad parameters and their associated deadlines in a chronological manner. The second is a detailed schedule that lays out the tasks and deliverables in an itemized day-by-day manner.

The overview schedule shows the team what the forest looks like. Depending upon the complexity of the project, it can be a formal or an informal document. Still, an overview shows the major milestones as the project progresses, and the work due at each milestone. This schedule can break the project into weeks or months and, in certain instances, can be further segmented to illustrate phases of the project. It should also be included in any proposals presented to the client and circulated to every member of the team.

Dealing with Deadlines

Just short of having everybody, including the client, sign a blood oath to meet the dead-lines, it is critical that every member of the team understand the effect of missed dead-lines.

This might not be as large an issue for the team as it could be for the client. Nothing causes a Project Manager to rip out clumps of hair faster than a client who consistently misses deadlines for approvals or content delivery. Apart from having weapons on the desk when you broach this subject with your client, position it in terms the client under-stands, which usually involves the client clearly understanding the goals of each event as well as the financial and time implications of tardiness. In certain instances, it will not hurt to ask the client to appoint a back up person with the authority to approve, sign, and date documents, should the client be unavailable.

One of the authors tells the story of dealing with a tardy client. Content always arrived three or four days late and approvals inevitably conflicted with cross-country business trips. Naturally the project missed the deadline by about six weeks.

After the project was completed, the author sat down with the client for a post-mortem to review the process. On the whole, the client was extremely satisfied with the work, but one comment in particular stands out. "You know," said the client, "you guys do great work. The only problem I can see is that it seems to take forever to get anything out of you."

The detailed schedule shows the client and the team what each tree in the forest looks like. This document serves to move the team forward to the final goal. It is detailed for a reason—by breaking down the production process into a day-by-day continuum, all the players are presented with a daily To Do list.

This document is spawned from the overview and should always take into account scope creep. In many ways it is a living document in that it is always changing as tasks are added or subtracted, or deadlines expanded or contracted.

The last thing a Project Manager needs is to have the client or team member searching for a deadline. This is why many developers post the detailed schedule to the client site or staging area to provide a clear communications vehicle that tracks and presents the progress of the project.

Project Scheduling Tools

Project schedules run the full gamut from a piece of paper taped to a wall, to full bore, full color, multi-page missives that resemble the launch schedule for the space shuttle.

Strange as this may seem, one of the most common tools used is a simple word proces-sor. Even the simple word processor packaged with your PC or Macintosh does a great job, though some developers will use word processors for the overview and create the detailed schedule using a spreadsheet.

The calendar templates or extensions that are available for many word processing, page layout, and drawing applications are also quite useful. Many agencies use customized versions of these sheets, while others prefer to develop their own.

When the project is complex, many developers use a project-management application. Regardless of the method or software chosen, after the team and the client buy in, the project moves from a nebulous project to a focused continuum, from concept to delivery.

Using the Dreamweaver Calendar Extension

Over the years software manufacturers have realized the users of their products are constantly clamoring for more and more features. To satisfy this craving, many of the more popular applications have the capability to use small, side applications that extend the functionality of the main application. Dreamweaver MX uses extensions. Fireworks MX uses commands and extensions.

Extensions can be either created by you or downloaded from a variety of sources. Writing a custom extension is well out of the scope of this book, so we will be concentrating on adding a third-party extension.

One of the better sources for these is none other than Macromedia. At the time of this writing there were more than 500 Dreamweaver extensions available for download. Before you head over to the Macromedia site and merrily start downloading, you need to obtain a copy of the Extension Manager, if it isn't already installed on your machine.

The Extension Manager is a utility developed by Macromedia for the installation and management of extensions for Dreamweaver MX, Fireworks MX, and Flash MX. Extensions use the .mxp format and, when downloaded to your machine, they are opened by the Extension Manager and then put into the proper Dreamweaver folders. Double-clicking an extension after download opens the Extension Manager, and starts the installation process.

Dreamweaver MX users will already have the Extension Manager installed, which means you only have to download extensions.

If you have the Extension Manager installed, follow these steps to download and install the Calendar extension.

1. Open your browser and point it to `http://www.macromedia.com/exchange/Dreamweaver`. If this is your first visit to the Macromedia Exchange, you will be prompted to register. This happens only once. After you register, you should be at the main page.

Note

You can get to Macromedia's Dreamweaver Exchange directly from within Dreamweaver MX. If you have the application open, select Command, Get More Commands. This launches your default browse, and takes you into the Dreamweaver Exchange's main page.

2. Enter **Calendar** in the Search Extensions text box, as shown in Figure 1.2. Selecting the pop-down list in Search Extensions shows a variety of categories for the extensions. This can be rather confusing, especially if this is your first visit. To avoid confusion, do a keyword search—**Calendar**—rather than hunting through the categories. It is a lot quicker.

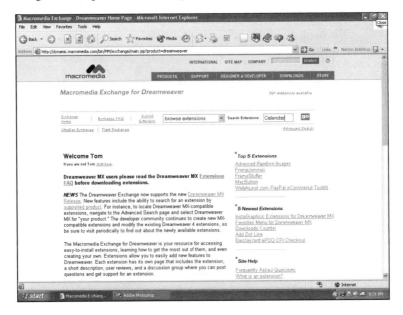

Figure 1.2   The main page of the Dreamweaver Exchange. Unless you know the category for the extension for which you are looking, do a keyword search.

3. Click the Go button. You are presented with a list of the extensions that contain the keyword you entered.

4. Click the Calendar hyperlink to be taken to the extension's page and then click the Download button for your platform, as shown in Figure 1.3. Although many prefer to save the downloaded extensions to the desktop, you can have them download into the Downloaded Extensions folder located in the Dreamweaver MX application folder.

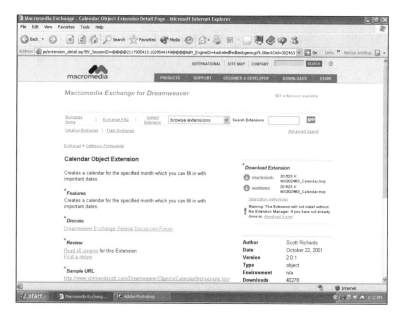

Figure 1.3   After you have located your extension, choose your platform.

The extension is now downloaded to your machine. To install the calendar, follow these steps:

1. Double-click the .mxp file on your desktop to open the Extension Installer. If that doesn't work, open the Extension Manager application and select File, Open. If Dreamweaver MX is already open, select Commands, Manage Extensions to open the Extension Manager. Use the File button to browse to your Extension folder and then select the extension to install. Click the Install button.

Note

When installing extensions in Flash MX, be aware that some of the components require you to quit and then restart Flash MX.

2. The next screen you see contains an Agreement and a Disclaimer. Extensions are third-party software, and being asked to carefully review the Licensing Agreement is standard operating procedure during the installation of any software. Click the Agree button.

Note

The majority of the extensions available are not developed by Macromedia; thus the third-party software designation. The Calendar extension was actually developed by a Macromedia employee in his spare time.

At this point of the process, the Extension Manager takes over. One of its functions is to ensure all the files contained in the package are placed in their proper locations on your computer. After this process is completed you will be notified if the installation was successful, and you should see the screen shown in Figure 1.4.

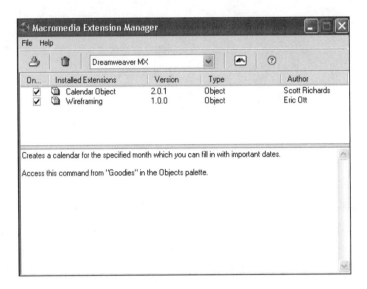

Figure 1.4   The Macromedia Extension Manager installs, loads, and activates any extensions containing .mxp in the filename. Selecting the extension name reveals the information at the bottom of the Extension Manager window.

The Calendar extension is installed into your Extensions folder located in the Dreamweaver Configuration folder. To use the Calendar extension, follow these steps:

1. Open a new Dreamweaver document.

2. Select Calendar at the bottom of the Insert menu.

The Insert Calendar dialog box appears, as seen in Figure 1.5. You can customize the appearance of the calendar by making a few intuitive selections. Click OK when you finish.

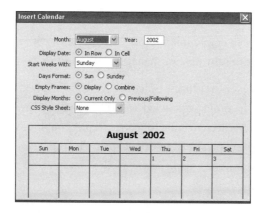

Figure 1.5   The Insert Calendar dialog box allows you to customize the look of the calendar.

A calendar reflecting your preferences appears in the page, as seen in Figure 1.6. To add an event or schedule item, simply click in a date and then type in your entry.

August 2002						
Sun	Mon	Tue	Wed	Thu	Fri	Sat
				1	2	3
4	5	6	7	8	9	10
11	12	13	14	15	16	17
18	19	20	21	22	23	24
25	26	27	28	29	30	31

Figure 1.6   The Calendar extension allows you to create detailed schedules and, thanks to its HTML formatting, can be easily added to a project site.

Summary

As you have seen, the web development process doesn't start with software. It starts with careful planning and a healthy dose of management expertise.

The scope sets the stage for the process by letting everyone involved in the process understand the purpose of the project and what has to be produced. Anything added or subtracted from the project will contribute to scope creep. A couple of ways of managing the effects of scope creep were presented in this chapter. Planning the project, managing the team and the process, and the establishment of clear lines of communication were also covered.

The team's marching orders are usually contained in the creative brief. The Project Manager or even the client can prepare this document. The brief could be as simple as an email to all involved, or as complex as a multi-page printed document. Regardless of size, the brief has to bridge the gulf between the client's expectations and the team's pragmatism.

After the brief is prepared, content should be identified and planned. From there, the team is assembled from in-house or external sources. Though the web development community is rather freewheeling, a distinct division of labor has arisen and many specialized skills are brought to bear upon the project.

Having identified what needs to be produced and by whom, the project moves into the scheduling phase. There are a number of tools available, and this chapter discussed how the Dreamweaver Calendar extension can be used for this purpose.

With the site development plan in place and the team focused on the goals and the deadlines, you have completed only half of the job. You now have to put into place protocols for how the content will be managed when it is in production. As you will see, two of Macromedia's MX products—Dreamweaver MX and Fireworks MX—contain some powerful tools for this important aspect of the process.

Chapter 2

Content
Management

If you don't have content, you don't have a

site. It's just that simple. If you have the

right content and you manage it properly,

your chances for successful completion of

the project are increased immeasurably.

What is the "right content?" It is anything on the page that supports the client's message and goals.

It can't be overlooked that web creators work in a team-based environment. In this case communication among the team members is crucial. Using Dreamweaver MX's Assets panel and Check In/Check Out feature as well as Dreamweaver MX's Cloaking feature and Design Notes and Reports, the team will have been handed a full suite of collaboration tools.

Use these tools and you avoid having two people doing two different things to the same images when Check In and Check Out are enabled. All of the common site elements—from colors to code, from Flash to QuickTime—are in one place: the Assets panel. This panel enables easy access throughout the design process. By attaching Design Notes to their changes, designers leave a record of their work for others in the group. The Cloaking feature prevents the wrong people from accessing folders they have no reason to be using.

These features give everyone involved a sense of the forest—the project—when they usually tend to concentrate on the trees—the content.

Using Available Management Tools

Taking the time to carefully organize the management of your site even before you light up a pixel will pay huge dividends in time gained at the end of the process. Regarding your hard drive as the repository for your files is a fatal error. Something will get lost. Instead, always think of where the hierarchy of the files will be, how they will be named, and where they will be saved.

Folders

Most sites start with a single folder, sometimes referred to as the *local site*. The files residing in the folder are usually edited and manipulated from within that particular folder. The advantage to you, the developer, is the ability to test the site locally without going live. This applies primarily to static sites. Dynamic sites can be tested locally, but the rules are slightly different.

As the project grows in complexity, a hierarchy of folders inevitably develops. Though there is no standard method of folder hierarchy, there are some general guidelines you should consider.

- If the site is complex, break it into categories. For example, the JCT site we build could have a folder named Shoes, and all the pages relating to that product can be found in that folder. As the site grows subfolders named Men's Shoes and Women's Shoes can be added.

- If the site contains a lot of media, such as images and sounds, put those files in one folder. Again, many developers have a folder named Assets. Inside that folder might be subfolders for Sound, Video, Images, Line Art, Text, and so on. If the site is complex, each section of the site could have its own Assets folder.

- Don't change the structure mid-game. Your local and remote sites should have exactly the same structure. One of the advantages to using Dreamweaver MX is that when you upload the local site to the remote site, the local structure will be precisely duplicated.

- Use Dreamweaver MX's Cloaking feature to ensure each team has access to only those files and folders that they are permitted access.

Media Asset Management

In today's environment of wide broadband access, rich media, such as sound and video, are becoming ubiquitous and not the novelty they once were. Managing these assets is just as critical as managing folders. Again, there are no rules regarding their management, other than some general guidelines.

- Separate the media by type. For example, put all the sound files in one folder. If a particular sound is being used by another media source, make sure a copy of that file is with the file in which it is used.

- For video and Flash MX animations, separate all the files used by media type. For example, a folder named Flash holds all the Flash files. Inside of that folder is another that holds all the MP3 sounds used in the Flash animations, and so on.

- If rich media files—QuickTime, Director, and Shockwave files—are being delivered by outside sources, have the files delivered on optical media, such as a CD. By doing this you have a back up that is readily available. The worst possible delivery medium is email attachment. Rich media files are huge—300Mb is common.

- Back up your files. If you are particularly fastidious, back them up onto magnetic and optical media. If there is a chance a file will become corrupted or lost, the odds are good that is exactly what will happen.

Using the Dreamweaver MX File Management Tools

It's important to understand that web design, like graphic design in print media, requires consistency of design throughout the entire site. Far too many web designers focus on individual pages at this point, and wonder why their designs lose their effectiveness. To avoid this, ask the simple question, "How does the site work?" Contrast this with, "How does this page look?"

A web site is a collection of documents, ranging from copy, HTML documents, JavaScript documents, digital video, Freehand, and Fireworks images and Flash animations, which must be carefully managed. It is the prudent web designer who creates the assets before creating the pages. Still, creating a shell document at this stage helps to identify any potential design problems and creates a single storage area for the management of all the assets created and used in the site.

Another aspect to consider is workflow. Issues such as file storage, document management, and so on should be dealt with sooner rather than later, and the MX Studio has an abundant number of tools for this purpose, which all come into play when you define a site in Dreamweaver MX.

Defining a Local Dreamweaver MX Site

When working with Dreamweaver MX, the term *site* can refer to one of two things: a web site that you are creating, or the local storage area for all your content from text to interactive Flash MX files. In either case, the file storage area has to be built before you can build a web site. By building the storage site, you first need a location where the files are organized and accessible. As well, Dreamweaver MX enables you to track files through the process, share them with others in the team, and eventually load them to the server.

The standard workflow protocol is to create the pages on a local machine and then upload them to a remote server, making them available to the public.

There are three ways to define a local site when you launch Dreamweaver MX. The first is to select Site, New Site. A window opens with two tabs—Basic and Advanced. Clicking the Basic tab launches a wizard, as shown in Figure 2.1, that offers you the choice of using a basic or advanced method to define a site.

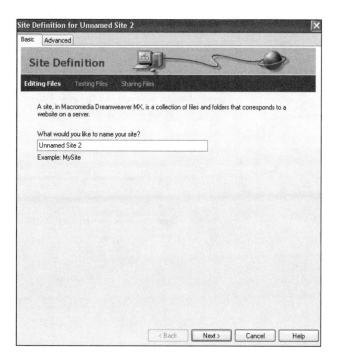

Figure 2.1   Selecting the Basic tab launches a wizard that walks you through the process of creating a local site. If you don't have a lot of experience building sites, this is a great choice.

If you select the Basic tab, you are walked through the steps necessary to create the site. You are asked what you want to name the site, and to identify the folder where the site's files are located. The next screen asks if your data is dynamic—constantly changing—or static. After those questions have been answered you are then asked if the files will stay on your machine or be uploaded to a server accessible by the work group. If you answer Yes to the work group question, Dreamweaver MX prompts you to tell it how the files get to the server, and to identify the folder on the server where the files will be placed.

The second method is to click the Advanced tab and then select Local Info from the Category area, as shown in Figure 2.2.

The first field to fill in is the name of the site. Next, select the folder being used for the files by typing in the name of the site, or by navigating to the folder on your system and selecting either Choose (Mac) or Select (PC).

Leave the Refresh Local File List Automatically option selected. By leaving it selected, you ensure any new files are automatically added to the list of local files. This also ensures that you aren't constantly selecting View, Refresh (PC) or Site, Site File View, Refresh Local (Mac). The final input area asks you to identify a default folder for your media assets.

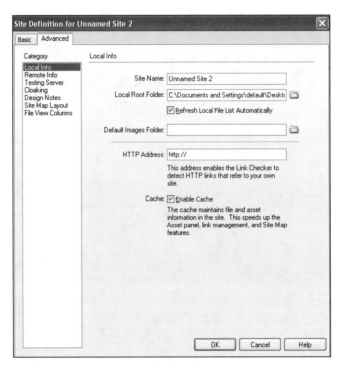

Figure 2.2   Defining a local site using the Advanced options sets the path to the site files on your computer.

Enter an HTTP address. If you have it, this would be a good time to enter the full address, such as http://www.domainname.com. By specifying the URL, Dreamweaver can use the address to verify whether absolute links refer to pages on the web or pages within the site.

Ensure the Enable Cache option is selected. Dreamweaver, in certain respects, mimics a web browser in that it automatically tracks certain files and assets in your site. The most common advantage you receive from this feature is a speed boost when it comes to link updates.

Defining a Remote Dreamweaver MX Site

The site you design is eventually going to move from your computer to a server that is regarded as the remote site. This step determines the information Dreamweaver needs to publish your pages to a web server.

Select Remote Info from the Category options in the Advanced panel and then select the category that applies to your site. The Site Definition dialog box opens, as shown in Figure 2.3.

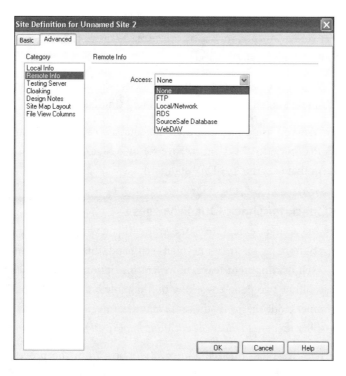

Figure 2.3   Defining a remote site sets the path to the site files on your server.

Choose None—the default if the site is being developed on your computer and is not being uploaded to a server until the end of the process. Select FTP if you connect to the server using the File Transfer Protocol (FTP). If you select FTP, you are prompted for the following information:

- **FTP Host**. The name of your FTP connection to the web server. This is in the form of www.mysite.com.

- **Host Directory**. The path to the directory holding your files. If you are unsure of the location, check with your ISP or network administrator.

- **Login**. The user name assigned to your account.

- **Password**. This is obvious.

- **Use Passive FTP**. If you are behind a firewall, you might have to select this. Check with your network administrator.

- **Use Firewall (in Preferences)**. Selecting this tells Dreamweaver to use the firewall preferences with the correct host and port information to connect to an FTP server.

You choose Local/Network if the server used to publish your pages to the web is located on the same network as you are, such as a Large Area Network (LAN). Make sure Refresh Remote Files List Automatically is selected.

The choice RDS stands for Remote Development Services. Select this option if your remote folder will be located on a computer running ColdFusion server.

Choose WebDAV if you use a Visual SourceSafe database (Microsoft Visual SourceSafe Client 6.0 on a PC or MetroWerks SourceSave 1.1 on a Mac), or you use a collaborative authoring system that uses the WebDAV standard.

Setting the Check In/Check Out Privileges

Each of the remote options, except for None, presents you with the Enable File Check In and Check Out option. If you are a one-man web band, this option is unimportant. If you work on a web development team, however, this option is critical. The worst case scenario here would be two people working on the same bit of JavaScript. We all know no two programmers code in exactly the same manner. Imagine the huge frustration, not to mention hostility that could ensue, if each one kept overwriting the other's work.

Dreamweaver removes this potential source of friction from the process. If a file is checked out, you see a check mark next to the file's name in the site window. If the check mark is red, one of your team members is working on the file. If the check mark is green, you are working on the file. As well, the site window displays the name of the user. If each team member has supplied an email address, you can click that person's name in the site window and send an email directly to that individual.

Checked-in files are treated a bit differently. They are, initially, read-only files, as indicated by the padlock icon. This prohibits unauthorized personnel from making changes to the file without the appropriate permission to edit it.

The following scenario illustrates this process:

Chris is the graphic designer. He has opened the remote site and has checked out a page because he wants to place a Fireworks file named image.jpg on it. He can do this by clicking the Check Out button on the Site Window toolbar, or by opening the file. If he opens the file directly, he will be asked if he wants to check out the file. Chris will also be asked if he wants to check out any files that are dependent on the file that he is checking out, such as gif's, jpeg's, or Flash movies.

Tom, the Project Manager, wants to see the page as well. He opens the remote site and notices a red check mark beside the file. He clicks Chris' name and sends an email asking Chris to let him know when he finishes his work.

Jordan is also in need of the file because he wants to finish up the HTML. He clicks Chris' name, and asks Chris to notify him when he finishes.

Chris finishes his work and clicks the Check In button to transfer the files back to the remote server. Both Tom and Jordan automatically receive emails to this effect.

Jordan checks out the file and makes his changes. The check marks on Tom's and Chris' remote sites turn red. When he finishes, Jordan clicks the Check In button and all the files associated with the page are returned to the remote server.

Tom opens the remote site and notices the padlock, but still can open the page because it is read-only. What he can't do is make changes to the files.

If you are using the Check In/Check Out feature, it is vital that all members of the team have Check In/Check Out set up on their computers.

Setting Up the Check In/Check Out Protocols

Setting up the Check In/Check Out procedures is relatively simple. To do so, follow these steps:

1. Select Site, Define Sites to open the Site Definition dialog box. Select your site and then select Edit in the pop-up window. If you are working on a new site, select New to define a new site.

2. Select Remote Site from the category list. All the options for remote sites, except for None, will have a button at the bottom that allows you to enable the Check In and Check Out feature. Clicking the button opens the Check In/Check Out options shown in Figure 2.4.

3. Click Check Out Files when Opening if you want to automatically check out a file when double-clicked from the Site window.

4. Enter your name in the Check Out Name box. The standard procedure here is not to simply enter your name. Many users also add a location or computer they are using. For example, Tom has a portable computer, an office Mac, and a home PC. He would enter **Tom-Office**, **Tom-Home**, or **Tom-Portable** to let the others in the group know not only that Tom has checked out a file but also where he is working on the file. Enter your email address in the Email Address text box. This allows one-click communication within the work group. Finally, click OK to enable this feature.

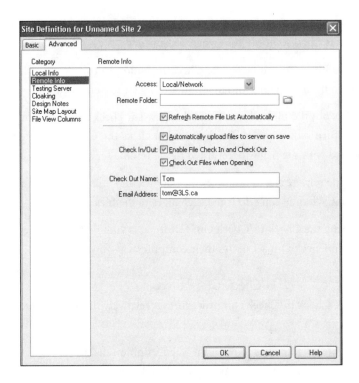

Figure 2.4   After Dreamweaver MX is told you want to enable Check In/Check Out, all you have to supply is your name and email address.

Checking Files In and Out

After you enable Check In/Check Out, working with files and notifying the group that you have the files is virtually automatic. To check out a file, follow these steps:

1. Open the site, select the file or files you want to check out, and select Site, Check Out. The files are marked as being checked out.

Note

The great thing about working with computers is that there are always six other ways of doing the same thing. In this case, you could also select the files and click the Check Out Files button on the window's toolbar. You could select the files and right-click on a PC, or Control-click on a Mac to bring up a context menu. You could select the files and use Ctrl-Alt-Shift-D on a PC or Command-Option-Shift-D on a Mac, or you can double-click the file in the Site Management window.

2. If you want to check out the files associated with the page or pages being checked out, select Yes when prompted.

When finished with the files, make sure the site you are working on is active and the files you want to check in are selected. There are a number of ways to "Check In" a file. They include the following:

- Select Site, Check In.

- Select the files and click the Check In button on the window's toolbar.

- Select the files and right-click (PC) or control-click (Mac) to open the context menu. Select Check In.

- Select the files and press Control-Alt-Shift-U (PC) or Command-Option-Shift-U (Mac).

If you want to check in the dependent files as well, select Yes, when prompted in the Check In dialog box.

Tip

The first rule of Dreamweaver Physics is in play here. The rule states: That which is checked out must be checked in. If you ignore this rule and use Site, Put instead, you will still update the remote file but it will not be regarded as checked in and remove the checked out status. Thus, it is extremely important that everybody involved in the site use Dreamweaver to transfer files to and from the remote server.

If you select the wrong file for check out, or simply change your mind, select the file and choose Site, Undo Check Out. In this case the file is returned to the server in exactly the state in which it was checked out.

Using Design Notes

If ever there was an unsung feature of Dreamweaver MX, Design Notes just might be that feature. When you are in a collaborative work environment, you can make no assumptions. You can't expect your team members to look at a page and instantly know what you have done.

Design Notes can best be thought of as those ubiquitous Sticky Notes. They can be "stuck" on pages or page elements. As the pages or elements move through the production process, the notes attached move with them. This includes physically changing the location of files. In fact, the only way to get rid of a note, after it is attached, is to delete the file.

Finally, if each computer has the Check In/Check Out feature configured, ensure that each computer is also configured for Design Notes. Never have one without the other.

To configure Design Notes, follow these steps:

1. Open the Site Definition dialog box, select Edit, and select Design Notes in the Category section of the window. The Design Notes window opens, as shown in Figure 2.5.

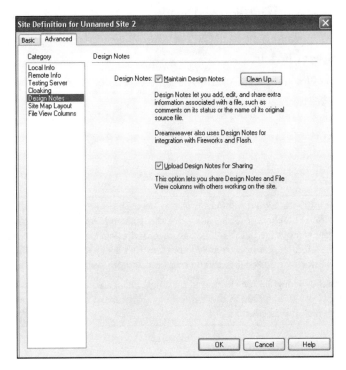

Figure 2.5   Enabling Design Notes in the Site Definition dialog box allows the team to attach and share notes with each other.

2. Select Maintain Design Notes.

3. If you have a group of coworkers involved, select Upload Design Notes for Sharing.

The Clean Up button in the Design Notes window serves a great purpose. Click it, and all notes that are not attached to a page or page element are deleted by answering Yes to the alert.

Adding Design Notes

Adding Design Notes is a simple procedure. To add Design Notes, follow these steps:

1. Select File, Design Notes to add a note to a page. (You can also right-click (PC) or Control-click (Mac) an element on the page and then select Design Notes from the context menu to attach a note to a page element.) Whatever action you choose, the Design Notes window opens, as shown in Figure 2.6.

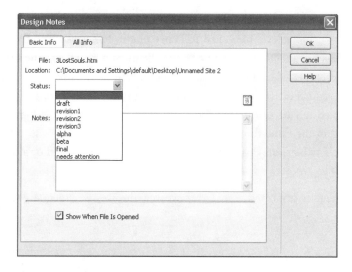

Figure 2.6   The categories in the Status pop-down menu are a comprehensive listing of current file status.

The Basic Info tab is a Project Manager's dream come true. The Status pop-down list options includes Draft, Revision1, Revision2, Revision3, Alpha, Beta, Final, or Needs Attention. Select one of these and you instantly know the status of the page or element per the note attached.

2. To date the note, click the Calendar icon and today's date appears on the note.

3. Create your note in the Notes field.

If you would like the note to appear every time the file is opened, select Show when File Is Opened. Be aware this feature only works for pages. It will not work for elements on the page with notes attached to them.

The All Info tab shows all the notes "stuck" on a file, and their status set through the Basic Info tab. To add a note, click the + sign. To delete a note, select the note in the Info field and click the − sign.

Fireworks and Design Notes

One of the key features of Macromedia's suite of web products is their capability to work with each other. For example, double-click a Fireworks image in your Dreameweaver page, and Fireworks is launched. You can then make your changes, export the image, and quit Fireworks. When you look at your Dreamweaver page, you see that the changes automatically are reflected in the document. This is referred to as a *roundtrip feature*, which is the capability to move between the applications and have any changes appear instantly in Dreamweaver.

For example, Chris creates a file called JCTLogo.png in Fireworks. The file is placed in the Dreamweaver page. The next day he realizes he made a mistake in the file—the logo should have been placed as a GIF image. He double-clicks the image in Dreamweaver, and Fireworks launches. Chris re-exports the JCTlogo.png as JCTlogo.gif. Fireworks creates a file named JCTlogo.gif.mno. (The .mno extension indicates a Design Note). This note is placed in the same directory as the JCTlogo.gif file. Along with giving you an absolute path, any hotspots or rollovers that might have been created or altered are also saved in the Design Note.

When the image is imported into Dreamweaver, the Design Notes are also brought along.

Creating Workflow Reports

Design Notes and Check In/Check Out can, in many respects, be regarded as a micro view of the process. Most of the information is passed between individuals. Reports offer a macro view, giving a Project Manager an overview of the entire process.

Introduced in Dreamweaver 4, the reports feature lives on the remote site so this requires the capability to connect to the remote site.

How does a report work? You simply connect to the remote site and then choose from a variety of options ranging from the status of the current document and selected files in the site, to a report regarding the status of the entire site. After you have selected the required report, you select the elements to be included in the report. You run the report that appears in a separate window. From there you can select the information you need.

Reporting on Checked Out Files

This report allows you to see who is currently working on a specific file. You can check to see all the files that have been checked out and by whom, or even narrow the search to a particular individual. To generate a report on a checked out file, follow these steps:

1. Select Site, Reports and then choose what documents to review from the Report On pop-down menu, as shown in Figure 2.7.

2. Click the Checked Out By option and then click the Report Settings button at the bottom of the window. Enter the name of the team member in the window that appears. Be careful here. The search is case-sensitive. If you are looking for the files checked out by Chris Flick, you could enter Chris or Flick. If you have a number of people named Chris on your team, they will show up in the results. If you leave the field blank, everyone who has a checked out file will appear. When you are finished, click OK and then click Run in the Reports dialog box.

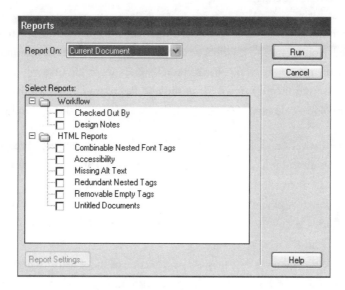

Figure 2.7   The Reports window is available through the Site menu, and allows you to choose the type of report to run.

Dreamweaver runs the report, and opens the Results dialog box that contains a list of the requested information. You can then double-click an entry to view it onscreen or select Save Report. If you select Save Report, the document is saved to the remote server as an XML document, which can be added to a web page, database, or spreadsheet.

Reporting on Design Notes

This robust area allows the Project Manager to review Design Notes, according to the criteria they set up in the Report settings. Again, if no criteria are set, all the Design Notes appear. To create a Design Notes report, follow these steps:

1. Select Site, Reports and then select Design Notes in the Workflow category, as shown in Figure 2.8. Click the Report Settings button.

Figure 2.8   Setting the criteria for a report.

2. The window that opens is a bit non-intuitive. Notice three columns that aren't named. Notice also the middle column is a pop-down menu containing the criteria for the note. Enter the name of the Design Note in the first column. Select a criterion from the pop-down list in the middle column. Enter a value for the Design Notes field being searched. Click OK and then click the Run button.

Here's a hypothetical example of how the process works. The Project Manager needs to know what files are completed. To obtain the list, he enters Status in the first field of the search criteria. He then selects Is or Contains in the second field. (Selecting Is is a bit more precise than Contains.) Finally, he enters Complete into the third field and clicks OK.

The Assets Panel

Introduced in Dreamweaver 4, the Assets panel is one of those features of an application that makes you wonder how you ever worked without it. Simply put, this panel tracks every asset in the site, including images, colors, templates, media files, and anything else that can be added to a web page. The assets include

- **Images**. These are the .gif, .jpg, and .png files on the pages.
- **Colors**. All the colors used for links, text, background, and so on.
- **URLs**. All of the site's links are listed, including http, HTTPS, FTP, JavaScript, gopher, email links, and local file.
- **Flash movies**. These are the .swf (pronounced "swiff") files used. You will not see the source files that have the .fla extension.
- **Shockwave**. Animations and interactive presentations created by Director for web use.
- **Movies**. QuickTime and MPEG movies.
- **Scripts**. JavaScript or VBScripts you use in the site. Be aware that HTML files will not appear in the Assets panel.
- **Templates**. Any templates used in the site.

- **Library items**. Any item that is used across multiple pages of a site can be placed into a Library. The neat thing about these items is the change to the instances is reflected across the entire site. For example, the designer omits the copyright symbol from a logo. He adds it to the Library item, and all instances of that image throughout the site are updated to include the copyright symbol.

To open the Assets panel, select Window/Assets or press F11. When it opens, notice that the panel offers you the opportunity to review the Site Assets or Favorites Site, which is the default—and lists all the assets for the entire site. Favorites are where you can do some customization. This view is a listing of all your favorite assets, such as logos, images, or illustrations. Use this for quick access to these often-used objects because the assets in the Favorites view are also found in the Site view. Two elements that can't be added to the Favorites are a template or a Library item. The Assets panel works a bit differently than you might expect. Things do change, and the Assets panel uses the Site Cache to track these changes. Each time you open the application and open the Assets panel, Dreamweaver has to parse the Site Cache to create the listing. It is, therefore, extremely important that Site Caching is enabled in the Site Definition dialog box.

If an asset does not appear in the panel, check your Site Definition dialog box to ensure Site Cache is enabled, or check to see if the Site radio button has been clicked and not the Favorites radio button. Another method is to click the Refresh button on the Assets panel.

Viewing site assets is simple. Click the name of the asset, and it appears in the viewing pane above the Assets list, as shown in Figure 2.9.

Figure 2.9   The Assets panel for the JCT site.

Inserting an Asset on a Page

The easiest way to add an asset to your page is to simply drag and drop the object from the Asset panel onto the page while you are in Design view. Here is how to use the Asset panel to do the same thing:

1. Open the Assets panel and then select your view—either Site or Favorites. Select the Asset category.

2. Place the cursor on the page where the asset is to be located.

3. Click the asset you want to place on the page and then click the Insert button. You can also right-click (PC) or Control-click (Mac) the asset, and do the placement from the context menu. You can also drag and drop your asset onto the page.

Adding or Removing an Asset from the Favorites List

It is convenient to have an Assets panel that is so robust. Here is how to add, rename, or remove an asset from the panel.

1. Open the Assets panel and then select Site.

2. Select one or more files, and click the Add to Favorites button.

This can also be done using the context menu, which appears through a right-click (PC) or Control-click (Mac). Select Add to Favorites from the context menu.

To remove an asset from the favorites area, select the asset(s) and then click the Remove from Favorites button at the bottom of the panel.

Renaming a Favorite Asset

Sometimes the name of a file seems to have no relation to the file itself, or is so ubiquitous as to be useless. For instance, assume a company has three colored variations of the logo that are used in specific instances. They give you the files named Logo1.gif, Logo2.gif, and Logo3.gif. They are a red version, a blue version, and a black version of the file. Do you really think you can distinguish between them when you are looking at them in the Site view? The prudent designer will address this issue elsewhere, but assets can be renamed without changing their appearance. Macromedia calls these new names Nicknames. To change the name of an asset, follow these steps:

1. Open the Assets panel, select the category for your asset in the Favorites view, and click once on the asset.

2. Click once more on the asset. (Be careful here. These two steps are not a double-click. Double-clicking launches an editor.)

3. Type in the new name, and press Enter (PC) or Return (Mac).

Your can also right-click (PC) or Control-click (Mac) to open the context menu, and select Edit Nickname from the choices.

Moving Assets from One Site to Another

The Assets panel is quite robust. You have to be aware that the Assets panel makes assets available to the whole site, not just the assets in the currently open document. For example, if Redlogo.gif is displayed in the Assets panel from the JCT Sales site, it belongs not only to the document currently open but to the entire site. This means that if you are currently working on a document from the site JCT Corporate, you also see Redlogo.gif in this site's Assets panel.

This is somewhat non-intuitive, but the learning curve is really short. In this case you can copy that logo from the JCTSales site to the JCT corporate site by selecting the assets, including entire folders, you want to copy; then right-click (PC) or Control-click (Mac), and select Copy to Site from the context menu. Navigate to the target site from the submenu that appears and release the mouse.

The asset is now copied to the specified site and placed in the appropriate folders. If the folders don't exist, Dreamweaver will create them.

Cloaking Files and Folders in Dreamweaver MX

The Cloaking feature is new to Dreamweaver MX. When a folder is cloaked, it is excluded from a number of normal operations that may be performed in your regular day-to-day workflow. The operations excluded are

- Put, Get, Check In, and Check Out
- Reports
- Site-wide operations, such as search and replace or checking and changing links
- Synchronization of files
- The contents of the Assets panel and the updating of libraries and templates

With all those operations unavailable to the file, why would you want to cloak it? Assume you have a folder full of videos and sounds, and you don't need to waste your time uploading the files to the server each day. You could cloak the folder, and the system would exclude the folder from any site operations you might want to undertake.

Be careful with this one. You can cloak folders, but not individual files. If you want to cloak a particular .png file, think twice because Dreamweaver MX will cloak all of the .png files in the site. Also, if an item is cloaked, you can still work on it by selecting the item in the Site panel. By doing this, you are overriding the cloaking.

Tip

Another use for cloaking involves protecting Flash MX files. Set up a cloaked folder for the .fla files and upload the .swf files to an uncloaked folder. In this way, the original Flash MX files are protected.

Enabling and Disabling Cloaking

Site cloaking is the default option meaning, cloaking is enabled when you create the site. To enable or disable the Cloaking feature, follow these steps:

1. Open the Site panel, and select the site you want to work on.

2. Select Site, Cloaking to display the submenu and then make your choice as shown in Figure 2.10. Other methods are to select the folder in the Site panel and right-click (PC) or Control-click (Mac) to open the context menu.

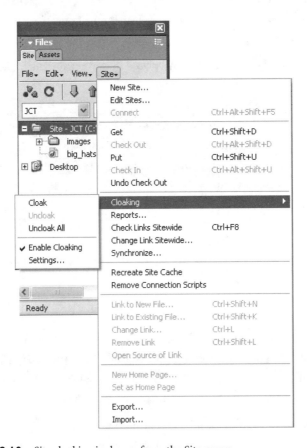

Figure 2.10   Site cloaking is chosen from the Site menu.

To cloak a particular folder, select the folder and select Site, Cloaking, Cloak. A red line appears through the folder that has been cloaked.

Cloaking and Uncloaking Files

Again, be careful with this one. The files are cloaked based on their file type, and all files in the site that have that extension will be cloaked. To cloak or uncloak files, follow these steps:

1. If the Site panel is already open, right-click (PC) or Control-click (Mac) on the Site window. If it isn't, simply open a site and then select Edit.

2. The Advanced Options opens, as shown in Figure 2.11. Select Cloaking and then select Cloak Files Ending With. Enter the extension of the file type and then click OK. A red line appears through all the files ending with that particular extension. To remove the cloaking, simply deselect the Cloak Files check box.

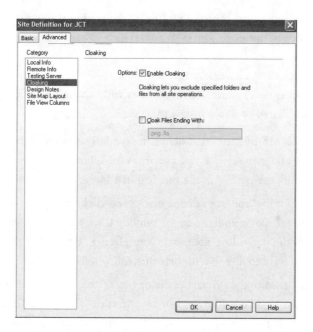

Figure 2.11   Cloaking files types in Dreamweaver MX. Exercise caution when enabling this option because, according to this dialog box, all the .png and .fla files in the site will be cloaked.

To uncloak all files and folders in the site, open the site, select Cloaking, and select Uncloak All. This removes cloaking from the entire site.

Shared Libraries in Flash MX

When working on the web always keep in mind that small is good. When it comes to Flash, the smaller the file size the better. The use of symbols in a library cuts down on bloat, and the capability to share those libraries among multiple Flash movies also cuts back on size. A little-known management aspect of Flash is the ability to manage library assets across multiple movies. This Shared Library feature can be used when the movie is playing back through a browser to make library assets available at run time.

Shared Libraries can also be used at author time—to use a Macromedia term. For example, one logo can be shared across multiple movies on the site. These shared assets can allow the team to update or replace any symbol in a movie with any other asset on the network. For example, you could change the color of a logo in a Shared Library. When that is complete, the symbol keeps its name and properties but the symbol change is reflected in all of the movies using the symbol.

If you do use this technique, consider placing all the common assets in an empty Flash movie that consists of nothing more than the assets being shared.

Updating or Replacing Shared Symbols

Web development is never static. Items are constantly changing or being removed. To update or replace shared symbols, follow these steps:

1. Open a Flash MX movie that contains the symbol you want. Select the symbol in the Library and then select Properties from the Library pop-down menu. The next steps link the symbol in the movie to the Library of another.

2. When the Library Properties dialog box opens, click the Browse button and then navigate to the movie containing the symbol. Click Open. A dialog box containing a list of the symbols in the movie you selected opens. Click the name of the symbol you want to link to and then click OK (see Figure 2.12).

3. You are returned to the Properties dialog box of the original movie. Choose Select Always Update Before Publishing, and click OK. By selecting the Always Update option, the symbol automatically updates if a new or changed version of the file is located in the source library.

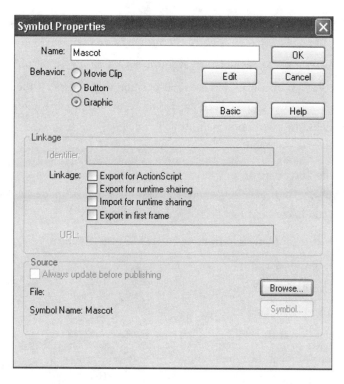

Figure 2.12   Sharing symbols in a library is a good way of automatically reflecting changes across all movies using that symbol.

Naming Conventions

With assets ranging from video to code coming together in a web site, it is absolutely critical that a file-naming convention be established and rigorously adhered to. What you need here is consistency because you can't always rely on icons to identify the file. For example, QuickTime plays many file types, ranging from sound to .swf's. Every now and then, the computer will toss off a blank icon as it somehow loses its association with the file. If the file is named Buzz and there is no application icon, you will not know if it is a sound, a graphic, or a .swf.

Again, there are no formal rules here. Use what best works for you and adhere to it. If you are looking for a system, here are some rough guidelines. When naming web sites, consider the following list:

- Use lowercase lettering for all names, and add the four-letter file extension to the name, such as pageone.html.
- Always name the index page either index.html, index.cfm, or index.jsp.

- If you have both an index page and a home page, name the home page home.htm.

- If a frameset is used, use filename_set.html, such as home_set.html.

- The parts of a frameset should use their position in the name. If the home page is broken into three frames, each one would be named home_top.html, home_right.html, and home_left.html.

Common File Extensions

Files should always indicate their source. Occasionally, the icon disappears and the extension lets you know what type of file you are looking at.

- html: Use the four letters to indicate an HTML page, not htm.

- cfm: ColdFusion script.

- css: Cascading Style Sheet.

- jsp: Java Server Page script.

- asp: Active Server Page.

- pdf: Adobe Acrobat document.

- swf: Flash MX movie.

- gif: Gif image.

- png: PNG image.

- txt: Plain text file.

- mp3: MP3 audio file.

- rm: Real media file.

- mov: QuickTime movie.

- avi: Windows Media file.

Image-Naming Conventions

Many images, such as buttons, require at least three separate files—Up, Over, and Down—to work. Others should be named according to function.

- btn_name.gif: A non-rollover button.

- btn_name_up.gif: Up state of a rollover button.

- btn_name_over.gif: Over state of a rollover button.

- btn_name_down.gif: Down state of a rollover button.
- logo_name.gif: Logo. If multiple sizes are used, add the size after the name.
- icon_name. png: Icons, custom or standard, used throughout the site.

Directory Conventions

Name folders in such a way that they clearly indicate the section of the site they represent. A file named Shoes doesn't work. A file named JCTSportShoes is much clearer and more identifiable.

If you have an Assets folder, create subdirectories for each grouping. For example, use the names Assets/Images/Employees. If you don't have an Assets folder, place the images folder off of the main directory, and group them in a rational manner, such as /images/shoephotos/images/icons.

Use naming conventions that make sense to everyone involved. For example use Home or Index instead of Main.

Version Control

Change is always guaranteed. The client wants the background taken out of a photo; then he wants the image cleaned up, and so on. All the while, that same image is moving into the site for review, back into Fireworks MX for more work, and then back into the site. It can get quite confusing.

Again, there are no rules regarding how to track versions of pages, images, and so on. Some shops use a numbering convention as they move through the process. For example, the original JCT logo is named logo_JCT_small_1.png. If a change is made, it is renamed logo_JCT_small_2.png. Others will retain the original name but make a copy of the file for offsite storage named logo_JCT_small_1.png. The reason is simple: You will eventually encounter a situation where you present the fourth iteration of the logo and, after review, it is decided the second iteration is the one to be used. By keeping the various versions handy, the change can be made relatively quickly. After the project is completed, all of the iterations can be discarded.

Another technique is one used by one of the authors. In short, when it comes to web page files, before he makes any changes to a page, he makes a copy of it and then adds a date to the end of it. If the file is named tom_and_jord.htm, tom_and_jord.htm is copied into into a backup folder and re-named tom_and_jord_3_20_02.htm. In this way he knows exactly when the last modification took place.

This might seem odd but he got into this habit when he was a print production designer for a local newspaper designing those car ads. Car ads take a long time to build, and dealerships like to use virtually the exact same layout but change the cars and prices. To contend with this situation, he started saving his files in this manner.

This also had another unexpected benefit. As you know, car dealerships love to have sales during certain holidays. By tagging the file with an actual date (as opposed to the date generated by the computer), he could easily pull up the St. Patrick's Day ad by searching for a March 17 (or close to it) date.

This technique doesn't have the same kind of benefits when it comes to web design, but if there is ever a dispute about when the last change occurred, he has the file tagged with the modification date.

Summary

Content management protocols and procedures are absolutely critical to the process of web design. As you have seen, the MX Studio contains a number of management tools that aid workflow, but there are also a number of items around naming and versioning that have to be put in place and rigorously enforced.

This chapter discussed how to set up a site in Dreamweaver MX, and how to create the local and remote sites, where you will be working, and where content will reside. You learned how the Notes Feature of Dreamweaver MX and Fireworks MX can aid the process, especially when it comes to versioning, and how those Notes can become a management tool through the production of Reports through Dreamweaver.

This chapter also covered access to files and explained how to implement Dreamweaver MX's Check In/Check Out feature along with the new Cloaking feature. By implementing these two features, you can control who has access to what files.

This chapter also explained how Dreamweaver MX's Asset panel can be a huge aid in the management of site-wide assets. There was also an explanation of Flash MX's powerful Shared Library feature and how it, too, can be used in the production process at author time.

Finally, you learned naming and versioning protocols. Though there are no standard methods for these two subjects, you learned ideas that you can quickly and easily implement into your workflow protocols.

As you can see, asset management is an important aspect of the design workflow process. Equally important is the communications process. The next chapter shows how to create a staging site in Dreamweaver and the creation of a project site in SiteSpring. Whichever method you choose, it can be that all-important determining factor in keeping the communications between team members, or between the client and the company, clear, concise, and focused. If you don't have those, you are heading for an unpleasant experience.

Chapter 3

Communicating Through Sitespring or a Client Site

At its heart, the web is a communications medium. Web pages communicate with the viewer, and in certain instances, the viewer can communicate with the page.

An important aspect of the process of developing web sites is communication. In the previous chapter we dealt with how a variety of management tools and features of Dreamweaver MX and Fireworks MX are used to manage content.

This chapter deals with how to manage communication. Communication can include how the members of the team communicate with each other, how the client communicates with the project leader, or how the client communicates their approvals to proceed to the next step of the development process.

The primary vehicles are a site you build where the client can view the progress of the project and communicate with the team. The other is a new product from Macromedia—Sitespring—that encompasses a rather complete set of client, project, and team management tools. Though Macromedia will not be updating the product in the near future, both Fireworks MX and Dreamewaver MX contain direct links to Sitespring. In Fireworks MX select Window, Sitepring. In Dreamweaver MX select Window, Others, Sitesping or press the F7 key. These links are invaluable and, as you start to use them on a regular basis, Sitespring will become an invaluable managent tool.

Using Sitespring for Workflow and Client Management

Sitespring is a typical Macromedia product, loaded with features that meet the needs of the company's clients. These features range from work group collaboration tools geared toward today's team-based approach to web development, to communications tools that lay down that all-important paper trail between the developer and the client as they move through the process of meeting the client's needs.

They key to Sitespring is recognizing the most important feature of the application isn't built into the software. The feature is *collaboration*. This tool enables everyone—from the web design shop's pixel monkey to the client who pays the bills—to work together to achieve a project's communications goals.

Your first exposure to this product, especially if you are a small company, might suggest that this tool is too complex for your workflow or client management needs. That would be a big mistake. The authors of this book are spread out across North America. Two of us live in Canada, and the other in the U.S. After we became comfortable with Sitespring, we quickly discovered how easy it was to manage all aspects of producing this book—from simple communication, to trading and commenting on manuscripts and graphics. We developed that important paper trail that allowed us to review each other's work far more quickly and efficiently than if were we to follow the typical workflow of swapping emails and so on.

To accomplish this type of communications management, we needed a tool that:

- Offered clear lines of communication
- Provided an easily accessible location for file storage for graphics and copy
- Supplied version control of each element of this project
- Gave us a focus point that was easily accessible to all of us so we could communicate with each other

Macromedia's Sitespring fit the bill for us. Take a close look at this application, and see if it's right for you and your company.

A Brief Tour of Sitespring

The beauty of Sitespring is that it is a web-based application. This means no proprietary software is necessary for the team and the client to start using the application. All they need is a 4.0 or higher browser with a JavaScript capability, Cascading Style Sheets support, and the Flash 5 plug-in.

There is also a small side application—Sitespring Helper—that allows the visitor to enter the Sitespring project site using a browser, and select and open files from within Sitespring. This application is downloaded to the user's computer the first time they attempt to open a file from within the application.

After logging into Sitespring, the interface appears on screen as shown in Figure 3.1.

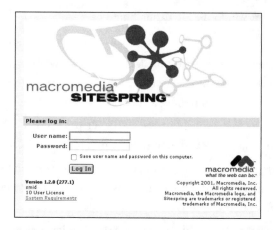

Figure 3.1 The log in page for Sitespring. The site administrator assigns the user name and the password.

Viewing the Sitespring Home Page

After you gain access to the site, you arrive on the home page, shown in Figure 3.2. At first glance it could be seen as quite confusing. In actual fact, it is quite simple to understand because the page is essentially divided into two parts—the toolbar and the modules.

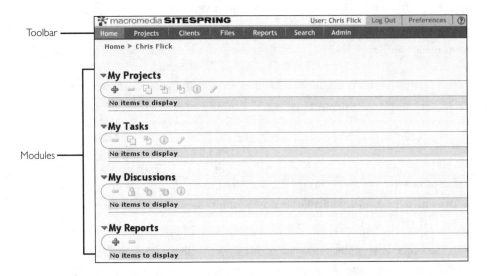

Figure 3.2   The Sitespring home page shows all the application's various choices.

The toolbar sits across the top of the page, and is used to navigate throughout a Sitespring site. The buttons on the toolbar are intuitive, and include the following:

- **Home**—Returns you to the Sitespring home page.

- **Projects**—Lists all the projects the team currently has under way.

- **Clients**—Presents you with a list of all the clients for whom you are working. This is a robust area because you can add clients, modify their information, view their information, or even remove a client.

- **Files**—Click here to open the File page. The File page shows a file tree in which you can open project files and even publish files to the project site.

- **Reports**—Opens the Create Report page. From there, you can build custom reports that can be shared with the team as well as the client. Reports can be saved and run again.

- **Search**—Projects in this business can get very complex very quickly. The Search area enables you to locate a file based on a keyword and an extensive range of search options, more commonly found on many of the web's search engines, are available to you to do more specific searches through the site.

- **Admin**—If you have been assigned Administrator or Project Manager permissions when the project was set up in Sitespring, you will see this button. Members of the team assigned User status will not see this. Click this button to go to the Admin screen where you can do everything from assign or delete team members to reassign passwords.

The name of the current user as well as a Help button, which looks like a circled question mark, which launches an online Help screen, is located under the toolbar. Under the bar is another navigation tool that Macromedia calls *breadcrumbs*. This tool operates in much the same manner as a traditional file path, only an arrow is used as a separator instead of a backslash. Each item between the arrows is a breadcrumb. In this interface, clicking one of the breadcrumbs to go backward is actually more efficient than using the browser's Back button because clicking the browser's Back button usually results in you going back to Sitespring's main page.

Sitespring Modules

The heart and soul of Sitespring are composed of the modules. They are My Projects, My Tasks, My Discussions, and My Reports. A module follows workflow, but only shows users the information to which they have been granted access. For example, discussions can be set up in such a way that the client can participate only when their direct role in the process is affected.

Navigating around the modules is simple and intuitive. Click the arrow beside the module name to expand or collapse the module. If you click the check box beside the module name, all the items in the module are selected.

Clicking the check box beside an item in a module selects that item; clicking the item hyperlink opens or goes to the area referenced by the link; and clicking any of the column headers sorts the items in ascending or descending order.

A module can display up to 10 items. If there are more than 10, a page number hyperlink appears in the bottom-left corner of the module. Click the number to go to the rest of the items in the module.

Setting the Rules with Sitespring

The first step in making Sitespring work for you is undertaken by the Sitespring administrator. The administrator is the individual charged with setting the rules for who has access to the site, what those users can do, and what they can't do. The administrator is also responsible for the installation and maintenance on the server.

One of the first rules that needs to be set is who has access to the site. The site administrator, who registers on the site with his own user name and password, undertakes this procedure. The only difference between the administrator and the others is that the administrator has an Admin link on the Sitespring home page.

The Administration options, as shown in Figure 3.3, allows the site administrator to manage who sees what, but also manages how projects and tasks are added. As well, the administrator sets up the notification schemes, email, and other system items related to Sitespring.

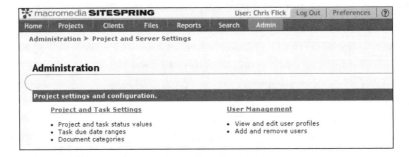

Figure 3.3   The Sitespring Administration page is accessible only to the site administrator and the Project Manager.

Adding a New User

One of the tasks assigned to the administrator is adding new users to the Sitespring site. Building the list of users or adding to the team is a simple task. To add a new user, follow these steps:

1. Click the Admin link on the home page to open the Administration page; then click the User Management link on the Administration page to open the User Management list.

2. Click the + sign on the User Management button bar, as shown in Figure 3.4, to add a new user. The page is broken into two areas. The top of the page is the typical contact information. The bottom half is where the user's name and password are set to grant the new user access to the Sitespring site. Enter the user name that the new user will enter when logging onto the site. Enter the user's real name. Assign a password to the user and confirm the password.

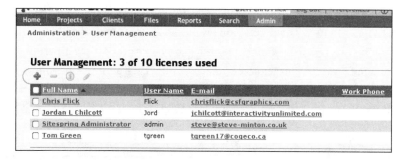

Figure 3.4   The User Management page of Sitespring enables you to add new users.

3. The boxes with asterisks have to be completed. The others are optional. It is extremely important that each user be made aware that both the user name and password are case sensitive, as shown in Figure 3.5, and must be entered exactly as entered in this area. If not, the user will be the recipient of a number of login errors when trying to access the site. Also, when you enter the password, it shows as a number of stars. If the entries for the password assigned and the password confirmation are not exact, Sitespring will toss up an error message.

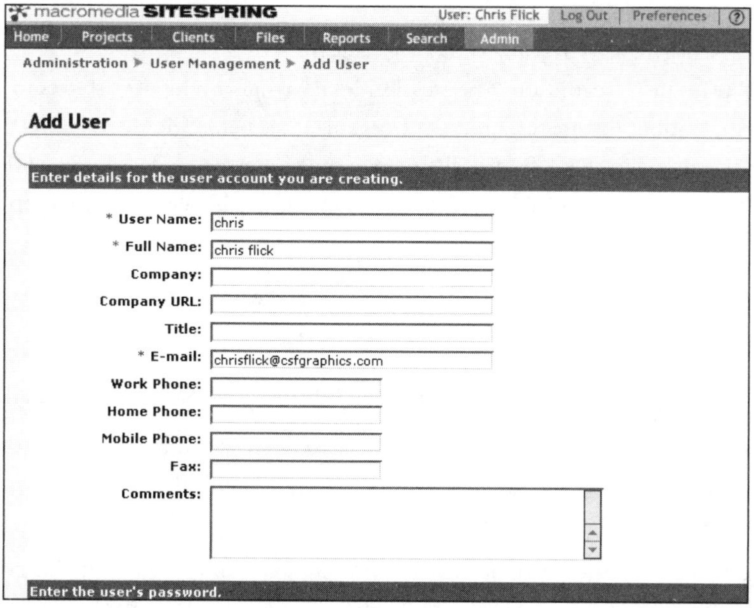

Figure 3.5   The Add User dialog box shows the user information and password for site access.

4. To allow access to the files, the administrator must select one of two permission levels for each user. The permission level is what limits the access to various parts of the site, such as the Administration page. The Project Manager permission allows the Project Manager access to everything. User permissions simply permit the user to view the various aspects of the Sitespring site as well as add, modify, and delete tasks. Having set the permissions, click the Save button.

Adding a Corporate Hierarchy

The importance of the permission levels of Sitespring can't be understated. There have to be clear lines of responsibility, authority, and communication between the team members as well as between the team and the client. Though a formal hierarchical management structure is a bit of an anathema in this industry, a flat management structure when it comes to project execution, is a guaranteed recipe for failure. The site administrator and the Project Manager should sit at the top of the pyramid. Everyone else should have user permissions.

For complex projects, it is common to assign a project management role to an individual who is responsible for the completion of an area of the site. After the scope of the project is nailed down and the team members are determined or roles defined, it's a good idea to pull out a sheet of paper and create a simple organization chart.

Creating and Modifying a Sitespring Client

With the team in place and their permission levels assigned, the next step is to create a client organization. By creating the client organization before doing anything else, you are able to select the client from a list when you create the project in Sitespring. The client information is simple to access. Should something change, such as a client's URL, there is one place to make the change and have it reflect across the whole Sitespring site.

Sitespring is a web-based product, meaning that the creation of a client organization is the creation of an index or home page for the project site.

To create a client organization in Sitespring, follow these steps:

1. Click Clients on the Sitespring home page to open the Client Organization page; then click the Add icon to open the Add Client Organization page, as seen in Figure 3.6.

2. Add the client information, such as name, address, and so on, in the text boxes. When you have completed the information, click Save. The client organization's name appears on the Sitespring home page.

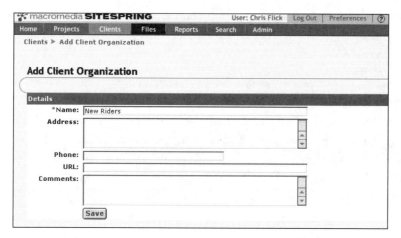

Figure 3.6   Setting up a Client Organization in Sitespring. The Text input area with an asterisk has to be completed. The remaining areas are optional or can be filled out later.

If the client information changes at any time, it can be easily changed to reflect the new status. Click Clients on the Sitespring home page to open the Client Organization page, and click the check box beside the client whose information needs to be changed. Click the Edit icon, make the change, and click Save.

Clients can also be deleted from Sitespring. Again, click Clients on the Sitespring home page to open the Client Organization page, select the check box beside the client to be deleted, click the Delete icon, and click the Delete button.

Caution

Be careful when deleting clients. Although deleting a client does cut down on information overload—and there is a certain perverse satisfaction gained from selecting a problem client and clicking the Delete button, there can be a problem with deleting a client before deleting a project. This tends to turn the project into an orphan: The Sitespring site will not have a client, and may lose all functionality. Don't delete a client until after you complete the associated projects.

Setting Up and Using the My Projects Module

Having set up the client site, the tasks for the various team members can now be assigned. In Sitespring a project holds all the information relating to the development of a site. This information is defined by the company building the web site for its client and can include all the information relating to one site or, for complex projects, the information can be broken down into manageable chunks. The information can include tasks, discussions, team, and other modules. If the JCT site were to be large, we could set up projects for each of the products, such as hats, jeans, shoes, and so on.

The best way to manage complexity is from a position of simplicity, and it is the prudent Project Manager who is able to break a complex project into a series of small, manageable projects in Sitespring.

The Project Manager naturally assigns the various levels of responsibility as well as information access in Sitespring. In this manner only the team members with the Project Manager designation can create and modify projects. Though a number of individuals can have this level of access, it makes sense to have as few people as possible with these responsibilities. A Sitespring project is also multi-dimensional. The basic unit of a project is a task with one team member assigned its completion. Many web developers believe in the axiom of creating complexity from simplicity. If a complex project is broken down into a logical progression of small, easily completed tasks, it only makes sense to assume the completion of the last task results in the completion of the project.

To add a project in Sitespring, follow these steps:

1. With the Sitespring home page open, click the My Projects button on the Sitespring toolbar. Click the Add (+) button to open the Add Project page, as shown in Figure 3.7

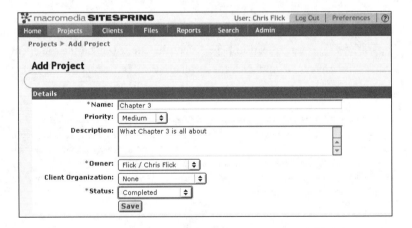

Figure 3.7   Setting up the projects in the Sitespring Add Project page is restricted to administrators or project managers.

2. In the corresponding text boxes, you can name the project, assign a priority to it from the Priority pop-down menu, and add a project description.

3. Choose an owner from the Owner pop-down menu. The owner name is that of the Project Manager. Choose the client organization from the pop-down menu, and select a project status from the Status pop-down menu.

4. Click the Save button. Having defined the project, the next step is to assign members of the team to the project. This, again, is done through the My Projects module.

5. Open the My Projects module, and click the project's hyperlink to open the Project page. Click the + sign under the Team area to open a list of registered users in a page named Add Team Members. Click the check box beside the team members you need to add.

6. Click the word Add at the top of the page to return to the Project page. The names chosen appear in the team area.

Now that you have assigned the team, a folder for file storage is created. Click the + sign in the Folders section of the page, and navigate to the folder on the server where the files will be stored. Click the check box beside the folder name to be used for storage purposes. Click the check mark at the top of the page. You are returned to the site, and the folder appears in the Folders area.

The Discussion Module

Clear lines of communication are critical in the development process. Though most communication in the development of web sites is traditionally done in either face-to-face meetings or through email, Sitespring adds the dimension of the threaded discussion to the process. In simple terms, a threaded discussion is a listing of all the posts and replies pertaining to a given topic. The Sitespring Discussions module, if used properly, can be a lifesaver.

Imagine that Jack has been asked to repair an image. He replies that he is too busy, and hands the task, via email, to his associate, Marty. Marty reviews the email but doesn't understand the nature of the request. Marty gets side tracked and forgets to reply to Jack's email. A couple of days later, the image still hasn't been repaired, and Jack asks Marty for the status of the image. Marty has a blank look on his face and asks Jack, "Didn't you get my email?" You can see where this discussion is going.

By threading the conversations, a virtual paper trail is laid down, and everyone with access to the discussion is able to participate.

In Sitespring, there are actually two forms of discussions that can take place. One form is strictly between the members of the team. In some respects, these are private discussions, and are usually internal communications between team members as they cope with issues, deadlines, trade ideas, and techniques.

The other type of communication—the public form—occurs only when the thread is published to the site. In this instance, anyone with the appropriate privileges—including the client—can participate. The Discussions module is the place where a client can review the work and then make suggestions or changes.

For example, the client reviews a page and suggests some rather significant changes. These changes are negotiated through the Sitespring discussion, and the client gives approval to proceed. Four months later, those changes are reflected in an invoice, but the client questions the added charge, claiming they were never authorized. (Sound familiar?) The Project Manager can simply refer the client to the threaded discussion regarding the change and the permission to proceed. In this instance, Sitespring just paid for itself.

The interface for the Discussion module is simple to use, and includes the following options:

- **Topic**—The summary of the discussion taken from the subject line in the first post of the discussion.
- **Owner**—The name of the individual who started the discussion.
- **Posts**—A listing of how many messages are included in the discussion.
- **Latest Post**—The date and time of the most recent addition to the thread.
- **Status**—Of the two possible options, open discussions are continuing; closed discussions have ended.
- **Published**—Indicates whether the discussion has been posted to the project site.

To start a discussion, open the My Discussions module on the project site, and click the + sign to add to the discussion. The Add Discussion page, shown in Figure 3.8, opens. Enter a topic, a message, and click Save. The discussion is added to the list, and anyone with the appropriate privileges will receive an email notifying them of the new discussion.

The icons on the Discussion button bar are also useful. These include the following:

- **+ (Add) or – (Delete) icon**—Adds or removes a discussion.
- **Padlock**—Closes a discussion.
- **Globe with + sign**—Posts the discussion to the project site.
- **The Globe with – sign**—Removes the discussion from the project site.
- **i button**—Opens the Help feature.

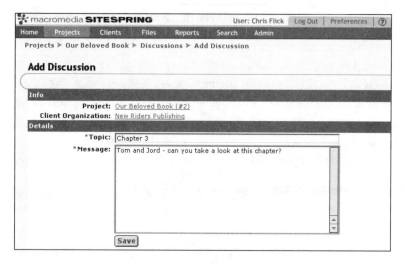

Figure 3.8   Adding a discussion in the Add Discussion page of Sitespring.

Keep a close eye on the Discussion button bar. If you are on the Sitespring home page, the + icon is not available. Click a project, and the icon becomes visible. This tells you that discussions can be deleted from the home page, but can't be initiated here. The other item to be aware of is the check box. If you click the check box beside the Topic option, all discussions are selected. Clicking the – icon on the button bar deletes all the discussions.

Starting a Discussion, and Participating in the Treaded Discussion

To initiate a discussion, open a project in the user's main page and then click the Add icon under My Discussions. Enter a subject header in the Subject field, and type your message. Click Save.

To reply to a message or add to a threaded discussion, open the My Discussions module from the Project site, click the name of the recipient of the message and then click the Post Reply button.

Tip

Not all discussions have to be public. You can send a personal email to anyone involved in the discussion by clicking the name shown in the Posted By line. This opens your default email application with the recipient's address appearing in the To area of the email.

Sitespring and the Communications Process

As discussed earlier, Sitespring adds a whole new dimension to communications between the client and the team, as well as among the team members. The Sitespring application can be used by the development team as a central communications vehicle as well as for those all-important communications between the client and the developer. The ability to communicate through Sitespring usually starts with the creation of a project site in Sitespring.

A project site is a web site created for communication between members of the team, as well as those appointed by the client as being responsible for the project. This site is not the same as a regular Sitespring site. It is a separate communications vehicle designed to allow the client to monitor the progress of the project. Through this site, the client can approve or reject ideas, suggest changes, and generally communicate with the team.

There are some rules regarding project sites of which you should be aware. These rules include the following:

- Each project site is linked to a specific project. For example, if a client has the team working on a site for a sales campaign and another team working on a new product, the campaign and the product projects would be linked to specific project sites. In this way confusion is avoided. This is a good method of breaking a complex site into a series of manageable projects.

- A project can be created without a linked project site, but a project site cannot be created without a linked project. This makes sense. A project site is a communications vehicle. When a project is created, it is given a name and parameters in the Project module. When the assets are created and ready to be approved by the client, the project site can be used for this purpose.

- Project sites can be used to share information with the client, such as scheduling, task status, discussions, and so on. They are also used to show the client any work that is in progress.

Creating a Project Site

The first step in creating a client project is to add client organization. In Sitespring, a client organization is the corporate information for your client that includes the name of the company, the address, and other contact information. After the client is identified, the information regarding the client's Project Manager or representative is added. This is one area of Sitespring that could use a name change. Your client's representative is called a Client User. There can be any number of Client Users, but it would be a good idea to keep the number relatively small to prevent confusion later down the road. The information required here ranges from the person's name to their fax number. After this information is entered, the individual is then assigned a password to permit access to the project site.

For example, if we were to create a site for the authors of this book, our Client Organization would be for a mythical company, possibly named Three Lost Souls. The users would be Tom, Jordan, and Chris. After all the information is entered, an internal database is created so that if Jordan's information changes, or Three Lost Souls moves to a new address in mid-project, the new information only has to be a changed in one place.

To create a project site, follow these step:

1. Click the Clients button in the Sitespring toolbar to open the Client Organizations page. To add a client simply, click the + button to open the Add Client Organization page, shown in Figure 3.9.

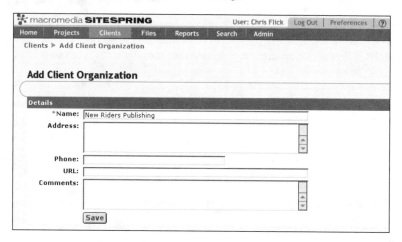

Figure 3.9   The first step in creating a project site is to identify the company for whom you are working.

2. Enter the organization name in the Name text box; then enter the address, phone number, and company URL in the appropriate input areas. If there are any comments you would like to enter, add them in the Comments text box.

3. Click the Save button to save the information you entered and be taken to a Confirmation page.

The users are created from the Client Organization page. (This is the company that employs the client users.) When the Client Organization page opens, click Add User to open the Add Client User page, shown in Figure 3.10. Add their names, addresses, and phone numbers in the appropriate areas. This is also where the login and password privileges are assigned. When finished, click OK.

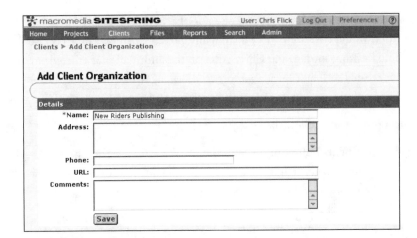

Figure 3.10   The Add Client User page can help keep the number of client users to a manageable level.

Creating a Project Site

Having identified your clients and their company, you can now create the project site through which you can communicate with your clients and they with you. To create a project site, follow these steps:

1. Open the My Projects module and then click the Create hyperlink to open the Create Project Site page. Review the project information and make any changes, if necessary.

2. You can now select a design template from the Design Template pop-down menu. These templates are web pages that can be used to add an element of design to the project site. Teton is shown in Figure 3.11.

3. In the Create Project Site page, you are also asked to specify the path to the site folder. In the Project Path text box, enter the name of the folder that will be used as both the project folder and the site URL, as shown in Figure 3.12. Click Save, and the path to that folder is now established site wide. After a template is chosen, all members of the project and the client's team who are authorized to access the site will be able to start communicating with each other.

4. Having created the project site, you can now determine who, from the project users list, has access to the site and what modules they are able to view. To enable these permissions, click the Details hyperlink in the project site name to open the Project Site (Details) page.

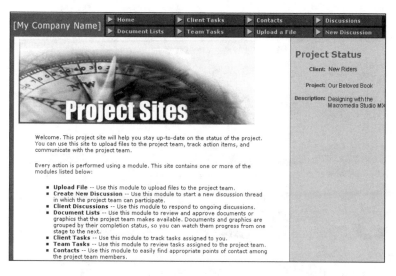

Figure 3.11   The project site created for this book used the Teton template.

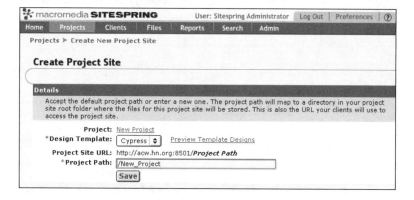

Figure 3.12   The Create Project Site page allows you to choose a site template.

5. When the Details page opens, click the Grant Project Site Permission icon on the Permitted Client Users module. To add a user to the site click the + sign in the Grant Permission to View Project Site module, as shown in Figure 3.13. Click the check box next to each client you want to add.

6. To add a client, click the hyperlink under the name of the users listed and then enter the necessary information, including a password as shown in Figure 3.14.

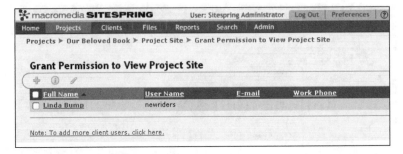

Figure 3.13   A new user now has access to the project site.

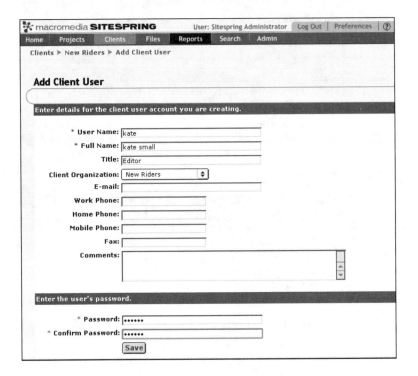

Figure 3.14   Kate Small was added to the list of authorized users.

7. When you have finished, click the Save button. The new user appears on the project site as shown in Figure 3.15.

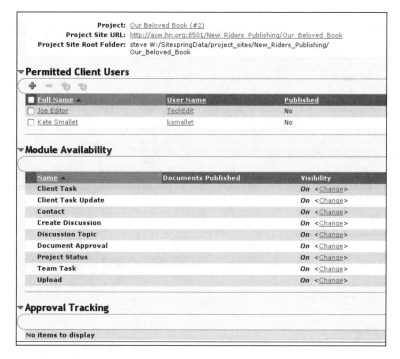

Figure 3.15   The project site window showing the site details and the client users with access to the site.

To remove a client user click the check box beside their name and then click the minus sign. Click Remove when prompted.

Selecting Modules for the Project Site

Sometimes all the modules available for viewing aren't necessary. If, for example, the client has no tasks to perform, the Client Task module is not necessary. Sitespring enables you to show only the modules you will use. This is useful because the application's default, as shown in Figure 3.16, shows them all.

In the My Projects area of the project site, click the Details hyperlink to open the project site. When the site opens, scroll down to the Module Availability module and then click the Change hyperlink in the Visibility section. The page refreshes, and the modules that are unavailable show their status as Off.

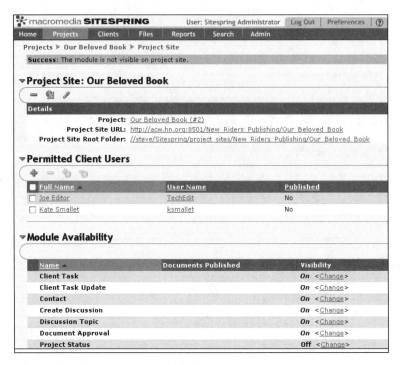

Figure 3.16   The project site showing details, users, and visibility.

Adding Document Categories

Document categories, according to the Macromedia documentation, are groups of files published to a project site. This definition is a bit vague.

To publish any document to the project site and have it available for viewing, as shown in Figure 3.17, the document must fall into a series of categories that can only be set by the Project Manager or site administrator. Any document that doesn't meet the category criteria will not be published to the project site. These criteria appear as their own modules on the project site.

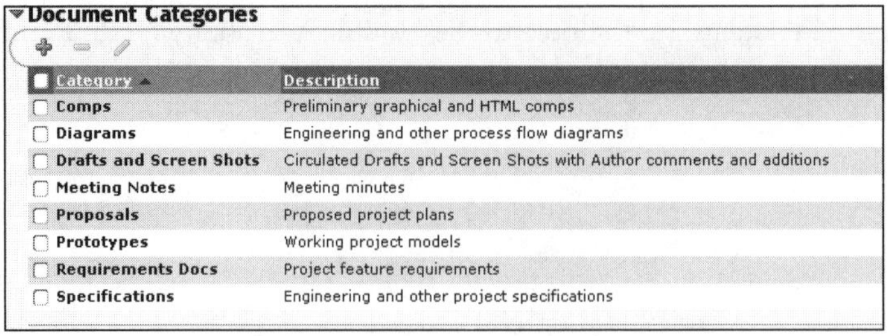

Figure 3.17   The project site before the document categories are set.

If you have administrative privileges, click Admin on the Main toolbar at the top of the site page and then click the Project and Task hyperlink to open the Status Values page. Click the + icon to open the Add Document Category page, as shown in Figure 3.18.

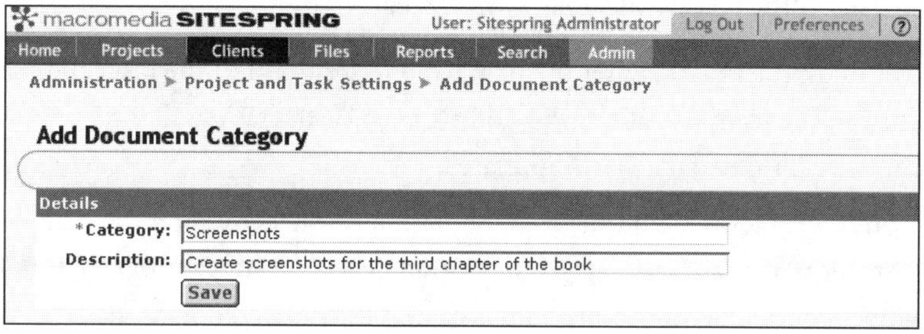

Figure 3.18   A document category is added by the administrator.

Enter a name and a description of the category in the corresponding text boxes. If the information is correct, click Save and your changes are reflected in the Document Categories module as shown in Figure 3.19.

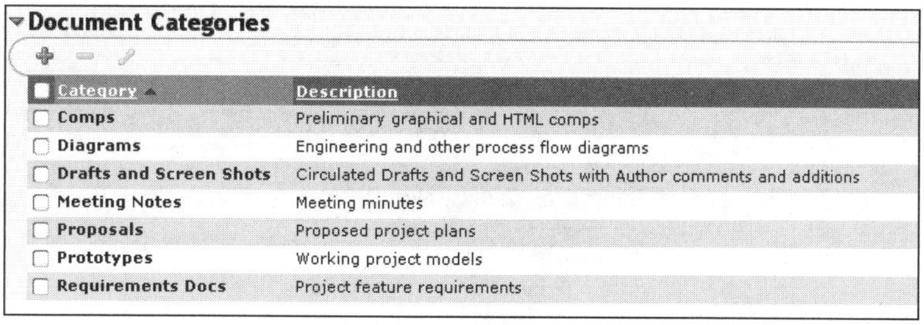

Figure 3.19   Drafts and Screen Shots has been added to the Document Categories.

Adding Your Team Members

Having pulled the project site together, you now have to add the names of the members of the team who will be working on the project.

To add team members to the project site, follow these steps:

1. Click the Add button under the Team module and then click the check box beside each team member you want to add. Deselecting a check box removes the team member.

2. Click the Add button. When the button is clicked, all team members receive an email letting them know that they are on that particular team along with URLs and instructions.

Assigning Tasks to Team Members

With the team in place, they need to have their duties assigned to them. Here's how to assign tasks in the project site.

To assign tasks in the project site, follow these steps:

1. Click Add under tasks. Enter the name and description of the task, and assign it to one of the team members. Provide a status for the task and, if there is a deadline, enter it in the Due Date input area.

2. If you have an estimated time for completion of the task, enter the date. The completion of a task is a part of the overall deadline. For example, if Tom is assigned a deadline to complete the imaging for the site, one of the tasks leading up to that deadline would be the completion of the color corrections. If your team member has a URL, enter the address. Click Save, and the task is assigned to the team member. A sample task window is shown in Figure 3.20.

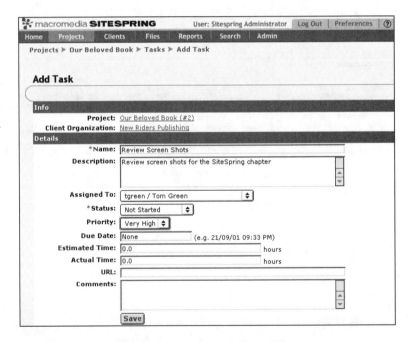

Figure 3.20   Tasks and deadlines are assigned to members of the team.

After you click Save, Sitespring automatically emails the team member with the assigned task. Another thing it does is notify team members with open tasks that their work is almost due.

Keep in mind that any uploaded content pertaining to the task can be linked to the task by clicking the add sign in the Linked Content section. Choose your content to link by clicking the check box beside the filename. You can even add discussion threads by clicking the + under Discussions to add a new thread. When completed, team members and clients are notified of the discussion. Replies can be posted by clicking the Post Reply link within the discussion thread.

Setting Up a Client Site in Dreamweaver MX

Though Sitespring can be regarded as an all-in-one package, you can also build a client site in Dreamweaver MX to perform many of the same tasks as those shown in Sitespring. Just as with Sitespring, a client site built in Dreamweaver MX can be regarded as Communications Central—a place where the team and the client can interact with each other. If you are setting up a client site through Dreamweaver MX, consider dividing the site into areas for the client and the team—and, of course, password protect the client site. In this way, the team can interact with each other, but you can control, on the client side, who talks to the client. When set up properly, signals don't get crossed and the communications lines are tightly controlled.

When you decide that a client site is necessary, there are some features that should be incorporated.

- Consider security. The last thing you need is for the client's work to be available to the world before the project is completed. Password protection to permit only authorized viewers to see the site—to prevent leaks and protect the confidentiality of the clients' information—is highly important.

- Ensure that all communications remain on the site. The threads built into Sitespring are there for a reason, and this capability should be incorporated in the site you build in Dreamweaver MX. Emails or instant messaging should be your absolute last choice.

- All members of the team should have access to everyone else's contact information. In the case of contract workers, this should include phone numbers as well as email addresses. On the client side, contact information regarding the project management team is all that is needed.

- Build in a critical path capability or some other scheduling capability that is common to both the client and the team. The Dreamweaver MX Calendar extension discussed in Chapter 2, "Content Management," is a good starting place.

- Ensure there is the capability to make important project documents available to the team and to the client.
- Make certain of the ability to present work to the client.

Explaining in great detail how to build a client site in Dreamweaver MX would be counter productive at this point because client sites are typically designed by the developer, and no two sites are the same. For example, Kelly Goto in her New Riders book, *Web Redesign: Workflow that Works*, uses a rather simple design for a client site; however, Todd Purgason in his New Riders book, *Flash deConstruction*, demonstrates an extremely complex client site. Both work, and both meet the needs of their company.

So rather than explaining how to build a client site, we now deal with two issues common to client sites.

The first issue is how to handle images that are under construction. Dreamweaver MX has a clever feature that enables you to build the pages with image placeholders. When the images are finished in Fireworks MX, they can be automatically posted to the client site for review.

The second issue is security. We show how to limit site access to the client site built in Dreamweaver MX.

Creating a New Fireworks MX File from a Dreamweaver MX Placeholder

Images that have yet to be created or are currently under construction in Fireworks MX should not hold you back from creating the pages in Dreamweaver MX and then linking them to the client site. This is accomplished by using placeholders in Dreamweaver MX.

1. Open the Dreamweaver MX page that will contain the image. Select Insert, Image Placeholder to open the Image Placeholder dialog box, shown in Figure 3.22. Name the placeholder, set its size, and add an alternate text description, such as **To Macromedia**. Click OK to display a gray box with the name and size on the Dreamweaver MX page.

Tip

If you click and drag on a corner handle of the placeholder in Dreamweaver MX, the image size you set in the Image Placeholder dialog box updates and the exact numbers are shown inside the placeholder. The updated size communicates itself to Fireworks when it is launched.

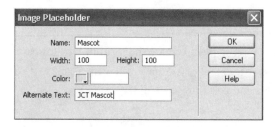

Figure 3.22   To add an image placeholder in Dreamweaver MX, give it a name, size, and
alternate text that appears when the cursor is over the image in the browser.

2. To add the image to the placeholder in Dreamweaver MX, you have three choices.
   You can right-click (PC) or Control-click (Mac) the placeholder and then select
   Create Image in Fireworks from the context menu. You can also press the Ctrl
   (PC) or Command (Mac) key and then double-click the placeholder, or you can
   select the placeholder and click the Create button in the Dreamweaver MX
   Property inspector. Each method launches Fireworks MX and opens a new docu-
   ment to the size specified in the placeholder.

3. When you finish the image in Fireworks MX, click the Done button at the top of
   the image to return to the Dreamweaver MX page. When you return to
   Dreamweaver MX, the image replaces the placeholder. If the page is available
   through a link in the client site, the image appears on the page.

If you want to edit the image, simply Ctrl-click (PC) or Command-click (Mac) the image
to launch the image in Fireworks MX. When you finish, click the Done button.

Limiting Access to Your Client Site

The suggestion to consider security was made for a good reason: In today's web development environment papered with non-disclosure agreements, confidentiality is
supreme. This section demonstrates how to restrict access by assigning user names and
passwords to the client site after it is built.

In Sitespring, this feature is built into the site, and is controlled by the site administrator
who assigns the user names and passwords. In Dreamweaver MX, the process is quite a
bit different.

Start with a database table of authorized users that contains the user names and passwords. It also would be a good idea to have fields for the individual's first and last names in the database. The next step is to create the form in Dreamweaver MX that asks for a user name and password. Finally, you have to create a Log In User server behavior to ensure that the name and password are valid.

Creating a Login Using Dreamweaver MX

Creating a log in is really not as complicated as it may first appear. Essentially, you open a new Dreamweaver MX page and then create a form. To do so, follow these steps:

1. Place the insertion point on the page where you want the form to appear, and select Insert, Form. If you don't see a red-dashed box indicating the Form area, select View, Visual Aids, Invisible Elements. The Property inspector changes to reflect the new object on the page.

2. Name the form in the Property inspector, and don't worry about filling in the Action and Method boxes. The Log In User behavior handles this.

3. Add two new text fields that allow the user to enter their user name and password. Select Insert, Form Objects, Text Field when the text fields are added to the Dreamweaver MX page label the fields in the Property inspector.

4. Add a Submit button by selecting Insert, Form Object, Button. A button appears on the page, and the text in the button will read Submit. If you want to change that text, select the button on the page and then change the label in the Property inspector. The text for buttons in Dreamweaver MX is changed by simply entering a new name for the button in the Label area of the Dreamweaver MX Property inspector.

Having created the form, you can now add the server behavior—Log In User—to ensure the text entered in the fields is correct.

1. Open the Applications panel, and select the Server Behaviors tab. Click the + button to add a behavior, and select User Authentication, Login User from the list in the User Authentication pop-down menu.

2. When the Login User dialog box opens, enter the requested information, or select it from the Login User pop-down menu.

3. In the Get Input from Form field, enter the name of the form from step 1 of this exercise. Be sure to enter paths for the successful and unsuccessful log in. The unsuccessful login could go to a page that says the Log In was unsuccessful, and prompt the visitor to click a button that goes back to the Login page. When you have finished, click OK.

Summary

The focus of this chapter was the communications process in today's collaborative web-production environment.

You have seen how Sitespring can become a powerful management and communications tool through its robust suite of project management and communications tools. In fact, Fireworks MX and Dreamweaver MX have direct hooks to Sitespring built into them. For Fireworks MX, select Window, Sitespring and for Dreamweaver MX , press F7 and you will be taken to the team's Sitespring project site.

We also discussed the creation of a client site built using Dreamweaver MX, as well as some of the features the site should contain. Recognizing that no two client sites are ever the same, we demonstrated a couple of techniques that allow you to post images to the client's site, and how to restrict access to the client site after it's completed.

We showed you how to create a Fireworks MX image using a Dreamweaver MX place-holder. We also showed a rather nifty Command or Ctrl key double-click combination to launch Fireworks MX from your Dreamweaver MX page.

Finally, we explained how to add the element of security to the client site by creating a Login page in Dreamweaver MX that uses server behaviors to check a database of authorized users and their passwords.

The next chapter deals with pulling your ideas together on paper, and modeling them in Dreamweaver MX.

Part II

Developing the Site Concept

Chapter 4

Testing Your Ideas with Site Models

The web design process starts with a developer sitting at his desk, sketching out ideas on a blank sheet of paper, and working out how the navigation elements will work as well as where they will be placed.

This blank sheet of paper might be used to draw a series of squares showing the flow from page to page. That same blank sheet of paper can be used to draw the design of each page or the placement areas for dynamic content.

This can seem to be a rather daunting task…and it is. Yet, in many respects, it will be the most valuable time you can invest in your project. This is the stage where you bring the numerous discussions, the briefings, and the time spent staring off into space or wandering around thinking about the project—to life.

Although we work in an environment where technology is king, it has absolutely no role in the planning process. In fact, you can't get more low tech in this business than a pencil and a sheet of paper. The planning stage of any project is where the site strategy is developed. This strategy isn't located on a few sectors of your hard drive, or included on the installation CD of Dreamweaver MX. It resides in your mind and comes to life only as you start to define and confront the goals for the task at hand.

Just as no two businesses are the same, there is no common web design strategy. There is also no one correct way of developing that strategy. Think of a web design strategy in terms of a trip from your home to the local mall. Your strategy for the trip is simple: Get there in as short a time as possible. This involves planning the most efficient route from your front door to the mall. If you have never been to the mall, this may require using a map or asking people in your neighborhood for directions. You then review the information, and plan the route. It is a time-consuming process.

There is what might appear to be a faster method. Simply jump in the car and drive in the general direction of the mall. If you get lost, you can always ask people on the street for directions. By the time you get to the mall, however, I will have already been there, made my purchases, and departed. The odds are very good you will arrive late (thanks to wrong directions from people on the street), not find what you were looking for, and repeat this entire process—in reverse—for the trip home.

The strategic planning process, therefore, is the same whether it is planning a trip to a mall or planning a web site. You gather information, set your goals, and execute the plan.

Done correctly, the strategy uncovers a straight path through the entire design process. A poorly designed strategy will leave you wandering aimlessly, making it up as you go along, and the final product will reflect this lack of direction. The first step after all the information has been gathered is to model your site. A well-developed site model starts with a storyboard that presents the initial designs—a site model that shows how a user navigates through the site to obtain the necessary information for the creation of a site map, which will focus the direction and thinking of both the team and the client.

Planning the JCT Site

The site that we build throughout this book is for a fictional company named JCT. The interesting thing about the site is that it follows a strategic plan. The process started with our need for a site that would demonstrate the principals of the web design process from concept to FTP upload to an ISP. Any web designer should be familiar with this process because the process always starts with a client contacting the developer and asking, "Do you design web sites?".

After the client retains the designer, the planning process starts.

Talk to anybody in sales and they will tell you the key to a successful sale is not a great-looking outfit, perfect teeth, or great jokes. The difference between success and failure is in taking the time before the presentation to do some very careful fact finding. When it comes to developing a web strategy for your client, the fact-finding process involves determining the answers to such questions as the following:

Who is the client's audience?   Obviously, the design strategy for an employee web site on a corporate intranet is going to be profoundly different from one developed to be the company's storefront on the web. The intranet has a very narrow audience, but the web's audience is extremely broad and must be accessible to anyone with a browser.

In the case of the JCT site, the audience will be somewhat broad. It will consist of teenagers and college students who are somewhat net savvy, and who can get to the mall. In this case, the audience, though broad, is similar to that of an intranet because it is, in the context of the web, a narrow market.

What does the client want to say?   Never forget that the web is a communications medium. Its original purpose was to allow scientists to trade information with each other. If you visit a site for an advertising agency, they are simply saying, "We really know our stuff." If you visit an online retailer, they are saying, "Buy what you need right here."

In the case of JCT, the client wants the kids to visit the store.

Does the client have a corporate design standard?   On the web, branding is becoming paramount. Visit the Nike site, and you see the "swoosh." Visit the Coca-Cola site, and you see "red." Visit Disney, and the stylized mouse ears are there. With larger, multinational corporations, it is quite common to encounter a corporate design standard that encompasses both print and the web. The same image the client projects to the market through brochures, print ads, and annual reports now has to appear on the web. In this way, the company is managing how it is viewed by the market. In the case of Nike, for example, that swoosh says to anyone seeing it, "This is Nike." Even then, by carefully managing the brand and the look, you could hit any page on the Nike site and know you are visiting Nike. Same goes for their apparel and the print material. They present a consistent image to the market.

In the case of JCT, brand identity will be through the use of the logo and the mascot.

What does the client need?   It is extremely important for you to listen carefully to the client, and be able to discern between what the client wants and what the client needs.

continues ▶

There is an acquaintance of ours who is currently being driven crazy by one of his web clients. He presented the client with a rather elegant site design solution. He has completed the design, and now the client, as he puts it, "is nickel-and-diming me with changes that are going to ruin my design." In this case, the designer and the client have lost sight of the original goal of the design—the need—and are now focusing on extraneous matters that run counter to the goal. In one case, it was the addition of lines to the design of a couple of pages.

You have a rather odd job. You not only have to develop and execute a design, but also spend a lot of time with your client not as a designer but as a teacher. In the case of this client, the designer should have patiently explained how those lines may ruin the fidelity of the design. Those lines, suddenly appearing, could be a source of confusion with the visitors and force them to leave. Then again, if the client makes it clear, as one did to us, "that I am paying for this, and if I want a thick line, I get a thick line," you have some decisions to make about the relationship.

It is a classic case of artistic integrity colliding with client demands. At this point, that delicate minuet we talked about earlier in the book becomes critical as the client and the designer negotiate the validity and rationale of the request. The best way of dealing with this is to put it in terms the client clearly understands: "Here is how much it will cost to meet the request."

The Storyboard

After the general plan is put into place, and you and the client are in agreement, it's time break out that sheet of paper and start sketching out your ideas. A storyboard can uncomplicate your life. We have seen storyboards that could be framed and hung in galleries, and others that were simple doodlings on the back of a paper placemat in a diner. The purpose of a storyboard is to give you and, ultimately, your client an idea of how the site will look and work.

The JCT site's objective is to give you a comprehensive overview of how the suite of Macromedia web tools work together. As such, we decided designing a four-page site would give us the chance to demonstrate our objective. This raised an obvious question: "How do the pages work together and what do they look like?"

It is important you answer the first part of that question before dealing with the second part. If you worry about how the pages will look before you concern yourself with how the user will move through the site, you are setting yourself up for potential problems. One of the buzzwords in the web community is *usability*. It's a ubiquitous term that can have any number of definitions. The common thread running through all of the definitions is a focus on the user, not the technology. In this case, you want to make it easy for users to get to the information they need. Thus, it is important to decide ahead of time what sort of navigation model will be used for the site before you start drawing the storyboards.

Navigation Models

Just as the human body is built upon the framework of a skeleton, the framework of a well-designed site is built upon a clearly defined structure. To do this, you must invest a lot of thought into this phase. A well-conceived and executed navigation model will be the difference between a site that meets the needs of the visitors or one that meets the need of the designer to create a work of art. When it comes to web design, the user wins out every time.

The site map is the document that identifies all of the pages in the site and, most important of all, shows how each page relates to every other page in the site. The term *document* is relative when it comes to web design. We have seen the site map done on a single sheet of legal paper. We have seen the pages represented by Post-It™ notes on a wall or white board. We have seen site maps constructed through the use of index cards laid out on the floor. Regardless of the method chosen, jumping right into the design before considering the relationship between each unit of information on the site is, in computing terms, a fatal error.

Finally, the web is a vibrant place where nothing remains static. Don't box yourself into a corner where the addition of more pages at some future date is difficult. Your client may extend the product line to include left-handed widgets along with the full line of right-handed widgets four months after the site goes live. If you haven't planned for this contingency, the site may have to be completely restructured and the odds are highly favorable that you will lose your client.

Linear Navigation Model

The linear navigation model in Figure 4.1 assumes a straight line through the site from the home page to the last page. A good example of this would be a series of pages containing pictures from a family vacation. The user simply clicks through each page in a straight line.

Figure 4.1   A linear model is comparable to a slide show.

Use this model if you decide to control the user's movement through your site, but always be sure to include a Back button on each page except for the home page. Search engines can't tell which page is which in this model, and you have to be aware the user could potentially enter the site through any page.

Hierarchical Navigation Model

The hierarchical navigation model is one of the more common on the web. It starts with a home page at the top of the model, and the content branches off from there. If you have ever seen your company's organization chart with the chairman of the board sitting at the top of the pyramid and everything else spreading out from under him, you understand hierarchical navigation. The lines between the squares show who reports to whom. On the web, those lines show how the user can get from page to page in the site.

The advantage to this model is that users always knows where they are, and can easily move through the site. With the home page accessible from each of the major categories, the other advantage is that users control movement through the site.

Figure 4.2 shows how the JCT site would work using hierarchical navigation.

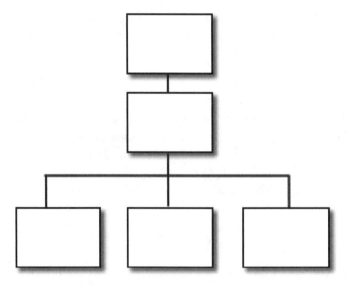

Figure 4.2   The hierarchical navigation model displays the information in order of increasing or decreasing importance.

Hub-and-Spoke Navigation Model

The hub-and-spoke navigation model takes full advantage of hyperlinks built into web pages. The user enters the hub—the home page—and can then access all of the spokes, which are the major pages in the site. The advantage here is ease of navigation. The user is always within one or two clicks of the home page; however, the advantage to this model can also be its drawback.

Imagine you want to fly from New York to Raleigh, NC, Macon, GA, and St. Petersburg, FL all in the same day. If you map out the trip, it looks like a straight line. If you add a hub—Atlanta—it becomes a huge frustration. Your trip is New York to Atlanta, Atlanta to Raleigh, Raleigh to Atlanta, Atlanta to Macon, Macon to Atlanta, Atlanta to St. Petersburg, St. Petersburg to Atlanta, and Atlanta to New York.

Figure 4.3 shows how the JCT site would use a hub-and-spoke model.

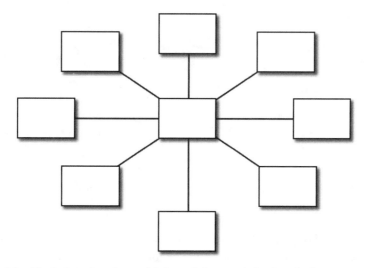

Figure 4.3   The hub-and-spoke model always brings a user back to the home page.

Full Web Navigation Model

The most free form model is full web navigation. It works just like the web—everything is connected to everything else, as shown in Figure 4.4. Use this model if the site is topic-specific, and you are encouraging the visitor to explore at will. The problem here is that the user could easily get lost in the site. If you use this model, it would be a good idea to have a link to a site map.

Choosing the Right Navigation Model

Our medium is the web, and no specific model works best. In fact, most sites are a combination of the models. As you go through the process developing the site you may discover there are far more main categories than can be easily managed. In this instance, look for an opportunity to bring the categories together into fewer subsets.

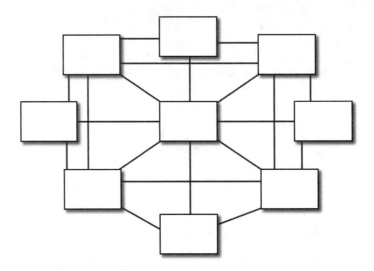

Figure 4.4   The full web model links virtually every page in a site with every other
                  page in the site.

For example, the JCT site has a number of categories for shoes. It would be silly to create main pages for children's shoes, sneakers, boots, women's shoes, men's shoes, outdoor shoes, and specialty sports shoes. It makes better sense to have them linked to one Shoes page. In this regard, department stores provide you with a great lesson in information design. If done properly, the store directory has a listing for Shoes—in web terms, this is regarded as a top-level link—and under it are the specific categories and locations for men's, women's, and children's shoes. If the shoes are easy to find on the directory, you will go to that section of the store. If they are spread out all over the directory, you will most likely get frustrated and leave the store. It is no different on the web.

Figure 4.5 offers some of the sketches an artist used as the site plan was thought through.

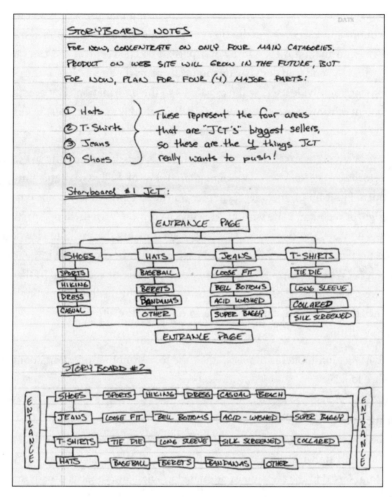

Figure 4.5   Some preliminary navigation sketches for the JCT site.

Designing a Page to Present Information

Every page on the web is a graphical representation of information. Each element of the page presents information as text, icons, images, links, and so on. How all of that information works without lessening the brand and confusing the reader is a black art. The design process is a delicate balance between how people use the web and how information is graphically designed.

The key to successful design, at this stage, is recognizing that the web is a communications medium, and users are looking for the building block of communication: information. The information is everything on a page. It is called *content* and can range from images to links. A good web designer methodically plans the site, as well as the placement of the content, to provide users with easy access to the information they need. Planning the placement of content is called *information design*, and is a system you create to ensure the user can quickly obtain the desired information in as short a time as possible.

There have been several excellent books written about web design and site structure. One of our favorites, *Web ReDesign: Workflow that Works*, by Kelly Goto and Emily Cotler (New Riders Publishing), includes a chapter on site structure. They point out that you can't design, or redesign, a site without viewing the project from three perspectives: content view, site view, and page view. Content is what makes the site. Site view looks at a site from the perspective of a site map, and page view, which uses a wireframe (discussed in Chapter 5, "Wireframing a Site"), looks at the structure of each page. In the previous chapter, we raised the issue of looking at a project in its entirety before starting. This section refines that issue, and starts zooming in on the entire site to the point where each page is now distinct.

After the navigation model is in place, it is time to ask another question about the site: How will it look?

Creating Storyboards

Storyboards simply block out the look of each page. They range from the simple—a series of roughly drawn sketches showing the composition of each page—to the multi-volume tomes used in the creation of animated movies. Storyboards usually start out as a series of doodles—called *thumbnails*—on a page

A thumbnail is a quick sketch of the basic page layout showing the placement of graphics and text. These can be done on a piece of paper, and represent the ideas and concepts for the design rather than the final design. We reviewed a number of concepts for the JCT site, but the one that kept catching our attention was the one shown at the bottom of Figure 4.6.

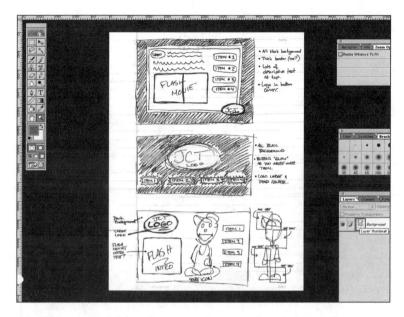

Figure 4.6   The top two didn't grab our attention as much as the bottom image.

After much discussion, we asked the artist to flesh out the concept, as shown in Figure 4.7.

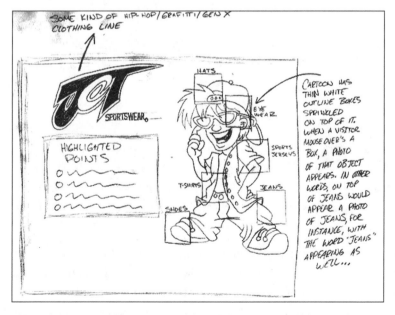

Figure 4.7   The mascot and logo came to life, and the artist included some ideas regarding the use of the mascot.

We liked what we saw and then asked our artist to develop a linear drawing of the home page. He submitted a few sketches, but the one that got things moving is shown in Figure 4.8.

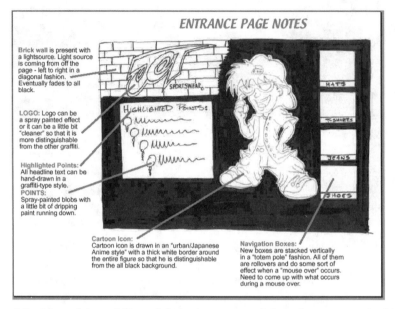

Figure 4.8   Many of the usability and design issues we needed to solve were contained in this initial composite drawing.

After much internal discussion about the design, we made a couple of changes based around usability. The boxes on the mascot were not intuitive. The design called for a box with a hairline. A visitor wouldn't instinctively know if one of those boxes was a part of the graphic or a link. The requested changes were made, and once we were comfortable with this look, we then asked how it would work with the other pages.

There are any number of ways to create storyboards, but one of the best methods acknowledges that we work on the web and that the content will be viewed through a browser. We first encountered a rather interesting approach to developing the storyboards a few years ago, and it also appeared in Lynda Weinman's New Riders book, *Designing Web Graphics.3*.

It is simply a screen shot of a blank browser window, and the linear is created in the window. In this way, you get a real sense of how the various elements will work in the browser window onscreen. The other important advantage to this approach is that designers tend to overlook the fact that the typical web page is not 11 inches wide by 8.5 inches high.

You can create a browser template in Fireworks. To do so, follow these steps:

1. Open your browser and maximize the window to fill the screen. Open all of the browser bars. Never assume your visitor will not have all of the browser bars open. Always plan for the worst so that you can avoid surprises.

2. Move your cursor to the middle of the browser window and, if you are using a Macintosh, turn off the Control Strip (Apple Menu, Control Panels, Control Strip. Select Hide Control Strip and then close the window). Sometimes the screen shot will include the cursor and, on Macintoshes, the Control Strip always sits in front of the window. If the cursor is in the middle of the browser window, you can remove it quickly in Fireworks. Take the screen shot and quit the browser.

3. Open Fireworks MX, and open a new Fireworks document. A PC screen shot sits on the clipboard, and when you open a new Fireworks document on the PC, the Canvas Size will default to the size of the image on the clipboard. On a Macintosh, the screen shot is automatically placed on your hard drive and named Picture 1, if it is the only one there. Navigate to your hard drive, and open this image. In the Fireworks tool panel, set the fill color to White and the stroke to None. Select the rectangle tool, and click/drag from the upper-left corner of the content area to the bottom-right corner. Do the same thing in the URL area. Name and save the file.

Now all you have to do is to print out a number of copies of this document.

Obviously, we made decisions without client input. This is where writing a book will never mirror the real world. The site map and the compositions (referred to as *comps*) are always submitted to the client for approval and sign off.

Structuring Your Site

There are millions upon millions of web users out there, and no two will use your site in exactly the same manner. Some will simply scoot in, have a quick look around, and leave just as quickly. Others will methodically browse through the site, looking for something of interest. Still others will be there for a reason, meet their goal, and move on.

This section focuses on site mapping, the first step to helping viewers achieve their goals. The site map is that all-important first step in the process. At this point, the team and the client start to comprehend the flow and the placement of the pages in the site.

The Importance of Site Modeling

A few months back, the daughter of one of the authors had missed her bus from one city to another. She had phoned and left a message that she would be leaving on the 5:00 p.m. bus, and someone would need to pick her up at the local bus station. The important piece of information that she didn't give was her arrival time. Rather than call the bus company, the author went to the bus company's site to find the arrival time.

At first glance, he couldn't find a link for the schedule. He found it buried in a bunch of links at the bottom of the home page. He clicked the link, and in the middle of the page was a drop-down list of cities. He clicked and selected the city from which his daughter was departing. Then nothing. Expecting a listing of destinations, he waited for the page to appear. It wasn't until he closely examined the page that he noticed a new category had appeared—the To category. He selected the destination city from another drop-down list.

Another page loaded, and the author quickly discovered the importance of this chapter. The page showed the list of departure times, but the list under the heading Arrival Time was blank.

In this instance, the company not only made it difficult to find the needed information, they never supplied it. He had to call the bus company and wade through complicated voicemail menus to discover the average travel time was about 2.5 hours. Even then, the local number given by the web site was wrong.

Had the bus company properly planned the information design, the author would have obtained the information with one or two clicks. Instead, his experience was both confusing and frustrating. The unfortunate aspect of web design is that spending the time necessary to properly structure a site is often neglected. It isn't a cool aspect of the design process. If you find yourself making that assumption, assume you are running that bus company. How many people each day visit your site to look for a simple piece of information, such as the arrival time of a bus? If they can't find the information, will they start patronizing a company that provides the necessary information?

What the company did not do was view their site as a user would view the site. Their site was designed from a corporate perspective, and the most important information, according to the site, was the departure time, not how often the buses departed and the fare. They never asked a few key questions, such as "What are our customers looking for?," "Are we meeting that need?," and "How can the site be structured to accomplish that goal?".

Had the site been modeled, this oversight would have become glaringly obvious. The model in Figure 4.9 shows the information on the page. You can see there is a huge hole under the Arrivals section. Information is missing. By not creating a model of the site, and going right into the design, a critical piece of information was completely overlooked in the rush to get the site online.

The war cry on the web is *usability*, and until clients are prepared to pay for usability studies and testing, the job falls on the shoulders of the team.

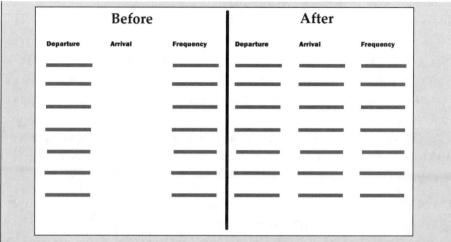

	Before			**After**	
Departure	**Arrival**	**Frequency**	**Departure**	**Arrival**	**Frequency**

Figure 4.9   Note the missing arrival times in the original. Had they put themselves in the shoes of a passenger, they would have provided the information shown in the After category.

Site Mapping

When we do seminars, a common question we ask is, "How many people in this room create site maps?" A few hands will go up in the air. We then ask, "How many people in this room use software to create their site maps?". Even fewer hands are raised. Finally, we ask, "How many people in this room don't have a clue as to what we are talking about?". Inevitably, several hands are raised.

A site map is much like your skeleton. It is the underlying structure of the body. A properly completed site map shows the organization, flow, content grouping, and information. At this stage of the process, the designer, your client, and you will be able to zoom in on the project from a macro view as a collection of pages to a micro view as individual elements on a page.

This map is a document that needs to be submitted for client approval As such, whether you use a client site, pieces of paper, a three-ring binder, PDF files, or whatever, ensure the client signs and dates the map. In many respects, this is an awkward process, but you can be sure the client will carefully review the map before signing on the dotted line. As well, the site map is a living document that changes as the site structure changes. If this happens, the client will have to provide their approval before you move any deeper into the project.

Building a Site Map in Fireworks MX

There are a variety of site map solutions available to the web developer. You could use a software solution such as Inspiration (`www.inspiration.com`) or Visio (`www.microsoft.com/office/visio`). You can create site maps by simply using a drawing program such as FreeHand 10. You could use a page layout applications such as QuarkXPress and PageMaker 7.0. Another solution would be to use web development applications such as Dreamweaver or go totally low tech and use simple boxes drawn on a sheet of legal paper. The method chosen usually reflects the complexity of the project. A software solution such as Inspiration or Visio is ideal for sites composed of hundreds of pages, while the sheet of legal paper is great for a site with a dozen or so pages.

One of the advantages to using Fireworks is the fact that it is a web graphic design application. Any files created here, providing they are .png files, can be quickly assimilated into a web page and posted to the project site for client or team review. Using an imaging or drawing application for this purpose is a cumbersome process involving compatibility, version issues, and conversion issues, along with a host of other considerations that make you wonder why they even bother.

The elements of a site map aren't terribly complex. You need to create a rectangle, a line, and an arrow. The rectangle represents the page, and the line and the arrow show the path the user travels from one page to another. What makes the map complex are the number of boxes, arrows, and lines required. Drawing each one, as needed, will inevitably bring us to that "Why bother?" question. Fireworks offers a rather nifty Library feature where you can store objects having the "draw once, use many times " property.

Before we get deeper into this subject, it would help to distinguish between a symbol and an instance. These two terms run through many of the applications in Macromedia Studio, especially Flash. That phrase "draw once, use many times" succinctly describes the concept.

A symbol is the master blueprint of an object. In our case, it is a square used in the site map. In relation to Fireworks, a symbol can be anything from an object shown as the square, a group of objects shown as the square with text inside it, or a block of text. The neat thing is symbols in Fireworks can contain objects, layers, and frames. In many respects, it would be correct to view a symbol as being anything drawn in Fireworks.

When an object is converted to a symbol, it is automatically placed in the Fireworks Library, and attached to that particular document. That isn't all. These libraries can be made available to any Fireworks document. By simply opening the Library and then dragging the symbol onto the page, you have created an *instance* of that symbol. This instance is a reference back to the symbol itself, as opposed to making a copy of the object.

Creating and Using a Fireworks Symbol

One of our favorite phrases regarding digital workflow is, "Let the software do the work." In this example, a little bit of time is spent at the start of the project to save a lot of time at the end of the project. In Fireworks MX, one of the great timesavers is the use of symbols and instances for repetitive objects on a page.

To create and use symbols in Fireworks MX, follow these steps:

1. Open a new Fireworks document by choosing File, New. Using Control-N (PC) or Command-N (Mac) to open the New Document dialog box, as shown in Figure 4.10, set the measurement system for the document's width and height to inches: the width to 14, and the height to 8.5. This gives you a legal-size page with a landscape orientation. Select White as the background color, and click OK.

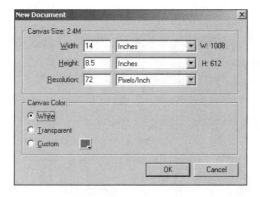

Figure 4.10   The New Document dialog box in Fireworks.

2. Select the Rectangle tool from the toolbox, and draw a rectangle on the canvas. With the rectangle selected on the canvas, set the fill to None, the stroke to Basic, Hard Line, and the stroke color to Black using the Fireworks MX Property inspector.

3. With the rectangle still selected on the canvas, select Insert, Convert to Symbol, or press F8. The Symbol Properties dialog box appears. Name the symbol **Box**, click the Graphic radio button, and click OK.

4. Open the Library panel by selecting Window, Library, pressing F11, or selecting the Library tab in the Assets panel. You will see your square in the Library.

Notice how your object on the page has changed. As seen in Figure 4.11, the arrow symbol in the bottom-left corner of the object and the bounding box indicate the object on the page is an instance.

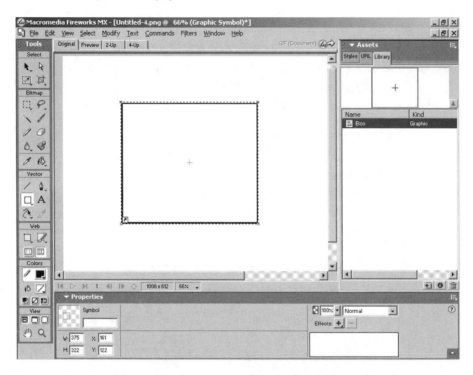

Figure 4.11   The object on the page has been converted to a symbol, which is automatically placed in the Library. Note that the Library panel has been undocked and is floating loose on the canvas.

5. If you need another box on the canvas, open the Library panel and then scroll to the symbol you need. Click/drag the symbol onto the document, and deselect the resulting instance on the page.

 Note

If you are a long-time Fireworks user, the movement of the Library to the Assets panel is new. The introduction of panels in Fireworks MX is Macromedia's response to the frustration Fireworks users had with window clutter on their screens. To undock the Library, simply drag the Assets panel onto the canvas. To return it to the panel, click and hold on the triangle of dots pointing to the word Assets on the panel. Drag the Assets panel onto the panel group, and when you see a thick line appear, release the mouse.

You can even make the Library its own panel. Select Panel Options, Group Library with, New Panel Group. To put it back, repeat the previous step and then select the name of the grouping from the list rather than New Panel Group.

Alternately, here's another method that is a bit less convoluted. Select Edit, Insert, New Symbol. Use Control-F8 (PC) or Command-F8 (Mac) to open the Symbol Editor window. Name the symbol and select Graphic. Draw the square and, when you are finished, close the Symbol Editor.

Using and Modifying Fireworks MX Symbols to Create a Site Map

By creating a series of primitive shapes and saving them as symbols in the Fireworks MX Library, you can create models of the pages by dragging and dropping the needed images onto the page. To do so, follow these steps:

1. Open the JCTmapex.png file located in the Chapter 3 Exercise folder on the book web site, and open the Library. Locate the Box symbol in the Library and then drag two instances of the box onto the document.

   The box is much bigger than the other boxes on the page. You will now discover the difference between making changes globally and locally to symbols. A global change affects all instances of the symbol on the page. A local change affects only the one on which you are working.

2. Double-click the image of the Box symbol in the Library to open the Symbol Editor. Select the Pointer tool, and click once on the rectangle in the Symbol Editor. Select the Scale tool on the toolbar, and click/drag a corner point to change the size of the box. Close the Symbol Editor.

3. All the boxes on the page changed size to reflect the change in the symbol. This is a global change—modify the symbol, and all instances used in the document are updated to reflect the change. Select Edit, Undo Edit Symbol to put the box back to its original size.

The next part of this exercise focuses on that old business adage, "work smart, not hard." You resize the box. This time you do it by the numbers. Remember, you can't hope to match the size of the boxes on the page by using your eyes.

1. Delete one of the two big boxes on the page and then select a small box on the page. The Property inspector shows you the width and height of the selected object, as seen in Figure 4.12.

2. Click on the big box, and change the width and height to those of the small box; then press Enter. The box changes to reflect these new dimensions. Now delete the box.

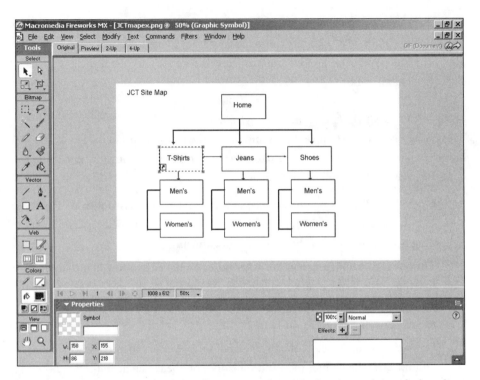

Figure 4.12   The Property inspector allows you to change the location and size of selected
objects "by the numbers." It is a lot more accurate than doing it by "eye."

With the image open, you should see there is a whole section of the map missing under
Shoes. You could build it by dragging and sizing elements from the Library; however,
here is a much faster way, as shown in the following steps:

1. Click/drag to select all of the elements, including the arrow, under the Jeans
    section.

2. With all of the elements selected, hold down the Alt (PC) or Option (Mac) key.
    The cursor changes to a hollow arrow. Press the Shift key. With both the Shift
    and Alt or Option keys held down, drag all of the selected elements to the right
    until they are under the Shoes box. Release the mouse, save the image, and quit
    Fireworks MX.

By pressing the Alt or Option key, you told Fireworks to copy all of the selected items.
Pressing the Shift key and dragging horizontally, you are constraining the movement of
the copy to only a horizontal move. The drag moves the copy, not the original, to the
final position.

Creating a Site Map in Dreamweaver MX

The Macromedia Studio is filled with tools and features that have secondary uses that, in some cases, are just as powerful as their primary purpose. A prime example of this is the Site Map window. This window is primarily used to view the flow and linking of the various pages in a site.

Site Map view presents the site in the format we have been talking about in this chapter—a form of organizational chart represented by a series of boxes linked with arrows. In the case of the Site Map feature, the boxes are replaced with an icon of the page. If pages have secondary pages linked to them, you see either a + or − symbol if you are working on a PC, or a pop-down arrow on a Macintosh. Pages with good links are blue. Pages with broken links are red. You sometimes see a globe icon that indicates an external file on another site, or a special link such as :mailto:". Also, if Check In/Check Out is enabled, you see the red or green check mark or the Lock icon. When you look at a site map, you see the home page at the top, and all of the other pages are linked with a connecting line or arrow.

Opening the Site Map Window

The introduction of panels to Dreamweaver MX reduces the onscreen clutter of windows in previous versions of the application. The Site Map feature is now contained as an option in the Files panel. It can be opened from the Window menu.

To open the Site Map window, follow these steps:

1. Open Index.htm in the SiteEx folder on the book web site. Select Window, Site Map. You can also open the Site Management window by pressing F8.

2. When the window opens, select Site View from the drop-down list. The site map opens and is constricted to the width of the panel, as shown in Figure 4.13. To make the view wider, click the Expand/Collapse button above the Map View.

The site map's primary purpose is to give you that macro view of the site. In typical Macromedia fashion, that isn't all it can do. Follow these steps to build a site map by linking new or existing pages to pages in the map.

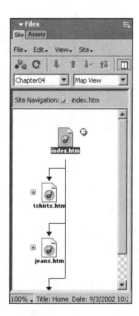

Figure 4.13
The site map opens in the panel. Clicking the Collapse/Expand button expands the view to full screen.

1. Open the site map, and select the Index Page icon. Select Site, Link to a New File (Control-Shift-K on the PC, or Command-Shift-K on the Mac). You can also accomplish this by right-clicking (PC) or Control-clicking (Mac) the icon and then selecting Link to New File from the context menu that appears. Either method will open a new dialog box.

2. In the Link to New File dialog box, enter the name of the new file, being sure to add either .htm or .html to the end of the name. Press Tab to go to the next input box. Enter **Sox Page** as a title for the new page and then press Tab. Enter a word or phrase to describe the link in the Text of Link text box, and click OK. A new page named Sox appears on the map, as shown in Figure 4.14.

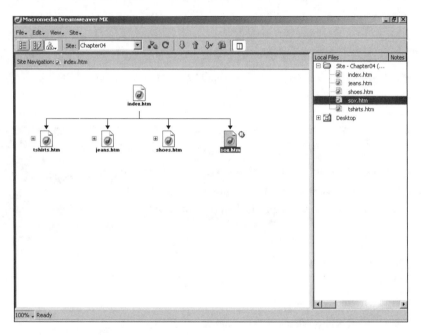

Figure 4.14   Pages can be added to the site in Map view either through the use of the Site menu or by right-clicking (PC)/Control-clicking (Mac) on a page and selecting Link to New File from the context menu.

3. To remove an unwanted page, select the Page icon on the map, and press Delete. Close the document, and don't save the changes.

Turning a Site Map into a Deliverable

Turning a site map into a document that can be submitted for client approval is a little-known feature of Dreamweaver MX. A user could turn the site map into something to be submitted for approval through a series of screen shots. This can be a somewhat convoluted process, usually involving a number of screen shots that have be stitched together in Fireworks. But now Dreamweaver MX makes this possible by doing the screen shot for you.

Open the Index page in the SiteEx folder, open the site map, and select File, Save Site Map to open the Site Map dialog box. Select BMP or PNG. (On the Macintosh, the choices are Pict or JPEG.) Click OK.

The map is saved in the format chosen and, best of all, is automatically sized to contain all of the icons. This file can then be opened in Fireworks for further manipulation, or added to a Dreamweaver MX page. The Fireworks MX or Dreamweaver MX document can be sent via FTP to a web server or Sitespring for client review, or attached to an email and sent to the client.

Note

After reviewing this section, one of the authors asked a rather interesting question. Why use Fireworks for a site map when it is much easier to accomplish this task in Dreamweaver? The Dreamweaver map is similar to an organizational chart for a corporation. The information is delivered in a top-down manner. When it comes to more freeform concepts, Fireworks offers a huge degree of flexibility. For example, the capability to color code would be a great productivity boon.

One of the ways of building a site map without software is to stick a bunch of those yellow sticky notes on a wall. The great thing about this is the capability to move them around to get a more logical flow and representation of movement through the site. Fireworks is a lot like the sticky notes. You can move the elements around.

Still, the question illuminates a fundamental principal of web design. Clients doesn't care how you did it; they simply care that it gets done!

Creating a Site Map in FreeHand

One of the most overlooked tools in the process is FreeHand, yet FreeHand offers some features unavailable in either Dreamweaver MX or Fireworks MX. Apart from the robust tool set unavailable in either application, FreeHand allows you to create multi-page documents. The pages could include specific areas of the site. You also have the ability to move the pages around to follow the site map as well as the ability to save the file as a .pdf document that can be used as a deliverable and submitted for client approval.

To create a site map in FreeHand, follow these steps:

1. Open a new FreeHand document. Select Window, Inspectors, Document, or click the Document tab in the Inspector panel to open the settings for the pages. Select

Custom from the Page Size drop-down menu. Set the length to 600 pixels, and the width to 400 pixels.

2. Set the orientation to Landscape, and add six pages to the document by selecting Add Pages from the Palette drop-down menu. Enter **6** into the Number of New Pages area. Click OK, and set the View to 6%.

3. Select the Page tool. Click on page 1, and drag it to the top of the window. Drag pages 2, 3, and 4 to form a horizontal row under page 1. Drag pages 5, 6, and 7 to form a vertical row under page 2. When you finish, your layout should resemble Figure 4.15.

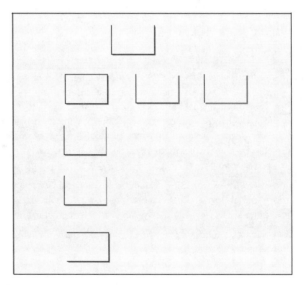

Figure 4.15   Site maps are easily created in FreeHand by using the Page tool to move the pages around to match a site map.

4. To keep the layout, select View, Custom, New and then name the view **Site Map**.

You have just set up the pages of the document to resemble the hand-drawn site map. The advantage to this approach is the ability to simply click a page, expand the view to 100%, and add the content. If you were to then select Site Map from the Custom view, you would see your content and be able to select the next page to work on.

Creating a FreeHand PDF File

After saving the document, select File, Export. Select PDF from the Save as Type drop-down menu (PC) or the Format pop-down menu if you use a Macintosh. Click the Set

Up button. If you have URLs embedded in the document, ensure you select Export URLs. If you are using custom fonts, you want the viewer to select Embed Fonts and click OK. Click Save (PC) or Export (Mac) when you return to the Export dialog box.

By choosing the Export URLs and Embed Fonts options, you preserve any links that may be in the file. You also ensure that the document looks the way you intended it to. The resulting PDF can then be printed, mailed to the client, or even made available to the client through the client site. The big advantage here is PDF documents are non-platform specific. Acrobat PDF documents can be opened on either a Mac or a PC providing the user has either the Acrobat browser plug-in or Acrobat Reader on their computer.

Summary

As you have seen in this chapter, building a site involves more than simply opening the appropriate applications and starting to work. It requires careful planning and testing to ensure the issues of usability and ease of navigation are addressed.

We have presented a number of web models, ranging from the simple to complex, and explained how they provide the structure upon which a site is built. We also walked you through the creative process behind the JCT site to show the process really does start with a piece of paper and a pencil.

You have seen how Fireworks MX can be used to create a site map, and how to create a Library of primitives in Fireworks MX by using symbols and instances that can be used for subsequent modeling requirements. We also demonstrated how to modify the symbols, both globally and locally, to reflect changes in client need or workflow.

Dreamweaver MX contains a number of unsung features that can help you deal with navigation, chief of which is site map creation and modeling. We reviewed how to open the Site Map feature in Dreamweaver MX, how to add and subtract pages from the map, and how to turn that map into a deliverable using the Save Site Map option.

Finally, we demonstrated how to turn multi-page FreeHand documents into site maps that can be used throughout the development process. We also explained how to turn those FreeHand pages into a deliverable by exporting them from FreeHand as .pdf documents.

Knowing how the pages will flow is the first step in the process. Planning where the content is placed on the pages is the subject of the next chapter.

Chapter 5

Wireframing a Site

In the previous chapter, we focused on the development of a storyboard. As you learned, a storyboard is the sketch or drawing of a web page. The site looks fine on paper, but you have to understand that moving from one medium, such as paper, to another, such as the web, rarely works without compromises.

These compromises involve a range of issues, from overall design of a page to the colors chosen. These issues rarely become noticeable when building the site map. A wireframe takes the design team and the client from the macro, or site, view to the micro, or page, view. Mistakes in the design of information have a tendency to be miniscule, but as you get deeper into the process, these flaws grow. In some cases, they will require major changes to such things as the navigation chosen and even the layout of the page. Dealing with them late in the design process will be expensive.

In Chapter 4, "Testing Your Ideas with Site Models," we related the experience one of the authors had in discovering when his daughter would arrive home on the bus. Eventually the bus company is going to hear that its clients find it difficult to find the information they need. The result will be someone from the bus company given the job of solving this oversight, and discovering the site needs to be redesigned.

After the bus company employee discovers that the cost of fixing this error is the same or even greater than the cost of the original design, someone is going to wonder why they didn't address this at the start of the process. No one likes to pay for the same thing twice. The rest of the story is self-evident and, in some cases, is forming the basis for a completely new area of legal case law. The courts are now being asked to decide whether it is the client or the designer who must bear the costs associated with these oversights.

Wireframing Defined

A wireframe model is a digital rendering of the storyboard. Wireframe models are digital representations of the site's pages using primitive shapes and text that illustrate the navigation, text placement, graphics, headlines, and other elements that demonstrate how a page works. As well, a wireframe can be used to model the information hierarchy. At a more practical level, a wireframe model of the page sets the graphical layout of the page and provides a visual framework for the writing of the HTML code, which describes a web page. Web designers who use these models traditionally build them for the major, secondary, and template pages. Designers also build wireframe models for any pages on a site that are perceived to be outside of the design. This type of page, for example, could be one designed to gather visitor information, or one to show the arrival times of buses.

Wireframes represent content, but wireframes aren't content. The shapes represent elements on a page, and can vary from the very simple, such as layout and navigation, to the complex, such as actual copy, rough approximations of pop-down menus, or graphics. They also set the basis for the production workflow, and can be designed to model navigation between pages. When you design a wireframe, include all of the elements, as well as navigation elements, called for in the original paper comprehensive.

Where do you start? Start with the home or index page of the site and then work your way out from there. How many wireframes do you build? For complex sites, you may be modeling over 100 pages. This number is driven by the scope and budget of the project. The absolute minimum should be the home or index page, as well as all major pages. If you have a number of secondary pages that use a slightly different design, build those models as well.

Planning the Elements of Navigation

Navigation has to be intuitive. Visitors to your site aren't willing to spend time to learn that really cool navigation system you have devised. If they don't understand how to get around your site to access information, they will go somewhere else.

This raises an important aspect of navigation. Navigation is not only the elements of navigation, such as buttons, links, anchors, image maps, and menus. It is also the shortest distance, measured in time, to the information. Therefore, planning how people will navigate around the site involves not only planning what will be used to get them to the information—the elements—but also how they will get to the information—the temporal element.

The elements of navigation must be consistent. A good example is the placement of a navigation bar. We have all encountered sites where the navigation bar at the top of a number of pages on the site suddenly moves to the side of the page elsewhere in the site. Immediately, the consistency of the design disappears and the user loses his orientation. The designer may have had a rational argument for that one, but visitors to the site will make the final decision. If they can't figure out what changed, they will leave. The design of buttons, navigation bars, and other elements must be intuitive. Flash designers, in their never-ending quest for cool, are among the worst transgressors. We have encountered Flash sites where the navigation bar is hidden until the user rolls over a miniscule object on a page. When the links appear, the text on the links requires a magnifying glass to read.

Finally, design the elements of navigation around the audience. Josh Davis and Yugo Nakamura are regarded by many Flash designers as being among the hottest web and Flash designers on the planet. Their sites, www.Praystation.com (Josh) and www.yugop.com

(Yugo), are designed for their peers and feature highly experimental work. Their navigation elements are designed for designers and, as such, their visitors are there to invest their time in exploring Josh's and Yugo's experimenting with new ways of presenting navigation elements and interface designs. If you were to apply their navigation elements to an ecommerce site aimed at retirees, you will encounter huge problems.

Buttons

In the early days of the web, buttons were the primary method of interactive navigation. Even now, they haven't lost their appeal.

Buttons traditionally have three states—Up, Over, and Down. Each is triggered by an obvious event, and in certain cases, is code driven. Javascript is the primary vehicle here. If you create your buttons in Fireworks MX and then export the resulting code with the button states, that code is Javascript. Dreamweaver MX, through its Javascript behaviors, allows you to not only assign actions based upon mouse events, but to also roll your own in the HTML editor.

In Flash MX, buttons have moved beyond the realm of simple items meant to be clicked to be able to go somewhere on the site. Although this is still the primary purpose of buttons, developers have discovered that embedding buttons in movie clips provides the user with a visual clue such as the pointer changes, thus the clip is live. Others have discovered that embedding movie clips in buttons provides the user with not only visual feedback, but also animations that can change depending on the event. Finally, there are a number of buttons contained in Flash MX's new user interface (UI) Components panel.

Dreamweaver MX also enables you to create Flash buttons directly out of the toolbar, and place them on your page. Selecting the resulting Flash button on the page and clicking the Flash Edit button on the Property inspector launches Flash MX, and allows you to tweak the button or perform major surgery.

Fireworks MX has completely revamped its powerful Button Editor. The Button Editor is still symbol driven, meaning that the button object must first be converted to a symbol. The major workflow change is the capability to set the object's behavior as a symbol, as shown in Figure 5.1. Double-clicking the symbol on the Stage or in the Library launches the Button Editor. From there, the various states are created easily by clicking a button in the interface that makes a completely editable copy of the previous state.

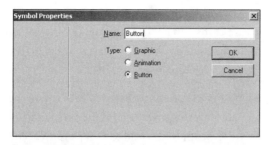

Figure 5.1   Fireworks MX buttons are no longer created through an Insert menu. Their behavior is set when they are converted to symbols.

Finally, don't forget Fireworks MX and FreeHand are tremendous tools for creating the artwork for the buttons. Fireworks MX, through its many textures and LiveEffects, can create visually attractive buttons. FreeHand not only allows you to create the artwork for Flash buttons, but also can be used to create its own Flash buttons. It enables you to export a .swf file. Dreamweaver MX also contains a feature for creating Flash buttons and Flash text. Though a welcome addition, this is a redundant feature if you own Flash MX.

Menus

In many respects, menus can be regarded as a series of individual buttons that have been strung together. For example, a button bar created in Fireworks MX contains a series of button states, each with a predetermined Up, Over, and Down state. In Flash MX, invisible buttons are traditionally used to provide the visual clue, such as a cursor change, that the strip on the menu is active.

Pop-down menus are a bit more difficult to create. At their best, well-designed pop-down menus created in Dreamweaver MX, Flash MX, or Fireworks MX closely resemble their counterparts contained in a Graphical User Interface (GUI). They are both recognizable and predictable. Fireworks MX automates this process through the use of a wizard, and the ComboBox component of Flash MX automates the process in Flash. Still, the best precision is driven by the capability to code the JavaScript in Dreamweaver MX, or Actionscript in Flash MX.

Links

Moving around in a web page is still within the realm of HTML. Whether it be a hyperlink on a Dreamweaver MX page or an image map created in Fireworks MX, the common question springing from the change in the cursor is one posed by taxi drivers all over the world: "Where to?"

Links can be absolute, such as the example `http://www.gosomewhere.com/whereto/`
`thispage.html`, to relative paths that navigate throughout the document. In cases where
you are working on a site that uses a number of servers, or your server hosts a bunch of
sites, you might want to consider root-relative paths.

A root-relative path establishes a relationship between each file on the site and the root of
the site. If we were to create a root-relative path for the preceding link, it would look like
`whereto/thispage.html`. The path would lead to `thispage.html` located in the `whereto`
subfolder of the site's root folder.

Dreamweaver MX and Flash MX also use anchors for navigation. Anchors allow you to
navigate within a page or number of pages by taking you to precisely where you want to
go. For example, assume you are looking at a page on a cooking site. There is a description of using Granny Smith apples as an ingredient in an apple pie. The words *Granny
Smith* have a link under them. That link is to an anchor instead of URL or a page in the
site. Click the link to be taken to the precise spot on the page elsewhere in the site where
Granny Smith apples are discussed. Dreamweaver MX uses anchors for this purpose. In
Dreamweaver MX, an icon that uses an anchor in a yellow shield represents an anchor.
Flash MX anchors are a bit different. They are new to Flash MX, and represent a fundamental approach to the user experience with Flash. Prior to Flash MX, Flash sites essentially stole the Back and Forward buttons from the browser. Since version 1 of Flash, this
has been the most common complaint from people attempting to navigate through a
Flash site. The addition of Named Anchors to the Flash MX Property inspector allows
the user to use the browser's Forward and Back buttons to navigate between keyframes
on a Flash timeline.

Creating an anchor in Flash MX is simple. Select a keyframe in the movie, name the
frame, and click the Named Anchor button in the Property inspector. Figure 5.2 shows
an anchor. When the movie is ready to be published, click on the HTML tab in the
Publish Settings dialog box. In the Template pop-down menu, select Flash with Named
Anchors as well as the code necessary to move the Flash presentation with the browser's
Forward and Back buttons.

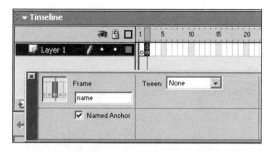

Figure 5.2   Giving frames a name and clicking the Named Anchor button in the Property inspector allows users to use the Back and Forward buttons of their browsers to navigate through a Flash MX movie.

Building a Wireframe for JCT in Fireworks MX

Up to this point, the JCT site is a paper-based project. Moving into a digital format involves either the use of Fireworks MX or Dreamweaver MX. This section focuses on Fireworks. The advantage to using Fireworks and not a drawing or page layout application, such as FreeHand or QuarkXPress, lies in its function as a web-imaging application. The resulting file can be saved in a web-ready format, such as .png or .gif. This means that it can quickly be dropped into a Dreamweaver MX web page and posted to a client site for client review. The other advantage lies in the capability to create slices that allows a visitor to navigate between the pages of the site. This enables you to test the navigation, and determine if the paths chosen are the right ones. As well, using a Library allows you to draw the bits and pieces prior to building the wireframe and then assemble the pages.

How we built the wireframe for the JCT site is a classic example of that old adage, *work smart, not hard.* We could have built the page the hard way, based on the paper drawing (storyboard). Rather than that, however, we decided to scan the color drawing and place the wireframes, using the Fireworks MX feature, over the comprehensive. Another real timesaver was using a standard set of symbols for the content that resides as symbols in a Library.

Symbols

There is always going to be content that is used in a number of places. An obvious piece of content would be a logo. In this case, rather than constantly adding the logo to a document, it can be converted to a symbol and used many times. The key point about converting objects to symbols is that any changes made to a symbol are reflected in every copy of that particular symbol within the document. Symbols reside in the Fireworks MX Library, and, in cases where copies of the symbol have to be shared among the workgroup, the Libraries containing the symbols can be exported out of a document and then imported into other Fireworks documents. To create a symbol in Fireworks MX, follow these steps:

1. Copy the Chapter 5 Exercise folder on the book web site to your desktop, and open the file named Frameit.png. A scanned linear comprehensive of the JCT Shoes page is the bottom layer. Lock the layer and then add another.

2. Open the Assets panel by choosing Window, Assets; then click the Library tab. The Assets panel is a great place to keep textures, styles, and even URLs that will be used multiple times. Note that we have included a number of primitive items.

3. One symbol—a graphic—is missing. To create the graphic symbol, select the Rectangle tool and then draw a square with a black stroke and a white fill on the canvas. Select the Line tool, and draw a black line from the upper-left corner to the lower-right corner. Draw another black line between the remaining corners. Don't worry about the size of the square. It is composed of vectors and is scalable.

4. Select the square and the lines, and press F8 to open the Symbol Editor. Name the symbol **Graphic/Image**, and click the Graphic property button on the Symbol Editor. Click OK.

Check your Library, and you see a new symbol—Graphic/Image—has been added to the list. If you click on it in the Library, you see the symbol. Also, the object on the canvas has a small arrow in the lower-left corner, indicating the object is an instance of a symbol.

After a symbol is created, it can still be edited. For example, you decide to fill the Graphic/Image symbol with a powder-blue color instead of the white fill we used, or the text in a symbol needs to be edited. There are three ways to edit a symbol. You can double-click the symbol's icon in the Library, or you can double-click the symbol's image in the Library. You can also double-click the symbol on the canvas.

You can change a symbol's name and property by double-clicking the symbol's name in the Library to open the Symbol Properties dialog box. After you have finished with your changes, click OK.

Exporting and Importing a Fireworks MX Symbol Library

Symbols, such as logos, are not limited to the document you are working on. If you have a series of symbols that can be used in other documents or need to be shared among the team, you can use the Library options to export them as a .png document. Here is how to export a symbol Library for use by other members of the team:

1. Select Export Symbols from the Panel Options pop-down menu. The Export Symbols dialog box opens, as shown in Figure 5.3. The top box shows you the content of the symbol, and the bottom lists all of the symbols in the Library. You can export selected symbols, or you can export all of them.

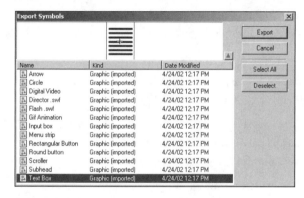

Figure 5.3   Symbols in the Library can be exported for use by other members of the team by selecting the symbols and then clicking the Export button.

2. Click the Select All button and then click the Export button. Navigate to the folder where the file is to be saved, and click OK.

3. The other members of the team can then select Import, Symbols from the Library pop-down menu, or select Edit, Libraries, Other, navigate to the folder containing the file, select the file, and click Open.

Instances

Symbols are original pieces of art that reside in the Library. Instances are copies of that art used on the Fireworks MX canvas. The best way of thinking of an instance is as an alias of the original. It is no wonder that the instance on the canvas always contains a curved arrow in the lower-left corner of the object on the canvas. The arrow can be regarded as pointing to the original in the Library. As you have already seen, double-clicking an instance on the canvas opens the Symbol Editor, and any change to a symbol is immediately reflected in all of the instances on the canvas.

After you get into the habit of using symbols, the building of wireframe models based on linear comprehensives becomes a relatively short task.

In the case of our file, the artists drew the page, referred to as a linear comprehensive, which was then scanned and placed into the Fireworks MX document. Instead of drawing each graphic and then copying and pasting copies of the graphic throughout the canvas, you simply drag the appropriate symbol into its position on the canvas and resize the instance. To work with symbols and instances in Fireworks MX, follow these steps:

1. Open the Frameit.png file and then open the Library. Drag the Library from the panel set, and open the panel until you can see all of the symbols. If you are working on a new copy of the Frameit.png file, add a new layer named Layer Two.

2. Open the Layers panel, select Layer Two, and rename the layer **Wireframes**; then, lock the layer containing the background image.

3. Select the Rectangle tool, and draw a rectangle the same size as the one surrounding the content on the linear. Set the rectangle's stroke to 1 point and the fill to None in the Property inspector.

4. Click on the Graphic/Image symbol, and drag a copy onto the canvas over the logo area in the upper-left corner. With the symbol selected, click once on the Free Transform tool, and scale the instance to roughly fit the logo area.

5. You could now drag and size any number of instances of the Graphic/Image symbol from the Library, but that would be a waste of time. Instead, click and hold the symbol on the canvas. Press the Option (Mac) or Alt (PC) key, and with this key pressed, drag a copy of the instance over the JCT guy at the right of the page. Release the mouse and scale to size.

6. Using Figure 5.4 as your guide, drag, place, and size your symbols. When you have finished, select the frame for the page and then fill it with the color white. Save the wireframe image to your Exercise folder on your desktop.

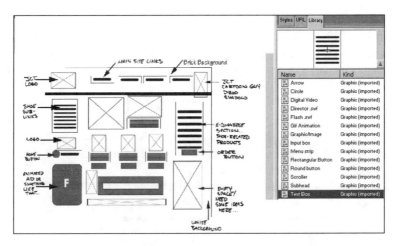

Figure 5.4   The wireframe is assembled from the symbols residing in the Fireworks MX Library.

Using Dreamweaver to Test Wireframe Navigation

Moving around a site is just as important as the ability to see the pages. Dreamweaver has a couple of tools that allow you to test or simulate how a user might move around a site. You can add hotspots—invisible areas on a page that change the cursor from an arrow to a pointing finger, indicating the capability to navigate elsewhere—in Dreamweaver MX to your navigation elements on the wireframe. This gives you the opportunity to ensure the navigation is both understandable as well as, in a temporal sense, short. You can also create a site map in Dreamweaver and then use it to navigate between the pages.

To add hotspots to a wireframe, follow these steps:

1. Open the Index.htm page in the FrameNav folder located in the Chapter 5 Exercise folder on your desktop in Dreamweaver. If the Properties panel isn't open, select Window, Properties, or press Control-F3 (PC) or Command-F3 (Mac) to open the panel.

2. To add a hotspot to the wireframe, you must first click on the image. The Property inspector changes to reflect the graphic properties. The hotspot tools are in the lower-left corner of the inspector.

3. Select the Rectangular Hotspot tool. Click once and then drag a hotspot over the first subhead button at the top of the page. As soon as you release the mouse, the Page Properties panel changes to the HotSpot Properties panel. If the hotspot is the wrong size, simply click on it and drag a corner handle in or out to adjust the size.

4. Click the folder beside the Link Input area to the Select File dialog box that lets you navigate to the page to which you will be linking. Navigate to the FrameNav folder on your hard drive, and select Hats.htm. Click Select in the dialog box, and the file chosen appears in the Link Input area, as shown in Figure 5.5.

5. Test the page in your browser. It should link to the Hats page.

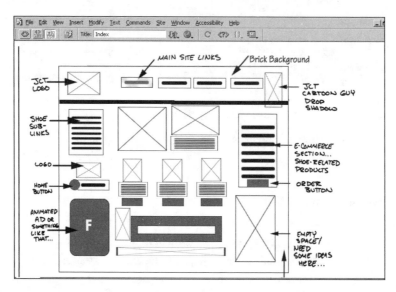

Figure 5.5   The Dreamweaver MX Property inspector changes to reflect whatever is selected. In this case, it reflects the hotspot added to the wireframe.

As you can see, navigation suddenly takes on a whole new dimension. This is a great time to consider whether any of the page elements are in the wrong place. In certain cases, you may even discover a couple of links that go to the same place. In this case, you should reconsider your navigation routes because multiple methods of getting to the same place are a traditional source of frustration for users.

Combining a Site Map with a Wireframe

As mentioned earlier in Chapter 4, mapping out the site gives both the designer and the client a look at the forest as opposed to the trees. You can now use the site map as a quick entry point to the individual wireframed pages. In this way, you can swiftly open any page on the site without having to drill through the site to get to the page you need to see. To use a Dreamweaver MX site map as a navigation tool to access the wireframes, follow these steps:

1. If necessary, open Index.htm. Select Site, Site Map, or press Option-F8 (Mac) or Alt-F8 (PC) to open the site map. You can now convert the map to either a .jpg or BMP image. BMP files are equivalent to .pict files on a Mac. If you are going to use the file on both a Mac and a PC, use the .jpg format. If it is used only on a PC, use the .bmp image. If it is used exclusively on a Mac, use the .jpg format.

Note

You may be asked to define the site when you open the Index.htm page. Use Index.htm as your root file when defining the site. If you are unsure as to how to define a site, see "Defining a Local Dreamweaver MX Site" in Chapter 2.

2. If you are using the PC version of Dreamweaver MX, select File, Save Site Map from the menu. If you are using the Mac version of Dreamweaver MX, select Site, Site View, Save Site Map. When prompted, choose the image format—.jpg or .bmp—and then navigate to the FrameNav folder on your hard drive. Click Save.

3. Adding the page to the site is relatively simple. Open the site map and then click once on the Index.htm page. If you are using a PC, select Site, Link to New File; Mac users should select Site, Site Map View, Link to New File. You are asked in the Link to New File dialog box to name the file—main.html—and to give the file and the link a name. In both cases, use the name **Main**. Click OK in the dialog box.

4. An icon for the new page appears on the site map. Double-click the icon to open this new page. Place the site map file, and add hotspots to the index page as well as a couple of others, as shown in Figure 5.6. Save the page and open it in your browser. This allows you to navigate to the various pages of the site using real names for the files, rather than the iconic representations on the wireframe.

Tip

Step 3 in the previous exercise involved a bit of mousing. Another way of adding a link to a new file is to select the file in the site map and right-click (PC) or Control-click (Mac) to open a context menu. Choose Link to New File Command; when the Link to New File dialog box opens, navigate to the file and click OK.

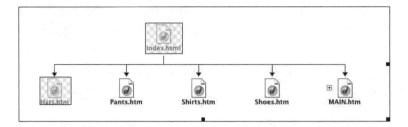

Figure 5.6   The site map image is imported into a new linked page, and hotspots are added.

Wireframing and FreeHand

The power of the MX Studio is apparent if you develop your wireframe drawings in FreeHand. The key productivity boosts for the developer are as follows:

- Paper-based deliverables—FreeHand's roots are in print, and the capability to print vectors through a laser printer gives you a crisp deliverable.

- Symbols—As you saw in the Fireworks MX exercise at the start of this chapter, symbols are a huge productivity boost. In FreeHand, symbols retain their vector characteristics.

- Fireworks MX compatibility—FreeHand documents can be opened in Fireworks MX, and if there is a symbol Library attached to the document, that Library will also open in Fireworks. You can also import FreeHand documents and their symbols into Flash.

- Symbols reduce file size, and it is virtually impossible to accidentally change a symbol. If it is correct in the first instance, it will be correct in all subsequent instances. Best of all, if a change has to be made, you can make it to the symbol and see it instantly applied to all of the instances.

Is it any wonder, then, that many developers regard FreeHand as their tool of choice for this aspect of the production process? Wireframe development becomes a round trip. The wireframe is built in FreeHand. The image is sliced or hotspots added in Fireworks MX and the results placed in Dreamweaver for client review.

Building the Wireframe in FreeHand

There are a number of features in FreeHand that lend themselves to the production of wireframe models. When building the wireframe, the most important production feature is the Layers panel. If you look at the panel, it appears to have been divided into two parts. The content you place in layers above the division will print. The content placed under the division is, for all intents and purposes, regarded by FreeHand as being non-printing. By putting a scan in the non-printing area, you can build or draw over it, and it will be ignored when you print a hard copy of the page. In this case, it makes sense to place the scan of the linear in the non-printing area, and build the wireframe model above it. To build a wireframe over a scanned image in FreeHand, follow these steps:

1. Open Wireframe.fh from the Chapter 5 Exercise folder on your hard drive. If the Layers panel isn't open, open it by selecting Window, Panels, Layers, or by pressing Command-6 (Mac) or Ctrl-6 (PC).

2. Notice that the scan appears to be grayed out. This is a visual indication this object is contained in a non-printing layer. To see this, click the check mark beside the Linear layer. The image disappears. Click the check mark again to make it reappear. Click the Lock icon. When a layer is locked, the content on that layer is unavailable for editing.

3. Open the Library panel by choosing Window, Library. You see the same set of symbols used in the FreeHand exercise presented earlier in this chapter; however, the Graphic symbol is missing. Creating a new symbol in FreeHand is remarkably similar to the process used in Fireworks MX. Select the Rectangle tool and then draw a rectangle on the page.

4. Select the Line tool, and draw one line from the upper-left corner of the rectangle to the lower-right corner. Draw another line from the upper-right corner to the lower left to create an X. Select the Pointer tool and then select the square and the two lines. Drag this object into the Library, and release the mouse. Name the new symbol **Graphic/Image**. Your Stage and Library should resemble Figure 5.7.

Sharing FreeHand Libraries with the Team

As in Fireworks MX, symbol Libraries can be shared among the members of the work group. For example, in the Library, you can create a folder named Wireframes, and place all of the wireframe elements you need into that folder. You can then add logos, color swatches, master pages, and anything else that would be needed by the group to their respective folders. To save the symbols or selected symbols, open the Library's popdown menu and then select Export. The Export dialog box opens, containing all of the symbols in the Library. Shift-click to select the items to be exported and then click the Export button. Name the file, navigate to the location where the file is to be saved, and click Save. When the file opens in FreeHand or Fireworks MX, it opens with a blank page. When opened in either application, the symbols in the exported Library will be placed in the new document's Library.

 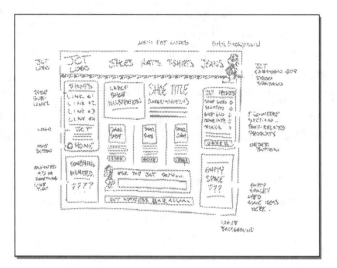

Figure 5.7   The scan is placed in the non-printing area under the bar in the FreeHand Layers panel. The symbols are set up and ready for use in the Library.

5. Add a new layer named **graphics** to the Layers panel. Drag a copy of the Graphic/Image symbol onto the page and then position it over the JCT logo area in the upper-left corner. Select the Scale tool, and resize the symbol.

6. Again, "working smart not hard" comes into play. Select the symbol over the logo, press the Alt (PC) or Option (Mac) key, and with the key pressed, drag a copy of the symbol over the JCT guy on the right side of the page.

7. Release the mouse and the Alt or Option key, and a copy of the symbol drops into place. Repeat this step for the remaining graphics, including the area named Empty Space at the bottom of the page.

Working with content on a FreeHand layer can become frustrating due to the way this application handles layers. For example, if an object is selected and you add a new layer, that object will move to the new layer from the layer where it currently resides. A great habit to get into with this application is to deselect everything on a layer by choosing Edit, Select, None, or Control-D (PC) or Command-D (Mac); then lock the layer. Deselect everything on the Graphics layer, and lock the layer. Add a new layer named **Text**, and add text symbols wherever text is called for. Keep locking and adding layers until all of the content has been covered. Name your final layer **Frame**, and draw a rectangle around the content. If you turn off the visibility of the Linear layer, your drawing should resemble that shown in Figure 5.8. Save the document as **Fhframes** to your Exercise folder.

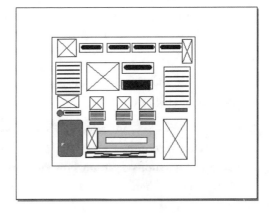

Figure 5.8   The symbols have been added to their layers and resized, and the page framed. By adding symbols to their own layer, you have quick access to them as changes occur.

At this point in the process, you have a single page constructed. To identify the objects, you could drag out a number of the arrow symbols and then add text that identifies each element on the page. You could also print this document to paper, and use it as a deliverable for client approval. If you have a number of pages that need to be built, FreeHand gives you the capability to create multi-page documents, unlike many drawing applications.

To add pages in FreeHand, you can select Window, Inspectors, Document and then select Add Pages from the panel's pop-down menu. Another method would be to select the Page tool from the toolbox, zoom out to 50%, and click on the edge of the page to select the entire page The page will look just like a selection on the page. Hold down the Alt (PC) or Option (Mac) key, and drag a copy of the page to another area of the pasteboard. After that is done, you can delete all of the content on the page's various layers, place a copy of the new page in the non-printing area of the Layers palette, and go to work.

Tip

If you are using FreeHand pages as a printed deliverable, consider adding a symbol to the Library that follows your normal approval sign-off design and wording. In this way, you can drag and drop the Approval symbol onto each page.

FreeHand to Fireworks MX to Dreamweaver MX

When you have two applications that can work with vectors but each has a specific purpose, you have an unbeatable combination of tools. FreeHand can be used to create the wireframes and the printed deliverables. Fireworks MX, however, can transform those files into a web-ready form. In this way, you deal with a production continuum. You work your way through the applications without having to lose time by recreating everything two or three times. By doing this, efficiency is injected into the process.

In the Fireworks MX exercise earlier in this chapter, you dropped the drawing into Dreamweaver MX and added the hotspots. In this exercise, you add the hotspots in Fireworks MX and then export the file to Dreamweaver.

1. Open Fireworks MX, and select File, Open. Navigate to the wireframe document you created previously in FreeHand and then click OK. You are presented with a number of questions regarding how Fireworks MX will handle the document. There is nothing here that requires special treatment, so click OK. The document opens on the page, and if you run the mouse over the various elements on the page, they are bordered in red.

2. If the canvas is transparent, change the canvas color to white—FFFFFF—using the Property inspector. If you don't have the Library open, select Window, Library, or press the F11 key on both the Mac and PC. Notice all of your FreeHand symbols are in the Fireworks Library, and the FreeHand layers have moved, intact, to Fireworks MX. What didn't move was the material on the non-printing layer.

Tip

An alternate method of opening the FreeHand file is to open a Fireworks MX document with the same page dimensions, select Edit, Select, All, or Control-A (PC) or Command-A (Mac), and drag all of the objects from the FreeHand page over to the Fireworks MX page. You know you are over the Fireworks MX page when the objects turn into a hollow rectangle. Release the mouse; the objects and the symbols drop into place. Unfortunately, reversing the process, such as Fireworks MX to FreeHand, does not result in the Fireworks MX Library moving into FreeHand.

3. Select the Rectangular Hotspot tool, and add hotspots to each of the four sub-heads at the top of the page. Don't worry about addresses or links—they will be prepared in Dreamweaver MX. Your Fireworks image should resemble Figure 5.9.

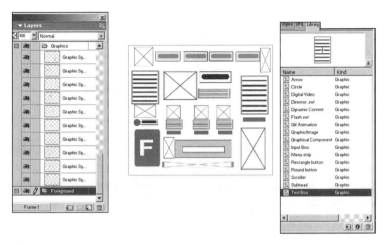

Figure 5.9   The FreeHand page, layers, and Library have been moved over to Fireworks MX, and the hotspots added to the image.

Tip

Another approach would be to assign the hotspots to the interactive areas of the page, convert the hotspots and selected items on the page into slices by selecting them, and select Edit, Insert, Slice, or Ctrl-Shift-U (PC) or Command-Shift-U (Mac).

4. Click the Fireworks MX Quick Export button in the upper-right corner of the Document window, and select Dreamweaver, Export HTML to open the Export Preview dialog box. Give the file a name, and save it to the FrameNav folder located in the FHFrames folder in the Chapter 5 Exercise folder on your hard drive. When the dialog box closes, save the image as a .png file.

Tip

Using the Export HTML command from the Fireworks Quick Export menu does not allow you to determine the image format for the Export. The default is a .gif. If the format is important, use File, Export Preview instead.

5. Click the Fireworks MX Quick Export button and then select Launch Dreamweaver from the pop-down list. When Dreamweaver MX opens, close the page and then open the HTML page you have just created in Fireworks MX, as shown in Figure 5.10. Click on one of the hotspots you created in Fireworks MX, and link it to one of the product pages in the folder. Repeat this for the remaining pages. After you have finished, test the page in a browser. By testing in a browser, you ensure the links are correct.

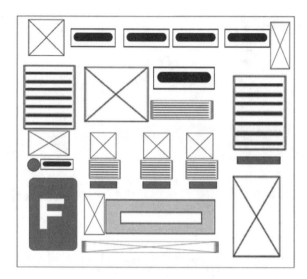

Figure 5.10   The page has moved from FreeHand to Fireworks to Dreamweaver where the links to the hotspots are assigned.

Building a Wireframe in Dreamweaver

Over the years, software manufacturers have seen their clients constantly clamoring for more and more features. To satisfy this craving, many of the more popular applications have the capability to use small side applications that extend the functionality of the main application. Photoshop does this through *plug-ins.* Dreamweaver' side applications or plug-ins are called *extensions.* Extensions can either be created by you, or downloaded from a variety of sources. Writing a custom extension is well out of the scope of this book, so we will concentrate on adding a third-party extension. One of the better sources for extensions is none other than Macromedia. At the time of this writing, there were more than 450 Dreamweaver extensions available for download. Before you head over to the Macromedia site and merrily start downloading, however, you have to obtain a copy of the latest version of the Extension Manager, if it isn't already installed on your machine.

The Extension Manager is a utility developed by Macromedia for the installation and management of extensions for Dreamweaver, Fireworks MX, and Flash. Extensions use the .mxp format, and when downloaded to your machine, they are opened by the Extension Manager and put into the proper Dreamweaver folders. Double-clicking an extension after download opens the Extension Manager and starts the installation process.

Installing the Wireframing Extension

Dreamweaver MX users already have the Extension Manager installed. The following exercise walks you through how to locate the Wireframing extension on the Macromedia web site, as well as how to install and use it:

1. Open your browser and point it to `http://www.macromedia.com/exchange/dreamweaver`. If this is your first visit to the Exchange, you need to register.

2. In the Search Extensions text input box, enter **Wireframing** and then click the Go button. Click the Wireframing hyperlink to go to the extensions page. Click the Download button for your specific platform.

3. Save the extension to your desktop. If you don't, the Extension Manager will launch automatically.

4. To install the extension, double-click the .mxp file on your desktop to launch the Extension Manager. You first see a disclaimer and licensing agreement. Click OK. The extension will be unpacked, and you will be notified if the installation was successful.

5. Quit the Extension Manager, open Dreamweaver, and go to work.

Tip

There is another way of installing extensions from within Dreamweaver. Select Help/Dreamweaver Exchange. If you are connected to the web, this will take you directly to the Dreamweaver Exchange, where you can locate and install extensions directly from within the application. The only caveat here is that some extensions require you to restart Dreamweaver for the extension to initialize. Wireframing isn't one of them.

Using the Wireframing Extension

This extension is simple to use. It essentially adds layers to a Dreamweaver document that function as the various boxes you can add to a site model. The following exercise builds the wireframe for the home page of the JCT site, and adds hyperlinks for site navigation. You will build the wireframes over the Fireworks wireframe image you created earlier in this chapter. This is done to give you the opportunity to work with this extension, and to place and size objects on a page. Normally you would build the model using a paper-based sketch of the site.

1. Open the DwWireframeEx folder in the Chapter 5 Exercise folder, and double-click the Index.htm document in the folder to launch Dreamweaver. When the page opens, select Insert, Wireframing to open the Wireframing pop-up menu. When the Extension Manager installed the extension, it was added to the Insert menu.

2. The Wireframing extension installs all of the bits and pieces necessary for a wire-frame, and makes them available to you through the Wireframing pop-down menu available through Insert, Wireframing. Select Button-Border=1 from the pop-down menu. A green box with a black border appears on the page. Drag the box over the Hats button and then resize, if necessary, by dragging a corner handle.

3. Inside the box between the brackets are the words Button Name. Select the words and type **Hats**. Without deselecting the word Hats, click the link area of the Property inspector, navigate to the Hats page in the DwNavFrame folder, select the Hats file, and click the Select button.

4. Select Insert, Wireframing, Gray Box with Label. A large gray box with words in the box appears on the page. This box is what is used to represent a graphic. Drag the gray box over the logo, resize the box, and replace the words in the box with **Logo**.

5. Add the Pants, Shoes, Shirts, and Home buttons. Add a gray box over the mascot, and label it **Mascot**.

6. Select Text Field with Label from the Insert, Wireframing menu. A white box with words at the top appears on the page. Drag over the text area, and resize the box to match the size of the text area at the left of the graphic. When you have finished adding the various elements, select the background image in the page and delete it. Your final page should look similar to Figure 5.11.

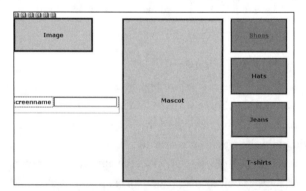

Figure 5.11   The wireframing is added to the page, and all the links are active.

This extension also contains a couple of important features. At the bottom of the wire-framing selections menu are two choices: the Page Title Bar and the Wireframing Disclaimer.

The Page Title Bar is a small box that you add to the first page, as shown in Figure 5.12. If ever a feature of an application had the wrong name, this would be a prime candidate. The title would have you assume you can add a title bar to the page. Not quite.

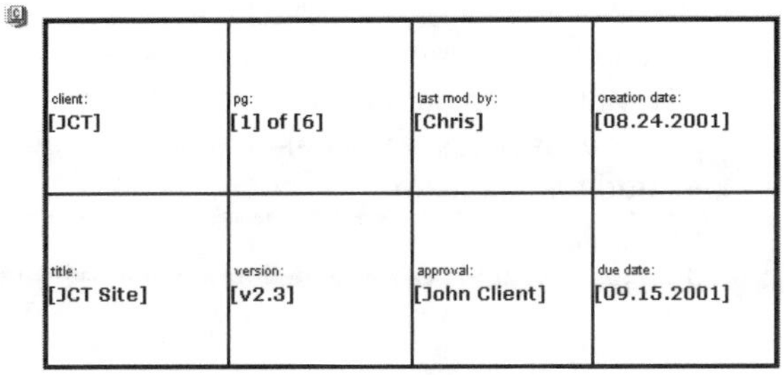

client: [JCT]	pg: [1] of [6]	last mod. by: [Chris]	creation date: [08.24.2001]
title: [JCT Site]	version: [v2.3]	approval: [John Client]	due date: [09.15.2001]

Figure 5.12   The inappropriately named Page Title Bar.

The Page Title Bar has a number of important areas that allow you to manage the client, project tracking, and the communications process. The areas of this feature are as follows:

- **Client.** Input the client's name.
- **Pg.** Input the page number and total number of pages in the site.
- **Last mod. by.** Input the name of the person responsible for the last modification to the page.
- **Creation Date.** Input the date the page was created.
- **Title.** Enter the name of the project.
- **Version.** This allows you to track major and minor site changes.
- **Approval.** The client's or project manager's name is entered here.
- **Due Date.** Enter the deadline.

The Wireframing Disclaimer is one of those little features designed to address potential disputes. You might encounter the client who thinks the wireframe is nothing more than placeholders for the final content. Rather than spend an inordinate amount of time explaining their function, you can add this rather concise disclaimer, as shown in Figure 5.13. Its function is to allow you to add a form of legal disclaimer that simply lets the client know how the model works, and that it is nothing more than a close representation of the site.

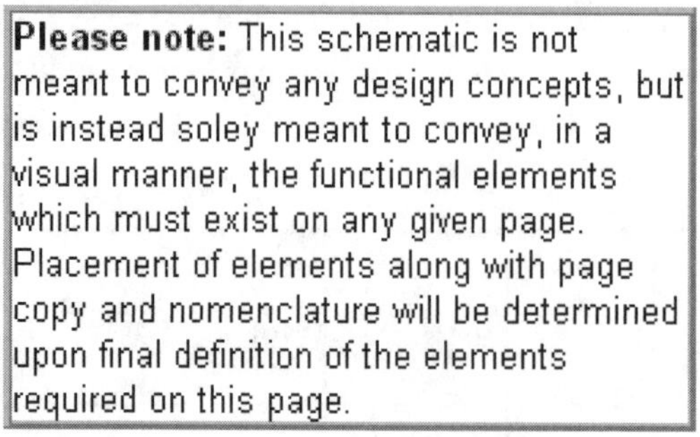

Please note: This schematic is not meant to convey any design concepts, but is instead soley meant to convey, in a visual manner, the functional elements which must exist on any given page. Placement of elements along with page copy and nomenclature will be determined upon final definition of the elements required on this page.

Figure 5.13   The Wireframing Disclaimer can be added to the first page of the wireframe.

Summary

As you have seen in this chapter, building a site involves more than simply opening the appropriate applications and designing the site. It requires careful planning and testing to ensure the issues of usability and ease of navigation are addressed.

You have seen how Fireworks can be used to create a wireframe model and how that model can then be imported into Dreamweaver MX, hotspots added, and the various links tested. We have also shown you how to create a Library of primitives in Fireworks that can be used for subsequent modeling requirements. You have seen how these Libraries of symbols can be shared among the members of the work group.

FreeHand is an excellent tool for the creation of wireframe models. Again, the Library feature is a huge productivity enhancement. It offers the ability to share the Libraries among the members of the group, add pages, and print hard copies for client approval.

The power of the MX Studio is evident when you start moving the documents between applications. You have seen the documents and symbols created in FreeHand move to Fireworks MX, where they can be converted to slices or have hotspots added to them. Using the Export button in Fireworks MX gives you one-click access to Dreamweaver MX by not only creating the HTML for Dreamweaver MX, but also launching the application. From there, the links can be added to the hotspots, and the final document tested in a browser.

You also discovered how the Wireframing extension can add a productivity boost to your efforts.

In the next chapter, we present how to prepare a site for the use of dynamic content using ColdFusion MX.

Chapter 6

Preparing for Dynamic Content

One of the great features of Dreamweaver MX is the capability to create dynamic web sites without an intimate knowledge of programming languages. What makes a site dynamic is the capability to load content on demand.

No longer do multiple pages have to be developed to display a variety of images or text. Instead, a variety of content can be flowed from a server into a single template as the content is needed.

In many respects, dynamic content opens up a new world within a web site—a world in which the content the viewer sees is constantly being updated. One advantage to this is that a greater amount of content can be displayed in significantly fewer pages. For example, a commercial photographer could display his work by category, and have only one page for each category rather than many pages. As the page is called from the browser, the content is loaded into the page from the server.

Dynamic sites work because they allow you to add, change, or remove data as required without affecting the web site. For example, the commercial photographer can have a site that categorizes many aspects of his work—sports, people, and so on—with several dozen photos in each category. The site may contain two or three template pages for searching and displaying the photographs. To the users who are sitting at their computer, each category of photos looks as though it has its own page, and each picture has its own details page. In this case, two or three pages are doing the work of dozens of pages. Best of all, the photographer can add, change, or delete images and photo categories without affecting the number of pages needed for smooth operation of the site.

A dynamic site also allows a greater degree of interactivity than ever offered on the web. Using our photographer as an example, a potential client could visit his page and choose to look at the portfolio. The page opens and images for each category appear. The client chooses his category—by clicking a picture—and then he can review the technical details behind the image or even the cost of the image. All of these interactive choices don't reside on a page. Their content resides in a database.

If you are planning to build dynamic sites, make sure a programmer is on your team. If the site involves a high degree of complexity, as in an ecommerce site, the margin of error available to you is minimal. Even though using Dreamweaver MX to build dynamic pages does not require mastery of programming languages, never forget that dynamic pages are code driven, which means they are in the realm of the team's programmer. Dreamweaver MX, through its user-friendly interface, does not make you a programmer. It is easy to make a mistake, and this mistake can be difficult to correct if you don't understand how it all works. As one of the authors is fond of saying, "It is like a book of spells: One wrong word, and you wind up with a million ducks."

Our intention is not to turn you into a coder, or explain how to build fully functional ecommerce sites for department stores. However, the direction taken by Macromedia in positioning their applications as rich, client-driven applications is significant enough that designers will not be able to avoid getting their feet wet in the area of dynamic site and content design.

In this chapter, we show you the techniques behind how you can build a dynamic site, and point out some of the pitfalls involved. Along the way, we show you how the Dreamweaver MX Suite is a powerful tool, and most important of all, how not to turn a web site into a million ducks.

Planning the Data

So far we have made it clear that web sites must be planned. This is basically the same process used when planning a dynamic web site. The only major difference you will encounter is that, along with planning content, you also have to plan the type of dynamic content to be displayed on your site. You have to define the purpose of the database, as well as the information categories needed and the subcategories. In the case of our photographer, he would define the purpose of the database as being to present samples of his work. The information categories would be areas such as image collection, clients, and visitors. The subcategories for image collection would involve Portraits, Sports, Landscapes, Corporate, and so on.

Presenting Data Quickly and Efficiently

When planning the data, you have to start thinking like a computer and considering how to create the databases in a logical manner. In terms of the web, confusion or contradiction simply adds time to the equation. For example, the online booksellers design their sites to reflect buying patterns. Every time a book buyer visits the Amazon.com site, the page that displays is different. Amazon always suggests books that reflect the buyer's purchasing pattern. Imagine what would happen if the suggestions included horticultural books, but all the buyer has purchased is murder mysteries. Suddenly confusion—*Am I really at Amazon?*—and contradiction—*What does gardening have to do with murder mysteries?*—come into play. The book buyer wastes time trying to find something that specifically meets his interests. If this happens often enough, the buyer will not return. Time is something users are not prepared to invest while they watch a spinning cursor as the server rummages through the database attempting to locate the appropriate data.

To get started, ask yourself a few questions:

- What is going to be stored in the database? Don't stop at a simple answer, such as "text" because this is too broad a description. Text could be a product description. It could be a list of names gathered from visitors. It also could be passwords permitting access into the site.

- What does each piece of data look like? By this, we are not talking about the font and point size of a piece of text. If it is a description of a product item, it would be a text field in the database. For example, if it is a name text field, it is a certain length. If it is a memo field, it would contain a lot more text.

- How will the data be presented? This involves a design decision because in dynamic sites, data is traditionally presented in a table-based layout. In this case, each cell of the table will hold content.

- Do you have a model that suits your needs? A model is a representation, or a definition, of how the data will be stored within a database. It consists of fields that hold each piece of data and tables, which are simply a logical group of fields within a certain function of a database. A good example of this is a shopping cart on an ecommerce site. As items are chosen, data is placed into various fields within a shopping cart table of the database. This data could be a product ID along with a mathematical calculation of the price and the quantity of the product. For example, a visitor decides to purchase two white shirts that cost $10.00 each. The final price would require a field that calculates the value of the purchase. Add in two pairs of pants at $25.00 each, and you would not only need a field for these items but also a line for the total cost of each of the pants and shirts in your shopping cart. What may work for a bulletin board model, such as a photographer showing his images, will not work for an ecommerce model in which the photographer sells his images. The biggest mistake you could make is to simply copy a model with which you are familiar and bend the technology around the model—that is inefficient. Make sure the model you are using is right for your needs.

- Is there repetition? If there is, you may find consolidation of data is necessary. For example, if you are collecting names and addresses, it will not make sense to store them in a different table if the information you are collecting is no different than someone who creates an account online. Down the road, this visitor's information can be reused when they become a paying customer, or if they enter themselves in a promotion that your company launches. Having 10 copies of the same data is poor data management.

Planning involves the present and the future. Situations change as products are added or dropped, and failure to plan for this flexibility will create a maintenance nightmare down the road. It is easier to plan to add shoes and ties while the model is being built. It is incredibly difficult and expensive to graft them onto a model that wasn't built to accommodate them. Again, if you are unsure of how to plan for a database that will meet your needs down the road, it's a good idea to consult a database developer for help.

Constructing a Database

After the plan is in place, it is time to create the database to hold the information that you can organize, sort, change, and update as changes occur. Though there are a lot of database applications available, we use one of the more common—Microsoft Access. This section is not designed to show you everything you need to know about creating and using databases. The purpose here is to demonstrate how to construct the document that will become the backbone of a dynamic site.

Creating the Database in Microsoft Access

As database applications go, this application is not the most difficult to use. The version we utilize is the one shipped with Microsoft Office XP Professional.

We should also mention that many ColdFusion hosts offer Microsoft Access hosting as a part of their package of services. This was the primary decision behind our using this database platform for our example.

To create a database in Access, follow these steps:

1. Open Microsoft Access. A blank page opens that contains a New File panel onscreen, as shown in Figure 6.1.

2. Select Blank Access Database. You are prompted to name your document and choose its location. Save your database in an area away from the web server. If this isn't possible, place the file in a password-protected folder to maintain the security of the data. Your web server administrator can help you do this. When you have named the database and decided where it will be located, click Create.

3. When the file is saved, the Database (Access 2000 File Format) dialog box opens, and asks you how the file should be formatted. Select Tables in the Objects menu on the left side of the dialog box, and click the New button on the menu bar to open the New Table dialog box. Select Design View, shown in Figure 6.2. A blank table opens.

Figure 6.1   To create a new database, select Blank Database from the panel on the right side of the screen.

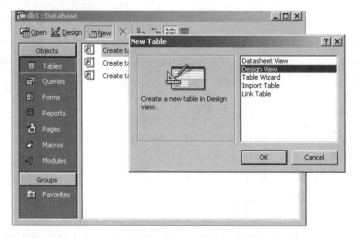

Figure 6.2   You start by selecting Tables from the Object menu, clicking New, and choosing Design View from the New Table dialog box.

4. Enter the following in the indicated areas:

Field Name: ProductTypeID

Data Type: AutoNumber

5. Click in the first cell of the second row and enter the following:

Field Name: ProductType

   Data Type: Text

6. Right-click ProductTypeID, and select Primary Key. Your table should resemble
    Figure 6.3. Close the table, and save it as **ProductType**.

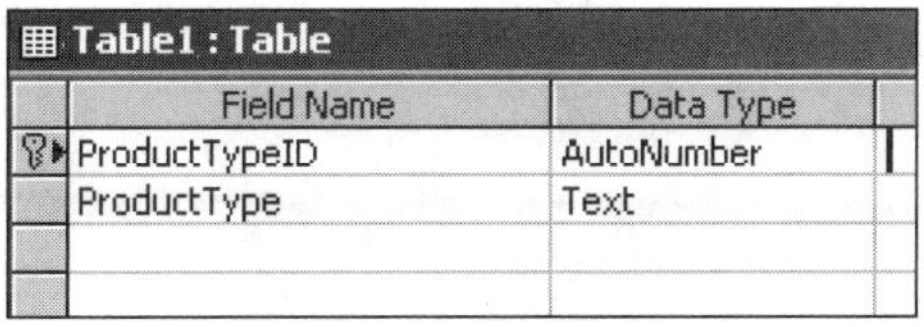

Figure 6.3   The database fields have been set, and the primary key added.

Note

A primary key in Access is a unique identifier for each record in the table, which will
help locate records faster when you need them. By setting the field as a primary key,
you are telling Access that each record in the table is unique.

7. The next table holds information regarding the JCT products. Create a new table
    using the earlier steps. When the table opens, enter the following information by
    clicking the appropriate column within the Design view window for each field in
    the table.

Field Name: ProductID

   Data Type: AutoNumber

Field Name: ProductTypeID

   Data Type: Number

Field Name: Product

   Data Type: Text

Field Name: Description

   Data Type: Text. Adjust the field size properties so that it can accommodate
           100 characters.

Field Name: Price

   Data Type: Currency

8. After the fields have been set up, right-click ProductID, and select Primary Key
    from the context menu that appears. Close the table and save it as **Product**. It
    should resemble Figure 6.4.

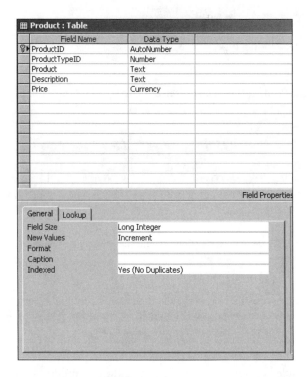

Figure 6.4   The Product table is now completed. Note the text area properties have been changed to accommodate a 100-character product description.

You now need to set the relationship between the ProductID table and the Product table. By doing this, you are able to associate information from one table with information within another table. You also need to be able to set up some rules within the database so that no stray records can be created. This ensures that you can effectively manage your data. The advantage to this is that repetitive information is excluded.

9. Select Tools, Relationships to open the Show Table dialog box. Select both tables, as shown in Figure 6.5, and click Add. The two tables appear in the Relationship window.

10. Two windows open in the Relationships window. To set the relationship between the two tables, select the ProductTypeID field in Product table, and click/drag it over the ProductTypeID field in the ProductType table. The cursor changes to a small rectangle when you are over the correct field.

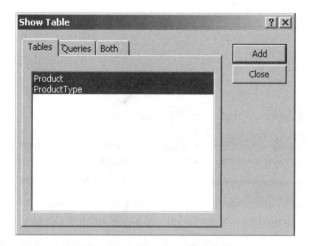

Figure 6.5   The relationship between tables is set in the Show Table dialog box. You are
prompted to select the tables that will be sharing data.

11. Release the mouse, and the Edit Relationships dialog box opens as shown in
Figure 6.6. Click the check boxes for Enforce Referential Integrity and Cascade
Delete Related Records.

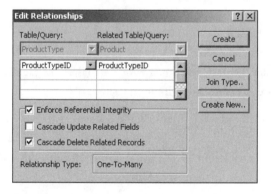

Figure 6.6   The relationship between the fields is determined in the Edit
Relationships dialog box.

12. Notice the One-to-Many option in the Relationship Type area. This means you
can have more than one product with the same product type. In our case, we are
going to have a number of shirts available in the Shirts category. Click Create,
and a line between the two fields in the tables is added. Close the Relationship
window.

Tip

One of the authors suggests printing a hard copy of the Relationship window. This gives him a handy diagram to use when designing a dynamic site.

Note

The Enforce Referential Integrity option sounds impressive, but essentially all it means is that records cannot be created in the main table without relating to a record in an associated table. In a one-to-many relationship, the field in the first table must be the table's primary key, and the field in the second can't be a primary key.

You have created a data model that will hold our various product types, such as shoes, shirts, hats, and so on—as well as the various products that will be tied to those types. You also looked to the future because the database is designed in such a way that you can add a new product type and then add new products under that type. Additionally, you designed the database in such way so that you cannot add a product that does not have a corresponding product type. This helps keep the data organized. You designed the database in such way that if you delete a product type, any products associated with that type will also be deleted. This explains why you clicked on Cascade Delete Related Records in the Edit Relationships dialog box. It is time to populate the database.

Populating the Database

Having designed the database and determined the relationships between the fields, you can now start to enter the data, or populate the database. This exercise creates the table for the shoes that are available through the JCT site.

1. Double-click the ProductType table in the Database window. This opens the table that will be used to set up the product categories. Because the ProductTypeID area automatically numbers the entries, click once in the field under ProductType and then enter **Shirts**.

2. Click in the field directly under Shirts, and enter **Hats**. The ProductTypeID fields now have numbers. Repeat this for Shoes and Pants.

3. Open the Product table, and enter the following into their respective areas. The key is the number under the ProductTypeID shown in Figure 6.7. It matches the ProductTypeID for Shoes in the ProductType table:

ProductTypeID: 3

> Product: Raven
>
> Description: Running shoe with racing stripe
>
> Price: 49.95

ProductTypeID: 3

> Product: Hawk
>
> Description: Basketball shoes
>
> Price: 59.95

ProductTypeID: 3

> Product: Falcon
>
> Description: Track shoes
>
> Price: 59.95

ProductTypeID: 3

> Product: Eagle
>
> Description: Tennis shoes
>
> Price: 79.95

4. Close the database and then quit Access. The database is now ready to be put online.

		ProductTypeID	ProductType
▶	+	1	Shirts
	+	2	Hats
	+	3	Shoes
	+	4	Pants
*		(AutoNumber)	

ProductType : Table

Figure 6.7   The products are entered into the Product table. The key is to have the ProductTypeID match the Shoes category in the Product table.

Note that there is no request to save the data. In Access, as in most databases, information is saved as soon as it is entered. The only time you may be asked to save something in Access is when you adjust the column size, filters, or sorting order. You are asked, in this instance, if you want to save the layout.

Going Online with ColdFusion MX

The most common reaction users have to ColdFusion MX, when they are first exposed to it, is "Where's the application?" There isn't one, because ColdFusion is a programming interface between the web server and your database. It takes the information from the database, and presents it to the user in either HTML or XML format. The only interface between you and ColdFusion is a web page. It's what is under the hood of that page that is so important and so powerful. Complex applications can be written using this application thanks to its framework-style approach to programming.

Though it may seem intimidating, ColdFusion MX is our intermediary between the database you just created and the Dreamweaver MX page that needs the information. For this exercise, you need to have ColdFusion MX installed and have assigned an administrative password.

To link up ColdFusion to your new database, follow these steps:

1. In the Start menu, open the ColdFusion Administrator page that appears in the browser and log in with your administrative password. Select the Data Sources link under the Data and Services heading to open the Add New Data Source window.

2. Enter **JCT** into the Data Source Name area and then select Microsoft Access from the Driver pop-down menu. Your screen should resemble Figure 6.8. Click Add to go to the Data Source details window for JCT.

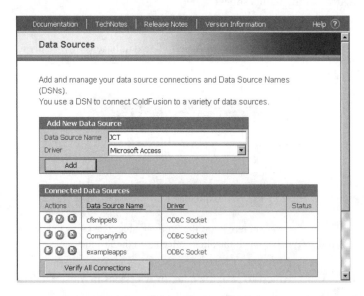

Figure 6.8   The first step is to tell ColdFusion MX what data source you will be using.

3. Click the Browse Server button in the Database File area to open the File selector box, and locate the JCT Access file. After it is located, as shown in Figure 6.9, select the file and then click Apply to select the database file.

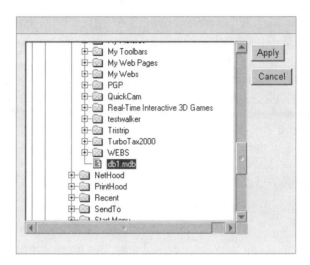

Figure 6.9   The database file has been located.

4. You are automatically returned to the Data Source window. Click Submit. The links are created and you are returned to the Add Data Source window. Your file appears in the list, as shown in Figure 6.10.

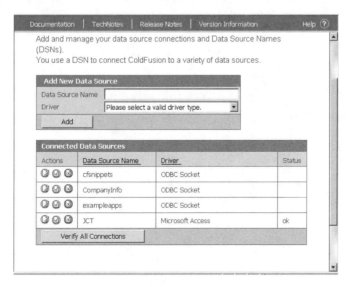

Figure 6.10   The JCT database created in Access is now linked as a ColdFusion MX data source.

Your database is now online and ready to be used with Dreamweaver MX and ColdFusion MX. Close your browser.

Creating a Test Dreamweaver MX Template for Live Data

This section demonstrates how to move data from the Access database created earlier through ColdFusion MX and then into Dreamweaver MX. The critical steps are to configure the site to talk to ColdFusion MX and then design a table-based page in Dreamweaver MX. If everything is done properly, the information flows into the table's cells.

1. Open your ColdFusion MX Administrator page from the Start menu. Select RDS Password under the Security heading. By setting a Remote Development Server (RDS) password, you can restrict access to ColdFusion MX servers by Dreamweaver MX.

2. When the RDS Password page opens, select the Use an RDS Password for Dreamweaver MX or ColdFusion Studio option. In the New Password text box, enter a password (up to 20 characters). In our case, because the ColdFusion server is not being used for hosting purposes, we used the admin password. This is strongly discouraged if you are online.

Note

Never use the admin password for development when you are online—ever; otherwise, you are offering any and all programmers with a browser free access to your entire ColdFusion MX server. It is just the same as not using the same access codes for your bank card and nuclear missile launcher.

3. Confirm your new password in the Confirm Password field. If the two passwords don't match, you get an error message. If your screen matches Figure 6.11, click Submit Changes. When you are notified the password has been accepted, quit ColdFusion MX.

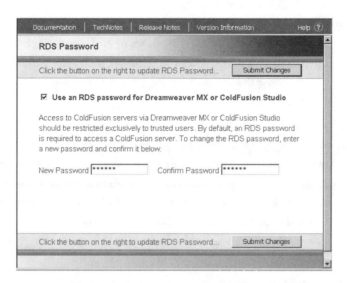

Figure 6.11   Setting a Remote Development Server (RDS) password in ColdFusion MX.

Building a Dreamweaver MX Page for Dynamic Data

You have set up the database, and configured the middleware. It is now time to design the pages in Dreamweaver MX that will pull the data from the Access database through ColdFusion, where it is placed on a page designed in Dreamweaver MX and then viewed through a web browser.

Dreamweaver MX has an abundant number of powerful tools that allow you to hook into ColdFusion and obtain the data in the database. Because the site you want to create uses dynamic data, you can create the site directly from the Dreamweaver MX Application panel.

1. Open Dreamweaver MX, and define a new site by selecting the Server Behaviors tab on the Application panel. Click Create a Site to open the Create Site window. Name the site **JCT** and then click the Next button at the bottom of the window. Complete instructions for creating a site are found in Chapter 2, "Content Management."

Note

For the purposes of this book and to get you familiar with Dreamweaver MX, use the Basic Site Configuration panel in the Site Definition dialog box. When you are more familiar with the advanced features of Dreamweaver MX site creation, you can easily navigate the Advanced panels. For now, the basic configuration will more than suffice in getting a test template up and running.

2. The next screen you see asks if you want to use a server technology. Underneath the question you are asked to click either a Yes or No button. Click Yes because you are using ColdFusion MX. After you select Yes, a pop-up menu appears that enables you to choose the server technology. Select ColdFusion from the list. Click the Next button.

3. This part of the Site Definition dialog box is important because it is where you set the location of your files. Your page is being built on a local computer that sits on your desk, and your ColdFusion MX server is on another computer, which could be on the same network or on another continent. In this case, you have a computer that is on the same network as ColdFusion, meaning your choice is limited to editing your files locally and then uploading them to a testing server at some other time. Select the Edit Locally Then Upload to Remote Testing Server option.

4. At the bottom of the screen is where you tell Dreamweaver MX where to put the locally edited files. Click the Browse button to open the File Selector dialog box. Navigate to the folder where your files are stored on your hard drive, select the folder, and click OK. Click the Next button to move to the next screen in the process.

5. This next screen of the Site Definitions dialog box allows you to set how you will be connecting to your test server. You are being asked, "How do you connect to your testing server?" The answer is in the range of choices in the pop-down menu. In this case, you are using RDS, so select RDS. A settings button appears beside your choice.

6. Click the settings button and fill in the Host Name (or IP address) of the server, the port you are using, which is usually kept at 80, the full host directory, which is the file path on your server's hard drive to the site root of your folder, and your user name and password to access the site. If you are the administrator or the only user, use the admin password. Again, this is not recommended in a live situation. Click the Save check box at the bottom of this dialog box if you want to save your password. Click Next when you are ready to move on.

Note

If you are using ColdFusion MX without a web server, such as Microsoft Internet Information Services (IIS) on a PC, you can use port 8500 as your port to talk directly to ColdFusion MX. 8500 is the ColdFusion MX default.

7. The next screen of the Site Definition dialog box allows you to set up the URL of your testing server's site root folder. This is important because Dreamweaver MX acts like a browser when connecting to your server for retrieving live data. Enter the URL to the server. We used `http://localhost/`. You might want to click the Test URL button to be sure your URL is valid. A small message box appears, informing you the test was successful. If the URL isn't valid, a different message box appears and offers you a number of possible solutions. If the test is valid, click the Next button.

8. You are now asked to choose whether you want to enable check in and check out. If you are the only one working on the site, select No, I Do Not Enable Check In and Check Out and then click Next.

9. You are now presented with a screen in the Site Definition dialog box that summarizes all the choices you have made. If all the settings are correct, click Done. You are now ready to create a new page, and test out your dynamic content.

Building the Dreamweaver MX Page for Dynamic Data

Having set the links to ColdFusion, it is time to start building the page that displays the information contained in your Access database.

1. Create a new page within your site, and make sure you are using a .cfm extension to enable ColdFusion to recognize and process the page. After you have created a new page, click the Server Behaviors tab in the Application palette to open the Server Behaviors panel.

2. Dreamweaver MX now provides you with a checklist of things to do in the Server Behaviors panel before you perform any dynamic content development with live data previews. You can perform the required steps by clicking the hyperlinked entries in the list. Follow these steps through the checklist:

   - If you have not already done so, set your Remote Development Server settings by clicking the RDS login hyperlink within the Server Behaviors panel. Use the password created in step 1.

   - Select your ColdFusion Data Source by entering the ODBC connection name to your Access database—JCT—that you created in the previous section.

   - You are now be prompted to create a RecordSet, which is how the requested data is pulled from the Access database. Click the + in the Server Behaviors panel, and add a new RecordSet. Give your RecordSet a name, such as **JCTProductList**. Select JCT as your data source.

3. You are now presented with a list of tables from which to choose. Select the Product table. In the columns area, click the radio button.

   When you get the hang of database handling, you can start filtering your data. There's also an advanced feature that allows you to enter your queries, but it is recommended that you learn about SQL, a database programming language, before using this feature.

4. Insert a table within the page that is two rows high by three columns wide. You can do this by selecting Insert, Table—or clicking the table object on the Object palette under the Common tab and then entering the number of rows and columns in the resulting dialog box. In the top row of the table, enter your desired headings. In this case, we used Product, Description, and Price.

5. Click the Bindings tab of the Application panel, select your Recordset—JCTProductList—and click the plus sign (PC) or the triangle (Mac) to open it. You see your database fields that you had set up earlier listed underneath.

6. Select the product field, and drag it to the first table cell under the Product header on your page. Select the description field, and drag it to the next table cell under the Description header on your page. Select the price field, and drag it to the next table cell under the Price header on your page. Your page should look like that shown in Figure 6.12.

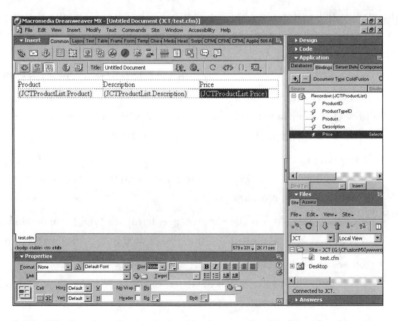

Figure 6.12   The data from the Access database is set to flow into the selected cells of the table.

7. Select the table row of your fields by dragging across the entire row, or by selecting one of the cells containing the field and then clicking the <tr> tag at the bottom of the page window. Click the + in the Server Behaviors tab of the Application palette, and add a repeating region.

8. You are now presented with the Repeating Region dialog box, in which you can enter the recordset and how you want the repeating records displayed. Make sure the defined recordset—JCTProductList—is selected. In this case, you want to show all the records, so click the All Records radio button (Figure 6.13) and then click OK.

Figure 6.13   Repeating regions simply increase the number of rows to accommodate the data in the recordset.

9. Click the Live Data View button on your page, and you see your data come to life. All the data is retrieved from the server and displayed on the page. By adding the repeating region in the table row, you have allowed a formatted table row to repeat itself, and display the data in a nice and neat fashion.

You have successfully created a working template, as shown in Figure 6.14.

Summary

This chapter focused on preparing for dynamic data. We discussed how dynamic data works, and presented you with some tips about planning for a dynamic site. Designers spend the time necessary to plan the site and the workflow, but it is also critical to take the time and plan what data you need. It's also crucial to determine how it will be presented to have it appear on the page quickly and efficiently.

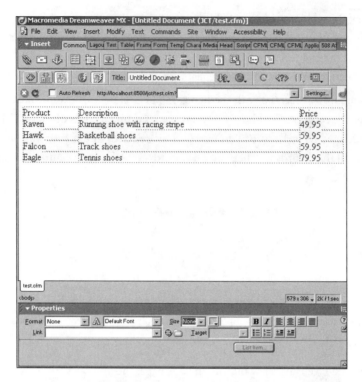

Figure 6.14   The data is live and the table in Dreamweaver MX grows to accommodate it. Don't be concerned if you prices grow to four decimal places; this page simply tests the dynamic data flow between Access and Dreamweaver MX.

We walked you through the steps necessary to create a database using Microsoft Access. We also discussed how to create the relations between the data tables in Access, and how to populate the tables with data.

After the database was created, we discussed how to configure ColdFusion MX to use the Access database. With that done, we showed you how to create a template in Dreamweaver MX that uses the dynamic data capabilities of the application as well as ColdFusion MX.

As you worked through this chapter, you discovered the process from creation of the database to having Dreamweaver access data that is fairly complex and, in certain instances, quite technical. This is why we strongly suggest a database developer or a coder be brought in as an integral part of your team.

In the next chapter, we start examining how to plan the look of the pages in your site. You will discover that MX Studio offers you a surprisingly comprehensive suite of tools that enable you to create content for your site.

Part III

Developing the Content

Chapter 7

MX

fireworks flash freehand coldfusion dreamweaver fireworks
eamweaver fireworks flash freehand coldfusion dreamweave
coldfusion dreamweaver fireworks flash freehand coldfusio
eehand coldfusion dreamweaver fireworks flash freehand
orks flash freehand coldfusion dreamweaver fireworks
weaver fireworks flash freehand coldfusion dreamweave

Planning the Look of the Pages

Everything on a web page either adds or detracts from the user's experience. Although obvious errors such as non-intuitive navigation controls, spelling mistakes, and irrational content placement will diminish the experience, type and color also factor into the mix.

Survey after survey finds that people don't surf the web to be entertained. The primary activity they undertake is reading the words on the web page .The images and animations on a page will draw the user's eye to the information, but the words on the page contain all the information. It is important that you make the words on the page as easy to read and understand as possible. Images and color may draw the eye to the content, but it is the words on the page that describe what the user is seeing. The issues of font choice, readability, and legibility are just as important as the placement of the content.

Color also impacts the user experience. In a perfect web world, color would be uniform across the platforms. Unfortunately, this is not the case. When working with color, a host of problems ranging from the color model to the computer display have to be defined and dealt with before proceeding with the creation of the content. A classic example is the client who uses a Pantone Blue for their print logo, and insists that same color be used on the web. The issue with that is the Pantone is an ink and the computer screen uses light to make a color. Neither color space—ink or computer—can make the transition to the other.

Each of the MX tools has a specific method of contending with these problems. The time to deal with these problems is before the content is created, not during the creation process. This is why many developers will rough out the content to give the pages their look. At this stage of the process, the financial implications of discovering and dealing with a major problem are negligible.

Typography

Type is not simply the grey stuff that goes around the pictures. It is an important element of the communications process, and far too many web designers have overlooked this in their efforts to pursue a cool and trendy look. Forget cool and trendy. People visit your site to read the information. If people can't read the information because the text is difficult to look at, how can they be expected to understand it?

The Internet has been with us for almost 40 years, but the web has been around for only about a decade. Typography has been around since the mid-1400's. It was when type moved from atoms of lead to bits on a computer that the problems started. The rise of desktop publishing also marked the decline of the typographer/typesetter. The craft, which usually involved a five-year apprenticeship, virtually disappeared, and the job landed on the shoulders of the designer. When the web arrived, the art of typography essentially disappeared because when it comes to the web, there is no typography. There is only type because typography is a creative art that can't be controlled by HTML.

Overview of Typography

The best you can hope for is that the users viewing your page have Arial, Verdana, Helvetica, or Sans Serif on their computers, thanks to the <font> and <Font Face> tags. Although Cascading Style Sheets (CSS) address the limitations of the tags, they are still rudimentary when it comes to typography. Even then, the older browsers starting at version 3 and lower don't always render CSS accurately. Fine typography, the use of fonts, and typographic technique to reinforce or present a message is now in the realm of artwork. This isn't to say that the type designer Matthew Carter didn't do some great work by designing Verdana and Georgia, but even these two fonts don't work all that well outside of a browser.

What happened? The pixel is a good starting point. Graphic designers who work in print media get to pack thousands of them into their images. They also have thousands of them come spitting back out at them through their laser printers and ImageSetters. We toilers on the web don't get to interface with our audience in a high-resolution universe. We get to light up a hundred or so pixels per inch, depending upon the platform, as we interface with our audience through a computer screen. At our resolution, the fine nuances of the serif on a Times Roman "T" looks roughly like a serif, and the distinction between Stone Sans and Univers is difficult at best to discern. The page that looks great at a screen resolution of 800 x 600 pixels may require a magnifying glass to read at a screen resolution of 1024 x 768.

Without Postscript and TrueType to help us along, enlarging type simply enlarges the pixels used to create the letterform onscreen. The result is a complete degradation of the typeface. Suddenly Times looks blocky and chunky. Loops lose their smoothness. The leg of a "k" starts to wander. In short, the type starts to break up…and then it gets worse.

To take advantage of vectors, web designers convert their type into artwork or, in the case of Flash MX, embed the font into their .swf files. Realizing this works, they then proceed to make a readable and legible line of type both unreadable and illegible. They toss fonts into their work, not for aesthetic or artistic reasons but because they are in the font folder and look cool. A bad situation starts to become ugly.

Although the intention in this section is to talk about some of the neat stuff you can do with type in Fireworks, Flash, and Dreamweaver, a brief overview of some of the fundamentals will help put much of what we are going to talk about into context.

Fonts, Faces, and Families

The terms *font* and *face* mean essentially the same thing. A *font* is a collection of all the letters, numbers, and special characters. For example, Times Roman is a font in the Times family. A family is a collection of related typefaces. The Times family on your computer could consist of Times, Times Bold, Times Italic, and Times Bold Italic. The Univers family, shown in Figure 7.1, is a good example of this.

Univers Light
Univers Light Oblique
Univers 55 Regular
Univers 55 Oblique
Univers 55 Bold
Univers 55 Bold Oblique
Univers 55 Black
Univers 55 Black Oblique
Univers 47 Light
Univers 47 Light Oblique
Univers 57 Regular
Univers 57 Oblique
Univers 67 Bold
Univers 67 Bold Oblique

Figure 7.1 The Univers family. Each of the faces is a font. Designed by Adrian Frutiger, there are 21 typestyles in the family. Univers 55 is the parent from which all of the variants were developed.

The Univers font family is extremely robust and flexible. Each font can be used with the others in the family, and the design won't be compromised. For example, mixing the fonts within a family can actually add expression to your design. This is referred to as giving words a voice. An example, originally developed by Carl Dair, would be the one shown in Figure 7.2. It is plain old Times. If you could describe the voice of the words, you could say they are a monotone.

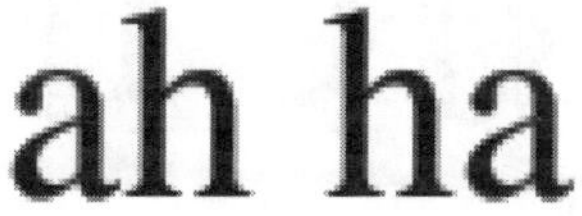

ah ha

Figure 7.2   By using equal weights, the voice of the font is a monotone.

Put Times Italic together with Times Bold, however, and you have the rather expressive phrase in Figure 7.3. The first word, *ah*, is set using Times Italic, and the word practically sighs. The second word, **ha**, is set in Times Bold, and it practically shouts at you. This example was developed by Carl Dair and used in his book, *Design with Type*, published by the University of Toronto Press.

ah **ha**

Figure 7.3   Notice how the phrase takes on a whole different meaning. The words are now expressive.

Readability and Legibility

When it comes to typography, the two words *legibility* and *readability* are rarely separated. Legibility is what makes type readable. In fact, the person reading the words will find it to be a pleasant experience because they don't have to work at deciphering the text.

When we read we really don't pay much attention to the individual letters. What we look for are the visual clues that make the letters familiar to us. For example, when we read, there are two areas of the letterforms that give us the clues to the letters. The first place we look is along tops of the letters in the word. In Figure 7.4, the capital letters are all a uniform size. In this instance, the reader is forced to stop and decipher each letter. That's work. The lowercase letters, however, are not uniform. The reader can quickly skim across the top of them and pick out the visual clues and unevenness, provided by the ascenders and descenders of the letters. This allows the reader to quickly discern each letter. Another example is included on the book web site. If you open the Legibility.swf file, you can see how one reads the words. When the file opens, you see the bottoms of the letters. If you move the blue box to cover the bottoms of the letters and show the tops, the word becomes quite distinct.

Figure 7.4   Notice how the tops of the letters make each one legible in the lower example.

The other area readers use for visual clues are the sides of the letters. In Figure 7.5, it is difficult to discern the word "condor" when the right side of each letter is hidden. You can see the word condor is easily understood when the left side of each letter is hidden.

Figure 7.5   The word condor is recognized, even when the left side of each letter is hidden.

Another factor to consider is the design of the letters in the chosen font. In certain instances, they can be either misread or misinterpreted due to their similarity to other letterforms in the font. Figure 7.6, for example, shows the uppercase letterforms of Univers 55 are quite similar. Note how the Q and the O have essentially the same shape. It is easy to miss the tail of the Q. The same goes for the F and the E.

OQFE
oqfe

univers55 60pt roman

Figure 7.6   Which is more readable, the upper line or the lower line? The captial Q and the capital F have essentially the same shape as the O and the E. The reader has to stop to decipher the letter.

Although the individual letters provide the visual clues, you can't overlook the fact that they are the building blocks of the words your user will read. If the clues are missing, or not given the opportunity to stand out, the word will form an unfamiliar pattern and can be difficult to read. A classic example is the extensive use of capital letters. Text set in all capitals suffers from a distinct loss of legibility, and the reader is left wondering what it all means. Essentially, what happens, as shown in Figure 7.7, is the letters all take on a uniform shape that removes the visual clues necessary to make the words recognizable. Set the whole thing in 6-point type with a light grey color, and you have a classic example of how to handle the small print that your clients don't want anyone to read, but the government says has to be there.

HOW WOULD YOU LIKE TO READ SOMETHING THAT WAS SET IN ALL UPPER CASE LETTERS? IT IS VERY DIFFICULT TO TO READ AND TAKES UP A GREATER AMOUNT OF SPACE THAN HAD THE LETTERS BEEN SET IN LOWERCASE. SOMETIMES YOUI CAN USE UP AS MUCH AS 35 PER CENT MORE SPACE ON THE PAGE WHEN YOU USE CAPITAL LETTERS. ALL OF THE WORDS HAVE EQUAL WEIGHT AND THE VISUAL CLUES AND CUES THAT DISTINGUISH THE LETTERS FROM EACHOTHER ARE OMITTED. THE END RESULT IS A BLOCK OF TEXT THAT IS VERY CLOSE TO BEING ALMOST IMPOSSIBLE TO READ. NOW YOU KNOW WHY THE SAMLL PRINT IN CERTAINS ADS IS RARELY READABLE. THE DESIGNER DOESN'T WANT TO YOU TO READ IT THUS THE PIECE IS HARD TO READ.

Figure 7.7   Text set in uppercase is almost impossible to read.

There is also a movement in the Flash community to use small dark grey letters on light grey backgrounds. Again, hopefully this is a fad because the type is both unreadable and illegible.

Another legibility issue is the spacing between letters and words. Typographers pay careful attention to this detail, and the space they remove is minute—try imagining the letter "m" and slicing off 1/1000 of the letter's width—but improves legibility due to the closeness of each letter. Remove too much space, and the letters touch, or crash, and form a single shape. Add too much space, and you lose the relationships between the letters that form the words. Try reading the text in Figure 7.8 to get a sense of the importance of this aspect of typography.

The space between letters and words is an important consideration. Notice how difficult this sentence is to read because the spacing has been reduced. I n c r e a s i n g t h e   s p a c e   c a n   a l s o m a k e   i t   d i f f i c u l t   t o r e a d .

Figure 7.8   Readability disappears when the letters (kerning) or words (tracking) are moved closer or farther apart from each other.

Choosing and Using a Font

Choosing fonts and using them properly requires subjective—not objective—decisions. Still, there are some very loose guidelines for font usage you might want to consider. You can also feel free to break them if the right opportunity presents itself.

- Always focus on the audience. That really cool typeface you saw on the snowboard ad probably won't work for your grandparents.

- You can't be taught how to use type. You can only learn how to use it. Prowl the newspapers, magazines, TV, the Internet, books, posters, movie titling sequences, and any other source of inspiration. Don't be afraid to look at what you determine to be poor type usage. By looking at it critically, you learn what not to do.

- If you have lots of text on the page, choose a plain serif font for the body text. Don't be chauvinistic and discount the use of Times, Times New Roman, or Century just because it seems like everybody is using them. Use the various fonts in the same family together, and your work will result in a surprising unity of design.

- The serif versus sans serif debate is right up there with the Macintosh versus Windows wars on the Net. If it works, it works. When in doubt, set the heads in sans serif and the body text in serif. If you are really picky, avoid serifs all together and use sans serif for the body text.

- If you must reverse type—white type on a black or colored background—do it sparingly. Even then, think twice about reversing a serif font. The fine details of these fonts tend to fill in. Go crazy with the sans serif faces instead and, if you do reverse a sans, space it out a bit to increase readability.

- Running a line of text from one edge of the browser window to the other is not a great idea. The text becomes nothing more than that grey stuff around the pictures, not information. Anywhere between 36 and 70 characters per line is a good length.

- If you don't know what you are doing, don't play with the font. If you need to condense it by squeezing the letters closer to each other, use the condensed version of the font, such as Franklin Gothic Condensed. The same goes for scaling. All you are doing is reducing legibility.

- Always use curly quotes and apostrophes.

- Always add one space after the period. Two spaces is a throwback to the typewriter.

- Use en dashes or em dashes, not hyphens. Leave the use of the hyphen to the amateurs. The use of the dash depends on where you live. En dashes are used in countries such as Canada where the British tradition is prevalent. Some designers get really picky and kern these spaces to suit the particular setting, especially in display type used for headlines and so on. The en dash is so named because it is roughly the same width as the capital letter N. Em dashes are used in the U.S. instead of the en dash. It is named "em" because it is approximately the width of the capital letter M.

The Origin of Serifs and Other Useless Information

Nobody can say with any accuracy how serifs suddenly arrived on the scene. The most plausible explanation has to do with the lettering in Rome.

During ancient Roman times, letters were carved into stone columns and walls. These letters were carved after a scribe, using a brush, painted the letters onto the stone. The serif appeared when the scribe stopped the brush and lifted it, leaving a bit of a brush edge on the letter. The carver, not seeing the error, simply chiseled that edge out of the stone as well—thus, the serif was created.

Another explanation is the serif was developed by scribes adding a stroke when the hand-drawn letter was finished.

Yet another of our other favorite explanations is the origin of the gibberish or Greek that is used for text placement—Lorem Ipsum. The origin of Lorem Ipsum actually goes back to the early 1500s when typographers would create specimen books of their fonts. Where did they get it? *Before and After Magazine*, Volume 4, Number 2 offered a rather interesting explanation.

According to the article, the phrase is Latin and is taken from Cicero's "de Finibis Bonorum et Malorum," written in 45 B.C. The actual phrase is, "Neque porro quisquam est qui dolorem ipsum quia dolor sit amet, consectetur, adipisci velit…" The early typographers simply scrambled it up.

Each of the letterforms in a font is there for a specific reason. Never forget for an instant that the use of certain marks can actually destroy the understanding of a word, or even change its meaning to something completely opposite of the original intent.

Typography and 94-Foot Lincolns

In the winter of 1994, one of the authors was sitting in an office he shared in Toronto with Dennis Mason. Dennis had developed quite the reputation in local typography circles due to his association with Mono Lino, an important Toronto type house, and his management of the Berthold Type Centres in New York and Los Angeles.

Dennis is a diminutive and unassuming Brit with a penchant for impeccable dress and pointy-toed boots. Dennis is also passionate about the proper use of type, and many hours were spent by the author listening to Dennis bemoan the lack of fine typography with the advent of digital media.

Dennis is a stickler for proper typography, and the author used to needle Dennis about this, claiming, "Gosh, Dennis, what has got you so upset? Everybody knows that type is just the grey stuff that goes around the pictures." Though the needling was good-natured, Dennis had taken on the role of mentoring the author regarding the nuances of fine typography. For the author, those twelve months of sharing an office with a master instilled in him sensitivity to the importance of typography that lasts to this day.

This particular day was a typical Toronto winter day. The slush was piled on the curbs of the streets, the sky was overcast, and the temperature was sitting just above freezing, meaning a steady cold sleet was falling and making a gloomy day even more intolerable. The morning papers were spread out on our desks and, to bring some cheer into the day, we were participating in our favorite sport of looking for really bad typography in the newspaper ads.

"Cripes," snorted Dennis, "look at this one. Obviously done by some desktop publisher." As you may have guessed, Dennis' opinion of desktop publishers was somewhere on the scale below contempt.

Dennis unfolded the paper and pointed to an ad placed by a local car dealership. They were trying to sell the last of their 1994 Lincoln automobiles. "Look at this," he said stabbing his index finger onto the ad, "this cretin can't distinguish between an apostrophe and foot mark." At that point the author, picked up the phone, hit the speakerphone button, and dialed the dealership.

When he finally was able to speak to a salesman, the conversation went something like this:

"I saw your ad in the paper," said the author. "Looks like you are clearing out your '94 models."

"Yes, sir."

"One, in particular, caught my eye, and I was wondering if I could see it?"

"Which one would that be, sir?"

"Well, it is just under the headline. According to your ad, you are selling 94-foot Lincolns, and that is something I just have to see."

To this day, Dennis never fails to relate this anecdote in his typography classes. In fact, one of his classes presented him with a small gift. The gift was a multiple-fold brochure. On the cover, it was written, "Your car is ready, Mr. Mason." When you unfolded the pages, it opened to reveal a perfectly proportioned 94-foot Lincoln.

In the case of our Lincoln, the use of the improper apostrophe—a foot mark—lengthened an automobile (see Figure 7.9). Learn to use the ASCII characters on your PC or Key Caps on your Macintosh. The last thing you need is to have one of the authors calling you about a car your client has listed for sale on the web. The last thing one of the authors needs is to have Dennis Mason stabbing his finger on your screen and saying, "You cretin."

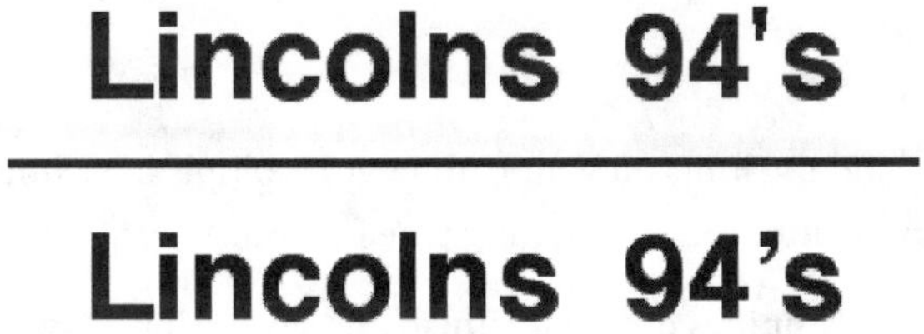

Lincolns 94's

Lincolns 94's

Figure 7.9   The use of a foot mark instead of an apostrophe changes the meaning. Is it distance, length, or a contraction? The apostrophe provides the access to understanding.

Web Type

The web, being screen based, is a low-resolution place when it comes to type. Eventually, those crisp Postscript fonts you see onscreen are going to have to be flattened, or *rasterized*. When a Postscript font is rasterized for print, it has thousands of pixels to work with.

The opposite occurs on the web. At best, you can expect roughly 100 pixels per inch. Not only that, but there is no Postscript on the web. There are only pixels. At such low resolution, the subtleties of the typeface are lost. To make things worse, the moment the type is converted to a graphic for use in a web page, the information—the text read by search engines such as Google, for example—is lost. Also, after a line of text is made into a graphic, unless it has an ALT tag (`<alt>`) applied to it, it won't be read by the screen readers used by visually impaired web surfers, either. You can't reuse them elsewhere in the page and, in certain worst-case scenarios, the art will grow or shrink depending upon the vagaries of the design and the browser. The core issue is one of copyright. The fonts on your machine are licensed through the company that owns the original font to the font manufacturer; thus, you don't have the right to make them available to anybody who visits your page. The result is today's reliance on the lowest common denominator when it comes to typography on the web. (See the sidebar, "How, After 371 Years, "Haas Neue Grotesk" Became "Swiss," later in this chapter for a more full discussion of the licensing issue.) The fonts used are those found on practically every desktop computer on the planet because they are installed along with the operating system. As well, dealing with bitmaps puts us right back to the beginnings of desktop publishing when all we had to use were screen fonts. Postscript fonts are relatively expensive to design and produce, meaning there will be very few fonts other than those developed specifically for the screen—Charcoal, Verdana, and Trebuchet, for example—that will take advantage of being displayed on a computer screen

The Technology of Digital Type

The technology behind the fonts on your computer is complex. It's important to understand what you have before you start setting type for your pages.

There are two major groupings of fonts: bitmap and Postscript.

Bitmap fonts build each character on a grid of pixels that are either on or off, depending upon the shape of the letters. This is where bitmaps fall apart. Being composed of pixels, they are extremely difficult to resize and shape without a serious loss of resolution. When you double the physical size of a bitmap, you aren't making the image larger; you are simply doubling the size of each pixel. The result are lines that wander, as seen in Figure 7.10, or letters that have a faint resemblance to their original character.

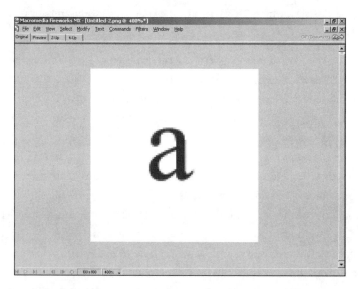

Figure 7.10   A Times bitmap letter. Note the jagged lines that indicate an attempt to accommodate some of the curves as well as the grid of pixels. The vertical rows render perfectly, whereas the curves display the square shape of the pixels.

Postscript fonts, on the other hand, are nothing more than a series of mathematical calculations for lines, curves, and subtle detail, as seen in Figure 7.11. This allows the text to become scalable with no loss of resolution because the math takes the size change into consideration. Even then, exercise caution. At small sizes, the calculations include hints regarding how to maintain the integrity of a curve in a serif, but they can become unreadable, especially on such low-resolution devices as a computer screen.

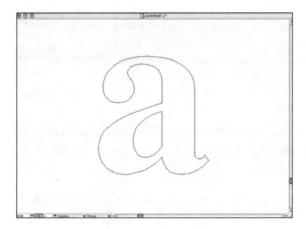

Figure 7.11   A Postscript Times letter. Note the nodes and the smoothness of the curves.

You would think the introduction of Postscript technology would solve the font headaches. Not quite. There are three types of Postscript fonts out there—Type 1, Type 3, and Type 5. Type 1 fonts are the standard Postscript fonts developed by Adobe many years ago. Type 3 fonts are those offered by third-party vendors, and Type 5 fonts are the fonts embedded in the ROM of your laser printer. Though there are no real functional differences between the three, the major difference is in how they build the letters. Type 1 and Type 5 fonts are built in the output device, such as a printer. Type 3 fonts are built in the font itself. The major problem is the current incompatibility of Macintosh fonts on the Windows platform. If you are using FF Confidential on the Macintosh, you can't simply drop the Postscript font into the Windows universe without first converting it to a format recognized by the PC.

Then, of course, there is TrueType. Postscript fonts essentially toss the printer or outline font around the bitmap onscreen when Adobe Type manager is installed. TrueType skips that step. Apple developed the TrueType technology when it introduced System 7.

The thinking was to simply store the outline and resolution hints in the system and then display them onscreen. The outlines are stored as a series of curves—B-spline curves, for you purists—that are far easier to compute and manipulate than the Bezier curves that make up Postscript fonts. The problem with this technology is there is no support for font encryption, which is why many of the classic fonts from the major type foundries are simply unavailable in a TrueType format. This explains, for instance, the origin of the TrueType font named Swiss. It looks like Helvetica, but isn't; Helvetica is based on the original font developed by Max Meidinger in 1951 and the foundry that owns the rights. Haas is protecting its property by putting the digital version into a format that includes encryption.

Don't for a minute think a TrueType font is somewhat substandard or less important than a Type 1 or Type 3 font. Both formats use PostScript and, especially on the Windows platform, TrueType is as close to being a de facto standard as one can expect. The typography explosion was kicked off by the introduction of TrueType, and innumerable web pages use this technology.

 How, After 371 Years, "Haas Neue Grotesk" Became "Swiss"

Max Meidinger designed and drew Helvetica in 1951 for the Haas Foundry, which is based in Munchenstein, Switzerland. The Swiss call Switzerland by the name Helvetia; thus, the origin of the font's name. Not being able to obtain the rights to produce a TrueType version of Helvetica, a version was created in the TrueType format and named Swiss.

Helvetica was initially released as Haas Neue Grotesk. Four years later, Walter Crunz, who worked for a company named Stempel, reworked the design for Linotype GmbH in Frankfurt, a major stockholder in Stempel. It wasn't until the Mergenthaler Linotype Company in New York adopted the design that Helvetica rapidly became the most popular sans serif in the world, replacing at the time the Futura font.

The Haas Foundry can actually trace its roots back to a type foundry founded by Jean Exertier in 1580, and can rightfully claim to be the world's oldest surviving type foundry.

Type and the Macromedia MX Studio

Typography as art is the only solution. Yet using type on the web simply breaks every rule of typography ever developed since Gutenberg started printing Bibles. A web page is, obviously, not a print page. The text is not fixed into place like it is on paper. What one person sees may not necessarily be what the individual in the next cubicle over sees, depending upon the fonts in his operating system.

Your layouts, therefore, should be designed to be fluid and to focus on the content, not the design. If you are putting text into a web page, concentrate on what you can control—size, color, weight, placement—and ignore the nuances of fine typography. Flash, being PostScript-based, is the only web tool that allows you to use the full gamut of typographic techniques from kerning to sizing type with no loss of resolution. This occurs because Flash allows the designer to embed the font's PostScript font outline into the .swf file. Thus, the kerning and tracking used for a line of text set in the font "Trixie" on the designer's computer appears on the viewer's computer.

Type controls in Dreamweaver MX for individual bits of text are rudimentary. The size of body text and headers is not dependent upon point size. Headers and body text range in size from 1 to 7, with 7 being the largest size, as shown in Figure 7.12. Bold or italic, set using the <B> and the <I> tags, is driven by HTML and not the font. What this means is that weight is determined by the system, not the design. Adding an <I> tag to Times does not load the Times Italic font; it simply slants the words. Adding color to your text is also problematic. You have to take into consideration the color space chosen—a web safe palette—as well as the background color when using type. The color of the text is also driven by HTML, although Dreamweaver does this for you.

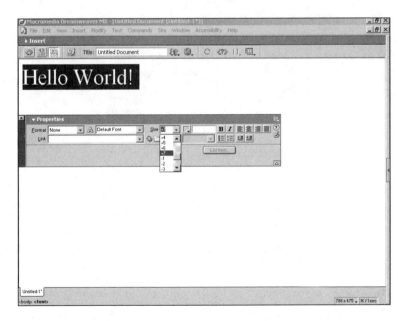

Figure 7.12   Type control in Dreamweaver is quite rudimentary when placed against page layout applications. The size of the text is driven by the size menu, which ranges from 1 to 7, with 7 being the largest.

In the print universe, columns of text are common. They aren't as common in the HTML universe, however. The major difference here is one of control. What you can't do on a web page, for example, is indent an entire column of text one or two points in from the edge without spending an inordinate amount of time tweaking the design. You are thus stuck with three basic alignments when it comes to type—Left, Right, or Center. Justification and even Force Justify are denied. When working with these alignments, it is absolutely critical that you pay close attention to the length of the lines of type or paragraph width. Anything more than 36 to 70 characters on a line will seriously affect the readability of the text.

Still, Dreamweaver contains some rather robust tools. There isn't space in this chapter to cover all of them, however. Instead we focus on the use of style sheets in Dreamweaver. Graphic designers using page layout applications, and even those of you who use word processors, are quite familiar with these. All of the formatting information for a particular bit of text is contained in the style sheet, and a click of the mouse applies the style throughout the document.

In Dreamweaver MX, there are two methods of applying text formatting styles to your pages. The first uses HTML styles, and the second uses Cascading Style Sheets (CSS). The former is not as robust as CSS and, in many respects, you could regard them as applying changes locally. For example, assume the word "Jordan" is used in several pages of the site. You notice the word is not bold and colored red. You could define an HTML style to accomplish this, but this style would only apply to the page where you made the change as well as all subsequent pages. You would have to manually go backward to find all instances of "Jordan" and reapply the style. CSS applies the changes globally. For example, you notice the same situation with "Chris." If you were to make the change in the CSS style, the change would be made (in other words, would cascade) throughout the entire site.

HTML Styles in Dreamweaver MX

We live in an imperfect web world where there is no predictability. Not only can we not predict what fonts the visitor has installed on his computer, but we can't even predict what version of the browser is being used. Style sheets add consistency to your layouts; the problem with CSS is that they only work in browsers that are version 4.0 or better.

The stop-gap solution is to use HTML styles until the demise of the 3.0 (or lower) browser. HTML styles in Dreamweaver are similar to their CSS counterparts, but they have one fundamental difference: Dreamweaver adds HTML tags to the style, not a CSS declaration. When using HTML styles, keep in mind these three important differences between HTML styles and CSS styles:

- If you change an HTML style attribute, the change is local not global.

- HTML styles use the HTML tags; for example, you can't remove the underline from a piece of text, which is quite common with CSS.

- A change to an HTML style is applied to a document on a site, whereas a CSS style change can be applied to all pages on a site through the use of an external style sheet.

Don't misunderstand these points. HTML styles are not something to avoid. They are a huge productivity enhancement, and have a relatively flat learning curve. Follow these steps to apply HTML styles in Dreamweaver MX:

1. Open Dreamweaver and then open Lorem.htm in the DWTypography folder in your Exercise folder on the book web site.

2. Next, open the HTML Styles panel. There are three ways of opening this panel— Select Window, HTML Styles; press Control-F11 (PC) or Command- F11 (Mac); or click the Design panel and then click the HTML Styles button when the Design panel opens.

3. Select New from the panel's pop-down menu to open the Define New Style panel. Use the following settings:

    Name. NewParagraph.

    Apply To. Selection.

    When Applying. Clear Existing Style.

    Size. 4.

    Color. FF0000.

    Style. Bold.

4. Click OK.

5. Select the first paragraph of the text and click on your New Style in the HTML Styles panel, as shown in Figure 7.13. The new style is applied to the selected text. To return the text to its original state, select the text and click the Clear Selection Style in the HTML Styles panel. To remove the style completely, select the style and click Delete in the panel's pop-down menu. To edit the new style, select Edit from the HTML Styles panel pop-down choices. The HTML Styles editor launches, and you can make your changes.

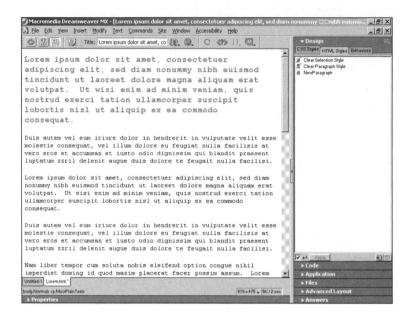

Figure 7.13   The style is defined and applied.

The Styles of HTML Style

You will notice you have a couple of style choices in the New Style dialog box. They are important.

If you select Paragraph, the style is applied to the entire paragraph regardless of where you click in the paragraph. The Selection option can be applied only if a block of text is selected.

To test this, click inside the second paragraph and then click your new style. Nothing happens because you wanted the change to be applied to a selection. Select a few letters of the text. Click your style. Note how only the letters selected now have the new style attribute.

Tip

The standard method of adding text to your page is to copy and paste from your word processor into Dreamweaver. For those of you with Microsoft Word 2000 or Office 2000, there is an even better way.

Open the Word file, and save it as a web page by choosing File, Save as Web Page. Click where you want the text to go in your Dreamweaver page, and select File, Import, Import Word HTML. A series of dialog boxes appear, asking how you want to handle the text. Go with the defaults.

Cascading Style Sheets in Dreamweaver MX

When you consider the fact that entire books and entire chapters of some excellent Dreamweaver books (such as *Inside Dreamweaver 4*, by Anne-Marie Yerks, New Riders, ISBN 0735710848) have been devoted to this subject, we can't hope to turn you into an expert in the short space allotted. The best we can do here is to explain how Cascading Style Sheets work and how to apply them using Dreamweaver MX.

As the term implies, the style sheet and the styles it contains "cascade" throughout an entire site. If you think of a waterfall with five shelves, you can quickly see how a style sheet is implemented through the various levels of styles, and how each level can be over-ridden by the level above it. Style priorities that are set on one level of the waterfall deter-mine the styles for the remaining levels. A change made locally takes precedence over a page-level style, which in turn can take precedence over a global style.

As pointed out earlier, CSS can be frustrating because the support for them in the browsers is spotty, at best. The text that looks great in Netscape may look totally differ-ent in Explorer. Still, from a production point of view, you can't beat CSS. For example, code-driven pages with lots of text formatting can really slow things down. If the code is contained in an externally linked document with the Dreamweaver page pointing at it, things tend to accelerate. Another timesaver is one change is instantly reflected across the entire site. From a typographic point of view, the size options are replaced by the more precise point and pica sizes used in typography, which allows you to use the absolute value, such as 12 points or 1 pica. The other size options are inches, centimeters, mil-limeters, and pixels, which, when it comes to type, really shouldn't be considered.

A style sheet is really nothing more than a series of rules. For example, a rule could be H1 (color: red). In simple terms, all you are doing is setting a rule that says all level 1 headlines will be red in color. This line of code also follows the syntax used for CSS. CSS rules contain two parts: a selector (H1) and a declaration (color: red). The selector sim-ply says which HTML tag is affected by the style, and the declaration says exactly what the style will be.

CSS styles can be either embedded into the HTML or contained in their own external style sheets, which are linked to the page. For example, the following code contains an embedded style sheet that normally appears before the <Body> tag for obvious reasons:

```
<HTML>
<HEAD>
<Style Type = "text/css">
<!-
H1 (color: red; font-size: 24 pt ; font-family : Times New Roman)
-->
</STYLE>
```

By putting the style attribute, <Style Type = "text/css">, at the top, older browsers that don't support CSS will hit the line of code, not understand it, and simply move on. By adding a comment - <!-- --> at the beginning and the end of the code, browsers that can't use CSS are stopped from trying to show the code.

To access an external Cascading Style Sheet, the code would look somewhat like this:

```
<HTML>
<HEAD>
<Link Rel = "aCSSstylesheet" HREF= "Integrationbook.css" Type =
➥"text/css">
```

And so on.

In this instance, the browser would start looking for a file named Integrationbook.css, and after it finds it, start executing the style instructions.

Having seen how CSS is code-driven, the best way of learning how to use these styles is to create them without code in Dreamweaver. You can then open up the code in your HTML editor, see how it is written, and follow the changes requested. In the following example, you create an external style sheet that enlarges the text and then apply that formatting to the text. You then do a similar action, only the new styles are embedded into the page.

1. Open the Lorem.htm file in the CSS folder in your Chapter 7 Exercise folder on the book web site.

2. Select Window>CSS Styles (or press Shift-F11) to open the CSS Styles panel. If you already have the Styles panel open, click the CSS tab.

3. Click the New Style button to open the New CSS Style dialog box, and name the style **.bigitup**. Don't forget the dot.

4. Select Make Custom Style (class) from the Type area, as shown in Figure 7.14; then select (New Style Sheet File) from the Define In area. This step creates the external sheet. Selecting This Document Only would embed the style into the page. You are prompted to save the page. Give the page a name, but don't omit the .css extension.

5. Having set the style, you are prompted to define the style. With Type as the category selected, use the following settings:

   Font. Times New Roman, Times, serif.

   Size. 14 points.

   Style. Oblique. This is another term for Italic.

Line Height. Normal. This is the leading setting and is traditionally set one or two points more than the size of the type.

Decoration. Ignore them. The decoration styles are self-explanatory.

Weight. Bold.

Variant. Normal. All this does is switch between upper- and lowercase, and small caps.

Case. Don't bother with this.

Color. FF0000. Click and hold on the color chip to select a different swatch.

If a category does not apply to the page, simply ignore it.

6. When you have finished, the Style Definitions for .bigitup dialog box should resemble those shown in Figure 7.15. Click OK.

Figure 7.14   The style is named, set to a custom style, and defined in an external style sheet.

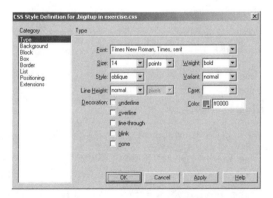

Figure 7.15   The formatting styles are extensive, and the categories available offer a tremendous amount of control over the formatting change.

7. Select the first paragraph of the text and then select .bigitup from the Styles panel. The text gets bigger, and becomes a red italic.

The next example involves a local change. This exercise asks you to change all of the bold text in a page to a sans serif Bold Italic with a blue color.

1. Close the open Dreamweaver document and then open the LoremBLD.htm in the CSS folder. Open the CSS Styles panel, and select New from the panel pop-down menu. Select Redefine HTML from the Type area, and select the b tag from the list in the Tag area. Select This Document Only from the Define In area and then click OK to open the Style Definition dialog box.

2.   When the Style Definition dialog box opens, use the following settings:

    Font. Arial, Helvetica.Sans.

    Size. 14 points.

    Weight. Bold.

    Style. Italic.

    Line Height. 16 points.

    Color. 000099.

3. Click OK, and all of the bold text on the page takes on the new formatting attributes.

Fireworks MX and Type

Fireworks MX, using both vectors and bitmaps, is a powerful tool when it comes to typography. The text editing features are available both from the Property inspector and the Text Editor found in the Text menu. The ability to play with the text—bevels, fills, strokes, and so on—makes it a great creative tool. What really makes this app shine, however, is the fact that even though you can add all of these effects, the text remains live, meaning it is fully editable at all times.

The application is still weak in the areas of kerning and tracking. The use of sliders to set point sizes and tracking amounts lacks the precision of the controls in other imaging or page layout applications. Use the Property inspector to change elements such as font, point size alignment, and so on. If you want to correct a typo, or add a word or two, you have to use the Text tool or the Text menu. About the only advantage the Text menu offers over the Property inspector is the ability to edit the text in the Text Editor dialog box, shown in Figure 7.16.

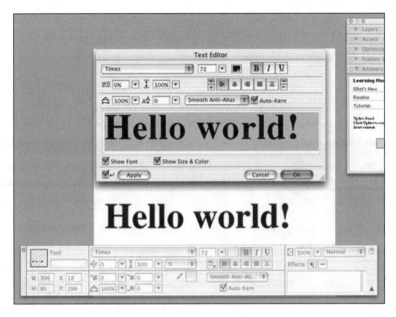

Figure 7.16   The Fireworks MX type controls are in the Property inspector and the Text
menu.

When it comes to using text as art, Fireworks MX, through its many effects and export
options ranging from .gif to .png, is the tool of choice. Keep in mind, however, if an
image is not converted from vectors to a bitmap, you run a risk of having your font sub-
stituted with Courier if the font you are using is not installed on the user's machine.

Flash MX and Type

Flash MX, being vector based, could be regarded as a solution to the resolution and substitution issues. The problem is that Flash MX was not designed to manage the large
amounts of static text you traditionally see scattered across web pages. Although Flash
MX can display dynamic, constantly changing text, such as stock quotes, and text can be
added into input fields in such elements as forms, those features are out of the scope of
this book.

The application is tremendous for accurately displaying fonts because it uses the vectors
to draw them. The nuances that distinguish one font from another are maintained at all
sizes and, providing the font has been embedded into the Flash projector, font substitution is not an issue.

Flash embeds the font into the .swf file, but not all fonts can be exported with the movie. To ensure the font is embedded, use the View>Antialias Text command. If the font looks jagged, Flash MX can't recognize the outline, and will ignore the font on export.

Another feature that straddles the Flash and HTML worlds is the addition of device fonts to Flash MX. These fonts are the traditional _sans, serif and _typewriter. These fonts are not embedded into the projector. Instead, when the movie plays, the Flash MX projector finds a font on the user's machine that most closely resembles the device font and displays that font. At sizes below 10 points, consider the use of a device font because they are more legible at playback. This is especially true if you have more than a dozen or so lines in the block of text.

On the downside, typographic controls such as kerning and tracking are rudimentary at best. If you are looking for the precision of the typographic control in a drawing or page layout application, you won't find it in Flash. In this case, it would be best to do the typesetting of the headline in FreeHand, convert it to vector outlines, and import those outlines into Flash as a symbol or a FreeHand 9 or 10 file. If the text is not to be animated or otherwise manipulated, you might consider not using Flash. In this instance, export the outline to Fireworks MX and manipulate it there.

The major change regarding how Flash MX handles text is the type controls being a part of the Property inspector, as shown in Figure 7.17. All of the fonts, including the device fonts, are now available in one easily accessible location.

Figure 7.17   The redesign of the Flash MX interface makes the formatting of text much simpler than in the past thanks to the addition of the Property inspector.

Note

If precise control of the lettering and spacing is an issue, don't discount the use of FreeHand 10. This would involve situations such as the client handing you the corporate logo as an .eps file on a disc or other media. You can create the text block in the application and, depending upon its final use, export the text block to Flash MX or Fireworks MX. You can also convert the block to PostScript outlines, which is the PostScript equivalent of text being converted to art, and import the file into the two applications as well.

Color

When the web first arrived, web designers were inevitably drawn from the print tradition. Most dealt in a universe that was somewhat predictable when it came to color. Cyan was cyan regardless of where the job was printed, and it was common knowledge that the color onscreen was not that which would appear on the printed page.

The arrival of the web presented the designer with a host of new problems. Instead of the predictability of dots of ink on a piece of paper, those dots became the phosphors of a computer monitor. When that happened, a host of issues ranging from monitor calibration, color spaces, and the gamma differences between the platforms arose. In the field of digital media, the concept of WYSIWYG (What You See Is What You Get) is the norm. Unfortunately, when it comes to color, WYSINNWYG (What You See Is Not Necessarily What You Get) is the rule.

Color Models

The terms *color model* or *color space* are somewhat interchangeable. Simply put, the model used on computers is the RGB space, which means the color the viewer sees is a combination of red, green, and blue light. The important issue is the number of colors that can be represented in the model. This is called *gamut*.

In the bad old days, we were limited to a gamut of 256 colors. This was 8-bit color. With the advent of more powerful computers and Windows 95, the gamut increased to 65,000 colors, and today we can present images using 16.7 million colors—which is technically referred to as the *true color space*.

Unfortunately, as web developers and designers, we really don't have the pleasure of being able to use all of those colors in our designs, nor do we get to view them accurately between the platforms. The reason is *gamma*, which refers to the overall brightness of a computer monitor. It is not consistent between the platforms. On the Mac side of the fence, an image created on a Mac appears darker on a PC, and images created on the PC appear to be somewhat washed out when viewed on a Mac. This is due to the Mac gamma being set to 1.8 and the PC gamma being set to 2.2. The larger the number, the darker the display.

Previewing Gamma Settings in Fireworks MX

Fireworks allows you to preview how your image will look under different gamma settings.

If you are using a Macintosh, select View, Windows Gamma. The image darkens to approximate how it will look on a PC. If you use a PC, select View, Mac Gamma and the image appears to brighten.

Don't be fooled by this. What you just did was to see how the image would appear on your monitor. What you did not do was to adjust the image's brightness. If the image appears to be too dark or too light, you can address this by selecting the image and then manually adjusting the brightness and contrast from the Effects area of the Fireworks MX Property inspector.

Color Palettes

If you have worked with color, you've inevitably developed a palette of colors you use on a regular basis. These colors appear throughout the site and add a high degree of consistency to the design effort. In many cases, the choice of color is dictated by the client through either a formalized Graphic Standards document, or from the colors in the corporate logo. Be careful with this one. Corporate color schemes inevitably spring from rigid print color systems such as Pantones or mixtures of printing inks. You will never be able to accurately reproduce print colors in a digital medium. The best you can do is to get close to the colors.

The choice of a personal palette can also limit your creativity. It tends to fit like an old sweater and give you the same feeling of comfort and safety. Instead, sit on a park bench and look at the grass in the park. Look at how the grass is composed of shades of green with maybe some tan shades where the grass has been worn down and the ground shows through. If you are stuck in traffic, look at how the color of the cars around you are affected by the sun and the physical shapes—curves and angles—of the car body and the glass. These activities can sensitize you to the color palette around you, and give you the opportunity to examine palettes other than yours.

Palettes can be either formal and informal. A formal palette is presented much the same way one would look at the page in a swatch book. The colors and their use are clearly presented. Samples of a formal color scheme for the JCT site in the form of FreeHand and Fireworks MX documents are included on the book web site.

Creating the Color Scheme in Fireworks MX

If you have ever wanted to relive the joys of your childhood, here's your opportunity. The creation of a color scheme in Fireworks MX is a lot like finger painting.

Select the Paintbrush from the Bitmap toolbar, and set the size of the brush, the color, and other properties in the Property inspector. With the properties set, you can now scribble across an area of a blank document. Change the color and scribble away. You also might want to change the opacity of the color and see how they mix. A more formal method is to lay down the colors into a rough approximation of the interface rather than rough "scribbles" across the screen. This is shown in Figure 7.18.

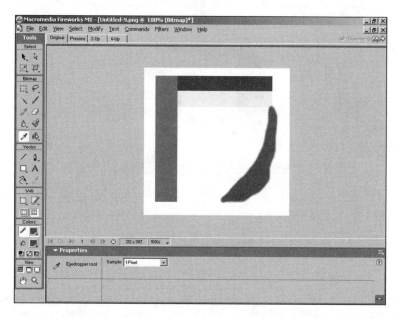

Figure 7.18   Setting the color scheme in Fireworks can be compared to finger painting. In this case, you are looking at how the colors work together.

Creating the Color Scheme in Flash MX

The process of creating a color scheme is a bit different in Flash MX, though the finger painting is the same.

Select the Paintbrush from the toolbar, and set the stroke color either in the Stroke Chip on the tools palette or the chip shown on the Property inspector. Set the brush options in the Options area at the bottom of the toolbar, and paint away.

The interesting point about this technique is that you are actually using Flash MX to sketch out your ideas, as shown in Figure 7.19. Don't be afraid to use filled shapes to add a bit more rigidity to your sketch.

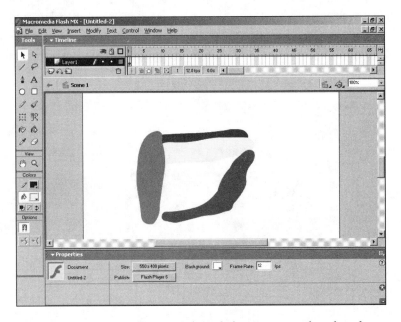

Figure 7.19   Use the bitmap and vector tools in Flash MX to create the color scheme.

Note

The colors in a swatch panel in FreeHand can be exported to other documents. If you are creating a formal color scheme, the color swatches can be used in other documents. It is done by creating a custom color library.

Choose Export from the swatches pop-down menu, and select all of the colors to be exported. Click OK; then enter a name for the Library in the Create Color Library dialog box, along with the number of rows and columns to be found in the Library. Click Browse to navigate to the folder where the Library is stored, and click Save. The JCT Swatch Library—JCTswatches.BCF—is included on the book web site.

Web Color

Although we can see millions of colors on a monitor, there are some interesting issues that arise when you move from a space containing millions of colors to one containing only thousands. When it comes to web development, it is not the computer but rather the browser that remaps the color to the browser's built-in color palette. The good news here is the color shifts are not as profound as those occurring when moving from millions of colors to 256 colors. If the browser were not managing the remapping, the color would shift to the system palette and the color in your pages would look profoundly different on a Mac and on a PC. This is not an issue if the browser is running on a 24-bit computer display; the palette is essentially ignored, and you get accurate color.

The problem here is not everyone with access to the web uses 24-bit monitors, or has computers that can show millions of colors. About half of the users on the web use 16-bit monitors, and the RGB colors specified in your HTML or graphics editor are moved to their closest equivalents on the palette. The result is a subtle shifting or dithering of color. This is especially evident if you try to match a graphic's background color to the background color specified in Dreamweaver MX.

The Web Safe palette solves this. The Web Safe palette consists of the 216 colors that are the same—thus the word "Safe"—on both the Mac and PC platforms. Though the colors in the palette can be expressed as decimals or percentages, hexadecimal notation is more reliable and accurate. The Hex values use a base-16 system, and only need six characters to describe an RGB color. The MX Studio, in fact, uses the Hex values as its default for all of the applications.

Gradients

If any one aspect of content creation can trip you up, it is the use of gradients. As the colors shift from one color to the next, they sometimes change completely. In fact, moving gradients between applications is like opening a Christmas present—you never know what you are going to get until you open the document.

Thankfully, the MX Studio solves this problem for you. Using a common color palette and the ability to drag and drop between FreeHand, Flash MX, and Fireworks MX, or to move from Dreamweaver MX to Flash MX and Fireworks MX at the click of a button ensures fidelity to the original colors. Still, there are a couple of pitfalls of which to be aware when moving between FreeHand and Flash.

FreeHand's color palettes do include a web palette that is available from the Fill menu. Eventually the image is going to have to hit the web, meaning it will have to be exported as a bitmap. If you make this choice, the only export format that includes a web palette is the .gif option. If you are going to directly import a gradient into Dreamweaver MX, be aware that your choice of palette and file format can produce startlingly different results, as shown in Figure 7.20.

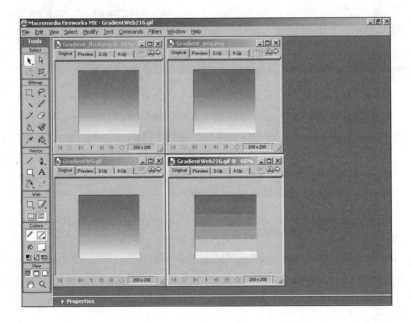

Figure 7.20   Graphic proof that careful attention to a color palette can have a profound effect on the final product.

The original FreeHand gradient is shown in the upper left of the figure. Exporting the image as a .png file, upper right, maintains the fidelity of the color. At the bottom, things fall apart. The FreeHand gradient has been exported as a GIF file with the color being set by two different web palettes. The image in the bottom left uses the GIF with a Web Snap palette, which pulls all of the color in the gradient to its web safe equivalent. The image in the bottom right uses a simple Web Safe palette using 216 colors.

If color fidelity between FreeHand and the web is an issue, the format is .png. If it must be a .gif, use the Web Snap palette.

Roughing Content

Having supplied the client with a variety of art, ranging from pencil sketches to wireframes, now is the time to start bringing your ideas to life. Roughing content is a low-risk method of providing the client with an idea of how the elements will look on the page and, in certain instances, how they will function. From your perspective, roughing content gives you an opportunity to produce the content with an eye to potential problems such as placement of graphics, color, and type. If problems are uncovered, they can be addressed and solved.

The advantage to you, the designer, is that you can present the client with a document that demonstrates many of the concepts you have presented up to this point of the process. In many cases, this is the stage where you discover just how carefully you have presented your ideas. There is an old maxim in the graphics industry: "The client never knows what they want until they see it." This will be their first look.

If you have done your job, the client will instantly understand what you have been presenting and give the all-important approval to proceed. If there are problems or changes, your investment in time is not jeopardized. You can make the changes quickly, based on client input, and then proceed. Either way, it is a win/win situation, and a low cost method of determining whether or not you and the client are reading from the same page.

The Macromedia MX Tools

The suite of MX tools, along with FreeHand, have been designed to produce content from concept to final form. To help you along, the engineers at Macromedia have included a number of wizards and other helpful features. The job of these tools is to help the fledgling developer create some interesting effects in a low-stress manner. Among the pros, these tools are regarded as rather lightweight, but they are ideal for this step of the process.

For example, you can rough out a Flash animation to show the client how it would work. If the client likes the idea, you have a green light to drop the content from Fireworks MX and FreeHand into the Flash MX files and go to work. If the client has objections, you really haven't invested a huge amount of time in the piece, and can quickly make the changes requested. You can create simple pop-down menus or slices in Fireworks MX to demonstrate how the navigation works. You can create simple Flash buttons in Dreamweaver MX and then use the application to place the rough content in pages that are subsequently submitted to the client for approval.

These pages could be anything from a collection of various menu schemes for the site to working comprehensive designs. Their complexity should be driven by the importance of the job, not your personal convenience.

In this section, we demonstrate how to rough a pop-up menu in Fireworks MX, how to rough out an animation in Flash MX using elements created in FreeHand, and how to assemble and test this content in a Dreamweaver MX page for submission to the client.

Creating a Rough Pop-Up Menu in Fireworks MX

The Pop-up Menu Editor was introduced in Version 4 of the application. The original intention was to give the users of the product the capability of producing some very complex pop-up menus for their web designs. These menus are triggered by an event such as a rollover or mouse click. The advantage of the wizard is that it generates the HTML and JavaScript when the menu is exported out of Fireworks. To create a pop-up menu in Fireworks MX, follow these steps:

1. Open a new Fireworks MX document that is 25 pixels high and 200 pixels wide. Set the background to transparent and then set the resolution to 100 dpi.

2. Draw a box using the Rectangle tool in the Vector Tools section of the toolbox that is 50 pixels wide by 25 pixels high. If the box is larger or smaller, set the height and width to the measurements given using the Property inspector. In the Property inspector, set the background color to grey and then add a one-pixel black stroke around the box.

3. Select the Text tool, click once in the box, and enter the word **Shoes**. Set the font to Helvetica, the point size to 12, and the weight to Bold in the Property inspector.

4. Select both the words and the box. Hold down the Option (Mac)/Alt (PC) key, press the Shift key, and drag a copy of your selection until it is touching the right edge of the original image. Repeat this step two more times.

5. Select the Text tool, highlight the text in the second box, and enter the word **T-Shirts**. Repeat this step for the remaining two boxes, replacing the word Shoes with **Pants** and **Hats**. Finally, select each box and its word, and group the two objects.

The menu bar is now ready to become a pop-up menu. To accomplish this, each object in the menu must be converted to slice to generate the HTML and JavaScript that will allow it to function.

1. Select the Shoes panel. Select Edit, Insert, Slice, or use the keyboard command Alt-Shift-U (PC) or Option-Shift-U Macintosh. The panel turns green, indicating a slice, and the Web layer also has a new layer named Slice. Rename this layer **Shoes**. The slice could have also been done using the Slice tool. By inserting a slice over a grouped object rather than dragging a slice over it with the Slice tool, you avoid any overlap that may occur. This is especially important here because each object butts up against its neighbor.

2. Click once on the white dot on the Shoes panel, and select Add Pop-Up Menu from the menu that appears. This step launches the Pop-up Menu Editor.

   At first glance, the Content window may appear confusing. The + and - buttons add submenu items, and the buttons beside them determine whether the item is indented or not. The first item in the list is the main head, and can't be indented.

3. Click once in the first cell, and enter the word **Men's**. Click the next cell under the Men's cell, and enter the word **Hangin'**. Click the Indent button.

4. Click the + button. Add the text **Rad Red** and then click the Indent button. Repeat this step three more times, adding the words **Cool White**, **Gnarly Green**, and **Chillin' Blue** to the cells. The added items should line up under Rad Red. Your text should look like that shown in Figure 7.21.

Figure 7.21   The levels for the pop-up menu. Indenting a level moves it down in the menu hierarchy.

Note

If you were actually using the Pop-up Menu Editor to create your menus, you would add an URL, absolute or relative, to the Link cell. If the link already exists in the image, it will appear in a pop-up menu when you click the Link cell. If you were targeting a frame from the menu item, you would type the name of the frame into the target section.

5. Click the Appearance tab of the Pop-up Menu Editor. This page allows you to add texture and color to the menu, and even decide whether the menu pops down in a vertical or horizontal layout. For the purposes of this exercise, use a simple HTML layout and the panel defaults for color and font choice.

Note

If you really want to get fancy, you can create your own button styles. Simply create a button or some other object and then add it to the Style menu. Select the new object in the Styles menu, and select Export, Styles from the Assets panel Option menu. Navigate to the Nav Items folder on your hard drive, and save the file containing the .stl extension to that folder.

6. Click the Position tab in the Pop-up Menu Editor. This page allows you to determine how the submenu items will position themselves when the mouse is clicked. The decision is to have each menu roll down out of the selected item. Click the second icon beside Menu Position—Set Menu Position to Bottom of Slice—and then click the last one beside the submenu position—Set Submenu Position to Bottom of Menu. Click Done.

7. Select File, Export, Command-Shift-R (Mac), or Control-Shift-R (PC) to open the Export dialog box. Before clicking OK, ensure Save as Type: HTML and Images, HTML: Export HTML Files, and Slices: Export Slices: Include Areas without Slices are all selected.

8. Choose the folder where the files are to be placed, and click OK if you are using a Mac or Save if you are using a PC.

There is a one-click method of exporting a Fireworks MX image into Dreamweaver MX, as well. Fireworks MX has an Export button on the right edge of the menu bar. It looks like the Fireworks MX icon with an arrow shooting out of it. Press the mouse button on the icon and a pop-up menu appears. Select Dreamweaver, Export HTML, and the Export menu automatically opens. You can also launch Dreamweaver from this menu. We'll get to that next. For now, simply save the menu as a .png file to your folder, and quit Fireworks MX.

The Dreamweaver MX to Fireworks MX Connection

The hub of the MX Studio is Dreamweaver MX. It is a lot like the Chicago O'Hare airport version of the workflow process. Everything eventually arrives or departs from Dreamweaver. In past iterations of the products, moving between Fireworks to Dreamweaver and back to Fireworks was somewhat cumbersome and non-intuitive. The MX Studio, especially Dreamweaver and Fireworks (and to a lesser extent, from Dreamweaver to Flash MX), has been designed with ease of use in mind. In all cases, the applications are accessible via one click either in Dreamweaver's Launcher or through the Export button in Fireworks MX.

To demonstrate this, explore the Dreamweaver to Fireworks capability in the following steps:

1. Open a new document in Dreamweaver MX, and save the document with the name **menutest**. Click the Fireworks MX icon on the Insert toolbar to insert the Fireworks HTML. When the Insert Fireworks HTML dialog box opens, click the Browse button.

2. Navigate to the Fireworks HTML file and select it. The toolbar appears on the Dreamweaver page. To see if your menu works, select File, Preview in browser. This launches your favorite browser and allows you try out the menu.

3. There is a problem, however. The submenus all open on the wrong side of the bar, so you need to quit the browser.

4. Select the Shoes slice on the Dreamweaver page and then click the Edit button on the Property inspector. This icon on this button changes according to the file type selected. For example, the selection is a Fireworks object, and the Fireworks MX icon appears on the Edit button. If this were a Flash MX object, the icon would change to the Flash MX icon. Click the Edit button to launch Fireworks MX. The application opens, and you are prompted to select the file you want to open. Select the .png file you saved earlier.

Note

The next step assumes Fireworks MX is set as the default editor for .gif and .png files. To check this, open the Dreamweaver MX Preferences, as shown in Figure 7.22. When the Preferences open, select File Types/Editors. In the Extensions box, locate the PNG extension. Beside it, in the Editors area, Dreamweaver MX shows you the default editor for this file type. One of the authors, for example, is using a PC and his default editor is PHOTOED.

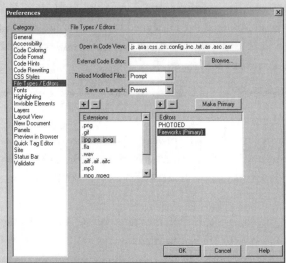

Figure 7.22   Fireworks MX is set as the editor for .png and .gif files through the Dreamweaver MX Preferences.

Select the editor and click the – button. The Editors area is now empty. Click the + button. You will be prompted to navigate to the Application folder for the editor. Navigate to the Fireworks MX folder, and double-click on the Fireworks MX Application icon.

5. When the file opens, click the white dot on the Shoes slice to open the context menu. Select Edit Pop-up Menu to launch the Pop-up Menu Editor. Select the Position tab and then select the last button of the submenu position choices to set the submenu to the bottom of the menu. Click OK (Mac) or Done (PC), and click Done at the top of the menu bar to return to Dreamweaver MX. Test in your browser, and you will discover the menu is now functioning properly, as shown in Figure 7.23.

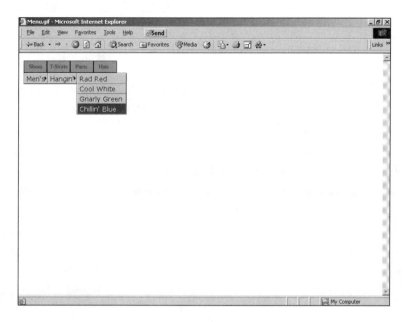

Figure 7.23 The pop-down menu previewed in a browser. The big advantage to the Dreamweaver to Fireworks connection is one click access to Fireworks MX out of Dreamweaver's Property inspector.

FreeHand to Flash MX to Dreamweaver MX

Pairing FreeHand with Flash is an unbeatable combination. If there is a major weakness in Flash MX, it is its collection of rudimentary of content creation tools when compared to the number of filters and so on that are contained in FreeHand. Although these tools do an adequate job, they just don't reach an industrial-strength standard. Flash MX's industrial-strength content creation tool is FreeHand.

FreeHand was originally designed as a vector drawing tool in the print universe. With the introduction of Flash and Macromedia's embracing of the web, more and more Flash artists are starting to discover that FreeHand offers a huge degree of flexibility, ranging from the capability to drag and drop images from FreeHand into Flash MX to the capability to create symbols in FreeHand that move seamlessly into Flash MX's Library.

Toss the Flash Edit button on Dreamweaver MX's Property inspector into the mix, and you have a virtual Flash round-trip ticket.

The purpose of roughing out content is to demonstrate concepts, not wow the client. In this manner, only one FreeHand document needs to be created for all of the Flash animation objects.

In this exercise, you rough out a small Flash animation that shows how these three tools work together:

1. Create a new document in FreeHand, and name it **JCTbits**. Select the Text tool, click on the page, and enter a 120-point Times, Bold, uppercase J. Create two duplicates of the letter, select each one with the Text tool, and then change one to a C and the other to a T.

2. Select the C and give it a blue fill. Select the Text tool again and enter the word **Shoes**. Set the size to 48 points. Now, select each of the letters as well as the word Shoes, and select Convert to Path from the Text menu.

   If you are at all concerned about whether the font is available on the viewer's computer, converting letters to outlines, is a good habit to develop. Converted text becomes fully editable artwork in Flash. In addition, you avoid some of the nastier font substitution issues that occur when you use a font that the user doesn't have installed on his computer. This technique is recommended for headlines and lettering used as a graphic. Don't use it for body text.

3. Select the Oval tool, and draw a small oval. Add the word **shoe** into the oval. The content is now in place.

   Flash loves symbols, so it only makes sense to convert each item on the page into a symbol.

4. Select the J and, if it isn't already open, select Library from the Window menu. Select Modify, Symbol, Convert to Symbol. A new document has been added to the Library.

5. Double-click the name in the Library and then rename the symbol **J**. Repeat this step for the other items on the FreeHand page. Save the image, but don't quit FreeHand or close the image.

Note

There is another method for symbol creation. Select the letter C, and drag it into the lower half of the Library. When you release the mouse, a new symbol has been created. Rename the symbol.

6. Open Flash. Unfortunately FreeHand hasn't been "MX'ed," which means you will have to open a new Flash MX document in the old way…by opening the application.

7. Create a new Flash document that is 364 pixels wide and 245 pixels high, and set the background color to white. Click on the FreeHand document to make it active, and choose Edit, Select, All, or use the keystrokes Control-A (PC) or Command-A (Mac). Drag all of the items on the page from FreeHand onto the new Flash MX document's Stage. Quit FreeHand.

   As you can see, all of the items are in the Flash MX document. If you open the Flash MX Library, you will see the FreeHand symbols have also traveled with the images.

8. One of the standard practices in Flash is to put each item of the content on its own layer. This provides you with an easy way to track each item of the Flash movie. Unfortunately, dragging the items from FreeHand to Flash puts everything in frame 1 of the first layer. To fix this, select Modify, Distribute to Layers, or use the keystokes Command-Shift-D (Mac) or Control-Shift-D (PC). Each item is now on a layer, and, best of all, each layer carries the name of the symbol.

9. Create a new graphic symbol and name it **Mascot**. When the symbol opens, draw a small colored square and then add the word **Mascot** inside the square. Click the Scene 1 button to return to the main movie. Add two more layers named **Actions** and **Mascot**.

10. Move the letters J and T to the upper-left corner, and the letter C to the bottom-right corner. Place the Shoe symbol on the pasteboard to the right of the Stage and then rotate it a bit.

11. Click once on the Free Transform tool in the toolbox, and move a corner handle when the tool turns into the Rotate icon. Your Stage should now look similar to that shown in Figure 7.24.

12. Click and drag through all of the layers at frame 25, and add a frame (F5). You are now ready to start animating.

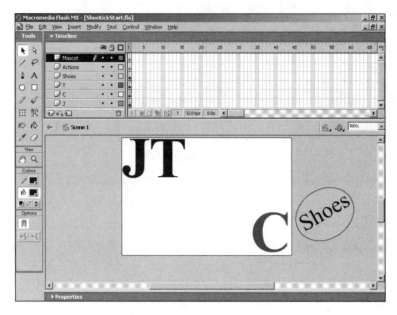

Figure 7.24   The stage is set in Flash MX. Much of the content is composed of symbols dragged from FreeHand 10, dropped onto an empty Flash MX stage, and added to layers by clicking on Distribute to Layers thorough Flash MX's Modify menu.

Frame-Based Animation in Flash MX

Animating in Flash MX is not terribly difficult. The key is to have the action occur between keyframes. In our rough, the shoe is going to kick the C into its final position. As the C moves across the Stage, the shoe moves into its final position and the word "Shoes" fades in along with the mascot. To get this animation up and going, follow these steps:

1. Click in frame 5 of the Shoe layer, and add a keyframe by selecting Insert, Keyframe. Add keyframes in frames 15 and 20 of the Shoe layer. Add keyframes in frames 5, 6, 15, and 20 of the C layer.

Note

You can also add keyframes by right-clicking on the frame and then selecting Keyframe from the context menu. Mac users can access the menu by pressing the Control key and clicking on the frame.

2. With the keyframes in place, you can quickly add the motion. Click once on frame 5 of the Shoe layer and then move the shoe symbol onto the Stage until it almost touches the C. Select the Free Transform tool, click on the shoe if it is deselected, and rotate it back to the horizontal.

Tip

There is another way to rotate the shoe back to its starting position. Select Window>Transform to open the Transform panel. Click once on the show symbol, and enter **0** for the rotation value in the Transform panel.

When something is kicked, it tends to distort. In the case of our C, it distorts out to the left to simulate this effect.

3. Select the C in frame 6. Select the Free Transform tool, click on the middle handle on the left edge of the symbol, and drag out to the left. The amount of distortion is up to you.

4. Click on the keyframe in frame 15 of the C layer, and drag the C to a point roughly in the center of the Stage. Select the shoe, and move it to a point just to the right of the C.

5. Click on the keyframe in frame 20 of the C layer, and drag the C to its final position between the J and the T. Click on the shoe and then drag it to a point about halfway down the left edge of the Stage.

6. Having created the keyframes, it is now a simple matter of letting Flash do the movement. Click once between frames 1 and 5 of the shoe layer. Select Insert, Create Motion Tween. An arrow appears between the frames. Add Motion tweens for the rest of the shoe layer. Click once between frames 6 and 15 of the C layer, and add a Motion tween. Add the remaining tweens on the C layer. If you move the playback across the movie, you see the animation.

Fading in a symbol, as a special effect, is also relatively easy in Flash MX. Transparency in Flash uses a term called *Alpha*. The amount applied is always expressed as a percentage, with 100% being fully visible and 0 being invisible. Be careful with this technique. It does tend to add weight to a Flash file and slow things down.

On the surface, adding a special effect may seem to be a bit much when you are using primitive shapes. In fact, it is quite useful. If the effect is determined to be unnecessary, finding out before the content is added will provide a saving in cost and time. To fade in a symbol, follow these steps:

1. Open the Library, drag an instance of the Mascot symbol onto the upper-right corner of the Stage in frame 1, and add a keyframe at frame 10.

2. Select the mascot in frame 1 by clicking on the mascot on the Stage. Set the selection in the Color pop-down menu of the Property inspector to Alpha, and set the percentage to 0. The mascot disappears.

3. Click once between the two keyframes on the Mascot layer and add a Motion tween. If you drag the playback head across the frames, the mascot appears to fade in over 10 frames.

4. Add a keyframe in frame 15 of the Shoes layer, and drag an instance of the Shoes symbol onto the Stage in frame 15. Add a keyframe in frame 20 of the Shoes layer.

5. Select the instance of the word "Shoes" in frame 15, set the alpha to 0, and add a Motion tween.

With everything in place, press Return (Mac) or Enter (PC) to play the animation. At this stage, the movie functions according to plan. If you were to place it in a web page, it would pose a big problem because the animation would loop continuously. To the user of the page, this could be a huge annoyance. Follow these steps to fix it:

1. Add a keyframe at frame 25 of the Actions layer.

2. Right-click (PC) or Control-click the keyframe to open the context menu. Select Actions to open the Actions panel. Alternately, select Window, Actions or to press the F9 key. This opens the Frame Actions panel.

Note

Frame actions are the code in the movie that control what happens when the playback head enters a frame.

3. On the left of the panel are a series of icons that resemble books with arrows. Click the Actions book and then double-click the word "stop". A line of code appears in the blank area to the right. The action you just selected tells the playback head to stay on frame 25. Close the Actions panel, and you see a small italic *a* in frame 25 of the Actions layer.

At this stage of the process, you have two choices: test the movie, or publish the movie.

Testing a movie will be covered in greater depth in Chapter 15, "Animation on the Web (Flash)." This step allows you to identify potential bottlenecks that will affect playback. Publishing enables you to create the HTML as well as the .swf file that will be placed into Dreamweaver. This will also be covered in greater depth in Chapter 15. For the purposes of rough content, save the movie and then select File, Publish (or press Shift-F12).

With the Flash MX movie created, it is time to place the .swf file you have just created into Dreamweaver MX. To add HTML code and the .swf created by Flash to Dreamweaver MX, follow these steps:

1. Quit Flash and then open a new Dreamweaver document.

2. Insert the Flash .swf file into Dreamweaver MX by selecting Insert>Media>Flash, or by pressing Command-Option-F (Mac) or Control-Alt-F (PC).

Tip

There is another way to add the .swf file to Dreamweaver MX. Instead of using Insert, Media, Flash, open the HTML page generated by Flash in Dreamweaver.

3. Test the movie in your browser. When it finishes, quit the browser to return to Dreamweaver MX.

4. With the Flash item selected on your page, click the Flash Edit icon in the Property inspector. Flash launches, and you are taken to the folder where your files are located.

5. Open the Flash file—the one with the .fla extension. When Flash opens, you see Editing from Dreamweaver in a box at the top of the Flash page.

6. Open the C symbol, break it apart (Control-B on a PC or Command-B on a Mac), and change the color of the C from blue to red. Click the Done button.

Flash re-exports the file, and when you test in the browser, the C is now red.

Summary

On the web, content is king. In this chapter we have explained how the words on the page contain the information. If that information is not clear, such as the text is neither readable nor legible, the visitors to your site will not have a pleasant experience.

The problem with type on the web is that there is no type. There is only art, and we discussed the use of Type tools in the MX applications. We also discussed how to apply simple HTML styles and Cascading Style Sheets in Dreamweaver MX.

Color also plays an important role. We discussed the various models, paying particular attention to the use of gradients in a web page. We also showed how to create color models in Flash and Fireworks. We showed you how one-click access to Flash from Dreamweaver can be a huge timesaver and productivity boost.

Having dealt with color, we then explained how the three MX tools and FreeHand can be used to rough out content, and to plan the look of various elements on your pages. We also explained how this technique is a low-risk method of bringing your ideas to life, both for you and the client.

In the next chapter, we move from the micro-page view to the macro-site view, and discuss how to build a protosite or working model of the site in Dreamweaver MX.

MX

fireworks flash freehand coldfusion dreamweaver fireworks
amweaver fireworks flash freehand coldfusion dreamweave
coldfusion dreamweaver fireworks flash freehand coldfusic
reehand coldfusion dreamweaver fireworks flash freehand
works flash freehand coldfusion dreamweaver fireworks
eaver fireworks flash freehand coldfusion dreamwea

Planning the Look and Feel of the Site

So far, you have moved through the project from concept to wireframing, and the time has now arrived to build a prototype of the site. This step gives you the opportunity to test basic functionality, content, and the navigation scheme.

At this point in the process, you start working out the kinks, such as awkward navigation, and modifying the look and feel of the site to resemble that proposed to the client.

The designers should now be looking at building the pop-down menus, any pop-up screens, rollovers, and so on that may be required for the site. As the designers work their way through this process, they need to test their work using a variety of browsers, such as the various versions of Netscape and Internet Explorer and (most important of all) the cross platform browser issues—such as how they display images, and how they work with JavaScript, Cascading Style Sheets, and HTML. One of the most common complaints encountered when designers gather are the cross-platform issues that inevitably crop up. For example, Internet Explorer version 6 is the latest iteration of the application. It is unavailable on the Macintosh platform. Developers, therefore, have to develop for one version of the application on the PC, and another on the Mac. Identifying and solving cross-platform issues at this stage of the process can result in a huge time and cost saving later on.

The coders and database developers should be working on the dynamic elements of the site. They should also be designing the databases and testing the dynamic elements in much the same manner as that presented in Chapter 6, "Preparing for Dynamic Content." They should be examining and testing designs containing JavaScript and DHTML menus, layers, pop-up windows, Cascading Style Sheets, shopping carts, and any other features that use server-side elements. Problems inevitably crop up and, again, solving them early in the process is to everyone's advantage and avoids scope creep.

At this stage of the process, you should consider building a *protosite*, or a working model of the site design with minimal content and navigation. As you construct this protosite, you discover how important the MX Studio can be in your development workflow.

Building a Protosite with the Macromedia MX Studio

The purpose of a protosite is not to build a fully functional working model of the final project. A protosite's primary function is to test how a user moves through the site, whether the pages flow in a logical manner, and review content placement. A protosite does not contain pop-down menus, animations, working buttons, and so on—though it is common practice to do some light scripting to permit navigation between the pages.

A protosite is sometimes referred to as an *HTML clickthru*. By being able to navigate through the site using simple mouse clicks, you get a real sense of the flow throughout the site. You are also able to determine if the information on the page is correct, or whether the content should be moved or changed. For example, you might discover that moving from the main Shirts page to each style of Shirts might not be a smart move because the content for each of the shirt styles is lacking. In this case, consolidating pages might be the best solution. Discovering this before actual production gets underway is a great method for staying on budget and on schedule.

Treat the protosite as a deliverable. By involving the client in the process, they inevitably start to take ownership of the project. Until this point, most of the work was nebulous, involving concepts and ideas. When the site starts to come to life, the client starts looking for the holes in the content and, in certain cases, discovers just how cumbersome numerous paragraphs of text can be. Don't be surprised if the client starts requesting changes regarding the content. This is the best time to accommodate those changes; they can be made quickly and inexpensively at this point.

In this chapter, we build a three-page protosite for JCT. The site consists of the main page, a home page for the Shoes page, and a shopping cart for the Shoes page. The workflow is fairly simple. The pages are built in FreeHand and then placed into Fireworks MX for optimization and slicing. The Fireworks MX slices are assembled in Dreamweaver MX, and made available to the client through the client site or SiteSpring.

Building a Prototype in FreeHand

As you discovered in Chapter 5, "Wireframing a Site," FreeHand offers the designer a high degree of precision and control that isn't available in Fireworks. Though we use essentially the same techniques to build the protosite pages, we also use a few new tools, techniques, and menus.

To build a protosite, follow these steps:

1. Copy the Chapter 8 Exercise folder from the book web site to your desktop. Open a new FreeHand document, and set the page size to 600 pixels wide by 430 pixels high using a custom setting in the Document inspector.

2. Select Edit from the Page Size pop-down menu on the Document inspector to open the Edit Page Sizes dialog box. Click the New button to create a page size that is added to the Page Size pop-down menu, enter the name **JCT** in the Page Size entry area, and click Close. The dialog box disappears, and the name of your new page is at the bottom of the Page Size pop-down menu.

3. Open the Layers panel. Import JCTCorporate.jpg from the Chapter 8 Exercise folder into the document, and drag it into the non-printing area under the bar in the Layers panel. After the page is placed in the non-printing area, it appears to fade, which indicates that you can now draw over it.

It is standard operating procedure in FreeHand to lock layers you aren't working on. This avoids having the work accidentally move to another layer. In the case of the JCTcorporate image, this isn't necessary. The image is actually placed under the document, meaning you can draw over the image, but you can't draw on the image. Change the name of the non-printing layer from Foreground to **Corporate Page**.

Tip

When you place a file, such as JCTCorporate.jpg, into a FreeHand file, ensure that the file being placed and the final FreeHand file are located in the same folder. If both files, in this case the FreeHand file and the JCTCorporate.jpg file, are not in the same folder you will be prompted to locate the image the next time you open the FreeHand file.

4. Select Window, Toolbars to open the Toolbars submenu. A number of choices are available to you. Select Main from the submenu, and the Main toolbar at the top of your window disappears. Select Main from the Toolbars submenu again, and the toolbar reappears. Select Text from the Toolbars submenu, and a toolbar showing various text formatting options appears. Select the Tools toolbar, and drag it onto the toolbar at the top of the page. You should now have three strips of tools—Main, Text, and Tools—at the top of the page under the menus. The top strip is the Main toolbar, and contains many of the common functions of FreeHand ranging from opening a new document (on the left) to opening the Layers panel on the far right. The Text toolbar contains a series of buttons and menus for the more frequently used text commands. This reduces the amount of mousing and keyboarding needed to open the Text panel when all you want to do is to change the font, point size, or alignment of a piece of text. Your toolbars and page should resemble Figure 8.1.

Note

The font used for the JCT site is Scrawlin SSI from Southern Software, Inc. It has a bit of a playful feel to it, which matches the tone of the site.

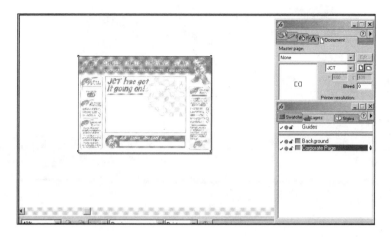

Figure 8.1   The FreeHand workspace can be customized by adding many common commands and tools to a series of toolbars at the top of the screen.

5. Add a new layer, and name it **Top**. Select the Text tool, click once anywhere on the page, and enter the word **Shoes**. Click the Text tab to open the Text inspector. If the Text tab is not visible, select Window, Inspectors, Text, or press Control-T (PC) or Command-T (Mac). When the Text inspector opens, set the word Shoes to 24-point Arial. If the Text toolbar is open, you can format the text using it.

6. Choose the Direct Selection tool, click the text block you just created, and drag the selected text block over the word Shoes in the image placed earlier in the non-printing layer. There are three other text blocks that need to be created, but rather than entering the text, formatting it, and moving it, let the computer do the work. Press Alt-Shift (PC) or Option-Shift (Mac) and then drag a copy of the text block over Hats. Repeat this two more times by dragging copies of the word Shoes over T-Shirts and Jeans.

7. Select the Text tool, double-click the text block with the word Shoes that is covering Hats, and change the selected word to Hats. Repeat this for T-Shirts and Jeans.

8. With the Text tool selected, click once on the document and then enter **CORPO-RATE HEADQUARTERS ADDRESS 1-800-555-1000**. Set this in 16-point Arial Bold, and change the color to #FFFF00 (yellow). Move the text block to its final position at the top of the page.

9. Select the Rectangle tool, and draw a rectangle that covers the brick area at the top of the page. Set the stroke to None and the fill to #993300 (brown). Move the rectangle into position over the brick area. If the rectangle covers the words, select Modify, Arrange, Send to Back to position the rectangle behind the words. Your page should resemble Figure 8.2.

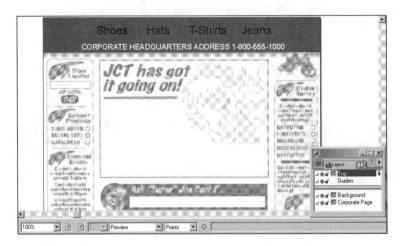

Figure 8.2   The top part of the main page is completed.

10. Add three new layers, and name them **Left Side**, **Center**, and **Right Side**. Add the content in the box in the Left Side layer. Add the content in the Center layer, using 36-point Arial, and add the content to the Right Side layer.

The rounded box at the bottom of the Center layer was created by drawing a rectangle filled with #993300 and no stroke. The Rectangle tool was selected, and the height of the rectangle from the Object inspector (Window, Inspectors, Object) was noted. A circle using the same width and height as the height of the rectangle was drawn, filled with the brown, and no stroke was added. The circle was put into position over the rectangle and then both objects were selected. They were joined by selecting Xtras, Path Operations, Union. Your page and layers should resemble that shown in Figure 8.3. If they do match, save the file as **JCTCoporate** to the Chapter 8 Exercise folder.

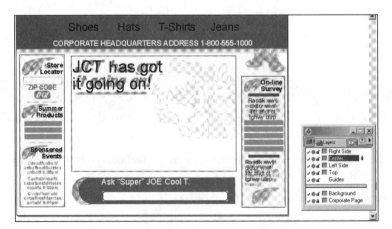

Figure 8.3   The home page of the protosite is completed.

Building and Using Master Pages in FreeHand

The content for each of the pages, excluding the shopping cart, uses the same content at the top and the bottom of the page. If the content—logos, images, words—is the same on each page, it makes sense to let the software do the work. The feature that does this for you is a *master page*. The interesting aspects of master pages in FreeHand is they can be applied to all or selected pages of a document, they can be created and applied at any time in the process, and you can create as many master pages as necessary.

To create a master page in FreeHand, follow these steps:

1. Select the banner and the words at the top of the page by unlocking the top layer in the Layers panel, and selecting all the objects in the layer. Unlock the center layer, and, with the Shift key held down, also select the banner, words, and box at the bottom of the page. Copy the selection by selecting Edit, Copy.

2. With the content for the master page on the clipboard, it is now a simple matter of creating the master page. Select Window, Inspectors, Document to open the Document inspector. Select New Master Page from the inspector's pop-down menu to open a blank master page document.

3. Paste the content from the clipboard onto the new master page. Ensuring everything on the page is selected, move the top-left corner of the top banner to the top-left corner of the master page. Your new master page should resemble Figure 8.4. Close the master page.

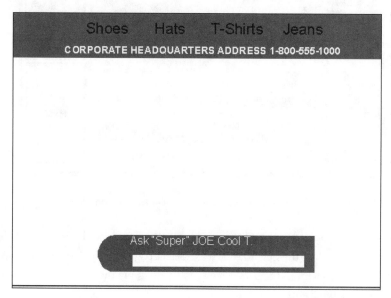

Figure 8.4   The master page elements are in place.

4. Select Add Pages from the Document Inspector pop-down menu. When the Add Pages dialog box opens, add two pages by entering **2** in the Number of New Pages text input box. To apply the master page elements to the new pages, click the Make Child of Master Page radio button and then select the master page from the pop-down list of master pages. Click OK.

5. The easiest way of seeing your new pages is to select View, Fit All, Three pages—one with all the content and two with the master page elements appears in the Document window. Select the middle page and then select View, Fit to Page.

6. Lock all your layers, and add a new layer named **Shoes**. Import the Shoes.jpg file from the Chapter 8 Exercise folder into the Shoes layer. Drag the Shoes layer into the non-printing layers.

7. Add three new layers named **ShoesLeft**, **ShoesCenter**, and **ShoesRight**. Just as you did in the previous section, build the page by adding the content to the respective layer. When you finish, your page should resemble the one shown in Figure 8.5. Save your FreeHand file.

Figure 8.5   The second page, including master page elements, is complete.

8. Create a new master page that contains only the banner and the words at the top of the page. Close the new master page. Select page 3 in the Document inspector by clicking its icon in the preview window, and apply the new master page from the pop-down list of master pages to page 3.

9. Add a new layer named **cart** to the document. Ensuring the new layer is the only one unlocked, import and center the Shoppingcart.jpg file in the Chapter 8 Exercise folder on your desktop onto the new page. To center the image, select Window, Align to open the Align panel. Select Align Center from both the Horizontal and Vertical pop-down menus. Click Align to Page at the bottom of the window and then click OK. The image snaps to the center of the page and overlaps the banner.

10. Move the image down the page with the Down Arrow key. This layer does not need to be redrawn; therefore, it isn't moved to a non-printing layer. The shopping cart page should resemble that shown in Figure 8.6. Save your FreeHand file as **JCTCorporate** in the FreeHand 10 format in your Chapter 8 Exercise folder.

Figure 8.6 The shopping cart page is added using a different master page.

Exporting a FreeHand HTML File

Though the pages are destined for Fireworks MX, there is an option in FreeHand that allows you to export the pages as a series of HTML files. You can even add HTML links to objects on the page. Here is how you attach HTML links and the HTML options available when exporting the FreeHand file as an HTML document.

1. Select page 1 of your FreeHand document. Open the Document inspector, and change the master page assigned to page 1 to None.

2. Unlock the Left Side layer on your Layers panel, and click the Go button on the left side of the page.

3. Select Window, Navigation. The Navigation dialog box opens, as shown in Figure 8.7. Click once in the Link area, and enter http://www.newriders.com/. At the top of the dialog box, enter **Go New Riders** in the Name area. Close the Navigation dialog box, and save the file as **JCTHTML**.

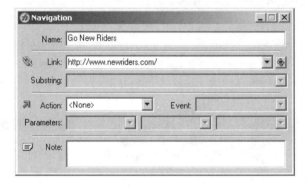

Figure 8.7   The Navigation dialog box in FreeHand allows you to assign URL's to objects as well as links to pages in the FreeHand document.

Caution

The Navigation dialog box also contains a pop-down menu in the Link input area. If you open the pop-down menu, you see a list of the pages in the document. Selecting a page assigns that link to the page. Be very careful with this feature. The links are relative links, meaning that they are assigned to the page. If you assign a link from page 1 to page 3 and then subsequently move page 3 into the page 2 position in the Document inspector, the link goes to the wrong page. If you must assign links to pages in FreeHand, do it as the absolute last step before saving the file or exporting it.

We also told you to remove the master page assigned to page 1. If you don't, it displays in Dreamweaver MX, resulting in a horrible jumble of images on the page. This also results in an HTML warning when the file is being exported.

4. To export the FreeHand document as HTML, select File, Publish as HTML to open the HTML Output dialog box shown in Figure 8.8. Use the following settings:

HTML Setting—Default. This is the only one available.

Pages—All. Notice you can also output a range of pages.

Show Output Warnings—Selected.

View in Browser or HTML Editor—Select Dreamweaver 6.0.1722 from this pop-down list. Dreamweaver 6.0 and Dreamweaver MX are identical. When you open Dreamweaver MX, note the version number is 6.0 on the Dreamweaver MX splash screen.

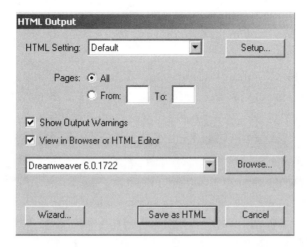

Figure 8.8   The HTML Output dialog box allows you to choose what pages are converted to HTML documents, and in which browser or editor the file are viewed.

5. Click the Setup button at the top of the HTML Output dialog box to open the HTML Setup dialog box, as shown in Figure 8.9. You use this dialog box to create a custom setting named MX Book.

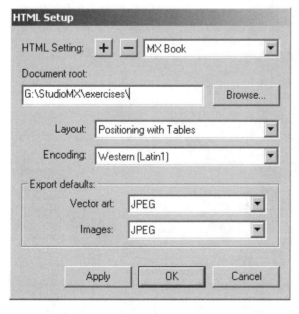

Figure 8.9   The HTML Setup dialog box allows you to choose how the resulting HTML file will be written and how the artwork will be exported.

6. Click the + button beside HTML Setting to open the New HTML Setting dialog box. Enter **MX Book** in the text box, and click OK. The new name appears in the HTML Settings.

7. Click the Browse button. When the Open dialog box appears, navigate to the folder that will hold the files. Select the folder and then click the Select button. The path to that folder appears in the Document root text box.

8. If you want the content placed in layers or tables, select either option from the Layout pop-down menu.

9. Select .jpg as the export default for both vectors and images from the pop-down lists in the Export defaults section of the dialog box. Click OK to close the HTML Setup dialog box. MX Book now appears as the HTML setting. Click Save as HTML.

10. Dreamweaver MX launches automatically. Create a site for the pages. When page 1 appears in Dreamweaver MX, as shown in Figure 8.10, test the page in a browser by choosing File, Preview in Browser. Click the Go button when the page opens in the browser, and you are taken to the New Riders home page. Quit Dreamweaver, save the file in FreeHand, and close FreeHand.

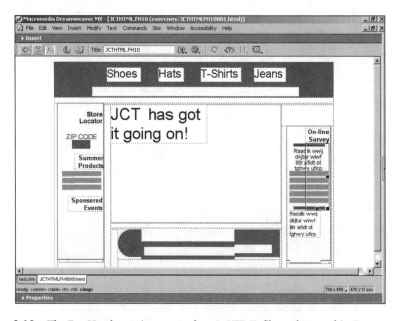

Figure 8.10   The FreeHand page is converted to an HTML file, and opened in Dreamweaver MX. The placement of the objects is not exactly the same as the original.

Note

Notice a number of items on the FreeHand page have shifted around in Dreamweaver MX. This is due to objects overlapping each other on the FreeHand page.

The creation of multi-page FreeHand documents and the use of master pages is a huge productivity boost when it comes to workflow. Rather than designing multiple pages using the same elements, the team or the designer creates the pages containing the common elements, and builds around them. By creating a multiple-page document, you can quickly create a .pdf document that can be added to the project file, or treated as deliverable. You can also create a quick HTML version of the FreeHand file. You are now about to discover the value of creating multi-page FreeHand documents in the next section, which takes the pages into Fireworks MX.

Optimizing the FreeHand Protosite in Fireworks MX

Though the movement of FreeHand documents into Fireworks MX can be accomplished by either copy and paste or drag and drop into Fireworks MX documents, there is a another method that allows the designer to import each page of a multi-page FreeHand document into a separate Fireworks MX page.

Again, this is a huge productivity boost. Instead of navigating through a number of individual FreeHand documents to find the document you want to work on, you simply tell Fireworks MX what page inside the multi-page FreeHand document you would like, and Fireworks MX does the rest.

To optimize a protosite created in FreeHand, follow these steps:

1. Open Fireworks MX and then open a new document. Set the width and height to 600 pixels wide by 430 pixels high, and set the background color to white. Click OK to display the new blank page.

2. Select File, Import, or press Control-R (PC) or Command-R (Mac); then navigate to your FreeHand file being used for the protosite, and open it. Fireworks MX immediately detects that you are opening a vector file, and the Vector File Options dialog box shown in Figure 8.11 appears, asking you how to treat the file in Fireworks MX. Select page 1 from the pop-down menu in the File Conversion area. This is a key step. The capability to import individual pages of a multi-page FreeHand document is critical. The great thing about this is the capability to choose the page you want to bring in rather than waste time importing a number of individual files. The cursor changes to the place cursor when the file is loaded.

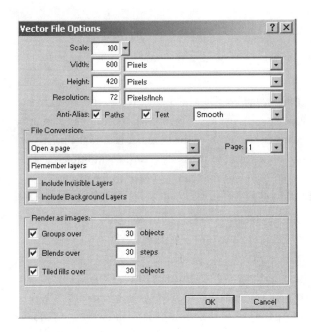

Figure 8.11   The Vector File Options dialog box enables you to import the individual pages of a multi-page FreeHand document.

3. Place the cursor in the upper-left corner of the Fireworks MX page, and click. The FreeHand page drops into place.

Note

One of the quirks of this technique is that some of the objects—especially text—will not place in precisely the manner as the FreeHand document. It is more in the area of a minor irritant than anything else. Always take a minute or two to review the page and make any needed adjustments.

4. Import the Logo.png file from your Chapter 8 Exercise folder, and place it in the upper-left corner of the page. With the placed logo selected, press Alt (PC) or Option (Mac). When the cursor turns white, drag a copy of the logo down to the Store Locator area on the left side of the page. Place the logo in the upper-left corner of the box defining the Store Locator, and resize the logo to fit.

5. Repeat the preceding step by dragging copies of the resized logo to the Sponsored Events and Online Survey areas. Import the Mascot.png file from the Chapter 8 Exercise folder, and place it on the right side of the page. When finished, your page should resemble that shown in Figure 8.12.

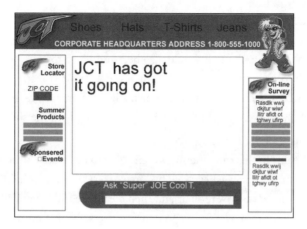

Figure 8.12   Page 1 of the FreeHand file has been imported and tweaked. The logos and the mascot are all in place, as well.

6. Attempting to open a big graphics file in a browser will result in a delay. Select the following items on the page:

Shoes

Hats

T-Shirts

Jeans

Mascot

The box on the left side of the page

The Go button

The large box in the center of the page

The Ask graphic at the bottom of the page

The box on the right side of the page

7. With these items selected, select Edit, Insert, Slice, or press Alt-Shift-U (PC) or Option-Shift-U (Mac). You are asked, through a dialog box, if you want to create multiple slices. Click Multiple. The page is then divided up into a series of slices.

8. With the slices in place, you can now export the slices and corresponding HTML file out of Fireworks MX for eventual placement in Dreamweaver MX. Select File, Export Preview. Select .gif with a Web Snap Adaptive palette and then click Export to open the Export dialog box.

9. When the Export dialog box opens, name the file **Home**, select HTML and Images from the Save as type pop-down menu, and choose Export Slices from the Slice pop-down menu. It would also be a good idea to consider putting all the slices into a separate Images folder. If you do, be sure to click the Browse button, and either create a new folder or navigate to an existing folder to hold the slices. Click Save. The HTML file is created along with the slices.

10. Import page 2 of the FreeHand file, place the mascot.png and logo.png files, and tweak the page. In this case, the slices aren't able to be created automatically because the master page is regarded by Fireworks MX as a graphic. Select the Slice tool on the Fireworks MX toolbar and then create the slices manually by clicking and dragging the tool over Shoes. In many respects, this is a bit more efficient than the previous method because fewer slices will be created. After you have sliced up the image, as shown in Figure 8.13, export the slices and save the file.

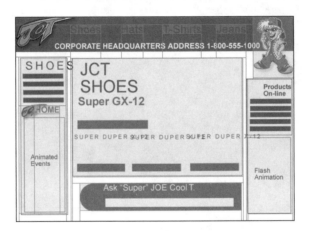

Figure 8.13   The Shoes page is imported and manually sliced. Note the Property inspector and the toolbar are showing the Slice tool has been selected.

11. Import page 3 of the FreeHand file, place the mascot.png and logo.png files, and manually create and export the slices. Save the file. Select Quick Export, Dreamweaver, Launch Dreamweaver to open Dreamweaver MX.

Note

The instruction regarding the slicing of the FreeHand page is a case where editorial necessity wins out over workflow efficiency. This was great opportunity to quickly review slice creation in Fireworks MX, and to demonstrate a couple of methods of achieving the same goal.

To have access to the artwork from the top layer from FreeHand that was turned into a master page, all you have to do is select the entire top artwork and ungroup it. The text (shoes, T-shirts, and so on) is then editable, and can be auto-sliced.

Assembling the Protosite in Dreamweaver MX

The process of creating multi-page documents in FreeHand and then moving them into Fireworks MX is a relatively smooth process. It is no different from when you move those same documents from Fireworks MX into Dreamweaver MX. In fact, with the addition of the Quick Export button to the Fireworks MX menus, the process is uncomplicated and seamless. After Dreamweaver MX opens, the steps required to assemble the pages are relatively simple to accomplish.

To define the site and create the links to the pages created in Fireworks MX follow these steps:

1. Open Dreamweaver MX and select Site, New Site to define the site for the pages just created in Fireworks MX. Name the site JCTProtoSite, and set the home page as the HTML document named **Home** created in Fireworks MX.

2. Open the Files panel and then click the Site tab. Select Map view from the pop-down menu in the Site panel.

3. Double-click the home page to open it in Dreamweaver MX. When the page opens, select the Shoes slice and then set the link in the Property inspector to the Shoes.htm page created in Fireworks. Save the page as **JCTHome**.

4. Double-click the Shoes page in the site map to open the file in Dreamweaver. Click once on the Order Online Today button to select the slice in the center of the page.

5. Click once on the Rectangular Hotspot tool in the Property inspector, and draw a hotspot over the Order Online Today button. Set the link for the hotspot to the ShoppingCart.htm file created in Fireworks MX. Add another hotspot to the Home button, and set its link to Home.htm. Save the page.

6. Open the ShoppingCart.htm page. Add a hotspot over the Continue Shopping button, and link it to the Home.htm file. If you look at your site map, all the links are now reflected. Open the Home.htm page, shown in Figure 8.14, and select File, Preview in the browser to test the various links.

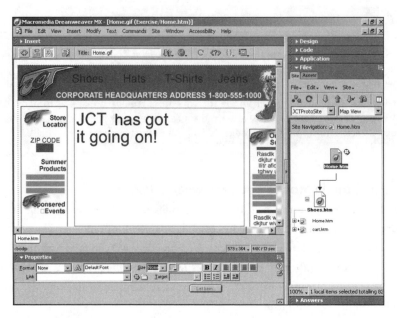

Figure 8.14   The home page with the links reflected in the site map. Note that the link to the
Shoes.htm page in the Property inspector is associated with the selection—
Shoes—at the top of the page.

Tip

You don't have to double-click a page in the site map to access the various pages in the
site. You can click the tab with the page's name at the bottom of the page window, or
select the page from the bottom of the Window menu.

Summary

This chapter has reviewed the creation of a protosite using FreeHand, Fireworks MX,
and Dreamweaver MX. This is an important step in the process because it is at this stage
that the site starts to take form. Though not intended as a full working model, the addition of light scripting to a protosite in Dreamweaver MX can give the team and the
client a sense of not only how the pages look, but whether the navigation is relatively
simple to use.

We showed you how the process can start in FreeHand, and how master pages and multi-
page FreeHand documents can actually result in huge productivity boosts for the team.
Rather than creating a variety of individual FreeHand documents for each page of each
section of the site, all the pages can be assembled quickly in a single FreeHand document.

As well, elements that are common to each page can be turned into individual master pages that can then be applied to the various pages in the document.

We also showed you how to add a link to a FreeHand object using the Navigation dialog box, and how to export the pages in the document as HTML pages from within FreeHand.

After the FreeHand pages are created, they are imported into Fireworks MX as individual Fireworks MX documents through the Vector File Options dialog box. When the pages are tweaked in Fireworks MX, they can be sliced automatically by turning selections into slices, or manually sliced with the Slice tool. The slices are then exported out of the file, along with an HTML document, and are ready for assembly in Dreamweaver MX.

We showed you how to create the site in Dreamweaver MX, and using the site map, Fireworks MX slices and Dreamweaver MX's Hot Spot tool, how to link the various HTML documents together. Finally, we tested the links from Dreamweaver MX in a browser.

After the team is satisfied with the pages, the resulting site can be uploaded to a server and then linked to either the project site or the SiteSpring project site for client review.

In the next chapter, we examine many of the imaging features of Fireworks MX—from color correction and special effects to efficient slicing of images.

fireworks flash freehand coldfusion dreamweaver fireworks
reamweaver fireworks flash freehand coldfusion dreamweave
coldfusion dreamweaver fireworks flash freehand coldfusio
freehand coldfusion dreamweaver fireworks flash freehan
orks flash freehand coldfusion dreamweaver fireworks
eaver fireworks flash freehand coldfusion dreamweave

Imaging in
Fireworks MX

Fireworks is one of those odd tools the

market had a hard time understanding

when it was first introduced. To some, it

was a Photoshop wannabe. To others, it was

toy. What both groups missed was that the

purpose of the application is the creation

and optimization of images for the web.

At the time, it was an odd hybrid of vector and bitmap tools that did some pretty amazing things. Over the years, Fireworks has quietly established itself as an integral member of the Macromedia MX Studio.

To understand the application, you first need to understand what you are working with, and the format—whether it is GIF, JPEG, or any other format that Fireworks MX can export—for the final use of the image.

Vectors

Vector objects are the heart and soul of the application. Although there are a number of great features from bitmap handling to LiveEffects, vector objects are what give the developer and web artist the precise control and editability of practically every aspect of an image.

In Fireworks, a vector floats in space, which is similar to FreeHand. Its location on the canvas is determined by a series of mathematical coordinates, rather than fixed in place with pixels. As well, these mathematical calculations determine the shape of the object (the path) and its fill color. This is why vector objects have remarkably small file sizes.

What makes Fireworks MX really shine is the fact that the surface of a Fireworks MX image is composed of pixels. When a vector object is modified, such as changing the shape of a circle and a marble fill is applied, the path is first changed and then the surface is changed to the marble fill. This is what makes LiveEffects, such as bevels and embosses, so important to Fireworks MX.

As well, the ability to use vectors allows you to create rather complex drawings in FreeHand and then bring them into Fireworks MX for subsequent editing or optimization.

Bitmaps

You can't avoid bitmaps because images, regardless of their source, are composed of pixels on a grid. In many respects, after the image is created, those pixels are like energy—they can neither be created nor destroyed. If you add pixels to an image to increase its resolution, a process called *interpolation*, image quality inevitably degrades along with an increase in file size. This is because the computer is making a best guess as to the color of the new pixel, and the addition of the pixels adds information to the file, which increases file size. Remove pixels, a process called *down sampling*, and you wind up with a smaller file size and a degraded image because information has been removed and can't be replaced.

When creating images for the web, the issue of resolution inevitably raises its ugly head. Resolution, in simple terms, is the number of pixels per linear inch necessary to accurately reproduce an image. If the image is off to print, it is not unheard of for the image to have a resolution of 1,200 pixels per inch. If it is being viewed only on the web, the resolution should match the monitor. The problem here is Macs and PCs use different screen resolutions. The Mac is 72 pixels per inch, whereas the PC is 96 pixels per inch. The difference is absolutely negligible, and a good compromise is to work with images that have a resolution of 100 pixels per inch. The web also uses the RGB color space, so images should be saved using the RGB model.

Formats

There are a number of imaging formats available to you through the Macromedia MX Studio. Knowing which format is best suited to the task at hand is critical to the success of the process. In fact, for certain applications in the Studio, some of the more common formats, such as TIFF, PICT, and BMP, are unworkable. The three most common formats—PNG, JPG, and GIF—are able to be used by every application in the Studio, and can be created by either Fireworks MX or FreeHand.

PNG

One of the most diverse formats available, the Portable Network Graphics (PNG, pronounced "ping") format is also one of the least understood. PNG was originally developed as a royalty-free alternative to the Compuserve GIF. It really hasn't caught on, not because it isn't superior to the GIF and JPG formats, but because of a lack of support among the older browsers. Still, it fills a huge hole in the graphics community because of its capability to store a lot of information in a relatively small space with no loss of image quality. As well, PNG is the only web format offering true transparency.

The PNG format can be used to store 24-bit or 8-bit color data. When compared to a JPG image, though, the PNG format has a larger file size because it is lossless; thus, the files are larger than JPG, but have a higher image quality.

What really makes PNG so important to the web developer is its support of transparency. The transparency information is contained in an alpha channel, which is a lot more robust than the 1-bit transparency offered by the more common GIF format. The other advantage PNG offers over a transparent GIF is the capability to use opacity. The downside to adding a transparent alpha channel to a PNG image is that not all of the major browsers support it without the aid of a plug-in, such as QuickTime. If you have a transparent background in a PNG image, about the only application that can best use it on the web is Flash MX.

PNG is the default format for Fireworks MX. If you are preparing images for use in Flash MX, whether you are using transparency or not, this is the format to use. If the PNG contains transparency, Flash automatically interprets the transparency channel and applies it to the Flash symbol for underlying objects to show through. The other advantage Fireworks MX offers to Flash MX is that Flash recognizes most, if not all, of the layers, vectors, and so on that travel with the PNG image.

GIF

Graphic Interchange Format (GIF) files are best used for flat colored images, which are relatively small due to their limited color palettes ranging from 2 to 256 colors. Photographic GIF images often appear to be of lower quality because they can't accurately represent gradients or photo-realistic data. As well, slices are traditionally exported as GIF files.

If you need transparency, you can create a transparent GIF, but be aware it is one-bit transparency. This means that there will be no feathering in the image.

JPEG

The Joint Photographic Experts Group (JPEG) format is the de facto standard for imaging on the web. The files are relatively small when compared to their PNG counterparts, but there is a trade-off for this advantage: The JPEG format is lossy. When the image is compressed, color data is shifted away from its original state, which is why you can never get the background color of a JPG image to match the hexadecimal color on a web page. Also, it does not support transparency.

Still, JPG is the way to go for photographs that are going to be used on a web page. If this is your intention, it is important to work on an image that has been scanned and saved in a non-lossy format, such as TIFF . Apply the JPG compression only when you save the image. If you work on a JPG image and then save it again as a JPG image, you experience color degradation and artifacts. This is why placing a JPG image in Flash is the absolute worst thing you can do to an image.

When a JPG image is created, the color shifts and degrades. Compressing a JPG file again, either in Flash (Flash compresses the image at runtime using JPG compression) or Fireworks MX, only compounds the problem. The colors shift and degrade, yet again.

Color Correction in Fireworks MX

When an image is created by either a digital camera or through a scanner, the image is never perfect. A color cast—which is when an entire image is contaminated with a certain hue, tilting the color balance in the direction of that hue—is inevitably created, and the contrast is usually muddy. Although there are a number of better applications for color correction, especially for high-resolution print images, Fireworks MX does an excellent job of color correction for the low-resolution images used on the web. In fact, the steps to correcting color, whether for print or web use, are essentially the same. They are as follows:

1. Identify the key type.

2. Adjust the highlights and shadows.

3. Adjust and fine tune the contrast.

4. Adjust the color balance.

5. Apply Unsharp masking.

Tip

Many of the color correction decisions you make are subjective—such as, "The flesh tones look about right"—rather than objective—such as, "The flesh tones must have specific values." With this in mind, be aware you may have to redo the work if the team questions your color decisions. Always, always, always work on a copy of the image, and not the original.

Color Correcting an Image Using the Fireworks MX Tools

In this exercise, you'll correct an image created by a digital camera at a Flash event in Toronto, and follow the five steps from the previous section. What makes this whole process so simple is the color correction tools are all located in the Filters menu. When correcting images, never forget that small changes are needed. The objective is to improve the image, not to compound the problems you are attempting to fix.

To correct the color of an image, follow these steps:

1. Open FlashGathering.tif from your Chapter 9 Exercise folder on the book web site. If you were to eyeball the image, you wouldn't be able to tell whether it is High Key (bright), Mid-Key (good midtones), or Low Key (dark). Correctly identifying the key type can determine your correction strategy.

2. Select Filters, Adjust Color, Levels. The graph that opens is a histogram showing pixel distribution in the image. A big bump on the left says the bulk of the pixels are in the dark area of the image. A bump on the right indicates they are clumped in the white area, and a bell curve shows they are distributed over the midtones. In this case, the image's pixels are primarily distributed over the dark area of the histogram, seen in Figure 9.1. This means some of the pixels need their values shifted toward the midtones and white area.

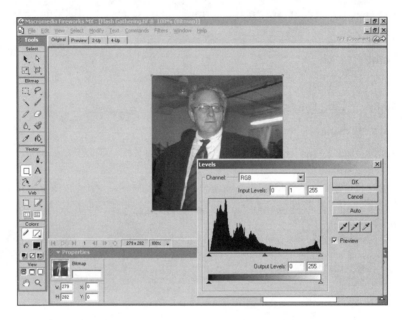

Figure 9.1 Setting the white point and black point using the Levels sliders allows you to redistribute tonal values more evenly throughout the image.

3. Click the Black Point slider, and drag it to the right to a value of 10 in the Minimum Intensity box above the histogram. Click the White Point slider, and drag it to the left to a value of 240 in the Maximum Intensity box. Click OK.

What you did was to redistribute the tonal values in the image. All black pixels with values between 0 and 9 are remapped to a value of 10—shifted toward the midtones—and all the white pixels with values between 241 and 255 are remapped to a value of 240. You should notice a bit of detail appearing in the jacket and the white shirt. The midtones, located in the face, should also become a bit more vibrant.

4. Having completed the first three steps, you now need to fine tune the brightness and the contrast of the image. Select Filters, Adjust Color, Brightness, and Contrast to open the Brightness/Contrast dialog box that contains the Brightness and Contrast sliders. Move the sliders to get a sense of what they do. Move the Brightness slider to -3 to tone down the white shirt. Move the Contrast slider to 6, as shown in Figure 9.2. This action brings out a bit more detail in the jacket. Although you can enter values directly into the boxes, use the sliders for more precise control.

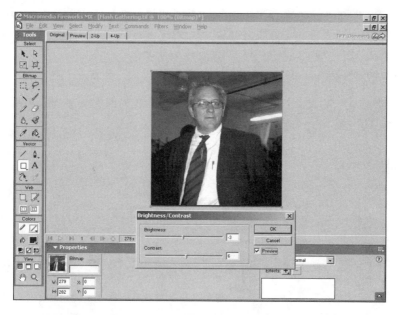

Figure 9.2   The Brightness and Contrast sliders simply brighten or darken pixels. Pay close attention to the changes in the image when using the sliders.

5. Adjusting the color balance requires you to identify the color cast and remove it. A color cast is a predominant color that is affecting the entire image. A color cast is always easiest to catch in the image's midtones. What you can't do, at this point, is simply look at the image onscreen and decide that there is too much green in the image. What you have to do is sample a range of pixels, and then determine which color in that range is predominant and needs to be reduced. Select the Eyedropper tool, and set the sample to 3x3 Average in the Property inspector. The other two options—Point Sample and 5x5 Average—are not

appropriate. Using Point Sample shows you the values for only one pixel. The 5x5 Average grabs five pixels around the sample point, examines their colors, and presents you with an average color for the pixels sampled. In this case, the result is too vague because the sample is large.

6. Move the cursor onto the flesh tones of the image, and look for an area that would fit into midtones. Click the mouse, and the resulting color for the sample appears in the Fill Color chip of the toolbox.

7. Click the chip to open the Swatches pop-down menu and then click the Color Picker icon to open the Color Picker. Select RGB. The color is shown as a swatch, and the sliders show you the percentage value. Based on the values of the sampled color, red seems to be the color cast, as shown in Figure 9.3. The objective is to remove some of the red from the image. Close the Color Picker.

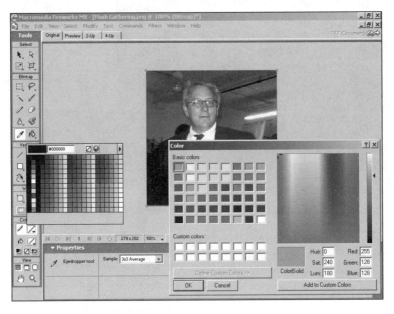

Figure 9.3   A pixel in the flesh tones is sampled, and the color is examined in the RGB Color Picker. It is determined that red is the color cast.

The rule for color reduction is quite simple: Reduce the value of one color, and you increase the value of its complement. For example, reducing the red in the image increases the cyan values in the image. In this case, subtle changes are needed.

8. Although you can use the Hue and Saturation option for this task, it is not rec-
    ommended because you do not have the precise control necessary. Levels or
    Curves are your best choices. Select Filters, Adjust Color, Curves to open the
    Curves dialog box. Notice a straight line moving upward from the bottom-left
    corner of the graph to the upper-right corner, and how the graph is divided into
    quadrants. These are the quarter tones. Think of this line as being a more precise
    tool than the slider in the Levels area.

9. Because the red needs to be reduced, select Red from the Channel pop-down
    menu above the curve. To see what the curves can do, click the line where it
    intersects the midpoint of the graph. A handle appears where you clicked. Drag
    the handle to the bottom of the graph. The image turns a ghastly green because
    you have removed all of the red from the highlights and the midtones. Move the
    handle in the opposite direction, and you simply keep adding red. Drag the han-
    dle back to the intersection point and then drag it downward until the Output
    value reads 115, as shown in Figure 9.4. Click Cancel.

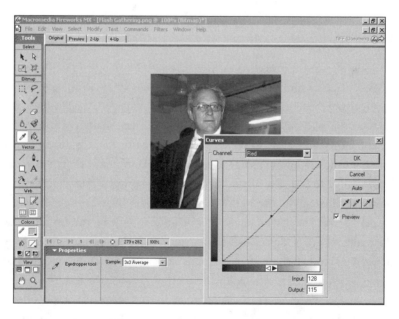

Figure 9.4   Use Curves to remove a red color cast from an image.

10. Select Filters, Adjust Color, Levels to open the Levels dialog box. Select the red
    channel from the Channel pop-down menu, and move the Gamma slider to the left
    and the right. You see the same effect as using Curves. Move the slider to the right
    until the value in the Gamma box reads .93, as shown in Figure 9.5. Click OK.

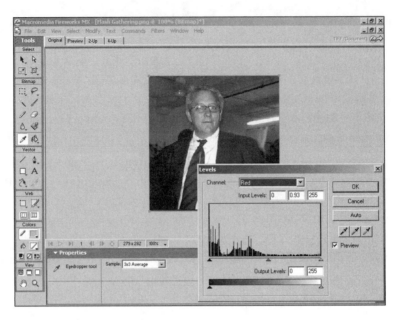

Figure 9.5   Use the Gamma slider in the Levels dialog box to remove a color cast in the red channel.

11. The final step of the process is to apply Unsharp Masking (USM) to the image. USM adjusts the contrast levels of adjoining pixels where strong color changes occur, giving the illusion of a sharper, in-focus image. What USM does not do is bring an out-of-focus image into focus. Select Filters, Sharpen, Unsharp Mask to open the Unsharp Mask dialog box, shown in Figure 9.6. The three sliders in this dialog box need a bit of explanation. The Sharpen Amount slider has values that range from 1 to 500. The higher the amount, the more drastic the change. If you move the slider all the way to the right, you see this effect. You never need to use a value of 500. The Pixel Radius slider determines how far out from the edge of the change—1 to 500 pixels—the filter will go. The higher the radius, the more noticeable the change, so try to keep this value low. The Threshold slider determines which pixels are affected by the contrast change. The lower the threshold, the less picky the USM filter is about what pixels it affects. This is not necessarily a good thing, because some pixels contain noise or dust that was scanned in, and shouldn't be sharpened. For most images, a value around 12 is about right, but you have to experiment to determine that on your own for each image. Use the following settings on the image:

Sharpen Amount: 48

Pixel Radius: 1

Threshold: 42

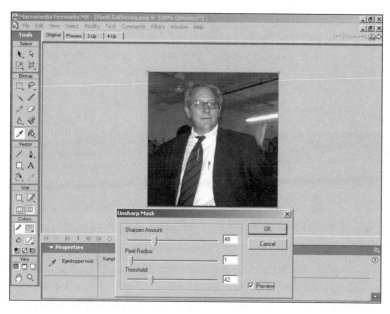

Figure 9.6   Unsharp Masking applied to an image.

12. Click OK and save the image. Open the original image and compare the two. A side-by-side comparison is shown in Figure 9.7.

Figure 9.7   The final image has a lot more detail, and the colors aren't as washed out as they were in the original image.

Using the Paint Tools to Touch Up an Image

There is something on the subject's tie that really should be removed. There are a number of techniques for accomplishing this. This exercise looks at the use of the Rubber Stamp and Pencil tools.

Using the Rubber Stamp Tool

Sometimes referred to as the Clone tool, the Rubber Stamp tool simply copies pixels from one area of an image to another.

To use the Rubber Stamp tool to touch up an image, follow these steps:

1. Open the image you just corrected, select the Magnifying Glass, and zoom in on the area of the tie where the artifact is located. Click once on the Rubber Stamp tool.

2. When you bring the Rubber Stamp tool onto the image, the cursor icon changes to a bullseye. Place the cursor in the red area of the tie (below the second stripe), press Option (Mac) or Alt (PC), and click once. A crosshair appears where you clicked, and the cursor changes to a circle. The crosshair indicates where the pixels to be copied are located, and the circle is their final destination.

3. At the extreme, magnification of the image using the default settings for the tool is unwise. In the Property inspector, set the Size option of the crosshair sample area to 2, and the Edge option to 1. Click and drag the tool to move some of the red pixels to the area just under the stripe. Keep doing this until most of the area is covered.

4. Repeat the previous step for the area above the stripe. To match the stripe, place the cursor over the third stripe, press Option (Mac) or Alt (PC), and click/drag along the second stripe. Fix the first stripe using the same technique. Your image should resemble that shown in Figure 9.8.

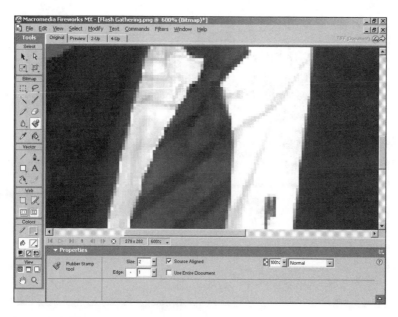

Figure 9.8   The tie and the stripes have been cloned. Note the settings for the Rubber Stamp tool in the Property inspector.

Using the Pencil and Subselect Tools

There are still a few pixels that need to be fixed. The reason these areas weren't touched with the Rubber Stamp tool is because there was a risk of copying some of the red over the stripes, or even moving part of a stripe into the red area. In this case, the Pencil tool is an ideal touch-up tool. Though regarded as a drawing tool, the ability to set the width of the tip allows you to sample a color, apply it to the Stroke chip, and click the pixels that need to be colored.

To use the Pencil tool to touch up your image, follow these steps:

1. Select the Eyedropper tool, click once on the stroke chip, and click in the red area of the tie.

2. Select the Pencil tool. Click the pixels that need to be colored red. Sample the stripe, and click the pixels that need to match the stripe color. When finished, your area should resemble Figure 9.9.

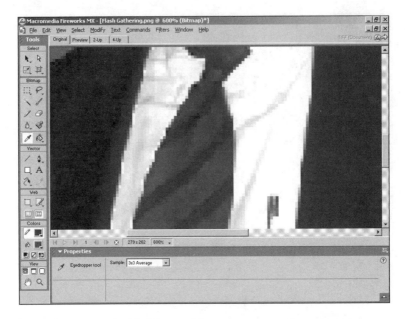

Figure 9.9   The Pencil tool is ideal for touching up areas as small as one pixel.

When you zoom out to 100% size by double-clicking the Magnifying Glass, you can see the results of your handiwork, as shown in Figure 9.10.

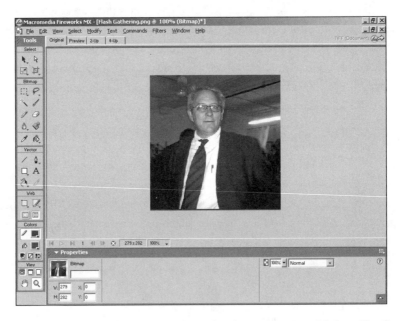

Figure 9.10   Using the Rubber Stamp and Pencil tools removes an unsightly artifact from an image.

3. To remove the pen, zoom in on the image in the area where the pen is located. Notice there is not a lot of detail in the area. Select the Lasso tool, and select an area of the white shirt that approximates the size of the pen. Select the Subselect tool, and drag the selection over the pen. The Subselect tool, when applied to a pixel selection, copies the selected pixels and allows you to move them to their final destination. Save the image and leave it open for the following exercise.

Cropping an Image

When you work on the web, your biggest concern when it comes to images is the final size. One of the quickest ways to pare down the physical size and the file size of an image is to crop it. Fireworks MX offers two tools for this purpose.

1. To learn the first method for cropping an image, open your image and select the Crop tool. Click-drag over the gentleman in the image, and release the mouse. As seen in Figure 9.11, the area inside the selection is what you need to keep, and the area outside the selection is what you discard.

Figure 9.11   The image is ready for cropping. Drag the handles to adjust the crop area.

2. To adjust the crop area, drag the handles to reduce or expand the area. When you are satisfied, press Enter (PC) or Return (Mac). The image outside of the handles is gone, and the final size of the image is much smaller. To undo your cropping, Select Edit, Undo Crop Document, or press Ctrl-Z (PC) or Command-Z (Mac). Leave this image open for the next exercise.

The second method does not remove any of the images. To use the second method to crop your image, follow these steps:

1. Place the cursor over the Crop tool, and click/hold the mouse button. The Tools option open. Select the Area Export tool.

2. This is an interesting variation on a crop. Instead of removing an area of the image, only the image inside the selection area is exported. Click/drag the tool across the area to be exported and then press the Return (Mac) or Enter (PC) key. Fireworks MX launches Export Special menu, as shown in Figure 9.12, and you can export the selection in any of Fireworks MX's formats. At this point, save your image and leave it open for the next exercise.

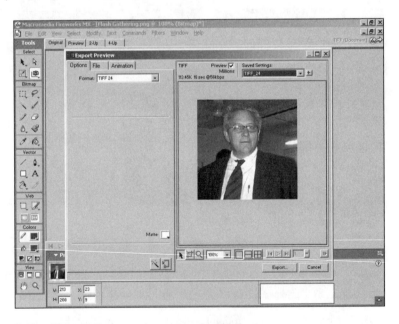

Figure 9.12   The Area Export tool exports only the selection.

Sizing Images

If any one issue will consistently pose problems for your imaging efforts, it will be that of resizing an image. When it comes to vector-based art, this isn't a problem because of the nature of vectors. The dilemma occurs when bitmaps are involved.

As pointed out earlier in this chapter, bitmaps are collections of pixels. When you see a bitmap image such as a photograph scaled larger, you are actually seeing an illusion. Assume you have an image that is 3 inches wide by 5 inches high. The intention is to scale the image to a size of 6 by 10. When this happens, the image doesn't double in size—the pixels double in size to fill the area. The result is the dreaded jaggies that cause a pixelated image. We all have seen this done deliberately, and to great effect, by extremely skilled artists. For the average user, however, scaling an image upward is not advised.

Scaling down an image has the opposite effect. The same number of pixels are jammed into a smaller area, resulting in the illusion of a higher resolution image. Faced with these two issues, the rule is simple—set the size of the image at the time it is captured.

Scaling By the Numbers

If there is any form of life in the image, never scale the image unless you maintain the proportions. In this case, the best precision is obtained by doing it by the numbers.

To scale an image to maintain proportions, follow these steps:

1. Using the previous image, click the image to select it. Select Modify, Transform, Numeric Transform to open the Numeric Transform dialog box.

2. Select Scale from the pop-down menu at the top of the dialog box. Select Scale Attributes and Constrain Proportions, and enter **200%** as the Scale amount. Click OK. The image doubles in size and pixelates. Note that the canvas does not grow to accommodate the change. Undo the change.

3. Select Modify, Transform, Numeric Transform again to open the Numeric Transform dialog box. Select Resize from the pop-down menu. In this case, rather than selecting a scaling percentage, you are given the opportunity to scale the image to precise dimensions. Set the width of the image to 150 pixels, as shown in Figure 9.13, and click OK. Undo the change.

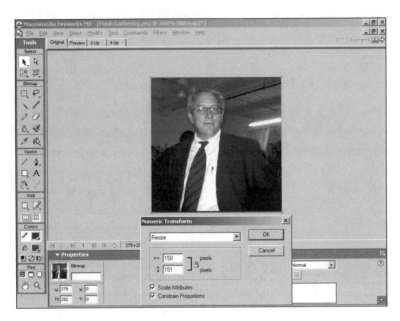

Figure 9.13   The pop-down menu in the Numeric Transform dialog box allows you to scale an image to a precise percentage (Scale) or precise height and width (Resize).

Using the Scale Tool

The Scale tool is used to adjust the size of an object by hand. Although not precise, it is a handy tool for making an object bigger or smaller. The Scale tool works on vector and bitmap objects as well as groups combining both vectors and bitmaps.

To adjust the size of an image, follow these steps:

1. Using the image from the previous exercise, select the rectangular marquee from the toolbox and then select an area of the image. Click the Scale tool in the tool-box, and the marquee changes to include handles. Be careful with this. Only the corner handles will allow you to scale. The others will distort the image.

2. Press the Shift key and, with the Shift key held down, click/drag on a corner handle in or out to enlarge or shrink the selection.

 Tip

There is a way of doing it by the numbers using the Scale tool. Make your selection, click the Scale tool, and change the width and height attributes on the Property inspector as shown in Figure 9.14. Just be aware that the proportions of the change won't be constrained. If you change your mind, press Escape to turn off the scale handles.

Figure 9.14   Use the Scale tool to scale a selection on the canvas. You can also change the
height and width attributes in the Property inspector.

Selective JPG Compression

A feature added to version 4 of Fireworks makes you wonder how you ever lived without it. Selective JPG compression is simply applying a different JPG compression level to
a selected area of an image. In the image you have been using, for example, the subject is
important but the background isn't. If you were to lose some of the detail in that area,
no one would really notice. The reward is an even smaller file size.

Creating the Mask

Selective JPG compression is a masking technique. An area of an image is selected, and
the JPG compression for the selected area is set to a different level than the rest of the
image. In this instance, you are not only applying selective JPG compression, but desaturating and blurring the background to draw the eye to the subject of the image.

Saving a Selection

There will be instances where you will have to make a complex selection to isolate a particular area of an image and nothing else—for example, selecting the face of a subject. In
this case, the background and other features can't appear in the selection. This takes

time, and Fireworks MX gives you the ability to create complex selections and to then save them for later use.

To save a selection, follow these steps:

1. Open your image and select the Lasso tool. The background is going to be changed, so it is important to have a gentle transition between the subject and the background. This is accomplished by adding a 1-pixel feather to the selection.

2. Select Feather from the Edge pop-down menu on the Property inspector, and enter **1** as the feather value.

3. Select the background, taking care to follow the outlines of the subject. If you need to add or remove a part of the selection, hold down the Shift key to add to the selection (a small + sign appears under the cursor), or hold down the Alt (Mac) or Option (PC) key to subtract from the selection (a small minus sign appears under the cursor). Choose Select, Save Bitmap Selection to save the area. Click the mouse to deselect.

4. Choose Select, Restore Bitmap Selection, and your selection appears. The neat thing about this feature is that if you save the image, quit the application, and open the image at a later date, you can select Restore Bitmap Selection and the selection appears. The file, JPGSelect.png, has a selection embedded into it. That's the good news. The bad news is, unlike other applications, you can't save multiple selections.

Blurring and Desaturating a Selection

Sometimes, you want to create a background that will not interfere with any foreground graphics. A great technique for creating such a background is to blur an image and then remove some of the color tonality. The process of removing the amount of color is called desaturation. This technique is also known as popping color.

To blur and desaturate a selection, follow these steps:

1. With your selection loaded, select Filters, Blur Gaussian Blur to open the Gaussian Blur dialog box. Select Preview, and then set the blur amount to 3. If you are going to be blurring selections, use this feature, not the Blur command. You can control the blur amount using Gaussian Blur. Simply selecting Blur applies a preset blur amount to the selection. Click OK.

2. Select Filters, Adjust Color, Hue and Saturation to open the Hue/Saturation dialog box. The Hue slider can be used to change the color of selection. The Saturation slider governs the intensity of the colors in a selection, and the Lightness slider governs how light or dark the selection will be. Selecting Preview shows you the changes as you make them. Colorize is normally used to add color to grayscale images.

3. Select Preview and then deselect Colorize. Move the Saturation slider to the left until a value of -55 appears in the input box. The color of the background is removed, as shown in Figure 9.15. Save the image.

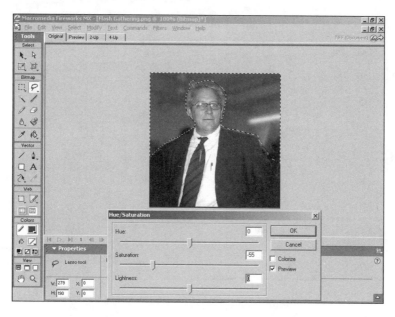

Figure 9.15   The background has been blurred, and some of the color in the selected area has been removed using the Saturation slider.

4. If your selection is not visible, load it. Select Modify, Selective JPEG, Save Selection as JPEG Mask. The selection becomes tinted to indicate the mask has been applied. To manage the compression, select Modify, Selective JPEG, Settings to open the Settings dialog box. Set the compression to 30%. This lower setting compresses the selected area more than the rest of the image. Click OK.

5. To see the results of this setting, click the Preview tab of your document. The area is pixelated. To remove the mask, click the Original tab and then select Remove JPEG Mask from the Selective JPEG menu. Another method for adding

the compression is to use the Optimize panel. Open the Optimize panel, and load your selection. Select JPEG-Better Quality from the Settings pop-down menu. Click the Edit Selective Quality button to open the Selective JPEG Settings dialog box. When the dialog box opens, select Enable Selective Quality, and set the level to 70%, as shown in Figure 9.16. Click OK and then click the Preview tab in your document window. Use the Export Special option to save the image as a JPG image with 80% compression. Save the image to your folder. The original .tif image is 448K. The file we just saved is 12K.

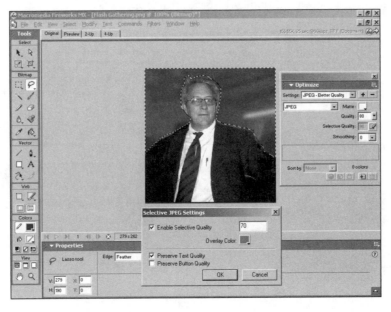

Figure 9.16   The Selective JPEG Settings can be set through a menu or by using the Optimize panel.

Tip

Selecting Preserve Text Quality and Preserve Button Quality overrides the selective compression levels. Use this feature if text items or button symbols are in the affected area.

Special Effects

From changing the color of a selection using a blending mode to creating composite images using bits and pieces of photos, your imagination is the only limit to what kind of web graphics you can create. There are any number of special effects you can create using the Fireworks MX tools. Three of our favorites are creating sepia tone images, adding an effect we call the Granny Feather, and adding a frame to an image.

Special effects can be used for various purposes. You can make images look old, or create a specific mood. Moods can range from washing the image with a dark color for a mysterious, sinister look to adding a drop shadow to give the illusion of depth. As always, exercise moderation when using these effects. Overused effects can be worse than not applying an effect at all.

Creating a Sepia Tone Image

If you have ever been to an amusement park, and have gone to the old-time photo studios to dress up in a costume and have your picture taken, you notice that the picture you get is not only black and white, but it looks like it has been well aged for the past 100 years. You look at the picture, and you start believing that this could be how your ancestors looked. A modern digital technique for making new images look old is called adding a sepia tone.

To create a sepia tone image, follow these steps:

1. Open the FlashEvent.png file from your Chapter 9 Exercise folder. Click once on the image, and select Filters, Adjust Color, Hue/Saturation to open the Hue/Saturation dialog box.

2. Click the Preview and Colorize buttons. The image turns blue, and the Saturation slider will move to the left. Move the Hue slider to the left until you obtain a value of 40, as seen in Figure 9.17. Click Cancel so your changes won't be saved.

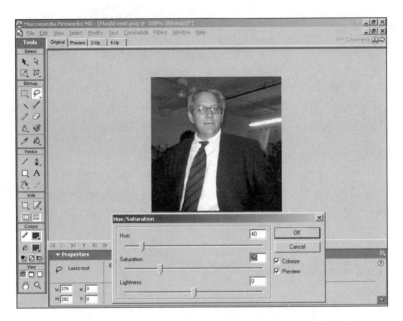

Figure 9.17   Sepia tone images are created using the Hue/Saturation dialog box.

Another way to create a sepia tone image is to select the image and then choose Commands, Creative, Convert to Sepia Tone, but we prefer step one simply because we can control the color.

Creating a Vignette Effect

Most of us have seen photographs in antique stores or hanging on the walls of our grandparents' houses that look as though the image is an oval and the image fades off at the edges. This is an old photographic technique that our grandparents were used to—thus the name Granny Mask.

To create a vignette effect, follow these steps:

1. Open the image created in the previous exercise. Select the Oval marquee and select Feather from the Edge pop-up menu in the Property inspector. Set the feathering amount to 10.

2. Place the cursor on the gentleman's chin; then press and hold the Option (Mac) or Alt (PC) key to draw out from the center and create an oval selection.

3. Choose Select, Select Inverse, or press Ctrl-Shift-I (PC) or Command-Shift-I (Mac) to select everything in the image except the original selection. Press the Delete key twice to create an interesting feathered edge, as shown in Figure 9.18. You can press the Delete key more to enhance the feathering effect.

Figure 9.18   A vignette effect is accomplished by adding a high feather value to the tool in the Property inspector.

Adding a Frame to an Image

Why settle for boring white frames around images when you can get some pretty spectacular frames in only two steps? Frames can be useful in situations where you want to call attention to the subject by surrounding it with a graphic that is more visible than a straight line.

To add a frame to an image, follow these steps:

1. Open the FlashEvent.png file from the Chapter 9 Exercise folder, and reduce the image to 75% size.

2. Select the Rectangle tool from the Vector tools, and draw a rectangle from the top-left corner to the bottom-right corner.

3. On the Property inspector, use the following Fill and Stroke settings for the rectangle:

   Fill: None

   Stroke Color: 0000FF

   Tip Size: 10

Stroke Category: Unnatural, Viscous Alien Paint

Edge: 30

Texture: Chiffon

Texture Amount: 26 percent

How about a framed picture? Rather than using smeared pixels for the stroke, Fireworks MX gives you the ability to add a texture to the stroke. These textures can be readily applied by using a predefined pattern from Fireworks MX, or by using one you create yourself. In this case, you are shown how to add a wooden frame around an image.

1. Revert the image to its previous saved state by choosing File, Revert, and reduce the image to 75% size. Open the Layers panel.

2. Draw a rectangle that is larger than the image. Set the stroke to None and the fill to Pattern, Wood Pattern 2.

3. Move the layer with the pattern under the layer containing the image. Select the Wood layer, and add an inner bevel from the Effects section of the Property inspector.

Masking

Masks in Fireworks MX can be either bitmaps or vectors. In Fireworks, the mask is not applied directly to the image, but rather the mask is applied to an object under the mask. The part of the image that shows through is dependent upon the gray value of the over-lying mask pixels. If the pixels are white, everything is visible. If they are black, every-thing under the black pixels is hidden.

The way a mask works is to hide everything on the underlying image that lies outside the boundaries of the masking shape. The shape can be either a bitmap created using the paint tools or a vector. Vectors are traditionally used to create complex masks such as having an image appear through some text. The text is composed of vectors.

This is a useful technique to master because the effective use of a mask draws the viewer's attention to the image. It also opens up a number of creative possibilities for fills using photographs or graphics, rather than solid colors or gradients.

To create a bitmap mask, follow these steps:

1. Open Mask.png from the Chapter 9 Exercise folder. Open the Layers panel, if necessary, and notice there are two layers—one with the image, and another black and white layer over it.

Note

The Mask layer was created by selecting the subject and then copying and pasting. The copied image was converted to grayscale using Commands, Creative, Convert to Grayscale, and the Lasso tool with a one-pixel feather was used to select the subject. The selection was then filled with black, and the colors inverted by selecting Filters, Adjust Color Invert.

2. Select both layers and then choose Modify, Mask, Group as Mask. The background disappears, and the two layers are merged into one with a chain link between them in the Layers panel, as shown in Figure 9.19. That chain link indicates a mask.

Figure 9.19   A bitmap mask has been applied to remove the background of the image.

Vector masks are a bit more robust because they are always editable. All of the editing features from fills to effects can be applied as well. Shapes are not the only images that can be used as masks. Text objects can also be used, as you will see in Chapter 12, "Using Type." In the previous exercise, you merged two layers to create a mask. In this exercise, you use a slightly different technique to achieve the same effect.

To create a vector mask, follow these steps:

1. Open Vmask.png. Select the Rectangle tool from the Vector tools, and draw a rectangle that covers the image.

2. Using the Property inspector, set the stroke to None and then fill to Linear Gradient. Select the Direct Selection tool, click the gradient, and move the handles so the gradient colors run from white at the top to black at the bottom.

3. With the gradient selected, select Edit, Cut. Click the image, and select Modify, Mask, Paste as Mask. The Property inspector changes to reflect the application of a vector mask, as shown in Figure 9.20.

Figure 9.20   Note the change in the Property inspector when applying a vector mask to an image.

4. Select Grayscale Appearance in the Vector Mask properties of the Property inspector. The image appears to fade out as it approaches the bottom of the image. To adjust the effect, drag the round handle of the gradient adjustment handles to the tip of the subject's nose.

Adding an Edge to a Mask

Masks don't always have to be used for fades or contain straight edges. You can add some special effects to a mask, just as you did for images. Using the Edge effect, you can create various types of weird and wonderful framing effects.

To add an edge to a mask, follow these steps:

1. Open Edgemask.png. Select the Rectangle tool from the Tools palette and then draw a white square that covers the image. Draw a black square, about the size necessary to let the face show through, on a layer above the white square.

2. Select the black square, and select Filters, Alien Skin Splat LE, Edges. A message box opens, asking if you want to convert the object to a bitmap. Click OK.

3. Select Torn Paper from the Edge Mode pop-down menu, and click OK. The shape of the object on the Stage is radically altered.

4. Select the white and the black square layers on the Object panel, and then select Flatten Selection from the Panel Options pop-down menu. The two layers are now merged into one layer.

5. Select the new layer and the image layer, and create a bitmap mask. If the mask doesn't reveal the face, click the chain link between the object and the mask on the layer strip. The chain disappears.

6. Click the mask icon on the strip to select the mask on the canvas. Change to the Direct Selection tool, and move the mask into position. Click between the two panels on the strip to put the chain link back, and save the image. Your final image should resemble Figure 9.21.

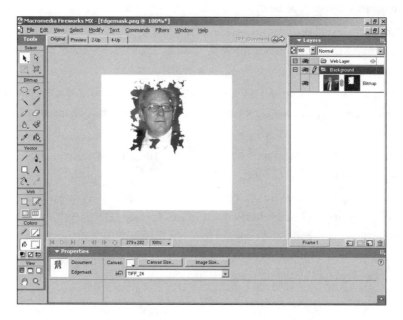

Figure 9.21   The Alien Skin Edges filter from the Splat collection has been applied to the mask to add a bit of drama to the mask.

Creating Masks in FreeHand for Use in Fireworks MX

Don't forget you are working with some powerful tools when it comes to the MX Studio. FreeHand contains a host of Xtras and Modification tools that are unavailable in Fireworks MX. If you do use the FreeHand tools, place a copy of the image to be masked into FreeHand's non-printing area of the Layers panel. Create your shape, distort or otherwise modify the shape to your liking, and drag the shape from FreeHand into your Fireworks MX document. You may want to refer to Chapter 11, "Creating Line Art for the Web," for some information about FreeHand.

To create a FreeHand mask for use in Fireworks MX, follow these steps:

1. Open Flashgathering.png in Fireworks MX. When the image opens, launch FreeHand, and create a new document.

2. Click the Fireworks MX image, and then drag it into FreeHand. Open the FreeHand Layers panel by choosing Window, Panels, Layers, or use Ctrl-6 (PC) or Command-6 (Mac).

3. After the Layers panel opens, click the image and then drag its layer to the non-printing area of the Layers panel. (This technique is explained in Chapter 5, "Wireframing a Site.") The image appears to fade.

4. Select the Ellipse tool, and draw a circle over the faded image to identify the mask area. Select the circle.

5. You now need to distort the circle and give it a jagged effect. Select Window, Toolbars, Xtra Tools to open the Xtra Tools toolbar. Double-click the Roughen tool to open the tool options, as shown in Figure 9.22.

6. Enter a Roughen value of 12, select Rough for the edge, and click OK. With the object selected, place the cursor inside the object. The cursor changes to a crosshair.

7. Click/drag the mouse to apply the Roughen settings to the object. Release the mouse, and deselect the object.

8. The big productivity boost with the Macromedia Studio is its integration. Objects created in one application can be quickly added to the other applications. Select the shape, and copy it. Open the Fireworks MX image and select the image you will apply the mask to. Select Modify, Mask, Paste as Mask. The mask is applied, but it's in the wrong place.

9. Open the Fireworks MX Layers panel, and click the chain link between the image and the mask on the layer strip. Click the mask image on the strip to select the mask object on the canvas. Select the mask, drag it into its final position, and click the link area between the image and the mask to put the chain back in place.

Re-establishing the link allows the mask and the underlying image to move around the canvas as one unit. If you are feeling really creative, add a drop shadow effect from the Property inspector to the image, as shown in Figure 9.23.

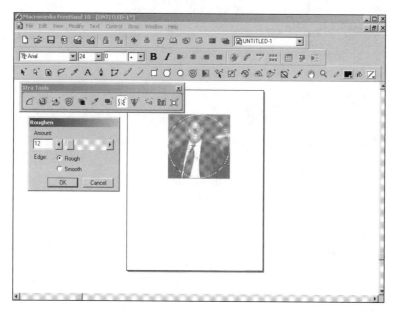

Figure 9.22 The Roughen tool is selected and its settings established.

Figure 9.23   The mask object from FreeHand is applied as a mask in Fireworks MX by selecting Paste as Mask from the Modify menu.

Filters

No discussion of imaging in Fireworks MX would be complete without a review of filters. In Fireworks MX, the filters are found in the Xtras menu. If you use Photoshop, for example, you are familiar with using image filters. When you launch Fireworks MX, any bitmap filters in the application's Xtras folder are loaded into the Xtras menu. To add your Photoshop filters to Fireworks MX, you can simply set a path to the Photoshop Plug-ins folder through the Fireworks MX preferences.

To accomplish this, open the Preferences, select Folders, Photoshop Plug-ins, and click the Browse button. Navigate to the Photoshop Plug-ins folder, and click Choose.

Caution

Only Photoshop filters for version 5 or lower of Photoshop will work in Fireworks MX. Other filter collections, such as Alien Skin's Eye Candy 2000 Splat, or KPT (Kai's Power Tools), will work with Fireworks MX. If you are at all concerned as to whether the plug-in will work with Fireworks MX, the best resource is the manufacturer.

As you saw in the previous exercise, filters are available through the Filters menu; however, that isn't the only place where you can access them. If you have an object selected, the filters and plug-ins are accessible from the Property inspector by clicking the + sign in the Effects pop-down menu. The other aspect of using filters is they primarily work on bitmaps. Again, as you saw in the previous exercise, applying a filter to a vector object requires converting that object to a bitmap.

Image Maps and Rollovers in Fireworks

Image maps are simple images that have been sliced in Fireworks. Rollovers use those slices to identify what image replaces what slice. While it sounds complicated, creating rollovers that swap one image with another is actually simple to accomplish in Fireworks MX. Rollovers are used for providing tactile effects to a user, such as changing colors when you position your mouse pointer over a button. Image maps can be used for combining multiple URLs on a single image. For example, if you had a bar with three icons on it, you can add an image map to the bar to give each icon its own URL. The next three examples demonstrate how to create a simple rollover that swaps one image for another, how to create a disjointed rollover that uses one image on a page to trigger a swap on another image on the page, and how to use an image external to Fireworks MX to trigger a disjointed rollover.

To create a simple rollover, follow these steps:

1. Open Rollover1.png in Fireworks. Click once on the image, and select Edit, Insert, Slice. Open the Frames panel by pressing Shift-F2, or click Frames and History and click the Frames tab.

2. Open Rollover2.png, click the image, and copy it to the clipboard. Close the image.

3. Select Add Frames from the Panel Options menu to open the Add Frames dialog box. Enter **1** in the Number input box, select After Current Frame in the Insert New Frames area, and click OK.

4. A new frame appears under frame 1. With this new frame selected, paste the image from the clipboard into this new frame.

5. Select frame 1, click the slice, and click the behavior handle (the white dot) on the selected slice. Drag the handle to the upper-left corner of the slice. A blue line extends from the handle to the upper-left corner of the image, as shown in Figure 9.24.

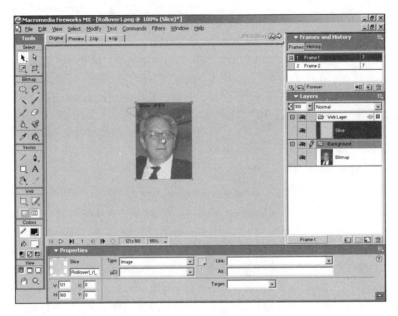

Figure 9.24   Drag the behavior handle to the point in the image where the swap is to occur. The square handle at the end of the line indicates the registration point of the replacement image.

6. The Swap Image dialog box appears, asking you where the image replacing the original is located. Because there is only one extra frame, you see frame 2 in the Swap Image From pop-down menu. Click OK.

7. Click the Preview tab to view and test the rollover, or press the F12 key to preview the rollover in a browser.

Creating a Disjointed Rollover

This is an interesting effect. The user rolls over one image on the page, and another image on the page changes. The image that is rolled over is called the *trigger*, and the image that changes is called the *target*. You might use this when you mouse over a button with a name on it; a picture on the other side of the page can change to show an image of the person connected to that button.

To create a disjointed rollover, follow these steps:

1. Open Disjoint.png. The trigger is the image on the left, and the target is the black square on the right. Open the Frames panel, and click frame 2. Note the target has been replaced with an image. Click frame 1.

2. Click the behavior handle, and drag it to the upper-left corner of the target, as shown in Figure 9.25. A Swap Image dialog box appears. You are prompted to identify the Target frame—frame 2. Click OK in the Swap Image dialog box, and test your rollover by using Preview to test in Fireworks MX, or pressing F12 to test in a browser.

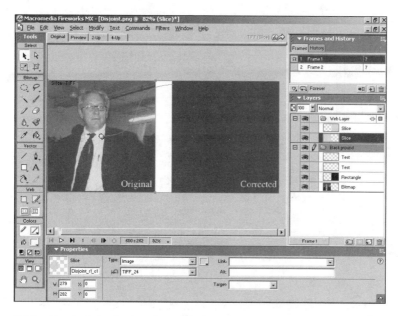

Figure 9.25   Use the behavior handle to identify the trigger image and the target image.

Tip

To remove a rollover, click once on the line starting from the behavior handle. An alert box asks you if you want to remove the behavior. Click OK, and the line disappears.

Using External Files in Rollovers

The two previous examples demonstrated a swap using an image located in a frame of the Fireworks MX image. You can use an image outside of the currently open document as the source for the rollover. Be aware that this technique only works with GIF, animated GIF, PNG, and JPG images.

To use an external file in a rollover, follow these steps:

1. Open the External.png file, and add a slice to the image. Click the behavior handle, and select Add Swap Image Behavior from the pop-down menu in the Behaviors tab to open the Swap Image dialog box, shown in Figure 9.26.

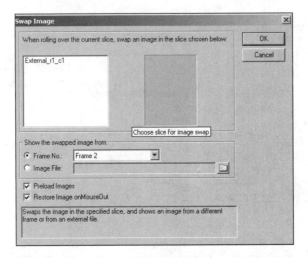

Figure 9.26   The Swap Image dialog box opens to enable you to use an external image as the target.

2. Select Image File, and click the Browse button. Navigate to the External2.png file in the Rollover folder of the Chapter 9 Exercise folder, select the image, and click Open. Deselect Preload Images, if the file is an animated GIF.

3. You can't test this using the Preview window of Fireworks MX. Press F12 to see the effect in action.

Caution

This is one of those techniques that requires a bit of caution on your part. When the image is placed into Dreamweaver MX and then viewed through a browser, make sure you have the target file located in the local site. If not, your visitor will experience a missing image icon because Fireworks MX creates a document-relative path to the target file.

Another nasty side effect is the size of the target image. It must be the same height and width as the trigger image, or the browser will resize the image for you.

Slicing and Dicing Issues

The primary objective behind slicing images is to minimize the download time into the browser. For example, you can build entire pages in Fireworks MX. If those pages are loaded into a browser, the poor user—especially those with 56K modem connections to the Internet—will spend an inordinate amount of time waiting for the image to load.

Slicing cuts up an image into manageable pieces that are quickly read and assembled in the browser. The other great feature of slices, as you have seen, is the ability to turn them into interactive elements on a page. Dreamweaver MX assembles the slices by building a table using the HTML generated by Fireworks MX for the slices.

Don't get ambitious when creating slices. If you have far too many slices, Dreamweaver MX builds an unnecessarily complex table that can actually take longer to build than a non-sliced page because of the demand put on the server. When planning your pages, slices should be taken into account and a simplified layout can help you avoid tables that don't build well.

To add the slices to the JCT home page, follow these steps:

1. Open the Sliceit.png file in your slices folder to open Fireworks MX. If you roll the cursor over the image, you notice it is one large bitmap. To develop your slicing strategy, don't look at the image. Look at the geometry instead. The best slices are those that are composed of rows and columns.

2. Select the Slice tool from the toolbox, or press **K** to switch your current tool to the Slice tool. Draw a slice over the mascot.

3. Draw another slice that encompasses the banner at the top of the page and its drop shadow as well as another slice over the box containing the *JCT has got it going on!* text. Draw another slice over the Ask area at the bottom of the page. Draw another slice over the Store Locator, and draw a final slice over the Survey.

4. You can expand or contract slices by switching to the Selection tool, and placing the cursor over the edge of a slice. Depending on whether the edge is horizontal or vertical, the cursor changes to a vertical or horizontal line between two arrows. Click and drag the edge. Your final sliced image should resemble that shown in Figure 9.27.

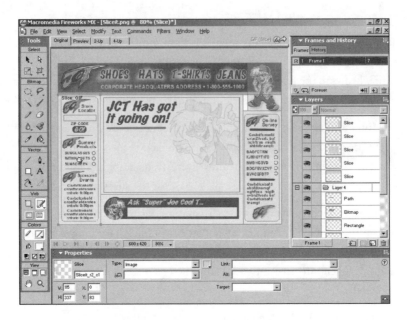

Figure 9.27   The slices follow the geometry of the page.

5. Open the Web layer to reveal all of your slices. Depending upon the complexity of the slices and their use, it makes good sense to name each one. In this manner, it is quickly identifiable. Select the slice covering the banner, and double-click its strip in the Web layer. Name the strip **Wall**. Repeat this step for the remaining layers using the following names. You screen should look like that shown in Figure 9.28.

Wall

Mascot

Survey

Going_On

Ask

Locator

Note

Notice the name for the Going_On slice. Fireworks MX does not allow spaces between words in the Web layer because they are referenced in the HTML code. If there is a space in the name, Fireworks MX responds with an Alert box, giving you the rules. Either truncate the name, such as GoingOn, or add the underscore between the two words. If you don't truncate or add an underscore, Fireworks MX adds the underscore for you after you click OK in the alert box.

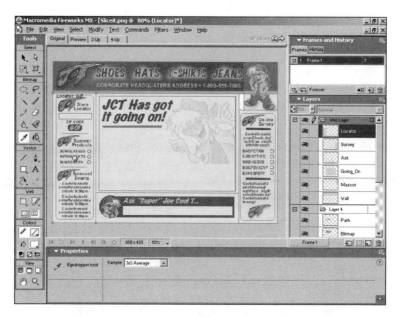

Figure 9.28   Naming the slices in the Web layer makes it easier to add interactivity and other behaviors to the slice.

6. With the slices completed and properly named, select File, Export, or press Ctrl-Shift-R (PC) or Command-Shift-R (Mac) to open the Export dialog box. Slices are converted into images and an accompanying HTML document; therefore, it makes sense to develop the habit of putting the images and the HTML file in one easily accessible location rather than having a bunch of files sitting in a folder or on the desktop. In this way, the HTML and the images can be quickly shared with the team with no risk of the loss of an image slice.

Create a folder called FWSlices for the page, and have another folder named images for the images inside that folder. When the page is to be assembled, the individual charged with that task can open the FWSlices folder, and see the HTML file and the images folder. Inside the images folder is all of the slices. The other advantage to this method is if files are being transferred either through an FTP site or as an email attachment, only one file needs to be compressed.

7. If you do not have a folder for the page, create one from the Export dialog box by clicking the New Folder button. You should also create an images folder inside the folder you just created. To ensure you are saving to your first folder, use the following settings:

File name: MainPage.

Save as Type: Select HTML and Images from the pop-down list.

Slices: Select Export Slices from the pop-down list.

Select Include Areas without Slices: There is a small area of the image that isn't sliced.

8. Select Put Images in Subfolder and then click the Browse button to open the File Selector dialog box. Navigate to the folder that contains the slices, open it, and select the Select button to select your folder and close the File Selector dialog box. The name of the folder chosen appears after the word Select on the button, as shown in Figure 9.29.

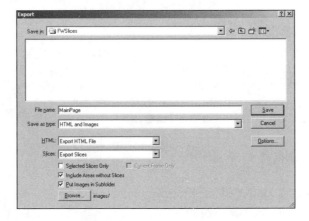

Figure 9.29   The folders for the page and the slices are identified.

9. Click the Options button to launch the Options dialog box that specifies how the HTML file is formatted. Click the General tab and then select Dreamweaver HTML from the list in the HTML Style pop-down menu.

10. Click the Table tab. This area determines how the space between the table cells is handled and the color and contents of cells that are empty. Select 1-Pixel Transparent Spacer from the selection in the Space with pop-down menu. Select Use Canvas Color and then select Spacer Image from the Contents pop-down menu. Click OK and then click Save.

11. Before you leave Fireworks MX for Dreamweaver MX, save the sliced image as a .png file located in the same folder as the HTML file. In this manner, if the file needs subsequent editing from Dreamweaver MX, the .png file with all of the slices is easily located. Click the Fireworks MX Quick Export button, and select Dreamweaver, Launch Dreamweaver.

12. When Dreamweaver MX opens, navigate to the folder containing the HTML document generated by Fireworks, and double-click the document to open it in Dreamweaver MX. Clicking on the image in Dreamweaver MX selects each slice.

An alternative to selecting each slice individually is to open the Insert panel, click the Common button, click inside the blank Dreamweaver MX page, and click the Insert Fireworks HTML button as shown in Figure 9.30. The Insert Fireworks HTML dialog box opens. Click the Browse button and navigate to the HTML document generated by Fireworks MX.

Figure 9.30   The HTML document generated by Fireworks MX is opened in Dreamweaver MX, and the Mascot slice has been selected.

To insert the HTML code, double-click the file in the Insert Fireworks HTML dialog box, or select the file and then click the Open button. The dialog box closes, and the path appears in the Fireworks HTML File area. Click OK; the file appears where you clicked the cursor.

> **Caution**
>
> The Insert Fireworks HTML button is great for inserting an image and its code into a specific location on a web page. Using it to open a full-page Fireworks MX image is a bit of overkill.
>
> The Options button at the bottom of the Insert Fireworks HTML dialog box should be approached, initially, with a bit of caution. Selecting Delete File After Insertion deletes the Fireworks MX HTML file just placed.

Alternate Tags

Alternate text, or *alt tags*, used to be important because they were the text that appeared on a page if an image failed to load. In the newer browsers, alt tags appear almost as a tooltip if the cursor remains over a slice.

Alt tags are important in today's development environment. It is quite common for visually impaired individuals to use screen readers that convert the alternate text to voice when the tag appears onscreen.

To add an alt tag to a slice in Dreamweaver MX, follow these steps:

1. Click the Mascot slice on the page that is currently open. Click inside the Alt area of the Property inspector, and enter **Company Mascot** in the Alt text box, as shown in Figure 9.31.

Figure 9.31   Adding an alt tag to a slice is done in the Property inspector.

2. Test the page in a browser. When the page appears, place the cursor over the mascot and the alt tag appears.

Optimizing Fireworks MX Slices for Export

In the "Slicing and Dicing Issues" section earlier in this chapter, you learned how to create slices, manage them for export to Dreamweaver MX, and place them into Dreamweaver MX. This section explores how the Fireworks MX Property inspector is a new and valuable tool for preparing slices before you select the Export menu.

1. Open your sliced Fireworks MX image, and select the Mascot slice.

2. The Property inspector changes to show you the properties for the selected slice. Make the following changes to the Mascot slice properties:

   Edit the Object Name: Change the name to **Mascot1**. Press Enter (PC) or Return (Mac), and note that the new name appears in the Web layer strip for the slice.

   Slice Color: Click the color chip, and select FF0000 to turn the slice from green to red.

   Slice Export Settings: Select GIF Web Snap 128 from the pop-down menu in the Optimize panel. This allows you to apply selective compression, somewhat like the selective JPG compression used earlier in this chapter. This is especially useful for slices containing few colors.

   Link: `http://www.newriders.com`. Clicking on the slice in the browser now takes you to the New Riders site.

   Alt: Enter **Go to New Riders** as the Alternate text for the slice.

   Target: _blank. The New Riders site loads into a new, unnamed browser window.

   When you finish, you Property inspector should resemble Figure 9.32.

3. Press F12 to test your changes in your browser. Quit the browser, and select File, Export to export your image slices and HTML.

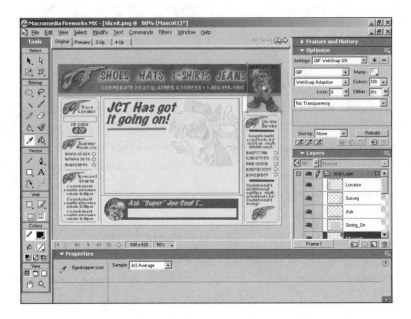

Figure 9.32   The Property inspector allows you to preview your slices before they are exported.

Summary

This has been a rather comprehensive overview of the imaging process in Fireworks MX.

We demonstrated, through the color correction of an image, how the various color management tools of Fireworks MX that range from Levels to Unsharp Masking can improve an image.

We also demonstrated how several of the Paint tools—Rubber Stamp and Pencil—are ideal for major and minor touch-up work for your images. We also showed you how the Cropping tool can be used to not only crop an image, but to directly export a cropping area.

The chapter covered several issues concerning sizing and resizing images, and how to use the various tools for that purpose. We also showed you how to pop color by desaturating an area of an image, and discussed in some depth how to apply selective JPG compression to an image.

You can't discuss imaging without demonstrating a few effects, and we showed how these effects can be done.

Masking has always been a strength of Fireworks MX, and we discussed how to create a bitmap mask and a vector mask, how to apply a filter to the edges of a mask, and how to use the Xtra tools in FreeHand to create a mask that is used in Fireworks MX.

Rollovers were covered, and you were shown how to create a simple rollover, a disjointed rollover, and a rollover that calls an external image file for the swap. We finished the chapter with a comprehensive review of many of the issues surrounding slicing images and exporting them to Dreamweaver MX, and how to use the new Fireworks MX Property inspector to set up your slices from naming to compression, prior to exporting them to Dreamweaver MX.

The next chapter deals with another form of bitmap—digital video. We will explore how the new digital video feature of Flash MX allows you to add video to your Flash sites and animations.

fireworks flash freehand coldfusion dreamweaver fireworks
amweaver fireworks flash freehand coldfusion dreamweave
coldfusion dreamweaver fireworks flash freehand coldfusic
reehand coldfusion dreamweaver fireworks flash freehand
orks flash freehand coldfusion dreamweaver fireworks
eaver fireworks flash freehand coldfusion dreamwe

Video and Flash MX

Prior to the release of Flash MX in early
2002, the holy grail for Flash developers
was the ability to play video in Flash. Prior
to the MX release, that ability was rudimentary—some would say primitive—at
best.

You could bring video into Flash, but controlling it was a hit and miss proposition. The best a user could do was to import it and either live with each frame of the video being translated into a Flash frame, or trace the frames you needed and delete the video frames.

Those days are over. Flash MX now includes its own codec—Spark, developed by Sorenson Media—that has Director developers drooling. The video in Flash is decompressed and compressed when the video plays, at run time, in the .swf. This means a digital video can now be treated as a symbol in the movie, rather than as an object the movie uses when it plays.

Before you fire up your camcorders and load a ton of video through Firewire into your computer, it is important that we review digital video and how clips are prepared for Flash MX.

Digital Video Overview

Digital video has been around on the web for several years. When it first arrived, however, the best results always seemed to be reserved for those with high bandwidth connections such as a T1 line, a DSL line, or a cable modem. The issue was not the technology but rather the cost of the service. The situation is a bit different today. As more and more users satisfy their need for speed, the price for bandwidth has become affordable. At the same time users were satisfying their speed craving, video compression technologies, especially in the area of streaming such as the Sorenson Video codec, were dramatically improving.

Still, the creation of digital video is one of the most technically challenging and time-intensive processes in the creation of web content. To do it right requires an investment in time, measured in weeks or months, from the second the Record button is pushed on the camera to the video stream appearing on the client's web site. It also requires a high level of skill involving the mastery of a number of specialized applications as the developer attempts to achieve an elusive balance between movie quality and file size.

When you get right down to it, digital video is a series of bitmaps that are synchronized, if there is a sound track, to audio. Flash developers are familiar with both video and sound. Still, there are a number of issues around digital video that have to be considered before pressing the Record button on a camcorder.

Video Issues

In the previous chapter, we covered a number of important points to consider in the manipulation of bitmap images. If you are simply plugging a Firewire cable between the camera and your computer, and then working with the resulting raw footage, the issues of color depth and resolution are unimportant. This rarely occurs, however. Special effects, such as explosions created in 3D software, are added. Titling sequences are created. Track mattes are used to give the illusion of an individual walking across an interface created in Fireworks MX, for example. Soundtracks and effects are added. These are all video elements, and the prudent web designer will possess knowledge of resolution, color depth, and alpha channels before attempting to undertake a video project.

File Formats and Compression

Flash MX supports a number of common file formats, as listed here. When choosing a format, keep in mind platform differences because certain formats are supported by QuickTime 4 or DirectX 7 on the Windows platform.

- Audio Video Interleaved—AVI files are supported on both platforms and by most video editing applications. The format is a bit volatile on a Mac in that image, sound, and playback quality is inconsistent; therefore, it is not recommended on the Mac.

- Digital Video—The .dv format is supported by both platforms, and is the standard file format for digital video cameras.

- Motion Picture Experts Group—The MPEG standard is the most common format for streaming video through the Internet.

- QuickTime—The .mov format is supported by the QuickTime 4 or higher player on the PC, and is the standard for the Macintosh.

- Windows Media File—The .wmf or .asf format is supported only by DirectX 7 or higher on the Windows platform, and is playable on the Macintosh. Use this format for really long videos, live streaming broadcasts, or web streaming.

When it comes to working with digital video, all of the video media you receive should be uncompressed or generated using a lossless compression method.

As we pointed out in Chapter 9, "Imaging in Fireworks MX," compressing a .jpg file through Flash's .jpg compression results in a distinct lack of quality. It is no different with digital video, but there is one added side effect of which to be aware. Recompressing an already compressed video source file can, in certain instances, actually increase the size of the final file, so any video you receive should use lossless compression or no compression at all.

If you are shooting your own video or contracting the shoot, insist the video be captured digitally rather than on traditional videotape. When video is transferred from tape, there is always noise on the captured file that can't be removed.

Frame Size

The physical size of digital video on the web is small for a reason. A video that is 320 pixels wide by 240 pixels high requires a significantly higher amount of bandwidth to load and then play than a movie that is half that size. Although today's high bandwidth connections can handle a 320 by 240 video, a 160 by 120 size loads and plays a lot quicker.

When deciding the frame size of the video, always put yourself in the user's position. When a video plays, data is being fed to that individual's computer. A high data rate can actually clog a user's system as the user's computer processor attempts to play the movie, play the sound, and run the operating system and any applications that are open at the time. The most common symptoms of this are choppy playback, dropped frames in the video, or sound that drops out.

Movie Length

Bottom line? A five-minute digital video has a larger file size and bandwidth requirement than a two-minute video. Again, the audience will vote with its mouse if it has to wait two or three minutes for a video, even when it is prepared to stream, than one that takes 15 seconds to load and plays back flawlessly. If they decide to wait, long videos that experience a streaming lag—the playback head catches up with the stream—that interrupts the playback will hand the viewer a less than pleasant experience.

If you must have a long video, you should make the client aware of the potential problems that could occur, especially in low-bandwidth situations. When it comes to video on the web, the shorter the better.

Frame Rate

Frame rate is essentially the speed at which the video plays. The higher the rate, the larger the file size and the greater the processor demand on the viewer's computer. On television the rate is 29.97 frames per second (the NTSC standard). On the web, the rate is between 12 and 15 frames per second. In fact, 12 frames per second is the default playback rate for Flash MX. If you have a video that is the classic talking head where there is very little change in the background, you could get away with a rate that is as low as 10 frames, or less, per second.

Compression

A never-ending source of amazement for those experiencing digital video for the first time is that the size of three minutes of raw, uncompressed digital video is measured in terms of gigabytes, not megabytes or kilobytes. This is why all video, whether it is being used for the web or not, is inevitably compressed. As we pointed out in the previous chapter, when compression is applied to a data source, information is inevitably lost. Choosing the correct compression method manages the degree of the loss.

Compression can be broken down into two forms: spatial and temporal.

Spatial compression essentially shrinks each frame of the movie by looking for colors that are redundant in each frame and then removing them. This type of compression is commonly used where there is a lot of camera movement or movement of the subject. For example, a video that pans across a crowd of people in a busy intersection would benefit from spatial compression.

Temporal compression, used by the Spark codec in Flash MX, ignores the individual frames and looks at the changes between specified frames of the video. These frames are called, just like in Flash, keyframes. The frames between the keyframes are called *difference* or *delta* frames. The greater the number of keyframes, the more accurate the quality of the video and the larger the file size. A delta frame, for the purposes of comparison, is significantly smaller than a keyframe. This is because the pixels that don't change between keyframes are, in very simplistic terms, removed; therefore, temporal compression results in significant file size reductions. The downside is that finding the correct balance between quality and file size can only be done by trial and error, and is one seriously time-consuming process.

Temporal or spatial compression is achieved through the use of a *codec,* which is short for *Co*mpressor/*Deco*mpressor. When watching a digital video, people rarely understand that the QuickTime, AVI, or MPEG videos they see can have a variety of compressors used, or none at all.

The more common codecs are Cinepak, Sorenson, and Indeo Video. For the purposes of this chapter, we will be concentrating on only one: the Sorenson Spark compressor used and supported by Flash MX. When you add video to your Flash MX movie, Spark compresses the file. When you play the movie through the web or other media, the Flash player uses Sorenson Spark to decompress the movie. This is an important distinction. When you play back a QuickTime movie, a separate helper application—the QuickTime

Movie player—is launched and undertakes the decompression duties. In Flash MX, this capability is built into the .swf file, which reduces the load on the computer's processor and demand on RAM.

There is also a third-party tool offered by Sorensen—Squeeze—which is one amazing tool for the preparation and integration of digital video into Flash MX. We will explain how this utility works later on in this chapter.

Data Rate

This is the single most important aspect of the digital video creation process. Data rate, sometimes referred to as *bit rate*, is the speed at which the information passes from the modem to the processor. Depending on the connection, this rate can vary anywhere from 1.5 Kbps to as much as 50 Kbps.

The biggest mistake you can make is to set the data rate too high. Though quality inevitably improves as the data rate increases, you will inevitably hit what Sorenson calls the quality ceiling. The clip looks uncompressed, and the quality levels out. When using Squeeze or Spark, that quality ceiling is achieved with a lower data rate.

A good starting point is to use this formula from Sorenson: Data rate = Width x Height x Frame rate/48000. Using this formula, a 240 x 180 movie set to play back at 15 frames per second requires a data rate of 13.5 Kbps. This rate would be good for a talking head. It would most likely double if you were to use a clip from, say, a Formula One race.

Even though the number seems low, when data streams into the computer, you will have to wait for the video to either fully load or wait for enough information to load to ensure the playback doesn't over take the download stream. To ensure this doesn't occur, seriously consider the use of a preloader using Actionscript.

In this instance, you tell Flash MX how long to wait before playing the video. The standard formula for this calculation is: Preload time = download time – movie length (seconds) + 10% of the length.

Assume you have a one-minute clip that is 900Kb in size and is targeted for playback through a 56Kb modem.

Download time = file size / (bandwidth of modem/8) = 900/(56/8) = 129 seconds

Preload time = 129 - 60 + 6 = 75 seconds

Using these formulas, your preloader will need 75 seconds to allow the data to move into the processor for playback, and the days of users willing to watch a 75-second progress bar in Flash MX are over. In this instance, the preloader needs more time than the movie length before the video plays. If the file size is cut in half, which Squeeze and Spark can easily accomplish, the time reduces to 10 seconds.

Using Sorenson Squeeze to Prepare Video for Flash MX

Squeeze is a stand-alone application offered by Sorenson Media. You can find a trial version of this application at `http://www.sorenson.com`. Although it prepares video for a number of other uses, we will be looking at the advanced controls it has in preparing video for Flash MX. Even though you can place video directly into Flash, the Spark codec that comes with Flash MX does not give you the ability to match the compression to a variety of bandwidth situations, for example, or create an .flv (this is the native video format for Flash video.) or .swf from the footage.

In addition, Squeeze can be used for capture directly from your digital video camera. It can also be used to prepare QuickTime movies, and to prepare and deliver video for Sorenson's online storage and playback service called Vcast. In the following exercise, we walk you through the interface and prepare an uncompressed clip as an .flv file for insertion into Flash MX.

Preparing Footage in Squeeze

The key to working with Squeeze is to start with an uncompressed source for the footage. Using already compressed footage—Cinepac or Sorenson—will only degrade the quality of the final product. There are a couple of subtle differences between the platform versions of this application.

To create your footage using Squeeze, follow these steps:

1. Open Squeeze. If you are using a Mac, Squeeze will ask you to locate the file sources, seen in Figure 10.1, that include batch processing of clips in a folder, an individual clip, or digital video camera capture. Click Movie File, navigate to the Chapter 10 Exercise folder, and open Subway.mov. The Squeeze interface opens, and the first frame of the clip appears in the preview window.

Figure 10.1   Mac users are first asked to identify the source of the uncompressed clip and are taken to the interface shown in Figure 10.2.

If you are using a PC version of Squeeze, the source controls are contained in the interface. Click the file folder at the top of the Squeeze interface, navigate to the Chapter 10 Exercise folder, and open the Subway.mov file. As with the Mac, the first frame appears in the preview window of the interface as shown in Figure 10.2.

Figure 10.2   PC users go right into the interface and can navigate to the clip by selecting Open from the File menu, or clicking the file folder button in the upper-left corner of the interface.

Mac and PC Difference in Squeeze

There are some very subtle differences between the Mac and PC versions of Squeeze. For example, in the PC version of Squeeze, you can change the Estimated Bandwidth setting of a modem; you can't in the Mac version.

In the PC version, the icons on the initial Mac screen shown in Figure 10.1 are built into the interface, as shown in Figure 10.2. The Capture button on the PC version is located in the bottom-left corner of the preview area.

The menus on the PC version are more complete than the Mac version. This is not a huge issue because the design of the Squeeze interface is so simple that using menu items is not necessary.

Access to the custom settings for each of the output options is different. On the Mac, double-clicking a compression setting button opens the options for that button. On the PC, these options are available through a menu item.

These differences don't affect the creation or quality of the .flv, but you should be aware of them all the same.

2. Click the .flv button to select the output format. Click the Modem preset button shown in Figure 10.3. This is quite an interesting set of buttons. You can choose to prepare the video for a variety of bandwidth situations. For example, clicking the Modem, ISDN, and Low Bandwidth buttons tells Squeeze to prepare three separate versions of the file, as you can see in Figure 10.3. If you want to remove one of the files, PC users should right-click the filename and then select Delete Output File from the context menu. Mac users simply have to click the preset button for the file to remove the file.

Figure 10.3   You can choose your bandwidth setting by clicking one of the presets at the top of the interface.

3. Squeeze automatically reduces the height and width of the file when the Modem preset is clicked. To change the setting to 240 x 180, you have to open the Compression Settings. Again, the platform differences come into play. PC users should right-click the Subway_Modem.flv setting in the Output Summary area to open the Compression Settings dialog box. Mac users should double-click the Modem Settings button to open the Compression Settings. Deselect Audio Output because there is no sound in the clip. Change the height and width to match those in Figure 10.4, and then click OK to close the Compression Settings dialog box.

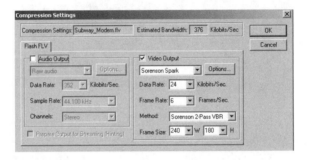

Figure 10.4   The Compression Settings are robust, and allow you to change a number of the defaults from audio compressors to data rate.

Note

The Compression Settings dialog box on the Mac platform is arranged a bit differently than the PC version, but the input areas are the same. The only major difference between the Mac Compression Settings dialog box and that shown in Figure 10.4 is an inability to change the estimated bandwidth. Is this a huge issue? Not really.

4. Click the SqueezeIt button. The application compresses the file and saves the .flv in the same location as the source file. When the compression finishes, click Close to return to the interface. Quit Squeeze.

If you open the Exercise folder where the original subway video is located, you see a rather remarkable saving in file size. The original file is 5.369MB in size. The .flv file weighs in at 40K.

An Overview of the Spark Pro Codec

Sorenson Spark is the video codec that comes bundled with Flash MX and enables you to add video to your Flash MX movies. Coming from the Sorenson Media company, the same people that brought you the Sorenson 3 codec used in web video situations, you can be sure the compression is strong with no loss of quality and a significant reduction in file size. A stripped-down version of the codec is included in Flash MX; however, Spark Pro, included with the retail version of Squeeze, offers you even more advanced features and a higher quality of video output.

The advanced settings for the Squeeze-based version of the codec are available by clicking the Options button beside the codec in the Compression Settings dialog box. When you click the button, you are presented with the dialog box containing three tabs—Summary, Encode, and Playback.

Clicking the Summary tab simply shows the Advanced settings that are currently applied to the codec.

Clicking the Encode tab allows you to set how the Spark codec encodes the information. The Encode Settings are:

- Quick Compress—Select this, and the codec compresses the video about 20 percent faster than normal. The trade off is the sacrifice of a bit of image quality. If you are compressing out of a .swf, don't select this option. Reduce the frame size or frame rate of the playback instead.

- Drop Frames—If you don't want to increase the data rate, select this option. If you do select it, if the video quality starts to reduce, Spark drops a frame and uses that data saving to increase the video quality. If it is hitting the minimum quality, Spark then returns to the specified frame rate.

- Automatic Key Frames—This slider determines how often Spark adds a keyframe to the video. The use of this slider also affects file size. The more keyframes in the video, the larger the file size. Sorenson Media recommends keeping this slider somewhere between the 35 and 65 range for optimal playback.

- Minimum Quality—Using this slider involves a trade off between image quality and data rate when streaming the video through a modem. If you select the check box, you force Spark to keep the image quality above the level specified by the slider. The trade off here is that Spark increases the data rate to meet your specification. If you don't want the data rate to increase, select Drop Frames.

If you click the Playback tab, you are presented with two options:

- Image Smoothing—As a video streams through the Internet, there are inevitable blocky areas during playback. Selecting this option smoothes them out. Select this only in low data rate situations, and never use it for high-quality video.

- Playback Scalability—Not everybody using the Internet has the best computer on the market. Select this option, and the clip is configured to drop frames, evenly, for low-end computers that have trouble managing the playback of the video.

Importing Video into Flash MX

Importing video into Flash MX is no different from importing another item into Flash MX. If the video has not been previously run through Squeeze, a stripped-down version of the codec opens and presents you with some options.

You also have to make a couple of decisions. Will the video import directly into the Library as a symbol? Will the video be embedded into the Flash movie? Will it be played externally? These are all new decisions. Still, what hasn't changed is how Flash MX manages a video. Drop it on the Flash MX Stage, and the timeline expands to accommodate every frame of the video.

To import an uncompressed video, follow these steps:

1. Open Flash MX. Select File, Import and then navigate to the Subway.mov file used earlier. You are asked if the movie is to be embedded into .swf or linked to an external file. We'll deal with each of these options in greater depth later on in the chapter. For now, select the Embed option, and click OK.

2. The Import Video Settings dialog box opens, as shown in Figure 10.5. Use the following settings:

   Quality: 80

   Keyframes: 36

   Scale: 100%

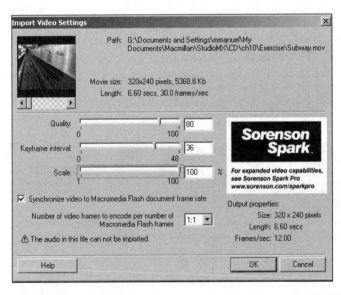

Figure 10.5   The Spark compression settings for the Spark codec contained in Flash MX are extremely basic.

3. Ensure the Synchronize box is checked, and leave the video frames to Flash MX frames ratio at 1:1. A more complete explanation of your options is contained in the "Using the Flash MX Spark Codec" sidebar.

4. Click OK, and a progress bar showing Spark compressing the video appears. When the compression is complete, you are prompted to expand the timeline of the Flash MX movie to accommodate the frame length of the video.

5. The video that appears on the timeline is embedded into the Flash MX movie, and a copy of the file is placed in the Flash MX Library. The key difference between a video asset and a graphic asset across the same number of frames on a Flash MX timeline is the appearance across the frames. The graphic asset has keyframes. The video only has one keyframe at the beginning of the sequence. Delete the video from the timeline and the Library. You now learn how to import an .flv created by Squeeze into Flash MX.

Note

The frame rate for the video and that for the Flash MX movie are not the same. The video is set to play back at 30 frames per second while the Flash MX movie is set for 12 frames per second. This difference between the rates is serious enough to make you consider opening the video editing software and setting the rate to 15 frames per second. (If you own QuickTime Pro, you don't need to do that. Simply open the Subway movie in QuickTime and then select File, Export. Compress the movie using the video codec with a 15 frames per second rate, and save.)

The difference between 15 frames per second and 12 frames per second is negligible.

If you do import video footage into Flash MX, make sure it is uncompressed—or at least compressed using a lossless compressor such as video.

6. Import the .flv file you created in Squeeze into the Flash movie. Because the .flv is already compressed and encoded using the Spark codec, Flash embeds the file directly into the movie without recompressing the file.

The two examples demonstrated here were simply to show how to import video into a Flash MX movie.

When you import a video, you should also decide whether to import the movie to the Stage or into the Library—File, Import to Library. This decision is in the realm of housekeeping decisions. You saw the effect of importing to the Stage. Importing into the Library places the clip in the Library, and keeps the instance off the Stage. In situations where you may be importing multiple clips or reusing the clip, use Import to Library.

Using the Flash MX Spark Codec

Think of the version of Spark in Flash MX as being Spark Lite. Still, when you import an uncompressed video, if you don't own Squeeze, you are going to have to make some decisions.

The Import Video Settings dialog box in Figure 10.5 presents you with a lot of information. At the top, for example, you are told the path of the file, its dimensions, and the file size. You are also shown the length of the video, in seconds, and its current frame rate.

The lower right corner contains the output properties. As you move the sliders, these values change.

The Quality slider controls the amount of compression applied to the clip. In many respects, it resembles the JPG compression slider in Fireworks MX. As you move the slider toward 100, the quality improves but the file size decreases. Lower values yield smaller files with a distinct loss of quality.

The Keyframe Interval slider controls the number of keyframes added to the clip. Again there is a distinct relationship between the number of keyframes, quality, and file size. The more keyframes in the video, the less compression can be applied.

The Scale slider controls the physical size of the clip. For example, raw footage is often captured to the NTSC standard, which is too large for web use. This slider lets you reduce or increase the size of the clip from 160 x 120 pixels up to 320 x 240. Frame size is intimately related to file size. Reducing a 320 x 240 file that is 1MB to 160 x 120 reduces the file size to about 750Kb.

The check box beneath the sliders is important. It synchronizes the video's frame rate to that of the Flash MX movie. Never leave this one unchecked.

The Number of Video Frames to Encode per Number of Macromedia Flash Frames option is also important. This was explained in a Note earlier in this chapter. Where this box really shines is in the area of raw video, where the frame rate is set higher than 15 frames per second. Use this pop-down menu to set the number of frames that appear on the Flash MX timeline.

An example demonstrates the perils of ignoring this area. Assume you import a video that is 30 frames per second, and put it on a Flash MX timeline set to play back at 12 frames per second. In this case, every 12th frame of the video on the timeline will be saved. The rest will be dropped. The result is a somewhat choppier version of a 30 frames per second video. If the ratio is set to 1:6, every sixth frame of the clip will be kept, and the video will be even choppier. In this instance, the only way to ensure smooth playback would be to increase Flash MX's frame rate to 30 frames per second, which is not at all recommended. When preparing video for Flash MX playback, always set the video's frame rate to that use in Flash—which is traditionally 12 frames per second.

Select Import Audio if you want to bring the audio track into the movie. This option is available only if the video contains an audio track.

Embedding Video

When video is embedded into a Flash MX movie, it becomes part of the resulting .swf file. Unlike QuickTime or other formats, you don't need a helper application of plug-ins to show the video.

To embed video into a Flash MX movie, follow these steps:

1. Open a new Flash MX document. Set the Stage size to 240 wide by 180 pixels high. Select Insert, New Symbol, and create a movie clip named **Subway**. Click OK, and the symbol opens.

2. Import the Subway.flv file into the symbol. Click the Scene 1 button to go to the main timeline.

3. Open the Library by choosing Window, Library, and drag an instance of the Subway Flash MX movie clip (not the video) onto the Stage. Align the clip to the center point of the Stage using the Align panel. The Stage should resemble that shown in Figure 10.6.

Figure 10.6   The video is placed into a Movie Clip symbol in Flash MX and then placed on the main timeline.

4. Select Control, Test Movie to view the movie in its entirety; then save the file.

Linking Video

Linking is considerably different from embedding. There are two serious drawbacks to doing this.

When a QuickTime movie is linked, the movie will not become a part of the .swf file. The Flash file must now be exported as a QuickTime movie. If you do choose to link, be aware that certain aspects of interactivity through Actionscripting will be lost.

The other drawback is the movie is now dependent upon QuickTime for playback. If the user doesn't have QuickTime or the QuickTime browser plug-in installed, they are essentially out of luck.

To link an external movie, follow these steps:

1. Open a new Flash MX movie, and select File, Import to Library. When the Import dialog box opens, select the Subway.mov file.

2. A message box opens, asking whether to link or embed the file; select Link. By making this selection, you bypass the Spark codec.

3. Open the Library, and drag an instance of the video onto the Stage. A message box opens, asking if you want to extend the number of frames. Select Yes.

4. To test your movie, press the Return (Mac) or Enter key (PC). If you select Control, Test movie, you would be presented with a blank Stage because the video is not embedded into the Flash file—it is external.

Video Properties in Flash MX

After a video is imported into Flash MX, your ability to manipulate the video is somewhat limited. If you select a clip on the Stage, the Property inspector offers you only two choices. If you double-click the video in the Library, you only have a couple of choices—adjusting the video size and swapping the video for another Flash MX video.

The Property Inspector and Video

When a video is selected on the Stage, the Property inspector changes to show you the video properties. They are the physical dimensions of the video, its location on the Stage, and a Swap button, as shown in Figure 10.7.

Never change the width and height of a video in the Property inspector, or consider scaling the instance. Video clips are bitmaps, and all you do when you scale a bitmap is make the pixels bigger. The result is a serious degradation of the video's image quality. Reduce the size of the video, and you develop another problem. The same number of pixels is in a smaller place, so you have more data in the area than is necessary. The problem is not the image quality. The problem is the increased CPU power needed to interpolate the pixels if resized on the Stage.

If you must scale a clip, do it in a video editing application or use Squeeze to accomplish the task. Even then, scale to exact dimensions, which should have the 4:3 aspect ratio used by digital video. If not, playback quality will be compromised. If you don't have the ability to scale before import, use the Scale slider in the Import Video Settings dialog box to accomplish this task.

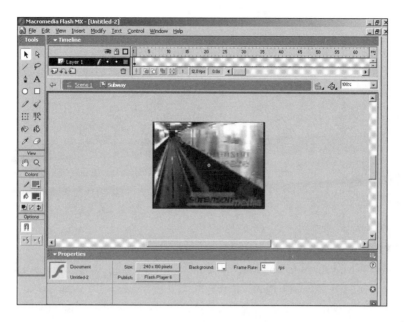

Figure 10.7   The video properties of a video on the Stage as shown in the Flash MX Property inspector.

The Swap button allows you to swap out instances of video clips with others. The only rule here is linked clips can only be swapped with linked clips. The same rule applies to embedded video clips.

Video Symbol Properties

Double-clicking the video symbol in the Library launches the Embedded Video Properties dialog box for the object, shown in Figure 10.8. The Embedded Video Properties dialog box allows you to export embedded movies as well as update re-import movies.

The Update and Import buttons don't need a great deal of explanation. Update is great when the video producer makes a change to the video. In this case, the Flash developer on the team would use this feature to update to the latest version of the video. Import allows you to replace the video with another.

The Export button has more to it than meets the eye. Export allows you to export the video clip out of Flash MX, and use it for other purposes. The great thing about this is it can be used as the Poor Man's Squeeze. The exported file is always an .flv.

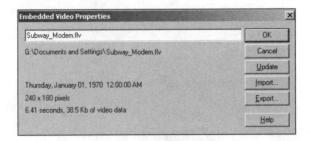

Figure 10.8   The Export button in the Embedded Video Properties dialog box allows you to export an imported .mov as an .flv file.

Creating a Flash MX Video with Preloader

The project we are about to build includes the creation of a preloader. The purpose of a preloader is to avoid the situation whereby the Flash movie waits until the content has been loaded for playback. Preloaders are common for large Flash presentations on the Internet. The problem a user encounters is that, in many cases, the user spends a long time watching a progress bar move across the screen before the actual movie starts playing.

The best preloaders do one of two things. If they are at the start of the movie, they load just enough content to be able to play the movie while the rest of the content loads. In this scenario, a movie would start when, say, 35 percent of the content has loaded. The movie starts to play and, while it does, the remaining 65 percent loads in the background. The other use for a preloader is to load content in mid-movie. Let's assume you have a section of a Flash presentation that uses bitmaps and sounds that could slow down the presentation. This section starts on frame 50 and ends on frame 75. In frame 49, you could have a small animation that plays until Flash has loaded frames 50 to 75.

The best preloaders are those that do not look like preloaders. They entertain the viewer with a simple animation or game while the real movie is loading. This way, the end user believes they are watching something that is meant to be a part of the entire movie, rather the look at something that is telling you that it is loading. Remember, what you are dealing with is streaming media, and properly organized material will present itself smoothly at any data rate. This includes the preloader.

Preparing the Clip in Squeeze

The uncompressed video you use is 3.5Mb and has a duration of 12 seconds. The sound in the video is 16 bit, 44KHz, stereo sound. Obviously it just isn't going to work in anything less than a very high bandwidth situation. To ensure that this movie will play back over a modem, we need to prepare the movie for modem playback. Preparing the movie for modem playback involves a combination of setting the compression, size, and playback rate to a level suitable for playing over the Internet through a modem connection. In the following exercise, the video is prepared as an .flv file for modem playback in Squeeze. You also import the video directly into Flash, for those of you who don't have Squeeze.

Preparing for Modem Playback

In this exercise, a file is prepared, in Squeeze, for Flash MX playback. If you do not have Squeeze, the resulting file, Converge.flv can be found in the Chapter 10 Exercise folder on the book web site. The next section, "Inserting the Clip in Flash MX," uses the QuickTime file for embedding into Flash MX. You can download a demo of Squeeze from Sorenson Media's web site (`http://www.sorenson.com`).

To prepare a video for modem playback, follow these steps:

1. Open Squeeze, and import the Converge.mov file from the Chapter 10 Exercise folder. When the video imports into Squeeze, click the .flv button and the Modem Output button. Open the compression settings. (If you need to review how to open the compression settings, see step 3 of "Preparing Footage in Squeeze" earlier in this chapter.)

2. Two issues need to be addressed in the Compression Settings dialog box. The first issue is the playback rate. Flash MX has a default rate of 12 frames per second, and the video will output at 6 frames per second. Change the frame rate in Squeeze to 12 frames per second.

3. The sound is currently inappropriate for web playback—the current settings are ideal for a music CD, but will add too much bloat to the file. Flash MX outputs sound as an mp3 file; therefore, it makes sense to set the compression to Fraunhofer MP3 in the Format pop-down menu. Set the sample rate to 22 KHz, the data rate to 112 kilobits per second, and the channels to mono. Cutting the sample rate in half and merging the stereo channels into one mono channel reduces the size of the sound track by about 50 percent. Using MP3 compression

for the resulting sound file as well as reducing the data rate can save even
more bandwidth on playback through Flash MX. Your screen should resemble
Figure 10.9.

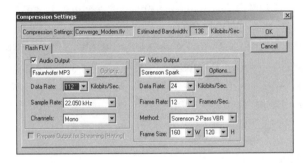

Figure 10.9   In low bandwidth situations, reducing both the sample rate and data rate, out-
putting as a mono file, and applying MP3 compression to the sound track results
in a more efficient streaming movie.

4. Click OK. When you return to the main menu, click the SqueezeIt button.
    When the file finishes compressing, quit Squeeze. The file size of the resulting
    .flv file should be about 800Kb.

Inserting the Clip in Flash MX

Placing a QuickTime file into Flash for web playback that is over 3Mb and contains CD-
quality sound is simply not going to work. Playback will be choppy, and will take a long
time to download and play.

To optimize the video using the Spark compressor built into Flash MX, follow these
steps:

1. Open Flash MX. Select File, Import, or press Command-R (Mac) or Ctrl-R (PC)
    to open the File Selector dialog box. Navigate to the folder containing the
    Converge.mov file, select it, and click Open. The Import Video dialog box opens
    and asks if you want to embed the movie or link it. Select Embed to open the
    Sorenson Spark Codec dialog box.

2. In the dialog box, choose these settings:

    Quality: 70%

    Keyframe Interval: 24

    Scale: 50%

3. Make sure the Synchronize video to Macromedia Flash document frame rate and Import Audio boxes are checked.

4. Set the ratio of video frames per number of Flash frames to encode as 1:1. Your settings should resemble those shown in Figure 10.10. If they do, click OK. Flash MX asks you if you want to add the video frames to your movie. Click OK.

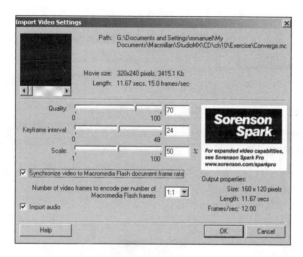

Figure 10.10   The QuickTime import settings for the Sorenson Spark codec in Flash MX. Note the values shown in the lower-right corner of the dialog box.

Note

As you can see, using Sorenson Squeeze offers a huge degree of control over the final output. This control is simply not available using the version of the Spark codec packaged with Flash MX. The fundamental difference is in the handling of the sound. Essentially, the Flash MX version of the codec imports the CD-quality sound. This needs to be dealt with later on in the process.

5. Double-click a frame in layer 1 of the timeline to select all the frames of the video. Drag these frames until the first frame of the video is in frame 10 of the timeline. This makes room for the preloader in the timeline. Name the layer **Video**.

6. Add two new layers named **Actions** and **Labels**. Adding these two layers does not add to the files size. These additions make it easier to find actions and labels that refer to frames. Although actions and labels can be added to frames that contain content, it has become standard practice in the industry to separate both from the underlying content.

7. Insert a keyframe in frame 10 of the Labels layer. You can do this in a couple of ways:

- Select the frame, right-click (PC) or Command-click (Mac), and select Insert Keyframe from the context menu.
- Select the frame and select Insert, Keyframe.
- Select the frame and press the F6 key.

8. Open the Property inspector and then enter **MovieStart** as the label name in the Frame area of the inspector. Your screen should resemble that shown in Figure 10.11.

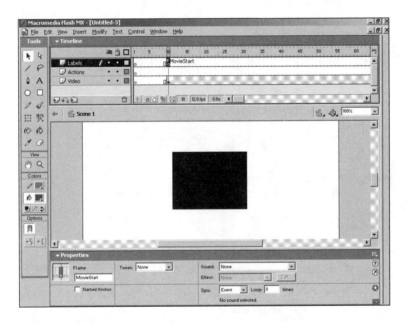

Figure 10.11   The video has been imported into Flash MX, and layers for Actions and Labels have been added. Note the label in frame 10 of the Labels layer and its name in the Property inspector.

Building the Progress Bar for the Preloader

As the content loads, it makes sense to give your viewer an approximation of how much time is left in the preload. This is usually done with a progress bar that moves from left to right.

To build a progress bar, follow these steps:

1. Select frame 1 of the video layer. This is the frame where the progress bar will be visible. Select the Rectangle tool. Set the stroke to None and the fill to a dark gray.

2. Draw a filled rectangle onscreen. Select the Direct Selection tool, and click once on the bar to select it. Open the Property inspector, and set the width of the selected object to 175 pixels and its height to 17 pixels. This rectangle will be the progress bar.

3. Select the progress bar and convert it into a Movie Clip symbol by selecting Insert, Convert to Symbol, or by pressing F8. When the Convert To Symbol dialog box appears, name the symbol **Bar**, select Movie Clip as its behavior by selecting Movie Clip from the Properties, and click the box in the upper-left corner of the Registration choices. This sets the registration point of the progress bar to the upper-left corner of the graphic.

   If the Convert to Symbol dialog box resembles Figure 10.12, click OK. Return to the main timeline, select the Movie Clip in frame 1, and name the instance **bar** in the Property inspector.

Figure 10.12   The progress bar is converted to a Movie Clip symbol, and given a name. Its registration point is set to the upper-left corner of the object.

4. Select the Bar movie clip on the Stage, and convert this into a Movie Clip symbol again. This encapsulates the Bar movie clip. Name the new movie clip **Progress Bar** and, in this case, name the instance of this movie clip **progressbar**.

5. Open the new Progress Bar movie clip by double-clicking on it in the Library. Add a new layer to the movie clip above the layer containing the Bar movie clip, and name the layer **Progress Bar**.

6. Change the name of layer 1 to **Bar Layer**. Select the Bar movie clip, and select Edit, Copy. Click in frame 1 of the Progress Bar layer and then select Edit, Paste In Place. This places a copy of the movie clip in the new layer.

7. Select the first frame of the Progress Bar layer to select your new object. Click once on the object on the Stage, set the instance name to **progress**, and select Color, Tint on the Property inspector to change the color of the bar.

8. A progress bar gives the user a rough indication of how much of the movie has loaded. This step lets the user see how much of the movie is left to load. Add a new layer named **Indicator** to the Progress Bar movie clip. Drag this layer under Bar Layer.

9. Click once on frame 1 of the Indicator layer. Select the Text tool, and draw a text box under the colored bar on the Stage. Set the text property to Dynamic Text and the font to 18 point Arial, and then name the variable in the var box **percentageDisp**. The variable name is important. It will be referenced in the code that controls the preloader. The Layers and Text properties of the Progress Bar movie clip should resemble Figure 10.13.

Figure 10.13   The elements and layers for the Progress Bar movie clip are in place. Note the variable name in the var area of the Property inspector.

Adding the Actionscript for the Preloader

A great technique for writing any code is to first write it as *pseudocode*. By this, we mean write out what has to happen and then write the code that accomplishes the tasks. In the case of the preloader, a lot has to happen. The main movie has to stop on frame 1. The preloader checks ahead to the StartMovie marker, and ask a simple question: Have enough of the frames in the video on the main timeline been loaded to be able to comfortably play this movie. Determining this can be done using the Bandwidth Profiler to see where the hiccups are. You can then determine how many frames or bytes need to be loaded before letting the movie play. In this case, we are demonstrating how many bytes need to be loaded.

If the correct number of frames has not been loaded on the main timeline, follow these steps:

1. Perform a check to see how many frames have been loaded. Calculate the percentage loaded by taking your number of frames loaded, dividing it by the total number of frames, and multiplying it by 100.

2. Scale the width of the progress bar in the Progress Bar layer of the Progress Bar movie clip to equal the percentage number.

3. Put the percentage number in the Dynamic Text box.

4. Keep the playback head in frame 1, and then repeat steps 1 to 3 until the percentage value equals 100%.

If the correct number of frames has been loaded on the main timeline, send the playback head to the StartMovie marker and then play the movie.

Here's how the Actionscript is used to manage the preload section that is added to the movie:

1. Select frame 1 of the Script layer in the main timeline. Right-click (PC) or Control-click (Mac) to open the context menu for the frame, and select actions. This opens the Actions panel.

2. Select Normal Mode from the Action pop-down menu. Open the Actions book in the panel on the left side of the window, open the Movie Actions, and double-click the Stop action.

3. You see `stop ();` in the code area of the Actions window. Close the Actions editor. The Stop action is added to the first frame of the Script layer, as indicated by the "a" over the keyframe.

4. Open the Progress Bar movie clip, and add a new layer named **Actions**. Move this layer to the top of the layers.

Tip

Here is another of those good Flash MX habits to develop. If you have an Actions layer and a Labels layer, the Labels layer always sits above the Actions layer. The Actions layer always sits above all the content layers. It helps to keep the timeline organized. Having the Labels layer on top allows you to immediately locate and use the proper label within a timeline. The Scripts layer is a central layer to store all your frame actions.

5. Open the Actions panel, and select Expert Mode from the panel pop-down menu. Expert Mode allows you to type directly into the Actions area of the window.

6. Enter the following script. The lines with the double backslashes in front of them indicate a comment. In this case, we are telling you exactly what each line of the code is supposed to do. Comments are ignored when the script runs.

```
this.onEnterFrame = function() {
        preloadAmount = _root.getBytesTotal() / 1.5;
// the number of bytes we want to load.
// this amount is worst case for 28.8 modems
        loadedWidth = bar._width; // the width of the progress bar frame

        if( _root.getBytesLoaded() < preloadAmount )
        {
                var percentage =( _root.getBytesLoaded() / preloadAmount );
// if we are still loading, get the percentage
// of how much is loaded
                progress._width = parseInt( loadedWidth * percentage );
// set the progress bar width by using
// the percentage of the full width
                percentageDisp = parseInt( percentage * 100 ) + "%";
// if a text display is present, get an integer
// representation of the percentage
// and put it in the text box
        }

        else
        {
                root.gotoAndPlay("MovieStart");
// if we did load enough to play,
// tell the main timeline to play the video
        }
}
```

The code is commented as to what each line does; however, the first line sets the Progress Bar movie clip so that it executes the preceding code every time Flash attempts to advance one frame according to its frame rate. After enough of the movie is loaded, the preloader jumps to the frame labeled Movie Start to play the video. After the video starts playing, the Progress Bar movie clip is forgotten along with the script.

7. Select Check Syntax from the panel's pop-down menu, or press Ctrl-T (PC) or Command-T (Mac) to open the Notification dialog box. You are notified if there are no errors. If there are no errors, click OK in the Notification dialog box, and close the Actions window. If there are errors, go to the line indicated and make sure you have no spelling mistakes or extra spaces, which are the two most common syntax errors.

8. Test your movie by selecting Control, Test or by pressing Ctrl-Enter (PC) or Command-Enter (Mac). The best test for the preloader in this case is to make sure that the Bandwidth Profiler and Streaming are on by selecting View, Bandwidth Profile as well as View, Show Streaming. This way, you can get an approximate feel for how the movie is loading under various bandwidth conditions.

Controlling Video in Flash MX

The movie sits on the timeline, which means it can be treated just like any item on the timeline. This allows you to add navigation controls on the timeline and control your movie. This section adds simple Stop and Play controls to the video.

To add Stop and Play controls, follow these steps:

1. Add a new layer, and name it **Controls**. Add a keyframe in frame 10 of the Controls layer.

2. Flash MX contains a number of pre-rolled buttons as well as other elements in an area called the Common Library. The Play and Stop buttons will come from the Buttons Library. Select Window, Common Libraries, Buttons. Open the Circle Buttons folder, and drag an instance of the Play and Stop button onto the Stage in frame 10 of the Controls layer. Your movie should resemble Figure 10.14.

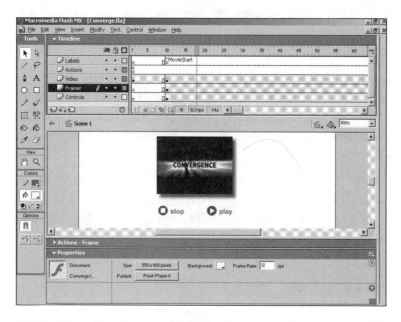

Figure 10.14   Play and Stop buttons are added to the movie to give the user the ability to control the video.

3. Select the Play button on the Stage, open the button's actions, and assign a Play action to the button. The code should read:

```
on (release) {
play();
}
```

4. Select the Stop button and add a Stop action to the button. Its code should read:

```
on (release) {
stop();
}
```

5. Test the movie. When it plays, click the Stop button. The movie will hold on the frame. Click the Play button, and the movie resumes playing. Save the movie.

Creating a Video Frame in Fireworks MX

The video just sits on the Stage. You can add a bit of depth to it using an object created in Fireworks MX.

To create a video frame in Fireworks MX, follow these steps:

1. Open Fireworks MX and then open a new document that is 175 pixels wide by 135 pixels high with a transparent background.

2. When the document opens, select the Rectangle tool from the toolbox, and draw a rectangle on the canvas.

3. With the rectangle selected, open the Fireworks MX Property inspector by selecting Window, Properties, or by pressing Control-F3 (PC) or Command-F3 (Mac). Set the width to 160 pixels, and set the height to 120 pixels. Set the stroke to None and the fill to Black. The size of the box matches the dimensions of the video.

4. Move the box to a point that is a few pixels from the top of the canvas and an equal number from the left edge of the canvas. With the box selected on the canvas, select Effects, Shadow and Glow, Drop Shadow on the Property inspector.

5. When the Drop Shadow dialog box opens, enter the following settings:

    Distance: 12

    Color: 000000 (Black)

    Opacity: 71%

    Softness: 5

    Angle: 315 degrees

    Your image should resemble Figure 10.15.

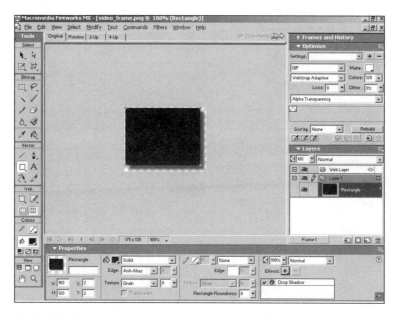

Figure 10.15   The framer box with a drop shadow is ready for placement in Flash MX.

6. There are a number of ways to get the image from Fireworks MX into Flash MX. Due to the simple nature of the image, here is the fastest method. Select the object on the canvas, and copy it to the clipboard.

7. Open the Flash MX movie, and create a new graphic symbol named **Framer**. When the symbol opens, pass the image into the symbol.

8. Return to the main timeline of the Flash movie, and lock the layer containing the video. Add a new layer named **framer** and then drag the layer under the locked layer.

9. Drag an instance of the Framer symbol onto the Stage in frame 1 of the Framer layer. Move the playback head to frame 10, and move the Framer symbol under the video.

10. The progress bar now has to be moved under the frame. Unlock the Video layer and double-click anywhere in the unlocked layer between frames 1 and 10. Using the arrow keys, move the progress bar under the frame. Your Flash movie is finished, and the Stage should resemble that shown in Figure 10.16.

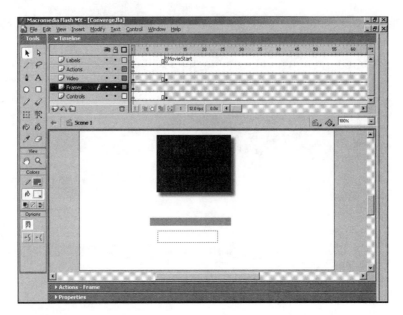

Figure 10.16   All of the assets are in place and ready to be published.

Publishing the Flash MX Movie

Earlier in this exercise, we mentioned that the Spark compression couldn't manage the compression of the sound in the same manner as using Squeeze. You can approximate the sound settings in the Flash movie to match those set in Squeeze. If you are using an .flv file, simply publish the movie without worrying about the sound settings in this section.

To approximate the sound settings, follow these steps:

1. Select File, Publish Settings to open the Publish Settings dialog box. Click the Flash tab.

2. Click the Set button beside Audio Stream. The Sound Settings dialog box opens. Use these settings:

    Compression: MP3

    Covert Stereo to Mono: Selected

    Bit Rate: 112 Kbps

    Quality: Fast

    If your settings match those shown in Figure 10.17, click OK.

3. Click Publish in the Publish Settings dialog box. Save the movie, quit Flash MX, and open the resulting HTML file in Dreamweaver MX. Test the file in a browser.

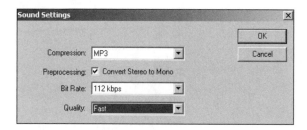

Figure 10.17 You can use the Sound Settings dialog box to approximate those of Squeeze. What you can't do is reduce the sample rate, or use the Fraunhofer MP3 compressor in Squeeze.

Summary

The ability to embed video in Flash MX and use it in Flash movies is a major addition to the Flash MX application.

We explained the inclusion of video into Flash requires more than using the insert command. It involves a lot of planning and technical knowledge to achieve optimal playback in Flash.

In this chapter, we explained how to use Sorenson Media's Squeeze to optimize video for playback in the new .flv format used by Flash MX. We also covered many of the subtle differences between the Macintosh and PC versions of the application. We also offered a detailed explanation of the advanced features of the SparkPro codec used by Squeeze.

We discussed many of the importing and playback issues involved in working with digital video in Flash MX. We also included a detailed explanation of the Import Video dialog box that appears when an uncompressed video is imported into Flash MX. We showed how videos are embedded into the Flash movie, and how videos can be linked to external sources.

We discussed the properties of digital video in Flash MX, and showed how to create an .flv file using Flash MX, not Squeeze. We then showed you how to use Squeeze to create an .flv file from a digital video with CD-quality sound. We explained how to create a Flash movie that imports the video in Flash MX, and how create and code a preloader that uses graphics and text. We also showed you how to create a frame for the video in Fireworks MX, and how to approximate the sound settings from Squeeze using the Sound Settings dialog box when the file is published in Flash MX.

The next chapter discusses many of the line art creation tools and their uses in Macromedia Studio.

Chapter 11

Creating Line Art for the Web

fireworks flash freehand coldfusion dreamweaver fireworks
amweaver fireworks flash freehand coldfusion dreamweaver
coldfusion dreamweaver fireworks flash freehand coldfusion
reehand coldfusion dreamweaver fireworks flash freehand
works flash freehand coldfusion dreamweaver fireworks
weaver fireworks flash freehand coldfusion dreamwea

A common question asked by people new to the content-creation process is, "What the heck is line art?" In simple terms, it is anything that can be drawn on paper using a pencil or pen.

This would include items such as logos, maps, illustrations, and even typography. Although much of this work has become digital, artists and illustrators inevitably start the process by sitting at a desk or drawing board, and sketching out their ideas.

Many web designers are currently bemoaning the fact that the Studio seems to shine when it comes to application development. They see the coder and the developer in the spotlight while they are relegated to a supporting role. This is a huge mistake. The Studio offers the designer an awesome suite of tools that range from the simple pencil to a variety of vector plug-ins and special effects that are simply unavailable elsewhere.

For example, one of the authors would create navigation buttons for his Macromedia Director presentations in Photoshop. It was a laborious process that involved masks, textures, and colors—and it could take up to 30 minutes per button. When he was exposed to LiveEffects bundled in Fireworks and discovered that the time he spent building buttons could be reduced by two-thirds, he immediately switched to Fireworks as his primary tool for this task.

In this chapter, we focus on many of the tools and techniques available to you in FreeHand, Fireworks MX, and Flash MX. We also show you the workflow one of the authors used to create the JCT mascot to demonstrate how the creation process moves from atoms of pencil lead on paper to digits on disk. Before we do, though, it is important to review the strengths and weaknesses of the file types traditionally used in line art creation.

Graphic Types

As discussed in Chapter 9, "Imaging in Fireworks MX," you really have only two file type options for graphics: You can create the graphic as a series of vectors, or you can create a bitmap graphic. Regardless of which graphic file type you choose, it inevitably becomes a bitmap graphic when it appears onscreen because a monitor can't display vector images without rasterizing them.

When you create an object in FreeHand, or animate the FreeHand object in Flash MX, the objects are rasterized to the screen as the computer turns the lines into the colored pixels you see onscreen.

Vector Artwork

FreeHand, Fireworks MX, and Flash MX use vector graphics. These are graphics defined using mathematical formulas rather than pixels onscreen. For example, if you draw a green circle inside of a blue box in FreeHand, you can move the circle to another location on the page. In simplistic terms, you are essentially changing the current mathematical x and y coordinates of the circle on the page to another set of coordinates on the page. If you change the line on the square from a straight line to a curve, you are simply changing the mathematical description of that particular line.

This is important to understand because vectors, being math-based, don't need to remember the location and color of every pixel of the object. This is why vector images are so small, and tend to load into a Flash animation a lot quicker than a bitmap.

Vector graphics can also be resized without you having to be concerned with the quality issue. Again, it is all math. When a vector object is made larger, you are simply changing the mathematical calculation to accommodate the new length of the lines that compose the object.

Moving Artwork Between Applications

When working with vectors in the Studio, you will discover the tight integration between FreeHand, Fireworks MX, and Flash MX. Vectors created in all three applications move freely between the apps, meaning there are no file-compatibility issues between them.

To move art between Macromedia applications, follow these steps:

1. Open Flash MX, and draw a simple square with a colored stroke and a contrasting fill. Select the square, and copy it to the clipboard.

2. Open a new FreeHand document and then select Edit, Paste. The square from Flash appears on the page.

3. Choose the Subselect tool, click once inside the fill, and click/drag a corner handle to the center of the square.

4. Click the stroke and then drag a corner handle out or in. Select this object, and copy it to the clipboard.

Note

Flash objects are not quite traditional vector objects. They contain a stroke that defines the shape of the object, as well as a fill color that is regarded, by Flash, as another object.

5. In your Flash MX document, paste the object onto the Stage. At first glance, it may appear that you have lost the fill. This is not the case. With the object

selected in Flash MX, select Modify, Ungroup. Choose the Subselection tool, click the line, and select Modify, Arrange, Send to Back. The fill appears because Flash regards the stroke object and the fill object separately.

6. Open a new document in Fireworks MX. When the New Document dialog box opens, click OK. The dimensions of the new document match the dimensions of the object on the clipboard. When the canvas opens, paste the object on the clipboard into Fireworks MX.

7. Select the Fireworks MX Subselection tool, click the object, and move a couple of points on the object. Select and copy the manipulated object, open Flash MX, and paste the object on the clipboard onto the Stage.

As you can see in Figure 11.1, the original shaped moved from Flash into FreeHand and then back into Flash. The FreeHand shape moved into Fireworks and then back into Flash. Other methods of accomplishing this task are to select the object and then drag and drop it between the applications, or save the vector object in FreeHand and Fireworks in a format recognized by Flash MX, such as .eps, fh10, fh9, or .png.

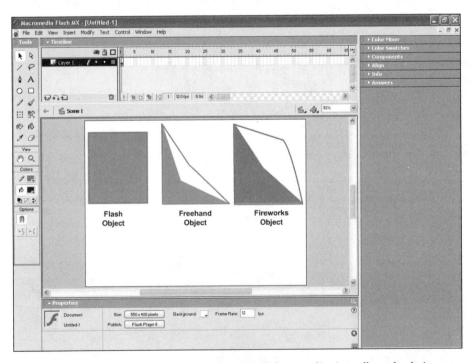

Figure 11.1   The ability to work on one object in all three applications allows the designer to bring the specific strengths of each one to bear upon the artwork.

Bitmap Artwork

All of the Studio applications can work with bitmaps. As you learned in Chapter 9, "Imaging in Fireworks MX," bitmaps are raster images composed of pixels on a grid. The problem with this form of image is that the file sizes can get very big, very quickly, and unlike vectors, you can't move selections around on the page; you can only move pixels. When that happens, the area where the original pixels were located fills with the background color.

The file-size issue is important. Bitmap images express their resolution as pixels per inch. The more pixels per square inch the computer has to map, the more information there is in the file, and the result is a large file size. On the web, this can be deadly because the browser needs to receive all of that information before it can display the image onscreen. The longer it takes to receive the information, the longer your visitors drum their fingers on the desk waiting for the image to appear.

To deal with the file-size issue, three formats—.gif, .png, and .jpg—are traditionally used for web-based line art. The .png and .jpg formats were discussed in Chapter 9. We now examine the .gif format.

GIF stands for Graphic Interchange Format, which is a standard developed specifically to deal with accurate color reproduction between the Mac and PC platforms. It has a limited palette of 256 colors, but you will rarely encounter a situation where all 256 are needed. This is one of the strengths of this format. By reducing the color palette to only those colors needed, you can achieve significant reductions in file size.

When would you use a .gif? Look for an image with solid colors and little shading. These images would include artwork such as plain type, logos with flat color tones, and some cartoon-like illustrations. The following gives some insight as to why .gif would be a better choice than .jpg in the preceding examples.

Similar to the .jpg format, you are essentially compressing the image when you create a .gif. There are two primary concepts you should know about .gif compression. Unlike using .jpg compression, .gif compression is generally a lossless compression scheme; however, modern-day .gif compression also allows the option for adding lossy compression schemes, similar to .jpg, to be applied to the image, thus reducing the size even further. Although the compression scheme is generally lossless, the conversion process isn't. Any time an image is moved from the RGB color space to an indexed color space—one that refers to a color palette by index number, as opposed to directly referring to the color value—there will be some loss. In the case of a .gif, the loss is minimal, and after the image is converted, there will be no subsequent loss of color.

Also, GIF uses LZW (Lempel-Zev-Welch) compression, which is the primary compression algorithm if you use a file compression application such as StuffIt. In essence, LZW compression looks for repetition in the data streams, meaning it is ideal for compressing rows of identical colors. For example, the JCT mascot has large areas of similar color, such as the red in the shoes. When the compression algorithm hits that row of 25 red pixels, the information is stored as 25 red. When the compression algorithm encounters a row that has a gentle gradation from blue to dark blue, such as that used in the JCT logo, each pixel has to be mapped. When you can replace 25 bits of information with one bit of information, you quickly realize why LZW is so efficient when it comes to working with GIF images.

Although FreeHand can export a file as a .gif, Fireworks MX may prove to be a better choice in most modern design scenarios.

Creating a .gif Image in Fireworks MX

The process of creating a .gif image is rather uncomplicated in Fireworks MX, and is managed in the Export Preview dialog box.

To create a .gif image in Fireworks MX, follow these steps:

1. Open the JCT_Dude.png file in Fireworks MX, and change the view to 100%. When deciding to convert an image to .gif, you can't look at the image as being the JCT mascot. Instead, look at it as areas of contiguous color. When you do that, apart from a couple of small shading areas on his hands, hair, face, and pants, you will see the colors are rather solid. The areas containing shading don't contain any gradient fills, which means the likelihood of a color being remapped to a different color is remote.

2. Select File, Export Preview to open the Export Preview dialog box shown in Figure 11.2.

   The key in this dialog box is the choice of color palette for the image. If you click and hold on the Palette pop-down menu, you are presented with a number of choices. When you choose a palette, pay attention to the numbers in the upper-left corner of the Preview pane. The numbers tell you the file size and the estimated download time for the image. The palette choices are:

   - Adaptive—This palette builds a color table from the actual colors in the image. This is the choice to make if image quality is paramount.

   - WebSnap Adaptive—This palette is built from the colors in the image, but any colors that don't fall into the Web Safe palette are converted to their closest equivalent.

Figure 11.2   Used for a lot more than creating GIF images, the Export Preview dialog box allows you to optimize the image for export.

- Web 216—The image is mapped to the Web Safe palette of the 216 colors that a browser will display equally on the Macintosh and PC platforms.

- Exact—This is an odd palette. It creates a color table of all the colors in the image. If the number of colors exceeds 256, it automatically defaults to the Adaptive palette.

- System (Windows) and System (Macintosh)—The image is mapped to the system palette chosen. This one is rarely used, and those of us who were there in the early days of color still recall the color shifts that occurred when an image created on a Mac was displayed on a PC. The reason was the palettes were quite different from each other. In fact, the Web Safe palette is composed of 216 colors because those were the colors that were similar on both platforms, as shown in the Web 216 palette.

- Greyscale—The color information is replaced with 256 shades of grey.

- Black and White—A throwback to the first days of computing when color was simple. You had black, and you had white.

- Uniform—A mathematical palette based in the RGB values of the image.

- Custom—This palette is derived from an external palette or GIF image.

3. Select the WebSnap Adaptive palette. If you look at the shading around the mascot's mouth, you won't see much of a change. Select the Web 216 palette, and the color around the mouth looks pixelated. What happened is the color for the shading does not exist on the palette. In this case, the colors in the palette are mixed—dithered—to approximate the color. As you move down through the choices, the dithering becomes more pronounced.

4. Another method of reducing the file size is to reduce the number of colors in the palette. If you click and hold on the Colors pop-down menu to the right of the Loss menu, you are presented with a number of choices ranging from two to 256 colors. Again, as you reduce the number of colors, the file size reduces. On the surface, this may appear to be a good thing. It is, up to a point, because as you reduce the number of colors in the image, the color in the image starts to degrade.

5. Close the Export Preview dialog box.

There is another method for applying the presets that is new to Fireworks MX. If your Property inspector is open, you see a list of choices in the Compression area of the inspector. As you select them, the image changes onscreen.

Another new area for applying .gif compression is through the Optimize panel, shown in Figure 11.3. If your Optimize panel is not contained in the panel grouping, select Window, Optimize, or press the F6 key to open the panel. The Optimize panel contains all of the controls necessary to ensure an image contains the right mix of color, compression, and image quality that yields the best file for the task at hand.

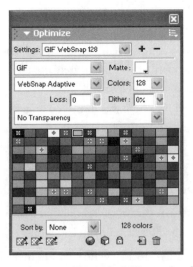

Figure 11.3   The Optimize panel, new to Fireworks MX, contains the critical image optimization controls.

Creating Line Art Using the MX Studio

Rather than rehash a lot of the work that has been and will be printed about using the various tools in the applications, you will now concentrate on how two pieces of line art were created for this book.

The section "Creating the JCT Mascot" deals with the creation of the JCT mascot, and follows author Chris Flick's narration of the workflow from paper to Fireworks MX. The section "Vectorizing Bitmaps in FreeHand" deals with the vectorization of the JCT logo as it moves from FreeHand to Fireworks and into Flash.

Creating the JCT Mascot

This section is not meant to be a drawing lesson, but merely to show the steps taken to create the JCT mascot.

As with the first conceptualization of the JCT site, pen and paper were initially used for some rough sketches. Although there are only two sketches here that will be highlighted, this process actually involved many sketches and character studies. Additionally, there was also a considerable amount of research that went into creating this character, such as gathering information on hip-hop type clothes, magazines, music videos, and so on. This represents the culmination of all that work.

The first sketch, shown in Figure 11.4, has some notes beside the mascot. With only one eye showing, he looked a bit too evil. Also, at this point, the thought of him wearing a hat had not entered the picture. And, with his arms crossed, it hid a very important feature behind the branding of the site…his shirt.

Figure 11.4   The JCT mascot starts as sketches on paper.

To feature his shirt, another pose would be necessary—in this case, a pose with a more open stance and his arms wider apart. Figure 11.5 shows the initial drawings of the little guy as a stick man, which helps establish the pose of the character. The second drawing on the page shows the progression of fleshing him out, and putting skin and muscle to his bones.

Figure 11.5   The drawing starts to approach the final image as the pose is established and the body is developed.

When satisfied with the drawing, the sketch is enlarged on a photocopier. The enlarged copy is put on a light table, and the image is traced with an ink pen. From there, the artwork was placed on a scanner to digitize the drawing. Even when images are going to appear on the web, it is better to scan drawings at a higher resolution than 72 dpi, preferably in the 150- to 300-dpi range so that after the image is colored and reduced to 72 dpi, all the lines and colors look crisp and clear. Figure 11.6 shows the results of the scan.

No matter how hard you try to have a clean scan, you will always have artifacts such as dust or scratches from the scanner glass. These produce spots and marks—called *noise*—on the page. It's now just a matter of cleaning up the scan. Areas where noise was introduced are circled. Rough lines that appear after scanning are not always satisfactory. Here is how to clean up the scan in Fireworks MX:

Note

If you want to work along with Chris, copy the files in the Chapter 11 Exercise folder on the book web site to your hard drive. Open the Flick_Dude.png file in your Chapter 11 Exercise folder.

Figure 11.6   The mascot is scanned at 150 to 300 dpi to work with crisp lines in
Fireworks MX.

1. Select the Magnifying Glass tool and then zoom in on the area—or areas—that
   looks rough. In this particular case, some lines around the shoe look rough.

2. In the Property inspector, select Fireworks MX's Eraser tool, and choose a small
   square brush setting of 1 to 2 pixels with no edge. This way, none of the illustration's lines are eliminated. You only want to eliminate the fuzziness caused by the
   scanner.

3. Carefully click and drag along the outside of the lines to eliminate the fuzziness,
   which are those gray patches outside the line in Figure 11.7. This step is best car-
   ried out with a graphics tablet and pencil; however, if you do not have these
   items, you can use your mouse. If you're not adept at drawing with the mouse,
   zoom in closer to ensure sure you aren't eliminating any part of the illustration.

Using the Painting Tools to Colorize Line Art

Many artists have different ways of working. Chris is no exception. His preference, when
it comes to coloring line art, is to lay down all of the base colors first—no complex, fancy
stuff such as complicated shadows and effects like that. The shoes are a simple red, the
shirt is a simple baby blue, and so forth. The tools used most often for this task are the
Paint Bucket, the Paint Brush, and for detailed work, the Pencil.

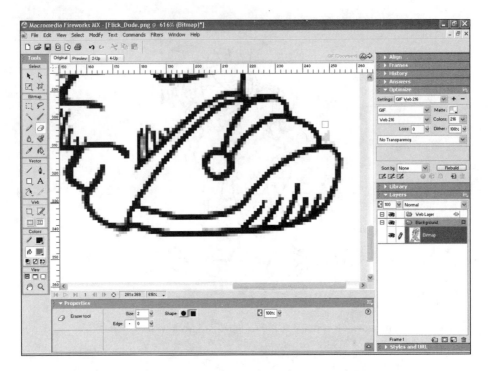

Figure 11.7   The noise is removed using Fireworks MX's Eraser tool.

With the noise removed, you can now go to work painting the illustration. If Photoshop were used at this point, you would have to select the black line of the JCT dude, duplicate it, and create a new layer before you could even start to colorize him. Not in Fireworks MX! It's simply a matter of selecting the Paint Bucket tool.

Before you start throwing paint into the image, it is important to understand that the Paint Bucket tool has an option on the Property inspector that will affect your work. If you select the Paint Bucket tool, you will notice there is a Fill Selection check box on the Property inspector. For this part of the exercise, you do not want to have a check mark in that box. If you do, you will be tossing paint over the entire canvas.

To paint the mascot, follow these steps:

1. Select the Magnifying Glass tool, and zoom in on the shoe area until the shoe almost fills the entire window.

2. Select the Paint Bucket tool and then select red (FF0000) as the fill color from the Property inspector, as shown in Figure 11.8.

3. Place the Fill Selection tool inside the shoe area and then click the mouse button. One aspect of Fireworks MX that you will likely find handy is the capability to

scroll around the image without changing the tool. To fill the other shoe, simply press the spacebar and the paint bucket cursor changes to a grabber hand. With the spacebar held down, simply drag the image until you see the other shoe and then fill it with red as well.

The jeans the mascot is wearing comprise a large area of the image; therefore, it doesn't make sense to work at such high magnification.

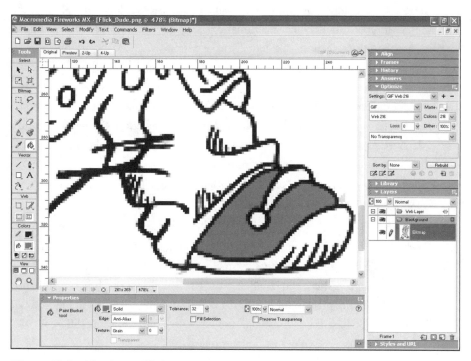

Figure 11.8   The shoe is filled using the Paint Bucket tool. Note the Fill Selection check box on the Property inspector is deselected.

> **Tip**
>
> After you get the hang of working with the application, constantly switching between the tools can become an annoyance. I use the keyboard commands to switch between tools. If you don't know the command for the Paint Bucket tool, roll the cursor over the tool to display a tool tip. The letter G is the keyboard command for that tool. The letter Z is the command for the Magnifying Glass tool.

4. Press the Z key to switch to the Magnifying Glass tool, and by holding down the Alt key on the PC or the Option key on the Mac, decrease the magnification by clicking in the jeans area. You can also choose from among a number of

preselected views by clicking in the Select Magnification area at the bottom of the window and selecting a percentage view from the presets in the pop-down menu.

5. With the jeans visible, press the G key to switch to the Paint Bucket tool and change the fill color to 3366CC, which has that blue-jean look. Click in the jeans to fill them with the blue. You may notice there are some small areas that were not fully painted inside the blue jeans.

6. Choose the Magnify tool, and zoom in on areas that were not colored. Next, use the Eyedropper tool (keyboard command: I) to pick up the color of the jeans just in case the color selections accidentally have gotten switched. To pick up color with the Eyedropper tool, set the sample to 3x3 Average in the Property inspector, place the cursor over the color you need and click the mouse. Selecting a 3x3 Average ensures you get a good read of the selected color. The application essentially looks at the colors of all the pixels, three pixels out from the selection, and calculates an average color. Sampling a single pixel is dangerous because you get that color, and only that color.

7. Select the Paint Bucket tool again—make sure the blue of the jeans is the fill color—and fill the empty areas as well.

8. If you are adept at using Fireworks MX, you could also switch to a paintbrush (keyboard command: B). In the Property inspector, select a 1-pixel soft-rounded tip with a small edge and fill the very small areas in that way. If you get down to filling in one-pixel areas, you could also use the Pencil tool (keyboard command: B) and click in the pixel to fill it with the blue-jean blue, as shown in Figure 11.9. The rest of the mascot was colored in the same way, only choosing different colors along the way. The colors used are as follows:

Pants Button: #FFCC33

Shoe Soles and Laces: #999999

T-Shirt: #FF3366

Shirt: #66CCFF

Flesh Tone: #FFCC99

Tongue: #FF0000

Glasses: #33CC33

Hair: #FFFF00

Hat Front: #0066CC

Hat Back: #000066

Hat Brim: #FF0000

Shaded Area of the Brim: #650000

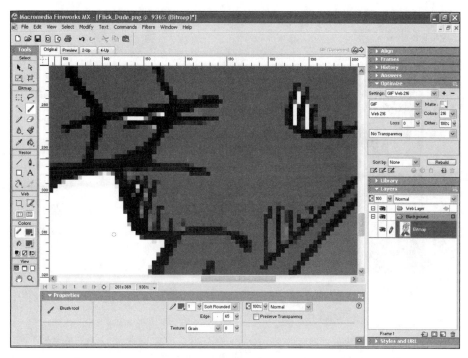

Figure 11.9   The Paint Brush is a great tool for touching up extremely small areas.

Creating Airbrushed Shadows

Adding shadows to an image gives the illusion of depth, and you can gain this effect by airbrushing the image.

To add shadows by airbrushing, follow these steps:

1. Select the Magnifying Glass tool, and zoom in on the area you want to airbrush.

2. Select the Brush tool. In the Property inspector, choose Air Brush—Basic from the Brush pop-down menu. Set the brush tip to between five and 10 pixels, set the opacity to 60%, and select Preserve Transparency. Choose a dark-blue color as the shadow color, such as 000066.

3. Click-drag the brush along the inside edge of the jeans. Each time you release the mouse button, you are essentially re-dipping your brush into ink. If you hold down the mouse button and drag over an area you have already airbrushed, you start to build darker shadows. You can see the result of airbrushing in Figure 11.10.

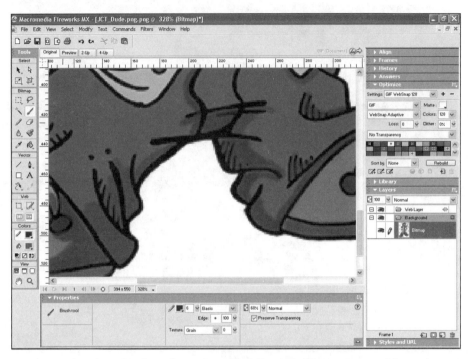

Figure 11.10   The airbrush can be used to add shadows to an image. Pay careful attention to the brush size and opacity settings on the Property inspector.

Note

This is where an individual's expertise and creativity comes into play. The airbrush is just one way that you can add depth to your illustrations. Some people may not even want to add depth and are perfectly content with large, flat colors. Both color versions of the JCT mascot are supplied in the Exercise folder on the book web site—the flat colored JCT mascot, and the more elaborate airbrushed version. Have fun!

Eliminating the Background and Reducing the Resolution

It's now time to eliminate the background. This is done in case our JCT mascot should ever appear on top of a colored background, which he does as part of the JCT site design. After the background has been eliminated, the image is essentially complete. The only remaining step is to reduce the image resolution to a more respectable web size—from a 150-dpi document down to a 72-dpi document.

To eliminate the background and reduce the resolution, follow these steps:

1. Open the JCT_Dudefinal.png file in your Exercise folder, but don't select anything just yet. The first thing you need to do is to set the canvas color to Transparent in the Property inspector.

2. Select the Magic Wand tool, and press the Shift key. With the Shift key held down, click in the white background area and the white areas between his arms. Release the mouse and the Shift key, and press the Delete key. A checkerboard appears, indicating transparency.

3. Deselect by pressing Ctrl-D (PC) or Command-D (Mac).

Note

Clicking the mouse or switching a tool won't deselect automatically. Although this may, on the surface, be an irritant, using the Deselect command is actually a great way of ensuring everything had been deselected.

4. With the background gone, you can reduce the resolution of the image. Select Modify, Canvas, Image Size, or click the Image Size button in the Property inspector. When the Image Size dialog box appears, as shown in Figure 11.11, make sure Constrain Proportions and Resample Image are both selected.

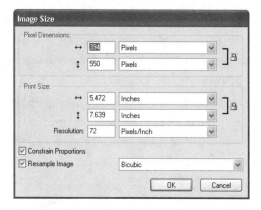

Figure 11.11   The size and resolution of an image can be set in the Image Size dialog box.

5. Change the Resolution setting from 150 pixels/inch to 72 pixels/inch. Click OK or Done, depending on which platform you are using.

The image can now be saved as a .png, or exported out of Fireworks MX as a .gif.

Vectorizing Bitmaps in FreeHand

This next part of the exercise deals with the creation of vector line art in FreeHand from a bitmap. Along the way, you will discover the close relationship between FreeHand, Fireworks MX, and Flash MX in their capability to both manage and work with vector line art.

Start with a bitmap of the JCT logo. Although FreeHand, Fireworks, and Flash can display bitmaps, they do have some limitations:

- They can't be scaled larger without experiencing image degradation.
- They add extra weight in Flash MX through their demand on the user's processor and streaming bandwidth.
- The elements of the line art can't be subsequently animated in Flash. You can't, for example, have an exploded view of the logo animate into position in a Flash presentation.

That's the bad news. The good news is that FreeHand removes those limitations. Best of all is through the use of layers in FreeHand, your artwork travels with both elements into Fireworks MX and Flash MX. Most bitmaps are converted to vectors by tracing over them using the pen tool.

To trace the JCT logo, follow these steps:

1. Open a new FreeHand document, and select File, Import. Navigate to your Chapter 11 Exercise folder and then import the Logo.png file. The cursor changes to what looks like a half-square. Click the mouse, and the JCT logo drops into the document.

2. Open the Layers panel by choosing Window Panels, Layers, or press F2; then drag the foreground layer into the non-printing area of the panel. Lock the layer by clicking on the Lock icon. Add a new layer and name it **Gradient**.

Note

One of the best pieces of advice ever given to one of the authors is, "Think like a computer." When you are planning to trace an object in a vector drawing application such as FreeHand, the worst mistake you can make is to concentrate on the art. If you think like a computer, you see the logo is actually composed of four objects: the gradient, the JT, the C, and the o. Building the logo should follow that layering order.

3. Select the Pen tool. Click once on the line of the gradient to establish your starting point; then continue clicking and dragging around the shape to follow the lines and curves of the object. When you place the pen over the first point, a small circle appears to the side of the pen tip to indicate you are closing the shape. You should have a rough approximation of the shape of the gradient object.

4. Select the Subselect tool. This is a great tool for touching up lines and curves. To adjust a curve, click and drag the segment. To move a point, click and drag the point into its final position. Your shape should resemble that shown in Figure 11.12.

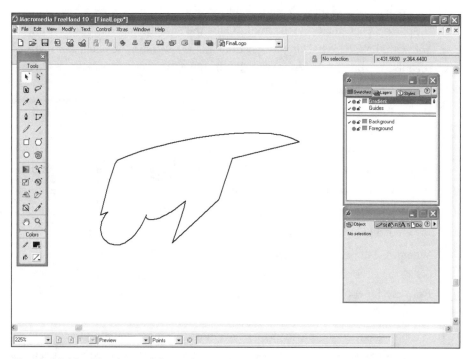

Figure 11.12   The shape of the gradient is drawn using the Pen tool and tweaked using the Subselect tool.

Stroking an Object and Creating a Gradient Fill

The next step is to add the stroke to the object, and to fill it with the gradient. In the case of our logo, we aren't sure what the gradient colors are. This requires a bit of work to get them right.

To add a stroke and fill to an object, follow these steps:

1. Click the gradient object, and select the Stroke inspector by selecting Window, Inspectors, Stroke. If the panel is already onscreen, click the Stroke tab. Set the stroke to Basic, the color to black, and the width to 2.5 points.

2. To create the gradient fill, you must first identify the colors for the gradient and add them to the selection of fill swatches. Deselect the gradient object, and lock

the gradient layer. Select the logo in the non-printing layer—it should be named foreground—and bring that strip back up to the printing layer under the gradient layer. Unlock the foreground layer.

3. Select the Eyedropper tool, and place it over the yellow in the upper-right area of the gradient. If you press the mouse button, you will see a square appear under the cursor. That square is the sample. Open the Swatches panel, click the sample, and with the mouse button pressed, drag the sample onto the panel and release the mouse. The sample is now added to the fill colors and you can see the RGB colors that make up the yellow.

4. Repeat the previous step for the red in the lower-left area of the gradient, the blue in the JT area, and the dark blue of the C. The Swatches panel now has the red and the yellow swatches of the gradient, as well as the other two colors used in the logo. Deselect the logo, lock the foreground layer, and drag it back into the non-printing area of the Layers panel.

5. Now that the colors are available, they can be used to create the gradient. Unlock the gradient layer, select the gradient object, and open the Fill panel.

6. When the Fill panel opens, select Gradient from the Fill Type pop-down list. Select the Graduated gradient icon above the Overprint area, and select Linear from the Taper pop-down list. You should have a gradient that runs from black to white.

7. It is now relatively simple to change the gradient color and angle. Open the Swatches panel, select the yellow swatch, and drag it on top of the black swatch at the bottom of the gradient panel. The gradient now runs from yellow to white.

8. Drag the red swatch over the white swatch on the gradient, and release the mouse. There is a bit more yellow than red in the original gradient. To adjust that, click the yellow swatch and drag the resulting copy to a point shown in Figure 11.13. Set the gradient angle to 230 degrees by either entering the value into the area under the Angle knob and pressing the Enter (PC) or Return (Mac) key, or by moving the knob until the angle appears.

Working with Layers in FreeHand

A common feature of today's drawing and painting programs is the inclusion of layers. What makes layers so great is the capability to create extremely complex drawings composed of rather simple shapes on their own layer. In this way, if an object needs to be changed, it can be done on a layer without affecting any of the other images in the drawing.

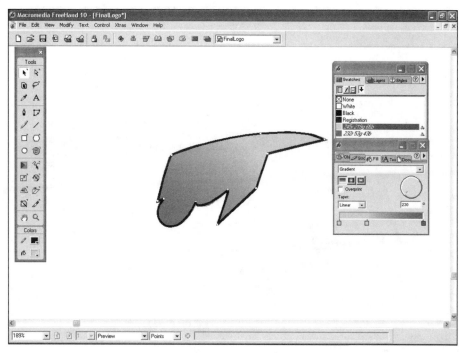

Figure 11.13   A custom gradient is created by sampling the colors in the original artwork and then adding the colors to the swatches. Those swatches are then used to create the gradient.

If any one aspect of FreeHand drives developers new to the application crazy, it is how FreeHand uses layers. One of the most common complaints is that items drawn on one layer almost magically appear on another. The key to maintaining your sanity is to recognize that working in one layer and selecting an object in another automatically moves the selected object to the chosen layer. If you remember to keep all non-active layers locked, you won't have this problem.

To draw the logo in a different layer, follow these steps:

1. Add a new layer named **JT**. The pen on the layer name indicates it is the active drawing layer. Lock the Gradient layer, and turn off its visibility by clicking the check mark beside the layer name.

2. Select the Pen tool, and trace the JT object. When you close the shape, it fills with a gradient because that was the last fill used. Open the Fill panel, and select Basic from the options. Click the light-blue color in the Swatches panel. The JT fills with the light blue, as shown in Figure 11.14. Turn on the visibility of the Gradient layer.

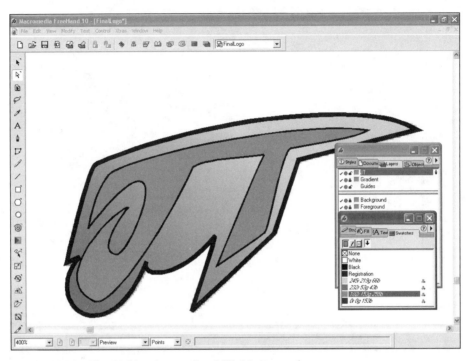

Figure 11.14   The JT object is created and filled in its own layer.

3. Repeat steps 1 and 2 to create the C and the o. When you are finished, save the image as a FreeHand 10 file.

FreeHand to Fireworks MX and Flash MX

There are a number of ways to get the logo into Flash MX and FreeHand MX. Each step in the following exercise demonstrates a different method. Choose the one with which you are most comfortable.

- Unlock your printing layers, and choose Edit, Select, All. Copy the selection to the clipboard. Open Fireworks MX and then paste the contents into a new Fireworks MX document. Notice that each layer moved into Fireworks MX as well. Open a new document in Flash MX, and paste the contents of the clipboard onto the Stage. If you click the logo on the Stage, you notice that each layer is treated as a separate object on the Stage.

- If you are using a Mac, you can drag the logo from FreeHand and then drop it into either Fireworks MX or Flash MX.

- Save the image and quit FreeHand. Open a new Fireworks MX document, select File, Import, and navigate to your FreeHand file. Open the FreeHand document. When the Vector File Import dialog box appears, deselect Background Layers and then click OK. The logo appears on the canvas, and the FreeHand layers appear on the Layers panel. If you were to leave the Background Layers box selected, the non-printing bitmap would also appear in the Layers panel.

- Open a new Flash document, select File, Import, and navigate to the Logo file. Open the file, and when the Import FreeHand dialog box appears, deselect Include Background Layers. Click OK. If you open the Library, you notice that a Brush Tips folder has appeared. We'll deal with that in Chapter 15, "Creating Assets with Flash."

Special Effects in Fireworks MX

Fireworks MX graphics are essentially composed of a stroke and a fill. Toss in the capability to turn those objects into beveled granite with a drop shadow, and you have added that essential wow factor that is so common on the Internet.

LiveEffects are unique to Fireworks MX. The key word is *Live*. The capability to automatically reapply or tweak an effect in real time is a huge productivity boost. Prior to the introduction of Fireworks, the creation of these effects—from drop shadows to bevels—in other imaging applications was a laborious, time-consuming process.

This section examines a sampling of the more common effects, plus a couple that were introduced in Fireworks MX. The best way of learning to use them is to play with them—you are only limited by your creativity.

The Effects Panel

In previous versions of Fireworks MX, LiveEffects were menu-driven. This has all changed with the move of LiveEffects from a menu to the Property inspector.

To add a LiveEffect, follow these steps:

1. Open the Effectslogo.png file in your Chapter 11 Exercise folder. This graphic is the JCT logo you created earlier using FreeHand.

2. Click the gradient object. The first object you see is the small arrow in the lower-left corner of the selection. This indicates the selection is a symbol. The great thing about symbols is that you can work on the instance on the canvas without

affecting the original artwork. Notice that the Effects area of the Property inspector becomes active.

3. Click the + sign in the Effects area and a pop-up window appears, as shown in Figure 11.15. This window is essentially broken into two areas. The top area is the new home of LiveEffects, and the lower area contains all of the filters and plug-ins used by Fireworks MX. The filters and plug-ins are also available through the Filters menu.

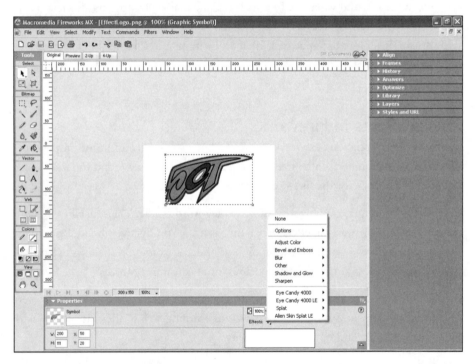

Figure 11.15   All of the Fireworks MX effects and filters are available by simply clicking the + sign in the Effects area of the Property inspector.

4. Select Bevel and Emboss, Inner Bevel. The effect is applied to the selection, and a box allowing you to control the features of the bevel from its color to its shape appears. Go with the default by clicking on the canvas. The gradient now looks like it is a button. To remove the effect, click the object to which the effect has been applied, select the effect name in the Property inspector, and click the – sign. The effect disappears.

Drop Shadows

Drop shadows are one of the most common effects on the web. They are used to present the illusion of depth, and are traditionally located under an object. Here's a way to add some drama to the logo that is a bit different from the traditional, shadow-under-object approach that is so common on the web today.

To add a drop shadow, follow these steps:

1. Select the C, and select Shadow and Glow, Drop Shadow from the Effects menu.

2. Set the Shadow Distance slider to a value of 50, and the Shadow Softness slider to a value of 12. Click the canvas. The C takes on a completely different appearance, as shown in Figure 11.16. The shadow of the selection falls across the objects under it, and is quite distinct on the canvas because the C no longer sits over the JT but appears to hover quite a distance above the logo.

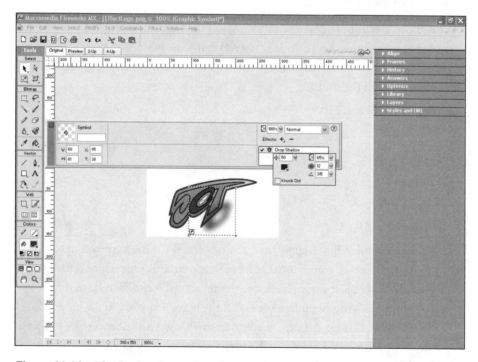

Figure 11.16   The depth, color, angle, softness, and opacity of a shadow are available through the Drop Shadow Effects controls.

3. To give the selection a glass-like quality, select the object and then move the Transparency slider to a value of 80%. Select the effect, and click the i button to open the Drop Shadow controls.

4. Select the Eyedropper tool, and click once inside the C to sample the color. The shadow color chip changes to the sample color.

5. Click once on the canvas, and the C appears to be a piece of glass. The underlying objects are visible, and the shadow is the color of the object.

Applying Bevels

Another standard effect on the web is the ubiquitous beveled button. Bevel effects are often used for creating the perception of depth within the object itself. Some examples include stamped or engraved effects. Bevels are odd in that your viewers are actually going to disagree on their appearance. Some will see the bevel as an "innie" while others will see it as an "outie." Don't ask us why. It is something we have wondered about for years.

To add a bevel, follow these steps:

1. Remove the drop shadow from the C. Select the Gradient layer, and select Bevel and Emboss, Inner Bevel. An inner bevel creates the beveled edge inside the selected object. The gradient takes on a distinct 3D appearance. Use the following settings in the controls:

   Bevel Edge Shape: Flat

   Width: 10

   Contrast: 50%

   Softness: 2

   Angle: 300

   Preset: Raised

2. Remove the inner bevel, apply the outer bevel, and use the same settings as those for the inner bevel. Notice the difference in appearance. One major difference is the ugly red beveled edge. This is due to the fact red is the default color in Fireworks MX. Another difference is that the bevel is applied to the outer edge of the selection. Change the edge shape to frame 1, and set the bevel color to a sample of the color in the gradient. The logo now looks as though it is inset into the beveled edge.

As you have seen, there are some striking differences between the Inner and Outer Bevel effects. They are all managed through the controls. Here is a brief explanation of what each control does:

- Bevel Edge Shape—Selecting one of the options will change the number, shape, or degree of the bevel. These are especially pronounced when applying an outer bevel.

- Width—This sets the thickness of the bevel's side or edge.

- Contrast—This slider controls the brightness of the lit and shadowed edges.

- Softness—This slider controls the sharpness of the edges using values ranging from 0- the strongest- to 10- the softest.

- Angle—This controls the angle of the light source for the object.

- Preset—There are four choices here that are traditionally used for buttons.

- Color—Only available to the Outer Bevel effect; use this to select a color for the border or edge.

Using the Fireworks MX Fills and Patterns

Sometimes a button or text effect needs more than a solid color as its fill. Fireworks MX ships with a large variety of gradient, pattern, and texture fills that you can use to create some rather interesting effects for vector or vector-based text objects. You can use the presets, or, if you are working in a team-based environment, you can create custom fills and patterns, which can then be shared among the group.

To add a fill and pattern, follow these steps:

1. Open a new Fireworks MX document, and set the background color to white. Select the Rectangle tool in the Vector tools, and draw a square.

2. With the square selected on the canvas, choose Cone from the Fill pop-up menu on the Property inspector. The square changes to a cone.

3. To edit the appearance of the cone, click the color box in the Property inspector. The Edit Gradient window opens with the gradient colors, called the Color Ramp, at the top of the window and the effect in the preview area. In the middle of the box are the preset gradients that ship with Fireworks MX. You can change the colors in the gradient by clicking on a gradient color and selecting its replacement from the color chips. You can change the effect by moving one of the sliders at the bottom toward the middle of the color ramp. You can even change the entire appearance by selecting one of the presets. Copper is one of our favorites.

4. To give the cone the appearance of rough copper, apply a 50% wood texture to the selection.

5. You can also adjust the angle of the gradient fill. Select either the Pointer or the Gradient tool, and click the object. The gradient handles appear. Drag the round handle to adjust the location of the cone's tip in the selection. Drag the square handle to adjust the skew and fill width of the effect. Try using the settings shown in Figure 11.17. The gradient can then be saved as a style (see Chapter 15 for more information on styles) and shared with the group.

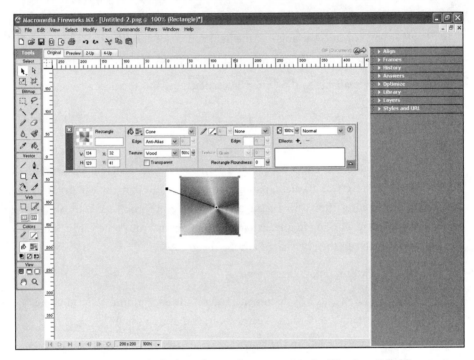

Figure 11.17   Gradients don't always have to be composed of solid colors. By adding a preset style and texture, a colored gradient takes on the look of weathered copper.

6. Select your object on the canvas and then choose Pattern, Illusion from the pattern's pop-up menu. The square fills with what looks like woven metal.

7. Choose Feather from the Edge pop-down menu on the Property inspector. Select Confetti as the texture and set the Texture Amount setting to 60%.

8. Click the object with the Selection tool. Two adjustment handles appear. Move the handles to change the angle and fill width of the texture. Add an inner bevel and a drop shadow. You now have the interesting object shown in Figure 11.18.

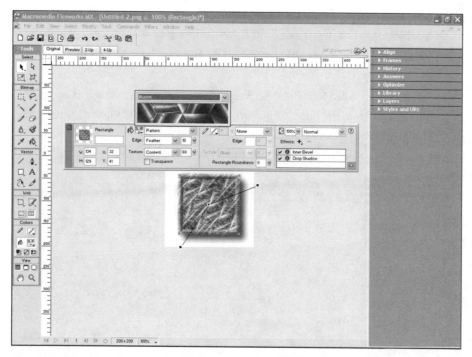

Figure 11.18 The effects and fills used together with your creativity create endless possibilities.

Note

You are not limited to the textures that ship with Fireworks MX. Any bitmap saved as a .png, .gif, .bmp, .tif, or .pct image can be used as a texture. To apply a custom texture, select the object on the canvas and select Other from Textures list. Navigate to the file you want to use, and click Open. The new texture appears at the bottom of the Texture list.

One of the neatest texture effects we have seen was done by an acquaintance who was designing a patch for an AIDS quilt. He scanned about 50 of those little red peppermint hearts that are so popular on Valentine's Day, and used them as his fill.

Using Splat and Eye Candy

Shipping with Fireworks MX is a sample of a new filter set from Alien Skin called Splat, and three of Alien Skin's Eye Candy 4000 filters. We could get all technical around them, but the amount of fun you can have with these filters should be illegal.

To apply the Splat and Eye Candy effects, follow these steps:

1. Draw a vector circle on the canvas, and apply a solid fill and a stroke to the object.

2. Select Effects, Eye Candy 4000 LE, Marble from the Property inspector. The Marble dialog box opens; the controls are intuitive. In the Settings menu, select the Green Marble preset and then click OK. You now have a green marble circle on the canvas.

3. Select Effects, Alien Skin Splat LE, Edges. When the Edges dialog box opens, select Pixels from the Edges pop-down menu, Transparent Fill, and set the angle to 300 degrees. Click OK. Apply an inner bevel effect, and your marble looks like the melted bottle cap shown in Figure 11.19.

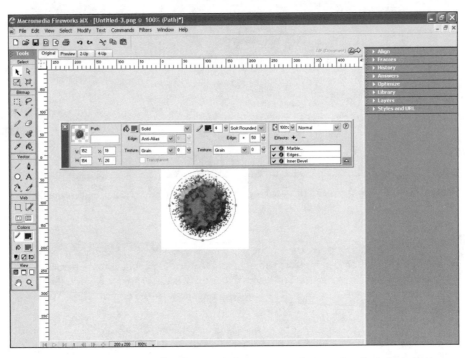

Figure 11.19   Applying two Alien Skin filters and a Fireworks inner bevel results in images such as melting bottle caps.

 Caution

Be careful with filters. If you are thinking of using the filters that ship with Photoshop versions 6 and 7, don't bother; they won't work in Fireworks MX. The Alien Skin 4000 and Splat filters are optimized for use in Fireworks MX. Splat is new to the market. It is an absolute riot to use because you can create everything from interesting edge effects to image frames composed of pennies. Other filter sets that works with Fireworks MX are the KPT filters from Corel and the Xaos tools.

Using the Twist and Fade Command

Inside the Creative Commands menu is an effect named Twist and Fade. Essentially, this command distorts and changes the opacity of the selected vector or bitmap object or objects based upon the settings in the Twist and Fade dialog box.

To apply some twisting and fading to a single object and a group of objects, follow these steps:

1. Open a new Fireworks MX document with a white canvas. Select the square Vector tool, and draw a rectangle on the canvas. Set the fill to None and use a fairly thick black stroke, such as five pixels.

2. Select Commands, Creative, Twist and Fade to open the Twist and Fade dialog box, as shown in Figure 11.20. Click once on the Options button to open the command's Options dialog box. Move the box to the position shown in Figure 11.20.

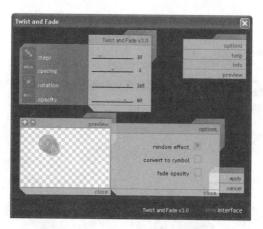

Figure 11.20   You can control the effect using the options in the Twist and Fade dialog box.

The controls are as follows:

- Steps—The number chosen using the slider determines how many copies of the object will be made to achieve the effect.
- Spacing—This slider sets how far apart the objects are from each other. It also controls the direction of the fade. Low numbers move up and to the left. High numbers move down and to the right.
- Rotation—Sets the angle of rotation, or the twist, of the object. The value chosen has a profound affect upon the final result.
- Opacity—Keep this value low for single objects, and for objects that overlap, you might want to consider a value as high as 100% so they can be seen.

- Preview—This shows you the effect before you apply it. If the object disappears out of the box, click and drag it back into view.
- Options—Random Effect: this does exactly what the name implies—the effect is randomly chosen for you. Click the check box to see the effect in the preview window. Click it again to apply a new effect, and so on.
- Options—Convert to Symbol: Converts the final result into a symbol that can be subsequently manipulated and placed into the Library for use by other members of the team.
- Options—Fade Opacity: Selecting this control changes the opacity between each step of the effect, and will fade it to almost invisible.

3. Use the following settings for the selected square:

   Steps: 8

   Spacing: -1

   Rotation: 55

   Opacity: 80

4. Click the Apply button, and you should see the effects shown in Figure 11.21.

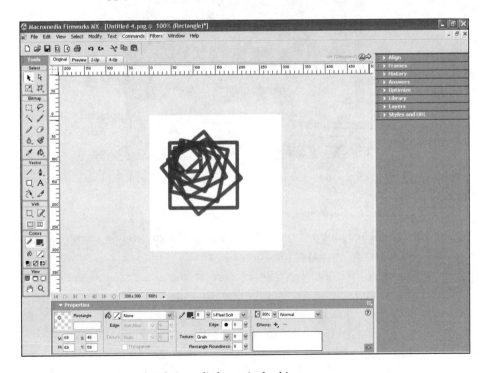

Figure 11.21   Twist and Fade is applied to a single object.

The Twist and Fade command creates some interesting effects to single objects. If you really want to let it rock and roll, apply it to multiple objects on the canvas.

To apply a Twist and Fade effect on multiple objects, follow these steps:

1. Open Dots.png from your Chapter 11 Exercise folder in Fireworks MX. Select the object on the canvas, and apply the Twist and Fade command twice. If you really want to get creative, open the options and select Random Effect before you apply the command.

2. Undo your changes, or revert the image. Select the object, and ungroup the dots. Select all of the dots and then apply the command twice using the Random Effect option. The effect is applied to each dot, which gives you a totally different effect than the previous step.

3. Select all of the dots. On the Property inspector, set the canvas color to black and then select Effects, Eye Candy 4000, Bevel Boss. Tweak the controls, including the light source, and click OK. Each dot now takes on a 3D look and resembles something the Hubble telescope would find in the deepest corners of space, as shown in Figure 11.22.

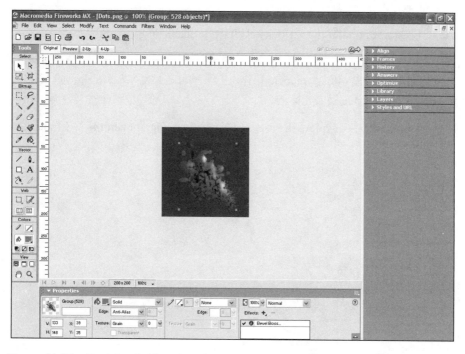

Figure 11.22   Don't be afraid to play what-if games. The result here is our asking, "What if we apply the Fade and Twist command and then apply the Eye Candy Bevel Boss filter to the result?".

Summary

This chapter has showed you a variety of techniques, from coloring line art to creating galaxies in outer space.

We began with a review of the various file formats available to you, and showed you how to move vectors between FreeHand, Flash MX, and Fireworks MX. We also discussed the various pros and cons behind the use of .gif images as they pertain to line art.

Chris Flick, our resident cartoonist, walked you through the steps he used to create the JCT mascot and also showed you how a variety of tools in Fireworks MX can be used to bring a sketch to life.

We discussed the conversion of bitmaps to vector art work in FreeHand. We covered how a user traces an object in the application—creates gradients using the colors in the tracing object, and discussed the uses and abuses of the Layers feature of FreeHand. We ended the discussion by demonstrating how a variety of methods ranging from copy and paste to drag and drop can be used to move the line art, intact, from FreehHand into Flash MX and Fireworks MX.

We moved on to creating objects using the various LiveEffects—bevels and drop shadows—in Fireworks MX. We showed the creative possibilities available to you through the use and customization of the various Fill effects available in Fireworks MX.

We finished the chapter by demonstrating the use of two new filters from Alien Skin—Eye Candy and Splat—that are included with Fireworks MX. We also showed you how to use the Twist and Fade command.

In the next chapter, we explore the use, and abuse, of typography in the MX Studio.

Chapter 12

Using Type

In Chapter 7, "Planning the Look of the Pages," you learned that when it comes to the Web, there is no such thing as typography. There is only type. This chapter explores how to use type and typography to create some rather spectacular designs using the tools in the MX Studio.

Done properly, typographic art is a powerful communications vehicle. The choice of font, layout, and effect can instantly communicate a mood or message in a manner that can be more powerful than a series of photos or images. This chapter examines the use of a number of typographic techniques designed to use words to convey meaning and mood. From the creation of a typographic logo and the design of a type-based splash screen, to some of the special effects you can create in Flash, FreeHand, and Fireworks, you discover how type can solve some communication problems.

Let's start building stuff.

Building Scrollable Text Boxes in Flash MX

With the advent of SmartClips in version 5 of Flash, the capability to "write once, use many" arrived. Until that point a lot of complex code was being written for single purposes, such as controlling the scrolling action of text. SmartClips introduced the concept of a special movie clip written in such a way that you could pass information to it to customize the clip's function.

Flash MX's components, which now replace SmartClips, take this concept out of the coding realm and put it squarely in the hands of designers. Mind you, coders are still required because, at heart, components are still SmartClips that allow the coder to set the methods at runtime. Why, then, are designers so happy? Components are graphical, meaning they can be dragged and dropped onto media and used right away. Their skins can then be changed.

Even more important is the fact components allow both the designer and the user to focus on the user interface. In the past, scrollbars in Flash were either intuitive, or the user was left to figure out if the splotch between the arrows would scroll the text. Components add an easily recognizable and, more importantly, usable element to a design.

This exercise uses the ScrollBar and ScrollPane components to make a scrollable text box.

The ScrollBar Component

This little gem allows you to add vertical and horizontal scrollbars to dynamic and input text fields in Flash MX. In this way you can add large amounts of text into a predetermined text box, and the user can quickly scroll through the text. Best of all, the designer doesn't have to do any coding.

To create a scrollbar, follow these steps:

1. Open a new Flash document, and use the Text tool to create a text field on the Stage. Select Dynamic Text from the Text Type pop-down menu on the left side of the Property inspector. This step also works for the Input Text choice of the Text Type pop-down menu. You would use this selection if the user were to input text such as a name or address.

2. Name the instance of the text box in the Instance Name field, under the Text Type pop-down menu beside the width and height section at the bottom of the Property inspector. We used Text, but you can use any name you want. Select Multiline from the Type pop-down menu on the Property inspector. (If you leave the line type at single line, the text will not scroll.)

Note

Flash MX has changed the way variables and instances are declared. An instance is always named on the left side of the Property inspector. A variable is the text that gets entered into the var box on the right side of the Property inspector.

3. Right-click (PC) or Control-click (Mac) on the text box and then select Scrollable from the context menu. Open the Lorem.txt file on the book web site, and copy a few paragraphs of the text. With the text tool selected, click once inside the Flash MX text box and then paste the text into the text box. The Property inspector should look similar that shown in Figure 12.1

4. If the Components aren't visible in your panels, select Window, Components, or press Command-F7 (Mac) or Control-F7 (PC). Click the Components panel. Select Flash UI Components, and drag a copy of the ScrollBar component onto the text near the right edge of the box. When you release the mouse, an instance of the component will snap to the right side of the text box, as shown in Figure 12.2. Be careful with where you release the mouse. Depending upon your position in the box, the component will snap to the edge nearest to the point where you released the mouse. If it is near the top of the box, you will get a horizontal scrollbar at the top of the text box.

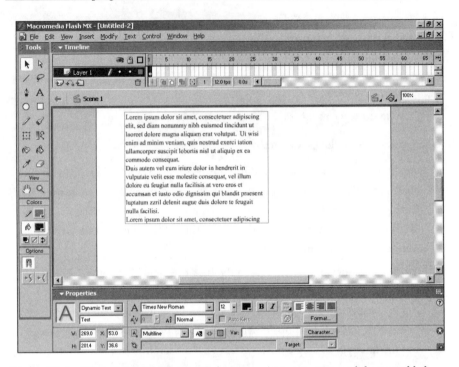

Figure 12.1   The text box has been created, given an instance name, and the text added.

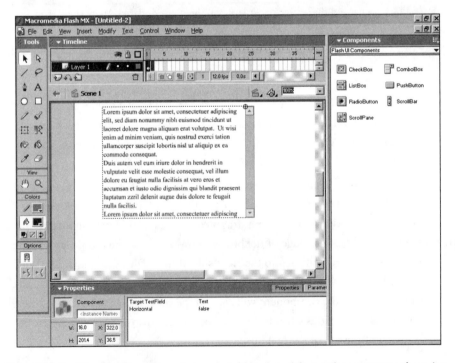

Figure 12.2   The ScrollBar component snaps to the edge of the text box nearest to the point where you released the mouse button.

5. Select Control, Test Movie to export as a .swf file and open in a separate window. The text with the scrollbar is onscreen. Scroll through the text. Close the window when you are finished.

Using the ScrollPane Component

The ScrollPane component is used exactly in the same way as the ScrollBar component, but you need to be aware of a subtle difference in how the text is handled. Instead of being attached to the text, this component uses a movie clip.

To create scrolling text using the ScrollPane component, follow these steps:

1. Follow steps 1 and 2 in the previous exercise to create the text box and give it an instance name. When the box is created and the instance is named, convert the text box to a Movie Clip symbol. Give the symbol a name, such as ScrollText, in the Create Symbol dialog box.

2. Click the Advanced button in the Symbol dialog box. The dialog box expands to include two new sections—Linkage and Source. Select Export for Actionscript from the Linkage section, and give it a name, such as ScrollText, in the Identifier text area. Click OK and then delete the text block on the Stage.

Tip

If you give the movie clip a name and then select Export for ActionScript, Flash MX enters the same name in the Linkage ID that you used for the movie clip name. This is convenient; however, if you change the name of the movie clip later on, the linkage name will not change with it. This is a tricky bit that is the subject of much discussion on various Flash MX discussion lists.

3. Drag a copy of the ScrollPane component onto the Stage, and right-click (PC) or Control-click (Mac) to open the context menu. Select Scale. When the handles appear, drag the handles to set the height and the width. The Property inspector changes to reflect the component with which you're working.

4. Enter the name **scrollIt** for the box in the Instance area of the Property inspector. Click once in the Scroll Content area of the Property inspector and then enter the name of the movie clip, which is also the name of the Identifier set in the Advanced Symbol dialog box. Click in the Horizontal Scroll area of the Property inspector, and select True from the pop-down menu. Click the Vertical Scroll area, and select True as well. By setting the Horizontal and Vertical Scroll values to True, the handles are visible at playback. If the text fits the scroll area, the handles will not be visible if Auto is selected from the Horizontal and Vertical Scroll pop-down lists.

5. If you were to test the movie at this point, the scrollbox would work, but the text would appear to scroll over the box. This component, because the text is dynamic, needs to have the text's font embedded into the movie. Open the movie clip in the Library and then select all of the text. Click the Character button in the Property inspector, and select All Characters from the options presented. Click OK, click the Scene 1 button to close the movie clip, and test the movie by choosing Control, Test Movie.

Note

If you test the movie without embedding the font, the display of the text inside or outside of the scroll pane depends on the size relationship between the movie clip's text field and the way you scaled the ScrollPane component. If the movie clip's field is larger than the scrollpane, the text will be outside the box. If the movie clip text field was smaller than the scrollpane, the text will scroll inside the box but will not fill the pane top to bottom.

There is another little gotcha here. In the first scrollbar example, the size of the text field sets the size of the area inside which you can see and scroll text. In the ScrollPane component, the size of the text field inside the movie clip should be big enough to show all the text you have copied and pasted into it. If that text field inside the movie clip is smaller than the amount of text pasted into the field, the scrollpane will stop displaying the text at the point where the text is cut off by the text field box in the movie clip.

Using the Type Tools in Fireworks MX

The text tools in Fireworks MX may, at first glance, appear to be rather rudimentary. Don't make this mistake. There is a lot of power under the hood and, if used properly, the type tools can expand your creativity.

The capability to play with type in Fireworks MX is a key productivity feature of the application. Providing the text is not converted to a bitmap, you can apply an astounding number of effects to the type, yet still retain the capability to edit the text. For example, you could turn the word Chris into a chunk of beveled marble. You could then copy the text with the effect, select the word, replace Chris with Jord, and the copy, too, would look like beveled marble.

The other aspect of working with type in Fireworks MX is the capability to format the text, right on the Stage using the Property inspector. This reduces the amount of time spent mousing around looking for the Type Editor. Though the Editor still exists, all of its tools appear on the Property inspector.

Creating a Typographic Logo

For the past few years, one of the authors has been a regular visitor to the site of Dmitry Kirsanov, a writer, artist, and web developer formerly based out of St. Petersburg, Russia but now located in Halifax, Nova Scotia. The first page of his former site—`http://www.kirsanov.com/old/`—contains the simple linked dk, as shown in Figure 12.3. This is a classic example of the use of the proper font as a design element. The logo is composed of two letterforms—d and k—that are linked at the serifs. Both letters are set in an italic font. What makes this logo so compelling is the use of the gradient on a solid background to force the eye to the logo and the serif of the d, which appears in front of the k. The effect is one of a subtle interlinking of the two letters to create a unified whole.

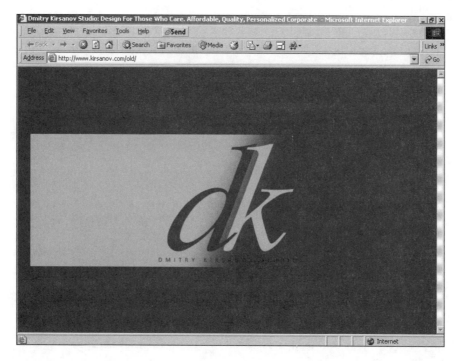

Figure 12.3   Dmitry Kirsanov's treatment of his logo.

Beneath the logo is the name of the studio, set in a sans serif font, which is tracked and colored black to provide contrast to the page. Note that the two most important elements on the page are visible, legible, readable, and contrast quite nicely with each other; yet there is not one graphic on the page, other than the type, that has been converted to a bitmap from its postscript origins.

To give you an idea of the passion people bring to typography, the two letters created by Dmitry are actually composites of Times and Garamond Italic fonts. Dmitry, for example, borrowed the stem of the Garamond Italic k and grafted parts of it onto the Times Italic letter. He then started adjusting the width of the letters to achieve the look and feel he was seeking.

To re-create Dimitry's logo, follow these steps:

1. Open a new Fireworks document, and set the canvas size to 528 pixels wide by 241 pixels high. Set the background color to transparent.

2. Select the Rectangle tool in the Vector toolbox, and draw a rectangle on the page that matches the canvas size. Make sure the X and Y coordinates on the Property inspector are set to 0.

3. With the rectangle selected, choose Linear Gradient from the Fill Options on the Property inspector. Click the Gradient Chip in the Property inspector.

4. Click the first slider arrow in the gradient window and then set the color to 99CC33. Click the second slider arrow, and set the color to 003300. Move the arrows to match those shown in Figure 12.4.

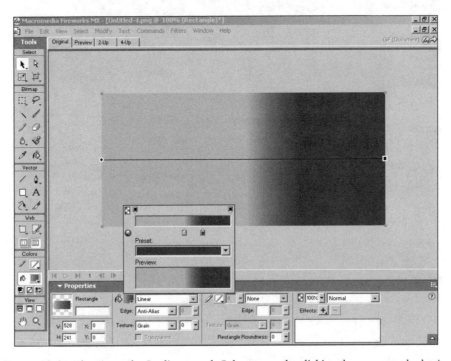

Figure 12.4   The Fireworks Gradient panel. Colors are set by clicking the arrows and selecting a color from the palette. The gradient can be changed by moving the arrows across the palette.

When you look at Dmitry's logo, you see the angle of the gradient approximates the angle of the italic text.

5. Select the Pointer tool and then click the canvas. A line with handles at either end appears on the object. This line shows the gradient direction.

6. Drag the left handle with the circle to the top left corner of the rectangle you just drew. Drag the handle with the square to approximately the middle of the page, as shown in Figure 12.5.

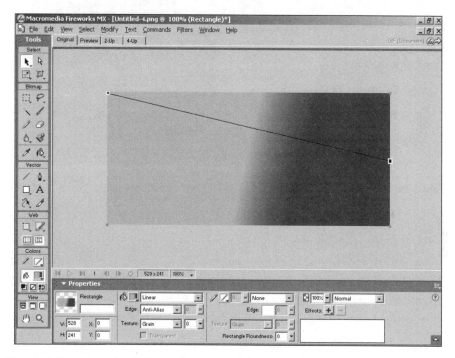

Figure 12.5   The angle of a Fireworks MX gradient is changed by dragging the round handle up and down on the page. Moving the square handle in and out changes the coverage of the gradient.

7. Open the Layers panel, and add a new layer named **dk**.

8. Select the Text tool or press T and then click the canvas. Click inside the text box, and type a **d**. Select the letter and set the font to Times Italic in the Property inspector. (If you don't have the Times Italic postscript font, use the italic version of Times New Roman.) Set the point size to 200 points and the color to 003300. Move the letter into the position as shown in Figure 12.6, and click OK.

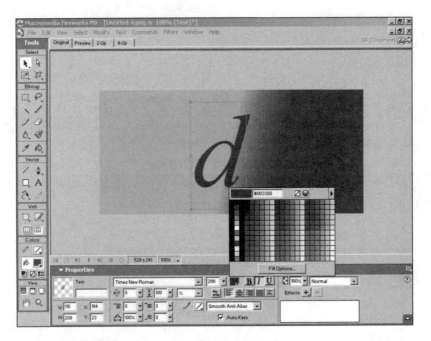

Figure 12.6   The letter is in place and formatted in the Property inspector.

9. Copy and paste the letter d onto the canvas. The letter is placed on its own sub-layer within layer one, the default layer for any Fireworks MX document. Select the pasted letter with the text tool and enter a lower case **k**. Use the same formatting as you did for the first letter, except use the color 99CC33. Move this letter into place and deselect. Name the sublayer **K**. Create a new layer in the layers panel, and drag the K sublayer into the new layer.

10. The fill and the angle of the gradient needs adjusting. The slant of the gradient matches that of the italic letters. Using the gradient handles and the color sliders for the gradient fill, match the angles and spacing shown in Figure 12.7.

    The text is currently in its postscript form. This is going to make it difficult to have the serif at the bottom of the d appear in front of the stem of the k.

11. Lock the k layer. Select the d layer, select the d, and select Modify, Flatten Selection. Alternately, you can press Control-Alt-Shift-Z (PC) or Command-Option-Shift-Z (Mac). This has the effect of rasterizing the postscript object, which is good news. The bad news is the letter is no longer editable.

12. Select the Rectangular marquee and click/drag across the bottom serif of the d. With the bottom of the d selected, select Edit, Cut. Unlock the k layer, select the layer, and then paste. The serif is pasted into the position from which it was cut from the d, as shown in Figure 12.8. Now would be a good time to save your work.

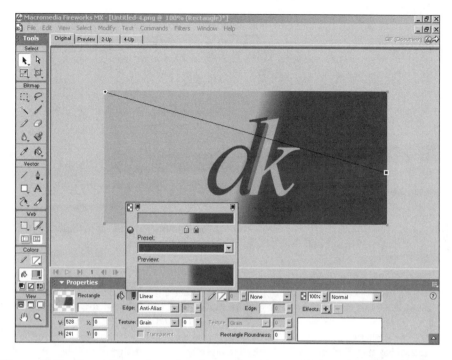

Figure 12.7   The gradient color and angle are adjusted to match the slope of the italic k. Use the stem of the k as your guide.

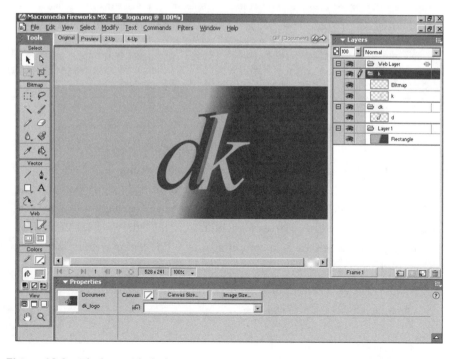

Figure 12.8   The logo with the layers.

Note

The previous series of steps essentially rasterized the art. The disadvantage here is the loss of the ability to edit the letter in the Text Editor. One of the authors caught this and, in true developer fashion, said, "That ain't the way I would do it!"

What he would do is turn each of the letters into a symbol and use an instance of each in the creation of the logo. This would retain the editability, should the client change their mind.

13. Select the Text tool, and enter **DMITRY KIRSANOV STUDIO**. Set the font to Helvetica (or Arial, if you're working on a Windows machine), the point size to 10, and the color to black.

14. Select the text in the Text Editor, and set the kerning to 31%. Move the text into position and then click OK.

The Kerning Control Slider

Typographers will quite rightfully look down their noses at the use of the kerning slider. Essentially, all this control does is spread out the selected letters or words. By selecting all of the letters and moving the slider, you in effect tracked out the letters and the words by adding space between them. Clicking between letters and moving the slider up or down has the effect of moving the letters (kerning) on either side of the I-beam closer or farther apart.

Classic typography kerns the pairs of letters by removing one one-thousandth of the width of a letter m between the two letters. This is far more precise than a percentage.

Leave the Auto kerning option selected in the Text Editor. Part of the information contained in a postscript font is how close pairs of letters in the font are to each other. For example, the first name of one of the authors is Tom. The font will determine how close the letter o in the "To" kerning pair is to the capital T. This information changes from font to font, which is why it is a good idea to never deselect this option.

15. Select the Crop tool, and trim off some of the top, bottom, and right side of the image. The amount to be trimmed is your decision.

16. Export the image as a .jpg. Use 80% as your Quality setting, and select No Smoothing from the Smoothing pop-down list in the Export preview window. You could save the image as a .gif image with an adaptive palette, but a .jpg version of the image adds a degree of smoothness to the letters you can't obtain with a .gif image. Selecting No Smoothing in the JPG options retains the crispness of the lettering. Smoothing tends to add a bit of a blur.

17. Click the Quick Export button on the menu bar, and select Dreamweaver, Launch Dreamweaver.

18. Create a new Dreamweaver MX page, and set the background color of the page to 003300. Add a new table cell that is 175 pixels high, and select Autostretch in the Property inspector. Import your Kirsanov image into the cell, and test in the browser. It should appear as shown in Figure 12.9.

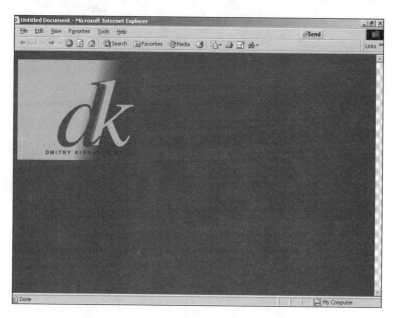

Figure 12.9   The logo placed in a table cell in Dreamweaver and viewed in a browser.

Creating a Typographic Introduction Page

The movie "Get Shorty" piqued our interest in author Elmore Leonard. When we originally visited his web site at www.elmoreleonard.com, shown in Figure 12.10, we could not help but notice the fine typography for the introduction page. What struck us was not only the use of negative leading, but the use of various weights of a font. Though the entire site, after this page, is done in Flash, this HTML page offers an excellent overview of how typography can serve both as an information element and as a design element.

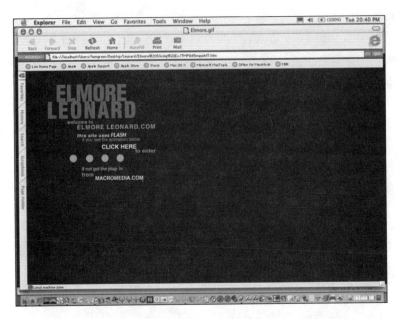

Figure 12.10   The former introduction page to the Elmore Leonard site.

Note

As is quite common these days, the site has been redesigned and the use of Flash discontinued. This means the introduction page, captured in 2001 and shown in Figure 12.10, is no longer available.

The font used for his name also deserves comment. Though it is a custom font, it is quite distinctive in that it has been distressed. Notice how it appears to have holes in it. This is common in a typographic movement called Grunge Typography that sprung up about five years ago. The other aspect of this logo is something many web designers overlook. If you go to your local bookstore or Amazon.com, you will see the font here matches that used on his books; thus there is continuity of design across multiple, unrelated media.

We will not be using the same font for Elmore's name but instead will focus on Helvetica. To create the introduction page shown in Figure 12.10, follow these steps:

1. Open a new Fireworks document that is 367 pixels wide by 310 pixels high, and set the background color to black. Add a new layer, and name it **Logo**.

2. With the Logo layer selected, choose the Text tool and then click once on the canvas. Enter **ELMORE** on one line, press Enter (PC) or Return (Mac), and enter **LEONARD** on the next line.

3. With the new text selected, set the font to Helvetica and then click the Bold button. We used the font Helvetica Black. In this case, you wouldn't click the Bold button because it would simply make a bold font thicker. If you don't have Helvetica, use another sans serif such as Arial.

4. In the Property inspector set the point size to 60 points, the alignment to Centered, and the color to #666666. If you do use Helvetica and set the weight to bold, add a 1-point Basic Soft Line stroke around the words. Don't worry about how it looks. We'll deal with that later.

5. Move the Leading slider down to a value of 75%. The two words move closer so the top of the word Leonard just touches the bottom of the word Elmore. This process—called *negative leading*—reduces the spacing between the two lines. While this is an interesting technique, use caution because the letters are set in uppercase type, and the objective is to maintain legibility. If they come much closer they will crash into each other, and lose their distinctive shapes.

6. The next step moves, or kerns, the letters to improve their readability. At present, some letters are directly above each other. Click between the L and the M, and move the Kerning slider to a value of -7%. Select the entire word LEONARD, and move the slider to a value of 7%. Notice the letters spread out a bit, as seen in Figure 12.11.

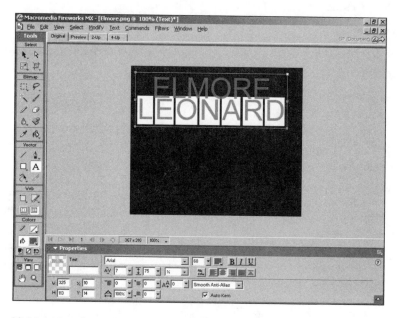

Figure 12.11   Note the tracking value of 7% applied to the line of text using the Property inspector.

Playing with Leading and Baseline Shift

The text block underneath the headline is interesting because it demonstrates the creative use of negative leading as well as moving text above and below the baseline.

Leading has its roots in the days of metal type. To separate the lines of text on a page, typesetters would add a strip of actual lead between them. The width of this strip determined how close the lines of text were to each other. A baseline shift simply moves the selected text above or below the imaginary baseline upon which all text sits. Superscript, the upper 2 in 2^2, moves the character above the baseline whereas the 2 in H_2O is a subscript that moves the character below the baseline. Again, the tools for accomplishing this in Fireworks lack the precision demanded by fine typography.

To create a baseline shift, follow these steps:

1. Add a new Layer, and name it **Text 1**.

2. Select the Text tool, click the page, and enter the following text :

    welcome to

    ELMORELEONARD.COM

    this site uses FLASH

    if you see the animation below

    CLICK HERE

    to enter

3. Select the first line of text, and in the Property inspector choose the following settings:

    Font: Helvetica

    Size: 12 points

    Color: FF9900

    Weight: Bold

    Alignment: Flush Left

    Tracking: 5%

    Leading: 100%

    Horizontal Scale: 100%

    Baseline Shift: 0

4. Select the second line, and choose the following settings in the Property inspector:

   Font: Helvetica

   Size: 16 points

   Color: FF9900

   Weight: Bold

   Alignment: Flush Left

   Tracking: 9%

   Leading: 91%

   Horizontal Scale: 100%

   Baseline Shift: 0

5. Click at the start of the second line and, using the spacebar, move the line until the E is under the o in welcome.

6. Select the words this site uses in the third line, and choose the following settings in the Property inspector:

   Font: Helvetica

   Size: 12 points

   Color: FFFFFF

   Weight: Bold Italic

   Alignment: Flush Left

   Tracking: 9%

   Leading: 148%

   Horizontal Scale: 100%

   Baseline Shift: 0

7. Select the word Flash in the third line, and choose the following settings in the Property inspector:

   Font: Helvetica

   Size: 14 points

   Color: FFFFFF

   Alignment: Flush Left

   Weight: Bold Italic

Tracking: -7%

Leading: 148%

Horizontal Scale: 100%

Baseline Shift: 0

8. Click in front of the third line and, using the spacebar, move it until it is under the E in the word Elmore.

9. Select the fourth line of text, and choose the following settings in the Property inspector:

Font: Helvetica

Size: 12 points

Color: FF9900

Alignment: Flush Left

Weight: Deselect Bold and Italic to get the Roman, or normal version of the font.

Tracking: 0%

Leading: 95%

Horizontal Scale: 100%

Baseline Shift: 0

10. Using the spacebar, move the fourth line until the i in if lines up with the i in the word this.

11. Select the fifth line of text, and choose the following settings in the Property inspector:

Font: Helvetica

Size: 16 points

Color: FFFFFF

Alignment: Flush Left

Weight: Bold

Tracking: 0%

Leading: 133%

Horizontal Scale: 100%

Baseline Shift: 0

12. Move the fifth line until the C is under the letter h in the word the.

13. Select the sixth line of text, and choose the following settings in the Property inspector:

Font: Helvetica

Size: 14 points

Color: FF9900

Alignment: Flush Left

Weight: Bold

Tracking: 0%

Leading: 79%

Horizontal Scale: 100%

Baseline Shift: 0

14. Move the sixth line until the "t" is under the last letter of the word HERE. Your text on the canvas should look like Figure 12.12.

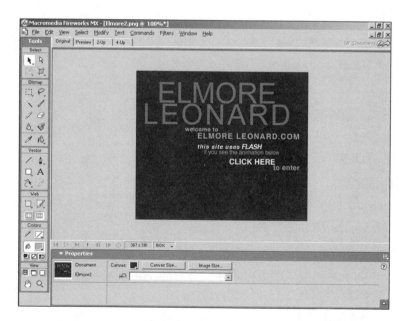

Figure 12.12   Using a variety of leading and tracking settings in the Property inspector results in some interesting effects.

15. Add a new layer, and name it **Text 2**. Select the Text tool, click the canvas, and when the Text Editor opens, enter the following text:

    if not, get the plug-in

    from MACROMEDIA.COM

16. Select the first line, and choose the following settings in the Property inspector:

    Font: Helvetica

    Size: 12 points

    Color: FF9900

    Alignment: Flush Left

    Weight: Bold

    Tracking: 0%

    Leading: 93%

    Horizontal Scale: 100%

    Baseline Shift: 0

17. Select the word from in the second line, and choose the following settings in the Property inspector:

    Font: Helvetica

    Size: 12 points

    Color: FF9900

    Alignment: Flush Left

    Weight: Bold

    Tracking: 0%

    Leading: 115%

    Horizontal Scale: 100%

    Baseline Shift: 0

18. Select the text MACROMEDIA.COM, and choose the following settings in the Property inspector:

    Font: Helvetica

    Size: 14 points

    Color: FFFFFF

    Alignment: Flush Left

Weight: Bold

Tracking: 0%

Leading: 30%

Horizontal Scale: 100 %

Baseline Shift: -10

19. Move the text to the bottom of the canvas. Add a new Layer named **Dots**. Select the Ellipse tool, and draw a circle on the page. Fill it with FF9900. Using the Alt-Click-Drag technique (PC) or Option-Shift-Drag (Mac), add three more circles. The page is finished, and should look like that shown in Figure 12.13. Save the image.

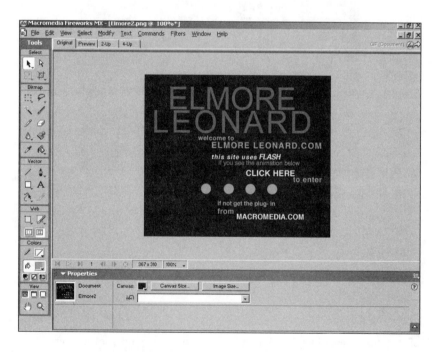

Figure 12.13   The finished page showing the kerning, tracking, baseline shift, and navigation dots

Exporting to Dreamweaver MX

The image you created in the previous exercise could go intact into Dreamweaver, but the decision is to slice the image. By creating slices in Fireworks MX, the page loads much faster into a browser because the page is now a series of small images rather than one large one.

To export the image to Dreamweaver MX, follow these steps:

1. Shift-click each of the text blocks, and select Edit, Insert, Slice, or press Alt-Shift-U (PC) or Option-Shift-U (Mac). The Insert Slice dialog box opens and asks if you want one or multiple slices. Click Multiple. Green overlays indicating the slices appear on the page and red lines indicate the slice guides. Adjust the slice guides to match those shown in Figure 12.14.

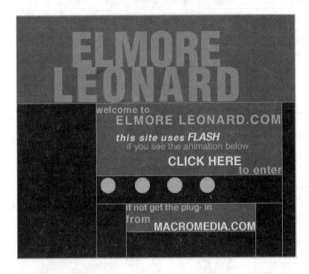

Figure 12.14   The page is sliced.

2. Select File, Export Preview and choose Gif with Adaptive Palette in the formatting options. Click Export, and choose the following settings:

   HTML and Images

   Export HTML

   Export Slices

3. Select Put images in subfolder and, if you don't have one for this exercise, create a folder on your desktop and select it. Click the Options button on the right side of the Export dialog box to open the HTML Settings dialog box. The General tab is already be selected by default. Choose the following settings:

   HTML Style: Dreamweaver

   Extension: htm

4. Click the Table tab and then select the following options:

   Space with: 1-pixel transparent spacer

   Color: Canvas

5. Click OK.

6. Click Save and then select Launch Dreamweaver from the Quick Export Button's submenu.

7. When Dreamweaver MX opens, open the HTML page saved with your Fireworks image. Name this page **Elmore**, and preview the page in your browser. Your page should resemble that shown in Figure 12.15.

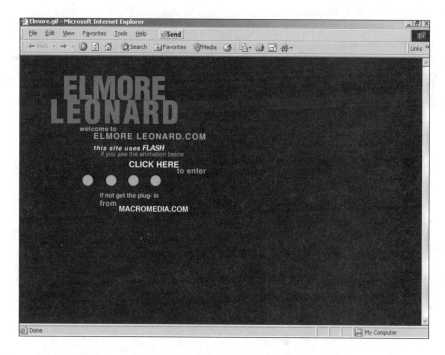

Figure 12.15   The page is placed in Dreamweaver and opened in a browser.

Text Effects in Fireworks

You can create some interesting effects with text in Fireworks. The three specific effects discussed in this section are:

- Masking with text

- Punching holes in objects

- Adding LiveEffects to text

These are great techniques, but never forget that you are working with type. This means that you can play with it all you want, but it must be both legible and readable.

Masking

Masking is technique where an underlying image shows through a shape above it. The effect is to give the appearance of a piece of text being filled with an image, rather than with a solid color.

There is a Provincial park named Obatanga on the North Shore of Lake Superior in Ontario. Obatanga is a huge park dotted with dozens of lakes and rivers, and is, in many ways, a canoeist's dream. In the following exercise, you manipulate an image taken at dusk on one of the lakes and use it as the fill for the title page of the park's site.

1. Copy the Chapter 12 Exercise folder on the book web site to your desktop. Open Obatanga.jpg from the Chapter 12 Exercise folder, and select the Text tool. Click the image and enter the word **Obatanga**. Use the following settings in the Property inspector:

   Font: Times or Times New Roman

   Weight: Bold

   Size: 120 points

   Color: FFFFFF

2. Move the text to the position shown in Figure 12.16, and set the Canvas color to White. Shift-click on the text and the image.

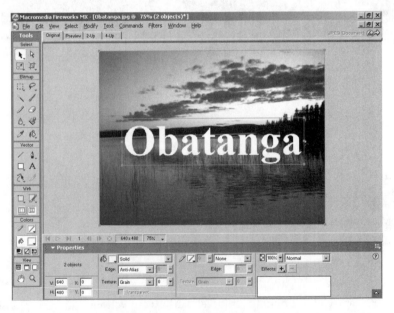

Figure 12.16   The text is placed over the image. By selecting both the text and the image, and then applying a mask, the image disappears and shows through the lettering.

3. Select Modify, Mask, Group as Mask. The image now appears through the letters.

4. Save the image.

Masks and Colors

A mask is interesting in that the black in a mask lets all of the image show through. This was the case in the previous technique. A mask uses the gray values to determine opacity; thus, a mask at 100 percent white has no opacity, and all of the image shows. If black were used, there would be nothing showing through the text. Based on this, the following are a couple of neat tricks to try with a mask:

- Select the objects in the Obatanga image and then select Modify, Ungroup.

- Double-click the text, and set the text color to 999999. Apply the mask, and note how the image appears to have faded.

- Ungroup the mask and then change the Canvas color to a rich blue.

- Select the text, and select a Black and White linear gradient from the Fill menu.

- Apply the mask. Note how the image fades in the direction of the gradient. To tweak the effect, you can ungroup the mask, move the gradient handles, and reapply the mask.

Punching Out Text

In the previous exercise, you used the text to mask an image. Sometimes, however, you need more than a flat color to fill the text. You might even need to use a second picture as the fill.

In this case, the lettering chosen is simply changed to a series of vectors. This is important because many times you simply can't provide the font, and changing to vectors gets around that problem.

Even then, exercise some care with converting fonts to a path. Sometimes the letterforms take on subtle changes. For example, one of the authors converted words set in Univers Black to a path. Univers Black is a strong and bold font. Upon conversion, a couple of the letters such as the b in Obatanga lost some of that boldness. A word to the wise: Pay close attention to the *before* and the *after* when you convert a series of letters to outlines.

To "punch out" text, follow these steps:

1. Open the Obatagna.jpg image from the Chapter 12 Exercise folder you copied from the book web site onto your desktop, and add a new layer to the image.

2. Select the Rectangle tool, and draw a rectangle that is slightly larger than the canvas. Select Fill, Pattern, Goo-Blue. Select the Text tool and then click the Goo-Blue. Enter the word **Obatanga**.

3. With the Obatanga text selected, select Text, Convert to Paths. This step creates the vectors based upon the postscript font.

4. At this point, each of the letters is a collection of paths. Select Modify, Ungroup (or Control-Shift-G on a PC, Command-Shift-G on a Mac) and then select Modify, Combine Paths, Join (or Control-J on a PC, Command-J on a Mac) to turn the letters into a single path.

5. With the letters selected, press Shift and click the Goo-Blue. Select Modify, Combine, Punch. Punch creates a hole through the selected object under the shape. The image shows through the letters, as shown in Figure 12.17.

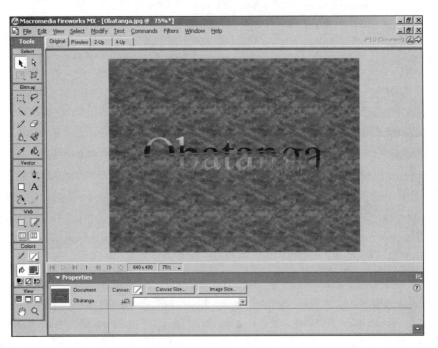

Figure 12.17   The word is cut out of the Goo-Blue fill pattern in layer 1, allowing the underlying image in the background layer to show through.

Tip

You don't always have to use layers to fill text with an image. You can convert the text to an outline and then simply paste an image into it using Edit, Paste Inside, or pressing Control-Shift-V (PC) or Command-Shift-V (Mac).

If you can't be bothered with a number of steps, here's another way to fill text (or any object) with a .jpg or .png image. Select the object, open the Fill menu, select Pattern, Other, and simply navigate to the image you want to add. Toss in a texture and add a color with opacity, and you can create some rather interesting effects.

Using LiveEffects

There are a number of special effects you can add to objects created in Fireworks. These effects are referred to as LiveEffects. The neat thing about LiveEffects is that even though an effect is applied to the text, the text is still fully editable. These are usually found in the Effects panel, and range from simple drop shadows to some neat bevels and embosses. Feel free to play around with them, but always ask yourself after the effect has been applied, "Will my user be able to read this?"

To apply a LiveEffect to text, follow these steps:

1. Open a new Fireworks file, and set the canvas size to 600 pixels wide by 200 pixels high. Set the canvas color to white—FFFFFF.

2. Click the Text tool, and enter the word **Obatanga**. Set the font to Times Extra Bold. If you do not have Times Extra Bold, select Times New Roman, set the weight to Bold, and set the point size to 120. Set the color of the text to black— 000000. Click OK.

3. With Obatanga selected on the canvas, click the plus (+) sign beside the Effects button on the Property inspector. This opens the Effect panel.

4. Click-hold the pop-down arrow in the Effects panel. When the Effects pop-down menu appears, select Shadow and Glow, Drop Shadow. Note the shadow that appears under the word. The Drop Shadow dialog box is quite robust. You can set the shadow distance in pixels as well as the color of the shadow. You can also set the shadow's opacity and softness, and the angle for the shadow. Go with the defaults and then click the image. The effect now appears on the Effects panel. If you want to change any of the settings, click the "i" icon in the effects area of the Property inspector; if you want to remove the effect, click the effect and then click the Trash icon at the bottom of the panel.

5. To add a little bit more drama to the effect, change the stroke color to 666666 on the Text Property inspector. Click the color chip in the stroke area of the Text Property inspector again, and click the Stroke Options button at the bottom of the chips. Add a one-pixel soft pencil stroke around the lettering.

   Now that you know how to play with the LiveEffects, let's really rock and roll!

6. Delete the effect by clicking the minus (−) sign in the Effects area of the Property inspector. Select the text on the Stage, choose Fill, Fill Options, Pattern, Other and navigate to the Obatanga.jpg image. Click OK.

7. The image fills the word and you see two arms, shown in Figure 12.18 that look like 3:00 o'clock on the image. These arms control the fill rotation. Drag the dot where the arms intersect to a point above the words. This moves the image inside the words.

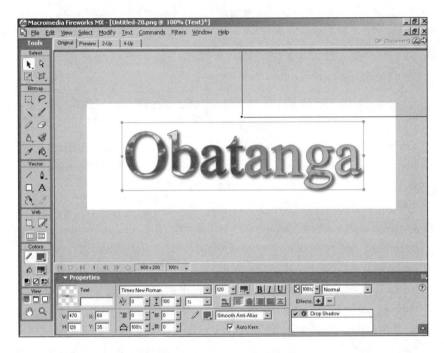

Figure 12.18   You can fill text with an image and manipulate the image in the text by moving the arms or the intersection point of the arms.

8. Select Bevel and Emboss, Outer Bevel from the Effects area of the Property inspector. The edge of the embossed area fills with an ugly, red color. To fix it, first select Sloped from the Beveled Edge pop-down menu, and then use the following settings:

Width: 4 pixels

Color: 999999

Contrast: 75%

Softness: 3

Angle: 135

Button preset: Raised

9. Add a drop shadow with a distance of 12 pixels. Your image should look like that shown in Figure 12.19.

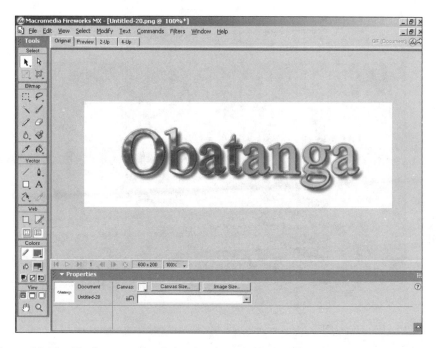

Figure 12.19   The letters are beveled and embossed, filled with an image, and set off with a drop shadow.

The FreeHand to Flash MX Connection

The site http://www.Art2life.ca, shown in Figure 12.20, passed across the radar of one of the authors when he was in, of all places, Hamburg, Germany. Considering the site is owned by one of the more famous Canadian art galleries—The McMichael Collection—and considering the gallery was 15 minutes up the highway from the author's office, one would think he had heard of it, or at least visited the site, if not the gallery.

What struck him was the use of fine typography on the site, including leading, font choice, and alignment. These are things you can't get in a browser or Fireworks MX. This exercise shows how fine typography can be used on the Web, if you use the right tool for the job. In this case, it happens to be FreeHand.

Before we begin, a disclaimer: We will not be using the same font as that used in the site. We will be using the Times family.

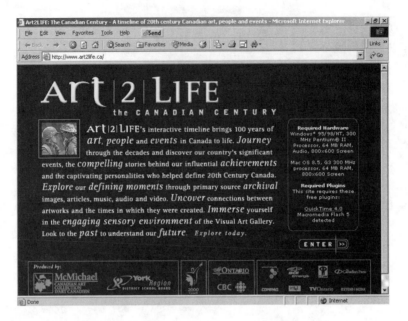

Figure 12.20   The Art2life home page, which is the entry point into a history of Canadian art.

To apply fine typography in FreeHand, follow these steps:

1. Open a new FreeHand document. Select the Text tool and then enter the text exactly as follows:

   Art 2 Life's interactive timeline brings 100 years of

   art, people, and events in Canada to life. Journey

   through the decades and discover our country's significant

   events, the compelling stories behind our influential achievements,

   and the captivating personalities who helped define 20th Century Canada.

   Explore our defining moments through primary source archival

   images, articles, music, audio and video. Uncover connections between

   artworks and the times in which they were created. Immerse yourself

   in the engaging sensory environment of the Visual Art Gallery.

   Look to the past to understand our future. Explore today.

2. Select all of the text, open the Text panel, and use the following settings:

    Font: Times

    Size: 16 points

    Leading: 24 points. To get precise leading, select the = symbol from the leading pop-down menu.

    Alignment: Justified

3. Select the first three words—Art 2 Life—but don't select the apostrophe and the letter "s" in the first line. Set the point size to 24 points.

4. In the second line, set the words "art", "people", "events", and "Journey" to 24 point Times Bold Italic. We used the font BI Times Bold Italic.

5. In the fourth line, set the words "compelling" and "achievement" to 24 point Times Bold Italic.

6. Repeat step 5 for the words "explore", "defining moments", and "archival" in the fifth line, as well as for the word Uncover in the sixth line, the word immerse in the seventh, "engaging sensory environment" in the eighth, and "future" in the last line.

7. Click once at the start of the first line and then press Tab three times to move the text to the 96-point mark on the ruler. Repeat this step for lines two and three. This leaves room for a small picture box that will be added in Fireworks MX.

    Moving text from FreeHand to Fireworks MX can be a bit tricky. The odds are very good you will lose the tabs and the line width of the text when the image is placed in Fireworks MX. Use the following steps to ensure smooth movement between the applications.

8. Click the Pointer tool and the click once on the page to close the Text panel. Click the text, and select Text, Convert To Paths, or use Command-Shift-P (Mac) or Control-Shift-P (PC). This turns the text into art as shown in Figure 12.21. Save the file, but don't quit FreeHand just yet.

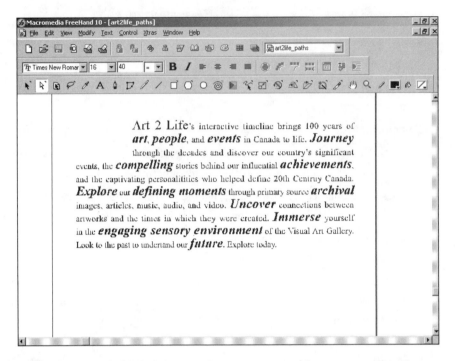

Figure 12.21 The text has been converted to its postscript outlines to ensure smooth movement to Fireworks MX.

Moving From FreeHand to Fireworks MX

With the text set properly and in a format that will not be affected by moving from one application to another, it is time to make the move. After the text is in place, you can add an image and a heading for the page. To do so, follow these steps:

1. Open a new Fireworks MX document. Set the width to 525 pixels, the height to 365 pixels, and set the canvas color to black. Click OK.

2. Click the text in the FreeHand document, and drag it on top of the new Fireworks MX document. Release the mouse, click the FreeHand document, and save it. Quit FreeHand.

3. Click the area where the text was placed in the Fireworks MX document. Obviously, black text on a black background is impossible to see. With the object selected select Filters, Adjust Color, Invert to turn the text white.

4. The heading and the subheading now have to be created. Select the Text tool, click once above the text, and enter **Art 2 Life**. In the Property inspector set the font to Times, the point size to 60, use a tracking value of 5%, and set the text color to 33CCCC.

5. Add a 2-point vertical line that is just a bit higher than the height of the capital letters between the words "art" and "2", and between the words "2" and "Life". Use the same color as in the previous step.

6. Select the Text tool, click once under the head, and enter the words **the CANA-DIAN CENTURY**. Set the text to 18 point Helvetica Bold, and set the color to 33CCCC. If you have it, use a bold condensed version of Helvetica. Drag the handles of the text box to span the width of the first line of text. Select Justified in the Alignment options of the Property inspector.

7. Select the Pointer tool and then select the headline as well as the lines and the text under the headline. In the Property inspector set the Effect option to Bevel and Emboss, Inner Bevel. Adjust the settings until the bevel on the text meets your approval standard.

8. You now need to add a placeholder for a small slide show of paintings. Select View, Rulers. Drag a horizontal ruler that lines up with the baseline of the third line of text. Drag another horizontal line that lines up with a point that is about half way between the top of the capital A and the baseline of the subhead.

9. Drag a vertical guide that lines up with the right edge of the letter A in the headline, and another that lines up with the left edge of the text block. Select the Rectangle tool, and draw a square in the area identified by the guides. Set the fill in the square to None, the stroke color to 33CCCC, and the stroke to 1 Pixel Hard in the Property inspector. Your finished page should look like that shown in Figure 12.22.

At this point, you can slice up the image, as you did in the previous exercise, and export the slices to Dreamweaver MX.

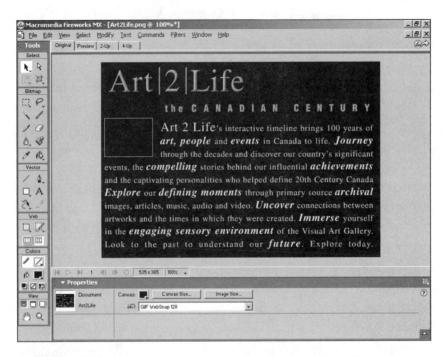

Figure 12.22   The key to this page is doing the bulk of the typesetting in FreeHand, saving it as outlines to maintain the formatting, and using the drag-and-drop technique to get the outlines from FreeHand into Fireworks MX.

Creating a Type-Based Flash Splash Page for the JCT Site

As we pointed out in Chapter 7 postscript fonts are the way to go. Being a vector-based application, Flash MX makes extensive use of vectors, but when it comes to fine typography, the tools are still rather primitive. Options such as kerning, tracking, and leading are there but don't offer the fine control one would expect from a vector application. Where Flash does shine is in the rasterization of the vectors for screen display. The lines are crisp and defined with very little evidence of the dreaded jaggies.

There are those who would suggest that Flash could be used as a web-typesetting tool. This would be a huge mistake. The typographic controls are primitive, and using Flash for static work—a block of text on an HTML page—is a waste of the application's power.

Keep in mind that any conversation regarding the use of type in Flash will include the use of postscript. Talk to any competent Flash developer, and the conversation will inevitably get around to efficiency or optimization. Flash developers always keep a close eye on the pipeline, that mythical wire that is dependent upon the bandwidth available to the user. A letterform is a postscript outline that uses Bezier curves, and anytime the direction of the curve changes, that curve will display between two points. Those points add weight to the file. The more points there are in a letter, the more curves there are and the larger the file size of the letter. Letters with fewer points are more efficient. So, what fonts have the fewest number of points? The sans serif fonts. This explains why a lot of Flash sites out there use sans.

We also can't ignore one of the biggest mistakes made by Flash developers when it comes to type. There will inevitably be an occasion where the Bold, Ultra Bold, or the Black version of a font is unavailable. The obvious solution is to add a stroke to the outline of the letters—big mistake. By doing this, you are distorting the font and, according to Fred Goudy, the designer of such fonts as Goudy and Goudy Sans, anyone that would do that would steal sheep. Also, adding the stroke in Flash may not be beneficial. If you must stroke a font, do it in Fireworks or FreeHand. These apps will simply thicken the stroke around the postscript outline. In Flash, it is a two-step process: The font is described with and without the outline, which defeats the whole purpose of optimization.

Inspiration

Working with and animating text offers infinite possibilities. Such noted Flash artists and New Riders authors as Brendan Dawes, Hillman Curtis, and Todd Purgason look to the work of Saul Bass for inspiration. Saul did a lot of titling work for Alfred Hitchcock movies with his most famous work being the titling for the movie "Psycho." In fact, Brendan Dawes maintains the premiere site for Saul's work—`http://www.saulbass.net`—and provides a list of links for sites that have drawn their inspiration from Saul. Apart from the work of Saul Bass, look to the movies for inspiration. Pour through your VHS and DVD collections, and study how the titling sets the tone and mood for the film. Look at the choice of font and then look to technique. A classic sequence is the Stars Wars opening, and another is the title sequence done for "Traffic," which can be seen at `http://www.apple.com/trailers/usa/traffic/`. In fact, a great source for viewing movie trailers is `http://www.apple.com/trailers/`.

A favorite of ours is Born Magazine. This avant garde site features some amazing Flash work, and the poetry section features some of the best Flash typography on the Web. Our personal favorite is "Flesh of a Mango," done by Peter Huang and Wil Arnott of Mod7 Studios to animate a poem by Nathan Barnett. Check it out at `http://www.bornmagazine.org/projects/mango/`. The poem has a delicacy about it that is made apparent by the choice of font used for the text.

Finally, don't discount the commercials on television, or what you see in print ads. There is a lot of creative work out there, and it may just provide the spark of inspiration you need to get yourself going.

Preparing the Splash Screen Scene

The JCT introduction page is designed to provide an eye catching and engaging entry into the site. The plan is to have the words for the various products appear on the Stage. The text for each product fades in randomly while a tag line at the bottom of the Stage appears to have a spotlight moving across it. The words are then split apart and fade out while the JCT logo grows and the whole tag line is revealed.

On the surface this may appear to be a complex procedure. While it is complicated, the advantage of Flash is that complexity can be broken down into a series of rather simple pieces, thanks to the use of symbols and instances in the application. There is a lot of technique employed here, but the whole focus is to maintain the legibility and readability of the text on the Stage while producing an extremely fast loading and engaging Flash animation.

To create a type-based Flash MX splash screen, follow these steps:

1. Open Flash MX, and open a new movie By choosing File, New. You can also use Ctrl-N (PC) or Command-N (Mac) to open a new movie.

2. When the New Movie dialog box opens, use the default Stage size—550 pixels wide by 400 pixels high—and the frame rate of 12 frames per second. Set the background color to black—000000—and click OK. You can also set these values in the Property inspector. Rename layer 1 as **Background**.

3. Add 11 new layers to the new movie above the Background layer. Use the following names and order from the top to the bottom of the timeline:

   Actions

   Logo

   Tag line

   ShoeFade

   Shoes

   PantsFade

   Pants

   ShirtsFade

   Shirts

   HatsFade

   Hats

   Background

4. Select the Rectangle tool, set the Stroke to None, and set the Fill to Black. Draw a rectangle that covers the Stage in the Background layer.

5. With the rectangle selected, set the width and the height of the rectangle to match the Stage size. Set the x,y coordinates on the Property inspector to 0,0. By doing this you are ensured the object is perfectly aligned to the Stage.

6. With the object selected, select Modify, Convert to Symbol, or press (F8). Name the symbol **Background,** and select Graphic as its behavior.

Tip

Get into the habit of converting everything that appears on the Stage into a symbol.

Note

What's with covering the Stage with the same color? This movie is inevitably going to be playing through Explorer, Netscape, or another HTML-driven environment thanks to the Embed tag. The result could be a background color or image that doesn't work with your design. By adding this symbol, you not only control the color as well as avoid the problems that could crop up, but you also now have an object that can be manipulated at a different point in the animation.

7. The decision is to work within an area that is 10 pixels smaller than the Stage. We also want to accommodate precise placement of the objects on the Stage. A grid can be built for this purpose. Select View, Show Rulers, or press Control-Alt-Shift-R (PC) or Command-Option-Shift-R (Mac). Drag a horizontal guide from the Ruler, and place it 10 pixels from the top of the Stage. Drag another horizontal guide onto the Stage, and place it 10 pixels from the bottom. Drag vertical guides onto the Stage, and place them 10 pixels from the right and left edges.

8. Add another two guides—one vertical and another horizontal— in the exact center of the Stage by clicking the Background symbol—not the crosshairs that indicate the center point of the symbol. Due to its size and location, the center point is the center of the Stage. Drag the guides to line up with the crosshairs. Lock the Background layer.

Note

When setting up your guides, zoom in on the upper right corner before dragging your guides onto the Stage. This makes it easier to see exactly where the guide is before releasing it. Zooming in makes the ruler's tick marks more visible, and shows smaller changes from tick mark to tick mark. Also, when a guide is exactly over a tick mark, it turns white. Another habit to develop when working with guides is to lock them into place. Select View, Guides, Lock Guides. This way, you will not be able to accidentally move a guide.

9. Create a new graphic symbol, and name it **logo**. Import the Logo.fh10 file from the Exercise folder, and place it into your symbol. Save the movie. Your screen should resemble that shown in Figure 12.23. Save the file, and leave it open.

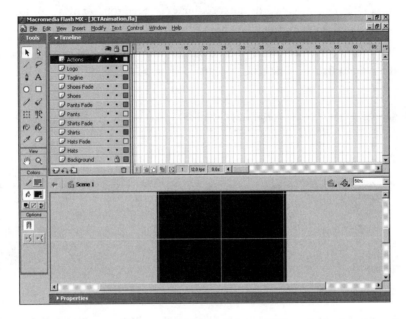

Figure 12.23   The Stage and layers are set. The rulers are visible, and your layering order should match the one shown here.

Creating and Animating the Text

Each text block is animated in its own movie clip symbol, which is then be brought onto the main Stage. Here, we explain how to create only one movie clip. The creation of the remaining movie clips follow these steps:

1. Open a new graphic symbol by selecting Insert, New Symbol, and name it **Pants**. You can also use Control-F8 (PC) or Command-F8 (Mac) to create a new symbol.

2. Select the Text tool, and roll the cursor onto the Stage. The cursor changes into an "A" with a crosshairs above it. Click once. Enter the word **Pants** into the text box and then select the entire word

Tip

If you want to select a word or all of the words in a text box after setting a word in type, select the Direct Selection tool, and click any part of the letters. That selects the whole box. You can then change the font, point size, or color all at one go.

3. In the Property inspector, set the text to 48-point, Arial Bold, and choose white for the color, FFFFFF. Use Arial Black as the font choice, if you have it, but don't select the Bold weight.

Note

Looking at the text, the space between the "P" and the a could be reduced. The left arm of the "a" can be brought a bit closer to the "P" to reinforce the relationship between the two letters. What we need to do is kern the "Pa" letter pair. In Flash the kerning tool is rudimentary—meaning that it uses percentages—and is named *tracking*. The Kern check box, which should never be deselected, maintains the kerning information within the font, much like that in Fireworks. Keep in mind that you can't kern in Flash. The best you can do is move a series of letters closer to each other or spread them out.

4. Select the P and then move the Tracking Control slider downwards. Note how the remaining letters move towards the P, and how the a crashes into the P, if you're not careful. Use a value of -4, as shown in Figure 12.24. This is an extremely small value, but kerning involves the art of subtlety.

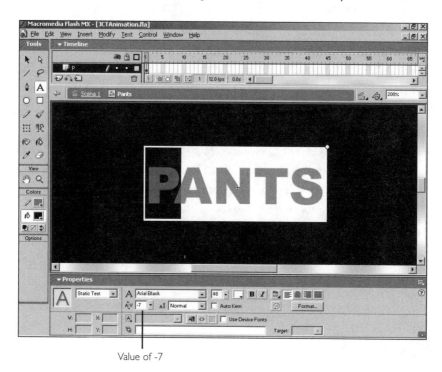

Value of -7

Figure 12.24   You can choose the various settings for the text in this area, including rudimentary kerning.

Tip

You can also click the Text tool between the P and the a, press and hold down the Alt (Mac) or Option (PC) key, and press the Right or Left arrow keys on the keyboard. Each press of an arrow key nudges the kerning between individual letters about one–half pixel.

5. With the text box selected on the Stage, select Window, Panels, Align, or press Control-K (PC) or Command-K (Mac). Click the To Stage button and then click the Align to Horizontal Center and Vertical Center buttons. This centers the text box on the Stage by aligning it with the crosshairs.

    With the text in place, it is now time to prepare the symbol for the animated text.

6. To animate the text, you need to turn it into artwork and then place each letter into its own layer. Select the text and then select Modify, Break Apart, or press Control-B (PC) or Command-B (Mac). Each letter is now in its own separate text box. If you select Break Apart a second time, each letter becomes nothing more than an outline and a fill.

7. All of the letters should be selected on the Stage. Select Modify, Distribute to Layers to assign a layer to each letter. If you have an extra layer, such as layer 1, delete it by clicking the layer name and then clicking the Trash can icon. If the names in the layer order bother you—stnaP, for example—drag the layer strips to a more acceptable order—Pants. Select each letter, and convert it to a graphic symbol.

8. Press the Control (PC) or Command (Mac) key, click frame 25 of the P layer, and drag down through the layers. Add a frame to set the duration of the animation by choosing Insert, Frame, or by pressing F5. At 12 frames per second, this animation will last for roughly two seconds. At this point of the production process, your Stage and layers should resemble that shown in Figure 12.25.

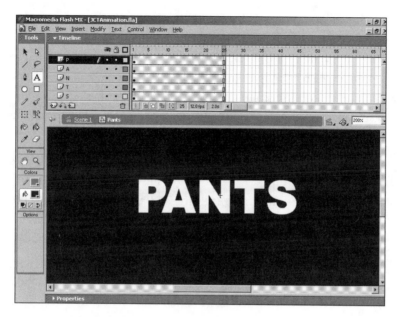

Figure 12.25   The layers are created, the letters have been converted to symbols, and the duration of the animation has been set to 25 frames.

The plan now is to have the letters grow and fade in over a series of frames. Here's how you do that.

1. Starting in frame 5 of the top layer, click and drag down to the bottom layer. Add a keyframe by selecting Insert, Key Frame, or by pressing F6.

Tip

You can spend a lot of time using the keyboard or the menus to add keyframes, motion tweens, frames, and so on. Keep in mind, however, that these items are also accessible in a couple of other ways. Right-clicking (Command-clicking on a Mac) on a frame opens a context menu with the available commands. Another method to access commands easily is to simply click and hold on a selected frame in the timeline. This action results in a pop-down menu with the commands showing.

2. Move the playback head to frame 1 and then select all of the letters, not the frames, on the Stage. Select Color, Alpha from the pop-down menu on the Property inspector, and set the value to 0.

   In Flash, Alpha determines opacity. Selecting the letters on the Stage opens the object Properties on the Property inspector. Selecting the frames opens the Frame Properties. If you can't see the Color button on the Property inspector, you have selected a frame.

3. With the letters in frame 1 still selected, choose Modify, Transform, Scale and Rotate, or press Ctrl-Alt-S (PC) or Command-Option-S (Mac). Set the scale value to 40%, and click OK. Click/drag anywhere between frames 1 and 5 of the top down to the bottom layer and select Insert, Create Motion Tween. An arrow appears between the keyframes. If you move the playback head across the frames, you see the letters grow and fade in. We chose a uniform value. To add more interest, use different values for each letter. You can also lengthen or shorten the tween by dragging a keyframe out or back.

This is a bit too uniform. The letters should appear to arrive randomly.

4. Shift-click the two keyframes in the P layer and drag the selection to frame three. Drag the remaining layers to random start points. If the duration of a frame goes beyond 25 frames, simply click the square at the end of the timeline, and drag it back to frame 25.

5. If you press Enter (PC) or Return (Mac), you can preview your animation. Your final symbol should look something like that shown in Figure 12.26.

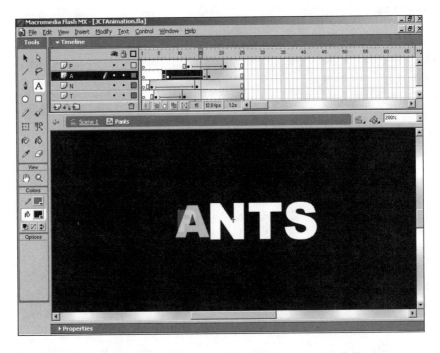

Figure 12.26   The final animation for the word PANTS. The letter P is fading in.

6. Repeat the previous steps for the remaining words.

Housekeeping

The letters in each of the words are converted to symbols. This isn't a bad thing, except there are a number of letters such as S and T that are common to each of the words being used in the animation. Simply replace the letter with the symbol if it already exists. Here's how:

Select the letter, and note the x and y coordinates of the selected letter on the Property inspector. Delete the letter, and drag an instance of the letter on to the Stage. Enter the x and y coordinates of the original letter into the Info panel, and press Enter (PC) or Return (Mac). The letter moves into place.

Another technique that prevents clutter in the Library is to put all of the objects in a folder. For example, click the New Folder icon in the Library to open a new folder. Double-click the new folder and name it **Pants Folder**. Move all of the symbols relating to the Pants animation into this folder. Double-click a folder to open it, and double-click it again to close the folder.

Creating a Mask in Flash

The use of masking was discussed earlier in this chapter, so you're familiar with this effect. Here, the decision is to have a flashlight-like effect for the tag line, "We have you covered with JCT!" This effect appears at the bottom of the Stage. Masking in Flash is a great technique, and with the introduction of version 5 of the application, a whole lot simpler to accomplish than in earlier versions.

To create a mask in Flash, follow these steps:

1. Create a new graphic symbol and name it **Tag Line**. Add three new layers to the symbol above the first layer. From the top to the bottom, name the layers Actions, Spot, Text, and Backdrop.

2. Enter the text **We have you covered with JCT!** on the Stage in the Text layer. Set the words as Arial, 24 points, set the tracking to 3, and the color of the text to white.

3. Select the Backdrop layer. Choose the Rectangle tool, set the stroke to None, and the fill to 333333. Draw a rectangle that is just slightly higher and longer than the text block. For this example, we used a height of 40 pixels.

4. Click the Spot layer. Select the Circle tool, set the stroke to None, and the fill to white.

5. Hold down the Shift key and draw a circle that is a bit smaller than the backdrop. For this example, we used a width and height value of 36 pixels. Convert the circle to a symbol. This object is going to be animated; symbols can be animated, objects can't.

6. Add a frame for all of the layers at frame 50 and keyframes in the Spot layer at frames 25 and 50. Create a Motion tween between the keyframes in the Spot layer.

7. Click your circle in frame 1, and move it into position just before the start of the text block. Note the y position in the Info panel, and drag it to a point just beyond the end of the text block. Check the y position on the Info panel; if it is different from the original value, change it.

8. Click the circle in frame 25, and drag it to a point just to the right of the end of the text block. Click the keyframe in frame 55; if the circle isn't in its starting position at the left side of the text block, move it there.

9. To create a mask, right-click (Control-click on the Mac) the Spot layer name, and select Mask from the pop-down menu. An icon consisting of a blue square with a turned up corner appears on the text layer, and a black square with a blue circle appears on the Spot layer. The blue circle indicates a mask, and the turned up corner icon on the layer indicates the layer that will show through the mask.

10. To add the Backdrop layer to the mask sequence, right-click the layer name, select Properties from the context menu, and select Masked in the properties.

11. If you want to see the mask as you scrub across the animation, right-click (Control-click on a Mac) the Spot layer, and select Show Masking from the context menu.

12. If you test the animation at this point, the spotlight moves forward and backward across the text block. To have the spotlight stop and the words appear, simply drag the end of the tween to frame 44 and then remove the frames between frames 45 and 50 on the Spot layer. If you simply remove the frames, the tween will break. A broken tween has a dashed line instead of an arrow between the keyframes.

13. Add a keyframe in frame 50 of the Actions layer, and add a Stop action. Your layers should look like those shown in Figure 12.27.

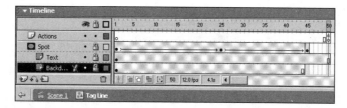

Figure 12.27   The masking layers and keyframes are in place for the Tag Line symbol.

Tip

Any object can be a mask in Flash. Just remember, the mask has to be above the layers being masked.

Producing the Animated Splash Screen

Now that you have created your assets, it is time to create and test the animation. The word symbols and the masked tag line are going to be added to the Stage, along with the logo. The following steps demonstrate a technique Hillman Curtis calls a Split Fade to get the words off of the Stage while the logo appears.

1. You are currently in a movie clip. To close the movie clip and return to the main timeline, click the Scene 1 button above the Stage. Drag through all of the layers at frame 70 and add a frame. You will not be using the Background symbol, so lock the layer by clicking the dot under the Lock icon in the Background layer. If content is not going to be moved, get into the habit of locking the layer after it is in place. This ensures you don't accidentally move something.

2. Drag an instance of the Hats symbol onto the Stage in the Hats layer, and drag the playback head across the frames until the word Hats is visible. Click the Hats symbol on the Stage to select it and then drag it to the upper left corner of the Stage so the top and the side of the letter H touch the upper left guides. Repeat this for the remaining clothing symbols in the Library. The placement should resemble that shown in Figure 12.28.

3. Drag the Tag Line symbol onto the Stage, and place it at the bottom. Drag the playback head across the timeline until all of the text is visible and then move it into its final position.

4. If you leave everything alone at this point, the various clothing symbols keep playing repeatedly. To avoid this, select the Hats symbol on the Stage, and select Play Once from the Instance properties under the Loop button on the Property inspector. Repeat this for all of the clothing symbols on the Stage, as well as for the Tag Line symbol.

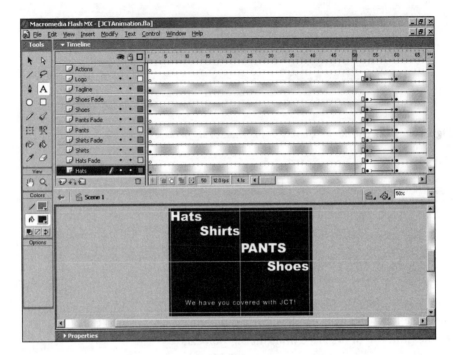

Figure 12.28   The final placement of the symbols on the Stage. Your layering and timeline
should resemble what is shown here.

5. Add a keyframe in frame 53 of the Logo layer, and drag an instance of the logo
   from the Library onto the Stage. Align the logo with the center of the Stage and
   then add another keyframe at frame 60. Add a Motion tween between the
   keyframes.

6. Select the keyframe in frame 53, set the Alpha of the logo to 0, and scale the logo
   down to 25%. Check the alignment on the first frame (frame 53) after the image
   is scaled because it sometimes moves.

The Stage is now set. The symbols are all in place and doing what they were designed to
do. The plan now is to have the clothing symbols leave the Stage at the same rate the logo
appears. To do so, follow these steps:

1. Add keyframes at frames 53 and 60 of the Hats layer. Shift-click the two
   keyframes to select the range. Press the Alt (PC) or Option (mac) key and then
   drag a copy of the selected frames up to the HatsFade layer.

2. Turn off the visibility of the Hats Fade layer. Select the instance of the hat symbol
   on frame 60 of the Hats layer. In the Property inspector, set the Alpha to 0. Click

again on the instance, and move the symbol using the Down arrow key on your keyboard, below the baseline of the text block.

3. Turn off the visibility of the Hats layer and then turn on the visibility of the Hats Fade layer.

4. Select the instance of the symbol on the HatsFade layer. To move it, use the Up arrow to move it up to a point above the Cap Height of the block. Turn on the visibility of the Hats layer.

5. Repeat steps 1 through 4 for the remaining three clothing layers.

6. Scrub the animation across frames 50 to 70, and you will see Hillman's infamous Split Fade. Save the file.

Summary

As you have discovered type is not simply that gray stuff that goes around the pictures. The Macromedia MX Studio offers you a complete set of tools that range from the rudimentary to the sophisticated.

You discovered how Flash MX components offer you a drag-and-drop solution to the creation of scrolling text boxes. By using familiar interface elements, you can offer your user an intuitive interface yet still create text that is both legible and readable.

We explored the creation of a typographic logo page that uses many of the text and graphics features in Fireworks MX. This showed you that communication doesn't always require a photograph or line art. In certain instances, two simple letters on a page can convey just as powerful a message. We also demonstrated how to create a text-based page that not only communicates a message, but uses a variety of traditional typographic techniques to add interest to a page. Along the way we also explained how to slice the page, and assemble those slices in a Dreamweaver MX page using one-click access to the application.

Fine typography is no longer in the realm of print design. We demonstrated how FreeHand can be used for this purpose. We also discussed how the conversion of text to art in FreeHand can maintain the integrity of a design. We showed how the LiveEffects in Fireworks MX, if used properly, can add some zing to a headline.

There are occasions where text can be used as the basis for some pretty spectacular special effects in Fireworks MX. These effects range from masking images to punch outs to masks with LiveEffects.

Finally, we walked through the creation of a type-based splash page in Flash MX. While creating this intro page, we made extensive use of Flash MX's type tools, as well as some interesting special effects designed to engage the viewer.

Though this chapter focused on the creation of typographic art, there is also line art. In the next chapter, we walk you through the creation of many of the line art creation features of the Macromedia MX Studio of tools.

Chapter 13

MX

Designing Dynamic Web Sites

The process of web development has undergone a profound change from delivering static, brochure-like information to real-time, up-to-the-minute information over the past few years, and Macromedia Studio MX has evolved to meet this change in web development.

Web sites have become *dynamic,* meaning content is delivered to a user's web browser, PDA, or even a Flash application on demand. Content is dynamically added to a web page as it is sent from the server to the user's browser. This is a fundamental shift away from pages where the content is fixed in place during the design process.

The evolution of dynamic web site development has also rippled through the teams that build web sites. Prior to the development of dynamic sites, the team was design driven. The members of the team who fell into the creative category developed the images, text, layouts, and all of the other visual and aural elements that comprised a web page.

The development of dynamic sites turns that model inside out, and rearranges its molecules. The coders and database developers are laying the foundations for dynamic sites. The specific needs of these developers in how content is created and pages are designed play a significant role in the new workflow.

In some respects, this has tended to polarize web development teams into two camps— the techies and the creatives. This separation of the two camps becomes an easy trap to fall into, and is a guaranteed recipe for failure. The rise of the dynamic site has merged these two solitudes to the point where the creatives can't work without an understanding of the coding and database constraints of web development, and the techs can't develop the site's infrastructure without understanding how the content being presented is created.

Web designers no longer simply build web pages. They develop the interfaces that tap the power of the content *systems* devised by their technical counterparts. Their work is no longer static. Their design elements shift and rearrange themselves in ways that explore the infinite possibilities and combinations of how their content will be presented. That can't occur without a mastery of the systems.

This chapter explores the process of designing dynamic web sites—specifically, the issues encountered as we took a static site and made it dynamic.

When this book was first presented to New Riders, the plan was to present how a series of tools developed by Macromedia could be used as a comprehensive workflow solution. We were halfway through the book when Macromedia did a 90-degree turn in the marketplace and announced the development of the MX Studio that was aimed squarely at building dynamic web sites.

Up to that point, the JCT site was static, being used to present techniques from the various chapters. We knew that ColdFusion MX was a part of the Studio, and kept quiet about it simply because we weren't willing to add yet another application to the list being covered. That all changed when one of our editors asked us why the JCT site was static when Macromedia was positioning the Studio as a great tool for the creation of dynamic content.

Two of the authors—Tom and Chris—who were on the creative side of the fence were less than thrilled. Jordan's response was the exact opposite: "Well, it is about time." The old way of doing things was over, and Chris and Tom were about to be introduced to Jordan's world! In retrospect, our resistance was eerily similar to printers adopting digital technologies in the early 1990's.

In 1993, while presenting digital prepress technologies to printers, one of the authors would start off the seminar by telling them, "Your choices with this new technology are real simple. You can choose to get digital or you can choose to live in the past and possibly lose work. Your call." When it comes to the new workflow, you have a similar choice: Get dynamic or get lost in the shuffle.

Getting Dynamic

The JCT site is a good example of the nature of dynamic web development. As a clothing retailer, the company is subject to the ever-changing fashion whims of its market. The shoes that were "hot" in June are just so "yesterday" in September. Developing and maintaining a site that kept abreast of these changes would be financially daunting. Add new clothing items to the list, and not only does the site constantly change, but it also constantly expands and contracts as product lines are added and subtracted from the mix.

The site is not complex; however, there are a number of specific pages that need to be created and maintained. For example, adding a new pair of shoes to the product line seems like a rather simple task; however, there are a number of fairly technical requirements for getting this job done. You need to ensure the image is the proper format and size for the page, and make sure there is consistency in the branding and navigation, not only to the page but also from the page to the rest of the site. You also need to make sure that the shoes are added to the product line in a cost-effective manner. These are many of the issues faced by any web developer charged with designing a site that requires constant updating.

The steps to building a dynamic site are rather straightforward:

1. Define the content.
2. Build the database to hold the content.
3. Design the templates that will hold the content.

4. Write the code that pulls it all together.

Defining the Content

Before you consider the design of the site, you need to precisely define the content needed. Spending the proper amount of time on this step ensures that nothing is over-looked. In the case of the JCT site, the structure of the content is pretty basic. There are shirts, pants, shoes, and hats. Were you to stop at this point, the project would be doomed. The definitions of the content are far too broad.

We went a bit deeper, as you saw in Chapter 6, "Preparing for Dynamic Content," and broke each product down into its smaller data pieces. They were:

> Item
>
> Description
>
> Price

Were we to take this even further, we could add the following:

> Color
>
> Size
>
> Men's
>
> Women's
>
> Image

At this point in the process, you need to be explicit and look at all of the possibilities. For example, the price is expressed in dollars. Are they U.S. dollars, or should Canadian dollars be used? Another example would be shoe size. If overseas orders are accepted, are the European sizes going to be made available, or should there be a conversion utility between the two size-measurement systems? As you can see, it is important to not only describe each piece of content in as concise a form as possible, but to also indicate the data type of each piece of content. Is it a date? A number? Text? An image? All of these questions need to be answered before the site design is considered.

Building the Database

Having described the content, you now create the database that will hold the content. Databases don't work in isolation on the web. To have the content flow from a database to the web requires the use of a system designed to make that happen.

These systems are sometimes referred to as *three-tiered architecture.* The term sounds quite impressive, but in fact describes how data moves upward through three steps that are the basic components of dynamic site development. They are as follows:

- A database—This is the place where the content is stored. Industrial-strength databases include Oracle, Sybase, and MySQL. In our case, we are using the latest version of Microsoft Access.

- Middleware—This is an application that sits on the server, processes the requests for pages, and feeds the content from the database to templates, created in Dreamweaver MX. ColdFusion MX is one of the more popular middleware packages.

- The interface—This is the server that feeds the templates, created in Dreamweaver MX, to the user's browser.

When looked at in these simple terms, building a dynamic site is available to anyone using off-the-shelf software from Microsoft and Macromedia. As one of the authors used to tell printers in how to adapt to the changes in their industry, "Nothing has really changed. The only change is how we talk about it."

We still need to build the pages in Dreamweaver using content from Word processors, Flash MX, FreeHand, and Fireworks MX. The only change is how we describe where that content is stored.

After you have documented the content and identified its data type, it is a simple matter of following the steps outlined in Chapter 6 to create the database that reflects the content list.

When building the database, the importance of adding a *primary key* can't be emphasized enough. A primary key in Access is a unique identifier for each record in the table that helps locate records faster when you need them. By setting a field as a primary key, you are, in essence, telling Access that each record in the table will be unique.

Finally, if you are adding text to the database from a word-processing application, strip out all formatting by saving the file as plain text. Use the template to provide the formatting information.

Building Templates to Hold Content

Templates are quite the time-saving tools. By allowing you to create pages with the same design but with different content, they are ideally suited to sites containing dynamic content. Although you will be dealing with the design of the templates in greater depth in

Chapter 20, "Connecting with ColdFusion MX," understanding how templates work in Dreamweaver MX and some of the design considerations behind their creation is important.

Templates are a combination of fixed content, such as images, buttons, and so on, mixed with a series of ColdFusion-driven areas for the content to be pulled off of the database or dynamically derived otherwise.

One of the great things about templates is they are somewhat chameleon-like. The user will think the site consists of dozens of different pages when, in fact, it is only one page pulling the information out of the database.

From a design point of view, templates are where the two solitudes—design and tech— either collide or collaborate.

When designing templates in Dreamweaver MX, be sure to do the following:

- Place all content that is common to every page of the site into the template.
- Place editable regions in every area of the template that will hold content. These editable regions are similar to placeholders.
- Test the template before creating the entire site.

Creating a Template in Dreamweaver MX

Template creation is surprisingly uncomplicated. You have two choices: Create the template from scratch, or modify an existing document.

To create a template from scratch in Dreamweaver MX, follow these steps:

1. Open Dreamweaver MX. You can either work with an existing site, or create a new site by choosing Site, New Site. Select File, New to create a new blank HTML document.

2. Add the images, tables, text, and so on that appear on every page. Anything that doesn't appear on every page has to be removed.

3. Select File, Save As Template to open the Save As Template dialog box, as shown in Figure 13.1. Save the document as a Dreamweaver template with the .dwt extension.

4. Enter a name for the template in the Save As text input field.

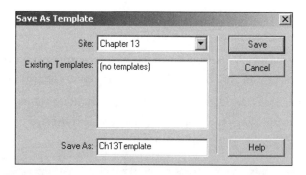

Figure 13.1   Save your template in the Save As Template dialog box.

5. Click the Save (Mac) or OK (PC) button. To use an existing document as a template, simply strip out the content that isn't common to every page and then select Save As Template from the File menu. Select the site with which the template is to be associated from the Site pop-down menu in the Save As Template dialog box, name the template, and save the template.

Adding Editable Regions to the Template

The content being pulled from the database is placed into specific areas of the page called editable regions. Editable regions on a template are the areas in which you can place page-specific data. The content in editable regions varies from page to page.

To add an editable region to your template, follow these steps:

1. On a template page that you have either created or opened, click an area where you would like to place an editable region. Select the Template tab from the Insert panel. The panel changes to show seven buttons under the Template tab. Click the Editable Region button to open the New Editable Region dialog box shown in Figure 13.2.

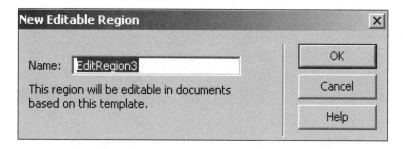

Figure 13.2   The New Editable Region dialog box is where the areas that hold the content are named.

2. Enter a name for the field and then click OK. The region containing a blue outline and the region's name appears on the page.

3. If you are using a table-based layout, create the table and then select the entire
   table by clicking it in your page. A black outline appears around the table.

4. With the table selected, click the Editable Region button, and name the region
   when the Editable Region dialog box opens. A table converted to an editable
   region resembles that shown in Figure 13.3.

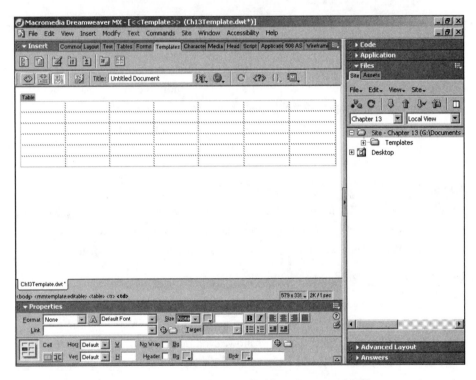

Figure 13.3   A table has been converted to an editable region named Table.

5. To remove an editable region, select the region to be removed and then choose
   Modify, Template, Remove Template Markup. The region disappears from the
   page.

Note

Saving a template not only creates a .dwt document, but also adds the template to the Dreamweaver MX Assets panel. To change the name of the template in the Assets panel, click the template name and then enter the new name. To open a template for editing, select the template in the Assets panel, and select Edit from the Assets panel pop-down menu. To apply a template in the Assets panel to a document, select the template and then select Apply from the Assets panel pop-down menu.

Writing the Code

Writing code inevitably falls into the realm of the tech. Although we present an extensive overview of the coding issues we dealt with in pulling the JCT site together in Chapter 20, it is important that the design accommodate the coding needs for dynamic data.

As we pointed out in the previous section, a template is driven by both graphics and HTML; therefore, it is important to keep this in mind when designing your pages. Some considerations would include

- If there is an area, for example, that will have content served into it, leave the area blank, or indicate in the design the areas on the page that will hold the dynamic content.

- If using editable regions in Dreamweaver MX, the appearance of the text will be code driven. The appearance of the text in these areas can be formatted in Dreamweaver MX's Property inspector. Your design should accommodate this limitation.

- Build flexibility into your design. The best way to accomplish this is to clearly understand what the coder needs to achieve regarding dynamic presentation of data, and how to balance those needs against the design objectives. The best time to have this discussion is before you start sketching.

- If there is code that is reused throughout the site, use the new Snippets feature of Dreamweaver MX to hold the code.

Working with Dreamweaver MX Snippets

Snippets are pieces of code that can be reused. The code could be HTML, JavaScript, CFML, ASP, and so on. Snippets are contained in the Dreamweaver MX Code panel, and the application ships with quite a few snippets to get you started.

A snippet can either be inserted into the code as a standalone block, such as a set of pre-formatted navigation tabs, or you can decide whether it wraps around a selected item on the page, such as adding a set of comments around an area of a page.

To insert a code snippet, follow these steps:

1. Select an object on the page and then choose Window, Snippets to open the Snippets panel shown in Figure 13.4. Alternately, you can choose Panels, Code, Snippets to open the Snippets panel.

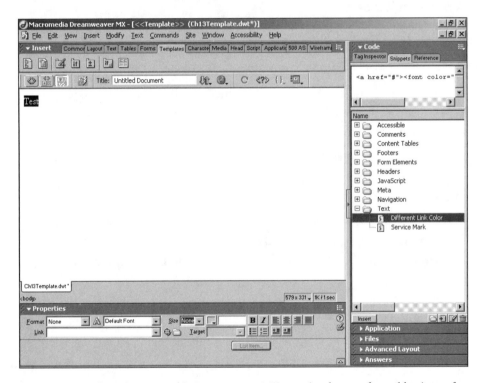

Figure 13.4   The Snippets panel in Dreamweaver MX contains dozens of reusable pieces of code, such as that used for changing the colors of links.

2. Scroll through the snippets in the panel to locate the desired code and then double-click the snippet to apply it to the object. Alternately, you can right-click (PC) or Control-click (Mac) the snippet and then select Insert from the context menu, or select the snippet and then click the Insert button at the bottom of the Snippet panel.

To add a snippet to the Snippet panel, follow these steps:

1. Select some code in Dreamweaver MX's code view.

2. Click the New Snippets icon at the bottom of the Snippet panel.

3. You can name the snippet, describe what it does, and decide whether to have the code wrap around an element (Wrap Selection), or simply insert it as a block of code (Insert Block). Click OK, and the snippet is added to your panel.

Snippets can also be shared among the members of the project team. This can be a huge timesaver because it saves your team members from having to write the same piece of code over and over again.

To share a snippet, follow these steps:

1. Locate the snippet you want to share in the Configuration/Snippets folder. This folder is located in the Dreamweaver MX Application folder.

2. Copy the snippet to a shared folder on your computer, or to a folder that is available to all of the team members on a network.

3. When the snippet is available, members of the team can simply copy the snippet to their computer's Configuration/Snippets folder.

From Static to Dynamic: Designing the JCT Site

The evolution of the JCT site from a static layout to a dynamic layout mirrors the dilemma many web designers are facing in today's production environment. Confronted with tools that make their job more efficient, they have to consider how to convert their work to accommodate the inclusion of dynamic data served into the site.

As has been stressed throughout this book, the building of web sites is a team effort that starts with a piece of paper and a pencil to sketch out the ideas and concepts for the pages. It was no different for the JCT site. As you saw in Chapter 4, "Testing Your Ideas with Site Models," the JCT site evolved from ideas to concept through a number of sketches on a sheet of paper.

As the process of developing the site moved along, it became apparent that a more corporate look was needed. The designs were changed, and the main pages were produced. Just as that process was completed, the client gently suggested the inclusion of a dynamic data feature to the site.

This section follows the process from the design of the new, more corporate look to the dilemmas faced by the designer when a great-looking design was adapted to accommodate the inclusion of dynamic data.

The designer and the programmer agreed upon creation of a navigation bar at the top of each page. The navigation bar is important because it is one of the elements common to each section of the site, and is thus an integral element in the branding of the site. Although each page may appear to have different content, the navigation bar remains the same throughout.

Going Corporate

The initial design was good, but we weren't pleased with how the site was developing. It looked cool, but it struck us that it really didn't further the brand, and that cool was giving way to ease of use. After some discussion, it was decided that the JCT site needs to be a bit more streamlined, and a more corporate look established.

After we came to this conclusion, new sketches were needed; therefore, new concept sketches are now needed. Working with pen and paper again, the new corporate look shown in Figure 13.5 is conceptualized and ready for approval.

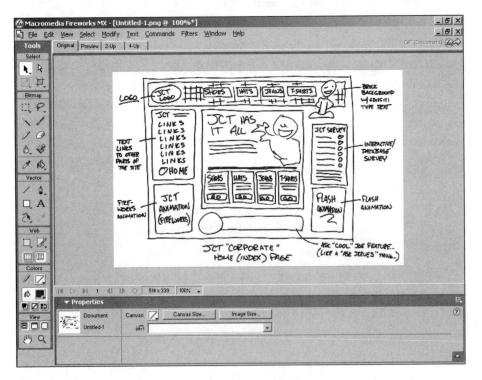

Figure 13.5   The new corporate look for the site is first presented as a sketch.

At the same time, we recognized we hadn't accommodated a page that would allow for online merchandise ordering in the future. We realized a new catalog-type design was required; as the overall site design was being conceptualized, so was the product catalog section. The final sketch, shown in Figure 13.6, is used for the product sections within the site. It is also, as it turned out, the design for the dynamic portion of the site.

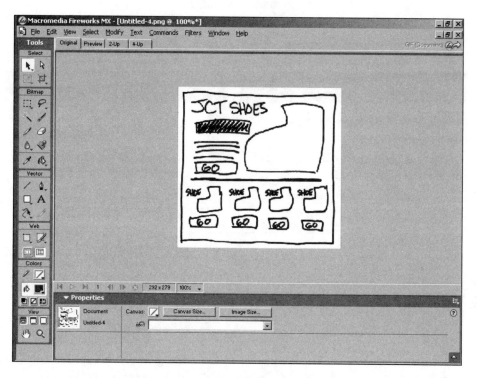

Figure 13.6 The final sketch for the ecommerce section, which inevitably formed the basis for the design of the dynamic area of the site.

After the final sketches for the new corporate look are approved, the designer can place the scan in its own layer in Fireworks MX and then build the page using the scan as a guide. The designer can also print out the page and use it as a guide. The final results for the home page and three of the product pages are shown in Figure 13.7.

Figure 13.7   The final designs for the home page and three of the product pages.

Notice that not all of the artwork has been totally disregarded. In fact, we used much of the older artwork previously created to establish the JCT navigation bar.

Note

Clients are notorious for changing their minds. When creating designs, it's a good idea to never throw out any of the artwork. The moment you do, you can expect the client to mention something in the file that was just trashed, and you will then have to recreate it.

Building the JCT Navigation Bar

When the decision to redesign the site was made, there was no discussion regarding whether the brick background for the navigation bar was to change as well. From the outset, we had wanted to include an edgy, urban graffiti look. The brick wall combined with the MarkerFelt font gave the site a specific feel, and we decided to keep it.

The other aspect of the navigation bar was the client has already specified that they would like the navigation bar to be interactive. This meant the text had to be treated as buttons. This also meant rollover effects for the four main sections of the JCT site had to be created.

The question was, "Do we create the buttons and HTML code using Fireworks MX?". Because we had a techie on the team, we had a brief discussion regarding the question and decided to forego creating the button HTML code in Fireworks MX. We decided instead to write the necessary HTML in Dreamweaver MX.

The reason behind that decision essentially came down to using the right tool for the job. Dreamweaver is a bit more forgiving, thanks to its Code view, in manipulating or modifying the HTML code should any of the rollover effects need to be modified. Were we to present our techie with the pre-rolled code from Fireworks MX (purists disdainfully regard the code produced by Fireworks MX as ugly code), we ran the risk of actually creating more work for our techie.

Note

Don't assume we are recommending ignoring the Button feature of Fireworks MX. It is extremely powerful. The decision to wire up the buttons in Dreamweaver MX was made because we had a technically minded member on the team who could react quickly to any changes or modifications to the code. In the final analysis, the buttons would have worked just as well using the Fireworks MX code because they would be hand coded in Dreamweaver MX. Why? Because when you get right down to it, the client doesn't care whether the code was done in Fireworks MX or Dreamweaver MX. The client only cares that the buttons do what they are supposed to do.

With that decision made, we simply had to create the buttons and their Up, Over, and Down states as separate images in Fireworks MX.

The following section details how our team techie went about creating the Up and Over images for the buttons, and how he dealt with the change from static to dynamic.

Creating the Rollover Effects

Before setting up any kind of slices for the rollovers, the rollover effect needs to be established. For the JCT rollover effects, the color of each word changes as the mouse rolls over it.

The main color of each section will remain red, as shown in Figure 13.8. In this case, the HTML color is #990000. This color represents our Up state. To remember small details such as individual colors, you might want to keep a small notebook handy. This can be used to note this type of information so you can keep track of all the details and changes a web site might go through before it is ultimately completed.

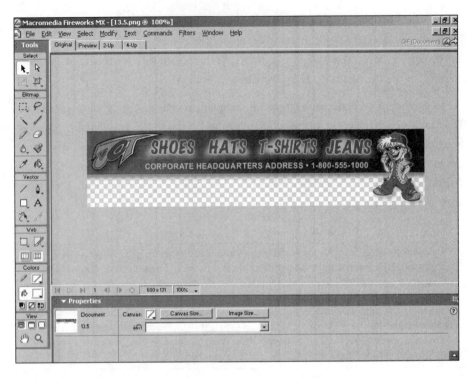

Figure 13.8   The Up state of each button will be red.

For the Over effect, we decided to go with a light-brown color. In this case, the HTML color is #996633. Again, you might want to jot these color numbers down in a notebook, should you be asked to change something later.

Having completed the Up state, you should now look at how the slices will be created.

Rather than use the Slice tool, you can draw the guides for the slices to obtain the tightest fit possible. To do this, use the page rulers to show whenever you create your guides (View, Rulers); then, simply drag a guide from the ruler onto the canvas. When you are happy with the way you have set up your guides, select the Slice tool in the toolbar, and carefully follow the guides, creating one slice area at a time. The slices created are shown in Figure 13.9.

Having created the slices, select all of the slices and then open the Optimize panel by choosing Window, Optimize, or by pressing F6. The Optimize panel, shown in Figure 13.10, allows you to set the optimization settings, from color depth to transparency, for all of the slices. You can use the panel to optimize one slice, or apply the settings to all of the slices.

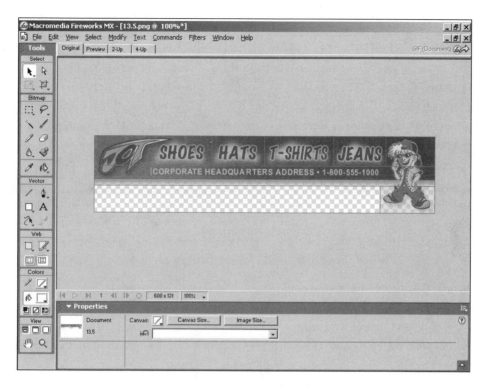

Figure 13.9   Using guides instead of the Slice tool to initially define the slice areas results in a tighter fit for the slice.

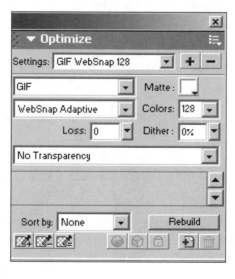

Figure 13.10   The Optimize panel allows you to prepare the images for export on the canvas rather than use File, Export Preview.

The Optimization setting of 128 colors may appear to be a bit much. The reason behind that decision is because the brick wall in the background has subtle shades and tones that may be lost if the color depth is reduced. Another reason for this decision is file size. The reduction in file size for small slices whose color depth ranges between 128 and 64 colors is marginal. GIF images aren't large, and the physical size of each slice is small enough to not result in a download-time issue when viewed in a browser. At this point, you have the option of letting Fireworks MX do all of the work for you—creating the HTML coding and exporting the artwork by selecting File, Export to open the Export dialog box. Select HTML and Images from the Save As pop-down menu. When you're creating individual rollover images for your coder, it is not necessary to create an HTML page along with the images. Select Images from the Save As pop-down menu, and select Export Slices from the Slices pop-down menu in the Export dialog box. Select Include Areas without Slices at the bottom of the Export dialog box.

Before clicking the Save button in the Export dialog box, make sure you have already set up the folder structure of your site, or you have at least created a folder where you will store all of your web-created images. By creating a folder, you can send that folder to the person who will be creating the actual HTML pages. Click the Save button, the Export dialog box closes, and you return to your image.

Now that all of the images with the red text have been exported to an images folder, Select the Hide Slices and Hotspots tool in the Web area of the toolbar to turn off the green overlay indicating a slice, and then select all of the red text using the Direct Selection tool.

In the Property inspector, change the color of the words to the light-brown color—#996633—by typing the number directly into the input area of the fill color pop-up color picker.

Having changed the color, click the View Slices and Hotspots tool again, and the slices reappear.

This technique of using the tools to hide and show slices is rather interesting. When you hide the slices, the eyeball indicating their visibility on the Web layer dims. If you click the eyeball in the Web layer to turn off the layer's visibility and then click it again to turn on the visibility, the eyeball is still dim and the green overlay doesn't reappear. If you want all of the slices in an image to disappear, use the Hide Slices and Hotspots tool. Use the Web layer when only individual slices need to be hidden.

If you export the image with the brown slices, you would duplicate many of the slices already created, and make life difficult for the coder. Fireworks MX has a neat little feature that allows you to export only the newly colored words.

Select all of the light-brown slices and then press Control-Shift-R (PC) or Command-Shift-R (Mac) to open the Export dialog box. Choose the folder containing the original slices; then rename the slices and select Images Only from the Save As pop-down menu. In the Slices pop-down menu, select Export Slices and Selected Slices Only, and deselect Include Areas without Slices. This ensures that only the words with the brown fill are exported. Click Save.

All of the images should now reside in a single image folder that can now be sent to the person creating the actual HTML coding in Dreamweaver MX.

JCT Goes Dynamic

Originally, the JCT site was conceptualized to be a static site, meaning there weren't going to be any database or dynamic features involved. Therefore, the JCT site was designed entirely in Fireworks.

At this point, HTML parameters or design limitations were not a huge concern. Because the site was static, a lot of little interesting visuals were planned. One of those visuals included rounded corners on all the side elements of the site, as shown in Figure 13.11.

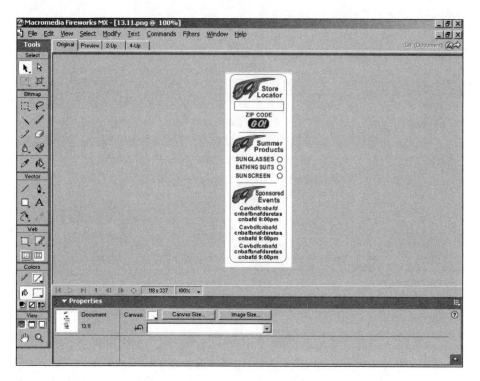

Figure 13.11   One of the interesting visual elements built into Chris's original design was rounded corners on many of the site's side elements.

With rounded corners, the image would have been sliced and exported from Fireworks MX and then reassembled in Dreamweaver MX within tables and cells; however, the discussion of making the site more dynamic came into play. The initial design had to be re-evaluated to determine what aspects of the original design would have to be changed to make the site more dynamic-friendly.

One change that immediately stood out was that all the nice little round corners would have to be eliminated because these sections would be created using HTML colors and tables. The main reason for this is because not only is the data dynamic, but the size of the table will vary as well. Allowing the table to be recreated in HTML will be a lot cleaner and less tricky than slicing up graphics to be manipulated on the screen using one of the many CSS tricks available. The side element images were changed, as shown in Figure 13.12.

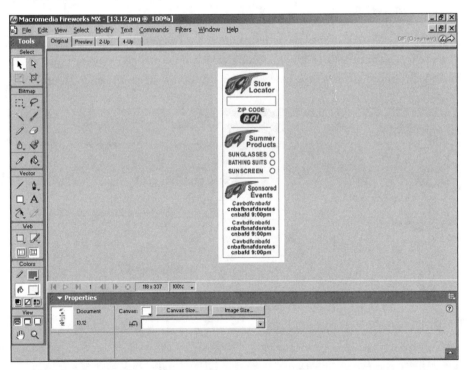

Figure 13.12   The design meets the realities of code, meaning the round corners for the side-bars had to change.

Because the side elements were now going to be created in HTML, there wasn't a need to maintain the side element graphics in Fireworks MX. These could easily have been eliminated, but then there wouldn't be a visual log of how the site will eventually look. All of the square boxes were kept in the side elements.

As Chris explains this, of course, became a new problem. I am the designer of the site. Jordan will be generating the dynamic portions of the JCT site. The problem is that I have no idea what he needs from me to complete his part in making the site dynamic.

To resolve this, I sent Jord an email asking him for a rough idea that will indicate what graphics (if any) he needs and what exactly he needs me to do. I want to make his job as painless as possible. Jordan responded by sending me the .png file, shown in Figure 13.13, indicating what he's envisioned.

Figure 13.13   Jordan sent this image to Chris to show Chris how the page should be designed.

The page looks interesting, but still doesn't indicate what Jordan needs. We traded several emails and ideas until we finally understood what the other needs. Jordan needed images; I needed to know which sections of the dynamic area would be HTML-based and which areas would be graphic. Figure 13.14 was the culmination of these discussions because it clearly indicates what parts of the dynamic area will be HTML-based, and what graphics Jordan needed to get to work.

Now that I know which graphic parts of the JCT site I need to create and send to Jordan, I open the JCT .png pages to start creating and optimizing my slices of the individual graphics. Basically, the only graphics Jord needs are some JCT logos, some titles, and the pictures of the individual JCT products (the shoe, hat, jeans, and t-shirt). My slices are already set up, so now I simply export the images to the folder that will be compressed as a .zip file and sent to Jordan.

From the perspective of the site designer, sending the files to Jordan is the most difficult part of the dynamic site-creation process. As soon as I send all of these individual graphics off to Jordan, the JCT site is, essentially, now out of my hands and no longer mine to control. I have to trust I not only sent Jord every graphic file he needs, but also through the magic of his programming skills, the dynamic results of the JCT site will still end up resembling the pages I originally conceptualized in Fireworks."

Figure 13.14   The page takes on a different dimension once it is determined which areas are graphic-based and which areas are HTML-based.

Chris Talks About Making the JCT Site Dynamic

For me, sending the files to Jordan was the hardest part in creating the JCT site. It wasn't so much the fear of the site becoming dynamic as much as it was not knowing what Jordan needed to create the dynamic features of the JCT site he wanted.

I have extensive experience working with database programmers and integrating database content into a web site. In almost all of these cases, however, very rarely did graphics ever become involved. Databases and HTML text was something I understood. Throwing graphics into the mix was entirely new to me.

Our geographical locations also proved frustrating as well. Because Jordan lives in Canada, and I am in the eastern United States, I simply could not get into my car, drive over to his house, and discuss face-to-face what we both wanted or needed from the other to make the dynamic aspects work for the site.

It wasn't until Jord sent me the sample JCT ecommerce page, and I saw what would actually be HTML text and what would be graphics, did I finally understand what he required.

Still, as a designer, it's sometimes hard to totally relinquish "your baby." I had to send one more email to Jordan confirming that he did, indeed, need only very specific graphics, and that everything else would be created dynamically with HTML text before I felt completely comfortable clicking the Send button.

Summary

As you have seen, when it comes to building dynamic sites, the old workflow and its division of labor simply doesn't work. A new workflow involving the collaboration of the design and technical side of web development is evolving.

As we pointed out at the beginning of the chapter, the steps to building a dynamic site are straightforward:

1. Define the content.
2. Build the database to hold the content.
3. Design the templates that will hold the content.
4. Write the code that pulls it all together.

Defining the content no longer involves determining the text, images, and interactive elements that are so common. The content has expanded to include precise definitions of the content. It is these definitions that determine how the database used to hold the content will be built.

After the content is defined, we explained how the dynamic web development process is a three-tier process with data moving from a database through middleware, such as ColdFusion MX, and into the pages developed in Dreamweaver MX.

We then showed you how to build a template in Dreamweaver MX, and how to work with the editable regions within the template to create the placeholders that hold dynamic content.

When it comes to code, the designer has to be aware of the needs of the coder or programmer on the team. We suggested a number of areas of which to be conscious when building your designs, ranging from clearly indicating which areas of a page are dynamic and which aren't to using Dreamweaver MX's new Code Snippets feature.

We then thoroughly discussed how the JCT site was built, as well as the decisions and compromises that had to be made to make it dynamic. We also presented an interesting method of creating rollover images that will be coded in Dreamweaver.

The chapter concluded with how our designer, Chris Flick, found the new workflow to be a bit disconcerting as he relinquished control of his design to our programmer, Jordan. Chris' comments regarding his adjustment to Jordan's needs are not unique and, in fact, will become increasingly important as the new workflow takes hold.

In the next chapter, we move back into more familiar territory as we examine how to create animation on the web using the tools present in FreeHand, Fireworks MX, and Dreamweaver MX.

Chapter 14

MX

Animation on the Web

The quality of animation on the web is inconsistent, at best. From those silly, blinking, Christmas lights that festoon family pages just after Thanksgiving to full-bore, Flash-based, animated cartoons with production values that would rival some of the Hollywood cartoon studios, animation has become a staple of the web. The main issue when considering an animation is asking yourself, "Do I need it?"

Animations can add weight to a site and slow things down. Poorly planned and, ultimately, poorly designed animations are what people will remember. For example, in the early days of Flash, when spinning globes were all the rage, one of the authors came across the site of a company in Akron, Ohio that sold tires. Taking up almost half of the company's home page was the ubiquitous spinning globe. The state of Ohio was highlighted, and a red dot marking the location of Akron was also prominent. The problem with the animation was threefold: the Akron dot was placed well south of Columbus, Ohio; Ohio grew to encompass large chunks of Pennsylvania and West Virginia; and the map inferred a global reach when the company was a neighborhood tire vendor. In this case, the planning was minimal because the size of the state and the location of Akron would have been caught in the storyboard phase. The state and city weren't necessary; a map of the neighborhood or a rotating tire animation would have been more effective and useful.

After you decide an animation is needed, you have to decide which tool is best suited for the job at hand. Though budget will dictate this—Flash animations are usually at the high end of the budget scale—it may just be that a more effective job can be done using a GIF animation created in Fireworks MX, or even one created in Dreamweaver MX.

When you have made the decision to produce an animation, the planning process takes over. The key tool here is a storyboard.

Storyboarding

A storyboard is a visual representation of the keyframes of an animation. It shows what will be seen, what sounds are heard, and what text, if any, appears onscreen. A storyboard presents two different kinds of information: a description of the images in the sequence through pictures and words, and a description of the spatial aspect of the sequence, such as movement.

The storyboard is the document the artists use to gather the information they need to do their job. It is also the document the client uses to envision the animation.

An obvious question is, "Why bother?" There are a number of valid reasons for producing a storyboard:

- It lays out the structure of the story. If the storyboard looks wrong, so too will the final product. Referring back to the tire store web site—Akron, Ohio, is in the north eastern part of the state, not near where the map indicated.

- It is a common point of reference for everyone involved in the project.

- Problems discovered here—a really big Ohio—can be easily and inexpensively addressed and resolved.

Format and Presentation

Preparing a storyboard is not a complex undertaking. It is all in the approach. You don't need to be a professional artist to create one. What you do need, however, is a great idea.

There are several different ways to present your storyboard. The average size panel, depicting what is seen onscreen, any audio, and written description of the frame can be done on a card that is 4 inches wide by 6 inches high. If more detail is required, some artists will devote an entire 8.5 inches by 11 inches page to the frame. As frames are created, they can be put into a three-ring binder for the really involved animations, or appear on a series of laser printed pages. By putting them on pages, you can simulate the pacing of the animation and editing. Pages or panels can also be removed or added as needed.

A sample blank storyboard is shown in Figure 14.1

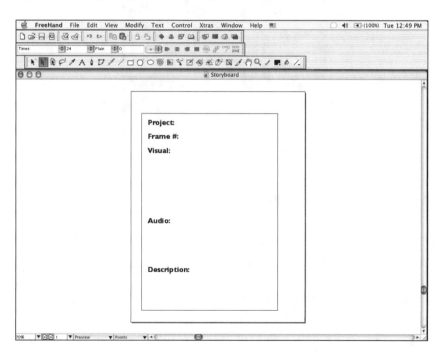

Figure 14.1   A storyboard shows the contents of the frame, any sound, and includes a brief description of the frame.

Another approach is one used by Sybil Worthington, a Toronto-based video editor. Figure 14.2 shows a storyboard Sybil created for a promo she produced for Counterforce, a show on The Learning Channel. The interesting aspect of this storyboard is how easily Sybil's ideas can work on the web. In 15 frames, from an ominous terrorist to the show's title, the art director for the animation and the client can quickly see how the concept for the promo develops. If you take an animation perspective, you can see how two elements—the noise on the right side of the screen and the gun sight—move and change over time.

Figure 14.2   It takes only 15 images to storyboard a video promotional trailer.

Animation in Fireworks MX

Animation in Fireworks MX is not far removed from those flip books we had when we were kids. If you rapidly flip through the pages, a horse runs or our favorite super hero flexes a muscle. As we know, this is an optical illusion. The drawings move faster than the eye can keep up, and the change in one image blends into the next, resulting in a smooth, continuous animation.

How Fireworks MX creates animations is no different from a flip book. Each drawing in the animation is contained in a frame. Frames are stacked on top of one another, and are displayed in rapid sequence on the monitor. What we see is an illusion that is no different from flipping through the pages of a flip book. This illusion is created with the Fireworks MX animation tools.

Animation Tools

Fireworks MX comes with a variety of tools that you can use to create exceptional animations. These tools, shown in Figure 14.3, make it easy to whip up some stunning animations.

Figure 14.3   There are a multitude of tools available in Fireworks MX that enables you to create animations.

The tools include the following:

- Frames panel—Accessible either through the Window menu—Window, Frames or from the Panel group on the right side of the canvas—frames are where animation occurs. Each frame is much like a single page of the flip book. The number of frames determines the duration of the animation, and the content on each frame can be manipulated.

- Layers panel—The Layers panel is where you manage the layering of each frame. A layer can hold objects that don't move, such as a background image, and share those objects across all of the frames in the animation.

- Frame controls—Found in the lower left corner of the Fireworks MX interface, these VCR controls allow you to do a frame-by-frame flip through the animation, or play the entire animation on the canvas.

- Property inspector—New to Fireworks MX, the Property inspector allows you to control the properties of an animation symbol—from movement to opacity—right in the Fireworks MX interface.

- Graphic symbols—Fireworks MX enables you to do the tweening between two instances of the same symbol.

- Animation symbols—Introduced in Fireworks 4.0, an animation symbol is a simple, self-contained, animation. Its properties are set when it is created and can be changed in the Property inspector.

Using Frames for Animation

The heart and soul of animation in Fireworks MX is contained in the Frames panel. Each frame of your animation can contain content that moves, or is otherwise manipulated.

To animate an object using the Frames panel, follow these steps:

1. Open a new Fireworks MX document. Set the canvas size to 300 pixels wide by 300 pixels high, and set the background color to Black.

2. Select the Text tool, click the upper-left corner of the canvas once, and enter your first name. Choose a strong font, such as Franklin Gothic Heavy, and set the text color to White.

3. Drag the Frames panel onto the canvas by clicking the panel gripper—the dots beside the panel name—and dragging the panel onto the canvas.

Tip

PC users get an extra added treat here. If you drag any panel to the left of the panel group or beside the tools on the left side of the canvas, a colored outline appears on the Stage. Release the mouse, and the panel sticks to the side of the panel group or to the left of the canvas beside the tools. It also expands to the depth of the interface. Drag it onto the canvas, and it will shrink and float, meaning it can be moved as needed.

4. Click the Frame Options pop-down menu in the Frames and History panel to open the Add Frame dialog box. Set the number of frames to 4, and select Insert new frames: After current frame. Click OK. You now have five frames in the Frames panel.

5. Click through the frames, and you will see your name appears only in frame 1. Select your name in frame 1, and choose Copy to Frames from the Frame Options pop-down menu to open the Copy to Frames dialog box. Select All frames and then click OK. Click through all of the frames and notice your name appears in each frame.

6. Select frame 2, select your name, and move it to another position on the canvas. Repeat this for the remaining frames. Your movement could resemble that shown in Figure 14.4.

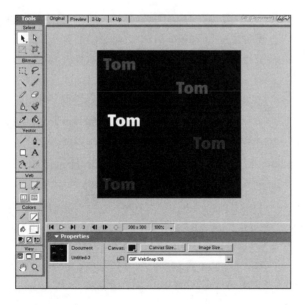

Figure 14.4   Moving an object in each frame gives the illusion of motion.

7. Click the Play control, or jog through the frames by clicking the Next Frame control in the Frame controls at the bottom of the Fireworks MX canvas. Your name appears to bounce around the canvas. Click the Play control again to stop the animation. Save the file.

Using Layers Within Animations

The name is animated and bounces around the stage over a span of five frames. What if there is content in the frame that doesn't move, such as scenic background? This is where the special relationship between layers and frames in Fireworks MX really shines.

To add a stationary object throughout the animation, follow these steps:

1. Open the Fireworks MX file you created in the previous exercise if necessary. Open the Frames panel, and select frame 2. Select the Rectangle tool, and draw a white square. Open the Layers panel, and notice the square sitting on a layer above your name.

2. Click on frame 1 of the animation. The square disappears from the Stage. Notice the layer holding the square in frame 2 of the Layers panel is also missing. This is an important aspect of the relationship between layers and frames in Fireworks MX.

   Each frame of an animation can be regarded as a separate piece of art; therefore, the layers for each frame pertain only to that frame. In the Layers panel, a pop-down menu of the frames appears in the lower left corner of the panel, as shown in Figure 14.5.

3. To share the layer across the frames of the animation, select the square. Open the Frames panel pop-down menu, and select Copy to frames from the Frame Panel option pop-down menu to open the Copy to Frame dialog box.

4. Select All frames and then click OK. If you click each frame of the animation, you notice the square layer also appears in the frame's Layer panel.

5. Layers in animation pertain only to the selected frame. This means you can choose an object on a layer in the frame, and change its color and position in the layers staking order. Select frame 1 in the pop-up menu at the bottom of the Layers panel. Click the box, and change its color. Move the layer in which the box is sitting under the text layer. Repeat this step for layer 3. Play the animation.

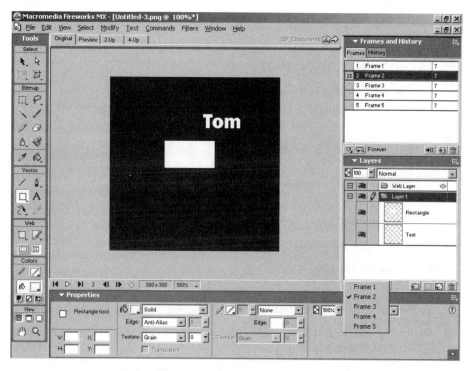

Figure 14.5   The frames in an animation are accessible from the Layers panel.

Object Animation

Now that you understand how layers and frames work together to create an animation, you can create the animation that makes up the last two frames of the Counterforce storyboard shown in Figure 14.2. The animation consists of a gun sight focusing in on the word COUNTERFORCE, which comes into focus in the last frame of the animation.

The purpose of this entire section is to give you an opportunity to work with the tools available to you, and to maybe spark a few creative synapses in the process. The animation is a great exercise, but not one you will likely build on a regular basis. It fits into an area of 300 by 300 pixels, and uses animated, progressive blurs. This type of animation places a huge demand on a browser as well as a computer. Still, the animation gives you an opportunity to use every animation tool available, which is the whole point of this section.

Preparing the Objects for Animation

The gun sight and the words should sit on separate layers. Also, the word COUNTER-FORCE requires a bit of work to get it to match what is called for in the storyboard.

To create the gun sight and the word, follow these steps:

1. Open a new Fireworks MX document. Set the canvas size to 300 by 300 pixels, and set the canvas color to Black.

2. To create the gun sight, select the Rectangle tool from the Vector tools, and draw a rectangle. With the rectangle selected, use the following settings on the Property inspector:

   W: 100

   H: 75

   Fill: None

   Stroke Color: 009933

   Stroke Thickness: 2

   Stroke category: 1-pixel Soft

3. Select the Line tool, and draw a line from the upper left corner of the rectangle to the lower right corner. Draw another line with the Line tool from the upper right corner of the rectangle to the lower left corner. The center of the rectangle is located where the lines intersect.

4. Draw a vertical line and a horizontal line through the center point of the rectangle. Select the diagonal lines and then delete them. Select both the horizontal and vertical lines, and set their stroke color, thickness, and stroke category to match those of the rectangle.

5. To reduce the number of layers, select all of the objects on the canvas and group them by pressing Ctrl- G (PC) or Command-G (Mac). Open the Layers panel, double-click the layer, and rename it **Sight**.

6. Select the Text tool. Click the canvas once and enter the word **COUNTERFORCE** using all uppercase letters. Click once between the R and the F. With the Shift key held down, press the Enter (PC) or Return (Mac) key. The word FORCE is shifted to the next line.

7. Select both words, and set them to 36 point, Arial, Black. If you don't have Arial Black, use Arial and then set the weight to Bold and the color to 009933. Select the word COUNTER, and set the range kerning to a value of 18.

8. Click once in front to the word FORCE, and set the Range Kerning value to 14. Select the letters O, R, C, and E, and set their Range Kerning value to -4. The edges of the N in and the F should line up, and the word FORCE should end under the R in COUNTER.

9. Select the Subselection tool, and click once on the horizontal line. Click-drag the right handle of the line, and drag it out to the end of the word COUNTER. Your screen should resemble those shown in Figure 14.6.

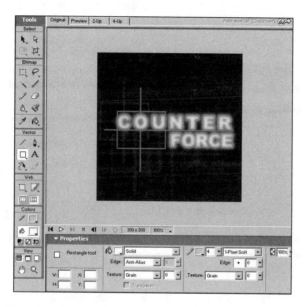

Figure 14.6.   The animation assets are in their layers and in place on the canvas.

Creating the Animation

With the assets in place, it is now time to create an animation that fades in over 11 frames. Also, the word has to fill with white as it comes into focus.

To create the animation effect, follow these steps:

1. Select the words and then choose Text, Convert to Paths. By converting the text to paths, you can now fill the letters with white while still leaving a green stroke around them. The letters also become editable art rather than text on the page.

2. Open the Frames panel. Select the first frame and then select Duplicate Frame from the Panel Options menu to open the Duplicate Frame dialog box. Enter **10** as the number of frames, and select After Current frame from the Insert new frames choices. You now have an 11-frame animation. The last frame will be the one that is in focus.

3. Select frame 1, and select the objects on the canvas. Open the Effects panel on the Property inspector, and select Blur, Gaussian Blur. Set the Blur value to 10. Click OK. Repeat this for frames 2 through 5, only set the blur values to 9, 8, 7, and 6 as you move through the frames.

4. Select frame 6. Select the words, and choose Modify, Ungroup. The letters become vector objects; if you look at the Layers panel, each letter is distributed to its own layer. With all of the letters selected, set the Fill to White and the Stroke to a 4-pixel Green (009933). Regroup the letters by pressing Ctrl-G (PC) or Command-G (Mac).

5. As mentioned in earlier chapters, one of the great rules of computer graphics is to let the software do the work. Rather than repeating the previous step for all the remaining frames, you can let Fireworks MX do the work for you. Open frame 7, select the words, and delete them. Do this for frames 8 through 11. Select frame 6, and select the words. Select Copy to Frames from the Frames Panel menu. When the Copy to Frames dialog box opens, set the range from 7 to 11. Click OK. The filled letters now appear in each frame.

Tip

There is another way to accomplish the sharing of static objects in Fireworks MX. Create a new layer and then move the object to the new layer using cut and paste. Double-click the folder beside the layer name, and select Share across frames in the Frame Options dialog box.

6. Select the gun sight and the words in frame 6, and apply a 5-pixel Gaussian Blur from the Effects menu in the Property inspector. Repeat this for the gun sights and words in frames 7 through 10, reducing the Gaussian Blur value by 1 until the value for the words in frame 10 is 1.

7. Click frame 1, and move the gun sight somewhere on the Stage. Repeat this for frames 2 through 9. By leaving the gun sight in place for frames 10 and 11, you end the blur animation with the sight in its final position and end in focus, on frame 11, with all of the assets in the final position. Your completed animation should resemble that shown in Figure 14.7.

A finished version of this animation—Counterforce.png—can be found in the Complete section of the Chapter 14 Exercise folder on the book web site.

As you may have noticed from the playback, the animation moves a bit too fast. Leave the file open, and you'll deal with a number of the animation controls in the next section.

Figure 14.7   The completed Counterforce animation.

The Fireworks MX Animation Controls

The capability to control an animation is important. Without this capability, you would not be able to set an animation's speed, or have an animation loop over and over. Fireworks MX contains four important tools for this purpose, shown in Figure 14.8.

These tools include:

- The Playback controls (sometimes referred to as the VCR controls)
- The Frame Delay controls
- Onion skinning
- Looping

Playback Controls

When building the Counterforce animation, you needed to be able to preview the animation to get a feel for the flow of the piece. To get a sense of flow, you would look at the animation and ask some questions such as:

- Does it play too fast?
- Is the movement of the objects smooth?
- Do the effects do what I originally intended, and what the storyboard called for?

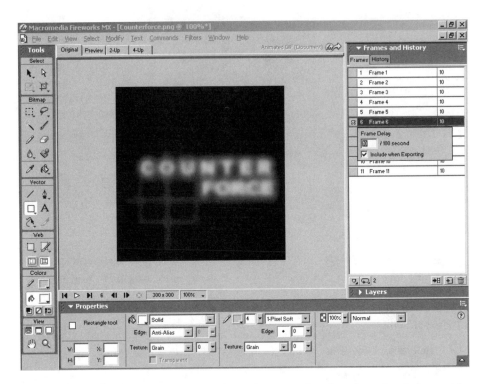

Figure 14.8   The animation controls in Fireworks MX are found on the main window and in the Frames panel.

The Playback controls, located at the bottom of the Document window, allow you to not only play the movie from start to finish, but to step through the animation, forwards and backwards, on a frame-by-frame basis.

When you click the Play button, the animation is played using the timing setting in the Frames panel. The default for Fireworks MX is 7/100 of a second. This can be changed and is discussed in the next section.

Finally, while the animation is playing, the Play button becomes a Stop button. You can stop the animation by clicking the button, or clicking anywhere in the Document window.

Frame Delay Controls

Unlike Flash MX or video editing software, Fireworks MX does not play animations at a fixed frame rate applied across the entire animation. For example, the default frame rate for Flash MX is 12 frames per second. This means each frame is visible onscreen for 1/12 of a second. Fireworks MX enables you to control how long each frame of the animation appears onscreen. For example, frame 1 could be visible for a 1/2 second, while frame 2 is visible for a full second.

Though this sounds great on the surface, understand the values used are nothing more than approximations. Eventually, the file is going to become an animated .gif. The timing will then be out of your hands and placed into those of the browser and the computer. Internet Explorer tends to play .gif animations faster than Navigator, and both play animated .gifs faster on faster computers.

To change the frame delay settings for the Counterforce animation, follow these steps:

1. Open the Frames panel, if it isn't already open.

2. Double-click the frame timing for the first frame. Frame timing is the number beside the frame name. A pop-up edit window, shown in Figure 14.8, opens with the frame delay settings. Enter **12** in the Frame Delay field. If you want this timing to be included in the animated .gif, keep the Include when Exporting check box selected. Set the frame delay for all of the frames to 12.

3. Play the animation. The gun sight moves more slowly than when you first viewed the animation. Try changing the delay to 5/100 of a second, or setting different rates for different frames.

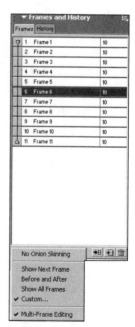

Onion Skinning

Your animation efforts usually involve working with a single frame, or moving between frames to review the location of an item that has moved. This is fine, but it is a rather crude method of testing. Onion skinning is an animation technique where very thin, nearly translucent, paper is used by a classical animator to show movement. By flipping through the sheets of paper, the animator sees the movement and how it affects the subsequent frames of the animation. By turning on the Onion Skinning feature in Fireworks MX, you get a precise view of the changes between frames and you can then edit individual or multiple frames.

The Onion Skinning button, as shown in Figure 14.9, is located in the lower left corner of the Frames panel. Clicking the button opens the Onion Skinning menu, also shown in Figure 14.9, which allows you to turn this feature on and off as well as selecting which

Figure 14.9
You can select a range of frames to onion skin using the Onion Skinning menu.

frames to view. When Onion Skinning is turned on, the current frame is shown at 100 percent opacity while the frames above or below the current frame are dimmed. When you click the Play button, Onion Skinning is temporarily turned off.

To use onion skinning, follow these steps:

1. With the Counterforce animation open, turn on the Onion Skinning feature from the Frames panel, and select Show Next Frame from the Onion Skinning menu. The current frame shows a down pointing arrow, and the frame below it shows an up pointing arrow. A line joins these arrows.

2. Click another frame, and the arrows move to the selected frame. Select Before and After from the choices in the Onion Skinning menu. The range of frames expands to three frames. Select Show All Frames, and the range selected includes every frame in the animation.

3. Select Custom from the Onion Skinning menu to open the Onion Skinning dialog box, shown in Figure 14.10. This dialog box gives you precise control over the number of frames to onion skin and their opacity. Enter **4** in the Show Before Current Frame area, and enter **3** in the Show After Current Frame area. The opacity settings determine the opacity of the frames above and below the selected frame. A value of 0 turns the frames invisible while a value of 100 turns off opacity. (The opacity settings don't affect the animation, but how the frames are seen when Onion Skinning is turned on.) Don't change the Opacity setting at this point.

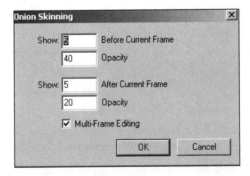

Figure 14.10   The Onion Skinning dialog box enables you to specify a range of frames to onion skin, and sets the opacity of the frames above and below the selected frame.

4. Click OK. Seven frames are now onion skinned in the Frames panel.

Note

The Onion Skinning feature asks you to select Multi-Frame Editing in both the Onion Skinning menu and the Onion Skinning dialog box. Selecting this feature enables you to select and edit objects on multiple frames of the animation. For example, you could select the gun sight in the Counterforce animation across all of the selected frames and then resize the object as a unit.

Looping

Looping is simple to understand. Do you want the animation to play forever or once? For example, if you had an animation of a spinning wheel, you would want it to spin forever. This is where you would want an animation to loop. On the other hand, with a Jack-in-the-box animation, you would probably only want to execute the animation once.

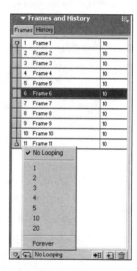

Figure 14.11
The Looping menu allows you to set how many times an animation plays.

To change the Looping settings for the Counterforce animation, follow these steps:

1. Click the Loop button at the bottom of the Frames panel to open the Looping menu shown in Figure 14.11.

2. In this menu, you can choose a specific number, or select Forever from the menu. Select 2. The menu disappears, and the number selected appears on the Frames panel next to the Looping button.

3. Play the animation. It plays twice.

4. Save the Counterforce animation and keep it open to use in the next section.

Tip

If you have a rollover button that triggers an animation, set the animation's looping to Forever. If you set the animation to loop once, you are playing with fire. It may not play, or you might even catch it in mid-play because different browsers handle preloaded .gif images in different ways.

Exporting a GIF Animation in Fireworks MX

Having completed the Counterforce animation, it needs to be exported to be playable in a browser. If it is to be played through a browser, it has to be exported as an animated .gif. If it is to be exported to Flash MX, you can simply save the file as .png file. If it is to be an Animated .gif, the file needs to be optimized for playback and then exported out of Fireworks MX as an animated .gif for placement in Dreamweaver MX. This section explores the creation of a .gif animation for browser playback.

Animation Optimization

The first step to optimizing animation is to set the looping options. You can then optimize the file to make it the smallest available for fast loading, and to reduce the wait time for the animation to load into the browser.

To optimize your animation, follow these steps:

Figure 14.12
The Optimize panel allows you to preflight an animation prior to export out of Fireworks MX.

1. With the Counterforce animation open, select Window, Optimize to open the Optimize panel shown in Figure 14.12. Alternately, you can press the F6 key, or open the Optimize panel, if it is visible in your panel group.

2. Select Animated Gif from the Settings pop-down menu. The various areas of the panel change to reflect your choice.

3. The quickest way to reduce file size is to reduce the number of colors in the image. This animation uses only three colors—black, green, and white. Select 4 from the Colors pop-down menu. The animation turns very ugly. If you use the Next Frame control in the VCR controls to click through the frames, you see the colors have totally washed out. This is because of the blur effect applied earlier. Set the number of colors to 64, and you see a significant improvement in image quality.

Tip

Many of the optimization decisions you make are subjective, not objective. We can guarantee one reader will agree with 64 colors, while another will disagree and insist on 128 colors. The technique of reducing colors is objective; the decision to use 64, 128, or 256 is subjective. Only experience will help you develop that all-important eye for what works for you and what doesn't.

Exporting an Animated GIF

Though most of the options for the animation, from frame rate to colors, can be set using the Frames and Optimize panels, the Export Preview dialog box puts all of the options in one place. The preview seen in the preview window is also more accurate than that shown on the canvas.

To export an animation using the Export Preview dialog box, follow these steps:

1. With the Counterforce animation open, select File, Export Preview to open the Export Preview dialog box. Click the Animation tab. The resulting window should resemble that shown in Figure 14.13.

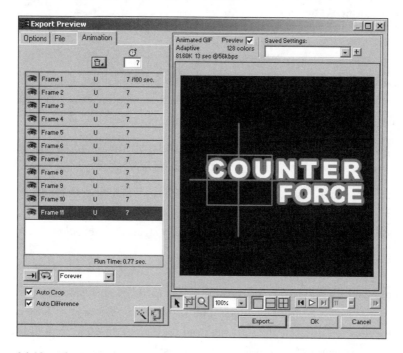

Figure 14.13   The Export Preview dialog box enables you to optimize the animation in one place rather than through the Optimize and Frames panels.

2. Click each frame of the animation, and you see the image for that frame in the preview window. You can play the animation by clicking the Play button in the lower right corner under the preview window.

3. Click each frame, and set the frame delay to **10** by entering the number in the Frame Delay field under the stopwatch icon at the top of the dialog box. If there are frames you choose not to export, click the View/Hide button beside the

frame. A frame is hidden when it isn't exported. When finished, click the Export button to open the Export dialog box.

4. Choose a target folder and name for your animation. Select HTML and Images from the Save as type pop-down menu, and select Export HTML file from the HTML pop-down menu. Click OK.

Note

You have a choice that is new to Fireworks MX. Do you do the optimization and so on using the Export Preview dialog box, or do you do it using the Optimize and Frames panels? If you choose the latter, click the Quick Export button and then select Dreamweaver, Export HTML. This launches the Export dialog box from step 4 without a stop in the Export Preview dialog box.

Animation Techniques in Fireworks MX

Now that you have the basics in place, you can create a few animations in Fireworks MX that unleash the power of the application.

Fireworks MX allows you to create a number of fascinating animations that can be posted directly to web sites or imported, intact, into Flash MX.

In this section, you use a tweening technique that uses graphic symbols and then sends the animation to Flash MX. This section focuses on fading objects in and out. You use an animation symbol to create a banner ad, and finally create an interesting reveal effect.

Tweening

Tweening, the process of letting the software fill in the changes between the start and end states of an object, is best done with Graphic symbols. For example, to have an object shrink requires you to create the start state and the end state—10 percent of the size—and then tell Fireworks MX, "You figure out the rest."

To add a tween, follow these steps:

1. Copy the Chapter 14 Exercise folder from the book web site to your desktop, if you haven't already done so. Open the Tweening.png file. You should see a big red shoe on the canvas. Click the shoe; the arrow you see in the lower left corner of the image tells you the shoe is an instance of a symbol in the Library.

2. Copy and paste the instance. The selected shoe on the canvas is the copy. Drag it off of the other instance, and leave it selected.

3. Click the Scale tool and then click/drag a corner handle to shrink the shoe. With the small shoe still selected, select Modify, Transform, Numeric Transform to open the Transform dialog box. Select Rotate from the pop-down list, and enter **270** in the text input area. The toe of the small shoe is now pointing to the bottom of the canvas. Click OK.

3. Move the small shoe to the center of the large shoe. Press the Shift key, and click the large shoe. With both instances selected, select Modify, Symbol, Tween Instances, or press Ctrl-Alt-Shift- T (PC) or Command-Option-Shift-T (Mac). This opens the Tween Instances dialog box, shown in Figure 14.14.

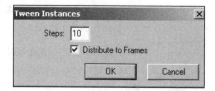

Figure 14.14   The number of steps and frames for an animation involving instances are set in the Tween Instances dialog box.

4. Enter **10** as the number of steps and then select Distribute To Frames. Click OK.

5. Open your Frames panel and notice you now have a ten-frame animation. Play the animation by clicking the Play control. The shoe rotates and shrinks.

You can edit and add to animations. For example, you can add the JCT logo to the animation, and have that small shoe continue to shrink while it moves off the canvas in the lower right corner.

To add a shoe animation, follow these steps:

1. Select the last frame of the animation. Press the Alt (PC) or Option (Mac) key and then drag a copy of the shoe instance to the lower right corner of the canvas.

2. Select the Scale tool, and reduce the copied shoe to as small as you can get it. Move the reduced shoe to a point just below the lower right corner of the canvas.

3. With the small shoe selected, Shift/click the shoe in the middle of the canvas. Tween these two instances over seven frames (Modify, Symbol, Tween Instances), and be sure to select Distribute To Frames in the dialog box. Play the animation.

4. Select frame 1 of the animation, and drag an instance of the Logo symbol from the Library onto the canvas. With the logo selected, select Copy to Frames from the Frames panel. Set the range from frame 2 to frame 20 in the Copy to Frames dialog box. Click OK.

5. Play the animation. The logo now appears in each frame.

You can also add to an animation in the middle of the animation. For example, you can have the word Shoes travel onto the canvas while the Shoe instance is moving off the canvas.

To add an animation, follow these steps:

1. Select frame 11. Select the Text tool, click the canvas once, and type the word **Shoes**. The text should be set in 36-point, Arial Bold.

2. Right-click (PC) or Control-click (Mac) on the word, and select Convert to Symbol from the context menu. The Convert to Symbol dialog box appears. Name the object and set its property to Graphic in the dialog box.

3. Move the instance of the word to a location just off of the left side of the canvas. With the instance still selected, create a copy of the instance and drag it to the middle of the canvas.

4. Shift-click both instances to select them and then tween the instance. Set the number of frames for the tween to 8.

5. Click OK and then play the animation. Save the file.

Playing Fireworks MX Animations in Flash MX

Fireworks MX integrates fully with Flash MX. You can export your vector drawings, animations, and button graphics to Flash MX with a single click of the mouse in Fireworks MX. This allows you the flexibility of designing in Fireworks MX, and using those designs in Flash. This flexibility comes in handy when you want to do bitmap and vector editing and effects.

To play your Fireworks MX animation in Flash MX, follow these steps:

1. With the shoe animation open in Fireworks MX, Click the Quick Export button, and select Macromedia Flash, Launch Macromedia Flash from the pop-down menu.

2. When Flash opens, select File, Import and then navigate to the shoe animation file. Select the file in the Import dialog Box and click Open to open the Fireworks Import PNG Settings dialog box shown in Figure 14.15.

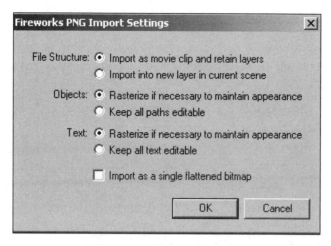

Figure 14.15   The Fireworks PNG Import Settings dialog box allows you to import your
animation directly into Flash MX as a movie clip.

3. Use the settings shown in Figure 14.15. Be sure to leave the Import as a single
   flattened bitmap option unchecked. Click OK.

   The movie clip is placed into frame 1 on the main timeline. If you open the Flash
   MX Library, you see two graphic symbols and a Fireworks Objects folder. The
   movie clip is in the folder.

Tip

Importing a Fireworks MX animation as a movie clip into Flash MX enables you to edit
the objects in the movie clip.

4. Open the Fireworks Objects folder in the Flash MX Library. Double-Click
   the movie clip in the folder. When the symbol opens, press Enter to play the
   animation.

Fading In and Out

Fading instances in and out is one of those effects that looks difficult to accomplish, but
is actually simple to create in Fireworks MX. Essentially, two instances of the same object
are placed in exactly the same position on the canvas. One instance has an opacity setting of 100 percent, and the other has an opacity setting of 0 percent. Where the invisible instance is located in the stacking order determines whether the effect is a fade in or
a fade out.

To create a fade, follow these steps:

1. Open Fade.png from the Fade folder of the Chapter 14 Exercise folder. The JCT mascot appears on the Stage. Click the mascot once, and notice that it is an instance of a symbol.

2. Select Edit, Clone to make an exact duplicate of the mascot on the canvas. Set the object's opacity to 0% on the Property inspector.

3. With the invisible instance selected, select Modify, Arrange, Send to back. By sending the invisible instance to a position behind the original, you are fading the mascot in. This means the animation will start with the invisible instance and then progress through the frames to the instance with 100 percent opacity.

4. Select both instances, and open the Tween Instances dialog box by choosing Modify, Symbol, Tween Instances. Set the Duration to 5 frames, and select Distribute to layers. Click OK.

5. Play the animation. The mascot fades up from 0 percent to 100 percent opacity. Stop the animation.

6. In the Frames panel, select the last frame of the animation. Select the instance, clone it, and set the clone's opacity to 100%.

7. Again, select both instances and tween them across five frames. Play the animation. The mascot fades in and then fades out.

8. You may encounter occasions where you decide a frame in the animation is redundant. For example, the last frame of the animation is exactly the same as the first frame. To remove the last frame—frame 13—select the frame in the Frames panel, and click the trash can icon in the lower right corner of the Frames panel. Play the animation.

9. The animation seems to zip through the frames. You need to have it hold on the frame where the instance is at 100 percent opacity. Select frame 7, and set the Frame Delay to 100/100 seconds.

10. Play the animation. The mascot fades in, holds at 100 percent opacity for one second, and fades out. Your final animation and Frames panel should resemble that shown in Figure 14.16.

Animation Symbols in Fireworks MX

Animation symbols are self-contained, reusable animations created in Fireworks MX. Though they have their uses, most developers prefer to animate by hand using instances, tweens, and the Frames panel. Still, they do offer a huge productivity boost for relatively uncomplicated animations.

Our Technical Editor, Dorian Nisinson, is an acknowledged Flash expert. One of her hard-core tutorials shows how to manipulate vector shapes using functions in Actionscript. The tutorial is called "V is for Vectory," and you use that title to demonstrate the use of animation symbols in Fireworks MX.

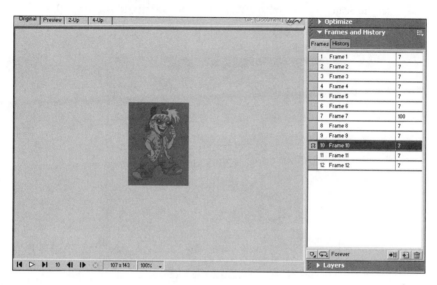

Figure 14.16   The mascot fades in and out, and holds for one second on frame 7 of the animation.

To use animation symbols, follow these steps:

1. Open a new Fireworks MX document, and set the size to 480 pixels wide by 60 pixels deep. These measurements are the standard size for a banner ad on the web. Set the background color to 000066 Blue.

2. Select the Text tool, click the canvas once, and enter **V is for Vectory**. Set the font to 48 point Times Roman Bold. Set the text color to 00FF33 Green. Select the word Vectory, and set the color to FFFFFF White.

3. To draw the viewer's attention to the word Vectory, you need to have it fade in. Because it is a part of a text block, that is going to be difficult to accomplish. The text, including the word Vectory, is one object. Select the text block with the Selection tool, and choose Text, Convert to Paths. This changes the text from an editable font to artwork.

4. Click the text once. All of the words are selected as one big block. Select Modify, Ungroup. Each letter of the text block looks like editable vectors. Select V is for, and choose Modify, Group. Deselect. Select the word Vectory and then group it as well. You now have two objects on the canvas.

5. Select Vectory. Choose Insert, Convert to Symbol to open the Symbols Properties dialog box. Name the symbol **Vectory**, and select Animation as its type. Click OK.

6. The Animate dialog box opens, shown in Figure 14.17. Set the number of frames to 5, set the Scale to amount to 125, and set the opacity to run from 0 to 100 (a fade in). Click OK.

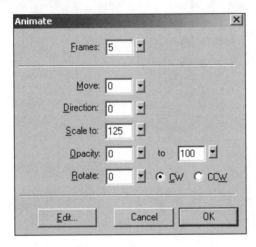

Figure 14.17   The Animate dialog box enables you to set a number of animation properties in one area.

7. An alert from Fireworks MX appears, stating the animation is longer than the number of frames in the image, and asking permission to add the frames. Click OK, and then play the animation.

8. The word fades in and grows, but the phrase "V is for" disappears. This is because it was not a part of the original animation symbol. Select frame 1 in the Frames panel, and select the phrase. Choose Copy to Frames from the panel options, and add it to all of the frames in the animation. Play the movie.

Using the Property Inspector to Control Animation Symbols

New to Fireworks MX is the capability to change many of the properties in the Animate dialog box, which appears when an animation symbol is created.

If you click the Vectory Animation symbol on the canvas, the Property inspector changes to offer the same categories as those shown In Figure 14.17. In fact, the Property inspector, shown in Figure 14.18, reflects the values you input into the Animate dialog box. This means you can change the duration of the animation, the opacity, rotation, and scaling properties right in the Fireworks MX interface.

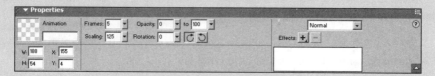

Figure 14.18   The Property inspector can be used to change the properties of an
animation symbol.

Another interesting feature is the capability to apply a LiveEffect to the animation. For example, if you were to apply the inner bevel effect—Effects, Bevel and Emboss, Inner Bevel—to the animation, the bevel is applied to the instances in each frame of the animation.

A Reveal Effect in Fireworks MX

Unlike Macromedia Director or video-editing software, there are no built-in transition effects in Fireworks MX. Here's how to build a reveal effect that gives the illusion of an object appearing out of a circle. It is accomplished by using the eraser in Fireworks MX.

To create a reveal effect, follow these steps:

1. Open the Reveal.png file in the Reveal folder of the Chapter 14 Exercise folder.

2. Select the Rectangle tool, and draw a rectangle that matches the canvas dimensions of 106 pixels wide by 142 pixels high. Fill the rectangle with 666666 Gray, and make sure there is no stroke.

3. Place a horizontal guide at the 70 pixel position on the ruler. Place a vertical guide at the 50 pixel mark of the ruler. The eraser won't work with a vector image, so select the rectangle and choose Modify, Flatten selection to turn it into a bitmap.

Tip

Use guides to set a common registration point for objects in multi-frame animations.

4. Open the Frames panel, and select Duplicate Frame from the panel options. Add nine frames. Click through the frames and notice the green guides appearing on every frame.

5. Select frame 2, and choose the Eraser tool. On the Property inspector, set the size to 10 pixels, the edge to 20 pixels, and the shape to round. Click once where the two guides intersect.

6. For the remaining frames, increase the size of the eraser by 20 pixels. Click at the intersection point and then select the next frame. Your eraser at frame 9 should be about 150 pixels in diameter.

7. Select frame 10. Select the rectangle and then delete it. Play the animation. Your animation should resemble that shown in Figure 14.19.

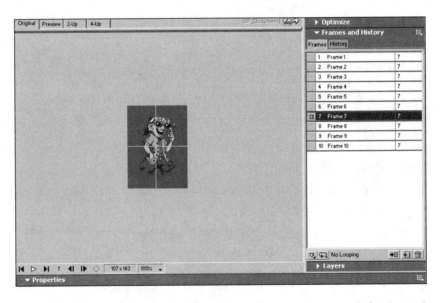

Figure 14.19   The use of a progressively large eraser allows you to create a rather interesting reveal effect in Fireworks MX.

Animation in FreeHand

Building an animation in FreeHand is a bit different than building animations in Flash MX and Fireworks MX. The objects to be animated are placed on their own layers, and the layers are subsequently exported as individual frames in the Flash MX .swf format for quick placement into Dreamweaver MX.

The process uses grouped objects, which are then subsequently assigned to individual layers using the Release to Layer Xtra.

Animating Text

In this exercise you use a text block and animate it across the page. Text animations are useful for animated logos as well as novelty items, such as flashing sale signs. There are as many uses for animated text as there are designers.

To create a text animation, follow these steps:

1. Open a new FreeHand document.

2. Select the Text tool, click the page once, and enter your name. Use 48 point Times New Roman Bold.

3. With the text selected, choose Text, Convert To Paths to turn each letter of your name into editable vectors. With the text still selected, choose Modify, Join to turn the vectors into a composite path. A composite path is an object composed of multiple paths.

4. Select the Direct Selection tool, click the object, and while the mouse button is down press the Option (PC) or Alt (Mac) key. Drag a copy of your name to its finished position to the right of the original image. Deselect.

5. Select both of the objects and then choose Xtras, Create, Blend. Copies of your name will run across the page from the original to the copy. With all of these copies, you can now animate them.

6. Select all of the objects on the page by choosing Edit, Select, All. Select Xtras, Animate, Release to Layers to open the Release to Layers dialog box, shown in Figure 14.20.

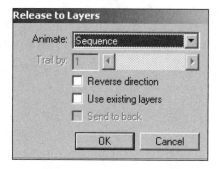

Figure 14.20   The FreeHand Animate Xtra controls how animations work in FreeHand.

7. Select Sequence from the Animate pop-down menu. Click OK. Open the Layers panel, and notice 25 layers have been added to the Layers panel.

8. Select File, Export to open the Export dialog box. Select Macromedia Flash (SWF) from the Save as type (PC) or Format (Mac) pop-up menu. Choose Open in External Application, and click the Browse button. When the Navigate to Valid Application dialog box opens, navigate to your FreeHand Application folder, and select the Macromedia Flash Player 6 application.

9. Click Open. When the dialog box closes, click the Save (PC) or Format (Mac) button. The Flash Player application launches, and your name moves across the screen.

FreeHand's Animate Xtra

The Xtra offers a lot of choices regarding how objects are released to layers. The choices in the Animate pop-down menu include:

- Sequence: Each object is released to a separate layer.

- Build: Creates a stacking effect. In the case of the name, one instance would be placed on layer 1. Layer 2 would contain a copy of the first object as well as the second object.

- Drop: Copies the objects to layers, but omits one from the sequence in each layer. If you select three objects, the second and third are placed on layer 1, the first and the third appear on layer 2, and the second and the third appear on layer 3.

- Trail: Select Trail if you want to specify how many layers comprise the animation. You can move the slider, or input a number directly into the Trail input box.

You also have three selection boxes at the bottom of the dialog box.

- Reverse Direction: The name moves from right to left.

- Use Existing Layers: Releases the objects to layers already created. This always starts with the current layer selected. If you leave it unchecked, the Xtra creates new layers.

- Send to back: Sends the selected objects to the back of the stacking order. For example, you may want to have the animation occur behind a static object.

Animating Objects

As you have discovered, FreeHand uses layers to create animation. When a file is exported as a .swf file, the layers in the FreeHand document are converted to the animation frames. This exercise demonstrates how to create a frame-by-frame animation using objects instead of text. You create an object that follows a circular path, and gives the illusion of random electrons bouncing around in space.

To create a frame by frame animation, follow these steps:

1. Open FreeHand. Select the Ellipse tool, and draw a circle that is 300 x 300 pixels. Don't fill the circle. This is the path the object will follow.

2. Draw another circle, 40 by 40 pixels in diameter. Fill it with a radial gradient by selecting Gradient from the pop-down list in the Fill panel and then clicking the Radial Gradient button.

3. In the View menu, deselect Preview to see the center point of the small circle. It will be used for accurate placement on the path. Drag the small circle to the top of the path, and align the center point of the circle with the path.

4. Press the Option (Mac) or Alt (PC) key and then click/drag a copy of the small circle to the bottom of the path. Align the center point. Repeat this two more times, placing copies of the circle at the 3 o'clock and 9 o'clock points on the path. You now have four circles on the path.

5. Place copies of the small circles between the four circles on the path. You should now have eight circles on the path, and the drawing should resemble that shown in Figure 14.21. When the drawing is finished, delete the big circle.

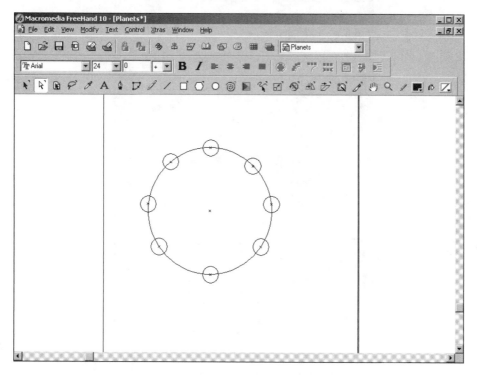

Figure 14.21   The objects are placed on the path and ready to be converted to an animation.

6. Select all of the objects on the page, and group them by pressing Ctrl-G (PC) or Command-G (Mac). Select Xtras, Animate, Release to Layers. When the Release to Layers dialog box opens, select Sequence and then click OK. Open the Layers panel, and notice each circle is now placed in its own layer.

Tip

For the Animate Xtra to work, all of the objects must be grouped as one object.

7. Select File, Export and then choose Macromedia Flash (SWF) from the popdown menu. Click the Set Up button in the Export Document dialog box to open the Movie Settings dialog box. The Movie Settings dialog box, shown in Figure 14.22, is divided into three distinct areas: Objects, Frames, and Publish. Objects is where you apply the compression settings, and either turn the text into vectors or retain the font. Frames allows you to determine how the animation plays, and at what speed. Publish sets the compatibility of the resulting .swf file with the Flash Player. (The current version of the Player is version 6. It will play a Flash 5 .swf.)

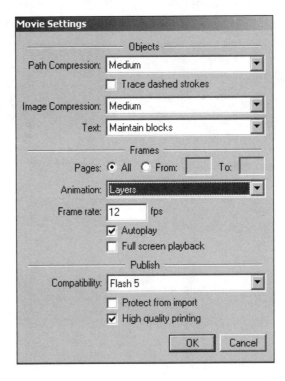

Figure 14.22   The Movie Settings dialog box lets you control a number of features, from compression to playback rate, prior to publishing the .swf.

8. Select Layers in the Animation pop-down menu, and set the frame rate to 12 frames per second. Click OK, name the file when you return to the Export dialog box, and click Save.

The Flash Player launches, and the electrons zip around the circle.

The Flash MX—FreeHand Connection

As you have seen, you can produce a Flash animation directly out of FreeHand. This is not terribly surprising, considering both applications are vector-based. A natural question at this point is, "Why use FreeHand if you have Flash MX?"

The answer depends on your preference. Yes, you can create animations in FreeHand, but the animation tools are less powerful. You have less control over the objects in each frame than you do in Flash MX, and there is no Actionscripting capability except for some basic actions that are accessible through the action area of the Navigation panel.

From our perspective, FreeHand is a great tool if you need to produce a rudimentary, down-and-dirty animation to test an idea, or for a quick banner ad. Other than that, from the perspective of a Flash developer, the capability to produce a .swf file in FreeHand is an interesting feature.

Also, don't forget that even though you can place the resulting .swf file into Flash MX, you can't edit it in Flash. What you produce is essentially what you get.

Where Flash and FreeHand really integrate is when the developer uses FreeHand for the development of the content and then uses Flash to animate the content. FreeHand objects are able to move seamlessly into Flash using methods ranging from importing to drag-and-drop with no degradation of image quality. Symbols created in FreeHand are also placed directly into Flash MX's Library when the FreeHand object is placed in Flash MX.

Animation in Dreamweaver MX

Animation in Dreamweaver MX is essentially code-driven. Using a form of HTML, called Dynamic HTML (DHTML), you can change the positioning of HTML elements on the page. Dreamweaver MX uses the content in layers for this purpose. Best of all, you don't have to be a coder to add an element of animation to the page.

Animation in Dreamweaver MX occurs on a timeline that closely resembles that of another Macromedia product, Director. By placing Dreamweaver layers on the timeline, you are able to control a layer's position, size, visibility, and position in the stacking order.

Before you dig into using a timeline in Dreamweaver MX, however, there is information about timelines you should keep in mind:

- They require a 4.0 browser or later.

- Any object being animated must be in a layer, or Dreamweaver MX will warn you about this in an alert box.

- The default frame rate is 15 frames per second. Don't for a minute believe you will achieve that kind of speed. The speed depends on the user's system. If they have a slower processor, or are running Photoshop, Premiere, FreeHand, and Fireworks at the same time they are viewing your animation through a browser, things really slow down.

Timeline Window

The Timelines window in Dreamweaver MX, shown in Figure 14.23, is simple to use. The current frame is always under the playback head, and you can drag the playback head back and forth to scrub through an animation. The frames move horizontally across the animation, and the content is in the numbered vertical channels. The animation bar is the line between the dots in a channel. The line indicates the duration of the animation, and the dots indicate keyframes in the animation.

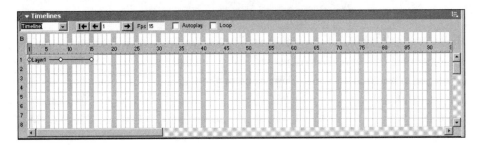

Figure 14.23   The Dreamweaver MX timeline closely resembles that of Macromedia Director.

Creating a Timeline Animation in Dreamweaver MX

In this exercise, you develop an animation of a shoe moving in a straight line across the page. You then learn how to move that same shoe in an arc.

To create a timeline animation in Dreamweaver MX, follow these steps:

1. Open the ShoeAnimate.htm file in the AnimationInDW folder of the Chapter 14 Exercise folder.

2. Click the Common tab on the Dreamweaver MX Insert panel, and click the Draw Layer button. Place the cursor on the page and then click/drag to draw the layer. When you release the mouse, the layer is indicated by a blank square with square selection handle at the top. There is also a layer icon placed in the upper left corner of the page, as shown in Figure 14.23. The Property inspector changes to the Layer inspector.

3. Click once inside the layer, and select Insert, Image. Locate the Shoe.png file located in the Graphics folders, and open it. The shoe appears in the layer. If you want to resize the shoe, click/drag a corner handle in to shrink, or out to enlarge.

4. Open the Dreamweaver MX timeline by selecting Window, Others, Timelines, or press Alt- F9 (PC) or Option-F9 (Mac). A blank timeline opens.

5. Select the layer with the shoe, and select Modify, Timeline, Add Object to Timeline. An animation bar, stretching across 15 frames, appears in channel 1.

6. To move the shoe across the page, select frame 15 in channel 1 of the timeline. Click/drag the Shoe layer to the right side of the page. When you release the mouse, a line appears on the page. This line shows the direction and distance of the movement between frame one and frame 15.

7. The three arrows at the top of the Timelines window serve as the playback controls. The arrow with the line to the left of it is the rewind button. Clicking the other two arrows moves you forward and backward, one frame at a time, through the animation. Clicking and holding the mouse button down on the forward or back arrow plays the animation at full speed. You can also drag the playback head across the animation to get a sense of the movement. Play your animation.

Moving the animation on an arc is not as complicated as it sounds. You need to add a keyframe to the timeline, and move the layer to its final position on the timeline. Dreamweaver MX then does all of the tweening.

To create an animation on an arc, follow these steps:

1. Right–click (PC) or Control-click (Mac) on frame 8 of the timeline. When the context menu opens, select Add Keyframe. A dot, indicating a keyframe, appears in frame 8.

2. Click the layer, and drag it down. The line on the page between the start and the end points of the animation will bend downwards, as shown in Figure 14.24. Play the animation.

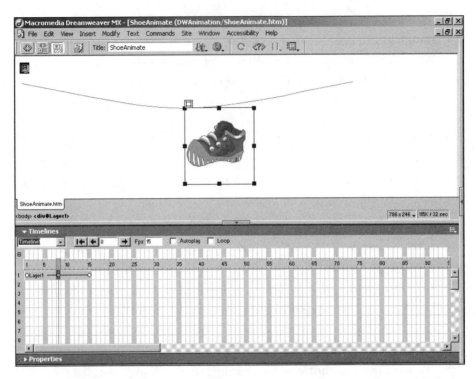

Figure 14.24   Adding keyframes to the timeline allows you to move away from straight linear movement across the page.

Recording Path Animation in Dreamweaver MX

When precision is essential, using the keyframes and timelines in Dreamweaver MX enables you to control smooth linear movement. There are occasions, though, where a more free-form approach is appropriate. Such occasions could include simulating a flight of a bumble bee.

To create an animation on a freeform path, follow these steps:

1. Open the FreeForm.htm file in you're the Chapter 14 Exercise folder. The shoe is already sitting in a layer. Select the layer.

2. Select Modify, Timeline, Record Path of Layer. If it isn't already open, the timeline appears.

3. Click the layer and then drag it around the screen. As it moves, a gray line follows the path of the movement. Release the mouse to stop recording when you are finished.

4. The timeline, shown in Figure 14.25, now changes to indicate the keyframes. Each dot represents a keyframe. The distance between them is related to how fast you dragged the object. The slower you drag, the closer the keyframes are to each other. The faster you drag, the farther apart they are. The path also changes to reflect the movement. Play the animation.

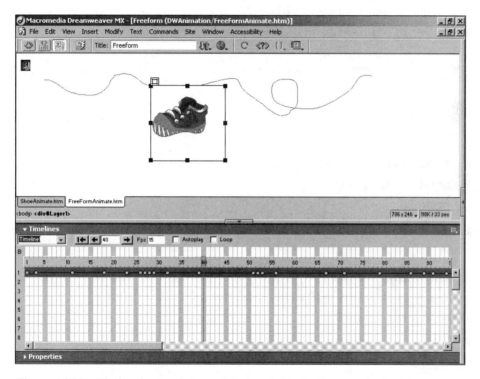

Figure 14.25   The layer's meandering path is recorded to the Dreamweaver MX timeline using the record path of Layer menu command.

Summary

This chapter looked at the animation tools available to you in Fireworks MX, Dreamweaver MX, and FreeHand.

We started off by discussing the importance of storyboarding an animation, and showed you a couple of techniques for accomplishing this.

We explained how a storyboard is a visual representation of the keyframes of an animation. It shows what will be seen, what sounds are heard, and what text, if any, appears onscreen. We also explained that a storyboard does is presents two different kinds of information: a description, through pictures and words, of the images in the sequence, and a description of the spatial aspect of the sequence, such as movement. The storyboard is the document the artists use to gather the information they need to do their jobs. It is also the document the client use to envision the animation.

We thoroughly reviewed the animation features of Fireworks MX, paying particular attention to the use of the Frames panel where animation occurs in Fireworks MX. We also walked you through how to optimize and export a .gif animation.

There was also a lot of technique presented. We demonstrated how to use Fireworks MX symbols to tween animation, and showed a number of special effects ranging from fading images and importing Fireworks animations into Flash MX to creating and using an animation symbol.

FreeHand also contains the capability to create animations using a frame-by-frame approach. We showed how to animate text and objects, and how create the Flash file from the FreeHand export menu.

The chapter finished with a demonstration of the timeline feature of Dreamweaver MX, and how to use the timeline to create linear, non-liner, and free-form motion for animation in Dreamweaver MX.

In the next chapter, "Creating Assets with Flash," we complete the animation overview by looking at how all of the applications in the MX Studio work together to create some incredible Flash MX movies.

Chapter 15

MX

fireworks flash freehand coldfusion dreamweaver fireworks
eamweaver fireworks flash freehand coldfusion dreamweave
coldfusion dreamweaver fireworks flash freehand coldfusio
freehand coldfusion dreamweaver fireworks flash freehan
works flash freehand coldfusion dreamweaver fireworks
eaver fireworks flash freehand coldfusion dreamwea

Creating Assets with Flash

If ever there were an application that simply oozes cool, Flash would be the hands-down winner. This application arrived in the web development community with subtlety of an earthquake, and we haven't-stopped feeling the aftershocks.

The first couple of versions of the application weren't all that spectacular, but the ability to create small, interactive animations on web pages or entire interactive web sites created in Flash was the hook. The introduction of Flash 3 shook the foundations of the web community to its core. We were suddenly able to code interactivity and animation using a primitive point-and-click interface, and some amazing work starting appearing around the world. Flash 4 refined the language—Actionscript—and turned Flash into a serious tool for site development, animation, and anything else that moved or responded to a user. In fact, Flash widened the scope of what was possible to accomplish in the very small space allowed by the web. Games and dynamic content started appearing, and the only limits were those imposed by the developer. Along the way, a new profession—Flash developer—arose.

Flash version 5 kicked out the jams and took interactive web site development to an entirely new level. Actionscript started to follow the JavaScript syntax by conforming to the ECMA-262 specification, which clearly sets out the rules and parameters of the JavaScript programming language. The result was the rise of yet another entirely new profession—Actionscript programmer. No longer was Flash only in the realm of the design community. The programmers could also roll up their sleeves and start producing some amazing applications and sites.

Before you dig into this chapter, you have to understand our intention is not to teach Flash, or promise to turn you into a Flash guru in 30 or so pages. Entire books have been written regarding Actionscript or designing in Flash, and there will most likely be a bunch more.

Note

Four recent titles from New Riders are excellent choices if you want to learn more about Flash. They are *Inside Flash MX* by Jody Keating and Fig Leaf Software, *Flash deConstruction* by Todd Purgason, *Drag, Slide, Fade: Flash Actionscript for Designers* by Brendan Dawes, and *Flash MX Magic* by Matthew David.

Our intention is practical, not artistic. We are going to show you a number of techniques regarding how to create assets in Flash MX, FreeHand, and Fireworks MX, turn them into a Flash animation, and then insert the animation asset into a Dreamweaver MX page. This may sound rather mundane, but there are a huge number of sites out there where the developer either forgot the information was moving through the Internet, used the wrong tool for the wrong job, or simply wanted to show off. The result, in the majority of these cases, is a site that can take up to two minutes to load into a browser. In today's Internet environment, two minutes is equivalent to an eternity. Among professional Flash designers, the benchmark for having something other than a pre-loader onscreen is no more than 15 seconds. Any longer, and these pros will strip the Flash animation down to its electrons to meet the 15-second limit. In fact, the animation we initially create is bloated. This will allow us to show you how to toss some of the data ballast overboard as we optimize a Flash animation for web playback.

Note

Our technical editor, Dorian Nisinson, has a practical measure of preload time. Load the file on the web, open the file on a computer that matches your target platform, and take a deep breath. If you pass out or turn blue before the page loads, you have a problem.

The Storyboard

A Flash animation usually doesn't start in Flash. The use of the word *animation* should tell you the process starts with a brainstorming session and then moves onto paper in the form of storyboards. In the case of our Flash animation, we needed something that would introduce the Shoes section. Many ideas were bounced around, but we kept coming back to a playful treatment of the logo.

"Wouldn't it be cool," we thought, "if the word "Shoes" is simply sitting in place. Then this giant running shoe drops out of the top of the animation and squashes the word. The word springs up and bounces off the top of the Stage before it settles into its final position."

At this point, after consensus is reached, you have to deal with the inevitable: "So what does it look like, and how do we explain it to the client?" A storyboard is the answer.

In this instance, a Flash storyboard is fundamentally different from the site storyboard mentioned in Chapter 4, "Testing Your Ideas with Site Models." A Flash storyboard is a visual representation of everything that is planned for a scene or movie. It shows what images will be seen and when they will be seen, and illustrates any text or audio that might be involved. For the money-is-no-object budgets, storyboards can be extremely detailed to reflect the complexity of the project. In this case, they are also a huge asset in the planning of the project. They can also be simple, involving stick characters drawn on a sheet of paper pulled out of a laser or ink jet printer. In either case, a storyboard provides everyone on the team, including the client, with a common hard copy point of reference. Hard copy is important because verbalizing a concept inevitably results in miscommunication—everyone forms a different mental picture of the project. Review our brainstorm at the start of this section. Now open the Finalshoes.swf file in the Completed folder in the Chapter 15 Exercise folder on the book web site. Was what you saw in your mind even close to what you just saw on your screen?

Apart from the previous example, there are a number of valid reasons for producing a storyboard:

- A storyboard points out flaws in the structure of your story. If the storyboard doesn't look right, you can bet your Flash animation will be less than compelling.

- You can isolate flaws in the visuals. We discovered the word Shoes stayed rigid, instead of compressing when the shoe hit it. When something soft is struck a blow, it tends to compress. We saw this mistake in our storyboard and made the change.

- You can see the "big picture." Novice Flash developers inevitably focus on bits and pieces of an animation, and rarely focus on the whole animation.

- Problems discovered at this stage are much less expensive to fix than problems found later down the road. Which costs less? Erasing and redrawing a shirt that falls in the Shoes section as a shoe, or spending an hour replacing the shirt with a shoe and then reanimating the shoe? We once saw a spinning globe (in the early days of Flash) where Akron, Ohio was located at the opposite end of the state. It cost somebody a few hours of billable time to fix that one, and it wasn't the client who paid the bill.

- If it is a simple animation such as ours, you don't need to spend an inordinate amount of time on this phase. You don't have to be a professional artist to produce a storyboard. In fact, one of the authors does them with stick people. All you need is a good idea.

Setting the Stage in Flash MX

The design calls for the Flash animation to sit in an enclosed area of the page. Obviously, producing a Flash animation larger than this would be a waste of time, and would present more problems than solutions. The questions here are: What is the size of the area that will hold the Flash movie, and what color will it be? If you look at the page shown in Figure 15.1, you notice there is a placeholder for the Flash movie. Follow these steps to learn the answers to these questions.

1. Copy the Chapter 15 Exercise folder to your desktop. Open ShoesPage.png, and select the placeholder for the Flash animation. The width and height for the placeholder are located in the bottom-left corner of the Property inspector, as shown in Figure 15.1.

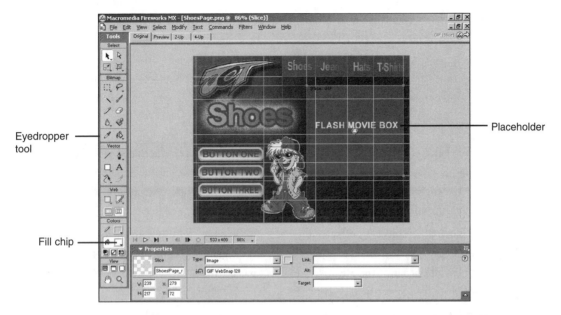

Eyedropper tool

Fill chip

Placeholder

Figure 15.1 The Property inspector gives you the exact dimensions of the Flash placeholder. The width and height are in the Flash movie.

2. The background color of the placeholder doesn't fit the overall design. The decision is to use a color from the blue in the C of the logo at the top of the page. Select the Eyedropper tool from the Tools panel, and click the blue part of the logo. Click the fill chip at the bottom of the Tools panel. The color swatch appears in the pop-down palette as well as the hexadecimal value of 0000C8. Note this color. Close the image, and quit Fireworks.

3. Open Flash. When a new movie opens, the Stage size defaults to 550 pixels wide by 400 high. To set the Stage to the required size, click the Size button in the Property inspector to open the Document Properties window. Set the width to 96 pixels and the height to 157 pixels. Leave the frame rate at 12 fps, and set the background color to white. Click OK. If the Stage seems too small, select the Magnifying Glass tool from the Tools palette and click once on the Stage.

Setting a Custom Background in Flash MX

As you may have noticed, the color you wanted from Fireworks is not available in the Flash palette. This is not as big an issue as it may first appear. Most developers simply leave the Stage color as the default color in Flash and then create a custom background using a colored rectangle the same size as the Stage.

There is another reason for creating the background rectangle. At its heart, Flash is an animation application, and sometimes you might want to distract a viewer while something changes elsewhere on the Stage. In this case, you could change the Stage color, or apply an effect that is quite striking. This inevitably draws the viewer's attention away from the other change that is occurring elsewhere onscreen.

To create the background rectangle, follow these steps:

1. Select the Rectangle tool from the Tools panel, draw a rectangle that covers the Stage, and then select it. Don't be afraid to make it larger than the Stage. With the rectangle selected, set the width and height in the Property inspector to match the width and height of the Stage. Press Enter (PC) or Return (Mac).

2. To ensure the object is perfectly aligned with the Stage, set the X and Y location in the Property inspector to equal 0. This step aligns the graphic perfectly to the upper-left corner of the Stage. If the object has a stroke, set the Stroke to None in the Property inspector, and set the fill to the color chosen from the logo.

3. With the rectangle still selected, select Insert, Convert To Symbol, or press F8 (Mac and PC) to open the Symbol Properties dialog box. This has the same effect as converting artwork to a symbol in Fireworks. The object on the Stage is now an instance of the original object residing in the Flash MX Library.

4. Name the symbol **Background** and then click the Graphic radio button in the Symbol Properties dialog box. Click OK. Double-click the Layer tab, and name the layer **Background**. Your Stage should resemble that shown in Figure 15.2. Save the Flash MX file, and quit the application. It is time to create the objects for the movie.

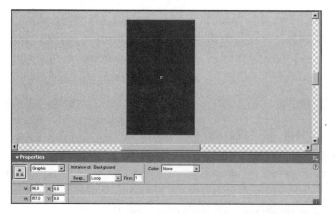

Figure 15.2   The Stage is set. The size of both the Stage and the background have been completed, the object has been turned into a symbol named Background, and the first layer has been given a name.

Creating and Assembling the Flash MX Assets

When visiting New York City a few years ago, one of the authors had the pleasure of attending a small presentation by Hillman Curtis to the New York Macromedia Users Group. One thing Hillman said really stayed with the author. "When you are working with Flash," said Hillman, "always pay attention to the pipe." By this, he meant always pay attention to the bandwidth of the average user. By paying attention to the pipe, you quickly learn to become a bit paranoid regarding everything in your Flash animation. *Everything.* Flash is a web animation application. Fireworks is a web imaging application. Freehand is a vector drawing application. Use the three together, and you have an unbeatable combination. That may be true, but Hillman's admonition, "Pay attention to the pipe," should always be there when working with Flash MX.

This is why it is so important to pay careful attention to artwork created in Flash, or artwork imported into Flash MX from Fireworks MX or FreeHand. The size of the file and its format will have a profound effect on the download time in Flash MX when being viewed through a browser. It makes sense, therefore, to carefully prepare and optimize the images in the originating application before placing them into Flash MX.

Preparing Fireworks MX Images for Flash MX

Fireworks MX images can be composed of combinations of vectors and bitmaps. It is the bitmap that concerns us here. Why? Flash hates bitmaps. Bitmaps clog the pipe, and add bandwidth and download time. Flash converts a bitmap to vectors, but the result, in many cases, is serious image degradation or a file larger than the original. When it comes to bitmaps in Flash, the fewer the better—and the smaller they are, the better they are.

Follow these steps to prepare our mascot for importation into Flash.

1. Open Mascot.png in your Chapter 15 Exercise folder on the book web site, select the image, and note the image size in the Fireworks MX Property inspector. The image is larger than the Flash Stage. Not only that, but there is a white background that doesn't match the Flash background color, and there is no drop shadow behind the little mascot guy. We'll deal with each issue in the order presented.

   A nasty feature of Fireworks MX is if you shrink the canvas smaller than the content on the canvas, that content will get trimmed. This happens even if you scale down the image after the reduction of the canvas size. Here's how to get around this:

2. With the mascot selected, cut the image. Using the Property inspector, set the canvas to the measurements of the Flash Stage, and click OK. Paste the mascot from the clipboard onto the canvas, and leave him selected. He is quite a bit larger than the canvas. Select Modify, Transform, Numeric Transform, or use Control-Shift-T (PC) or Command-Shift-T (Mac). This opens the Numeric Transform dialog box, as shown in Figure 15.3. Set the Scale percentage to 30%, and make sure Scale Attributes and Constrain Proportions are selected.

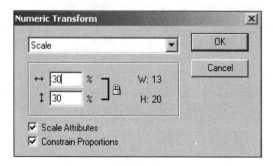

Figure 15.3   Doing it by the numbers in Fireworks ensures accuracy.

3. Move the mascot to the middle of the right side of the canvas, and apply a drop shadow using the Effects feature of the Property inspector. Note the wasted space.

4. Move the mascot to the upper-right corner of the canvas. Select the Crop tool and then click-drag around the mascot. Use the handles, shown in Figure 15.4, to adjust the crop. When you are satisfied, press Return (Mac) or Enter (PC).

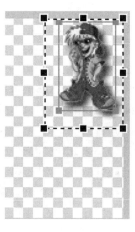

Figure 15.4   Applying a crop in Fireworks is extremely easy to accomplish.

5. Click the canvas and then set the Canvas color to Transparent in the Property inspector. Save the image.

Note

The purpose of the previous exercise was to introduce you to the pitfalls of canvas resizing, scaling by the numbers, and applying a LiveEffect—in this case, a drop shadow. There is, of course, a much easier way.

Select the mascot with the Subselection tool, and scale him to 40%. Cut him out of the image, close the image, and don't save the changes.

Open a new Fireworks document and then set the canvas size to 96 pixels wide by 157 pixels high. Fireworks always sizes a new document to match that of any content sitting on the clipboard. Select Transparent for the background, and click OK. Paste the image on the clipboard into the new canvas. Apply the drop shadow, and save the image.

Preparing a 32-Bit PNG for Export to Flash

The objective of this section is to get the image into Flash while still maintaining the transparent background. This should tell you the number of the formats available are limited. A .jpg will flatten the image and result in a white background. A transparent .gif will result in a white edge around the shadow. Both choices are inappropriate.

To place an image into a transparent background in Flash MX, you need a 32-bit image. A 32-bit image is simply a color image with a built-in alpha channel. Your two choices in Fireworks are TIFF 32 and PNG 32. Because Flash doesn't work with TIFF images, your choice is made for you.

To prepare a 32-bit PNG image for placement in Flash MX, follow these steps:

1. Select File, Export Preview, or press Control-Shift-X (PC) or Command-Shift-X (Mac) to open the Export Preview dialog box, as seen in Figure 15.5. Note the size of the file and the download time for a 56K modem. These are key bits of information.

2. Select PNG 32 from the Format pop-down menu, and click Export to open the Export dialog box.

3. Select Images Only from the Save As pop-down menu, click OK, and quit Fireworks.

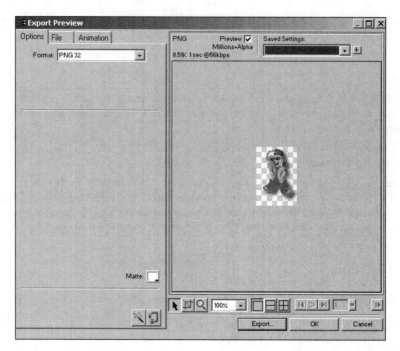

Figure 15.5   The export format for the image is set in the Export Preview dialog box.

Preparing a Transparent GIF for Flash MX

The shoe that will squash the words is a great candidate for conversion to a transparent GIF image. One reason for this is that it does not contain any sort of gradient effect on the edges of the shoe, such as glow or a drop shadow. Another reason is there are a limited number of colors in the image; by exporting to a limited palette, you have the effect of reducing the size of the file.

To create a transparent GIF, follow these steps:

1. Open the Shoe.png image in Fireworks MX. Select File, Export Preview to open the Export Preview dialog box, as shown in Figure 15.6.

2. Set the Format option to GIF, and the Palette option to WebSnap Adaptive. Select the eyedropper with the "+" sign in the Transparency area of the Export Preview dialog box, and click the white background. The background disappears. Click the Export button to open the Export dialog box. Name the image, click the Save button, and quit Fireworks MX.

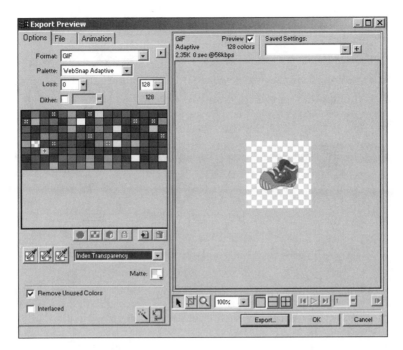

Figure 15.6   If an object has no gradient or feathered edge, consider the use of a transparent GIF when preparing for export to Flash MX.

Again, keeping an eye on the pipe is paramount. The image carries very little file size, thus minimizing the demand upon bandwidth.

Importing into Flash

Flash can import a number of formats, such as GIF, PNG, JPG, and Freehand 10 files. In previous versions of Flash, the importing of a 32-bit PNG file was a bit convoluted. It involved a separate Import dialog box and a long list of choices. No longer. The convoluted dialog box is reserved only for multilayer PNG images.

To import images with transparency into Flash MX, follow these steps:

1. Open your Flash animation, which contains nothing more than a symbol covering the Stage. Open the Library by selecting Window, Library, or press F11. When the Library opens, select New Symbol from the pop-down menu. Name the symbol **Mascot**, and select Graphic as its property.

2. Select File, Import, and navigate to the Mascot.png file you just created. Select it, click Add, and click OK (Mac) or Open (PC). The mascot appears on the Stage as a Flash symbol.

There are a number of other ways to import Fireworks MX images into Flash MX. You can select an image, copy it, open Flash, and paste the image into Flash. Another method is to select the image, click the Quick Export button, select Flash, and select Copy from the pop-down menu as shown in Figure 15.7. Our favorite way is to simply drag the image from Fireworks MX and drop it into Flash MX.

Figure 15.7   The Quick Export button is a new feature of Fireworks MX that allows you to export your images to variety of applications using a single click.

3. Import the transparent GIF of the shoe as a new graphic symbol. Create another symbol named **Shoe Words**. Enter the word **Shoes**. Set the font to 30-point Helvetica Bold, and set the color of the text to white. Save your work.

Preparing FreeHand Images for Flash MX

Flash uses vectors to create the objects seen on the Stage. The neat thing about vectors is they inevitably result in very small file sizes because vectors are simply mathematically described shapes (Bezier curves) with a fill color. Rather than mapping each pixel, which bulks up file size, the computer's processor simply does what it does best—crunch numbers—and then toss in a color. Those numbers result from the curve calculation between the nodes in a vector drawing. By keeping the nodes to an absolute minimum, the result is a smaller, more efficient image. Although this is an overly simplistic description of vector artwork, it does tend to illustrate the serious difference in file size between a bitmap image from Fireworks and a similar image from Macromedia FreeHand.

For our logo animation to work, an image exported from Fireworks would actually be counterproductive. The resulting file would be a bitmap that adds unnecessary overhead to the Flash project. If you inspect the properties of the Logo.png file located in the Chapter 15 Exercise folder on the book web site, you see the file is 64KB. In this case, we have included the Freehand drawing of the logo, Logo.fh10, in the Exercise folder. It weighs in at 24KB, a saving of 40KB or a saving in file size of just over 60 percent. This is significant.

This is why we included a FreeHand document in this exercise. Although we could have described how to do the animation using a Fireworks image, we kept coming back to the pipe. Yes, the animation would have worked, but it would have been simply yet another bloated Flash presentation. When it comes to Flash, using the right tool for the job takes precedence over all other requirements. In this case, a vector application has to be used.

Preparing the Logo for Flash MX

The introduction of symbols in FreeHand 9 solidified the Flash to FreeHand connection. A FreeHand symbol and a Flash symbol are virtually identical.

To prepare FreeHand symbols for export into Flash MX, follow these steps:

1. Open the Logo.fh in FreeHand. Note the FreeHand page size is smaller than the size of the Flash page. Again, the pipe comes into play. It is standard operating procedure for Flash developers to match the size of their FreeHand objects to the size of the Flash Stage…or smaller.

2. Choose Window, Library to open the Symbol panel. Select the gradient object by clicking the black stroke around the gradient, and drag the selected object to the bottom of the Library panel. Repeat this for the remaining three objects—JT, C, and the white O. After they are in the Library, double-click each symbol and rename them. Your Library should resemble Figure 15.8.

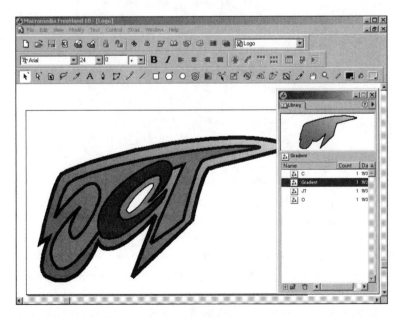

Figure 15.8   If everything is a symbol in Flash, it makes sense to import symbols from FreeHand into Flash.

Tip

An alternate method is to select the object and then select Modify, Symbol, Convert To.

Note

FreeHand symbols reside in the Library. The great advantage to using FreeHand 10 is that symbols can be edited. If the image is eventually destined for Fireworks MX, the symbol will move to Fireworks MX. Unfortunately, moving Fireworks MX symbols into FreeHand is not an option.

3. Open your Flash movie, and create a new graphic symbol named **Logo**. Select File, Import or press Ctrl-R (PC) or Command-R (Mac) to open the Import dialog box. Navigate to the folder containing the FreeHand logo, select the file, and click Open to display the FreeHand Import dialog box, as shown in Figure 15.9. Click OK.

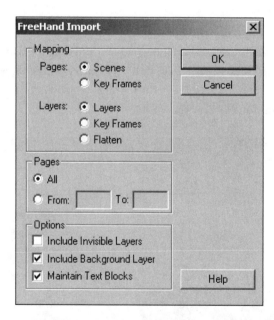

Figure 15.9   The FreeHand Import dialog box enables you to import everything from objects to pages created in FreeHand.

4. The Stage suddenly receives new layers, and if you open the Library panel by pressing Control-L (PC) or Command-L (Mac), there are new symbols. These objects—the symbols—were all created in FreeHand and moved seamlessly into Flash. To reduce the clutter in the Library, create a folder in the Library to hold

the logo art and symbols, and another folder to hold the art imported in with the shoe and the mascot. Save the file by selecting File, Save As. Name the file, and save it to the Chapter 15 Exercise folder on your desktop.

Preparing a Flash Animation

When working with an animation in Flash, it is best not to concentrate on the finished product. Look instead at the animation as a series of discrete units. In the case of our animation, the units are as follows:

- Elements that aren't animated, such as background, logo, and mascot.
- The shoe squashing the words.
- The shoe fading in and out.
- The two bitmaps—mascot and shoe—that may slow the animation. To ensure everything goes smoothly, a simple preloader ensures the content has been loaded before the animation starts.
- Animation that should play only once. This requires a Stop action on the last frame.

By looking at the animation in this manner, you cannot only simplify the assembly process, but you can also easily identify the number layers needed, as well as their position in the layering order.

Preparing the Stage

You are dealing here with the elements that don't move. You are also making room for the actions and the preloader. If an element is placed on the Stage and doesn't move, it simply needs to last for the duration of the animation and should be locked in place. In this way, these non-animated objects—the rectangle, the logo, the mascot—on the Stage don't get in the way, or are inadvertently moved out of position.

To prepare the Stage for animation, follow these steps:

1. Add two new layers to the top of the timeline by clicking the Insert Layer button. Name the top one **Labels** and the one under it **Actions**. Creating separate Labels and Actions layers is a common practice among Flash developers. In this manner, any actions that control the frame are accessible, and if the playback head is sent to a different location on the timeline, it moves to a frame with a name label

rather than a frame number. The reason for this is Flash movies do change as they are being created. Frames are added and subtracted. By going to a labeled frame, you avoid the risk of having serious problems later on in the process when a frame is added to the Flash MX movie.

For example, a picture of your daughter appears in place of the picture of your son. The image of the daughter was in frame 5. A frame is added in frame 4, meaning your daughter's image is now residing in frame 6. The image of your son is added in frame 5. Now you have to search through all of the Actionscript code that points to frame 5 and then change it to frame 6. This is tedious. If the Actionscript code points to a frame named Daughter, all you have to do is to move the marker to the appropriate frame.

2. Add four new layers above the Background layer and name them **Words**, **Logo**, **Mascot**, and **Shoe**. Make sure they are below the Actions layer. When you finish, your timeline should resemble Figure 15.10.

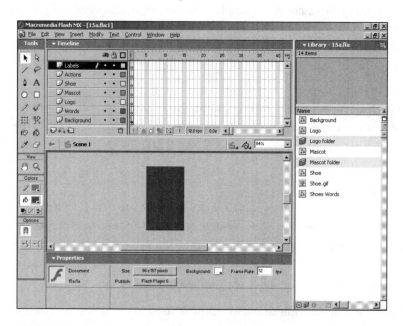

Figure 15.10   The layers in the animation are set up and ready to go. Note also how the symbols in the Library are accessible. Use file folders in the Library to reduce clutter.

3. Click in frame 30 of the Labels layer, and drag down to the bottom layer. Lines of frames are selected. Select Insert, Frame to set the duration of the animation to 30 frames.

4. Select frame 1 of the Mascot layer, and drag an instance of the mascot onto the Stage. Repeat this for the logo, the words, and the shoe, being sure to put each object in its respective layer. Move the objects to the positions shown in Figure 15.11.

Figure 15.11   The objects are in place, and the instances that don't move are locked into place. This ensures you don't accidentally move them.

4. Select the Background layer, and click the dot under the Lock icon to lock the layer in place. Repeat this for the Logo and Mascot layers.

Animating an Instance

To animate or manipulate an object on the Stage in Flash, you have to use a tween. A tween is all the steps between the start of the change and the end of the change, such as a movement or color change. The majority of the objects that you will tween are instances of symbols on the Stage.

To animate an instance in Flash MX, follow these steps:

1. Add keyframes in frames 3, 10, and 15 of the Shoe layer. Select the keyframe in frame 3. The shoe is selected on the Stage.

2. Select Modify, Transform, Free Transform to enable you to rotate the shoe, and then click the handle in the upper-left corner of the shoe. The cursor changes to the rotate cursor. If the cursor doesn't change to the rotate cursor, move the mouse until it does. When you see the rotate cursor, drag the shoe until the toe

is pointing upward. Deselect and select the shoe again, and then move it closer to the right edge of the Stage.

3. Select the keyframe in frame 10. Move the shoe until the toe of the shoe is touching the left edge of the Stage, and the sole of the shoe is resting on the bottom of the Stage.

4. Select the keyframe in frame 15, and select Modify, Transform, Scale, and Rotate to precisely scale an object using scale values. Alternately, you can press Ctrl-Alt-5 (PC) or Command-Option-5 (Mac). Set the scale value to 25%, and click OK.

5. Move the shoe to a point above the words. Right-click (PC) or Ctrl-click (Mac) anywhere between the keyframes in frames 3 and 10 of the Shoe layer, and select Motion Tween from the context menu. Your Stage and timeline should resemble that shown in Figure 15.12.

Figure 15.12   The shoe is ready to squash the words. Motion tweens are indicated by the arrows between the keyframes.

Tip

There are three other ways to insert a keyframe. Click frame 5 and press F6. If you own a Mac, you can also press the mouse button over frame 5 and keep it down. A context menu for the frame appears, and one of the choices in the resulting context menu is Insert Keyframe. Or you can right-click (PC) or Control-click (Mac) frame 5, and select Keyframe from the context menu.

A keyframe is any frame in which the object in the frame may change over time. For example, if an object is going to move from right to left over five frames, insert keyframes at frames one and five. A keyframe is easy to identify on the timeline: It is the solid dot in the frame.

6. Move the playback head until it is over the frame where the shoe touches the words. Insert a keyframe in the Words layer. Insert another keyframe where the shoe covers the word, and another where the shoe is no longer touching the words.

7. Select the first keyframe, select Modify, Free Transform, and drag a handle downward to start the squashing of the word.

8. Select the next keyframe to the right on the timeline and then drag down the handle until the word looks flat. Deselect the keyframe. Insert motion tweens between the keyframes in the Words layer.

9. You can test your work at this point by dragging the playback head to frame 1, and then pressing the Enter (PC) or Return (Mac) key. The shoe should step on the word and flatten it; then, as the shoe shrinks, the word bounces back. To have it bounce more, add keyframes to frames 20 and 25 of the Words layer. Select the instance of the word in frame 20, move it to the top of the Stage, scale it down, and give it a rotate.

10. Add motion tweens between the keyframes on either side of frames 15 and 20, as well as between 20 and 25.

11. Play the animation by pressing the Enter (PC) or Return (Mac) key. The words appear to spring out of place when the shoe leaves them, hit the top of the Stage, and drop back into position. Your timeline should now resemble that shown in Figure 15.13. Save the file to keep your changes.

Figure 15.13   The word "Shoes" has sprung out of position, as indicated by the keyframes in frame 13, 20, and 25 of the Words layer.

Creating Fades in Flash

The next part of the animation that needs to be created is the fading out and back in while the word bounces around the Stage. Having the object's opacity rise from 0% to 100% between frames 15 and 25 is how this is accomplished. When an object is transparent in Flash, it is said to have an alpha of 0. As objects become less transparent, their alpha value increases. The maximum value of 100 means no transparency is applied.

To create an alpha tween, follow these steps:

1. Insert a keyframe in frames 20 and 25 of the Shoe layer. Click the shoe in frame 20. Choose Color, Alpha from the Color pop-down menu on the Property inspector to change the color and alpha properties of the object. If you don't see Color on the Property inspector, click the Direct Selection tool in the toolbox.

2. Move the Alpha slider in the Alpha Amount box to 2%, or input the number into the Alpha Amount input box. The image fades out. Add motion tweens between frames 15 and 20 and between 20 and 25. If you move the playback head over the frames, the shoe appears to fade out and then back in. Save your file.

Tip

Alpha is one of those cool techniques that should be used sparingly. This technique slows down an animation because an alpha effect applied to a symbol instance will place an extra demand upon the user's processor. Keep an eye on the pipe. Another use for alpha is as a transition between scenes in a Flash movie—or even between Flash movies.

Adding Actions to Control Animation

Actionscript is the programming language for Flash. The language is robust, and a number of excellent books, referred to earlier in the chapter, have been written regarding the language and its uses. Obviously, a detailed discussion of the language is beyond the scope of this book. Instead, we explain some of the broader concepts behind what you are doing.

In very simple terms, actions control, for example, what occurs onscreen when the playback head moves into a frame. This is called a frame action. When objects are clicked onscreen and something happens, these are regarded as object actions. Actions are triggered by the fundamental truth of Actionscript: An action cannot be triggered unless there is an event. In the case of a Stop action, the event is the playback head leaving the frame to which the action is attached. When the playback head leaves the frame, the event is stopped on that frame. If we were to use the startDrag action, when the user clicks on the object and moves the mouse, the mouse movement event would trigger the action. The event is not the click, but rather the movement of the mouse while the button is depressed.

The Actions Panel

If you were to test the movie created so far, it would keep replaying. An animation that plays over and over is said to be a loop; however, we don't need that. The playback head should stop at frame 30, and stay there. The way to accomplish this is through the use of Actionscript.

To add an action to a frame, follow these steps:

1. Insert a keyframe on frame 30 of the Actions layer. If there is no keyframe, you won't be able to assign an action. Right-click (PC) or Control-click (Mac) the keyframe and then select Actions from the context menu to open the Actionscript Editor, as shown in Figure 15.14.

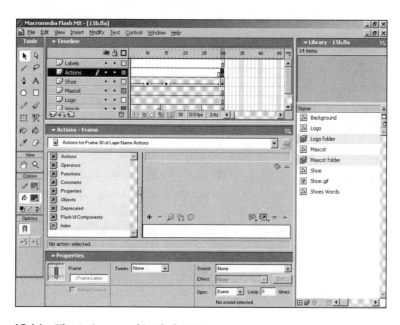

Figure 15.14   The Actions panel in Flash MX.

2. Click once on the Actions book. When it opens, click the Movie Actions book. Scroll down to the Stop action and then double-click the action. The Stop action is now applied to the frame. If you look at the frame, you see a small "a" in the keyframe, indicating a script is attached to that frame.

The Actions panel or Actionscript Editor is one of the more complex areas of Flash MX. Depending on your skill level, you can use it in Expert mode to directly enter the code from your keyboard, or simply point and click your way through the code in Normal mode.

The panel is also chameleon-like, changing to reflect the task at hand. For example, the action we just wrote was a Frame action, and the title of the window changed to reflect that. It also changes to reflect Button actions and Movie Clip actions.

The buttons on the left side of the panel are called *books*. Depending upon the action chosen—and in certain cases, the mode—the books also change. One book is especially important. It is the Deprecated Actions book. These are the actions from former versions of Flash that are, essentially, on their last legs and won't be supported by future versions of the application. That's the bad news. The good news is they are usually replaced with a new and improved equivalent.

If you are new to Actionscripting, get into the habit of checking the syntax when you have finished writing your code. This can be done by selecting Check Syntax from the Actions panel pop-down menu. If there is a mistake, the panel will tell you exactly where it is and the potential source of the problem, such as a missing or wrong bracket.

Hard-core coders can simply type up the code in Notepad or Simple Text, and copy and paste the code into the Editor. The Actions panel pop-down menu also gives you the ability to copy and paste the code into the panel, export the code as a text file, and even print the code. If you need this capability, it can only be accomplished through the Actions panel pop-down menu, not through the Flash MX menus. As well, you can number the lines of the code by selecting this option in the pop-down menu. This is especially useful if there is an error because the report will inevitably refer to the line of code containing the error. This is one of those options that you should leave on.

Building a Simple Preloader in Flash MX

There are two bitmaps in the animation. As you know, bitmaps can slow things down in Flash. To deal with this, we need to let Flash wait until frame 30 of the animation has been loaded before it proceeds. In this manner, we avoid any starts and fits that may occur while the browser waits for the image to be loaded.

A great habit to get into, when you approach Actionscript, is to use pseudocode. Pseudocode is simply writing, in English, what has to happen and then applying the Actionscript based on what you want to do.

In the case of our preloader, the pseudocode would be:

- When the playback head enters frame 1, check to see if all 30 frames have been loaded.
- If they haven't, go to frame 2 and come back to frame 1.
- If they have, skip past frame 2 and play the movie.

This tells us how to approach the writing of the code. We need an action that counts the frames loaded as the playback head leaves frame 1. If the number of frames is less than 30, an action in frame 2 sends the playback head back to frame 1. If all of the frames are loaded, the playback head is to skip frame 2 and carry on with the animation.

Frame 3, therefore, is an important frame. One thing you never want to do when programming is to send the playback head to a numbered frame. If you have added or subtracted frames, you are setting yourself up for problems. Flash allows you to *name* frames by adding labels.

In this exercise, you add a label named Go into frame 3 of your Flash MX movie. The code constantly references a frame named Go instead of frame 3. In this way, you add a degree of flexibility to your code because a label can be moved anywhere in the movie, and the code points directly to the label. Let's assume, for example, an animation is added between frames 2 and 10. Obviously, the content in frame 3 is now sitting in frame 11. Reference a frame number and, for especially complex projects, you will have to go through a lot of code and change every reference to frame 3 to frame 11. The odds are good you will miss one or two of the references. Reference a named label—Go—and all you have to do is move that label to frame 11 and the code will still work flawlessly.

Before you write code, here's how to add a label to a frame:

1. Click in frame 3 of the Label layer, and add a blank keyframe. A label needs to be placed in a keyframe.

2. Click inside the Text Input area under the word "Frame" in the Property inspector, and then enter the word **Go** in the Text Input area. Press Enter (PC) or Return (Mac). A small flag with the word "Go" beside it appears in frame 3, as shown in Figure 15.15.

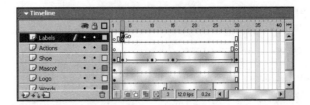

Figure 15.15   A label is added to frame 3 of the Labels layer. Labels always have a small flag.

3. Add a keyframe in frame 1 of the Actions layer, and right-click (PC) or Control-click (Mac) the keyframe to open the context menu. Select Actions from the context menu to open the Actions panel. Select Expert mode from the Panel Options pop-down menu, or press Ctrl-E (PC) or Command-E (Mac) to open the Expert mode Actionscript Editor. The Expert mode allows you to enter the code directly into Flash. Click once in the blank area of the panel and enter the following:

```
If_(framesloaded,=_totalframes){
GotoAndPlay ("Go");
}
```

   The first line asks if the number of loaded frames (`framesloaded`) total 30 or more (`,=`), which is the number of frames in the movie (`_totalframes`).

   The second line is the result of the first line being true. If 30 or more frames are loaded, the playback head goes to the frame labeled Go. If you are referring to names in Actionscript, they must be enclosed in quotes.

4. After you have entered the code, shown in Figure 15.16, select Check Syntax from the Panel Options pop-down menu, or press Ctrl-T (PC) or Command-T (Mac). Flash checks the code; if there is a problem, Flash will notify you.

5. For simple actions, you can double-click the command and then enter the information needed from the options presented. In this case, we tell the playback head, "When you enter frame 2, go back to frame 1." Add a keyframe in frame 2 of the Actions layer. Open the Actions panel and choose Normal mode, or press Ctrl-Shift-N (PC) or Command-Shift-N (Mac).

6. Open the Actions book and double-click GoTo. A GoTo dialog box opens at the top of the panel. Select Frame Number from the Type pop-down menu, and enter **2** into the Frame input area. The Actionscript changes to reflect your choices as shown in Figure 15.17.

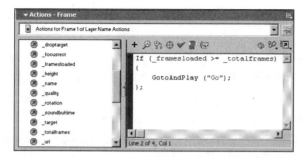

Figure 15.16   The script as shown. Note that _framesloaded and _totalframes can be found in the Properties book of the Actions panel. They are only visible in Expert mode.

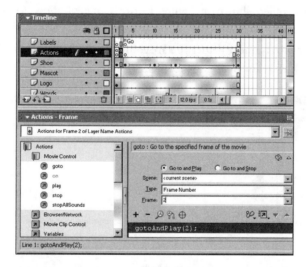

Figure 15.17   The GoTo action is attached to frame 2 of the movie. Double-clicking the action loads it into the script area. All you have to do is tell it what frame to go to and play.

Preparing for Export: Testing Animations and Optimizing Movies

The animation is complete, and now the real Flash work starts. To keep the animation as efficient and as small as possible, you need to wring every byte possible from the animation without compromising quality. Flash offers a surprising number of tools that can help you to accomplish your goal.

These tools allow you to measure the bandwidth to see where potential problems with the download will occur. You can optimize images. You can optimize sounds. All are designed to keep the file as small as possible without compromising playback. The following steps walk you through this process:

1. Select Control, Test Movie. This command creates a Flash .swf file, and opens the file.

2. As soon as the file opens, press Control-1 (PC) or Command-1 (Mac) to see your movie at its actual size, not the magnified view presented. The movie automatically starts to play.

3. To replay the movie, press Return (Mac) or Enter (PC). When you are finished, select View, Bandwidth Profiler or press Control-B (PC) or Command-B (Mac) to open the Bandwidth Profiler.

A Bandwidth Profiler Primer

The Bandwidth Profiler, shown in Figure 15.18, is one of those tools that rapidly becomes indispensable. Not only can you see your movie play, but you can also see the byte demands for each frame, whether you are going to have problems at various modem speeds, and even how many bytes the movie needs.

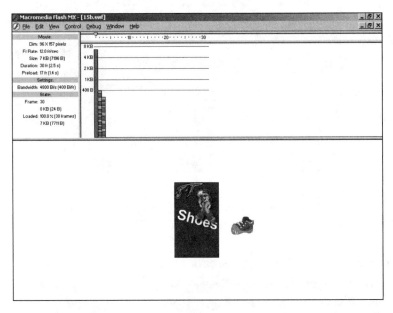

Figure 15.18   The Bandwidth Profiler in Flash MX provides you with a graphic representation of potential problems. In this example, the large spike in frame 1 indicates that a lot of information is being downloaded.

The first section of the Bandwidth Profiler, to the left of the graph, is divided into three sections. The top section, named Movie, tells you the physical size of the movie, how fast it is set to play, the size of the movie in kilobytes and bytes, and the duration and preload of the movie measured in frames and seconds. The middle section, called Settings, shows you the connection speed you are testing—in this instance, a 56K modem. The bottom area, named State, shows you the frame that is currently playing, how much of the movie has been loaded to that point, and the byte requirement for the frame.

The graph on the right gives you a frame-by-frame overview of how the content streams. The red line you see running across the graph indicates whether a frame will stream or stutter, based on the modem speed chosen.

In this case, you can see the impact of the bitmaps that load in frame 1. You can also appreciate the inclusion of the preloader. Were it not there, the movie would hang on frame 1 until the bitmaps are fully loaded.

To change the modem speed, select the Debug menu and choose a speed.

The content that enters on frame 1 is a potential bottleneck. Here's a method of shaving off a few bytes of bitmaps by optimizing an image:

1. Close the Bandwidth Profiler and then open the Library panel. The mascot is one of the bitmaps. Double-click the mascot.png image—not the graphic symbol—in the Library to open the Bitmap Properties dialog box, as shown in Figure 15.19.

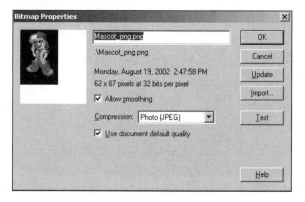

Figure 15.19   The Bitmap Properties dialog box allows you to optimize images within Flash.

When Flash renders a bitmap, it uses JPG compression. This is important to know because compressing an already compressed JPG can result in some serious image quality degradation.

2. Roll the cursor over the image in the Preview window. When you see a grabber hand, click and drag the image inside the window. Deselect Allow Smoothing in the Bitmap Properties dialog box. Note how the pixels along the outer edge of our mascot's left arm become a bit more distinct.

3. Click inside the name area at the top of the Bitmap Properties dialog box. Here you can change the name of the bitmap in the Library, not the original file. The information under the name area of the Bitmap Properties dialog box gives you the path to the image, its creation date, and the physical size and bit depth of the image.

   The Compression pop-down menu at the bottom of the Bitmap Properties dialog box offers two choices regarding how Flash compresses the image: Photo (JPG) or Lossless (PNG/GIF). Use JPEG compression for complex bitmaps, including photos. Use Lossless for bitmaps with large areas of flat color. Those are the guidelines, but you should not be afraid to explore and experiment.

4. Deselect Use Imported JPEG data (PC) or Use Document Default Quality (Mac, if visible), select the Lossless option, and click the Test button. Note the drop in the file size—30%. If you look at the image in the Preview window, there is no loss of image quality.

5. Select the JPEG option. Enter 20% in the Quality Text input box and then click Test. This produces a serious drop in file size, but an equally serious loss of image quality in the Preview window. Set the quality to 40%.

6. The image is starting to improve, but the blue in the shirt seems to fade. Set the quality to 45% and press Test. You'll notice a serious drop in size, and the quality is acceptable.

7. Set the Compression to Lossless and then click OK. The intention is to maintain quality. Do the same thing for the shoe.gif image.

If you want to edit the image further in Fireworks, this can be accomplished without re-importing the image. When you are finished working on the image in Fireworks MX, return to the Bitmap Properties dialog box, and click the Update button. The image is updated to reflect the changes made in Fireworks MX. Test the movie. The change in the byte hit on frame 1 is marginal. The reason is the amount of work done beforehand in Fireworks.

Optimizing Vector Images

Bitmaps aren't the only elements that could use a bit of efficiency. Each point on a vector requires processor power. The fewer the points, the lower the demand on processing power. The end result is a smoother flow to the animation.

In the case of our movie, the logo has quite a bit of excess baggage. To optimize a vector image, follow these steps:

1. Open the Logo symbol imported from Freehand, and break it apart by pressing Control-B (PC) or Command-B (Mac). Do this a couple of times to ungroup all the elements that comprise the logo. When the logo looks like it is composed of dots of color, you can stop breaking it apart. Breaking an object apart not only removes any symbol instances of the object, but it also reduces is to simple strokes and fills.

2. Select the Subselect tool in the toolbox, and click once on stroke around the gradient. Select the magnifying glass, and zoom in on the object. You see a rather large number of points.

3. Double-click the stroke of the gradient with the Selection tool. Select Modify, Smooth to remove points from the vector image. The object changes shape to reflect the removal of a few points. This is how a smooth works. By removing points, the curves travel a greater distance and lose a bit of definition.

4. Press Ctrl-Z (PC) or Command-Z (Mac) to undo the changes. Select Modify, Straighten. The curve changes. Selecting Modify, Straighten actually straightens out curves. Undo the changes. Select Modify, Optimize, and you open the Optimize Curves dialog box.

Tip

The Smooth, Straighten, and Optimize commands are also available by selecting the object on the Stage, and opening the context menu by right-clicking (PC) or Command-clicking (Mac).

When you select Optimize, you are presented with the Optimize Curves dialog box, shown in Figure 15.20. Optimize has essentially the same affect as smoothing, only you get to do it using a slider. Moving the slider to the right removes points; sliding it to the left reduces the severity of the change. Either way, there will be distortion.

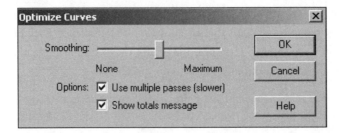

Figure 15.20   The Optimize Curves dialog box uses a slider to determine quality.

You also get a couple of choices in this dialog box. You can select Use Multiple Passes to repeat the smoothing process until no further optimization can be accomplished. Think of it as Auto Smoothing because you don't have to repeatedly apply it.

You can also select Show Totals Message to display an alert box that tells you how many curves there were when the process started, and how many were there at the end.

Optimizing Sound in Flash MX

As it currently stands, the animation is OK but a sound would really add to some drama to the piece and draw the viewer's attention to it. When it comes to sound, you have to exercise care because sounds add the most bloat to Flash MX movies. If you think adding a crystal-clear, stereo sound to Flash MX won't cause problems, think again.

Flash MX uses .aif, mp3, or .wav files. When it plays them, it converts them to mp3. Although two of the formats—.wav and .aif—are regarded as being somewhat platform-specific (Macs love .aif, and PC's adore .wav), this really should not be an issue. What is the issue is the size of the sound. A 16-bit stereo sound recorded at 44Khz will be immense. A 30-second sound in the same format will weigh in at 5.3 mb. Drop a channel, and the file size drops to 2.6Mb. Drop the sample rate down to 11kHz, and the file size sinks to 660Kb with little loss in the quality of the sound.

To add sound to the Flash MX timeline, follow these steps:

1. Import stomp.aif into the movie. It appears in the Library with a small speaker icon.
2. Double-click the sound in the Library to open the Sound Properties dialog box shown in Figure 15.21. Click the Test button to preview the sound.

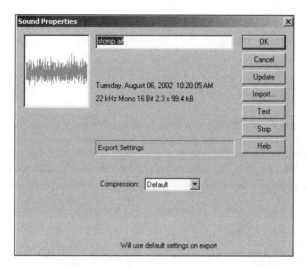

Figure 15.21   The Sound Properties dialog box allows you to control the compression settings as well as update sounds that may have been modified after import into Flash MX.

The top half of the Sound Properties dialog box tells you the type of file and when it was created, where it is located, the duration, and the size. The waveform is actually the sound itself. You can see that it is rather brief.

The bottom half of the dialog box, under the Export Settings, allows you to choose the file's compression scheme. The Compression pop-down menu gives you many choices, but the most common of all is the mp3 option. Selecting the mp3 option opens a couple of other dialog boxes that allow you to set the bit rate and quality of the sound.

The Update button in the Sound Properties dialog box has Flash check for a newer version of the sound file. The Import button enables you to bring another sound into Flash. You already know what the test button does. The Stop button stops the sound that is playing, and the Help button opens the Help menu.

Playing a Sound

Unfortunately, Flash MX is a bit weird in how sounds are added to the timeline. You would think that simply dragging an instance of the sound onto the timeline would be the procedure. Not quite.

To add a sound to the Flash MX timeline, follow these steps:

1. Add a new layer named Sound under the Actions layer and then add a keyframe in frame 10, which is the point where the show meets the word.

2. Drag the stomp.aif symbol in the Library onto the Stage—not onto the time-line—and release the mouse. The waveform in the timeline shows the sound has been added to your movie. Test the movie. The stomp should occur exactly as planned.

Note

One of the greatest sound applications ever developed for the Macintosh was SoundEdit16. The stomp sound was created in that application. Why are we telling you this? SoundEdit is a Macromedia product, and we can claim even the sound for this book was created using a Macromedia product. How's that for towing the party line?

Publishing a Flash Movie

Having eeked out every last byte from the images and sounds, and spent an inordinate amount of time with the Bandwidth Profiler, it is time to prepare the animation, as a Flash asset for placement in a Dreamweaver web page. The process of preparing a Flash movie for placement in Dreamweaver MX is called publishing.

Publishing a Flash MX movie converts it to a file format—.swf—that is a compressed, self-contained Flash file. This file is read by the browser's Flash plug-in. In this way, a Flash MX movie becomes the asset that is placed into the web page, and viewed by the user.

In Flash MX there are three Publish commands on the File menu: Publish Settings, Publish Preview, and Publish. Having three publishing choices tends to confuse developers who are new to the application. Publish Settings is the most important of the three. It is here that you make some specific decisions regarding how the resulting .swf file is handled by the browser. Publish Preview lets you preview the .swf file in the Flash Player, or launches Dreamweaver to allow you to view the file through a browser. Publish simply creates the files based upon the choices made in Publish Settings.

Using Publish Settings to Prepare a Flash Movie for Export

This is the single most important area of the application. It is here that you determine the format for the .swf and html files. You determine how the Flash MX movie streams through the web, how the assets in the movie load, what reports to generate, and how the bitmaps are compressed, as well as how the audio is compressed and streams. You also have to make some decisions regarding the HTML document ranging from how it appears when clicked or starts playing to the HTML template into which the resulting .swf will be embedded.

To set the Publish Settings for your Flash movie, follow these steps:

1. Select File, Publish Settings, or press Ctrl-Shift-F12 (PC) or Command-Shift-F12 (Mac). The Publish Settings dialog box opens, as shown in Figure 15.22.

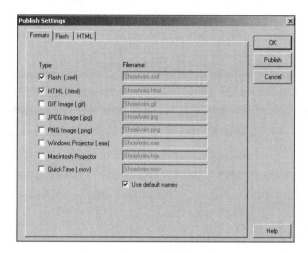

Figure 15.22   Choose how you want your file published. The choices range from .swf to an executable that can be launched from a CD.

2. Select Flash and HTML in the Formats panel. If you want to rename the files, deselect Default names and then enter your own.

3. Click the Flash tab of the dialog box. This tab, shown in Figure 15.23, deals with how the various elements in the movie are handled.

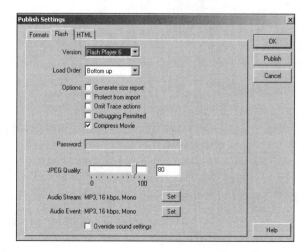

Figure 15.23   The Flash Publish Settings dialog box helps handle the various movie elements.

The Flash tab of the Publish Settings dialog box offers many options. Load Order simply indicates if the movie loads from the top layer down, or from the bottom layer up. If you have a lot of heavy media, generating a size report is a good idea. This report shows you, frame by frame, where potential problems exist. If you have a lot of code, you can omit trace actions and not have the Debugging window open when a code problem is encountered. Select Protect from Import if you don't want viewers copying your file to their computers, and deconstructing or altering them in Flash MX. Debugging Permitted, when checked, allows you to access the Debugger panel in the Debug Movie environment or from a web browser using the Flash Debug Player plug-in or Active-X control. If you permit debugging, especially over the Internet, be sure to assign a password to access the debugger panel.

Also in this tab, you can change the output quality of the JPG images in your movie, and you can set how sounds stream and the events that trigger sounds. If you want to override the settings for the sounds in your Library, click the Override Sound Settings button.

4. Click the HTML tab to see the options shown in Figure 15.24. These settings are self-explanatory. Of the lot, the Template pop-down menu is among the more important choices. If you click and hold on the choice presented, you are presented with a host of other choices. Essentially, each choice allows you to publish a predefined set of HTML tags to display the movie. If you want to learn about each one, select the option and then click the Info button beside it.

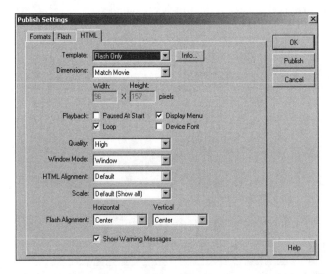

Figure 15.24   The HTML settings are intuitive. The most interesting is the variety of HTML templates available through the Template pop-down menu.

5. Click Publish, save the movie, and quit Flash MX. The published Flash files are placed in the same folder as the Flash MX movie, along with an .swf and an HTML file as shown in Figure 15.25. The .swf and HTML files will have the same name as the Flash movie.

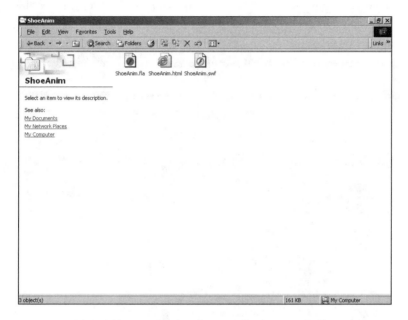

Figure 15.25   Published files are placed in the same file as the Flash file.

Inserting Flash Files into Dreamweaver MX

The process of inserting Flash files into Dreamweaver is simple. In the case of our page, you slice it up, open the file in Dreamweaver, and insert the Flash file into the place-holder. To accomplish this, follow these steps:

1. Open ShoesSlice.png in Fireworks MX. The slices are already in place. Select File, Export Preview, have the application export the slices and the HTML, and create the table with shims. Click OK.

2. Quit Fireworks and then open the Dreamweaver page created by Fireworks. Click once on the Flash placeholder, and delete it.

3. Select the slice containing the Flash Movie Box placeholder, and press the Delete key. Click inside the empty area of the placeholder, and then click the Flash button in the object menu.

4. Navigate to the .swf file you created in the previous section. Select it and then click OK. If the file is outside of the Dreamweaver page's root directory, you are asked if you want to move a copy to that location.

The Flash movie is nothing more than a gray box with a Flash logo, as shown in Figure 15.26. If you want to play the movie, click once on the gray box and then click the Play button on the Properties panel. You can also change the size of the Flash animation by changing the Height and Width values in the Properties panel. Test the movie in a browser.

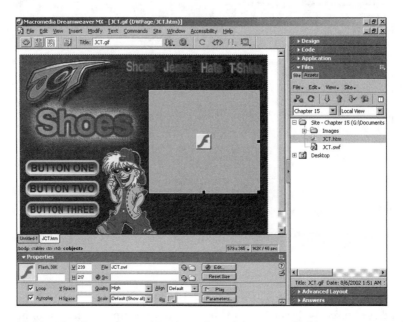

Figure 15.26   The slices are created in Fireworks and then assembled in Dreamweaver. The placeholder for the Flash movie is selected, and about to be deleted.

Summary

When it comes to web animation, the Macromedia MX Studio offers a set of very powerful tools. As we saw in this chapter, though, the tools don't come into play until after we plan our work. Fireworks MX can optimize images for placement into Flash and, for images requiring transparency, can export a 32-bit image to accomplish this. As well, we discovered the importance of creating the proper-sized images before importing them into Flash.

Flash, being a vector-based application, is tightly integrated with Freehand. One big productivity boost is the capability to create objects in FreeHand, save them as symbols, and then import those symbols directly into Flash.

There was a lot of ground covered in Flash. We saw how to prepare a Stage for animation. We demonstrated how to animate objects, how to control those animations using basic Actionscripting, and how to use the Bandwidth Profiler to isolate streaming and loading bottlenecks.

Seeing a bottleneck is one thing, but being able to unclog it is another. Using bitmap and vector optimization techniques, along with creating a simple preloader, we developed an animation that is small, quick-loading, and plays relatively quickly. We also reviewed the use of sound in a Flash MX movie, and thoroughly reviewed Flash MX's publishing options.

Finally, we covered how to place a Flash animation into a precise location on a Dreamweaver page.

Lots of practical advice was offered, but the most important remains, "When it comes to Flash, keep an eye on the pipe." In the next chapter, the pipe really comes into play as we create the animations used in the JCT site.

Chapter 16

MX

Preparing the Animations for the JCT Site

The web animation section of the book concludes by showing you how to create two animations for the JCT site. You also build a rather interesting Flash MX button that plays a video inside of the button when it is rolled over.

The animations that you create are a Flash intro to the site and a .gif animation that is slotted to play on each page of the site. The Flash MX button is a technique that mimics a flipbook animation. As the Flash MX playhead moves across the timeline, a series of still images from a video gives the illusion of a video playing when a user rolls over or clicks the button.

The theme running through this chapter is that an animation has to have a valid reason for being created and used. Using the rationale that "if the tool is there, use it" doesn't work in today's web development market. Chances are, if you build an animation into the budget, you will be asked to rationalize that suggestion.

In the case of the JCT site, the Flash intro is designed to act as a hook for visitors to the site, and to further the brand identity through the use of the logo and the mascot as outlined in the creative brief from Chapter 1, "Planning the Site." The .gif animations are a low-budget approach to reinforcing the brand identity.

If there is no rationale for the use of animation, the odds are very good that the animation's sole purpose is not to support the client's brand but rather to tell the developers' peers, "Aren't I clever?".

Splash Screen

When done correctly, a Flash-based splash screen is an extremely effective marketing tool. The viewer gets an entertaining preview of the site and, at the same time, a sense of the brand identity behind the site.

From a developer point of view, splash screens are labor-intensive. They require a comprehensive storyboard that plans, keyframe by keyframe, what the viewer will see and hear. The planning stage is also a great opportunity to articulate the purpose of the splash screen, and to ensure that everything needed for the presentation is absolutely necessary. Planning also allows you to create a listing of the necessary assets from imagery to sound.

In the case of our intro, the decision is to use the theme, "JCT is in the house." This is accomplished by having the JCT mascot appear to be dancing in a darkened nightclub, with the dancing effect enhanced by strobe lights catching him "busting a few moves." The sound is that of a house music loop; while the mascot is dancing, products from the site fade in and out.

Now that you have an idea and a concept for the intro, you have to identify what is needed.

Copy the Chapter 16 Exercise folder from the book web site to your desktop. The assets required for the animation can be found inside the Splash folder, and include the following:

- Various dance poses for our mascot
- A vectorized logo
- A mascot for the end shot (see Flash Dude.png)
- Product illustrations
- Flash Dancer Loop.aif
- Zap.aif
- Beam scan (located in the Flash sound library)

Creating the Dancing Mascot

The MX Studio contains a few surprises, one of which is the capability to create a Flash .swf animation as an export option in Fireworks MX. This makes life a bit simpler because the images we received from the designer were all bitmap images that will eventually have to be converted to vectors.

To create a .swf animation in Fireworks MX, follow these steps:

1. Open all seven of the dance pose files in the Dancer folder located in the Chapter 16 Exercise folder on your desktop.

2. Create a new file by selecting File, New. When the New Document dialog box opens, set the canvas dimensions to the dimensions 432 pixels by 475 pixels high. Set the canvas color to Transparent, the Image Resolution setting to 100 pixels per inch, and click OK. When the blank canvas appears on the Stage, save the file as **DancerSequence**.

3. Select the Dance1.png file, and click once on the mascot. The image is selected when you see the highlighted frame around the image, as shown in Figure 16.1. Copy the bitmap using Edit, Copy. Close the Dance1.png image, and paste it into the DancerSequence image.

4. When the image is pasted into the DancerSequence file, you may see the alert box shown in Figure 16.2. This alert tells you the resolution of the Dancer1 image is different from that of the DanceSequence image. If you click the Resample button, the image's resolution is either increased (upsampled) or decreased (downsampled). These choices would be a mistake if you were

working with a photograph. The result would be a loss of image quality because pixels are removed (downsampling), or the computer guesses the colors of the pixels to be added (upsampling). In the case of our mascot, you need only the lines so either choice is acceptable.

Figure 16.1   When you select an entire image in Fireworks MX, a blue highlight frame with handles at each corner of the image surrounds it.

5. The selected image is significantly larger than the canvas size. Select View, Magnification, 25% to fit the canvas and the image into the screen. On your tool palette, in the Select section, select the Scale tool. Sizing handles appear around the selected image. Resize the image to fit the canvas by clicking on a handle and moving it while holding down the Shift key to ensure the proportions of the image are maintained. When the image fits the height of the canvas, set the magnification back to 100%.

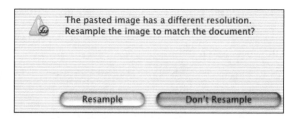

Figure 16.2   This alert box tells you the image about to be pasted into a document has a different resolution than the receiving document. Never click the Resample button if the image being pasted is a photograph.

6. You need to get rid of white area to reduce the image size when you export the .swf. In the Bitmap area of the tool palette, select the Magic Wand tool and then click on any one of the white areas of the image. The *marching ants* indicate the selected area.

7. Expand the selection to include all white areas by choosing Select, Similar. All of the white areas of the image, shown in Figure 16.3, are selected. Clear out the white area by choosing Edit, Clear. The white disappears, and the black lines remain.

Figure 16.3   All of the white areas surrounding the mascot are selected.

8. Open the Frames panel, click the drop-down menu, and select Add Frames to open the Add Frames dialog box. Add six frames and click OK. Your Frames panel should now have seven frames.

9. Go to frame 2 by either clicking the Frame Advance button, or by clicking the frame in the Frames panel.

10. Repeat steps 3 to 7 for each frame, adding a new dance pose from the open files in each frame.

Note

After all of the images are placed in frames, click the Play button to review the sequence. If they are not all aligned, the dancer appears to move. To fix this, turn on the Onion Skinning feature in the Frames panel, locate the frame that moves, and drag it into position. Another technique is to select each frame and, using the Property inspector, set each image's X and Y coordinates to 0.

11. After all of the frames are finished, export your frames sequence to a Flash MX .swf file by selecting File, Export. The Export dialog box appears. Export the resulting file to the Chapter 16 Exercise folder on your desktop. In the Save As pop-up menu, select Macromedia Flash SWF, as shown in Figure 16.4. Name the .swf file **Dancer Sequence.swf** and then click OK.

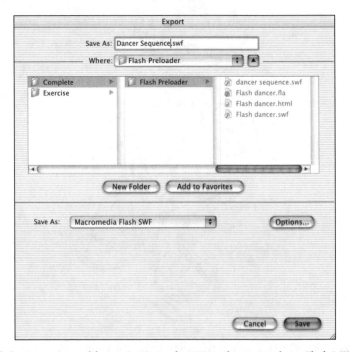

Figure 16.4   A sequence of frames in Fireworks MX can be exported as a Flash MX .swf file.

11. Save the Dancer Sequence.png file, and quit Fireworks.

Creating the Dancer in Flash MX

To create the dancer in Flash MX, you need to learn a little trick that we expanded from the New Riders book, *Flash Web Design*, by Hillman Curtis. You are going to convert the lines in the images to vectors and then get the dancer to dance by doing a form of roto-scoping. The end result is a series of seven silhouette images. This gives the shadowed look that's perfect for a nightclub scene.

Note

Rotoscoping is a video term for using a series of still images to give the illusion of movement.

To make the silhouettes, follow these steps:

1. Open Flash MX, and set the Stage size to 550 by 400 and the Stage color to #FFFFFF. Import the Dancer Sequence.swf file into your movie. The seven frames from the Fireworks MX document appear on the Flash MX timeline.

2. Select the first frame. The pose on the Stage should have a box around it to indicate your selection, and the Property inspector changes to indicate a grouped object.

3. Break apart the image to its bitmap form by selecting Modify, Break Apart. You may have to select Modify, Break Apart more than once to achieve the funda-mental image, as shown in Figure 16.5.

Figure 16.5   Breaking apart a bitmap in Flash MX turns the image into a collection of pixels.

4. Select the Lasso tool from the Tool palette. A set of options appears at the bottom of the Tool palette in the Options section. Select the Magic Wand option to turn the cursor into a magic wand. With the Magic Wand tool, Shift-click to select all of the white areas outside the dancer, and delete the selected background.

5. Choose Edit, Select All. Select the Fill Bucket and select the Black color chip in the Fill area of the toolbar or Property inspector. Click once inside the figure with the Fill Bucket to fill the figure with black. This also automatically changes the figure from a bitmapped image to a filled vector silhouette.

6. Select the Eraser tool, and clean up any rough edges or leftover lines. You might have to zoom in on the image for this.

7. When the edges fill the screen, press the spacebar to change the cursor to a grabber hand. Click with the mouse, and move the image to reveal a new area onscreen. When you release the spacebar, the grabber hand changes back to the Eraser tool. Your image should resemble that shown in Figure 16.6.

Figure 16.6   The dancing dude is now a vector object with a black fill.

Note

When you select the Eraser tool, the options at the bottom of the toolbar change to two buttons at the top and a pop-down menu underneath the buttons. The button at the top left, Eraser Mode, reveals a pop-down menu of Eraser Options from Erase Fills to Erase Inside a shape. The Spigot icon allows you to click on the stroke of an object and remove it. The pop-down menu under the buttons enables you to set the size of the Eraser.

8. Choose the Direct Selection tool in the Tools palette, and select the dancer. In the Options section at the bottom of the Tools palette, select the Smooth option. You may want to select this once or twice, unless you are happy with the image. Remember—a smoother image results in smaller bandwidth usage. Just don't make it unrecognizable.

9. With the dancer still selected, select the Free Transform tool in the Tools palette, and resize the dancer to fit the Stage. Move the resized image to the center of the Stage.

Tip

Hold down the Shift key to resize the image proportionally. Another way of resizing with a greater degree of precision is to do it "by the numbers." Select Modify, Transform, Scale and Rotate, or press Command-Option-S (Mac) or Ctrl-Alt-S (PC). When the Scale and Rotate dialog box opens, set the scale amount to a value anywhere between 65% and 80%. Click OK, and then move the object upward using the Up arrow on the keyboard to a point where the dude's feet are touching the bottom of the Stage.

10. Select frame 2, and repeat steps 3 through 9 for each frame of the animation. After you have created the silhouette figures, save the file and name it **Flash Dancer.fla**.

Tip

To get the images in approximately the same area, use the Onion Skin feature. This allows you to view the other frames to determine where the poses need to be, as shown in Figure 16.7.

Figure 16.7   The Onion Skinning feature of Flash MX works in exactly the same manner as the Onion Skinning feature of Fireworks MX.

Creating the Dance Animation

Now that you have created the silhouettes of the dancing mascot, it is time to get him moving. This is accomplished through the use of a movie clip and Actionscript to control the playback head.

1. With the Flash Dancer.fla file open, select all seven of the frames on the main timeline. Select Edit, Cut Frames, or Command-Option-X (Mac) or Ctrl-Alt-X (PC), to cut the frames from the Stage and place them on the clipboard.

2. Create a new movie clip symbol by selecting Insert, New Symbol to open the Symbol Properties dialog box. Select the Movie Clip property because part of bringing the mascot to life is making him move independently of the main timeline. Name the clip **Dancing Dude**, and click OK when done. You should be automatically in the Dancing Dude movie clip symbol for editing.

3. Select the first frame in the timeline window. Select Edit, Paste Frames, or press Ctrl-Alt-V (PC) or Command-Option-V (Mac), to paste the dancing mascot frames into the same positions on the movie clip's timeline as they were when cut from the main timeline. Rename layer 1 in the movie clip to **Dude**.

4. In the timeline window, create a new layer by clicking on the New Layer button located at the bottom of the timeline window. Name this new layer **Scripts**.

5. Select the first frame in the Scripts layer. After selected, click the Actions button on the Property inspector to show the Actions panel.

6. In the Actions panel, locate the Stop action and then drag it to the scripting area. stop(); appears in the scripting area. When done, close the Actions panel temporarily to keep it out of the way of our timeline editing.

 Tip

If you like to work in Expert mode rather than Normal mode, you can simply type **stop();** in your scripting area.

7. Exit editing the symbol by selecting Edit, Edit Document, or clicking the Scene 1 button at the top of the Stage. This takes you back to the main timeline.

Controlling the Dancer Movie Clip

You now need to create a dancing controller that will be placed on the timeline. This controller contains the Dancing Dude movie clip symbol, as well as a random script to control which frame of the dancing dude's timeline is displayed. By displaying a random frame, you can model the spontaneity of hip-hop dancing in real life where no two moves are actually the same. As well, selecting random frames ensures the clip never becomes predictable because the playback head is constantly moving around and displaying different frames in the Dancing Dude movie clip. Finally, by including a random function, the movie clip actually appears to be much longer than seven frames.

To create the dancing controller, follow these steps:

1. Add a new layer in the main timeline window by clicking on the Insert Layer button in the timeline window. A layer appears in the timeline window. Name the new layer **Dancin' Dude**.

2. Put the dancer into frame 33 to make room for a preloader. Click frame 33 of the Dancin' Dude layer. Insert a keyframe by selecting Insert, Keyframe, or by pressing F6 on your keyboard. A new keyframe appears on the timeline in the Dancin' Dude layer.

3. Open the Library panel by selecting Window, Library. Select the Dancing Dude movie clip symbol in the Library panel, and drag it onto frame 33 of the main timeline. Position the movie clip in such a way that the bottom of the Stage is used as the dance floor.

4. With the Dancing Dude movie clip symbol selected on the Stage, choose Select, Convert to Symbol to wrap the movie clip in a controller clip. The Convert to Symbol dialog box appears onscreen. Select Movie Clip for our type of symbol, and name the movie clip **Dancing Dude Controller**. The Dancing Dude movie clip is now wrapped in the Dancing Dude Controller movie clip.

5. To name the instance of the movie clip symbol you just created, click inside the text box of the Property inspector marked with a faint <Instance Name> on the inside. Type the name **dudeController**. The Property inspector should resemble that shown in Figure 16.8.

6. Double-click the Dancing Dude Controller movie clip on the Stage to open the symbol's timeline. Select the Dancing Dude movie clip that is in the controller movie clip. In the Property inspector, name the instance of the selected movie clip **dude**.

Note

The instance names—dudeController and dude—created in steps 5 and 6 are important because they will be referenced in the Actionscript. If you have a number of instances, note their precise spellings in a small notebook to avoid coding problems later on. Also note the spelling of the dudeController instance. The spelling is standard operating procedure when coding. Computer code does not recognize names with spaces. It is common to put two or more words together into one word. The first word usually starts the name using a lowercase letter, and the subsequent words start with an uppercase letter.

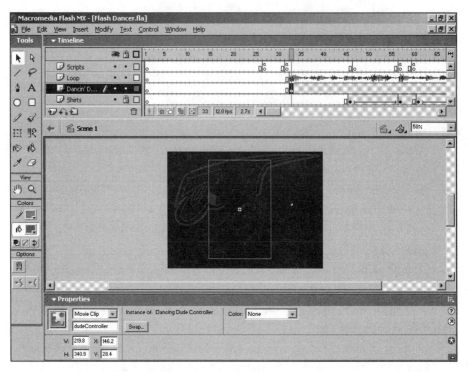

Figure 16.8   The instance of the Dancing Dude Controller movie clip on the Stage is named in the Property inspector.

7. Open the Actions panel by selecting Window, Actions, or by pressing the F9 key. The top of the Actions window should indicate Actions for dude (Dancing Dude), as shown in Figure 16.9.

8. Change the Actionscript Editor to Expert mode. The script you are about to write makes your dude appear to dance. This script is executed on every frame using the onClipEvent(enterFrame) handler. Enter the following script in the input area of the Actionscript Editor:

```
onClipEvent( enterFrame )
var theFrame = parseInt( Math.random() * 7 ) + 1; // pick a random
➥frame
this.gotoAndStop( theFrame );   // and tell our frame head to stop
➥here
}
```

In plain English, as the movieClip playback head advances to each frame, an event is triggered in the form of an onClipEvent(enterFrame). A local variable (var) named theFrame is created and assigned an integer (parseInt) which is a random number between 1 and 7 (Math.random () * 7) +1;. When the

variable is given the value, go to the frame with that number and stop
(this.gotoAndStop (_theFrame);. After the event is finished, the variable
theFrame is destroyed as it is no longer required.

9. When you finish entering the code, check the syntax to ensure there are no
errors. If there are none, return to the main timeline by selecting Edit, Edit
Document.

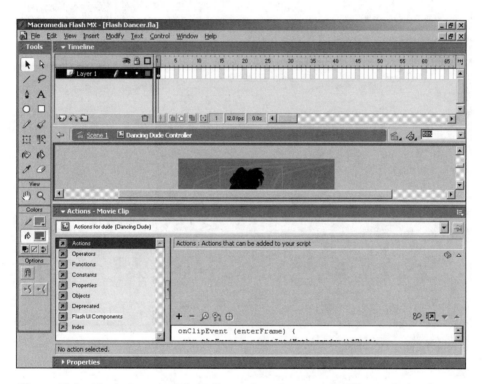

Figure 16.9   The Actionscript Editor tells you the code you enter will be attached to the
instance named dude inside the Dancing Dude movie clip.

Adding Music to the Movie

A dancer without music is rather useless. It is time to add a music loop. To add music to
the movie, follow these steps:

1. Select File, Import to open the Import dialog box. Locate and select the Flash
Dancer Loop.aif file in your Chapter 16 Exercise folder, and click the Open button. Repeat this step to import the Zap.aif sound effect. Both sounds should
appear in the Library panel.

2. Insert a new layer in the main timeline, and name it **Loop**. Click on frame 33 of the Loop layer and then insert a new keyframe. Open the Library panel, select the Flash Dancer Loop sound, and drag it onto the Stage in frame 33 of the Loop layer, as shown in Figure 16.10.

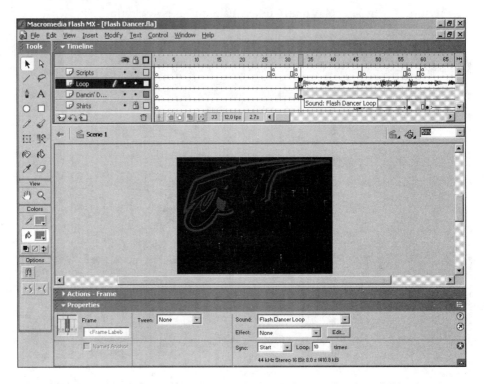

Figure 16.10   The sounds have been imported. The Flash Dancer Loop sound has been added to frame 33 of the Loop layer and assigned Synch and Loop properties in the Property inspector.

3. Select the sound in the timeline, and set the following properties for the sound in the Property inspector.

   Set Sync to Start.

   Set Loop to 10.

   These settings load the sound loop once, but play it 10 times. You also use the Synch property of Start because later on in the timeline, you use a Stop action to stop the movie rather abruptly.

Creating a Strobe Light Effect

A strobe effect is simply the effect of a light flashing from a dark color to a light color within a single frame. This is accomplished through the use of a movie clip.

To create a strobe effect, follow these steps:

1. Select layer 1 on the main timeline, and rename the layer **Background Strobe**. Click on frame 33 of the Background Strobe layer, and insert a keyframe.

2. Draw a rectangle onscreen that matches the Stage size of 500 pixels wide by 440 pixels high. Fill it with black, and set the Stroke property in the Property inspector to None.

3. Convert the rectangle to a Graphic symbol (Insert, Convert to Symbol, or press F8), and then name the Graphic symbol **Background Strobe**.

4. Select the newly created symbol, and again select Insert, Convert to Symbol. Select Movie Clip and name it **Strobe**. Double-click the Strobe movie clip symbol to open its timeline.

5. Select the Background Strobe symbol in the Strobe movie clip. Select Tint from the Color pop-down menu in the Property inspector. Create a dark color using the RGB sliders on the Property inspector by choosing values of 0, 0, 6. Set the Intensity slider to 100%.

6. Select frame 4 on the current timeline, and insert a new keyframe. Again, select the Background Strobe symbol in the Strobe movie clip. In the Property inspector, select Tint in the Color pop-up menu. Create a light color using the RGB sliders on the Property inspector by choosing values of 170,213 and 255 to change the color to a pale blue. Set the intensity to 100%.

7. Return to the main timeline (Edit, Edit Document), and then save the file.

What's a nightclub without a flashing neon sign in the background? We'll create the same strobe effect with the JCT logo created in Freehand.

To create the flashing neon sign, follow these steps:

1. Import the VectorizedLogo.fh10 file from the Chapter 16 Exercise folder on your desktop by selecting File, Import to Library.

2. Insert a new layer named **Logo Strobe** on the main timeline. Add a keyframe in frame 33 of the Logo Strobe layer. If the Logo Strobe layer is the topmost layer, drag it directly above the Background Strobe layer. This ensures the logo is placed behind the dancer.

3. Select the logo in the Library palette, and drag it to the Stage. It should appear on frame 33 of the Logo Strobe layer. Select the logo on the Stage, and then convert it to a graphics symbol named **JCT Logo Outline Graphic**. Select the newly created symbol, and convert it to a movie clip named **JCT Logo Outline**.

4. Double-click the JCT Logo Outline movie clip symbol to open its timeline. Select the JCT Logo Outline Graphic symbol in the movie clip. In the Property inspector, select Tint in the Color pop-up menu. Create a dark color using the RGB sliders on the Property inspector. Make it dark enough to remain visible; use the RGB settings of 0,26,85 to give the outline a blue color. Set the intensity to 100%.

5. Select frame 5 on the timeline, and insert a new keyframe. Select the JCT Logo Outline Graphic symbol in frame 5. In the Property inspector, select Tint in the Color pop-down menu. Create a light color (somewhat of a neon effect) using the RGB sliders on the Property inspector by using values of 0,255,61 to give the logo a green neon look. Set the intensity to 100%.

6. Having created a strobed logo, return to the main timeline by choosing Edit, Edit Document, and save the document.

Creating the Product Fade-Ins and Outs

The storyboard calls for a series of the products to fade in and out as the movie plays. To create the fade-in and fade-out effects, follow these steps:

1. Import the flash shirt.png, flash hat.png, flash shoe.png, and flash jeans.png from the Products folder located in the Chapter 16 Exercise folder on your desktop. Import them by selecting File, Import to Library.

2. Scroll to frame 155 of the main timeline. Click once on frame 155 of the topmost layer, and then drag down through the layers to select frame 155 of all the layers. Select Insert, Frame. The timeline for all the layers expands to 155 frames.

3. Add four new layers on the main timeline, and name them **Hats**, **Shirts**, **Shoes**, and **Jeans**. Select the Hats layer, and add a keyframe anywhere after frame 33. Remember, frame 33 is where the dancing begins. Drag the hat symbol from the Library to the Stage, and place it anywhere on the Stage you feel appropriate.

4. Select the Text tool from the Tool palette, and then click underneath the hat. Select the hat, and enter the word **Hats**. Use 24-point Verdana Bold with a white fill in the Property inspector, as shown in Figure 16.11.

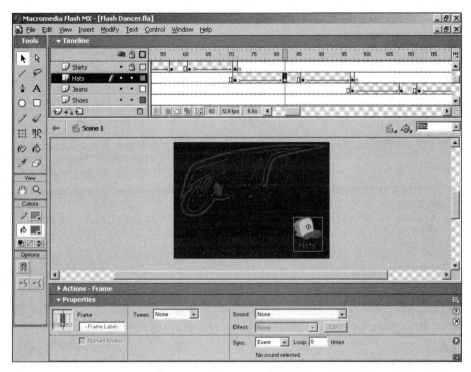

Figure 16.11   The hat has been added to frame 40 of the expanded timeline.

5. Select the Direct Selection tool on the Tool palette. With the Shift key pressed, click both the hat and the name to select them. Convert the selected objects to a graphic symbol and name it **Hats**. After converting to a symbol, the objects appear as one element on the timeline.

6. Select the newly created symbol on the Stage and, in the Property inspector, select Alpha from the Color pop-up menu. Set the alpha value to 0%.

7. On the same layer in the timeline, select a frame about 11 frames after the keyframe for the Hats symbol, and insert a new keyframe. A new keyframe appears with another instance of the graphic symbol of this product. In the Property inspector, Alpha should still be selected and set to 99%.

Note

Setting the alpha value to 99% may, at first glance, appear to be a bit odd. We use 99% instead of 100% because of color-shifting problems that occasionally occur within bitmap symbols. We have found that using a value of 99% alleviates this issue, for some bizarre reason.

8. Select a frame between the two keyframes in the Hats layer and then select Insert, Create Motion Tween. This is the fade-in. Doing the fade-out is exactly the same process; the only thing that changes is the alpha values are reversed.

9. On the same layer in the main timeline, select a frame about four frames after the last keyframe of the symbol, and insert a keyframe. In this step, we chose frame 55 for the new keyframe. A new keyframe appears with another instance of the Hats symbol. On the same layer in the timeline, select a frame about 11 frames after the last keyframe of our symbol and then insert a keyframe.

10. Select the new keyframe, click on the Hats symbol on the Stage, and set the Alpha in the Property inspector to a value of 0%. Click once between the keyframes and add a Motion tween. If you drag the playback head between the keyframes, the Hats symbol appears to fade out.

11. Repeat steps 5 through 10 for the remaining products. When you finish, the timeline should resemble Figure 16.12. Save the file.

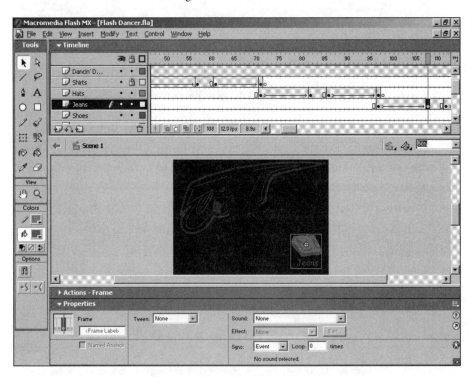

Figure 16.12   The timeline so far, including the fading products on their own layers.

Coding a Time Delay in Flash MX

You now create a simple time delay so the products stay onscreen without having to use more frames than necessary.

To create a simple time delay, follow these steps:

1. Insert a new layer named **Actions**. Insert a keyframe on the Actions layer in the same keyframe where the Hats symbol has just finished fading in; for example, add the keyframe to frame 56 of the Actions layer.

2. Open the Actions panel in Expert mode and then enter the following:

   ```
   timeDelay = 12;
   ```

   This creates a variable named `timeDelay`, and gives it a value of 12.

3. Close the Actionscript Editor. On the Scripts layer, insert a keyframe in the Actions layer on the frame just before the keyframe where the product fades out, such as frame 66.

4. In the Actions panel, enter the following:

   ```
   if( —timeDelay > 0 ){
   gotoAndPlay( _currentFrame - 2 );
   }
   ```

   If the value of the variable of `timeDelay` is 11 (the — means subtract 1 from the value; the term in programming terms is *decrement*) and the value is greater than 0, go back two frames.

   You are decrementing the `timeDelay` variable until its value equals zero. Until it hits zero, the playback head loops back two frames until the script is executed once more. When the value of `timeDelay` reaches 0, the playback head moves forward on the timeline.

5. Repeat this time delay for the remaining products.

6. Select the Dancin' Dude layer in the timeline, go to the frame that aligns with the end of the last product fade-out done earlier, and select the frame just after the product fadeout keyframe. Press the Shift key and click the last frame of the animation to select the range of frames.

7. Select Insert, Remove Frames, or press Shift-F5 on your keyboard, to reduce the number of frames for the Dancin' Dude layer. Do the same for the remaining layers.

8. Select the last frame of the Loop layer and then insert a keyframe. In the Property inspector, as shown in Figure 16.13, select Flash Dancer Loop.aif from the Sound pop-down list, and choose Stop in the Sync pop-down list. This stops the sound from playing. Save the file.

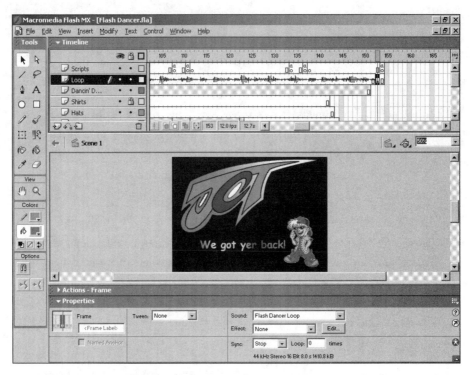

Figure 16.13   The sound properties for the Flash Dancer Loop change on the last frame of the animation to stop the sound from playing.

Creating a Punchy Ending

What's a production without a show-stopper ending? In our case, the logo lights up, and the dancing dude is replaced with the mascot.

To finish the intro, follow these steps:

1. Insert the following layers under the Actions layer in the main timeline: **Whoosh**, **Dude**, **Colour Logo**, **Slogan**, and **Rainbow**.

2. Select the frame number after the last dance frame for each of these layers, and then insert a keyframe. Your timeline should resemble Figure 16.14.

3. You are going to use one of Flash's stock sounds for the whoosh sound. Select Window, Common Libraries, Sounds.fla to open a Library of sounds.

4. Select the sound named Beam Scan, and drag it onto the keyframe just added to the Whoosh layer. You don't need to do anything further with this sound.

5. Select the keyframe added to the Colour Logo layer, and import the Logo.fh10 file from the Chapter 16 Exercise folder on your desktop. Place the logo on the Stage as desired.

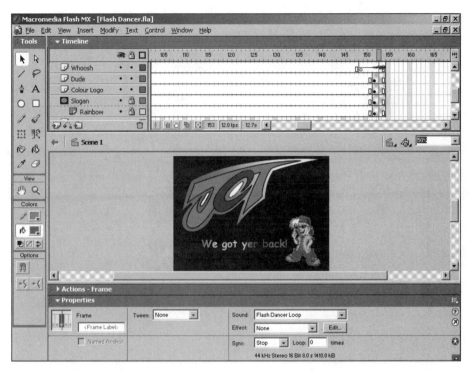

Figure 16.14   Keyframes are added to the end of the animation to start the ending sequence of the intro.

6. Select the new keyframe in the Dude layer, and import the file Flash Dude.png. If it doesn't appear onscreen, select it in the Library palette and then drag it onto the stage. Place the mascot on the Stage as desired.

7. Select the new keyframe on the Slogan layer. Select the Text tool, click once on the Stage, and enter **JCT is in 'da house!**. Set the slogan in 36-point Verdana Bold. Make sure the text property on the Property inspector is Static Text. This is important because you are going to turn this into a mask. The Stage and text properties should resemble those shown in Figure 16.15.

Creating a Mask in Flash MX

Masking in Flash MX is still a bit complicated. Essentially, you create a masking object and change it to a masking layer, and then any layer under the masking layer that is marked as masked shows through.

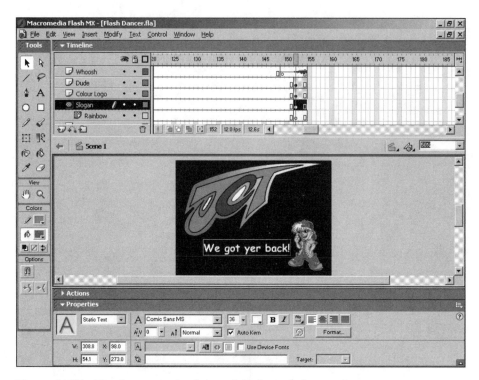

Figure 16.15   The elements are in place, and the slogan is formatted.

To create a mask containing an animated gradient, follow these steps:

1. Select the new keyframe in the Rainbow layer, and draw a rectangle slightly larger than the text.

2. With the rectangle selected, open the fill color chip on the Property inspector, and then select a linear rainbow gradient fill that has the same color at the beginning and the end. If you don't see a rainbow gradient that you like, feel free to make one. The trick is to have the same color on both ends. Convert the rectangle into a graphics symbol named **Rainbow Mask**.

3. Select the Rainbow Mask symbol on the Stage, and convert it to a movie clip named **Rainbow Rotation**. Double-click the Rainbow Rotation symbol to open its timeline. The logo and the mascot appear to fade, indicating you have opened a symbol on the main timeline.

4. Select the Rainbow Mask graphics symbol in the open timeline, and copy it. Insert a new layer and then select Edit, Paste in Place. This is the key to creating a seamless effect.

5. Select frame 96 for both layers, and insert keyframes in frame 96 of each layer.

6. Go back to frame 1 and select the gradient symbol in layer 1. Move the symbol so that it is on the right side of the graphic symbol in layer 2 and butts up against that symbol. Add a Motion tween.

7. Move the playback head to frame 96. Select the graphic symbol in frame 96 of layer 2, and move it so that it is on the left side of the gradient symbol in layer 1. Make sure it butts up against the symbol.

8. Drag the playback head across the animation, and the gradients should move in unison. The Stage and layer should resemble those shown in Figure 16.16.

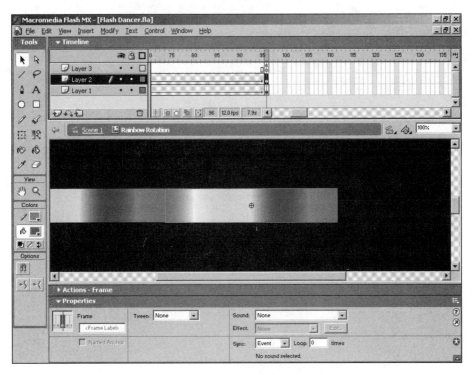

Figure 16.16   The gradients in the layers are set up in such way that they move in unison.

9. Insert a new layer named **Actions** and then add a keyframe in frame 96 of the Actions layer.

10. Open the Actionscript Editor, and enter the following:

```
gotoAndPlay(1);
```

11. You have now created the illusion of a seemingly endless rainbow transition. Return to the main timeline of the movie.

12. If necessary, move the Rainbow layer under the Slogan layer. The words fill with the moving gradient and, in Flash MX, the Masking layer—Slogan—has to be above the fill for the Mask—Rainbow.

13. Double-click the icon that looks like a turned-up sheet of paper on the Slogan layer to open the Layer Properties dialog box. Change the type to Mask, as shown in Figure 16.17, and click OK.

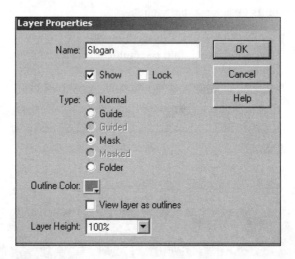

Figure 16.17   Double-clicking a layer's icon opens the Layer Properties dialog box.

14. If the Rainbow layer does not appear indented beneath the Slogan layer, double-click the icon on the Rainbow layer again to open the Layer Properties dialog box. Change the type to Mask and click OK.

15. Lock both the Slogan and the Rainbow layers by clicking the Lock property on each layer. The Stage and layers should resemble that shown in Figure 16.17.

16. In the Actions layer, insert a new keyframe that sits above the keyframes for the mask.

17. Open the Actions panel, and enter the following:

    ```
    stop();
    ```

    This stops the movie from looping to the beginning and also enables the rainbow to play.

18. Save the movie.

Creating a Unique Preloader

Flash preloaders fall into two categories. The first uses progress bars as well as other visual aids to indicate how much of the file has loaded into the browser. The other category includes the use of an animation to distract the viewer from becoming aware that content has to load. We have left frames 1 to 32 available for an animated preloader. For the intro, we have chosen to distract the user while the movie is loading. This type of preloader is preferred as opposed to the progress bar because it doesn't look like a preloader to the user. The user believes that this is part of the whole introduction.

To create the preloader, follow these steps:

1. Under the Actions layer, insert a new layer named **Logo Zap**, and select the first frame of the Logo Zap layer.

2. Select the JCT Logo Outline Graphic symbol from the Library panel, and drag it onto the Stage. With the symbol selected on the Stage, set its Alpha setting to 0 in the Color area of the Property inspector.

3. Select frame 24 on the Logo Zap layer and then insert a keyframe. Select the symbol and, in the Property inspector, select Tint in the Color pop-up menu. Set the color to a dark color, such as 0,20,18, and set the intensity to 100%. Create a Motion tween between the keyframes in frame 1 and 24 to have the logo fade in.

4. Insert a keyframe on frame 28 of the Logo Zap layer. Select the symbol in this new keyframe, and convert the symbol to a movie clip named **LogoZap**. Add a blank keyframe at frame 32 to ensure the instance is removed from the Stage at playback.

5. Double-click the LogoZap movie clip to open its timeline.

   You now create a random-type feel to the zapping in and out of the logo.

6. Insert a keyframe in frame 4. Select the JCT Logo Outline Graphic symbol. In the property inspector, select Tint in the Color pop-up menu. Select a light color chip, such as 255,255,251, at 100% intensity.

   With symbols manipulated, add a glow effect to the symbol in frame 4.

7. Select the JCT Logo Outline Graphic symbol at frame 4, copy it by choosing Edit, Copy, and insert a new layer below the current layer. Add a keyframe in frame 4 of the new layer, and select Edit, Paste in Place.

8. Break apart the new symbol by selecting Modify, Break Apart, or pressing Command-B (Mac) or Ctrl-B (PC). Keep breaking apart the image until it looks pixelated. Select the Subselection tool, and delete objects inside the outline.

When finished, change the color of the graphic to its original color by selecting FFFF00 in the fill color chip from the Property inspector.

9. Select Modify, Shape, Soften Fill Edges to open the Soften Fill Edges dialog box. Set the distance and number of steps according to yourpreference, such as 20 and 15, respectively. Click the Expand button in the Direction area and then click OK.

10. Convert the graphic to a graphic symbol by selecting Insert, Convert to Symbol to open the Convert to Symbol dialog box, and name it **Glow**. Click OK, select the new symbol on the Stage, and reduce its Alpha setting to 15%.

11. Insert two layers that contain a zap sound. Name them **Zap 1** and **Zap 2**. Select frame 3 of Zap 1, and insert a keyframe. Select frame 4 of Zap 2, and insert a keyframe.

12. Select the keyframe in frame 3 of the Zap 1 layer, and then drag the zap sound from the Library onto the Stage. Repeat this for the keyframe in frame 4 of the Zap 2 layer.

13. Select the sound in the Zap 1 layer. Click Edit in the Property inspector to open the Edit Envelope dialog box, shown in Figure 16.18. The handles above the sound graphs are volume controls for each channel. Set one channel to zero by dragging the square handle on the sound volume indicator to the bottom of the box. Set the other side to less than half. Click OK.

14. Repeat the previous step with the other sound, except set the opposite channel to 0. For example, if you muted the left side on the first sound, you would mute the right side on the other.

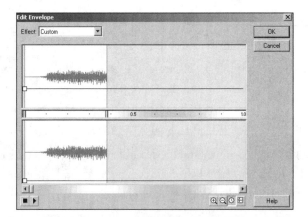

Figure 16.18   The Flash MX Edit Envelope dialog box for sounds. The Effect pop-down menu allows you to choose a number of pre-set effects.

Coding the Movie Clip and the Preloader

With all of the objects in place, it is time to add the code. You use a technique similar to the code used earlier in this chapter to slow down the playback of the animation for the LogoZap movie clip.

1. Add an Actions layer to the LogoZap movie clip. Select the first frame in the Script layer, open the Actions panel, and enter the following script:

```
theFrame = parseInt( Math.random() * 3 ) + 1;
// for a hint of unpredictability
gotoAndPlay( theFrame );
```

This script picks a frame at random between one and three, and then goes to it.

2. Insert a new keyframe in frame 6 of the Actions layer, and add the following code:

```
gotoAndPlay(1);
```

This simply tells the script to go back to the beginning.

3. Exit editing the symbol by selecting Edit, Edit Document to return to the main timeline.

4. Add keyframes to frames 27 and 32 of the Actions layer of the main timeline.

5. Select the keyframe on frame 27, open the Actions panel, and enter the following code:

```
if (_framesLoaded < _currentFrame + 1 )
{
        gotoAndPlay( _currentFrame - 2 );
}
```

This script checks to see if the next frame is loaded and ready to play. If it isn't, jump back two frames from where you currently are in the timeline and test again.

6. Enter the same script at frame 32 in the Actions panel.

7. Save the movie and test the file.

Creating an Animated GIF for the JCT Product Pages

The plan is to create an animation announcing a series of sponsored events offered by the JCT Company. Rather than produce a Flash animation with shoes squashing words or dancing mascots, the decision is to produce an animated .gif that draws the viewer's attention to the area. This is accomplished by creating an animated .gif that fades in and out.

To create an animated .gif, follow these steps:

1. Open a new document in Fireworks MX. When the New Document dialog box opens, set the canvas size to 89 pixels wide by 199 pixels high and the background color to white.

2. Open the Layers panel, and rename the existing layer **Mascot**. Select File, Import, or press Ctrl-R (PC) or Command-R (Mac), to open the Import dialog box. Navigate to the Animated _GIF folder in the Chapter 16 Exercise folder on your desktop, select the Mascot.png file, and click Open.

3. The cursor changes to the import cursor. Click once, and the mascot appears on the canvas, but he's a bit too large in size. Select Modify, Transform, Numeric Transform to open the Numeric Transform dialog box. If necessary, select Scale Attributes and Constrain Proportions. Enter **50** into the Width input field. The number 50 appears in the Height input field. Click OK. Move the mascot to the bottom of the canvas.

4. Add a new layer named **Logo**. Select File, Import, and import the Logo.fh10 image in the Animated _GIF folder located in the Chapter 16 Exercise folder on your desktop. Click Open.

5. The Vector File Options dialog box opens, as shown in Figure 16.19. Although vectors are scalable with no loss of resolution, the Vector File Options dialog box contains a rather interesting feature that allows you to scale the object prior to placement in Fireworks MX. Click and hold on the down arrow beside the Scale Input area. A slider appears. If you move the slider up and down, the values in the width and the height areas change to reflect the increase or decrease in the image size. Release the mouse.

6. A slider is a nice feature, but you can also obtain precise scaling by entering the scale amount into the Scale area. Double-click the number in the Scale area to select it. Enter **45**. The width changes to 90 pixels and the height to 49.95 pixels. Click OK; when the import cursor appears, click once. When the logo appears on the canvas, move it to the top of the canvas and then add a drop shadow using the Effects settings on the Property inspector.

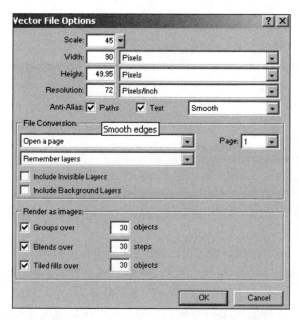

Figure 16.19   The Vector File Options dialog box enables you to specify the scale percentage
of a vector-based image prior to import into Fireworks MX.

7. Add a new layer named **Words**. Select the Text tool, and click once on the canvas.
    Enter **Sponsored Events**. On the Property inspector, use the following specifica-
    tions for the selected text:

    Font: Arial

    Weight: Bold

    Size: 16 points

    Color: 990033

    Kerning: -4

    Leading: 120%

    Alignment: Centered

8. Drag the words to a point just under the shadow of the logo.

9. Select the Words layer, and set the transparency of the layer to 25%.

10. Add a new layer named **Locations**. Select the Text tool and enter:

    August 4

    Blading Demo

    By J.C. Verde

Flick Gardens

Woodville, VA

11. Select the text in the Locations layer, and use these formatting settings:

    Font: Times New Roman

    Weight: Bold

    Size: 12 points

    Color: 000000

    Kerning: 0

    Leading: 130%

    Alignment: Left

12. Select Blading Demo, and set the selection's leading to 160 in the Property inspector. This moves the line down. Select Flick Gardens, and set the leading to 180.

13. Move the text block to the bottom of the screen, and turn off the visibility of the Locations layer.

Animation by the Numbers Using Frames and Layers

The ability to use frames and layers to create animations in Fireworks MX allows for the creation of some interesting effects in .gif animations. As you learned in Chapter 14, "Animation on the Web," each frame of an animation can be manipulated using the Layers panel without affecting any of the other frames in the animation. In this section, you will be constructing a 12-frame animation that fades our mascot and some text. It is a quick way for creating an animated events graphic for our web page.

To build a 12-frame animation, follow these steps:

1. Open both the Layers and the Frames panels. Having both open at the same time gives you easy control over all of the different aspects of the creation of the animation. Your screen should resemble Figure 16.20.

2. Select frame 1 in the Frames panel, and select Duplicate Frame from the panel options pop-down menu to open the Duplicate Frame dialog box.

3. Enter 1 in the Number area and then select After Current Frame. Click OK. Double-click the Frame Delay area of the first frame to open the Frame Delay dialog box. Set the delay amount to 45/100 of a second. Press Enter (PC) or Return (Mac).

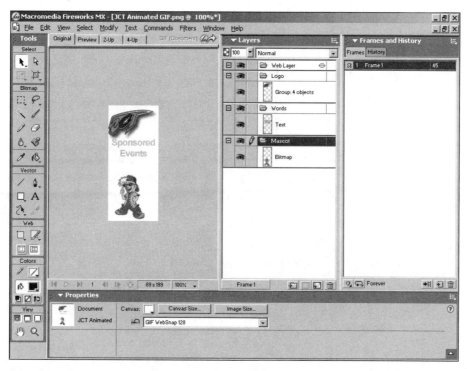

Figure 16.20   Placing the open Frames and the Layers panels beside each other reduces the amount of mousing between them, and saves you valuable productivity time.

4. Select frame 2, and set the transparency of the Words layer to 65%. Duplicate frame 2.

5. Select frame 3, and set the transparency of the Words layer to 75%. Duplicate the frame.

6. Select frame 4, reduce the Mascot layer's transparency to 65%, and increase the Words layer's transparency to 100%. Set the frame delay to 15. Duplicate the frame.

7. Select frame 5, and reduce the Mascot layer's transparency to 25%. Duplicate the frame.

8. Select frame 6, and set the frame delay to 50. Duplicate the frame

9. Select frame 7, and reduce the Mascot layer's transparency to 15%. Turn on the visibility of the Locations layer, and then move the text box downward until the first two lines of text are sitting on the bottom of the canvas. Set the frame delay to 65, and duplicate the frame.

10. Select frame 8. Select the Location text and then move it upward until four lines of text are visible. Duplicate the frame.

11. Select frame 9. Select the Location text and then move it upward until six lines of text are visible. Duplicate the layer, and duplicate frame 9.

12. Fireworks MX gives you the ability to add layers to your animations without having them appear in the previous layers. Add two layers named **Mask** and **More Info**.

13. Select the Mask layer. Select the Rectangle tool, and draw a white square that covers the last two lines of the Location text. Drag the Mask layer until it is directly above the Locations layer. The two lines of the text disappear. If necessary, move the Mascot layer above the Mask layer.

14. Select the More Info layer, and drag it above the Mascot layer. Select the Text tool and then enter the word **Info**. Set it in 18-point Arial Bold.

15. Change the Rectangle tool to a Circle tool. Draw a circle on the More Info layer using these specifications:

    Width: 22 pixels

    Height: 22 pixels

    Fill: FFCC00

    Effect: Inner bevel

    Bevel Edge Shape: Flat

    Bevel Width: 3

16. Set the frame 10 frame delay to 100, and create two duplicates of frame 10. If you click frame 9, you see that the More Info and Mask layers are not included on your Layers panel. Your frames and layers should resemble those shown in Figure 16.21.

17. Select File, Export Preview to open the Export Preview dialog box. Navigate to the folder where the animation will be saved, and use the following settings:

    Format: Animated GIF

    Palette: Web Snap Adaptive

    Loss: 0

    Dither: No

    Colors: 128 (due to the JCT logo drop shadow)

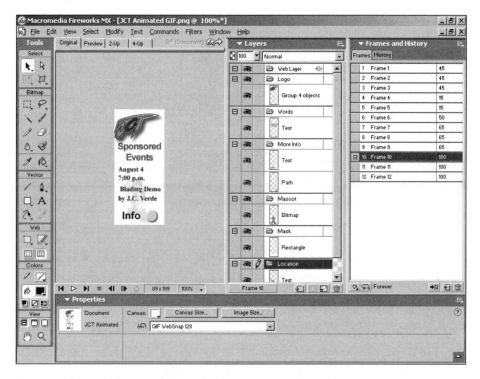

Figure 16.21   The layers and frames for the animation prior to export.

18. Click the Export button. When the Export dialog box opens, use the following settings:

Name: jct_animation_box.gif

Save As: Images only

Slices: None

Select Include Areas Without Slices

19. Click the Save button. When you return to the image, save the image and then quit Fireworks MX.

Creating Motion Graphics in Flash MX

Prior to the release of Squeeze and Flash MX, the inclusion of digital video into Flash movies was accomplished through the use of the rotoscoping technique mentioned earlier in this chapter. On the surface, it may appear that the days of this technique are over. Not quite. It is an awesome technique and, once mastered, adds yet another skill to your MX Studio skill set.

The technique involves exporting a series of frames from a digital video as individual images. These images are then resized using the Fireworks MX batch-processing feature. The images are imported into Flash MX and turned into a movie clip, and then that movie clip is used as a button.

This section shows you how to create a video button in Flash MX.

Capturing the Video Frames

The following steps require you to use some form of video-editing software. Although our preferred tools of choice are Adobe Premiere and Adobe After Effects, we are going to demonstrate the frame-capture technique using a far cheaper alternative: QuickTime Pro, which can be downloaded for $29.99 from Apple at `http://www.apple.com/quicktime/upgrade`. If you have the lite version of QuickTime, open the file menu in the QuickTime player. If you don't have a Save menu item, you have the lite version, and this technique will not work.

To capture video using QuickTime Pro, follow these steps:

1. Double-click your QuickTime player. When the Player opens, select File, Open and then navigate to the Subway movie located in the Video folder of the Chapter 16 Exercise folder on your desktop. Click OK.

2. Drag the Out slider, shown in Figure 16.22, until you see 00:00:02 on the timer to reduce the selected clip to a duration of two seconds.

Figure 16.22   Identify the footage you need and its duration by moving the In and Out point sliders in the QuickTime Player.

3. Select File, Export to open the Save Exported File As: dialog box. Navigate to the folder where the files are to be saved, and select Movie to Image Sequence in the Export pop-down menu, as shown in Figure 16.23.

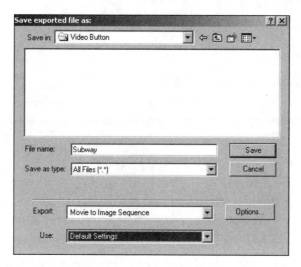

Figure 16.23   To export a digital video as a series of still images, select Export Image Sequence from the Export pop-down menu in the Save Exported File As: dialog box.

4. Click the Options button to open the Export Image Sequence Settings dialog box. Select PNG from the Format pop-down list, and set the frames per second to 8. Click OK to return to the Save Exported File As dialog box, and click Save. The files are exported to the folder chosen. Quit the QuickTime player.

Batch Processing Files in Fireworks MX

You now have a number of individual .png images in the folder. Each one is 320 pixels wide by 240 pixels high, which is far too large for use in a Flash MX button. Rather than resize each image separately, let the software do the work and use the Fireworks MX Batch Process feature to resize the images in one pass.

To create a batch operation in Fireworks MX, follow these steps:

1. Open Fireworks MX, and select File, Batch Process to open the Batch dialog box. Navigate to the folder containing the images you exported in the previous section. For those of you without QuickTime Pro, a series of the video capture images in the Batch Files folder is included in the Chapter 16 Exercise folder.

2. Click the Add All button, and the list of image filenames appears at the bottom in the file list window of the Batch dialog box, as shown in Figure 16.24.

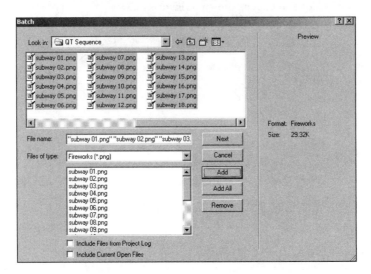

Figure 16.24   Clicking the Select All button in the Batch dialog box moves the contents of an entire folder to the bottom of the dialog box, indicating they will be manipulated.

3. Click the Next button in the Batch dialog box to open the Batch Process dialog box. Select Scale from the Batch Options list, and click the Add button. Scale appears in the Include in Batch area. Select Scale to Percentage from the pop-down list in the Scale area of the dialog box. Enter 20% as the percentage amount. If your settings match those in Figure 16.25, click Next to proceed to the next screen in the dialog box.

4. Select Custom Location, and click the Browse button to open the Select Images dialog box. Navigate to the folder where the batched images will be stored. The button at the bottom changes to indicate the name of the selected folder on the Windows version. On the Macintosh, the button at the bottom is labeled Choose. Click this button to select the folder and close the File Selector dialog box. Click Batch to start processing your selected files.

Tip

Always send batch-processed files to a new folder away from the original files. This way, you avoid the confusion of similarly named files or the potential loss of the original files.

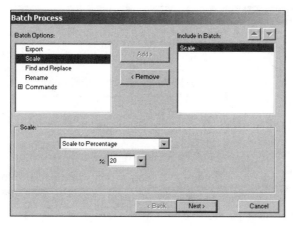

Figure 16.25   The images are scaled to 20% of actual size using the settings in the Batch
Process dialog box.

5. A Batch Process status dialog box opens, showing the progress of each file. Each
   file in the list from step 1 is automatically reduced in size and placed in the
   Batched Files folder. You are notified when the batch process is complete. Click
   OK to return to the Fireworks MX interface. Quit Fireworks MX.

Creating a Video Button in Flash MX

Having exported the frames out of QuickTime Pro and reduced them in size in
Fireworks MX, the image sequence is ready for placement in Flash MX. Note that each
image has a number at the end of its name. Those numbers are important because Flash
MX uses those numbers at the end of the filename to recognize and import all of the
images as an entire sequence.

To import an image sequence and create a video button, follow these steps:

1. Open Flash MX, and create a new movie clip named **Vid**. Select File, Import to
   open the Import dialog box. Navigate to the Batched Files folder containing the
   images resized earlier in Fireworks MX. Select the Subway 01 file and then click
   the Open button. A Flash MX alert appears, as seen in Figure 16.26.

2. The Image sequence alert is the key to the process. Flash MX detects a numbered
   sequence of images, and asks if you would like to have them all imported. Click
   OK to open the .png Import dialog box.

3. Select Import as a Single Flattened Bitmap and then click OK. The images appear
   on frames in the movie, and are placed in the same location in each frame. Move
   the playback head across the frames to see the effect.

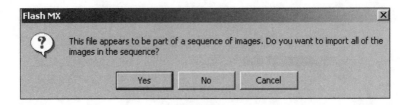

Figure 16.26   The Image sequence alert allows you to import a series of numbered images.

4. Create a new Button symbol named **Vid Button**. When the button timeline opens, open the Library and drag the image named Bitmap 1 onto the Stage in the Up keyframe and align the image to the center of the Stage. By using a static image in the Up state, you save the surprise for the Over and Down states.

5. Insert a keyframe in the Over area of the timeline. The image from the Up state appears. Delete it. Drag a copy of the Vid movie clip onto the Stage. Align it to the center of the Stage.

6. Add a keyframe to the Down frame and to the Hit frame.

7. To add some visual interest to the button, the video changes color when the mouse is clicked. Add a layer to the button timeline, and then add a keyframe in the Down frame of layer 2.

8. Select the Rectangle tool, and draw a rectangle over the image in the Down frame. Using the Property inspector, fill the rectangle with red (FF0000). Right-click (PC) or Control-click (Mac) on the red rectangle, and select Create Symbol from the context menu. When the New Symbol dialog box opens, name the symbol Matte and set the property to Graphic. Click OK.

9. With the Matte symbol selected on the Stage, set the Alpha setting to 30%. Copy the red square.

10. Select the symbol in the Hit area and then delete it. Select Edit, Paste in Place to put a copy of the red box on the clipboard into the same position it occupies on the Stage in the Down frame. Your finished button timeline should resemble that shown in Figure 16.27.

11. Return to the main timeline, drag a copy of the button symbol onto the Stage, and test the movie.

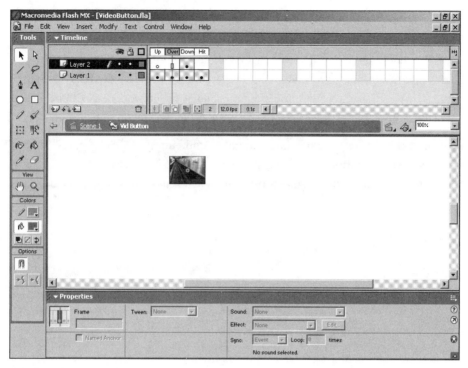

Figure 16.27   A video button is built using a still image in the Up state, a copy of the Vid
movie clip in the Over state, and a copy of the movie clip in the Down state.

Summary

This has been a rather complex chapter simply because creating effective animations is
not easy.

We started the chapter by pointing out that animations need to be planned out before
they are produced. This usually occurs right in the creative brief, or within the proposal
to the client.

We explained how to create a Flash MX intro for the JCT site. The key techniques were
the use of Actionscript to produce random images for the dancing dude, a rather interesting Actionscript preloader, and the fact the preloader doesn't use any watches,
progress bars, or other techniques to indicate content is loading.

We also reviewed how to create a .gif animation in Fireworks MX that uses the capability of layers and frames to work together in the creation of a .gif animation.

The last section showed how to create an animation generated from a series of video still images exported from a video, manipulated in Fireworks MX, and placed into Flash MX. We also showed how the batch-processing capabilities of Fireworks MX can be a huge productivity boost when the same actions have to be applied to a number of images.

In the next chapter, we cover building buttons. Round buttons. Square buttons. Buttons that pop down and buttons that move. We show you how the MX Studio can be used to build a variety of navigation elements from simple one-color buttons to mimicking the Aqua buttons in Apple's OS X interface.

Chapter 17

MX

fireworks flash freehand coldfusion dreamweaver fireworks
eamweaver fireworks flash freehand coldfusion dreamweave
coldfusion dreamweaver fireworks flash freehand coldfusio
freehand coldfusion dreamweaver fireworks flash freehand
works flash freehand coldfusion dreamweaver fireworks
eaver fireworks flash freehand coldfusion dreamweave

Building the
Navigation
Elements

This chapter deals with buttons—square

buttons, round buttons, buttons that pul-

sate. It also deals with menus that pop up,

pop down, and some that even act like

buttons.

Though we will talk about a lot of techniques, it is important to understand that a well-constructed button will make or break a site. These navigation elements are the items visitors use to navigate through a site. The key word in that last sentence is *use*; if the elements of navigation are non-intuitive, your visitor won't know how to use them—and might not try to use them at all. We have all visited ecommerce sites where the Submit button either made or killed the sale. What the button implies is that if you simply click the button, your order will be processed and sent almost, it seems, before you unclick your mouse button. The Submit button is usually beveled with a drop shadow, the cursor changes when placed over the button or the button looks like the ubiquitous blue, underlined HTML link. In sites where the button killed the sale, the opposite occurred. The wording was not clear—Buy. The button was not obvious—a bold word in a text block, or some sort of pale blue splotch that glowed when the cursor rolled over, or the word had an arrow pointing to it and no other indication the button was live. In short, the process is non-intuitive. If the navigation for a site is awkward, users will leave the site. In today's web development environment, usability is king. Buttons and menus are the elements of the site that your visitors will use, so planning these elements of navigation—which lend to the feel of the site—is just as important as planning the look of the site. Consider intuitiveness when designing buttons. If, according to Steve Krug in his book, *Don't Make Me Think*, the visitor has to think about their actions, you are putting up roadblocks and possibly preventing the visitor from doing what they want to do. These roadblocks multiply quickly, and will result in the visitor leaving. When designing buttons and menus, consider the following:

- The design must be consistent throughout the site. When buttons change shape from beveled to flat, the visitor will become disoriented.

- Wording must be intuitive. Which is more understandable—Submit, Place the Order, or Go for It.

- Menu placement must be consistent throughout the site. If a menu bar is placed across the top of one page but at the bottom of the other, the user will become disoriented.

- Use shared libraries. All of the applications have libraries that can be saved and shared among the members of the team, develop your buttons and place them in a shared library.

- Test. Test. Test. Just because you designed a button or a menu doesn't mean the rest of humanity will understand them. Ask friends, neighbors, and co-workers to try your button and menu creations.

Creating Buttons in Fireworks MX

Prior to the introduction of Fireworks, web developers and multimedia artists spent up to 30 minutes creating each of the various button states for their presentations or pages. Fireworks reduced that work effort to less than five minutes—but with the release of MX, there is more good news.

Fireworks MX allows you to create the buttons as symbols, meaning any graphic or text object on the canvas can be changed into a button that can be reused. The big change around the button symbols is that their instances can now be edited. For example, assume you created a beveled button with the word Home on the surface. If that button is dragged from the Library onto the canvas, an instance of the button is created. If you want to change the word Home to Shirts, you now have the ability to make the change without breaking the tight symbol-instance relationship between the Home button on the canvas and its parent in the Library. Suddenly, a button bar can us a number of the instances of the original symbol, not a number of copies of the original symbol.

Creating a Button Symbol and Modifying its Instance

The button creation process in Fireworks MX starts with the creation of a Button symbol. Declaring an object to be a Button symbol opens the Button Editor where the various button states are created. When the symbol is dragged onto the canvas, the slices are created automatically, and you can then play with the instance.

To create a button symbol, follow these steps:

1. Open a new Fireworks MX document. Set the Canvas size to 200 by 200 pixels and the background color to White. Click OK.

2. Select the Rectangle tool in the Vector section of the Fireworks MX toolbar, and draw a square that is 70 pixels wide and 70 pixels high.

3. With the square selected, open the Assets panel and then click the Styles tab. A number of preset button styles appear. Click the blue square—the rightmost square in the top row. The shape now resembles a piece of beveled blue marble.

Using the Fireworks MX Styles Palette

It is easy to overlook the power of the Styles palette, which is a collection of preset object and text effects. The Styles palette is also a location for standard effects that can be used throughout the site. For example, a number of buttons contain a custom marble fill with a beveled edge. In this case, you would create the object on the canvas with the fill and the bevel. With the object selected, click the New Style button at the bottom of the palette to open the New Style dialog box shown in Figure 17.1. Click the buttons in the dialog box that relate to the object, its effect, and the text. Name the style and then click OK. The new style will appear in the bottom of the Styles panel.

continues ▶

continued▶

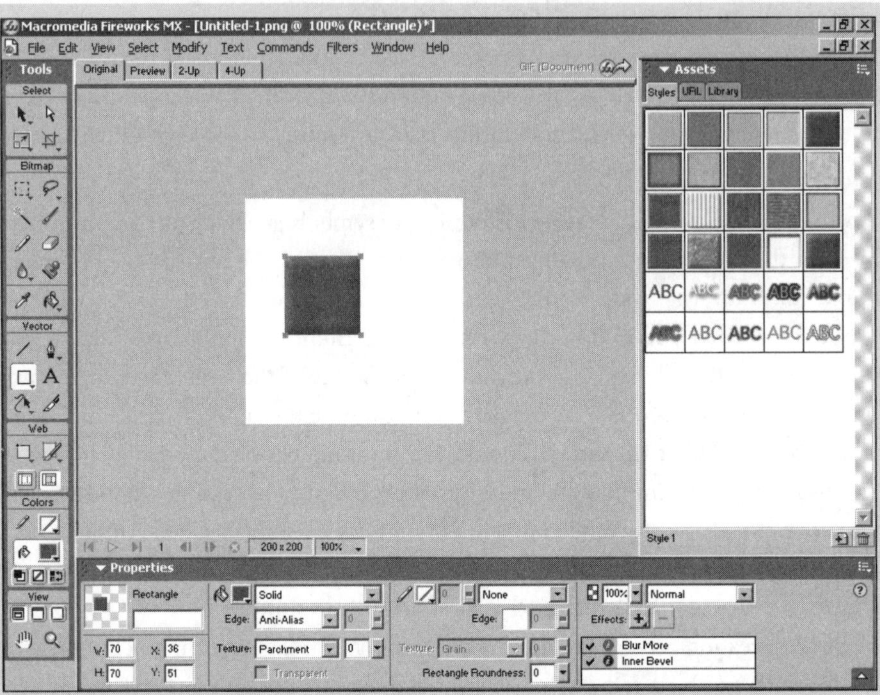

Figure 17.1   Creating a new style is not difficult when you use the New Style dialog box.

To delete the style, select an object on the canvas to which the style has been applied, and click the Trash icon at the bottom of the Styles panel. You can also press the Shift key, select the style on the panel, and click the Trash icon.

From a work group perspective, the capability to work from a common set of preset styles makes the process a lot more efficient. To share a set of styles, select the styles and then select Export Styles from Styles panel's Options menu. Give the document a name, and choose the location where the file will be stored. Click Save, and a Fireworks MX style document with the .stl extension will be created.

Other team members simply open the Styles panel on their copy of Fireworks MX, and select Import. They navigate to the folder containing the .stl document, and select it. Fireworks MX then places the imported styles into that user's Styles Library.

4. Select the Text tool, and enter an uppercase **A**. Set the font to 70-point, Arial bold. Click the Selection tool, and select both the shape and the letter.

5. Select Modify, Symbol, Convert to Symbol, or press F8 to open the Symbol Properties dialog box. Give the symbol a name, and select Button from the Properties list. Click OK. The object appears as a symbol on the canvas, the canvas will slice around the symbol, and a green Web layer indication appears over

the button. If the Web layer bothers you, open the Layers panel and turn off the visibility on the Web layer.

6. Click the button on the canvas. The Property inspector changes to indicate you have selected an instance of the button symbol. Hold down the mouse button, press the Alt (PC) or Option (Mac) key, and drag a copy of the button instance under the original instance. Release the key and the mouse, and the canvas slices changes to accommodate the new object. If the object is still selected, the icon in the Property inspector changes to indicate your selection.

7. Having two buttons with the same name can be quite confusing to the user. With the new button selected, change the A in the text area of the Property inspector to a **B**, and press Enter (PC) or Return (Mac). The new button reflects the change. The original and the symbol don't reflect the change, as shown in Figure 17.2.

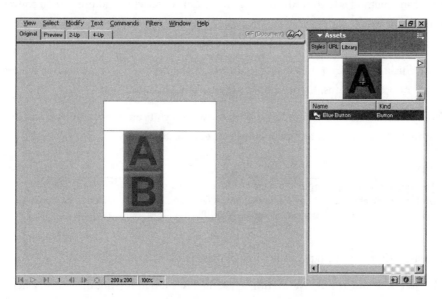

Figure 17.2   Changing the text property of an instance in the Fireworks MX Property inspector does not affect any of the other instances on the canvas or the original symbol in the Library.

Using the Button Editor

So far we have created a non-interactive button. That is, nothing happens when the mouse rolls over it or the button is clicked. These states are set in the Button Editor.

The Button Editor lets you create a button symbol that includes a two, three, or four state button. The states are self-explanatory. They are Up, Over, Down, and Over While Down, and each state contains its own window in the Button Editor. As well, the Button Editor window is divided into five tabs that walk you through the button creation process in an intuitive manner.

There are two common ways to open the Button Editor. If your canvas is blank, you can select Edit, Insert, New Button, or press Ctrl-Shift-F8 (PC) or Command-Shift-F8 (Mac) to import or draw a new button into the Up state window. The Up window is where the Button Editor always opens.

The second method is to draw the button on the canvas, select it, and press F8 to convert the object to a symbol.

Double-clicking on the image of the symbol in the Library will also open the Button Editor. Clicking Import a Button at the bottom of the Button Editor dialog box opens a Library of preset buttons. If you choose this, the states are already set.

If you prefer to create your button artwork elsewhere, you can import a FreeHand document into Fireworks MX and then convert it to a Button symbol.

Tip

There is another way to add an object on the canvas to the Button Editor. Open the Button Editor, and a blank Up window appears. Drag and drop the object to be converted to a button from the canvas into the Up Button work area.

To create a simple multistate button, follow these steps:

1. To create an Up and Over button, click the Over tab in the Button Editor. Click the Copy Up Graphic button to display a copy of the button's Up state in the work area.

2. Select the square, which is the copy of the Up state, in the work area, and select Effects, Adjust Color, Brightness/Contrast on the Property inspector. Move the brightness slider to a value of -25 and then click OK. Click Done in the Button Editor to close the Button Editor.

3. To test your new button, select File, Preview in Browser to check out your work.

   So far the button is interactive but it really does nothing. Adding the remaining two states—Down and Over While Down—will allow you to have an event occur when the button is clicked.

4. Open your new button in the Button Editor, and click the Down tab. Click the Copy Over Graphic button and then select the button in the work area. Click the Inner Bevel Property Info button on the Property inspector, and set the state of the effect to Highlighted to automatically lighten the button.

5. To add a link to the button's Down state, click the Active Area tab. The Property inspector changes to indicate a slice, as shown in Figure 17.3. In the Link area of the Property inspector, enter **http://www.macromedia.com** and then click Done in the Button Editor. Save the document as **ButtonTest**, and test in a browser.

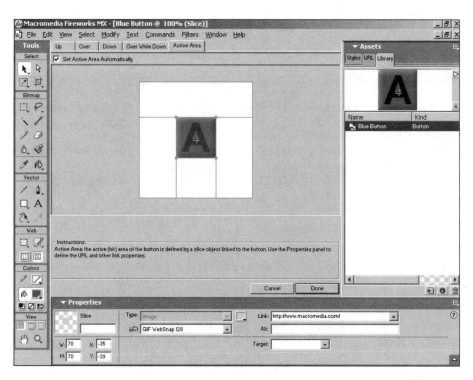

Figure 17.3   Adding an absolute or relative link to a button is done in the Active Area of the Button Editor. The actual link is added in the Link area of the Property inspector.

6. Open the Button Editor, and click the Over While Down tab; then click the Copy Down Graphics button. Set the property of this button to Inset in the Inner Bevel Effects area of the Property inspector.

Tip

This button state is somewhat specialized, and should not be used for a simple rollover. Over While Down is a state that assumes the mouse is pressed while over the button, and remains pressed. This state is inappropriate for a single button. It is designed for use with navigation bars.

7. Two buttons on a web page that go to the same place are also confusing. Select one of the buttons on the canvas, and change the destination for this button from Macromedia to `http://www.newriders.com`. Don't make this change in the Button Editor, or it will be reflected across all of the instances on the Stage. Use the Link area of the Property inspector for each of the instances chosen on the canvas.

Note

If a series of buttons are common to all of the pages in a site, there is a way to make them available to all of the members of the work group. Create all of the buttons, including their states, in one multilayer Fireworks document. Save the document as a .png file, and have the members of the team import the document into their Library panel. Alternately, each member of the team can place a copy of the file in the Fireworks MX Configuration, Libraries folder. The file is then accessed through Edit, Libraries. The file is included in the files listed in the Button Libraries menu. When the file is selected, the Import A Button dialog box opens, and you can select all of the buttons in the list as well as select only those needed.

Buttons in Flash MX

Creating a button in Flash MX doesn't require a degree in rocket science. Buttons in Flash MX are really nothing more than a movie clip with a four-frame timeline. Each frame contains an image of the Up, Over, or Down state of the button. The fourth frame determines the area of the button that will cause the cursor to change to a pointing finger when viewed in a browser.

As in Fireworks MX, any graphic or text object on the Flash MX Stage can be made into a button. As well, buttons with Up, Down, and Over states in Flash MX are always symbols. In this section, we review how to create and test a button in Flash MX. We wrap up the section with how FreeHand, Fireworks MX, and Flash MX can combine to create those really cool buttons used in the Apple Aqua interface.

It is important to understand that when it comes to Flash MX, the button symbol has two purposes. The first is, of course, to create interactive buttons that change color and navigate through the Flash movie or out to the Internet. The other purpose of Flash's button symbol involves usability. In certain instances, a mouse event—a click or rollover, for example—triggers an animation in a movie clip. Adding button behaviors and properties involving mouse actions to a movie clip will, when viewed in a browser, turn the cursor into a pointing finger to indicate the object is interactive. If those properties were not present, the cursor would have remained as an arrow.

Drawing Buttons in Flash MX

After you discover that virtually anything can be a button in Flash MX, the creative possibilities become endless. Text changes color, objects look as though they are depressed, and in certain cases, objects appear in different areas of the Flash Stage. Flash MX also allows you to import the button artwork created in Fireworks MX and FreeHand, as well as enables you to import the symbols and layers from a FreeHand document. In this way, if the tools in Flash appear limited for your needs, there is an abundance of equally powerful tools available to you.

To create a button in Flash MX, follow these steps:

1. Open a new Flash MX document, and set the Stage color to White. Add a new layer named **Text**.

2. With the Text layer selected, select the Text tool and then enter the word **Macromedia**. Set the text size to 24 points, and use your favorite font. Deselect the word, select the Text tool again, and enter the words **New Riders**. Place the words above each other on the Stage, and leave room for a round button above each word.

3. Select Insert, New Symbol, or press Ctrl-F8 (PC) or Command-F8 (Mac) to open the Create New Symbol dialog box. Name the symbol **Macromedia**, and select button from the Properties list to edit the button's timeline.

   The button's timeline is a bit different from the traditional Flash timeline. There are only four frames: Up, Over, Down, and Hit, which determines the area of the button the cursor has to be over to trigger the button events.

4. Add a keyframe in the Up frame, draw a blue circle, and align it to the center of the Stage. Add a keyframe in the Over frame. The Up symbol will appear. Change the color to Red and add a keyframe in the Down frame.

5. When the Over symbol appears, change its color to Green. Add a keyframe to the Hit frame; the Down symbol appears. You can draw a square over the object to indicate the active area, or just leave the button as is. Either way, the shape of the button or the square will be the hotspot that triggers the button event.

6. Your button should resemble that shown in Figure 17.4. Select your button in the Symbol Library and then select Duplicate Symbol from the Library pop-down menu. Rename the symbol **New Riders**.

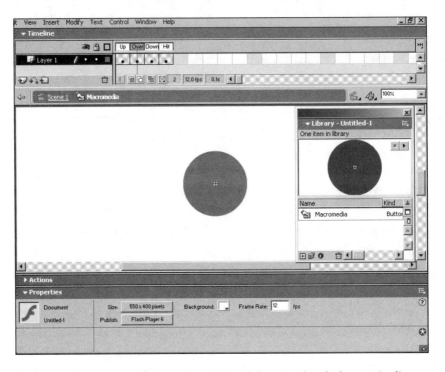

Figure 17.4   The various states of the button have been created in the button timeline.

7. Double-click the new symbol's image in the Library to open the Button Symbol Editor. Change the color for each of the states, and click the Scene 1 button just under the layers to be taken to the main timeline. Select frame 1 in Layer 1 of the main timeline, and drag an instance of the Macromedia button beside the word Macromedia on the Stage. Repeat this for the New Riders button.

> **Tip**
>
> To test the various states of the buttons, select Control, Enable Simple Buttons, or press Ctrl-Alt-B (PC) or Command-Option-B (Mac) to test your button. Roll the cursor over each button, or press the mouse to see the button change. This feature gets annoying very quickly because you can't select the button on the Stage when this feature is turned on. You should get into the habit of testing the states and then turning the feature off when you have finished.

Adding Button Behaviors

With the release of Flash MX, coding buttons with Actionscript became both easier and, in many respects, more difficult. In the previous version of the application, when you opened the Actionscript panel in Normal mode and a button was selected, you could choose specific mouse events. This has all changed. After an action is attached to a button, a default event—usually release—appears. Still, the Actionscript Editor, especially in Normal mode, is much more user friendly than past iterations.

One of the most common errors made by those who are new to Flash MX is adding the button code to the symbol instead of to the instance on the Stage. Always add the code to the instance on the Stage.

To add an action to a button, follow these steps:

1. Right-click or Control-click the Macromedia button on the Stage in the main timeline to open the context menu.

2. Select Actions from the context menu to open the Actionscript Editor. The little blue squares with arrows along the left side of the Actionscript Editor are more affectionately referred to as Books. Open the Actionscript Options pop-down menu, and be sure you are in Normal mode.

   The objective is to click the Macromedia button in the Flash movie, and be taken to the Macromedia web site; therefore, the event is a mouse press, and the action that is attached to that event is to navigate to the Macromedia main page.

3. Click the Actions book. When it opens, click the Browser/Network book to open the actions. To attach an action, double-click the getURL action.

   When you do this, the right side of the window activates. The top half of the window allows you to enter the URL of the web site to which you are navigating, and the window area enables you to choose the window or HTML frame into which the page will be loaded.

URL's can be entered either as absolute or relative paths. In the case of our button, entering **http://www.macromedia.com** is the preferred method because it is a web address. In the case of a frames-based layout, a relative path— myPage.htm—would be called for. When you enter the URL, notice that it has also been added between the quotation marks in the second line of the code that starts with getURL.

4. Check the code, and you also notice the event is wrong. The default for buttons is on (release). Our event is to be triggered when the mouse is pressed. Click the word release once, and the various mouse events appear in the pane where you entered the URL information.

5. Select Press and deselect Release. Your code should resemble that shown in Figure 17.5. If it does, close the Actionscript Editor. Repeat these three steps for the New Riders button. Enter **http://www.newriders.com** in the URL input area.

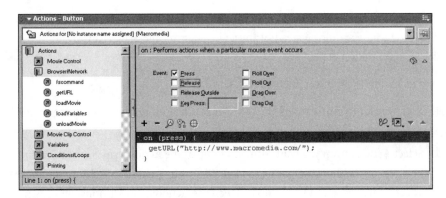

Figure 17.5   The URL and the event have been added to the getURL action. Though you can have multiple events that trigger an action, in this case, only one is necessary.

If you publish and test the movie at this point, clicking the buttons will take you to the URL you entered.

Using Actions to Navigate Through a Flash Movie

The capability to load web pages into frames and navigate to URLs is one use for buttons in Flash MX. Another use is to allow the user to navigate through the Flash movie. Though this may sound a bit complicated, it isn't. The Flash MX timeline is linear, meaning a button click moves the playback head to the frame or frame label specified in the Actionscript. Using frame labels, stop actions, and Actionscript attached to the navigation buttons, you can quickly enable the user to move through your movie.

To add an action to a frame, follow these steps:

1. Add two layers named Actions and Labels to your movie. The Actions layer will contain a script that stops the playback head on that frame. If that action was not there, the playback head would simply loop endlessly until a stop action is invoked somewhere else in the movie. The Labels layer will contain a label that will be used for navigation purposes.

2. Place the cursor over frame 10 in your top layer, and click/drag down to the Text layer. Release the mouse, and select Insert, Frames. Add keyframes in frames 5 and 10 of the Text and Actions layers. Add a keyframe in frame 5 of the Labels layer.

3. Select the Text tool, click in keyframe 1 of the Text layer, and enter **Go to Frame 5**. Click the keyframe once in frame 5 of the Text layer and then enter **Go to Frame 10**. Click the last keyframe once in the Text layer, and enter **Go to Frame 1**.

4. Select each of the text blocks you have just created, and convert each one to a Button symbol. To accomplish this, select the text block and press the F8 key to launch the Symbol Editor. When the Symbol Editor opens, name the symbol and give it a button behavior.

Tip

When naming button symbols, use a name that means something. A button named ToMacromedia is more relevant than a button named Button1.

5. Click the keyframe once in frame 5 of the Labels layer. Enter a name for the label in the Property inspector, and press the Enter (PC) or Return (Mac). A small red flag with the name beside it appears on the keyframe.

6. To stop the playback head over each of the keyframes, you add a Stop action to the frame. Right-click (PC) or Control-click (Mac) on the first keyframe in the Actions layer. Select Actions from the context menu. When the Actionscript Editor opens, double-click the Actions book, click the Movie Control book, and double-click Stop.

7. Rather than repeating the previous steps for the remaining two frames, do the following: With the Actionscript Editor open, click the keyframe in frame 5 of the Actions layer, and double-click the Stop action. Repeat this for frame 10. Close the Actionscript Editor.

8. Drag the playback head back to frame 1. Select the Text button on the Stage, and open Actions from the context menu.

9. Double-click GoTo in the Movie Control book, and change the event to Press. Click GoToAndPlay in the script. In this case, you will be navigating to a frame with a label—frame 5.

10. At the top of the Editor, select Frame Label from the Type pop-down menu. In the frame input area, you have two choices regarding how to get to the label named in frame 5. The first is to enter the name of the label. The second is to click and hold the button to the right of the input area. A list of all of the labels appear, and you can select the one to which you will be navigating. In this case, click the label name, and the name appears between the quotation marks in the brackets after GoToAndPlay.

11. Close the Editor, move the playback head to frame 5, and select the Text button. Open the Actionscript Editor, and double-click GoToAndPlay. In this case, you will be navigating to a numbered frame. Select Frame Number from the Type pop-down menu, and enter **10** in the Frame input area.

12. Close the Editor, select the button on frame 10, and use the Editor to navigate to frame 1.

13. Close the Editor. Your timeline should resemble the one shown in Figure 17.6.

Tip

The Actionscript Editor takes up a lot of screen real estate. Get into the habit of closing it when preparing to test your code.

14. Publish your movie, and test it in a browser.

Tip

The use of labels and not frame numbers for navigation is standard procedure among the Flash development community. A label is a graphic representation of a way point; when a script refers to a label, the playback always moves to that location regardless of whether or not the label has been moved on the timeline.

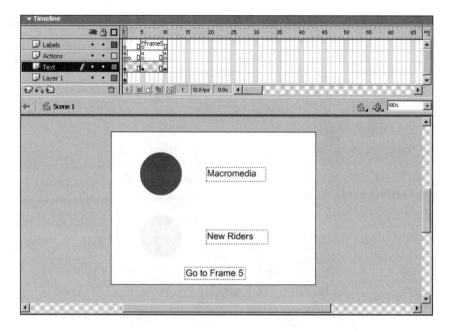

Figure 17.6   Navigating through the timeline requires you to plan how your user will move from one part of the timeline to the other. Use labels, not frame numbers, as your main navigation way points.

Building an Aqua Interface Button

When Apple introduced its new OS X, the news groups and other forums were suddenly inundated with users wondering how they can create those cool, pulsing, blue Aqua buttons.

A large image of the button can be found at `http://www.apple.com/macosx/technologies/aqua.html`, and can also be seen in Figure 17.7. If you examine the image, you see that it is composed of a series of discrete shapes. The basic shape resembles a capsule. The top of the button contains a reflection, and the bottom holds a glow. There is also a faint drop shadow under the text, and another under the button itself.

Building the button requires some basic shapes. The first shape is the button itself. Another shape is the area that holds the reflection, and yet another is the text. We will build these shapes in FreeHand and then exporting them to Fireworks MX. The button is built in Fireworks MX and then placed into Flash MX where it is given the capability to pulse when the user rolls over the button.

Figure 17.7   The Aqua button on the Apple web site.

Preparing the Button in FreeHand

Though the shapes could just as easily be done in Fireworks MX, FreeHand offers a degree of control over the shapes and text that is better than that the control offered by Fireworks MX.

To prepare a button in FreeHand, follow these steps:

1. Open a new FreeHand document, change the view from Preview to Keyline, and set the magnification to 200%. By switching to Keyline view, you can concentrate on the shapes and not be distracted by strokes or fills that may be added. Select View, Page Rulers, Show to open the vertical and horizontal rulers.

2. This step prepares the page for the precision drawing and placement of the shapes. Drag a horizontal ruler to about the mid-point of your screen. Set the 0,0 point to the guide you just placed. Drag a horizontal guide to the 20-pixel mark, and drag another to the 40-pixel mark. Drag a vertical guide onto the page and

set the 0,0 point to the intersection point of the top horizontal guide and your vertical guide. Place vertical guides at the 12, 20, 62, 104, 112, and 120 marks of the vertical ruler. Select View, Guides, Snap to Guides.

3. Add a new layer named **Button**. Select the Circle tool. Place the cursor at the intersection point of the center horizontal guide and the one at the 24-pixel mark.

4. Press and hold down Alt-Shift (PC) or Option-Shift (Mac), and click-drag a circle from the point outward to the left-most vertical marker. That key combination draws a perfect circle from the center point of the circle outwards.

5. Click the circle, press your Option/Alt -Shift keys, and click/drag a copy of your circle to the right edge of the drawing area. By holding down the Shift key, you constrain the move to horizontal, not vertical.

6. Select the Rectangle tool, and place the cursor at the point where the vertical guide at the 20-pixel mark intersects the top-most horizontal guide. Drag down to the point where the vertical guide at the 112-pixel mark intersects the bottom horizontal guide.

7. Choose Edit, Select, All, or press Control-A (PC) or Command-A (Mac), and select Modify, Combine, Union. The three shapes merge into one. Select this new shape, and ensure you have no extra control points. If you do have extra control points, select the Subselection tool, click the extra point, and press the Delete key.

8. Fill the shape with white, and if a stroke is present, set the stroke to None. Copy the shape and deselect the shape on the page.

9. Add a new layer named **Reflect**. Paste the shape on the clipboard into this new layer, and drag it over the original shape. With the Reflect object still selected, select the Scale tool, and by clicking the points at the top and the side, and click/drag until the object fits between the vertical guides at the 12- and 112-pixel marks and the height of the object is about 12 to 16 pixels. Deselect.

10. Add a new layer named **New Riders**. Select the Text tool, click the page, and enter the words **New Riders**. Select the text and open the Text panel by pressing Ctrl-T (PC) or Command-T (Mac). The text on the Apple button is a variation of the Lucida font. If you don't have the font, use a fine sans serif such as Arial, Futura, or a Bauhaus. Don't use a bold version of the font or set the weight to bold. It will be far too heavy for the button.

11. Set the point size to 18 points. The letters were a bit too spread out for our lik-
    ing. We tracked the lower case letters in at a setting of -5%. The Ne letter pair
    was kerned to a value of -7%, and the Ri pair was kerned to a value of -5%.

12. Change to the Selection tool, and move the words onto the button. Deselect the
    words.

13. Add a new layer named **Macromedia**. Select the Text tool and enter, format,
    track, and kern the word Macromedia and then deselect it. Your page should now
    resemble that shown in Figure 17.8. Save the image, and quit FreeHand.

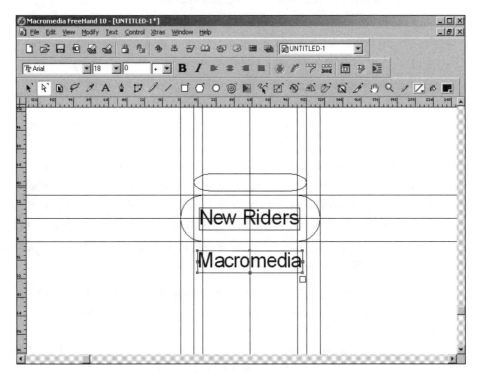

Figure 17.8   The shapes and the lettering have been created in FreeHand and are ready for
                   export to Fireworks MX.

Note

The shapes could have been filled with their respective colors in FreeHand. The problem is the Web Safe palette that ships with FreeHand does not allow for the creation of
custom hexadecimal colors, so it makes sense to create the images in FreeHand and
then export them to Fireworks MX for final assembly.

Assembling the Button in Fireworks MX

The old adage "Use the right tool for the job" applies here. Fireworks MX is a web application and, as such, the image can be prepared and optimized for export to the web through Flash MX. Along with the use of layers, opacity, and a variety of effects and filters, Fireworks MX exports the necessary 32-bit .png image that permits transparency in Flash MX.

To create the aqua button in Fireworks MX, follow these steps:

1. Open a new Fireworks MX document. When the New Document dialog box opens, set the width to 200 pixels, the height to 150 pixels, the resolution to 100, and the background color to White. Click OK.

2. Select File, Import, and navigate to the folder containing the FreeHand button. Double-click the file in the Import dialog box to open the Vector Options dialog box. Ensure that Antialias Paths and Text are selected, and choose Crisp from the Text Options pop-down menu. This ensures the text remains distinct when it is imported. Click OK.

3. Roll the cursor to the upper left corner of the canvas, and click once. The images appear on the Stage as well as in the Layers menu.

4. Select the Button shape on the canvas, and fill it with 0000CC. Drag the reflection into place over the button. If the Layers panel isn't open, open the Layers panel and create two copies of the Button layer. Be sure to give each layer a distinct name such as Button 1, Button 2, and so on. Turn off the visibility of the layers except for the Reflect layer.

Tip

If you don't feel like naming the button layers, let the software do the work. Drag a copy of the Button layer onto the New Layer icon at the bottom of the Layers panel. A new layer named Button 1 appears. Repeat this step one more time, and you have your three named copies.

5. The reflection of the button tends to fade off as it moves towards the center of the button. To create this effect, zoom in on the object on the Stage using the magnifying glass. Open the Reflect layer and drag the image strip under the Layer folder on top of the New Bitmap icon at the bottom of the panel. This creates a copy of the original image directly over the original.

6. Select the new image. Fill it with a linear gradient that goes from white to black by selecting the Paint Bucket tool and then moving the resulting handles so the square one is at the top of the image and the round one is at the bottom.

7. Select both images, and choose Modify, Mask, Group As Mask. Turn on the visibility of the Button and New Riders layers. The reflection fades from white to transparent as it moves towards the center of the button.

8. To create the illusion of the text curving with the button, drag the New Riders layer under the Reflect layer, and the slide the text under the mask. To see the final effect, double-click the magnifying glass to return to 100 percent view.

9. To create the glow inside of the button, select the Button 2 layer to select the object and to turn on its visibility. With the object selected, choose Modify, Transform, Numeric Transform, Scale. When the Scale dialog box opens, deselect both the Scale attributes and Constrain Proportions buttons.

10 Set the horizontal scale to 90% and the vertical scale to 40%. Click OK, and set the fill color on the Property inspector to #CCFFFF. Deselect.

11. Select the shape in the Button 1 layer. Set its horizontal scale to 95%, its vertical scale to 60%, and its color to 330099. Select both of the objects and group them.

12. Apply an 8-pixel Gaussian blur to the object from the Effects in the Property inspector. Select Effects, Brightness/Contrast, and set Brightness slider to 40 and the Contrast slider to 25.

13. To bring some of the underlying image in the Button layer through the glow, set the opacity of the grouped objects in the glow to 90%.

14. To finish the image, add a drop shadow to the words. Select the New Riders layer and then select the words. Click the Effects button on the Property inspect, and select Effects, Shadow and Glow, Drop Shadow. Set the Offset setting to 6 pixels, the Opacity setting to 50%, the Softness setting to 7, and the Angle setting to 270. The button is now ready for placement in Flash MX, and should resemble the one shown in Figure 17.9.

To prepare the button for export to Flash MX, the image needs to be carefully prepared for Flash MX. Because Flash MX can accept images with Alpha channels, you don't have to worry about the loss of detail that normally results from converting an image to a Transparent GIF. Still, the image is a bitmap, and bitmaps can slow down playback in Flash MX.

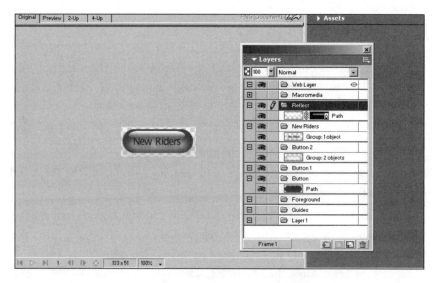

Figure 17.9   The button is complete, and your layers should resemble those shown.

To export the transparent button, follow these steps:

1. Select the Crop tool, and crop out the extra area of the canvas. Click the canvas once and then set its color in the Property inspector to None. This makes the canvas transparent.

2. Select File, Export Preview, and select PNG 32 from the format pop-down list in the Export Preview dialog box. This exports the Transparency to Flash MX.

3. Click the Export button. Name the file, and navigate to folder where the file is to be saved. Make sure Save As, Images Only is selected and then click OK. Quit Fireworks MX. If you are prompted by Fireworks to save the file, do so.

Creating the Pulsating Button in Flash MX

Getting the button to pulse is a three-step process. The button is first imported into Flash MX as a graphic symbol. That symbol is then added to a movie clip where the pulse happens. Finally, the movie clip is added to a Button symbol. Adding the clip to the Button symbol enables the button to pulse when the cursor rolls over it as well as allows it to go to the New Riders web site.

To create a pulsating button, follow these steps:

1. Open a new Flash MX document, and select Insert, New Symbol to open the New Symbol dialog box. Name the symbol, and give it a graphic behavior. When the symbol opens, import your Fireworks MX button into the symbol, and align it to the center of the Stage.

2. Select Insert, New Symbol to open the New Symbol dialog box. Name the symbol—for example, **ButtonMC**—and then select movie clip as its behavior.

3. When the symbol opens, drag a copy of the graphic button onto the Stage, and align it to the center of the Stage.

4. The intention is to have the button pulsate rather rapidly. Add keyframes at frames 5 and 10 of the timeline. Move the playback head to frame 5. Select the button on the Stage—not the timeline—and select Color, Brightness on the Property inspector. Move the brightness slider down to a value of -30. You can only darken the button if you are working with an instance of the Button symbol.

5. Click once between the first and fifth frames, and select Insert, Create Motion Tween. An arrow appears on the timeline between frames 1 and 5. Do the same thing between the keyframes in frames 5 and 10. If you press Enter (PC) or Return (Mac), you should see the image pulse. To ensure it pulses, add a new layer and name it **Actions**.

6. Add a keyframe at frame 10 of the Actions layer. Add a GoToAndPlay action to the keyframe with frame 1 as the frame to go to. The movie clip timeline should resemble the one shown in Figure 17.10.

7. To test the pulsing effect, click the scene 1 button and then drag a copy of the Button movie clip onto the Stage. Select Control, Test Movie. When you have finished watching the button pulse, close the test window.

8. Create a new button symbol. Drag an instance of the Button graphic symbol onto the Stage, and align the instance to the center of the Stage. Add keyframes in the Over, Down, and Hit frames.

9. Click the button in the Over frame, and press the Delete key to remove it. Drag an instance of the Button movie clip onto the Stage, and align it to the center of the Stage.

10. Select the button on the Stage in the Down frame, and reduce its brightness to -40 in the Property inspector. Click the Scene 1 button. Delete the movie clip that is on the Stage, and replace it with the new button symbol.

11. Test the movie. The button pulsates when the cursor is over it, and turns dark when pressed. Close the test window.

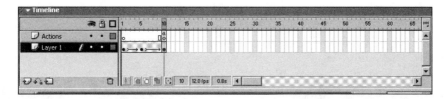

Figure 17.10   The pulsing effect is done in a movie clip. The instance at frame 5 is darkened and motion tweens are added between the keyframes.

Tip

Aligning the different instances is simple. After placing an instance of the button graphic symbol in frame 1 of the button, add a keyframe to frame 2, the Over state, and select the new instance of the button symbol. Go to the Property inspector, select the Swap button, and click the Movie Clip button symbol. Flash replaces the graphic with the movie clip with its animation. Be sure to change the symbol type in the Property inspector to Movie Clip.

12. Select the instance on the Stage and add a getURL action to the instance. Enter the URL **http://www.newriders.com**.

13. Have the New Riders page open in a new window in the browser. Select Window, _blank from the choices presented. Close the Actionscript Editor. Save the movie, and select File, Publish.

14. Quit Flash, and open the button's HTML page in your browser. Test the button. If you click it, the New Riders page opens, as shown in Figure 17.11.

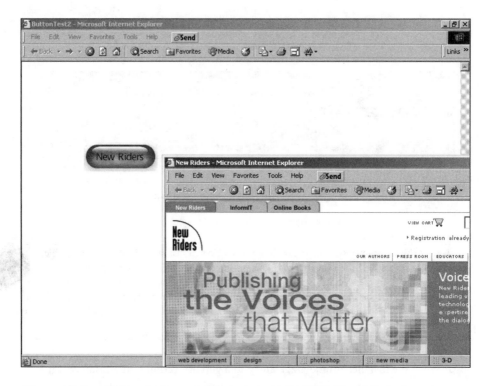

Figure 17.11   Clicking the button in a browser opens the New Riders web site in a new browser window.

Working with Buttons in Dreamweaver MX

As you have seen, there are a number of ways to build buttons. Eventually, though, these buttons are going to have to be incorporated into a page layout. Dreamweaver MX is a robust tool for accepting and managing a variety of media. Though Fireworks MX and Flash MX do an admirable job of creating buttons, Dreamweaver MX is another tool in the MX Studio production arsenal.

This section examines a number of Dreamweaver MX's button management capabilities. You start off with inserting a Flash button, using Dreamweaver MX's Flash Button feature. From there, you create a button in Flash MX and then learn how one-click access to Flash MX from Dreamweaver MX can be a real timesaver when changes have to be made. You also see how creating a button using artwork created in FreeHand, coding in Flash, and importing into Dreamweaver MX offers more creative flexibility that the Flash MX to Dreamweaver MX workflow. Finally, you create a JavaScript button using artwork from Fireworks MX that has a number of Dreamweaver MX behaviors attached to the button.

Flash Buttons in Dreamweaver MX

When Macromedia introduced version 4 of Dreamweaver, they slipped a rather neat feature into the application. The Flash Buttons feature offered the capability to create and use Flash buttons without the user having to own a copy of the application. Dreamweaver MX, quite wisely, has retained this feature.

Though Flash files are small, we suggest you approach the use of this feature in Dreamweaver MX with a degree of caution. As you saw in the previous example, the use of a symbol in Flash MX cuts back on bandwidth demands. The Dreamweaver MX Flash buttons don't use symbols; therefore, your trade-off for the elegance of this feature is a demand on bandwidth.

Using the Flash Button feature in Dreamweaver MX is great for a single button on a page. If you place five or six Flash buttons on the page, you will experience a bandwidth issue because processing resources will be consumed on the user's machine when the Flash Player is instantiated for each button. If you are going to be using the same button multiple times, consider creating it in Flash MX instead; however the Flash Buttons feature in Dreamweaver MX is a great tool to have available when needed.

To create a Flash Button using Dreamweaver MX, follow these steps:

1. Open Dreamweaver MX, and select the Media tab in the Insert bar. Click the Flash Button icon to open the Insert Flash Button dialog box shown in Figure 17.12.

Note

Flash buttons are placed only into named documents. If you open a new Dreamweaver MX document, you are prompted to save the document. There are two other methods available to insert a Flash button. The first is to simply drag the Flash button icon onto the page from the Insert bar. The second is to select Insert, Interactive Images, Flash Button to insert a Flash button into a named page.

2. Select the Chrome Bar button style from the list in the Style area. Enter **New Riders** into the Button text area and then select a font and point size for the button.

Figure 17.12   The Insert Flash Button dialog box presents you with a number of button choices and customization options. You can also make a few changes and test the button using the Property inspector.

Caution

Be careful with this with formatting text in a Dreamweaver MX Flash button. Not all fonts look good in a button. To examine your choice, enter the text, choose your font and point size, and click the Apply button.

3. In the Link area, enter the absolute link to New Riders—
   http://www.newriders.com. If you are linking the button to a page in the site, click the Browse button and then navigate to the page.

4. Having decided what page will load, you next choose the usual list of targets. The background color is a bit confusing. The color you select will not change the color of the button, but will change the color of the background where the button is placed. To try it, click the Bg Color chip once and then select #FF0000 (red) from the palette. Click the Apply button once. The rectangular background for the button turns red. Set the color back to White (#FFFFFF).

As you have seen, this feature allows you to match the background color of the area in which the button resides. If you are using a background image, or can't match the background color, select the No Fill option on the palette for a transparent background.

5. Give the button a name, and click OK. Preview the button by selecting File, Preview in Browser.

6. To change the properties of a Flash button, click the button once in the page, and enter new values for the button in the Property inspector. If you want to try the button without going to New Riders, click the Play button on the Property inspector and then click the button on the page. The Play button changes to Stop in the Property inspector. When a button is playing, it can't be selected. If you want to change the button type or the wording, click the Stop button, and double-click the Edit button to open the Insert Flash Button dialog box.

Tip

If you close the page with a Flash button and then reopen the page later, you may see the generic Flash Content icon in the button's location. To bring the button back to life, double-click the button to open the Insert Flash Button dialog box, click Apply, and click OK. The Get More Styles button also appears in the Insert Flash Button dialog box. Clicking this takes you to the Macromedia Dreamweaver MX Exchange where you can download more Flash buttons.

Using Buttons Created in Flash MX

As you learned earlier in this chapter, creating a button in Flash MX and navigating the web is not terribly difficult to accomplish. The first part of this section demonstrates how you can create a simple Flash MX button, place it in Dreamweaver MX, and edit the button in Flash MX with one click in Dreamweaver. From there, you create a similar button in FreeHand, export the file to Flash MX for the assembly and coding, and move into Dreamweaver MX. The final section shows how you can use a button created in Fireworks MX, which is turned into a Flash MX button symbol, and placed into Dreamweaver MX.

To create and place Flash MX buttons into Dreamweaver MX, follow these steps:

1. Open a new Flash MX document. When the document opens, set the size in the Property inspector to 80 pixels wide and 60 pixels high with a white background.

2. Open a new Graphic symbol and name it **Button**. Set the fill to the blue gradient at the bottom of the Fill Color palette, set the stroke to #999999 (light gray), and the stroke width to 4 pixels.

3. Select the Oval tool from the toolbar, press the Shift key, and draw a perfect circle. Click the circle once with the Arrow tool, open the Info panel by pressing Ctrl-I (PC) or Command-I (Mac), and set the circle's dimensions to 30 by 30 pixels.

4. Open the Align panel and then align the button to the center of the Stage.

5. Open a new button symbol and name it **toMacromedia**. When the Button Symbol timeline appears, drag a copy of the button graphic onto the Stage, and align it to the center of the Stage.

6. Select the Text tool, click once under the button, and enter **To Macromedia**. You can choose the font, but be sure to set the size to 12 points.

7. Add a keyframe in the Over frame. Select the Arrow tool, click the circle, and select Modify, Break Apart. This will separate the gradient from the stroke. Deselect the object in the Over frame.

8. Click the Fill Transform tool once and then click the gradient. When the handles appear, move the center point of the gradient to the top of the circle. The goal is to create an effect that illuminates the top of circle, giving the illusion that the ball rotated upwards. Add a keyframe to the down frame, and deselect the object in the Down frame.

9. Select the Fill Transform tool, and move the center point to the bottom of the circle. Deselect.

10. Insert a keyframe in the hit area. You need to ensure the cursor is over the ball before it starts rotating. Click the gradient once to select it, and copy the gradient. Select everything on the Stage, and press the Delete key. Select Edit, Paste In Place. A copy of the gradient is placed exactly where the gradient used to be.

11. Fill the gradient with a bright lime green color. Your Button Symbol timeline should resemble that shown in Figure 17.13. If it does, click the Scene 1 button.

12. Drag the Button symbol from the Library onto the Stage. Right-click (PC) or Control-click (Mac) the button on the Stage (not the frame), and select Actions from the context menu.

13. Add a getURL action, and set the URL to `http://www.macromedia.com`. Close the Actionscript Editor, and save the button.

14. After the save is complete, select Edit, Publish Settings, or press Ctrl-Shift-F12 (PC) or Command-Shift-F12 (Mac) to open the Publish Settings dialog box. Because the button is going to be placed in Dreamweaver MX, publishing an

HTML document along with the .swf isn't necessary. Dreamweaver MX will do that for you. Deselect the HTML check box, click the Publish button, and quit Flash MX.

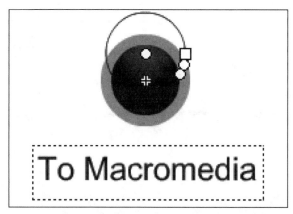

Figure 17.13   The various states of the buttons have been set. Note the position of the gradient's center point as set by the Fill Transform tool.

15. Open Dreamweaver MX. Set up a new site that saves the files to the folder containing your .swf file, and save the page. Open the Files panel, and click the Site tab.

16. Drag a copy of the .swf file onto the page. Click the Play button on the Property inspector to test the various states of the button, except for the link to the Macromedia site. Test the page in a browser. When you quit the browser, your Dreamweaver page should resemble Figure 17.14.

17. Now you need to change the link and destination to New Riders. Click the Flash button once on the page to select it. If it doesn't select, click the Stop button on the Property inspector. Click the Edit button on the Property inspector to launch Flash MX.

18. Navigate to the .fla file and then open it. Open the Button symbol, and change the word Macromedia to **New Riders**. Click the Scene 1 button.

19. When you return to the main timeline, select the instance on the Stage, open the Actions from the context menu, and change the URL in the getURL, action from `http://www.macromedia.com` to **`http://www.newriders.com`**.

20. Click the Done button above the timeline to quit Flash MX and return to Dreamweaver MX. If you click the Play button on the Property inspector, you see your change.

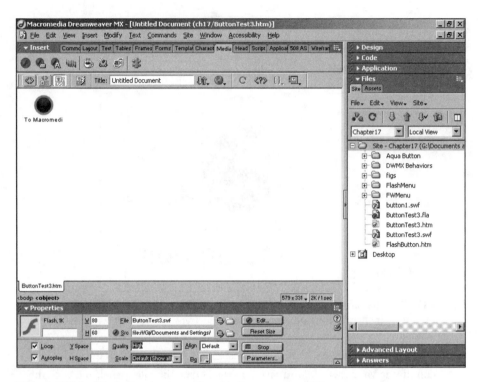

Figure 17.14   The button has been placed in Dreamweaver MX.

Understanding the Freehand to Flash MX to Dreamweaver MX Workflow

Flash MX's drawing tools are rather rudimentary when placed against those of FreeHand. In the previous exercise, you created a Flash MX button using a prebuilt gradient in Flash MX's Fill palette. This exercise teaches you how to create a similar button, but actually gives the illusion of a button being pressed.

To create a button in FreeHand, follow these steps:

1. Open FreeHand, select the Oval tool, and draw a circle that is 40 pixels wide and 40 pixels high. Fill it with a linear gradient that starts with #000066 (blue) and ends with #FFFFFF (white). Set the Gradient angle to 90 degrees. The circle should fill with dark blue at the bottom and finish with white at the top. If there is a stroke around the circle, click the Stroke tab and then select None from the Stroke pop-down menu.

Note

FreeHand's roots are in the print universe; therefore, when it comes to choosing color, the color pickers tend to resemble the ink swatch books that graphic artists purchase for their print work. It is no different for the Web Color Picker in FreeHand. The colors are treated as swatches from a book, and unlike Fireworks MX, the colors are not contained in the palette used in the Flash MX, Dreamweaver MX, and Fireworks MX interfaces. Hopefully, Macromedia will address this discrepancy in a future version of FreeHand.

2. Create a copy of the circle, select the Scale tool, and with the Shift key held down to constrain the proportions, scale the circle to a point where it is about 75 percent of the original size. Click the Fill tab, and set the gradient angle to 270%. Align the circles on the center points, group them, and convert them to a symbol named **Up**.

3. Open the Library, if necessary, and select the Up symbol. Select Duplicate, and rename the new symbol **Down**.

4. Make another duplicate of the Up symbol, and name it **Over**. Double-click the image of the Over symbol to open the Symbol Editor. Click the button once in the Symbol Editor to select it and then select Modify, Ungroup, or press Ctrl-Shift-G (PC) or Command-Shift-G (Mac).

5. Select the inner circle, click the Fill tab, and set the gradient angle to 0%. Open the Down symbol, and ungroup the circles. Change the inner circle's gradient angle to 90%, and the outer circle's angle to 270%. Close the Symbol Editor, place instances of the three buttons on the canvas, delete the Brush Tips folder from the symbol Library, and save the FreeHand document.

Tip

Exporting a FreeHand document that contains only the Up symbol will result in only that specific FreeHand symbol being exported to Flash MX. Also, FreeHand always adds a Brush Tips folder to the Library. Be sure to delete it before exporting any artwork containing symbols from FreeHand into Fireworks MX or Flash MX.

Tip

Placing gradients that go in opposite directions over each other create the illusion of one sinking into the other.

6. Open a new Flash MX document with a Stage that is 120 pixels wide by 130 pixels high with a white background color. Import your FreeHand document into Flash MX. If you have a couple of extra layers on the timeline, delete them.

7. Open a new Button symbol. Drag the Up symbol from the Library onto the Stage, and align it with the center of the Stage. Add a keyframe in the Over frame.

8. Delete the symbol on the Stage, and drag an instance of the Over symbol from the Library onto the Stage. Align the Over symbol to the center of the Stage, and add a keyframe in the Down frame.

9. Delete the button on the Stage, drag an instance of the Down button on to the Stage, and align it to the center of the Stage as shown in Figure 17.15. Add a keyframe in the Hit frame.

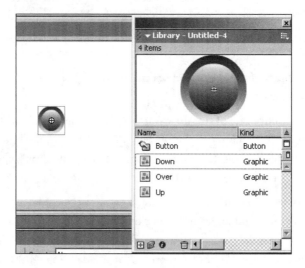

Figure 17.15   When using Flash MX to assemble the assets, you can simply import a FreeHand document composed only of symbols that will import directly into Flash MX's Symbol Library for use in a Button timeline.

10. Select the Oval tool. Set the stroke to None and the fill to a green color. Drag out a circle that is about the size of the inner circle and then place it over the inner circle. If it disappears behind the button, delete the button and align the green circle to the center of the Stage. Click the Scene 1 button.

 Tip

Another way of turning the inner gradient into the Hit area is to select the object, and press Ctrl-B (PC) or Command-B (Mac) to break apart the image into two circles. When you have the two shapes, delete the outer circle. Keep pressing the key combination until the inner gradient looks like pixels. Select the Paint Bucket tool, select a green fill on the Property inspector, and click the circle.

11.   Drag the Button symbol onto the Stage, select the Text tool, and click once under the button. Enter the words **To Macromedia**. Use a legible font and use a point size of between 16 and 18 points.

12.   Assign a getURL action to the button that sends the browser to `http://www.macromedia.com`. Test the movie, save the file, and publish the .swf without HTML. Quit Flash MX.

13.   Open Dreamweaver MX. Open a new page, and open the Insert panel, if necessary, by selecting Window, Insert, or Ctrl-F2 (PC) or Command-F2 (Mac).

14.   Click the Flash MX button on the Insert panel, navigate to the .swf file you have just created, and click OK to insert the button. Press the Play button on the Property inspector to test the states and then test the button in a browser.

Note

> Though we have covered a lot of techniques regarding how Flash MX and Dreamweaver MX work together, we have dealt with individual buttons. Remember—if you can create one button and get it to work, you can create ten buttons. The beauty of a Flash button is its physical size, meaning that a series of Flash buttons arranged into a button bar or placed in frames, tables or layers will not result in a bandwidth issue. Your only limitation is your creativity, imagination, and ingenuity.

Using Dreamweaver MX Behaviors

Behaviors are the Dreamweaver MX workhorses. Though a bunch get bundled with the application, there are a number of places, including the Exchange, where these power boosters can be obtained. What makes them so interesting is anyone, from the power coder who uses Notepad to design web sites to the designer who thinks Java is another name for coffee, can use them.

A behavior is a combination of an event and an action. An event can be rolling the mouse over a button, and the action is what happens when the cursor is over that button. In Dreamweaver MX, events can run from the click of a mouse to the loading of a page into a frame. When a behavior is added to an object on the page, it is said to be *attached* to that object. The neat thing about this is behaviors are just as easily unattached as they can be attached to objects. If you make a mistake, there is a bail out available to you. When you do attach a behavior to an object through the Behavior panel, you always see the Event on the left side of the panel and the action on the right side.

To create a Dreamweaver MX behavior, follow these steps:

1. Copy the Chapter 17 Exercise folder to your computer from the book web site. Open Dreamweaver MX and then open the Behaviors.htm page in the Dreamweaver MX Behavior folder of the Exercise folder. If your panels aren't open, press the F4 key to open them.

2. In the upper left corner you see a Fireworks MX button with the word Up in the center of the button. The Over and Down buttons are located in the Images folder. We will be using the Up button, which has the following events attached to it:

   - The button changes to the Over button when the cursor rolls over it.
   - The button changes to the Up button when the user rolls off of it.
   - The button changes to the Down button when the user clicks the mouse.
   - The Macromedia home page is loaded into the current browser page when the user releases the button.

Caution

When planning behavior actions, always think in a linear, logical manner. Creative types tend to think in terms of "1, 3, 5, 2, 4," which is fine in a creative environment; however, that process is deadly in a code environment.

3. The first event is to have the button change to the Over button. Select the image on the page. Open the Design panel, and click the Behaviors tab. Alternately, you can also select Behavior from the Window menu, or press Shift-F3. Click the Add Action (+) button and then select Swap Image from the Behavior pop-down menu to open the Swap Image dialog box. Click the Browse button, navigate to the Images folder, select the Over button, and click OK. Before you click OK in the Swap Image dialog box, make sure you have Preload Images and Restore Images onMouseOut selected. Click OK.

   Check the Behavior panel, to see that two events—onMouseOver and onMouseOut—have been added to the list.

4. Test the page in a browser. When you roll over the button, it changes to the Over button. Close the browser.

5. Adding the Down state is essentially the same as adding an onMouseOver event. With the button selected on the page, add a Swap Image behavior. This time, however, add the Down button to the behavior.

6. If you leave the behavior alone at this point, you lose the Over button because of competing behaviors. Select the onMouseOver event in the Behavior panel, and click the down arrow between the event and the action. From the pop-down menu list of choices, select onMouseDown. Test the page. Roll over the button, you see the Over button, and click the mouse to see the Down button.

7. Having the button navigate to the Macromedia site is a little bit trickier. Select the onMouseDown event in the Behavior panel, and click the Remove Event (–) button to remove the onMouseDown event.

8. Click the Add Action button, select the onClick event, and add the Down button. Click the Add Action button again, and select the gotoURL event to open the URL dialog box. Enter `http://www.macromedia.com` into the URL dialog box and then click OK.

   If you were to test the button at this point, clicking the button won't take you to the Macromedia site because the action uses a beforeUnload event, which is triggered by leaving the page. The event should occur with the press of the mouse.

Behaviors and Browsers

At this point in the process, being aware that your user's browser comes into play. For 3.0 and earlier browsers, the capability to click and go doesn't exist.

To see this for yourself, click the Add Event button and then scroll to the bottom of the pop-down list. Click and hold Show Events For, and select 3.0 and Later browsers. Select your URL action, and open the options. You are presented with two choices because the onClick event wasn't available in 3.0 browsers. Select the 4.0 and Later Browsers option, and you see an expanded range of choices, including the onClick event. This is because of the way browsers manage events. When a behavior is attached to a tag, an event is also inserted. The default event is based on two criteria: the browser type, and the tag.

If the browser can't manage the behavior, you are essentially locked out from access to the behavior. Browsers that fall into the category of 3.0 and later contain only 13 tags that can receive events. For example, Internet Explorer 3.0 can't handle a rollover because the browser hasn't been told how to handle an onMouseOut event.

When planning behaviors, it is critical that all members of the team understand the target browser, usually 4.0 or later, before they go to work.

9. Select the Go to URL event in the Behaviors panel. Set the default browser to 4.0 and Later and then select (onClick) as the event. Your Behavior panel should resemble that shown in Figure 17.16. Test the button in your browser, and save the page.

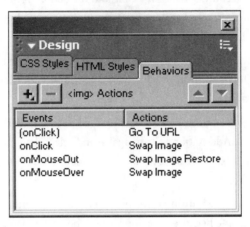

Figure 17.16   The Behaviors panel allows you to choose events that trigger actions. It is also the place where you pay careful attention to your target browser by selecting the version in the Show Events For list of browsers.

Creating a Pop-Up Menu in Fireworks MX

Pop-up menus are simply cool. Roll over or click a menu item, and a series of submenus are presented to the user. This technique was introduced to Fireworks as a command in version 4, and things have improved somewhat in Fireworks MX. The advantage is a pop-up menu hands you a rather simple tool for managing rather complex navigation.

The process of creating a pop-up menu is not complicated because the dialog box used to create theses menu is designed with the user in mind and carefully walks you through the steps necessary to create the menu. Though the focus of this section is the creation of the menu, you need to understand the artwork for the base menu can be created in Fireworks MX or FreeHand. The design of the submenus follows basic graphical user interface guidelines.

In this section, you work on a menu that could be used in the JCT site to not only navigate between the product pages on the site but to also allow the user to contact, through email, a list of people that work at JCT.

In the product category, the menu is designed in the following manner: When the user rolls over the Shirts category, a Men's and a Women's subcategory appears under the Shirts slice. Rolling over the Men's and Women's choices results in three more pop-up menus that enable the user to select a shirt color or shirt size.

Finally, menus are attached to the web layer of your document because they are code-driven. When you design a menu, it is a good idea to create a series of slices, each containing a menu category.

To create a pop-up menu in Fireworks MX, follow these steps:

1. Open the Menu.png file in the FWMenu folder, located in the Chapter 17 Exercise folder. The menu.png file opens to show series of slices, each covered with a green Web layer overlay.

2. Open the Layers panel, open the Web layer and then open Layer 1. The items in both layers contain identical names. It will make life much easier for the group if they get into the habit of giving the layers in the Web layer and the actual image layers the same name. If you click the Pants item in layer 1, notice it is a symbol. This is another great habit to develop.

3. Select Shirts in the Web layer. Right-click (PC) or Control-click (Mac) in the target that appears in the center of the overlay. Select Add Pop-up Menu from the context menu to open the Pop-up Menu Editor. The four tabs across the top of the dialog box control what is seen in the various choices, how the menu looks, where the menu is placed, and where the menu appears in relation to the slice when opened in a browser.

4. Click the Content tab. Three categories are available to you are:

   - Text—the words in the button.

   - Link—where to go when the button is clicked.

   - Target—the target for the URL. You can choose a preset target from the Target pop-up menu, or enter your own custom target.

5. Double-click the Text cell, and enter **Men's**. Double-click the Link cell and then enter **shirts.htm**. This action causes the Shirts page of the JCT site to open when the user clicks the Men's button.

6. The submenus for the Men's area are Colors and Sizes, and adding these submenus requires an amount of care. The Content area of the Pop-up Menu Editor displays hierarchy in the classic sense. Enter **Colors** under Men's to add the item directly under the Men's tab. This means that when the user rolls over the Shirt's item, Men's and Colors will be visible.

7. Click the Add Menu button, and double-click in the Text area. When the text cursor appears, enter the word **Colors**. Click the Indent Menu button once to indent the word just entered.

Note

If red were to be a submenu of Colors, you would click the Indent Menu button twice after entering the color in the Text cell.

8. Add a **Sizes** submenu for the Men's area. Press the Add Menu button, double-click in the Text area, and enter **Women's**. Add the Colors and Sizes submenus to the Women's area. Your content area should resemble that shown in Figure 17.17.

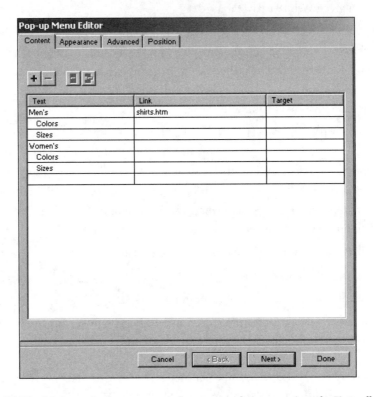

Figure 17.17   Menus and submenus are set by entering their names into the Text cell.

9. Click the Appearance tab. The Appearance area of the Pop-up Menu Editor sets the orientation, the text style, and colors of the content in the button as well as the appearance of the actual button. Click the HTML button, and select Horizontal menu from the Orientation pop-up menu. Selecting HTML allows the appearance to be set by code, resulting in a smaller file size for the final image. Selecting Horizontal from the Orientation menu sets the menu items on the page so that the Men's and Women's menus will be beside each other rather than one under the other.

10. Choose a font, point size, and color for the cell background and the text. We used
     the colors from the JCT palette set in Chapter 7, "Planning the Look of the
     Pages." If your Appearance menu resembles that shown in Figure 17.18, click the
     Next button or click the Advanced tab.

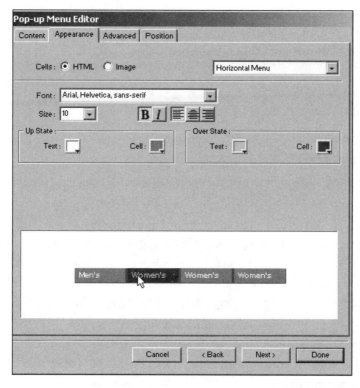

Figure 17.18   Appearance determines the orientation of the menu items, whether they are
code- or graphics-driven, and how they look on the final page.

Note

Clicking the Image button opens a series of graphic buttons that can be applied to the
item. If you find these to be limiting, create a button style using your own fill, stroke, and
LiveEffect, or create the style in FreeHand and then import it into Fireworks MX. Save
the object as a style using the Styles panel. Select the style, and export the style from
the Styles panel's Options menu to the Nav menu folder on your hard disk.

11. The Advanced area of the Pop-up Menu Editor allows you to control the size of
     the cells, the padding and spacing between the cells, how the text indents, how
     long to wait until the menu disappears, and many of the border properties. Use
     the following settings for your menu:

Cell Width: 65 pixels

Cell Height: 18 pixels

Cell Padding: 0

Text Indent: 5

Cell Spacing: 2

Menu Delay: 1,000 ms.

Pop-Up Border: Selected

Border Width: 1

Shadow: #666666

Border Color: FFFFFF

Highlight: FFFFFF

A preview of the choices appears in the Advanced dialog box. Click the Position tab at the top of the Pop-up Menu Editor, or click Next.

12. The Position tab allows you to set the location of the main menu and the sub menus. The position of the main menu can also be set by dragging its outline onto the canvas. The choices are simple. Click the Set Menu position to the bottom of slice in the Menu Position area to set the position to directly below the main menu. Your x value changes to 0, and the y value changes to 26.

13. Manually set the Submenu position using -67 as the x value, and 21 as the y value. Those two values open the menu directly under the menu item, and take into account the border added in step 11. Click Done and then press F12 to test the menu in a browser.

14. Coding up the Contact menu item at the far right of the menu bar follows the same steps with the only change being in the context menu. In the Text Input area, enter your name. In the Link area, enter **mailto:** and then enter your email address after the colon.

15. When you have finished, test the menu in a browser. If it works, export the menu slices as a series of .gif images. Save the menu as a .png image as well, just in case changes are needed. Quit Fireworks MX, and open Dreamweaver MX.

16. Open the Menu.htm page that you just created, and test the page in a browser. You might want to open the shirts.htm page, and add a link back to your menu page.

Using Components to Create a Pop-Up Menu in Flash MX

There are a number of methods for creating pop-up menus in Flash MX that range from the simple—jumps along the main timeline—to the complex—coded completely in Actionscript using movie clips. The newest method is to use the components that come packaged with Flash MX.

As pointed out in Chapter 7, components replace the Smart Clip technology that was introduced in Flash 5. This is such an advance in the technology that Macromedia was compelled to change the name to position components as an exciting new technology element of the Flash authoring environment.

In the menu that you create in this section, you use the Combo Box component. In many respects this component resembles the traditional pop-up menu created earlier in this chapter using Fireworks MX. Naturally, because it is Flash MX, it is far more flexible than it may appear at first glance. When added to your Flash movie, the combo box properties allow you to choose whether the component is a form that can be written to, or a pop-up menu—the combo box properties enable the component to be editable or not editable. You can also change the look of the box, the highlight color, size, and so on. This is an important point because when placement and size of a menu list—such as width— are important, you bump up against the limits of HTML.

This exercise shows you how to develop a pop-up menu that presents the user with a list of shirt colors. When the user makes the selection, clicking another component—the PushButton—places the selection on the page.

To develop a pop-up menu, follow these steps:

1. Copy the FlashMenu in the Chapter 17 Exercise folder on the book web site to your hard disk, and open the OrderShirts.fla file. The movie, which is only two frames long, has been set up for you. The first frame of the movie is where the user selects a style of shirt while the second frame is used to display the shirt chosen in the first frame. The selection is be passed, using Actionscript, to the Colors movie clip and then tells the movie clip which frame to display in frame 2. The Colors movie clip is a four-frame movie, with a label containing a colored shirt over each frame. You use the labels to display the shirt chosen.

2. Add three new layers named **Actions**, **Labels**, and **Components** to the movie. Add keyframes to each of the frames in the Labels layer; name the first label **Info** and the second label **Show**.

3. Move the playback head to frame 1 and select frame 1 of the Components layer. Open the Components panel and drag an instance of the PushButton and ComboBox components from the Flash UI selections onto the Stage.

4. Move the ComboBox component under the Pick A Style headline, and move the PushButton component to the bottom right corner of the Style area.

5. Select the PushButton component. To make components work, they must have certain properties assigned to them, and most important, they must have an instance name. Be aware of the change in the Property inspector. The icon in the inspector changes to let you know that you have selected a component, and a couple of input boxes appear in the Property inspector. Double-click in the Text input area for the label, and enter **Show**. Press Enter (PC) or Return (Mac), and the word you just entered appears on the button.

6. The next input area for the component on the Property inspector asks you to input how the user will interact with the button. Click the Click Handler input box, and enter **onClick**. Click the Instance area of the Property inspector, and enter **play_button**. Set the width of the button to 70 pixels. Your Property inspector should resemble that shown in Figure 17.19.

Figure 17.19   The PushButton component's name, event handler, size, and instance name can all be set using the Property inspector.

7. Navigate to frame 2 of the components layer, add a key frame, and delete the instances of the PushButton and ComboBox components in the layer. Replace them with another PushButton component and Set the label and the instance name to **Reset**, set the width of the Reset button to 70 pixels and an onClick event handler.

8. Move the playback head to frame 1, and select the ComboBox. You are now presented with a number of totally different options in the Property inspector. To ensure the box acts like a pop-down menu, click the Editable area and select False from the pop-down menu. Click the Labels property, and click the magnifying glass once to open the Values window. This is where you enter the various items for the menu. Click the Add button, click once beside the O, and enter **Green**. Add two more values—**Red** and **Blue**—and then click OK to close the Values window.

9. Check your Property inspector to see these values are now enclosed in brackets beside the labels. Name the instance **shirt_color**, and set the width to 100 pixels. When finished, your Property inspector should resemble that shown in Figure 17.20.

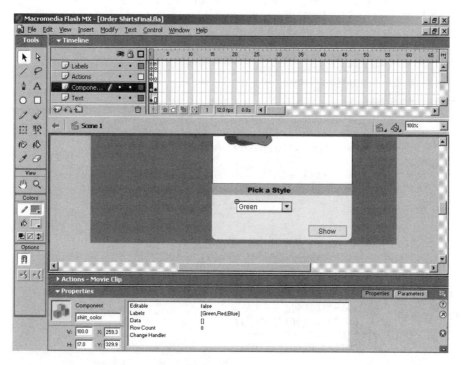

Figure 17.20   Clicking the Magnifying Glass and entering the categories into the resulting Values window will add the labels for the pop-down menu. Setting the "Editable" property to false ensures text can't be input into the ComboBox component.

Note

Be aware that the text added for the color names and all labels are case-sensitive. If the user types **green** instead of **Green**, the code in the Actions layer will not work. This is because Actionscript follows the ECMA standard for JavaScript, meaning labels and so on are case-sensitive.

Caution

If you are going to be passing values around using Actionscript, it is absolutely critical that the components be given instance names in the Property inspector.

10. The elements are in place. It is now time to wire up the interactivity using Actionscript. Open the Actionscript editor. Ensuring you are in the Expert mode of the Actionscript Editor, add the following code:

```
initValues();
// What to do if the "Show" or "Reset" buttons are clicked
function onClick(btn) {
        if (btn == play_button) {
            setShirts();
            gotoAndStop("show");
        } else if (btn == reset) {
            gotoAndStop("info")
        }
}

function setValues() {
        shirt_color.setValue(color_value);
}
function setShirts() {
        color_value = shirt_color.getSelectedItem().label;
}
\
```

Let's review each section of this script.

```
initValues();
function onClick(btn) {
        if (btn == play_button) {
            setShirts();
            gotoAndStop("show");
        } else if (btn == reset) {
            gotoAndStop("info")
        }
}
```

This piece of code sets all of the default values for the objects in the movie. It also drives the two buttons—play_button and reset instances of the PushButton component—by checking which one was clicked and then going to the appropriate frame label in the main movie.

```
function setValues() {
        shirt_color.setValue(color_value);
}
```

Components have to be told what to do. This piece of code tells the ComboBox component to take the selected color—in actual fact, it is the label selected from the three you input earlier—from the menu and then put that value into a variable named color_value.

```
function setShirts() {
        color_value = shirt_color.getSelectedItem().label;
}
```

That variable is then directed to the Colors movie clip used in frame 2 of the movie.

11. Insert the color_value variable into the movie clip by opening the Colors movie clip and then adding the following frame script to frame 1 of the clip's Actions layer.

```
if (_root.color_value == "Green"){
      gotoAndStop("Green");
} else if(_root.color_value == "Blue"){
      gotoAndStop("Blue");
} else if(_root.color_value == "Red"){
      gotoAndStop("Red");
}
```

When the playback hits frame one of the movie clip, it goes looking for a variable named color_value on the main timeline (_root.). It checks the value of the variable, and if that variable meets one of the three criteria, sends the playback head to the appropriate frame label in the Colors movie clip.

12. The main timeline should resemble that shown in Figure 17.21. If it does, test the movie, and save it.

Image Maps in Fireworks MX

The last thing designers need is to concern themselves with the intricacies of DHTML or JavaScript. From a designer's perspective, if something is hot, then something should happen. This chapter began by showing you how buttons created in Fireworks MX can make things happen. The chapter now concludes by showing you how properly prepared graphics that are sliced into image maps can also function as interactive navigation devices.

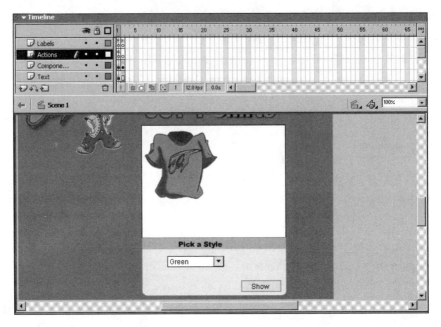

Figure 17.21   The final version of the OrderShirts Flash presentation. The Actionscript that drives the components is contained in frame 1 of the Actions layer.

The following exercise doesn't use the traditional map of the United States, south of the 49th. Instead, you create a series of hotspots that provide two types of visual feedback— the cursor change and a graphic change—along with the capability to click that graphic and navigate to a site. Along the way, you learn a couple of ways of working smart, not hard.

1. Open the Imagemap.png file in the FWMenufolder of your Chapter 17 Exercise folder. This image sets up in such a manner that the user rolls the mouse over one of the line of numbers. When the mouse is over the number, a red circle appears, and the user can click the number to navigate to another web site.

2. Select the Ellipse tool, and draw a circle with a red stroke (#FF0000) that encircles the number 1. With the circle selected, use the Property inspector to set the tip size to one pixel, the stroke to Soft Line, and the edge to 50. Deselect the Ellipse tool and then select the Slice tool. Draw a square slice large enough to cover the number and the circle.

3. Here is one place where you let the software do the job and make life easy for yourself. Click the slice once to show the target. Roll the cursor onto the green slice

area, press Alt-Shift (PC) or Option-Shift (Mac), and drag a copy of the slice over the number 3. This drags a copy of the slice straight up because pressing the Shift key during movement constrains the movement direction to either horizontal or vertical. Repeat this technique until all of the numbers are covered with a slice.

4. Turn off the visibility of the web layer, select the circle, and cut it out of the image. After the circle is removed to the clipboard, turn the visibility of the Web layer back on.

5. The circle moves due to the inclusion of frames in Fireworks MX. Open the Frames panel, and select the Frames tab. Select Add Duplicate Frame from the panel's pop-down menu. Enter **1** as the frame to be duplicated, and select After Current Frame. Repeat this until you have a frame named **Frame11**. You now have an 11-frame image.

6. If you double-click the frame name, you can enter your own name for the frame. In this case, where it is rather obvious what will happen, names are not necessary. Still, it is a good habit to develop. Turn off the Web layer visibility. Select frame 2, and paste the circle into place over the number 1. Select frame 4, paste the circle, drag it up over the letter 3. Repeat this step for the remaining numbers. Your image, with frames, should resemble that shown in Figure 17.22.

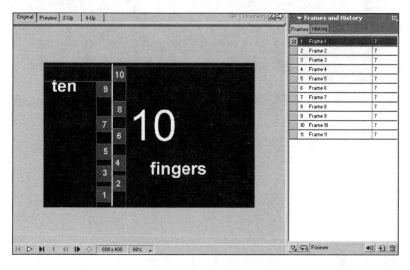

Figure 17.22   The frames have been created by duplicating the frame and moving the circle to its position in each frame.

7. The interactivity is accomplished on frame 1, which is the page seen in the browser. Turn on the visibility of the Web layer. Select the slice over the number 1, and click/drag the target to the left edge of the slice. Release the mouse. The Swap Image dialog box appears. Select frame 2 from pop-down list in the Swap Image dialog box. This simple maneuver is a quantum change from previous versions of the application. In Fireworks 4, you had click the slice, assign the behavior from a separate menu, and so on. It was rather cumbersome, to say the least. Repeat this step for the remaining slices, being sure to assign the correct layer to the swap. Your finished product should resemble that in Figure 17.23.

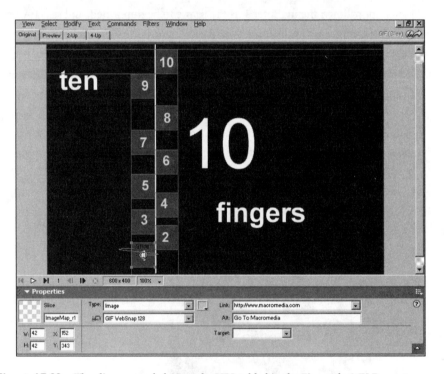

Figure 17.23   The slices are coded. Note the URL added in the Fireworks MX Property inspector.

8. These slices can also be used to navigate through the web, a site, or even to load content into particulars frames on a page. Select the first slice, and enter `http://www.macromedia.com` into the Link area of the Property inspector. To ensure accessibility, enter **To Macromedia Site** in the Alt (Alternate text) area of the Property inspector. Add a few more links to your buttons, put slices over the images, and test the image in a browser.

Summary

The creation of the elements of navigation using the creative applications in the MX Studio of tools is complete. From simple buttons created in Fireworks MX to menus using the new Components feature of Flash MX, the choices available to you are deep, indulgent, and varied.

In this chapter, we showed you how to create a button symbol in Fireworks MX and then explained how the instance of the symbol can be edited on the canvas without harming the symbol. In this way, an entire button bar can be built using one, not a number of, symbols. We also illustrated how the Button Editor in Fireworks MX, and how all of the buttons, can be built in the application and then shared among the members of the team.

Flash MX treats buttons not as swappable objects, but as simple four-frame Flash MX movie clips. Starting with a simple button, we progressed through building buttons that enable navigation through a Flash MX movie.

We also explained how FreeHand, Fireworks MX, and Flash MX can team up to build a pulsating button that resembles the ones used in the Macintosh OS X interface. Dreamweaver MX allows you to create Flash buttons in the interface, and we examined not only how to use this feature of Dreamweaver MX but also how to manage buttons created in Flash MX and then placed in Dreamweaver. We examined how the Freehand to Flash MX to Dreamweaver MX workflow can create buttons utilizing the powerful drawing tools of FreeHand as well as the scripting capabilities of Flash MX. We finished with buttons by examining the addition of behaviors in Dreamweaver MX that are added to button artwork created in Fireworks MX.

Pop-down menus are one of the cool tools used by developers as navigation aids. Fireworks MX improved upon their creation over previous versions of the application, and we thoroughly explored this feature. We also explained how you can create your own custom fills for pop-down menus in Fireworks MX, and share those fills among the members of the team.

If any one aspect of Flash MX represents a fundamentally different approach to development in this application, it has to be the inclusion of Flash MX components. It would be a huge mistake on the part of a developer to overlook these user interface bits and pieces. We examined how two of them—the PushButton and ComboBox components—can team up to create navigation elements driven by Actionscript.

We finished the chapter by looking at the creation of image maps in Fireworks MX, and saw how the creation of these vital navigation aids has actually been made even easier in Fireworks MX.

In the next chapter, we explore how the navigation principals and techniques are employed in the JCT site.

MX

fireworks flash freehand coldfusion dreamweaver fireworks
eamweaver fireworks flash freehand coldfusion dreamweave
coldfusion dreamweaver fireworks flash freehand coldfusic
freehand coldfusion dreamweaver fireworks flash freehand
works flash freehand coldfusion dreamweaver fireworks
eaver fireworks flash freehand coldfusion dreamweave

Transitions

This chapter marks the end of the creation

phase where we have created and assem-

bled our assets. You have covered many

production-related topics, ranging from

project planning to graphics creation. The remainder of the book shows you how to assemble all of the content into dynamic web pages; thus, we have reached a transition point in the web-creation process and the book.

A transition point is good place to stop and reflect upon the project so far, and review if there were tasks or decisions that could have been done more efficiently. For us, the central graphic focus of the site is the navigation bar, which appears on all of the pages of the JCT site. There were a number of decisions made regarding the bar, and we felt it would be valuable to share the thought process with you.

In staying with the theme of this chapter, we couldn't help but be struck by the fact that the introduction and development of Macromedia MX Studio marks the transition point between the workflow used to produce static web sites and the new workflow used to produce dynamic sites. The JCT site, using the static workflow model, would be a compilation of a few dozen pages. Each page is accessed through a predetermined link that takes the form of a navigation element, such as a button, a pop-down menu, or a hyperlink. The dynamic site you create is composed of only three pages, and the navigation is used to talk to a server that essentially pulls the requested content from a database and puts it in the appropriate box on the page. This is a fundamental shift, a *transition* for want of a better word, in how web developers approach their craft. In this chapter, we share our thoughts on this as well.

The last line of our introduction to this book concludes with the line from the *Wizard of Oz*. "We are no longer in Kansas." The line is uttered after Dorothy's house in Kansas has been buffeted inside a tornado and is put down in a foreign land named Oz. In many respects, the web design business has undergone a similar transition. We worked on static sites, the business went into turmoil, and now we are building dynamic sites in a place that is relatively unfamiliar and new to us. There are new workflows, new tools, new members of the team, and a new attitude on both the part of the clients and the developers.

This raises some interesting questions, which we explore in the last half of the chapter starting with "Getting Dynamic: Changing Workflow and Roles." Two of the authors— Jordan Chilcott and Chris Flick—have been involved in building dynamic sites, and offer their insights on a variety of topics including who does what, working with clients asking for dynamic sites, dealing with complexity and usability, and managing dynamic content.

Building the JCT Navigation Bar

Put three web developers in a room, and you will get three different opinions regarding your work. Each opinion usually starts with "That is not the way I would have done it…," and moves on from there.

The JCT navigation bar is one of those items that could just as easily have been produced as a GIF image as a JPG image.

When line art or photographs are produced, the artist inevitably has to contend with the final output device for the image. Print artists have it relatively easy because they have two relatively high-resolution formats—TIF and EPS—that offer somewhat predictable results. If the image is destined for web output, you still have two choices—GIF or JPG—but the results are unpredictable.

When web artists build an image, two primary concerns drive their decisions:

- Quality of the final image
- File size

In many respects, this is the paradox all web designers face. Think of the decision as being a seesaw. Quality sits on one side of the fulcrum, and file size sits at the other. The starting points at either end of the seesaw are super high-quality images and huge file sizes. Reduce the quality by moving it closer to the fulcrum, and file size moves as well. Reduce the file size, and quality moves towards the fulcrum, too. The hardest job designers face is finding that exquisite balance between quality and file size. And it isn't only imaging.

We have all encountered clients who have little or no experience building web sites, but they still believe they know the web because they know how to surf it. They can pull a site up on their browser and ask, "Why can't we do that?" or "Don't you think this web site looks cool?" or "Why don't we do something like this?" What they don't comprehend is the complexity behind the construction a simple site, much less that of a rich media site that uses Flash animations, QuickTime streaming video, and sound. Adding rich media doesn't improve the site. It simply creates more work as the team shuffles quality and file size on the seesaw.

JPG or GIF

All of the JCT images, especially those in the navigation bar, could just as easily been JPG images. The decision to make them GIF images was heavily weighted by the need to keep the file size small.

With the exception of the brick background as well as the gradient in the logo, the entire image is composed of flat, single colors that lend themselves admirably to GIF compression. For example, the shoes and pants of the mascot are prime candidates for GIF compression because they are essentially an area of single color. The bricks aren't GIF compression candidates because the pattern of color in the image has the wrong orientation. GIF compression works by compressing pixels on a horizontal line. The brick wall, with all of its color changes, makes compression a very difficult task to perform. A more complete explanation of GIF compression can be found in Chapter 21, "Image Optimization and the MX Studio."

Obviously, mixing compression in an image is not a good strategy. A compromise between image quality and file size has to be reached.

The brick background, logo, and mascot would have appeared cleaner and smoother had they been saved as JPG images. In general, when dealing with photograph-like art—such as the brick wall that contains multicolored blends, or the soft glow-like effects behind the lettering—JPG is the format because it tends to manage complex color blends better than GIF compression.

The Creative Factor

Surprisingly, the decision to go with the GIF format also has an artistic aspect to the choice. If you review the creative brief from Chapter 1, "Planning the Site," you see the site was to have an urban, hip-hop, graffiti-esque feel. Saving the images as GIFs added an unintentional urban roughness to the images, and even added a bit of character to the art.

As our artist, Chris Flick, described it, he got his inspiration from street art. "In some parts of Washington, D.C., you can find many examples of graffiti, some better then others. The *taggers*, as graffiti artists are known, aren't quite as good as the ones you can find up in New York though, but every now and again, you'll come across a tagger and think 'Wow! Too bad this guy's wasting his time on vandalism!'"

The decision to go with graffiti art was also about effect. When the GIF compression is set low, the pixels start to break apart. The result is what artists call a happy accident—an unintended effect that actually adds to the finished piece. In the case of the overall look, when the pixels started to break apart, they actually added an unexpected surface level to the image that made it look rough and chunky. In the logo, the effect of the GIF compression was to break up the blends inside the logo which, to the artist, gave the effect of sidewalk chalk. The yellow glows also ended up looking like spray paint instead of a soft neon glow.

This was one of those very rare situations where the artwork actually looked better in a slightly roughened state, as opposed to the clean and smooth appearance offered by JPG compression. In this case, jagged edges and overly compressed pixels weren't a bad thing.

Making the Decision to Go with the GIF Format

In books of this sort, there are always a lot of how-to steps, but little explanation of the reasoning behind the task.

As you have seen, there were a number of technical and aesthetic reasons behind the decision to go with GIFs, but the decision ultimately comes down to a graphic artist sitting at a computer and drawing from experience to make the decision. In this case, Chris Flick explains his thought process throughout this section.

As we said before, there were a great many reasons why I ultimately decided to create GIFs rather than JPGs. To walk you through the process, I will be using a comparison between a JPG version of the JCT navigation and a GIF version. In each case, I have highlighted four areas of each file format, and will take you through the reasoning behind my choices.

In Figure 18.1, you see an example of both navigation bars. The top was saved as a JPG with 75% compression. Below that, the navigation bar is saved as a GIF with a setting of 128 colors.

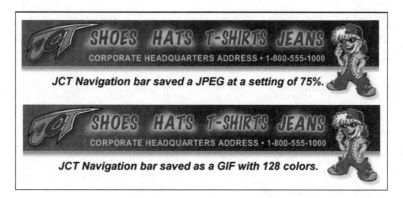

Figure 18.1   Two versions of the navigation bar are created and compared. (View the comparison on the book web site.)

Almost immediately, my eyes are drawn to the lower GIF version because its colors seem much more vibrant than the JPG. The JPG looks like it almost has a small layer of soot smeared across it. The reds of the words are much more intense in the GIF than they are in the JPG. Likewise, the baby blue color in the JCT logo seems much cleaner in the GIF format than it does in the JPG. Again, in the JPG format, it almost looks a bit dirty.

As mentioned before, though, there are some very subtle things going on between the two different file formats. These subtle things are shown in Figure 18.2. I have isolated four sections of both file formats to show exactly how subtle these things can be. The sections are labeled a, b, c, and d.

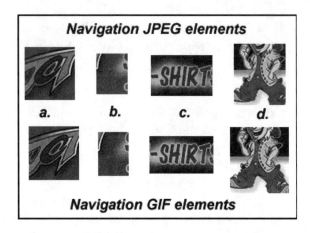

Figure 18.2   The images are remarkably similar because they are viewed at 100% magnification.

At first glance, differences don't become readily apparent. In fact, these images are quite similar. This is because the images are being compared at 100% magnification, which is why I rarely examine images at 100% magnification.

It is only when you zoom in, as shown in Figure 18.3, that the differences are revealed. I will be using this figure to walk you through the comparisons.

At first glance, section *a* seems as though it would be ideal for a JPG because the red, orange, and yellow gradient in the logo seems to have a much smoother transition than the GIF version below it. In fact, the GIF version seems to be choppy, and has a harsh transition between the three colors.

So, why didn't I save the JCT logo as a JPG file?

The JPG version of the logo didn't quite look graffiti-esque enough for my tastes. Normally, the roughness of the GIF color blend would bother me, and I would save it as a JPG. Because we were after a graffiti feel, however, I wanted the roughness of the GIF to resemble colored chalk, and it seemed to go hand-in-hand with the theme we were trying to create for the JCT site.

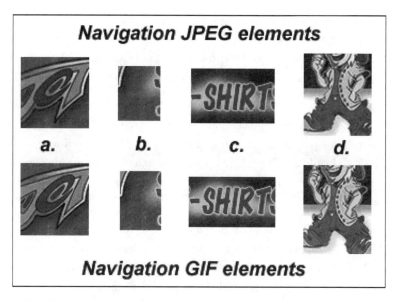

Figure 18.3   The images, when magnified, reveal their differences.

Likewise, the shadow had the same type of feel for me. The GIF shadow seemed rough and had a bit of texture to it. The JPG version has a much more serene softness to it, something you would never associate with spray-painted graffiti!

The brick background in section *b* also lost out.

Have you ever run your fingertips against the edge of a brick house? If you have, you know how coarse and bumpy the brick feel. There is a definite texture there. For me, the GIF file seems to really suggest that texture, especially along the diagonal lines where the pixels start to break up.

On the other hand, the JPG version simply looked similar to soft pastels—almost like smeared chalk. There doesn't seem to be any hard, coarse texture there. If I ran my hands across these brick walls, it looks as though my fingertips will enjoy it. That's not the case with the GIF version. It looks hard, rough, and coarse, and something I probably would-n't want to run my fingers over.

The glow in section *c* also factored into the decision. It was mentioned earlier that the colors in the GIF file seemed to be a bit more vibrant than those in the JPG files. You can readily see this in section *c*. In the JPG version, the red has a touch of maroon to it, which darkens the overall image. And, although we are trying to capture an urban, graffiti feel, we still don't want the images to look grungy or, in this case, almost polluted. The GIF format was an easy choice for this.

But what about the yellow glow around the letters? Again, the roughness of the GIF seemed to almost work to our benefit here, as well. The JPG yellow glow, much like the bricks in section *b*, seem to be too soft and smeared like pastel chalk. We're after a spray-painted feel here—something that looks as though it was done fast and on the fly.

Even though it is still compressed paint in a can, spray paint is not the same as air brushing. Spray paint, when applied in very quick strokes, tends to be heavily saturated in the middle and extremely rough at each end of the stroke. The JPG yellow glow looks as though it was air brushed. It has a nice subtle blend into the background, and looks as though it took a long time to create. Again, this is not something a viewer would typically see in graffiti art.

The GIF file, on the other hand, has all the characteristics you might find in a spray-painted stroke. The edges are extremely rough and break apart toward the end strokes. This is much more noticeable in the sample in section *b* than it is here because the word Shirts covers up most of the yellow stroke/glow in this instance.

When it comes to the mascot in section *d*, instead of doing a comparison between the two file versions, I am simply going to present a list of elements I see that make the GIF file the much preferred choice over the JPG version. They are as follows, and in no particular order:

- The flesh tones are a bit more accurate in the GIF version. The JPG file seems a little too much on the yellow side.
- The GIF colors are much more vibrant here, as well—especially in the magenta of the mascot's shirt.
- The red buttons show up in his jersey as red and not black.
- His shoes are bright red in the GIF file as they are supposed to be, not a dark maroon as they are in the JPG file.
- The line folds in his jeans are much more distinct in the GIF file than in the JPG file. In the JPG, they blend into the blue.
- His blue jeans appear much more blue-ish than in the JPG file. In the JPG, they are much darker.
- The outline around our mascot is much more prominent in the GIF file than it is in the JPG file. The JPG outline tends to blend into the background too much.
- The bill of the JPG hat looks as though it has turned a bit purple. The shadow isn't great in the GIF, but at least there is a much stronger sense that his hat is red—as it should be.
- The mascot's belt buckle shows up as yellow in the GIF, and off-white in the JPG.

Understanding Why the Mascot Was Not Produced in Freehand

Again, Chris jumps in to help you understand why we chose to not create the mascot in Freehand. Take it away, Chris:

Oh boy, we could write a whole chapter on this one.

The JCT mascot was created in a traditional illustration style. Basically, what that means is that I haven't quite gotten the hang of a drawing tablet, so I still prefer to create and color my illustrations using pen, paper, ink, and a scanner.

I know some digital artists, and even some cartoonists, that love the tablets. For me, however, I don't find them a time-saver at all. As such, I still use a bit of a comic book technique of scanning line art into Photoshop, layering my line art, and coloring it that way. This is the method that I learned when I was coloring Sunday comic strips for a local newspaper, and the technique—because I have used it for so many years—is fast and does the job.

Chapter 11, "Creating Line Art for the Web," we detailed the process of coloring line art using Fireworks MX. With that in mind, I am going to start making it a habit to color all of my line art this way, and see how I like the results.

Had we decided to make the JCT site Flash-based, however, I probably would have imported the JCT dude line art into Freehand and then colored him in there. The reason I didn't do is because I didn't want to use flat colors.

Had he been designed for a Flash site, he would have been colored without any blends or color shadows. This way, he would have been more acceptable and easier to manipulate in Flash MX.

Here is an old animator's trick to deal with the color limitations in Flash MX. If you pay attention to old animation, you'll notice that there are very few instances of characters having colored shadows. They are, for the most part, made up of large sections of flat colors. Some examples might include Yogi Bear's belly and fur, Popeye's sailor outfit, or Fred and Barney's skin, hair, and outfits. The exception would be the paw prints on Fred's fur clothing, though but it's still primarily made up of a single, flat yellow/orange.

In fact, now that I think about it, had he been Flashed, I might have even made the decision to color the mascot in Flash MX because the results would have been the same—large sections of flat colors, as opposed to the nice subtle color blends and shadows that currently exists from Fireworks MX. It would be an interesting decision."

Uses and Abuses of Flash MX Navigation

We could very easily have used Flash MX to create the navigation bars. There was a lot of discussion at the start of the project regarding this, and there were some valid reasons behind the decision to not use Flash MX (as Jordan Chilcott explains throughout this section).

Small files are not the be all and end all in this case. I have created two Flash navigation bars based on the graphics used by Chris. The files are in the Chapter 18 Exercise folder on the book web site. Of course, these files are not complete by any means.

The first file, FlashNav1, uses imported graphics from Fireworks MX with the settings set to rasterized, if necessary, to maintain appearance. To maintain the effect that Chris was using, Flash rasterized much of the graphics, and the result was a Flash file size around the same size as Chris' GIF image. Not to mention, there are no symbols or links. They have a negligible effect upon the final file size, but without them the file is already around the same size as the GIF.

The FlashNav2 file used imported graphics from Fireworks MX with the settings set to maintain editability. Much of Chris' effects were kept as vectors. Although it kept the file size down, it also destroyed the look. I'm sure there is a happy medium between the two because the mascot and logo were neatly converted to vectors in FlashNav2 while keeping the rasterized spray paint effect in FlashNav1. Mind you, I am not sure if the file size would be that much less than the GIF.

There's also the matter of the urban look. Remember, the urban look is important. It doesn't matter if we save a few kilobytes. If it doesn't have the look, forget it. You can save all you want on a client's site; however, if they don't like the look of it (and this is what they will be looking at), all of your work to push file sizes down is in vain.

Both of the exported files have a common problem: The bricks get overly smoothed out. This is one of the things that Chris was trying to avoid by using a .jpg. If we ease back on the compression, the file size grows. If we decide to use lossless compression, our exported file size shoots through the roof. Even at lossless compression, the bricks are slightly smoother. We wanted that rough look that the GIF image seemed to give us, and we didn't get it in Flash MX.

Had we developed the entire site in Flash MX, the site would have had a very different look. Everything would have been cartoonish. As it was, we wanted to give the site a bit of a realistic feel with the bricks, and show off the stuff Fireworks could do.

The use of Flash MX also has to meet client needs. For one of the writers, even though his client base doesn't have a huge need for Flash MX, one of his more prominent clients wants to do something with a part of their current site that absolutely has to be done in Flash. This will soon become the norm rather than the exception. When Flash development becomes part of your client's set of needs, it is the prudent developer who can successfully discover the balance between the flash of Flash MX and the solid working-class features in Fireworks MX.

Flash MX Pop-Down Menus Versus Fireworks MX Pop-Down Menus

The ability to create pop-down menus in Flash MX and Fireworks MX is a huge selling point for both applications. Which begs the question, "Why use Flash over Fireworks and vice-versa?"

Flash pop-down menus are great for using a standard component-based way of doing the everyday menus. As well, they are providing accessibility in accordance with Section 508, which we talk about in Chapter 23, "Working Out the Bugs and Going Live."

Flash pop-down menus are great, provided you allocate enough real estate in the HTML page to Flash to allow the pop-down to show. If you don't, the menu will get cut off.

Flash MX pop-down menus should be used like any other pop-down menu. You would want to group like items together under a menu. It's just common sense, as far as user interfaces go.

The JCT site design didn't lend itself well to using a Flash pop-down. Our navigation consists of four items, and we could have grouped them; however, we would have had to allocate the real estate for Flash, and there's a chance that the urban roughness would be lost in the .swf. Ultimately, the decision to produce navigation elements in Flash MX was a subjective one.

Fireworks MX pop-downs offer one slight advantage in this case: no plug-in required. As well, you would not have to allocate the extra real estate similar to what you would have to allocate to Flash.

Fireworks MX menu items appear as layers onscreen. They pop in and out over your content area, unlike Flash (unless you have defined your content area in the same Flash movie). They are a fast and easy way to construct a menu, and Fireworks MX makes that task even easier.

There is a twist to this, however, and it applies to using layers in general: If you have an .swf file, QuickTime, Real Media, Windows Media Player, or a form in the content area where the menu drops down, your menu gets lost in those areas. The above files have precedence because they are dynamically changing, and browsers render them on a continual basis. This means that anything on top of them gets drawn over.

Even so, pop-down menus in Fireworks MX are extremely easy to create, but they have to be created with care. If you can somehow educate your client to not be so concerned about the drop-down menu covering up part of the information on the web page, even if it is only momentary, drop-down menus are a great space saver, which seems to be why more and more pop-down menus are appearing on web sites.

Finally, the same interface rules apply to Fireworks MX pop-downs as they do to Flash MX pop-downs. We have discovered, through bitter experience, the best pop-down menus are short and sweet—not too many long selections under each category that inevitably makes a pop-down menu extremely elongated.

Getting Dynamic in Flash MX

Earlier versions of Flash allowed the developer to accommodate for the inclusion of dynamic data into the Flash site, provided the developer used an application called Generator.

The capability to create dynamic Flash sites within Flash MX has opened up a whole new world to Flash developers. As with any feature, it will get used and it will get abused.

Dynamic Flash sites are great for clients who are going to change their content on a continual basis. Flash MX has opened up a wide range of possibilities, from not only using dynamic text as did its predecessor, but also dynamic images and MP3s.

The main advantage to this is that the .swf can be smaller, allowing faster download time and streaming, while dynamically loading the text, sound, and images on the fly. With some creative planning, the user can start viewing the Flash movie almost immediately. With some real creativity, the user can be made to think that something is different each time the movie is played.

Another advantage lies with database developers and coders. It is only a matter of time before they come to regard Flash MX as the perfect front-end to various Internet-type applications. No more do visitors have to jump from page to page within a web application. Although the web application was a great innovation, it was a serious step backward in what computers are capable of doing.

Flash MX has taken serious and positive leaps forward. The user can remain on the same page, calling various web services in the background. They can shop online and not have to bounce from page to page, as they traditionally do on HTML sites. New features in Flash enable users to draw onscreen. This vector data can be stored dynamically in a database and recalled into a Flash movie. The possibilities are endless. We're finally seeing things start to resemble the applications on our computers as opposed to a series of pages loading and reloading as in the days of mainframe terminals.

Changing Workflow and Roles

You will eventually encounter the same situation we did when we were working on this book. The client changes his mind and everything changes along with it. Information on the site is now to become dynamic. The site evolves to a higher level of both sophistication and complexity as we go from numerous static pages to two dynamic pages and one index page, comprising a total of only three pages for our dynamic site.

As you will discover in the remaining chapters, the content essentially flows into a table-based layout. About the only thing that didn't change was the navigation bar at the top. Even then, instead of navigating to pages, the buttons loaded the content into the template. This is an extremely efficient method of building web pages.

What occurred to us, though, was the workflow had changed.

Not only did the designer design the site using linear and comprehensive drawings for the pages, but the design of the database also occurred at the same time. We discuss this change in the next chapter, "Building Dynamic Pages in Dreamweaver MX." What struck us was how easy it could be to relegate the designer to the task of creating the content that flows into the tables and nothing more.

On the surface, it would seem that Jordan, the programmer, was now calling the shots—directing Chris, the designer, how to create the content. Is this a by-product of building dynamic sites? Chris Flick and Jordan Chilcott explain how their roles really didn't change but how clear communication between the coders and the designers is critical:

"Actually, Chris' role didn't change," says Jordan. "He was still charged with creating images that are to be used for the site. They just don't appear on the page until called for. The only exception was the navigation bar. This appears on all of the pages. My role and Chris' role, as far as the navigation, were unchanged. His navigation bar provides the link to the page, and my responsibility is to make sure that the page exists."

Chris agrees. "My role didn't change I still had to figure out a modified layout for the new dynamic content, and prepare the graphics for Jordan. If anything, I think a lot of the confusion arose due more to our geographic differences than anything else. Had Jordan and I been in the same office, a great many problems could have been easily solved over a discussion at lunch."

Determining Who Does What

Making a static site dynamic is easier said than done. If you are planning a site, pick the model—static or dynamic—that best fits the situation. Do this at the start of the process, during the planning phase. At this point of the process, as Chris and Jordan point out, a delicate balance of design and code emerges only if the designer and the coder are talking to each other.

From the perspective of the database designer and coder, the roles involved in building dynamic sites require a complete understanding of the designer's intentions. As Jordan so eloquently describes it, "Chris may argue with me on this, but I believe that my role is a bit harder. I have to make the ColdFusion code look as if it doesn't exist to the user. To the user, the page has to come up as if it were a normal HTML page. This means building code around Chris' design. This isn't always a luxury when it comes to web application programming. Quite often, we (coders and database designers) are faced with building the application first and then we are given graphics. This makes the process a little more difficult as we sometimes have to rearrange our code in order to fit the designer's design."

"I think a lot of that depends upon which stage of the site creation you are talking about!" counters Chris. "There's no doubt that what Jordan had to do was hard. I, too, encounter this, because all of my clients have huge, database-driven web sites. Finding a way to mesh the two together—pretty pictures and ugly database information—isn't easy on either side. It just depends upon from which direction—coder or designer—you are approaching the problem. Both can be equally hard (or would that be frustrating?). Therefore, Jord is right in the sense that his job, in this case, was a lot harder than mine, due to the fact that we were trying to get the dynamic content to fit my design and my design did not accommodate dynamic data."

Even then, the proverbial trade-offs have to occur. The design has to accommodate how the data appears on the page, and in Chris's opinion, the design has to occur before the database information has been created. "It is never an easy task to design a site when the database information has already been created," says Chris. "Had Jordan first created all of the dynamic content, it would have been a pain in the butt for me to try and design a really nice looking site around that. So, it just depends on which way a designer or programmer's navigational needle is pointing during the planning phase. It just depends upon which side of the river you are sitting on."

"This is the importance of everyone on the team understanding each other's roles, especially when it comes to designing for dynamic data," says Jordan. "The old rules for designing static pages just don't apply when building dynamic pages. Designers will sometimes come up with a great design that works well for a static page, but doesn't for a dynamic page. Chris' original designs simply didn't lend themselves to the dynamic process. The result was a trading of emails and designs between Chris and myself that resulted in a compromise satisfactory to both of us."

Chris agrees with Jordan's observation. "This goes right into what I was saying earlier. The dynamic content was a surprise to me, so I had to scramble around for a Plan B. At times I even had to devise a Plan C, D, or even F. Had this been discussed at the very outset of the design process, I don't think this would have been all that great of an issue. And, although I can't say I foresaw the dynamic content situation on the horizon, I did consciously make an effort to create a site design that would be extremely flexible should any kind of Plan B be called for. This has more to do with the type of experience I sometimes have with intensive database-driven sites, so in that sense, experience really paid off in huge dividends for us."

Understanding the Client Factor

We wouldn't be designing dynamic sites if clients weren't asking for them. The interesting thing is, as we move through this period of transition, the process is just as new to the client as it is for the web developer. The process has become complex because of the client. They want people to stay on their site. They want traffic. They want to do business. They don't need an education. They need a site. As Chris and Jordan explain, this is easier said than done and makes listening to the client one of the most important aspects of the development process.

Clients are the reason things become complex. They want people to do specific tasks on their site. "If anyone needs to be educated," says Jordan, "it is the web development community. We need to be more attuned to what our clients are saying. When clients start talking about building a site that contains dynamic data, what they are really saying is they want users to buy things from them or to use their services. It is up to us to come up with ways that bring the client closer to the user."

Adds Chris, "For me, there are certainly clients out there that, if they don't specifically know what is involved with creating a web site, they certainly have a very good idea of the process."

Involving the client in the planning process, in Chris's experience does pay huge dividends. "I don't deal with a lot of ecommerce type of clients, so my perspective will be a little bit different than Jordan's. I suppose the cynic in me has come to expect a sort of 'Murphy's Law' of web designing…chances are, as a designer, if I create what I feel is a site that not only looks great but accomplishes exactly what the client wants, 9 times out of ten, they won't like the site—especially if they were never involved in the creation process. But, involve them in just one discussion and it's amazing how much more hands-off they become.

For me, this is amusing. I've come to the conclusion that despite the dot com bust, clients still think designing web sites is cool and hip. Somewhere deep down, they want to do the same thing—even if they might have an ounce of creative design capabilities within them. So, in some ways, as clients, they are living vicariously through me."

Still, faced with the complexities of building dynamic sites, clients continue to maintain an "I need it yesterday" approach to the project. What clients still don't understand is how long it can take to develop a dynamic site.

A proficient designer can put a site together in a relatively short time. Using Dreamweaver MX, we have created quality static sites in a matter of hours, thanks to all of the features available in Dreamweaver MX and Fireworks MX. Putting a dynamic site together takes a considerable amount of planning long before any code hits the page. This is something we made abundantly clear in Chapter 6, "Preparing for Dynamic Content." Dynamic sites bring everything to a new level of testing. Not only are we testing for links, but we are also testing for programming and database errors.

The "I need it yesterday" syndrome does infect the development community as well, and usually with disastrous results.

Jordan recalls one incident where he succumbed. He had been retained by a client with a stringent ColdFusion programming deadline. Jordan blindly took the challenge only to promptly fall flat on his face. The programming involved simply took more time than was available. Needless to say, Jordan lost the client because of bad planning. Still there was a positive outcome from the experience, and it's a lesson that he remembers, because he let his wanting to do this project get in the way of a realistic time schedule.

Ultimately, it comes down to the client. For Chris, if he comes across a client who wants to play at being a designer, he already knows there's going to be very little input they want from him, so he sucks it up and tries not to get too upset by the end results of the web site this unlikely collaboration has created. He just sort of shrugs his shoulders, and says to himself, "Hey, if it rocks your boat…"

Dealing with Complexity

Building dynamic sites is a complex process. Databases have to be built. Content has to be created and managed. Programmers have to ensure the content is moving from the database to the web site. ColdFusion MX programmers are ensuring the content is where it is supposed to be on the page, or doing what it is designed to do in the first place. As you can see, it is best to retain professionals rather than trying to do it yourself. Jordan and Chris discuss how they deal with complexity.

As Jordan succinctly puts it, "This is no longer a one-man show. Too bad there are many designers that are not seeing this. They believe that they can do it all. This is what is making it complex.

"It's not any different from any other part of the IT world. I don't know everything there is to know in the computing world, and I am grateful for it. If I had to know it all, I would freeze up. Yes, I will admit that I like to dabble in design, but that is because I like to do it, not because I feel that I have to do it. I have plenty of designers I can call on. When I have major projects from a client, I will often use those designers so that I can program. Why? Programming is what I love to do best."

From an artistic point-of-view, the same advice holds true. "I've long ago become accustomed to things I'm good at and things I'm not so good at and, when it comes to dynamic web design, these things are even more clear," says Chris. "For the life of me, even though I understand the concept of database integration, when it comes to putting it all into play, man, I am lost. The interest and focus just doesn't seem to come together quite like it does when I'm using Dreamweaver MX or Fireworks MX. Besides, I like to live by Dirty Harry's creed, that 'A man's gotta know his limitations.' This always seems to work best for me."

Is there a solution? "It doesn't have to be complicated," says Jordan. "It only gets complicated if you make it complicated."

Managing Content

The transition to a more modular approach to the design of web sites has understandably made the management of content an important issue for the team. In many respects, the ability to change the content at will is both an advantage and a disadvantage. Jordan has been involved with content management for a long time, and offers insight throughout this section.

I will go as far as to admit that I have written more CMS systems than in any other program for the web. There is a special reason for this from both the designer and the client point of view.

Designers are a finicky bunch of people. They get very catty when it comes to someone stepping on their code. They cringe whenever their client says, 'I want to be able to change the text at will…' I don't blame them. Some designers try to rationalize the acceptance of this request by thinking that if their client gets a copy of Dreamweaver MX, everything will be okay.

There is nothing worse than a client who suddenly believes that they can design because they have the tool without the training. This goes hand in hand with the designers who believe they are programmers because they have the tool and no training. I know this sounds harsh but it's a disaster that is waiting to happen.

Enter a Content Management System (CMS) system, which is a web application that allows the client to change their content at will without ever touching the design on a page.

A good content management system is one that works with the design and not against it. The designer should be able to work with the CMS system similar to working with a static page.

The ability to use dynamic content should appear no different than using static type. The client should be able to change the content on the back-end as quickly and simply as possible. When the client clicks Update, those changes should be reflected in real time.

If you are dealing with graphics, allow the client to upload to only one location in a site. If you are using ColdFusion MX, protect that area with an Application.cfm that redirects you away from that area immediately. This way, if someone tries to upload a .cfm page to try and take over the system, there's a better chance that an Application.cfm page will move you out of that area before any real damage is done.

If possible, don't allow a client to know where his area is physically located. As well, don't expect that the client knows HTML when entering their text. The designer should take care of all of the design formatting, while the client just worries about entering text. Use of Cascading Style Sheets today is great because you can define the formatting as you normally do and the dynamic content is seen as being no different than static content.

Keep the system modular, and keep the code as far from the layout as possible. Notable exceptions include the database fields and other ColdFusion tags necessary for display purposes within a page. The rest can be kept on a separate page. This way, the designer doesn't need to touch the code.

ColdFusion MX is great for modular programming. Various common application elements can be stored on a single Application.cfm. This page is loaded every time a ColdFusion MX page is called. This allows you to also keep your CMS application separate from any other ColdFusion MX web application (such as a shopping cart) you may have on your server.

Don't expect that one CMS application fits every need. You will find that clients have different needs and requirements. Work to meet those requirements, and make it easy enough for the designer to implement.

Designing Usability and Functionality

We also were struck by the fact that the move to dynamic designs makes the usability of a site and its functionality even more important than it was in the static way of doing things. With pages being essentially designed on the fly and the focus moving to web applications because of it, it is too easy to lose sight of the fact, during this period of transition, there is someone trying to use the site. Chris and Jordan explain how they always try to keep the user in mind when designing a dynamic site:

Why should this be any different with a web site than with any other application that you are using on your computer?" says Jordan. "It makes me laugh to hear people use web sites as the exception to the rule. It isn't. They are a living, breathing application just like anything else that you would run on your computer. What makes Apple's Mac OS a standard? It is easy to use and consistent. It shouldn't be any different with web sites.

We write users off because they don't know how to use our site, and rationalize by telling them, 'Well you just don't know the web, do you?' Talk about the biggest load of garbage you have ever seen. Again, we've seen sites that lack in either of the two principals. The end result is the same: an unusable site. Would you buy a desktop application that performs like this? I doubt it!

A good example is Macromedia's experience with Mac users. Mac users, at one time, made it very clear to Macromedia that their programs were similar to operating the control panel of a Klingon Battlecruiser. Macromedia listened, and took drastic measures to improve their user interface experience with their programs. It really shows on the Studio MX line.

We should be doing the same thing with our web sites. They should be easy to navigate and use. The end user doesn't get an owner's manual with the site. Then again, I can operate many Mac applications without ever cracking open the owner's manual. This is often the mark of a great application. It should also be the mark of a great web site. It often makes me wonder how many of the designers that are denigrating Jakob Nielsen, an advocate of web usability, are the same designers producing unusable web sites?"

Having heard from the coder, what about the guys who design the sites?

I try never to lose the fact that even though I design web sites, I also am a web surfer myself," says Chris. "I don't want people to be frustrated when they visit any of my web sites. I don't want them to ever say 'Huh? What's going on here?'

I want viewers to have a reason to visit and stay at my sites. Even if that reason is simply to be entertained. I think if you can offer some kind of service the visitor finds helpful, informative or even entertaining, they will keep coming back. But if you don't offer them something they find valuable, they won't come back.

Additionally, if there is something the visitor finds valuable, they will keep coming back regardless of the site's usability or functionality. My example? How many sites have you visited that looked absolutely horrid or were hard to navigate but had a great message board that met an entertainment or educational need? Therefore you keep returning to this horrid site."

Using Dynamic Sites to Reach Out

Visit the Amazon site, and you'll likely see that your Amazon home page is far different than anyone else's Amazon home page. The reason is dynamic design. The list of book suggestions reflects your buying patterns at Amazon. For example, one of the authors used to buy web and graphic design books through Amazon. Whenever he would return to the Amazon site, his recommended reading list contained the latest offerings from a variety of publishers. When he started thinking about web design as a communications medium, he purchased a few books from Amazon, and his recommended reading list changed to reflect this change in his buying pattern. Is this the wave of the future when it comes to dynamic design, and is it something we should embrace or reject as we build sites for our clients? We'll let Jordan and Chris bring their perspectives to bear on this question.

Writes Jordan:

"EMBRACE IT! It shouldn't be treated as some scary thing. In fact, it should be treated with great reverence here.

I remember going to a seminar by Stan Davis. He talked about using dynamic sites to give clients the personal touch and it had me thinking, this is what sites should be. In simple terms, the idea and purpose of a web site is to bring the company closer to the end user, rather than the opposite. End users want more than a cold, impersonal experience.

Amazon has it on the nose when they are looking at your buying patterns and seeing other people that have bought this book have bought other books as well in a similar vein. The company has brought themselves closer to you by recommending a few other books they believe that you may be interested in. They have done both you and themselves a favor. It's a mutual fulfillment.

They may have pointed out some other books that you may not yet own, but may find interesting. In return, you have given them the business of possibly buying more books. Not to mention that you are now on their list of preferred customers who may want to get an email letting you know when a special is coming, and who gets let in the front door (digitally speaking) to shop and save a little money.

It is no different from the time I wrote a reminder program for the web site of a major chain of jewelry stores. Visitors would request that the site remind them of events in their lives, such as birthdays and anniversaries. The site would drop an email to them a couple of days in advance, reminding them of the event as well as suggesting a gift from their store. The company has brought themselves closer to the user. It's a new form of marketing, and it is a powerful tool if used properly. Of course, improper methods include SPAM, and we all know about that.

This use of dynamic web design is still in its infancy. This is often where a marketing expert comes into play with a designer and programmer. Again, no one person can do it all."

Adds Chris:

"After seeing Sherlock III which is a component of Apple's new Jaguar Operating System at the recent Macworld Expo, I can really see Sherlock becoming a model of what other browsers (or sites) might try to duplicate. I'm not sure where this whole thing is taking us (I'm a lousy prognosticator—my football pools show that!—but I can certainly see much more customizing going on with the web). The use of dynamic web sites adds a degree of personalization simply unavailable through a static site.

Another aspect of the shift in design and purpose is the use of dynamic sites for mundane services. A really great example is going to the movies. I rarely purchase movie tickets at the box office. It's all done through the web—even though there might be a small fee attached to this service. For me, this is an extremely convenient method of buying tickets. And, what's even better, I can get tickets to blockbuster movies without having to worry about sold-out shows."

Summary

This chapter has been all about transitions—transitions in the book, and transitions in our industry.

With the completion of the content for the JCT site, the production process transitions from content creation to site creation. At this point in the process, you should take the time to review what you did well—and what you didn't do well.

We gave you a thorough insight regarding why we went with a GIF image for the navigation menu instead of the obvious JPG image. We discussed the technical and the creative reasons behind the decision. Chris Flick, the designer, offered further insight behind the decision.

We also discussed the uses and abuses of Flash MX in a dynamic universe, along with the uses and abuses of the improved capabilities in both Fireworks MX and Flash MX to create pop-down menus.

The move to dynamic site creation is also still in transition as developers and clients adjust to a new workflow. We examined a number of the broader issues behind this transition from workflow to usability, from making static sites dynamic to a little crystal ball gazing as to where the transition from static to dynamic web design is leading us. Both Chris Flick and Jordan Chilcott brought their years of experience to bear on all of these topics.

Next up? We show you how to build the pages that hold dynamic content in Dreamweaver MX.

Building Dynamic Pages in Dreamweaver MX

As pointed out in Chapter 13, "Designing Dynamic Web Sites," the design process is made much smoother when you use a template. The chief advantage to you, the designer, is that a template results in a locked page.

You can build editable regions into the page, and determine who has access to those regions, such as writers, designers, coders, and so on.

In the case of the JCT site, you will create the skeleton upon which the site is built in the next chapter.

As you have discovered, templates define the layout of a site. The difference between a template and a regular HTML page is quite profound. In today's web environment, sites inevitably grow. For example, the JCT site could grow to include backpacks, socks, jewelry, even skateboards and roller blades. If the site were based upon a static HTML design, individual pages for each category of a product would have to be developed and linked with all of the other pages in the site. This is a time-consuming and expensive process.

Template-based layouts that allow *scalability*—a techie web word for expansion—can accommodate these changes in a rather expedient manner because the purpose of a template is to accommodate change. If the site changes, all you have to do is change the locked region of the template and the change is reflected through the entire site.

There are two types of templates you can build. The first is a client-side template; the other is a server-side template.

This chapter deals with building client-side templates. Client-side templates, as discussed in Chapter 13, are used to define a consistent look and feel throughout the site using standard HTML. Content contained within the HTML-based pages are downloaded to the browser. A server-side template resides on the server, and the content is dynamically loaded into the page, depending upon the choices made by the viewer. This chapter deals with client-side templates. You'll learn about server-side templates in the next chapter.

Building a Navigation Bar

In this chapter you build the same navigation menu in two ways. The first way is to use a series of supplied slices that are placed in a table and have navigation behaviors applied to the buttons. The second way creates the tables and so on in Fireworks MX. You do this because there are still two ways of approaching workflow—the old way and the Studio MX way.

In either case, the navigation bar is placed into a ColdFusion MX template, and the content for the page is added into placeholders under the navigation bar.

Hand-Assembling a Navigation Bar from Supplied Graphic Slices

One of the more difficult jobs you will encounter is building a navigation bar from a sliced image. One of the authors, Jordan Chilcott, likens it to being handed the pieces of a jigsaw puzzle and then being asked to reassemble them to form the image. In this exercise, you assemble the navigation bar from the submitted puzzle pieces.

It is more difficult to hand assemble a navigation bar because the various states of the button require separate images. As you have seen in previous chapters, one button requires three or four separate images. In the case of the JCT site, there are four buttons at the top of the page, meaning there are either 12 images—an Up, Over, and Down state for each button—or 16 images if there is an Over While Down state, which is common with pop-down menus.

It is important for the individual tasked with the assembly job be given an image of how the elements are to appear on the page, as shown in Figure 19.1.

Figure 19.1   To avoid confusion, the person assembling the page should be supplied with a screenshot of the page they are working on.

To build the JCT navigation bar, follow these steps:

1. Copy the Chapter 19 Exercise folder from the book web site to your desktop. Create a folder to use as the site root on the desktop, and copy the navbar_images folder from the Chapter 19 Exercise folder to the folder you just created.

2. Launch Dreamweaver MX and then create a new site named **JCT Dynamic Site**. Open the Site view and notice the navbar_images folder located in the local site view on the right as shown in Figure 19.2.

3. Create a new HTML page by selecting File, New, or pressing Command-N (PC) or Ctrl-N (Mac). When the New Document dialog box opens, set the category to Basic Page and then select HTML in the Basic Page subcategory box, as shown in Figure 19.3. When finished, click Create, and a new HTML page appears. This is the page you use to assemble the navigation bar.

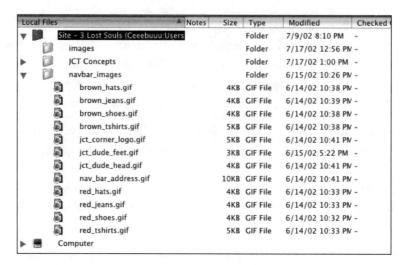

Figure 19.2   The navbar_images folder containing all of the slices for the navigation bar is located inside the root folder for the site.

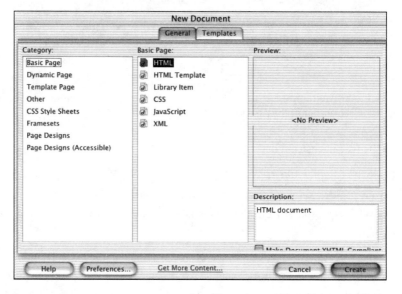

Figure 19.3   The Dreamweaver MX New Document dialog box allows you to choose the type of page you create.

4. To make it easy to build the page, open your site Assets panel by selecting Window, Assets, or pressing the F11 key. When the Assets panel opens, click the Image icon in the Files panel to see a preview of the image.

Tip

If you have a number of images in your site, you can sort your list by their full file path. To do this, click the Full Path title bar at the top of the list of assets in the Files panel. This groups all of the images together as shown in Figure 19.4.

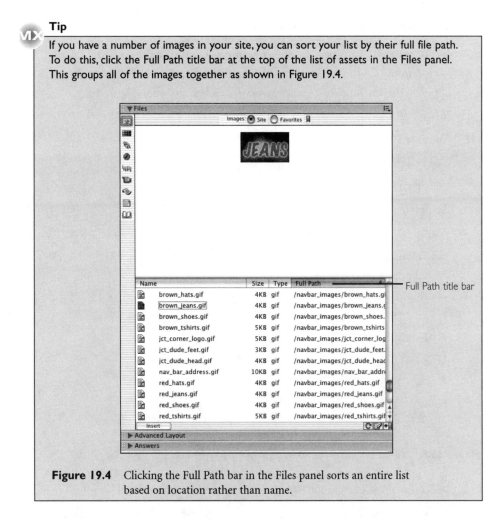

Figure 19.4   Clicking the Full Path bar in the Files panel sorts an entire list based on location rather than name.

Building the Navigation Bar

If you look at the list of navigation bar images in the Assets panel, you'll notice the whole image is composed of four menu choices, as well as the logo and the mascot. From this you can safely assume the navigation bar has a maximum of six slices going across it. It also appears that there are vertical slices because the address is in the center of the page, and the mascot's feet are at the bottom.

To build the navigation bar, follow these steps:

1. Insert a table on your page by selecting Insert, Table, or by clicking the Table button in the Common tab of the Insert palette. The Insert Table dialog box appears. Use the following values in the dialog box shown in Figure 19.5:

   Rows: 3

   Columns: 6

   Cell Padding: 0

   Cell Spacing: 0

   Border: 0

   Width: 100% (makes it easier to work with for now)

   When finished, click OK. A blank table showing six cells across and three cells down appears on the page.

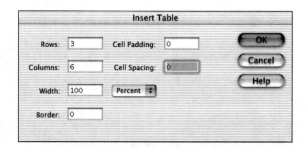

Figure 19.5   Tables are built in Dreamweaver MX using the Insert Table dialog box.

2. Select the top-left cell in the table, and make sure the Assets panel is visible.

3. In the Assets panel, select the jct_corner_logo.gif file and then click the Insert button, or drag the image icon from the Assets panel into the top-left cell of the table.

4. Select the next adjacent cell on the top row of the table, and select the navigation element that goes into this cell. Considering that you may have received rollover images as well, select the darker image—red_shoes.gif—to be placed in this cell.

5. Subsequent cells include hats, T-shirts, jeans, and the JCT logo, which goes in the corner of the navigation bar, and our mascot. Insert these navigation elements from the Files panel to their individual cells along the top of the table. When you have put your images in each cell at the top, the page should resemble Figure 19.6. Don't worry about the images appearing to be spaced apart; you will deal with that shortly. Save your page as **navbar.html**.

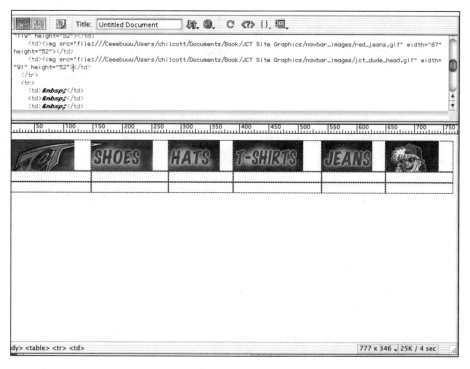

Figure 19.6   The top of row of cells contains the content to be used in the navigation bar. Note the split screen. The developer is using Code and Layout views to assemble the page.

6. The second row requires only one cell to hold the address slice. Select the entire row of cells in the second row, and click the Merge button on the Property inspector. Alternately, you can select Modify, Table, Merge Cells. The six cells in the second row become one long cell that spans the width of the table.

7. Select the nav_bar_address.gif image from the Files panel, and insert it into the second row. Again, don't worry about the disjointed look of the navigation bar.

8. Select the bottom-right cell of the table, and insert the jct_dude_feet.gif image from the Files panel. The page should resemble that shown in Figure 19.7.

9. There is a lot of space between the images. To address this, let the software do the work and tighten up the images in the table cells. Select the entire table. The Property inspector changes to reflect that you are editing the Table properties. Click once on the Clear Column Widths and the Clear Row Heights buttons on the Property inspector. The images in the cells neatly fit together. Save your file.

Figure 19.7   The slices have all been placed into their respective table cells.

Inserting Rollovers and Navigation Links

At this point of the design process, you either have an assembled navigation bar that you hand-built earlier, or the graphics designer was nice enough to hand us the completed file from Fireworks MX.

Having assembled the navigation bar, follow these steps to create the rollovers and navigation links for the buttons:

1. If necessary, open the Navbar.html page created in the preceding exercise in Dreamweaver MX.

2. Select the shoes image at the top of the navigation bar. The Property inspector changes to show the Image properties. In the Property inspector, enter **shoes** in the image name text box. For the link, because you know that you are using ColdFusion in the next chapter, you set up the link to ColdFusion by entering **shoes.cfm** in the Link text box as shown in Figure 19.8.

Figure 19.8   The show slice is named in the Image name area of the Property inspector and the Link area is named Shoes.cfm to prepare for a link to ColdFusion.

3. Repeat step 2 with the hats, T-shirts, and jeans images.

 Tip

Standard operating procedure is to have image names and their links reflect their categories. Also, it is not advisable to use the hyphen in T-shirts. Instead, use the name **tshirts**, and link to a page called **tshirts.cfm**.

4. Open the Design panel and then click the Behaviors tab, or select Windows, Behaviors. Select the shoes image in the table.

5. Add a behavior to the selection by clicking the + sign in the panel. A pop-down menu of behaviors appears. Select the Set Nav Bar Image behavior to open the Set Nav Bar Image dialog box.

6. Click the Browse button to the right of the Over Image area to display the selected image source dialog box. Locate the brown_shoes.gif in the navbar_images folder. Ensure Preload Images is checked in the Options area at the bottom of the Set Nav Bar Image dialog box. If the entries in the dialog box resemble those shown in Figure 19.9, click OK.

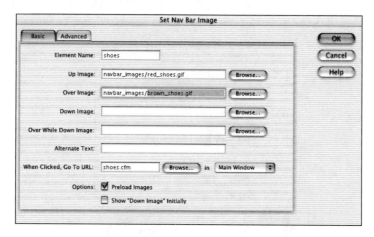

Figure 19.9   A nav bar rollover behavior is assigned to the shoe image in the table.

7. Repeat steps four to six for the hats, T-shirts, and jeans images.

8. The navigation bar is now complete. Save the file. If you want to test the page, press F12 or select File, Preview in Browser.

Building a Navigation Bar the Studio MX Way

You got a taste of the old workflow when you saw how to build a table-based page from a series of supplied slices. This workflow is still prevalent because many coders prefer to either roll their own code, or use the behavior features of Dreamweaver MX. In fact, in Chapter 13, one of the authors, Chris Flick, mentioned that he produced a series of slices in Fireworks because the coder, another author, Jordan Chilcott, preferred to do the behaviors in Dreamweaver MX.

In this exercise, you learn how to build a navigation bar the Studio MX way. You are going to produce the navigation bar, including rollover behaviors, in Fireworks MX. The navigation bar can then be used in Dreamweaver to produce a ColdFusion MX template.

To create the navigation bar in Fireworks MX, follow these steps:

1. Open the JCT New Corporate Nav Bar.png file in the Chapter 19 Exercise folder on you desktop to launch Fireworks MX. Notice the file has been built and sliced for you.

2. Open the Frames panel by selecting Window, Frames, and select Duplicate Frame on the Frame options pop-down menu.

3. When the Duplicate Frame dialog box appears, enter **1** in the Number text box and then click the After Current Frame radio button. If your Duplicate Frame dialog box resembles Figure 19.10, click OK.

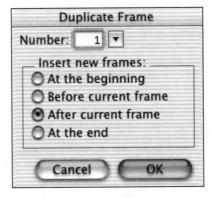

Figure 19.10   The image on the canvas is duplicated using the Duplicate Frame dialog box.

4. Select frame 2 in the Frames panel. The images that are on frame 2 appear; however, they won't be any different than frame 1 because you made a duplicate of frame 1.

5. The objective is to change the fill color of each menu item to a lighter color, which will indicate a rollover. Rather than doing each item, let the software do the work for you. With the Shift key pressed, click on each menu item on the navigation bar.

6. In the Property inspector, click once on the color chip to open the swatch palette. Select a lighter color, such as #996633. All of the menu items change color.

7. Select frame 1, and select the shoes slice. In the Property inspector, enter **shoes** as the slice name. In the link, enter **shoes.cfm.** This automatically puts the link in the HTML when you export the page. Repeat this step for the hats, T-shirts, and jeans slices.

8. Open up the Behaviors palette by selecting Window, Behaviors, or press Shift-F3. Shift-click each of the product name slices to select them.

9. Click the + button on the Behaviors panel to open a list of behaviors. Select Nav Bar Over behavior to open the Set Nav Bar Image dialog box, shown in Figure 19.11. All you need to do is to click OK to apply the behavior to all of the slices.

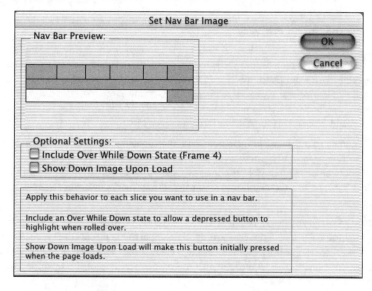

Figure 19.11   The nav bar behavior sets up the rollover so that only one button at a time can be selected.

10. Export the image by selecting File, Export. When the Export dialog box opens, use the following settings:

    Save As. Select HTML and Images from the pop-down menu.

    HTML. Select Export HTML file.

    Slices. Select Export Slices.

11. Click the Put Images in Subfolder check box. It usually defaults to images—leave it as such.

12. Name your HTML file **JCT_navbar.htm**.

13. Click Save, and quit Fireworks.

Fireworks has now exported the slices as well as created the HTML table that will hold your slices. Also, if you need to redo some of the images, you can switch back and forth between Dreamweaver MX and Fireworks MX, and any changes done in Fireworks MX are instantly reflected in Dreamweaver MX.

Tip

Don't forget that Fireworks MX has a new Quick Export button. Instead of selecting Export from the File menu, you can click Export HTML from the Dreamweaver MX pop-down menu after clicking the Quick Export button. This opens the Export dialog box. After the file is exported, you can click the Launch Dreamweaver MX button to open Dreamweaver MX.

Workflow the Studio MX Way

Dreamweaver MX and Fireworks MX can almost be regarded as Siamese twins. You create your link's image maps and slices in Fireworks MX, place them in Dreamweaver MX, and edit them from Dreamweaver MX in Fireworks MX. As well, the HTML code generated by Fireworks MX works seamlessly in Dreamweaver MX. The two applications, therefore, provide a streamlined workflow environment to the team for editing, optimizing, and placing HTML pages in Dreamweaver MX.

When it comes to working with dynamic data, the capability to place a Fireworks MX image placeholder into a Dreamweaver page is important. In this manner, you can create areas in your templates that hold the images created (or about to be created) in Fireworks MX, and use ColdFusion MX to place those images into the Dreamweaver MX templates.

The creation of dynamic sites requires tight integration of workflow. On the surface, it appears the job roles in the process are tightly compartmentalized: coders, designers, database developers, Flash developers. This is truly not the case. Each member of the team must coordinate their workflow with the other members of the team, and have input into the other's role.

To set up an integrated work environment, consider the following:

- Use Design Notes religiously. They move with the Fireworks files, appear in a Notes folder, and have the .mno extension. Design Notes contain information about the files exported from Fireworks MX. When you insert and edit a Fireworks image or table in Dreamweaver MX, Dreamweaver uses this information to locate the PNG file.

- Set Fireworks MX as the primary image editor in the Dreamweaver MX preferences. This allows Dreamweaver MX to launch Fireworks MX quickly.

- After the imaging files have been approved and completed, move them from the staging area or client site to the Dreamweaver site folder.

- Ensure each member of the team is familiar with the file-naming conventions. It is very easy to save a Dreamweaver MX file as an HTML page when it should have been saved as a ColdFusion MX template.

Creating a ColdFusion MX Template

All of the pages for the JCT site are built around one main ColdFusion MX template. From that template, you need to create only three pages for the site: the splash page, a product page, and a product details page. The rest of the site is handled with dynamic programming, covered in the next chapter.

In Chapter 13, you learned, in general terms, how a build a template in Dreamweaver MX. To learn how the content is added to a Dreamweaver MX template, follow these steps:

1. Launch Dreamweaver MX, and create a new template by selecting File, New. The New Document dialog box appears, as shown in Figure 19.12. Select Template Page from the Category area. The subcategory list box changes to a list of template pages. Select ColdFusion Template from the list and then click Create. A new ColdFusion template appears onscreen. Don't worry about the <<Template>> Untitled 2 name of the document; you can change that later.

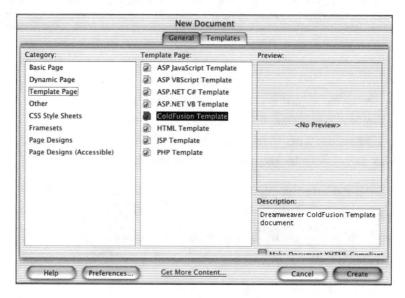

Figure 19.12   The ColdFusion template is chosen from a list of templates in the Dreamweaver MX New Document dialog box.

2. Click once on the Insert Table button on the toolbar. When the Insert Table dialog box appears, insert a two-row, one-column table on the page with no Border, Cell Spacing, or Cell Padding, and with a table Width of 100%. Click OK; the table appears on the template. The top row holds the navigation, and the bottom row enables you to enter your content.

3. Select the top cell of the table by clicking inside the cell. You are inserting the Fireworks MX navigation bar created earlier into this row.

4. Select Insert, Interactive Images, Fireworks HTML, or click the Fireworks HTML button in the Common tab of the Insert panel. The Insert Fireworks HTML dialog box opens.

5. Click the Browse button to open the Select the File Selector dialog box. Navigate to the Fireworks MX HTML file created earlier. Click Open to close the File Selector dialog box. The full path appears in the Insert Fireworks HTML dialog box.

6. Make sure that the Delete File after Insertion check box is unchecked before clicking the OK button in the insert Fireworks HTML dialog box.

Tip

By not selecting the Delete File radio button in the Insert Fireworks HTML dialog box, you avoid losing the HTML file driving the Fireworks MX navigation bar. If you accidentally insert the wrong file, you have to return to Fireworks MX and recreate the HTML.

7. You are now presented with an alert box telling you the template does not contain any editable regions. They are added later. Click OK.

8. You are now prompted to save your template. Name your template **main**. The Fireworks MX table from the HTML created earlier containing the navigation bar is inserted as a nested table into the top cell of the table, as shown in Figure 19.13. The nested table keeps everything contained.

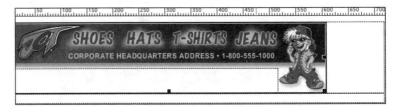

Figure 19.13   The navigation bar created in Fireworks MX appears in the top cell of the table in the ColdFusion MX template by inserting the HTML file created when the image was exported from Fireworks MX.

Inserting an Editable Region into the ColdFusion MX Template

You now create an editable region within your template. As explained in Chapter 13, an editable region is the only area of a template in which content can be updated or changed.

To create an editable region in the ColdFusion MX template, follow these steps:

1. Select the bottom cell of the table.

2. Select Insert, Template Objects, Editable Region to open the New Editable Region dialog box, shown in Figure 19.14.

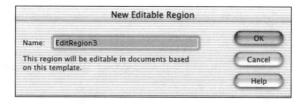

Figure 19.14   An editable region is added to a template by selecting Editable Region from the Template Objects area of the Insert menu. A name is also given to the newly defined editable region.

3. Name the editable region, and click OK when done. The page is now marked with a new editable region indicated by the region's name in a blue tab and inside the table cell. It is inside the cell, as shown in Figure 19.15, so that the integrity of the table is protected.

Figure 19.15   An editable region in a template is indicated by a blue tab containing the region's name in the table cell into which it is placed.

4. Select the outer table by clicking on the table outline, or by clicking on the outermost table tag on the bottom of the template window. The Property inspector changes to indicate you are editing the table.

5. Change the width of the table to 600 pixels. This matches the width of the Fireworks MX navigation bar. Center the table by selecting Center from the Align pop-down menu in the Property inspector.

Adding a Cascading Style Sheet to the ColdFusion MX Template

There may be a time when text will be input into the editable region. In this case, the event the text style needs to change, it makes sense to add a Cascading Style Sheet (CSS) to the editable region. Because the Style Sheet is contained within the template, you make it inline on your template for now, as opposed to making an external CSS file.

To add a Cascading Style Sheet to the ColdFusion MX template, follow these steps:

1. Open the CSS Styles panel by selecting Window, CSS Styles.

2. Click the New CSS Style button at the bottom of the CSS Styles panel to open the New CSS Style dialog box.

3. Click the Redefine HTML Tag radio button in the Type area.

4. In the Define In area, select the This Document Only option.

5. In the Tag text box, enter **td** as shown in Figure 19.16, or select the td style from the pop-down list. The **td** tag was chosen because we want to define a default text format for our table cells. Click OK to open the CSS Style Definition dialog box.

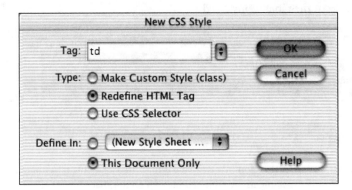

Figure 19.16   A Cascading Style Sheet named td is added to the editable region of the ColdFusion MX template.

6. Select Type in the Category list of the CSS Style Definition dialog box.

7. Select the font, size, and whatever characteristics you want. Whatever you don't want to change, leave blank. You are using this method rather than the old font tag because of the migration to W3C standards. This keeps your font styles constant from cell to cell in your table. Set your choices as shown in Figure 19.17.

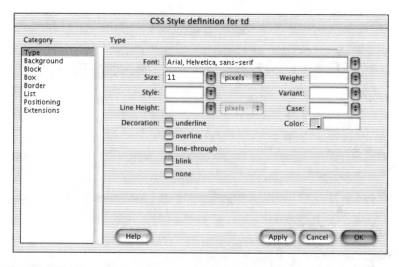

Figure 19.17   The font styling choices made for the Cascading Style Sheet are attached to the ColdFusion MX template.

8. Click OK when done. The words inside the editable region and the region's name changes to match the newly defined style.

9. The template is now complete. Save the template, and close your Template document.

Creating a ColdFusion MX Product Hit List Page

You now create a ColdFusion product hit list page from the template. A list of returned results matching a database search query is commonly known as a hit list. This page is used to display a list of selected products in the editable region of the template just created. The list of products is defined by a database search query that will be discussed in Chapter 20, "Connecting with ColdFusion MX."

To create the hit list page, follow these steps:

1. Select File, New to open the New Document dialog box. Click the Templates tab to change the dialog box to a New from Template dialog box and you will see a list of sites, as shown in Figure 19.18. Select the JCT Dynamic Site you created earlier in this chapter. A list of templates appears in the middle list box, and an image of the template page appears in the Preview pane. Select your template named main. Click Create when done.

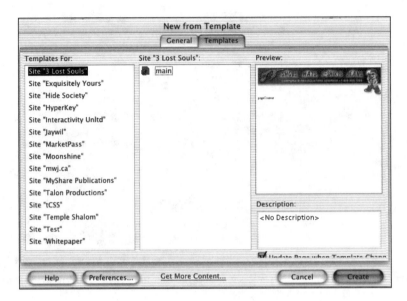

Figure 19.18   A template is applied to a Dreamweaver MX document by selecting the template from the list in the New from Template dialog box. (Clicking the Templates tab changes the dialog box from New Document to New from Template.)

2. When the new page is created, the template appears and the name of the template appears in a yellow box in the upper-right corner of the page. In the Title box of the new page, enter **Product Listing**.

    You now create an image placeholder for the main graphic in the pageContent region of the template. This is filled in when you connect, dynamically, to the server. You also create the placeholder table for a product list when you query the Access database.

3. Roll the cursor over the navigation bar. The cursor changes to circle with a line through it. This indicates this area of the template is locked. Click once inside the pageContent region, select the word pageContent, and press the Delete key.

4. Select Insert, Table to open the Insert Table dialog box. Create a four-column, three-row table that with 100% width and 0 in the Cell Spacing, Padding, and Border input areas. Click OK when done. This places a table in the pageContent region.

5. Shift-click each cell in the top row of the table, and select Modify, Table, Merge Cells. The top row is now a continuous cell.

6. In the top cell, create a placeholder image. Select Insert, Image Placeholder to open the Image Placeholder dialog box.

7. Name the image **productpict**, and set the dimensions of the image placeholder to 158 x 121.

Tip

If the images are going to be loaded dynamically, try to keep them a uniform size.

8. Click OK when done. An image placeholder appears as shown in Figure 19.19.

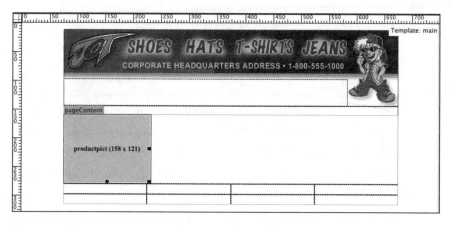

Figure 19.19   Use image placeholders in pages into which the image content will be loaded dynamically.

9. Enter the following text into the middle row of cells, starting with the second cell from the left. The first cell is left blank because it is used to hold the images.

    Product

    Description

    Price

10. Select File, Save As. Save the page as a ColdFusion template by selecting ColdFusion Template from the Save as Type pop-down list. Name the page **productlist.cfm**. Close the template.

You complete the template in the next chapter when you hook up to the ColdFusion MX server.

Creating a ColdFusion MX Product Details Page

You now create a ColdFusion product details page. This page not only shows the products chosen in the previous template, but also acts as a shopping cart allowing the consumer to purchase the product.

To build the product details page, follow these steps:

1. Select File, New to open the New Page (or New from Template, depending on whether the Template tab was selected previously) dialog box, and select the Template tab, and Notice a list of sites. Select JCT Dynamic Site. A list of templates appears in the middle list box. Select the main template. Click Create when done.

2. When the new page is created, enter **Product Details** in the Title box.

3. Click once inside the editable region of the template. Select and delete the word pageContent. Select Insert, Table to open the Insert Table dialog box. Create a two-column, two-row table that is 100% width. Enter 0 in the Cell Spacing, Padding, and Border areas. Click OK when done. This places a table with two columns and two rows in the pageContent region.

4. Select the entire right column of the new table, and select Modify, Table, Merge Cells. The right column becomes one big cell.

5. Click the right cell. Select Top in the vertical alignment pop-up menu of the Property inspector. This places the cell content at the top, no matter how big the table stretches.

6. In the right cell, create a two-column, three-row table with 100% width. Enter 0 for the Cell Padding, Spacing, and Border settings.

7. Open the Image Assets panel. If it isn't visible in your panel grouping, select Windows, Assets. Locate the three images named shopcart_blue_finger.gif, shopcart_red_finger.gif, and shopcart_yellow_finger.gif in the site's images folder.

8. Click the shopcart_blue_finger.gif and then drag it to the top-left cell of the two-column, three-row table you just created.

9. Click the shopcart_red_finger.gif and then drag it to the middle-left cell of the table under the blue finger image.

10. Click the shopcart_yellow_finger.gif and then drag it to the bottom-left cell under the red finger image.

11. Click once inside the right top cell. Enter the text **Your Security**.

12. Click once inside the right middle cell. Enter the text **Exchange Policy**.

13. Click once inside the right bottom cell. Enter the text **Your Gift Packages**.

14. Select the jct_animated_events.gif and then drag it just underneath the inner table. Click the inside of the cell containing the animated GIF, and select Right in the Horizontal Alignment pop-up menu. Save the page as **productdetails.cfm.** This saves the file as a ColdFusion template.

15. Select top-left cell of the outer table in the pageContent editable region, and insert an image placeholder that is 151 pixels wide and 128 pixels high. Name the placeholder **productPict**. Your page should resemble that shown in Figure 19.20. Save the page and close it

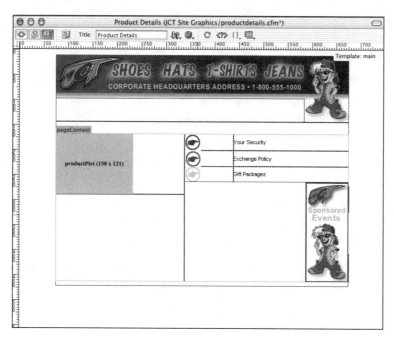

Figure 19.20   The completed design of the Product Details page is shown before the dynamic content is added.

This page is now complete. You learn how to add in the dynamic content in the next chapter.

Creating a Page to Hold the Flash Introduction

The site starts with the animation of the dancing mascot created in Chapter 16, "Preparing the Animations for the JCT Site." After the animation finishes, the browser loads in the first page created in this chapter.

To create a page to hold a Flash intro, follow these steps:

1. Select File, New to open the New Document (or New from Template) dialog box. Select the Template tab and notice a list of sites. Select the site you named JCT Dynamic Site. A list of templates appears in the middle list box. Select the main template. Click Create when done.

2. Click once inside the Title box of the new page, and enter **Welcome to JCT**.

3. Click once inside the pageContent area of the template and then select Insert, Table to open the New Table dialog box. Enter the appropriate data for a one-column, one-row table with a width value of 100% width and a value of 0 for Cell Spacing, Padding, and Border. Click OK when done. This places a table in the pageContent region.

4. Click inside the newly created table. In the Property inspector, click on the Bg color chip and then select the black chip from the swatches in the pop-down menu.

5. In the Property inspector, select Center in the Horz alignment pop-up menu, and Middle from the Vert alignment pop-up menu.

6. Ensure the cell used to hold the animation is selected. Select Insert, Media, Flash, or click the Flash button in the Common tab of the Insert panel to open the Select File dialog box.

7. Navigate to the flashdancer.swf file created in Chapter 16, or use the version in the Chapter 19 Exercise folder on your desktop. Select the file then and click Choose. The intro is now inserted onto the page into the one-cell table.

8. To preview the intro, click once on the .swf file on the page and then click the Play button in the Property inspector (see Figure 19.21).

9. Save the file as **index.html**. This is the splash page.

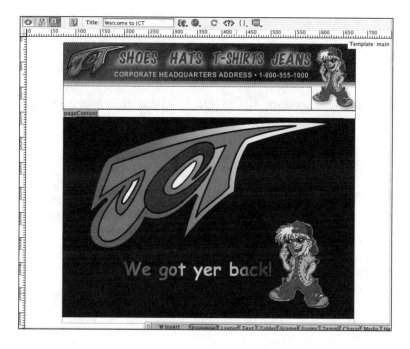

Figure 19.21   The completed splash page with the Flash intro playing in Dreamweaver MX.

Summary

In this chapter, you built an entire site consisting of only three pages. This is because the rest of the information and content for those three pages are served into them through ColdFusion MX.

We started the chapter by building the JCT navigation bar using the traditional method of building a table using named slices. We showed you how to assign rollover behaviors in Dreamweaver MX to the slices being used as buttons. We did this because there are occasions when you or the coder might feel the HTML code generated by Dreamweaver MX is needed.

We then followed the Studio MX workflow by adding the slices and rollover behaviors in Fireworks MX, and exporting them and the resulting HTML to Dreamweaver MX.

We showed you how to create a ColdFusion MX template in Dreamweaver MX, and how to place the navigation bar created in Fireworks MX into the template. We also showed you how to create an editable region in the template, which is used to hold the content.

Having created the ColdFusion template, we showed you how to apply that template to a Dreamweaver MX page, and how to nest tables inside the editable region of a page with a temple. In this manner, you created three pages that change to reflect the choices of the visitor.

In the next chapter, we show you how to load dynamic content into these pages.

Part IV

Testing and Delivering the Final Product

MX

Connecting with ColdFusion MX

This chapter builds on the fundamentals presented in Chapter 6, "Preparing for Dynamic Content." Using the three pages built using ColdFusion MX templates, you learn how to load the content from the Access database created in Chapter 6 into the various pages of the JCT site.

In many respects, this chapter picks up on the theme of the preceding chapter (Chapter 19, "Building Dynamic Pages in Dreamweaver MX"). Throughout this chapter, you'll see that the MX Studio way of performing tasks is starting to take hold in the industry.

If you go back to the beginnings of the Internet, you discover it was initially developed as a communications transmission vehicle that allowed scientists to trade papers and documents with each other. At that point in history, the web was a static medium characterized by long text-based pages. As well, each page was separate and distinct from every other page in the site. As the web gained in popularity, the need for more current and, in many respects, immediate information drove workflow. This resulted in a rather cumbersome and expensive process that involved constantly updating and modifying sites to accommodate changes. The constant updating and modifying sites gave birth to storing the information on a database, and presenting that stored information through a dynamic web site. These sites are capable of displaying time-critical content in an easily understood and navigable format.

Database connectivity and the inclusion of the database developer into the work team is a fundamental fact of life in today's web development environment. The rise to prominence of ecommerce and news services, such as CNN and the BBC, would not have occurred without this connectivity.

The importance of this connectivity was truly driven home on September 11, 2002, when the towers of the World Trade Center in New York were attacked and subsequently collapsed. The demand on the CNN site was so huge it overwhelmed the company's servers. This was also true for many other major news organizations with a web presence. What made this so remarkable was that it showed people now regard the Internet as a primary source of information, whether it is the latest hat from JCT or a video feed from a news event. All of this would not be possible without a database feeding information into a web page.

In this chapter, you learn to place the content for the JCT site into a Microsoft Access database and then feed that content through ColdFusion MX into the Fireworks MX placeholders and other content areas of the editable regions of the ColdFusion MX templates. How the content is placed in the database and the processes used to move it from Access to the web is no different than that used by CNN and Amazon.

ColdFusion and Macintosh Users

To be blunt ColdFusion MX, despite its Java nature, does not run in Mac OS X. This is one of those rare cases where an application is platform specific.

If you are a Mac user, you need one of the following to test the various bits and pieces created in this chapter:

- A provider that runs ColdFusion MX. This option is acceptable; however, you will not be using a local server, and unless you are paying for an extra virtual host, your remote server is also your test server.

- A separate PC to run ColdFusion MX. This is the optimal choice because you can use the PC as a separate test server, and the PC is local to your network. This choice is recommended if you are running ColdFusion MX on a PC running Windows NT or greater.

- A little patience. It is possible to run Virtual PC on a Mac in order to run ColdFusion MX; however, it may be slow as molasses.

Without ColdFusion, Mac users can't use the live data preview or the server behaviors because they relay the existence of ColdFusion MX on the network.

In this situation, the best you could do is to hand code the ColdFusion behaviors, without seeing the results because there will be no previewing of the page in a browser.

Preparing for Dynamic Content (Revisited)

In Chapter 6, you learned how to integrate Dreamweaver MX and ColdFusion MX. In that chapter, you learned a little about databases, created a database for use online, and learned how to connect ColdFusion MX to your database. Chapter 6 also covered how to create a ColdFusion page in Dreamweaver MX and preview your live data stored in your database. This chapter builds on Chapter 6 using the pages created from Chapter 19. If you haven't created your testing setup covered in Chapter 6, it is highly recommended that you review that chapter before proceeding.

Check your admin setting for the RDS password and the ODBC datasource connection. Also, check your site settings for testing the server URL. Dreamweaver MX uses these settings along with ColdFusion MX to preview your live data within Dreamweaver MX.

Again, it is emphasized that if you are unsure of the ColdFusion MX and Dreamweaver MX setup, please refer back to Chapter 6 to review setting your site definitions for dynamic capability.

Expanding the Access Database's Capabilities

The database created in Chapter 6 is rather rudimentary. Though you were able to feed text from the various fields in the database to a Dreamweaver MX page, it still doesn't allow you to add images to the page or even connect to the pages created in Chapter 19.

Adding the capability of displaying images dynamically gives the end user the perception that they are looking at a different page. The database will not hold the images themselves for two reasons: They will increase the size of the database and create possible maintenance nightmares, and you wouldn't be able to readily update the images without uploading an entire database. Instead, the filenames of the images will be stored in the database.

To incorporate dynamic images into the web site using our database, follow these steps:

1. Copy the Chapter 20 Exercise folder onto your desktop, and open the Access database file named jct.mdb to launch the main JCT window. Better yet, if you have been following along from Chapter 19, use your completed files from that chapter—or the completed files from that folder on the web site. They are part of the foundation for this chapter.

2. Double-click the Product file in the list to open the Product table.

3. Switch to Design view by selecting View, Design View. Click once in the empty cell under price in the Field Name column to add a new field. Enter the following information:

   - Field Name. GraphicURL (the name of the field to hold the name of an image).
   - Data Type. Text.
   - Allow Zero Length. Yes.

4. Your screen should resemble Figure 20.1. Save the changes and then close the window.

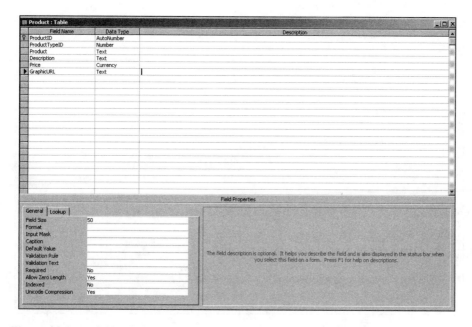

Figure 20.1   A field to hold the name of the product has been added to the Product table.

Having added a field for the name of the product, it makes sense to also add one to describe the product being shown on the web page along with a graphic for the product.

To add a field for the graphic file and product description, follow these steps:

1. Open the ProductType table, and switch to Design view.

2. Add a field, and use these settings:

   - Field Name. GraphicURL (the name of the field to hold the name of an image).

   - Data Type. Text.

   - Allow Zero Length. Yes.

3. Add another field, and use these settings:

   - Field Name. ProductDescription (holds the description).

   - Data Type. Memo.

   - Allow Zero Length. Yes.

Your table should resemble that shown in Figure 20.2.

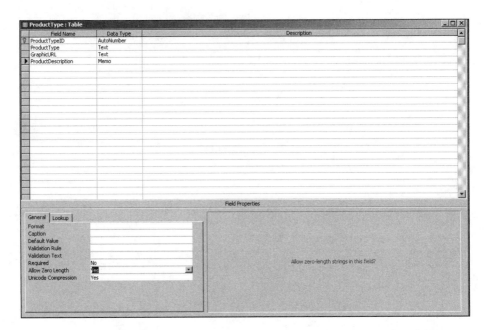

Figure 20.2   A description of the product eventually appears on the web page.

4. Open the Datasheet view (View, Datasheet View) of the open table, and save your changes.

Note

In the ProductDescription field, you set the text to Memo. A memo field is similar to a text field. Where it differs from a text field is that the memo field is variable and can hold up to 64,000 characters where a text field reserves and holds a fixed size predetermined by the user. This is useful because you don't know the length of the final product description, where text fields are good for information of known sizes, such as telephone numbers or zip codes.

Adding the Images and the Text to a Database

When you changed to Datasheet view, a list of the products appeared along with a product number and blank areas for the graphic URL for each product and a blank product description area. The order of the products is not important. What is important is the ProductTypeID's for the Product table. The ProductTypeID ties the product with the product type. There should be T-Shirts, Hats, Shoes, and Jeans in the ProductType fields, and numbers in the ProductTypeID fields.

To add the images and text in the empty fields, follow these directions:

1. In the GraphicURL field of Shoes, enter **shoe_shopcart_image.gif**.

2. In the GraphicURL field of Jeans, enter **jeans_shopcart_image.gif**.

3. In the GraphicURL field of T-Shirts, enter **tshirt_shopcart_image.gif**.

4. In the GraphicURL field of Hats, enter **hat_shopcart_image.gif**.

5. Write your own product description in each of the ProductDescription fields. In this case, you can have a little fun by opening up a clothing store catalog and using some of their ideas for writing your product descriptions. When you finish, the table should resemble that shown in Figure 20.3. Keep the table open; you will use it to look at the ProductID's.

ProductTypeID	ProductType	GraphicURL	ProductDescription
1	T-Shirts	tshirts_shopcart_image.gif	Sporty t's for the active teen. Made from durable cotton, these t's can stand almost an
2	Hats	hats_shopcart_image.gif	Hat's for any occasion from fad to fancy. We're the trendsetters in the field and we beli
3	Shoes	shoes_shopcart_image.gif	You won't know how great you feel until you have walked a mile in our shoes. Made fro
4	Jeans	jeans_shopcart_image.gif	Rugged and durable, our jeans were built for punishment. You will be able to wear us,
(AutoNumber)			

Figure 20.3   In the populated ProductType table, the filenames of our graphics along with product descriptions are entered into the table.

6. Open the Product table. Enter data, such as graphic URLs, more products, and descriptions for specific items. An example might be the various Shoe products offered by JCT.

7. Add the graphic filenames in their appropriate field. The images are available in the site folder path/images/shoppingcart_images/hitlist_images/. However, you will not be entering the folder path in the field because if you wanted to change the location of the files, you would have to update every field in the database. It is far easier to update your web page because you only need to make changes in one or two spots. Working from the top record down, enter the following graphic filenames in the GraphicURL field:

limegreen_drkgreen_shoe.gif

blue_red_shoe.gif

yellow_liteblue_shoe.gif

oceanblue_yellow_shoe.gif

8. Add new products by making entries with matching product type ID's. To create a proper search, make sure yours match with the ProductTypeID field in the ProductType table. Entries are made in the following order: ProductTypeID, Product, Description, Price, GraphicURL. Input the data shown in Figure 20.4 into the correct fields. When finished, your table should resemble that shown in Figure 20.4.

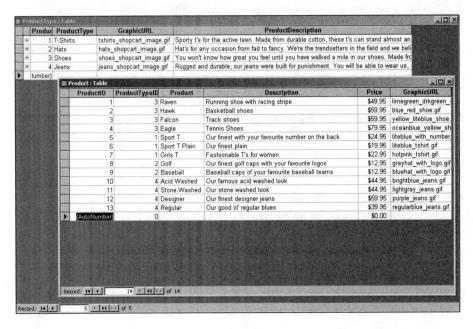

Figure 20.4   Extra products are added to the database. Note the relationship between the items in the ProductID table and the Product table.

You now have enough data to build a dynamic site with Dreamweaver MX and ColdFusion MX. Save the changes, and quit Access.

Getting Dynamic: The Dreamweaver MX/ColdFusion MX Connection

The inclusion of ColdFusion MX into the PC version of the MX Studio dropped the ability to create dynamic sites squarely into the laps of web developers. Suddenly, developers are able to create dynamic sites using the tools on their computers.

To create a dynamic site using Dreamweaver MX and ColdFusion MX, follow these steps:

1. Open Dreamweaver MX, and create a new site named **JCT Dynamic** using the JCT site folder in the Chapter 20 Exercise folder on your desktop as the site root.

Note

One template page serves many products. This is similar to designing a single template used in the design of many pages as shown in Chapter 19. The advantage to the developer is that the layout is done once, and any changes made to the template are reflected throughout the entire section.

2. Create a new text document by selecting File, New. When the New Document dialog box opens, click the General tab; then select Other in the Category area, and Text in the Other area of the dialog box. If your dialog box resembles that shown in Figure 20.5, click the Create button. A blank page with a colored stripe down the left side of the page opens. This type of document accepts only text.

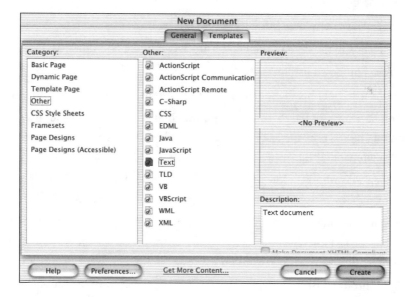

Figure 20.5   A text-based document is created.

3. Work on the shoe products first. Save the new text document as **shoes.cfm**. This turns the page into a blank ColdFusion page. You don't want anything on the page because this page is for your ColdFusion code. This page includes the template containing the page layout for the dynamic content.

4. Open the Server Behaviors panel by selecting the Application panel and then clicking the Server Behaviors tab. Click the + button, and select Recordset (Query) from the pop-down list to open the Recordset dialog box.

5. Enter the following information into the various areas of the Recordset dialog box:

   Name. Enter **getProductType.**

   Data Source. Select jct from the pop-down list. Dreamweaver displays a message telling you it is getting the JCT schema, meaning that it is opening the tables in the database.

   Table. Select ProductType from the pop-down list.

   Columns. Choose the All option.

6. In the lower half of the dialog box, there are four boxes that ask you how you want to get the records in the database. Set the filter in the Recordset window in this manner:

   In the Filter pop-down list, select ProductType.

   In the box to the right of the Filter list, select = in the pop-down list.

   In the pop-down list under the Filter list, select Entered Value.

   In the text input box beside the previous pop-down list, enter the word **Shoes**.

   You have now set the parameters for a search of the database. If you follow the input areas as presented and put them into plain English, you make a rather simple command: If the ProductType equals the word Shoes, do something.

7. If your Recordset window resembles Figure 20.6, click OK to write the query to the ColdFusion page. The recordset is listed in the server Behaviors panel.

8. The next recordset you need to create is a bit more complex. Click the + sign in Server Behaviors. When the Recordset window opens, click the Advanced button. A more involved recordset window opens.

9. Enter **productList** in the Name text box, and select jct from the list of choices in the Data Source pop-down window. An alert telling you the database schema is loading opens. When it closes, a list of items from the database appears at the bottom of the window in the Database Items box.

10. Click the + sign beside the Table icon in the Database Items box, and notice two tables created for the JCT database. Expand the Product table by clicking its + sign. A list of the fields in the Product table appears. Select ProductID and then click the SELECT button. Two lines of text are added to the SQL area of the Recordset window.

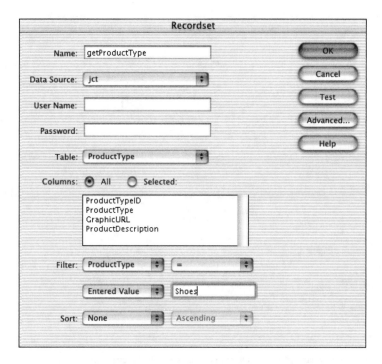

Figure 20.6   You access the information in the database by creating a recordset (query) in the Recordset window.

11. Click Product, Description, Price, and Graphic URL; click the Select button after you click each item.

12. Collapse the Product table in the Database Items area by clicking the – sign, and expand the ProductType table.

13. Click ProductType inside the ProductType table and then click the Select button. Notice the ProductType table added to the FROM clause in the SQL box.

14. Collapse the ProductType table.

15. Click once under the FROM line in the SQL input box, and enter the following two lines of text:

WHERE ProductType.ProductTypeID = Product.ProductTypeID

AND ProductType.ProductType = 'Shoes'

The first line joins the two tables together with a common field. In this case, the fields are related by their ProductTypeID. This give you the ProductType name with the returned record.

The second line sets the filter. You want to return only records that are Shoes. The Recordset window should resemble that shown in Figure 20.7.

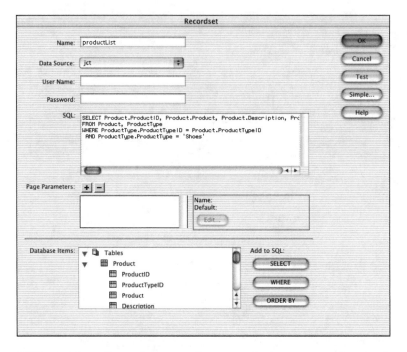

Figure 20.7   An advanced recordset query allows you to be even more precise when it comes to the information shown on a page.

16. If you want to test the SQL statement, click the Test button. A test window, shown in Figure 20.8, appears with your results. Click OK to close the test window.

Test SQL Statement

Record	ProductID	Product	Description	Price	GraphicURL	ProductType
1	1	Raven	Running shoe wit	49.9500	limegreen_drkgre	Shoes
2	2	Hawk	Basketball shoes	59.9500	blue_red_shoe.gi	Shoes
3	3	Falcon	Track shoes	59.9500	yellow_liteblue_s	Shoes
4	4	Eagle	Tennis Shoes	79.9500	oceanblue_yellow	Shoes

Previous 25   Next 25   OK

Figure 20.8   You can test your SQL query by clicking the Test button on the Recordset window to open a results window.

17. Click OK to close the Recordset window, and to add the productList recordset to the server Behaviors panel.

Moving Code from One Page to Another

The code you just produced can also be used temporarily on the site's productlist.cfm page, so you can complete your dynamic layout. Rather than repeat all the steps involved in creating the two recordsets, you can temporarily copy the code you just produced to the product list page.

To copy code from one page to another, follow these steps:

1. In the shoes.cfm page, select View, Code. The code for the two recordsets appear on the page. Select all of the code and then copy it.

2. Open the Files panel, and double-click the productlist.cfm page to open it.

3. When the page opens, open the Code and Design view, by selecting View, Code and Design.

4. Click the mouse once in line 1 of the Code view at the top of the page just before the <html> tag.

5. Paste the code and press Return (Mac) or Enter (PC). The code appears in the first eight lines of the Code view.

Linking Database Content to a ColdFusion Page

Having added the database queries to the page code, you can now start linking the various editable regions of the template to the Access database. To do this, follow these steps:

1. Double-click the productPict placeholder image in the template to open the Select Image dialog box.

2. Click the Data Sources button, and expand the getProductType recordset.

3. When the list of the fields appears, select GraphicURL, and prefix it with the following text in the URL text input area: **images/shoppingcart_images/**.

4. Click OK, and the image on the page now reflects that you have selected a dynamic image source by showing a lightning bolt on the image icon in the template.

5. In the Code view, select the table row (the <TR> tag) at the bottom of the window. The entire row is highlighted, indicating it is selected.

6. Open the server Behaviors panel, click the + sign, and select Repeat Region from the Behaviors pop-down list. Name the behavior **getProductType** in the Repeat Region dialog box, select All Records and click OK. By adding a repeat region, you can add more items in the repeating region.

7. Click the Bindings tab, and expand RecordSet (getProductType) in the bindings list.

8. Select ProductDescription from the list, and drag it onto the page beside the productPict image. Select the productPict image, and set the Align to Left option in the Property inspector. The template should resemble that shown in Figure 20.9.

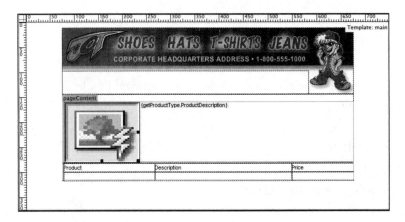

Figure 20.9   The image is dynamic as shown by the lightning bolt on the icon.

Creating a Dynamic Flash Text Box

Images aren't the only items on a page that can be made dynamic. In this exercise, you learn to create a dynamic text box in Flash. The interesting thing about this text box is that it is blank, and the text that appears in it is the product descriptions written in the Access database.

To create a dynamic Flash text box, follow these steps:

1. Open Flash MX, and set the document size to 300 pixels wide by 50 pixels high.

2. Select the Text tool from the Tools palette. Click once on the Stage and then drag a text box that fills the entire width of the Stage.

3. Click once inside the box, and press the spacebar to put something in the box.

4. In the Property inspector, set the text type to Dynamic Text and the variable name (Var) to ourTextBox.

5. Set the alignment to flush left, and set the font and size to a graffiti-like font, such as MarkerFelt. If you do not have MarkerFelt, feel free to substitute the font with any available font (there are plenty of free fonts on the Internet) that will suit your taste. Set the size to fill the Stage. If you are using MarkerFelt, set your size to 43 points.

6. Click the Character button on the Property inspector, and select All Characters from the Character dialog box. Click OK.

7. Click frame 5, and press F5 to insert a frame on the timeline. Add a new layer, and name it **Scripts**.

8. Select frame 5 in the Scripts layer and then press F6 to insert a keyframe. Select the keyframe in frame 5 of the Scripts layer, and open the Actions panel.

9. Select Expert Mode from the panel options pop-down menu, and enter the following into the code input area:

```
_root.ourTextBox = _root.theText;
```

This sets the text box to the incoming text, which is passed from ColdFusion MX once the page is generated.

10. Save the file as **flashtext.fla** and then publish it.

11. Quit Flash. You have now made a simple Flash dynamic text box asset that you can use on the page.

12. Return to the productlist.cfm page in Dreamweaver MX.

13. Insert the new Flash text box in the cell beside the dynamic image. With the Flash asset selected, click the Parameters button in the Property inspector to open the Parameters dialog box.

14. Enter **theText** for the parameter in the text input area of the dialog box.

15. To give the parameter a value, click the lightning bolt beside the parameter you just entered to open the to Dynamic Data Sources dialog box.

16. From the list of recordsets expand Recordset (getProductType), select ProductType, and click OK. Your Parameters dialog box should resemble that shown in Figure 20.10.

17. Position the Flash text box as shown in Figure 20.11, and size it according to your liking.

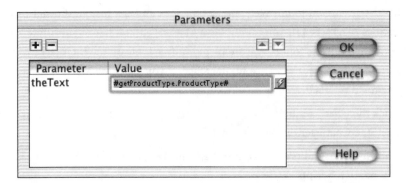

Figure 20.10   Parameters always need to have a corresponding value when they are set.

Figure 20.11   The Flash text box is placed in its final position and resized.

Tip

The capability to resize or otherwise change the properties of the text is the beauty of using Flash text. If you want to change any characteristics of your Flash movie, you can always click the Edit button to jump back and forth between Flash and Dreamweaver MX. Remember that this affects all of the product listings, however, because this is going to be a server template after you are finished.

Creating the Data Bindings

Data bindings, simply put, are the database assets that you use on a dynamic page. They define the sources of the content that are added to the page.

To create the data bindings for the Product Listing table, follow these steps:

1. Open the Bindings panel by choosing Window, Bindings, and expand the ProductList recordset.

2. Drag the Product field into the cell underneath the Product heading.

3. Having placed the Product field, you need to link it to the details page. Select the Product field binding on the page, and click the folder in the Link section of the Property inspector to open the Select File dialog box.

4. Select the productdetails.cfm file, and click the Parameters button in the Select File dialog box. The Parameters dialog box opens.

5. Enter **ProductID** in the name area, and press the Tab key to go to the value area. Click the Lightning Bolt button to open the Data Source dialog box. The link is now applied to the Product field on the page.

6. Expand the productList recordset, click the ProductID field, and click OK to return to the Select File dialog box. Click OK.

7. Drag the Description field into the cell underneath the Description heading.

8. Drag the Price field into the cell underneath the Price heading.

9. Undock the Application panel to allow it to float on the page. Expand the Bindings panel by clicking and dragging the right edge of the panel to the right. You should now see a format area in the panel.

10. Click the Price link in the table to select it. Set the format for Price as Currency, Dollar format by clicking the pop-down arrow. This formats the price in U. S. dollars and cents.

11. Select the lower-left cell, and select Insert, Image to open the Select Image Source dialog box.

12. Click the Data Source button to open the Data Source dialog box.

13. Expand the productList recordset, and click the GraphicURL field. In the URL text box, enter the path prefix of **images/shoppingcart_images/hitlist_images/**.

14. Click OK, and a dynamic image placeholder appears.

15. Select the row containing your data bindings, open the server Behaviors panel, and insert the repeat region named productList.

You can now test the page before making it a server template. Click the lightning bolt at the top of the window. Everything should appear except the Flash text. This is normal. If you want to test the Flash text, press F12 to preview the test page in a browser.

Making the Product List Page a Server Template

In the previous steps, you have created a dynamic product listing page that accesses and displays the shoes; however, you cannot forget the fact that the JCT site carries more than just shoes. The simplest solution would be to make copies of the product-listing page for each product. This is also the most inefficient solution because you would now have more than one product listing layout page to maintain. A more efficient solution is to have one layout to handle all of our product listings. In this way, changes to a single page affect all the pages that use it. This is known as a *server template*. The server template gets included into the product pages that are querying the database for various products. The only thing that changes, as you will see further in this section, is the SQL statement within the CFQUERY tag on the other product pages.

Caution

BE VERY CAREFUL WITH THIS! In fact, you might want to save a back-up copy of the page just in case you make a mistake. If you do make a mistake, you have to start over.

To change the product list page into a server template, follow these steps:

1. Open to the server Behaviors panel, and select the getProductType recordset.

2. Press the – button to delete it. You are notified that other behaviors depend on it, and asked if you would like to proceed with this anyway. Click OK.

3. Select the Recordset (productList).

4. Press the – button to delete it. You are notified that other behaviors depend on it, and asked if you would like to proceed with this anyway. Click OK.

5. Save the page and then close it. You now have a server template that is used in all of the product listings.

   Make sure that the productlist.cfm template is now uploaded to the test server.

6. Click the testing server button in the Site Definition dialog box and then click the Connect button.

7. Select your files, and click the Put Files button.

8. Open the shoes.cfm file, if necessary, and select View, Code and Design View.

9. Click in the design area; a chunk of code is selected.

10. Go to the code area, and click the line following your last </cfquery> tag. This is important for the following directions to work.

11. Select Insert, ColdFusion Basic Objects, CFINCLUDE. The Cfinclude dialog box appears, as shown in Figure 20.12. Enter **productlist.cfm** in the Template text box. Click OK.

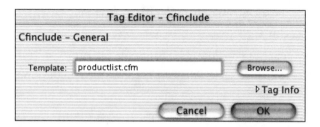

Figure 20.12   The Cfinclude dialog box appears after you insert a CFINCLUDE tag in your page.

Using the CFINCLUDE tag in the preceding case, you are telling ColdFusion to process your productlist.cfm page as if it were part of the shoes.cfm page. Thus, the productlist.cfm page is included in the shoes.cfm page. Including files allows ColdFusion applications to be written in modules.

Note

The <cfinclude> tag appears in the code section while the productlist.cfm template appears in the design section. It is important that this tag appears as the last line in your code; otherwise, you show the page before you are able to get your data. You must get your data first.

12. You can now test the page by clicking the lightning bolt on the top of the window. It should look similar to the test you made when you were constructing this page. Save the shoes.cfm page.

Creating the Hats, T-Shirts, and Jeans Pages

Having created a page for the shoes, a page has to be created for the hats. To create a second page for the site follow these steps:

1. Open the shoes.cfm file, and select File, Save As. The File Selector dialog box appears. Name the file hats.cfm and then click Save.

   Most of the work has been done for you. All you need to do is change the filters from Shoes to Hats.

2. Do a search and replace by selecting Edit, Find and Replace to open the Find and Replace dialog box.

3. Select Current Document. Select Source Code, and enter Shoes in the Search For text box. Enter Hats in the Replace With text box. Click Replace All.

4. Open either the shoes.cfm or hats.cfm page, select File, Save As, and name the page **tshirts.cfm**. Click Save.

   Again, all you need to do now is to change the filters to T-shirts by using Find and Replace to change shoes or hats to T-shirts; then do the same thing for the jeans page.

   All of the product list pages are done. The best part is that you used the productlist.cfm page only once, thanks to the CFINCLUDE tag.

5. Open the productdetails.cfm page, and open the server Behaviors panel.

6. Add a Recordset (Query) server behavior. When the Recordset window opens, click the Advanced button.

7. Enter getProductDetails in the Name area.

8. Expand the Tables in the Database Items, and expand Product.

9. Click Product and then click the Select button.

10. Click Description and then click the Select button.

11. Click Price and then click the Select button.

12. Click GraphicURL and then click the Select button.

13. Collapse Product, and expand ProductType.

14. Click ProductType and then click the Select button.

15. Click ProductDescription and then click the Select button.

16. Collapse the ProductType table, and manually type the following in the SQL text box under the FROM clause:

    WHERE ProductType.ProductTypeID = Product.ProductTypeID

    AND Product.ProductID = #ProductID#

    The first line joins the two tables together with a common field. In this case, you know the fields are related by their ProductTypeID. This gives you the ProductType name with the returned record.

    The second line sets the filter to #ProductID#. This was passed in the URL from the product listing page.

17. Click the + sign in the Page Parameters section. When the Page Parameters dialog box appears, enter **ProductID** in the Name text box and **0** in the Default text box. Click OK.

    This ensures that if you call this page without a ProductID, it defaults to 0.

18. Click OK when done. The server behavior is added to the page.

19. Select the productPict image placeholder, open the Bindings panel, and expand the getProductDetails recordset.

20. Click the GraphicsURL binding, and drag it over the placeholder. The image changes to a dynamic image.

21. Add a path prefix of **images/shoppingcart_images/hitlist_images/** in the Property inspector, and set the image alignment to Left.

    While we are at it, let's add the dynamic Flash text box.

22. Insert flashtext.swf using Insert, Media, Flash. Click the Parameters button in the File Selector dialog box to open the Parameters dialog box.

23. Enter **theText** for the parameter.

24. For the value, click the lightning bolt to open the Data Sources dialog box.

25. Expand the getProductDetails recordset, and select ProductType. Click OK and then click Choose when done.

26. Go to the next line in the cell by pressing Shift-Return (Mac) or Shift-Enter (PC).

27. Add one more flashtext.swf, and enter the following in the Parameters dialog box:

    Parameter. **theText**.

    For the value, click the lightning bolt to open the Data Sources dialog box. Expand the getProductDetails recordset, and select Product.

28. Click OK and then click Choose when done.

29. Resize the lower Flash text box so that it is smaller than the top one. Grab one of the handles, and resize it to your taste. Align your Flash text box in your cell as you see fit.

30. Select the Bindings panel, and drag the ProductDescription binding to the lower-left cell of the page.

31. Create a new paragraph on the page by pressing Return (Mac) or Enter (PC). This way, your product description won't look as though it is crashing into your Flash text and picture.

32. Drag the Description binding to the lower-left cell of the page.

33. Create a new paragraph on the page by pressing Return (Mac) or Enter (PC).

34. Drag the Price binding underneath the Description binding.

35. In the Bindings panel, set the format for Price as Currency, Dollar by clicking the pop-down arrow. A menu appears. This formats the price in U. S. dollars and cents. Set the vertical cell alignment to Top in the Property inspector.

36. Select the entire table inside the pageContent editable region, and add a repeat region server behavior. Enter **getProductDetails** in the name and then click OK.

37. Save the page, which should resemble the one shown in Figure 20.13.

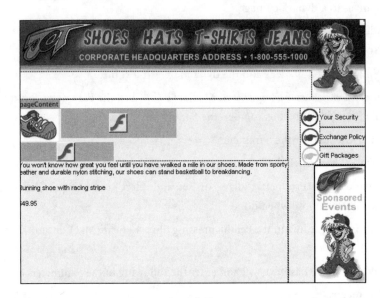

Figure 20.13   The pages are complete and ready to go live.

You can do a live data preview of this page. The main difference between this page and the product list page is that you have to supply a product ID in the query string text box in the URL, as shown in Figure 20.14. In this case, the page is expecting a ProductID as its page parameter.

Enter **ProductID=1** in the text box, and click Refresh.

You have just created an entire dynamic site with only three web pages.

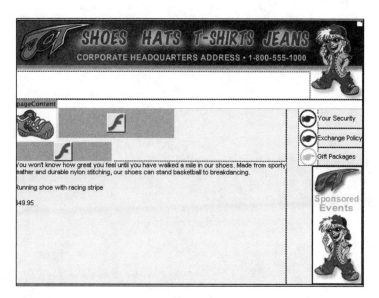

Figure 20.14   A live preview of the product list page appears.

Summary

When you think about it, creating an entire web site using only three pages is quite the achievement, and as little as five years ago was nothing more than a dream.

We started the chapter by creating the database that holds the data needed by the site. From there we examined how Dreamweaver MX and ColdFusion MX combine to create the pages that access the data in the database. We showed you specifically how to create the recordsets that refer directly to the database, and how to create the hooks into the data, called bindings, to have the text and images appear in the pages.

We showed you how to create a Flash MX text box that dynamically uses the product descriptions in the database and format them on the fly.

We also showed you how a single page can easily be turned into several pages by simply using search and replace.

We also discussed how to turn a page into a server template, and finally how to finish the pages for the inclusion of dynamic content.

In the next chapter, we start tweaking the site to make it more efficient. This is accomplished by working on many of the images in the JCT site to make them as small and efficient as possible.

C h a p t e r   21

Image Optimization and the MX Studio

Surfing the web today is almost as natural to the end user as using a telephone or television. What end-users don't see is the behind-the-scenes work presented up to this point that goes into making a web site work on the numerous platforms in use today.

Making images work on those platforms is no exception. Those amazing images and drawings you have produced will not necessarily be seen by users because you are essentially limited to three graphical formats: .gif, .jpg and .png. Even then, only the .gif and .jpg format are universally accepted. The .png format came to the party late, and will only receive wide acceptance after the older browsers are relegated to the trash heap of Internet history. Too, the Fireworks MX .png format might be a bit unwieldy because .png images created in Fireworks MX have Fireworks-only information, such as vectors, added to them.

Web site developers have to be sensitive to the fact that the base reference speed for Internet access is still pegged at a baud rate of 28.8Kb per second. This is painfully slow, and is comparable to attaching a garden hose to a fire hydrant. The encouraging news is the increasing numbers of surfers using DSL (Digital Subscriber Lines), cable modems, and even 56.6 dial-up modems. Over time, these connections and devices will increase the reference speed.

Being limited to only two graphic formats in a low bandwidth universe makes image optimization absolutely critical. To be viewed, your image needs to be saved in the proper format and then reduced to the smallest size possible.

In this chapter, you review the optimization features of Freehand and Fireworks MX. You then walk through the steps used to optimize the JCT navigation bar. The bottom line in each process is to think small.

Image Optimization in FreeHand

As a vector application, a designer wouldn't think the images produced in Freehand would need to be optimized. In fact, if you have a print or prepress background, you have been optimizing your images for years. Vector art, when converted to printing film, usually passes through a Raster Image Processor (RIP) to turn the vectors into a bitmap. To ensure the time spent RIP'ing the file is kept to an absolute minimum, artists and prepress professionals are accustomed to removing vector points, and smoothing lines to reduce the complexity of the file. It is no different on the web.

The key is to reduce the file size to accommodate bandwidth restrictions, and to simplify the image to accommodate processing restrictions on the user's computer.

Changing the Color Space in FreeHand

You will inevitably encounter this situation. The client hands you a CD containing all of the logos and illustrations for a print brochure, and asks you to put them on the company web site.

The problem is that the files are enormous—500 to 750KB—when placed against the needs of the web.

The quickest way to reduce the size of an image is to change its color space. For example, the web's output device is a computer monitor. Computer monitors use only three colors—red, green, and blue, which is shown as RGB—to render the image on a computer screen. FreeHand, with its roots in the print universe, needs four colors—cyan, magenta, yellow, and black. Which is shown as CMYK—to render its colors on paper. Simply changing the color space from CMYK to RGB reduces the files size by about 25 percent because there is one less color channel of information to be processed.

To change the color space of a FreeHand image, follow these steps:

1. Copy the Chapter 21 Exercise folder from the web site to your desktop. Open the LogoPrint file from the Chapter 21 Exercise folder.

2. On the surface, the image looks acceptable. Not quite. The designer used Pantones for the colors in the image. Click once on the gradient shape and then open the Fill panel. Notice the colors for the linear gradient at the bottom of the panel.

3. Click once on the yellow swatch. A Swatches panel opens, showing you the colors in the image. Roll the cursor over the yellow swatch and you are informed it is Pantone Process Yellow CVC, as shown in Figure 21.1.

4. Click the Swatch pop-down menu, and select Color Cube to open the RGB/Hex Swatch panel used by the MX Studio. Select the yellow swatch—FFFF00—and click it. This changes the Pantone color to an RGB color.

5. Open the Swatches panel again, and drag the yellow gradient swatch from the Fill panel to the Swatches panel. When you see a small + sign appear under the swatch, release the mouse and the color is added to the Swatches panel.

6. You no longer need the Pantone Yellow. Select it in the Swatches panel and then choose Remove from the Options pop-down list. Your Swatches panel should resemble that shown in Figure 21.2.

Figure 21.1   The logo is composed of Pantone colors, which are used for print and not web production.

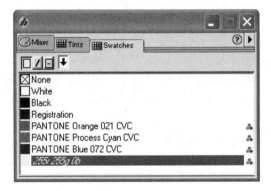

Figure 21.2   The RGB/HEX yellow is added to the Swatches panel, and the Pantone Yellow is removed.

Optimizing Vectors in FreeHand

Vectors are, in simplistic terms, composed of curves or lines that join two anchor points in an object. Anchor points are the bane of your existence because the more anchor points contained in an image, the bigger the demand on processing power on the user's computer. This is because the line drawn between the points is a mathematical calculation. The computer has to identify each point, do the math, and render the line. Efficient vector images use as few points as possible.

To optimize a vector object, follow these steps:

1. Open the LogoPrint file, if necessary, and deselect Preview in the View menu. Deselecting Preview shows only the lines that comprise the image. Click once on the gradient object. The points appear as shown in Figure 21.3.

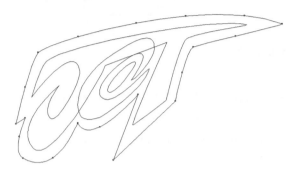

Figure 21.3   The best way to view points is to deselect preview in the View menu and then click the object.

2. The key to removing points is to follow the geometry. For example, the big, sweeping curve at the top of the gradient object has six points, but it needs only three points—one at the start, one in the middle where the curve changes direction, and one at the end.

3. There are two ways of removing points from an object. You can Select the Subselect tool, click a point, and press the Delete key. The point is removed, and the line adjusts to accommodate the removal of the point.

   Alternately, you can select Modify, Alter Path, Simplify to open the Simplify dialog box, shown in Figure 21.4. Moving the slider to the right or the left increases the severity of the change to the selected object. Click OK to apply the change. If it is too strong, undo the change and then reapply the Simplify dialog box.

Note

Removing points typically involves both methods.

Tip

A good habit to get into is removing stray points. These are points on the page that are connected to no other points. If the image is to be placed on a web page, these points travel along with the image and can waste bandwidth and processing time.

Figure 21.4   Use the Simplify dialog box to remove various points and for smoothing out your graphics.

The FreeHand to Fireworks MX Editing Connection

Throughout this book, you have seen a number of ways to move FreeHand images to Fireworks MX. There is also a way of using FreeHand to call Fireworks MX to edit a placed .png or .gif file.

To edit a Fireworks .png image from FreeHand, follow these steps:

1. Open a blank FreeHand document. Select Edit, Preferences to open the Preferences dialog box. Select the Object tab.

2. In the External Editors section of the Object tab, select PNG Image from the Object pop-down list. Select Fireworks MX from the Editor pop-down list. If Fireworks MX isn't listed, browse to it by clicking the Browse button and selecting Fireworks MX from the Choose an External Editor dialog box that opens. Select Fireworks MX and then click OK. Your preferences should now resemble those shown in Figure 21.5.

3. Repeat step 2, and use Fireworks MX as your .gif editor.

4. Select File, Import, and import the Logo.png file in the Chapter 21 Exercise folder into the document. When the cursor changes to the Place cursor, click once. The logo, along with an ugly red background, appears on the page.

5. Right-click (PC) or Control-click (Mac) on the placed image to open the context menu. Select External Editor from the menu. A Launch Edit alert box appears, asking if you really want to launch another application. Click OK.

6. An Editing in Progress alert box appears. It is important for you do nothing at this point. Sit back and let Fireworks launch.

7. When the image opens in Fireworks, set the canvas color to white. Save the image, and quit Fireworks MX.

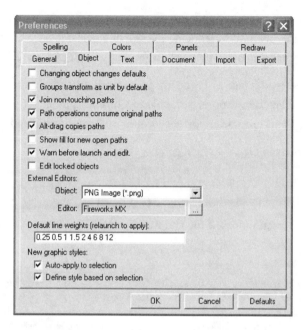

Figure 21.5   External editors for a variety of file formats are set in the Object panel of FreeHand's Preferences dialog box.

8. The image, with a white background, appears on the FreeHand page as shown in Figure 21.6. Click Done in the Editing in Progress dialog box to save the change.

Figure 21.6   The ugly red background is removed in Fireworks MX after Fireworks MX is launched from within FreeHand.

Using File Formats to Reduce File Size

There is yet another method to reducing file size in FreeHand. Save the file in a format that results in a smaller image. The two best formats are .gif and .png.

If you save a FreeHand image as a .png image, be aware that the vectors are unavailable in Fireworks MX. FreeHand converts the file to a bitmap .png file. If you need the vectors, use the drag-and-drop or import techniques we have shown throughout the book.

To convert a FreeHand file to a .png file, follow these steps:

1. Select File, Export to open the Export dialog box.

2. Select .png from the Save as File Type pop-down list, and name the file.

3. Choose the location for the file and then click OK.

Tip

If you want to go from FreeHand directly to Fireworks MX after saving the .png image, select Open in External Application at the bottom of the Export dialog box. As soon as you click OK, FreeHand references your list of external editors in the application preferences, discovers Fireworks MX is the .png editor, and launches Fireworks MX.

To convert a FreeHand file to a .gif file, follow these steps:

1. Select File, Export to open the Export dialog box.

2. Select .gif from the Save as File Type pop-down list, and name the file.

3. Choose the location for the file and then click OK.

If you check the file sizes, the original FreeHand document is 20KB, the .png document is 8KB, and the .gif document is 4KB.

Image Optimization in Fireworks MX

The image optimization process involves a fine balance between image quality and file size. Increase the image quality, and the file size increases. Reduce the file size, and the image quality reduces. Thankfully, Fireworks MX takes a lot of the guesswork and frustration out of this process by providing you with four side-by-side views of the image resulting from changes in the various settings.

Here's a brief overview of the steps to use when optimizing an image for web output:

- Always think small. Keep the physical size of the image as small as possible, and try to use as many areas of flat color as possible.

- Use the file format best suited to the final use of the image. Use the .gif format for line art, and the .jpg format for photographs.

- Remove any colors that aren't used in the image. The fewer the colors, the smaller the file size.

- When creating .jpg images, the quality slider is the primary tool. The lower the quality setting, the lower the file size and the higher the amount of image degradation that occurs.

Using the Optimize Panel for Line Art

Ground zero for your image optimization efforts is located in the Optimize panel. This panel contains all of the controls used to export an image. The best thing of all is the capability to compare the settings against each other to make the decision regarding which settings result in the best image quality prior to export.

To use the Optimize panel, follow these steps:

1. Open the Mascot.png image from the Chapter 21 Exercise folder. When the image opens, expand the Optimize panel in the panel group. If the Optimize panel is not contained in the panel group, select Window, Optimize or press F6 to open the Optimize panel.

2. Click the 4-Up tab at the top of the Document window. The canvas is broken into four panels containing the image of the mascot. Each image panel allows you to set individual optimization settings for the image in that particular panel. You can also move the images around inside the panels to compare the changes in areas other than those visible in the panel.

3. Place the cursor in the panel containing the original image. (It is the one in the upper-left corner.) Press the spacebar, and the cursor changes into a grabber hand. Click and drag the image until the mascot's face is in the panel. The three other images also move.

4. Select the magnifying glass at the bottom of the toolbar, place it over the mascot's nose, and click once. All of the images zoom into the point selected.

5. With the magnifying glass still selected, press the Option (Mac) or Alt (PC) key and then click the mouse twice. The images in all of the panels zoom out.

6. Select the Pointer tool on the toolbar, or press the V key to change the magnifying glass to the Pointer tool. Select the image under the original image. The window is outlined to indicate it is the active window.

7. Use the following settings in the Optimize panel:

Web File Format. GIF.

Indexed palette. WebSnap Adaptive.

Colors. 64.

Loss. 0.

Dither . 0%.

Transparency. No Transparency.

The information under the image changes. In this case, the image is 30.84KB in size, and will take about four seconds to load using a 56KB/s modem. The color, dither, and palette settings chosen in the Optimize panel also appear at the bottom of the pane.

8. Select the image to the right of the original image, and use the following settings in the Optimize panel:

Web File Format. GIF.

Indexed palette. WebSnap Adaptive.

Colors. 256.

Loss. 0.

Dither. 0%.

Transparency. No Transparency.

Note how the image size increases due to the increased number of colors in the image. The download time has almost doubled, too.

9. Select the remaining image, and use these settings:

Web File Format. GIF.

Indexed palette. WebSnap Adaptive.

Colors. 128.

Loss. 0.

Dither. 0%.

Transparency. No Transparency.

Notice how the file size is exactly the difference between the image with the small palette of 64 colors and the one with 256 colors. Also, the difference in download times between the 256-color image and the 128-color image is marginal.

If you start looking at the images from a quality perspective, the differences are startling. Zoom in on the mascot's face, as shown in Figure 21.7, and compare the shadow area on the right side of his face. The sacrifice you make when you reduce the number in colors is image detail. With a palette of 64 colors, the results are simply unacceptable. Your choice, therefore, lies between 128 and 256 colors, and the decision you make is subjective, meaning you should choose the image that looks best to you.

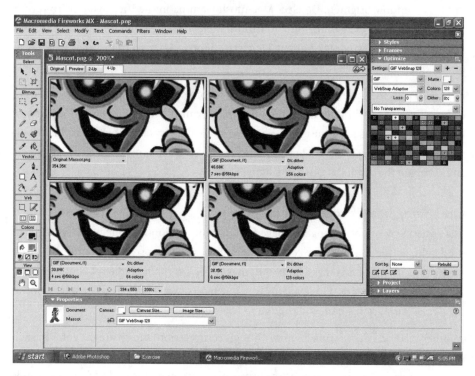

Figure 21.7   Image quality starts to degrade as the .gif color palette reduces from 256 colors to 64 colors.

Cross-Platform Gamma in Fireworks MX

Along with being able to preview the file prior to export, Fireworks MX gives you the opportunity to see what the file will look like on the other platform. It does this by mirroring the default monitor brightness or gamma setting on another platform. Windows platforms use a gamma setting of 2.2. Macintosh uses a gamma setting of 1.8. The difference means the image looks a lot brighter on a Mac than it does on a PC. By previewing the gamma, you avoid a potential nasty surprise, especially when viewing the Windows gamma from a Mac, of discovering the image is much darker than planned.

To preview the Mac gamma on a PC, select View, Macintosh Gamma. All four images in the 4-Up window brighten. Deselect Macintosh Gamma in the View window to turn it off. To preview the PC gamma on a Macintosh, select View, Windows Gamma. All four images in the 4-Up window brighten. Deselect Windows Gamma in the View window to turn it off.

Be careful with the gamma preview. The best it is going to show you is an approximation of how the image will appear on the other platform. If there is a startling difference between the two images, adjust the Brightness and Contrast settings in the Adjust Color area of the Effects area of the Property inspector. Even then, make small adjustments, and compare the results as you move along.

Optimizing Images to the .gif Format

The easiest way of optimizing an image for .gif compression is to include large areas of solid color in the image. If the color changes from pixel-to-pixel, the compression will not be as efficient. This is why a lot of .gif images don't contain gradients. Gradients only serve to increase file size. This explains why our mascot with large areas of solid color in the pants, the shirt, his hair, and cap is an ideal candidate.

Another method of preparing an image for .gif compression is to create the color in such a way that the solid areas are primarily horizontal, going across the images, rather than down the image. This is because of the way a .gif compression is undertaken. The pixels are read and compressed in a horizontal line moving from left to right. Which is more efficient: Reading each blue pixel in the pants and remembering its location, or replacing all of that with a line of code that says, "There are 600 blue pixels here."?

Another technique for preparing an image for .gif compression is to remove any stray pixels that might be present. These pixels might not be obvious when viewed at 100%, but when you zoom in on the image you might discover areas of pixels that are one or two shades different from the surrounding colors. One of the more common ways these pixels are introduced is when the client hands you the infamous CD of line art, and the image you need has been compressed as a .jpg image. From the client's perspective, the company has done you a favor and made your life easier. From your perspective, well, let's not go there.

To remove stray pixels, follow these steps:

1. Open the image, select the magnifying glass, zoom in on an area of the image, and look for splotches of faint pixels in the solid areas of color.

2. Having found a splotch, select the Eyedropper tool from the Tools palette. With the Stroke Swatch selected on the Tools palette or the Property inspector, click once on the main color in the area. This is your stroke color.

3. Switch to the Pencil tool. Depending upon your magnification, set the tip of the pencil to one or two pixels. Click on the pixels in the splotch to replace them with the stroke color.

Optimizing .jpg Images

When you optimize a . gif image, you shrink the file size by removing colors. The .jpg format compression is a bit more brutal in that its compression is achieved by removing pixels altogether, based on a sliding quality scale. This is why the compression is called *lossy*.

Still, it is the compression of choice when working with photographs. The reason is that .jpg images are capable of displaying more than 16 million colors, which means they are capable to reproduce the subtle tonal changes of a photograph. That's the good news. The bad news is, unlike a .gif image, there can be no areas of transparency in the image. If the image needs, for example, a transparent background, .gif is your only alternative.

It is critical that you exercise caution when considering using a .jpg image in Flash MX. When you create a Flash .swf file that includes photographs, those images are compressed as .jpg images. Compressing an already-compressed file, in computing terms, is a fatal error. The image seriously degrades. If the image is destined for use in Flash MX, set the quality of the Fireworks MX image to 100% (no compression) and then let Flash do the compressing. This is also why, if the client offers to supply the photos for the site, you should request they be in the .tif format. They will be uncompressed, and you can do the compression work, confident that the quality of the image is not being degraded.

Finally, if the image is to be viewed while it downloads, you can store the image using Fireworks MX as a Progressive .jpg file. Even so, be aware Internet Explorer is not exactly Progressive .jpg-friendly. The image will be treated as a regular .jpg, and rendered accordingly.

To compress a photograph using .jpg compression, follow these steps:

1. Open the Obatanga.tif file from the Chapter 21 Exercise folder in Fireworks MX. Click the 4-Up tab on the Document window to have four views of the image and then open the Optimize panel.

2. Select the panel under the original image, and use the following settings in the Optimize panel:

   Export File Format. JPEG.

   Quality. 100%.

   The file has shrunk from over 900KB to just over 118KB.

3. Select the panel to the right of the original image, and use the following settings in the Optimize panel:

   Export File Format. JPEG.

   Quality. 50%.

   The file has shrunk from over 900KB. Note how the sky in the upper-left corner of the image has started to pixelate and show artifacts, as shown in Figure 21.8. This is the first symptom of a data hemorrhage.

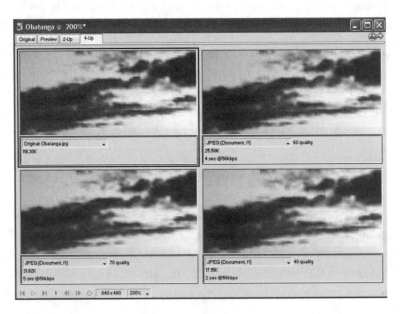

Figure 21.8   Never compress an already compressed .jpg image. The image degradation occurs sooner than if the image was never compressed.

4. Select the remaining panel, and use the following settings in the Optimize panel:

   Export File Format. JPEG.

   Quality. 30%.

   The file has shrunk from over 900KB to just under 10KB. Unfortunately, the image is pixilated and laced with artifacts. Were you to use this setting for the export, the image would be dead on arrival.

5. Close the image, and don't save the changes. To examine the effect of compressing an already compressed .jpg image, open the Obatanga.jpg image in your Chapter 21 Exercise folder.

6. When the image opens, change to the 4-Up view and then set the Quality setting for each of the three preview panels at 70%, 60%, and 40%.

The sky in the upper-left corner, as shown in Figure 21.7, starts to degrade at 70%. At 60% quality, the image pixelates, and at 40% the image should be taken out back and put out of its misery.

Chris Flick on .jpgs and .gifs

Basically, the standard here is that all photographs should be optimized as .jpgs. As pointed out earlier in this chapter, the choice is essentially made for you because all of the subtle color changes in a photograph can be handled only by a .jpg image.

A photograph, optimized as a .gif, will inevitably result in a substandard result due to the loss of essential detail. Line art—or, in this case, the art produced for the JCT site—optimizes well as a .gif because of all the large areas of flat colors.

Ultimately, it comes down to the experience of the web designer. We are in the awkward position of having to make some subjective choices when it comes to optimization. The choices inevitably involve a trade-off between the quality of the image and the speed of the download.

Optimizing the JCT Navigation Bar

This chapter concludes by pulling together many of the concepts presented earlier in this chapter, in Chapter 9, "Imaging in Fireworks MX," and Chapter 11, "Creating Line Art for the Web." Rather than present a how-to section, we felt it would be more meaningful if our resident graphic artist, Chris Flick, walked you through the process of image slicing and optimization.

In this example, Chris discusses not only how he created the slices for the navigation bar, but also shares several tricks and tips he has picked up over the years. Chris highlights a few of the features in Fireworks MX that make him more productive.

Chris begins his discussion at the point a project has received client approval for the artwork as shown in Figure 21.9. At this point, Chris starts to map out his strategy for creating and optimizing the slices, and preparing the slices for assembly in Dreamweaver MX.

Figure 21.9   The approved image is ready to be sliced and optimized by Chris Flick.

Creating the Slices

Now that the final design for the JCT navigation bar has been approved, I set up my guides to help determine the slices. My objective is to keep the number of slices to a minimum, yet leave each of the product slices at the top of the page capable of having a Swap Image behavior applied to them in Dreamweaver MX.

I find the Slice tool useful, but it gives me neither the precision nor the control I can obtain from actually dragging guides from the rulers and manually placing them on the page. In this way, I can visually break up the image, and look for potential problems, such as small pieces of the lettering or images appearing in two different slices. My final slice order is shown in Figure 21.10.

Figure 21.10   Chris drags guides from the horizontal and vertical rulers, and moved them around on the page to create his slice guides.

After I am happy with the guides, I can now create the slices. I usually zoom in on the image, select the Slice tool, and click/drag a slice from the upper-left corner of the slice area on the grid to the lower-right corner of the slice area. The final slices are shown in Figure 21.11.

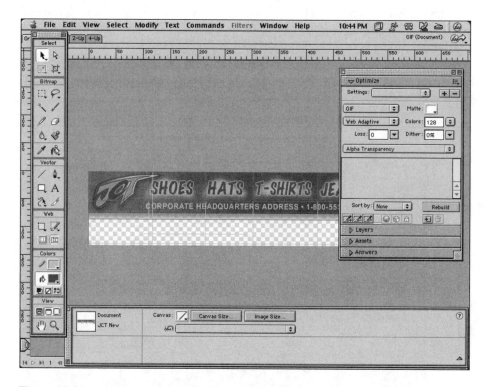

Figure 21.11   The slices are created using the Slice tool.

Another really great slicing tool is the Polygon Slicing tool, which is obtained by clicking and holding on the Slice tool in the toolbar. The Polygon Slice tool pops down, and I can select it. This tool is great for creating slices around irregularly shaped objects. For example, if I wanted to use the mascot as a rollover but didn't want a lot of the brick wall to appear, I would use this tool.

For tight slices, don't forget that you can draw a path around the irregularly shaped object on the canvas using the Pen tool. This creates a vector shape around the selected object. You can then select Edit, Insert, Hotspot, and convert the hotspot to a slice by selecting Edit, Insert, Slice.

Optimizing the Slices

Now that the slices are created, they need to be optimized for the web. When it comes to optimization, my goal is straightforward: Obtain the best image quality with the lowest file size possible. In an ideal world, I would be able to have both quality and image size; but with bandwidth constraints being as they are, I have learned my users are impatient. They want the page to load…and load fast.

To achieve my objective, I use the Optimize panel shown in Figure 21.12. The opportunity to see the effects of my decisions on the image, without changing the image, is invaluable.

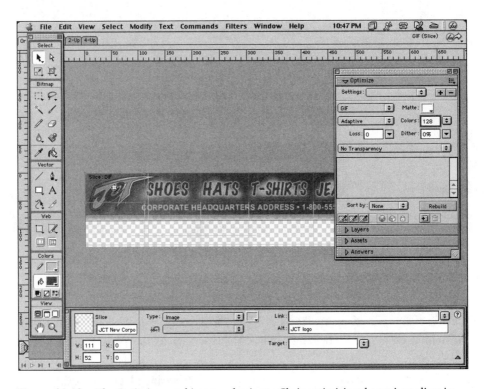

Figure 21.12   The Optimize panel is opened prior to Chris optimizing the various slices in the navigation bar.

One big change between the previous version of Fireworks 4 and Fireworks MX is the Rebuild button at the bottom of the Optimize panel. Clicking it rebuilds the image's color table to display the swatches in the document's Export palette. This button used to be at the top of the Color Table panel options. The Color Table command has been removed from Fireworks MX, and its various commands and functions incorporated into the Fireworks MX Optimize panel.

The Optimize window allows you to approach optimization from two viewpoints. You can optimize individual slices, as shown in Figure 21.13. This allows you to apply individual optimization settings to each slice. The advantage to this is that slices consisting of a single color can really be compressed.

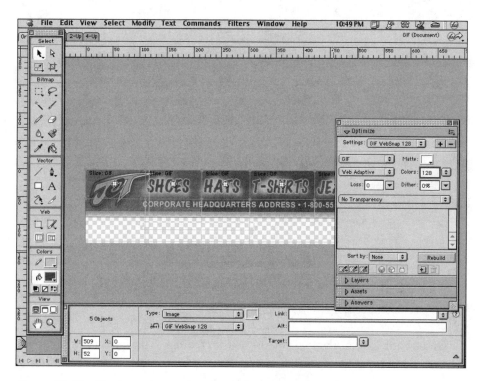

Figure 21.13   The Optimize panel can be used to optimize individual slices allowing various degrees of compression throughout the image.

You can also select multiple slices, as shown in Figure 21.14, and optimize them all at the same compression settings. The advantage to the designer is uniformity of compression across all of the slices.

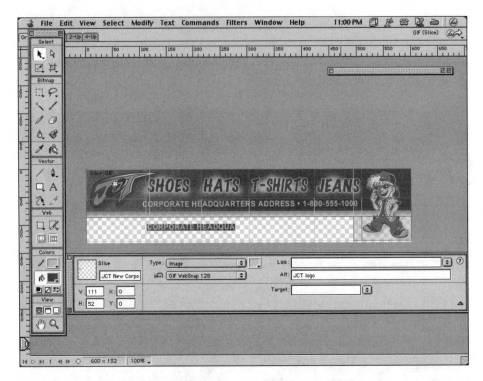

Figure 21.14   The Optimize panel can also be used to optimize all of the slices using the same compression settings for all of the slices.

The Optimize panel also allows you to easily switch settings or file formats for your optimized images. Simply select your sliced image and then make the adjustments inside of the Optimize panel.

One of the biggest changes in Fireworks MX is removal of the Objects palette window. Now, all of your image optimization occurs within your Property inspector. Click one of your slices, and the Property inspector changes to reveal all the old optimize objects selections, including Link, Alt, and Target.

The familiar choices are still here, such as:

- Type—Tells you if your selection is an image or html text.
- Color Box—Allows you to change the color of your slices.
- Clamp Tool—Tells you what web compression settings your image is set for.
- Link—Allows you to set up an http URL link to any of your graphics.
- Alt—Lets you name your graphics for easy recognition.
- Target—Allows you to control the JavaScript action of your image.

You can now export each of your slices individually. I used the Property inspector to determine the properties of each slice. With the slices optimized and the properties set, I simply select File, Export. When the Export dialog box opens, I make sure Selected Slices Only is selected. I then choose the folder where the slices will be placed, and I click Export.

Optimizing Non-Sliced Images

Not every image I work on is going to be sliced and the slices optimized. In this instance, I open the Optimize panel and then select the 4-Up tab in the Document window as shown in Figure 21.15. The beauty of this feature is that I can compare image quality at a variety of settings. After I decide which setting offers the best quality with the fastest download, I can export that image.

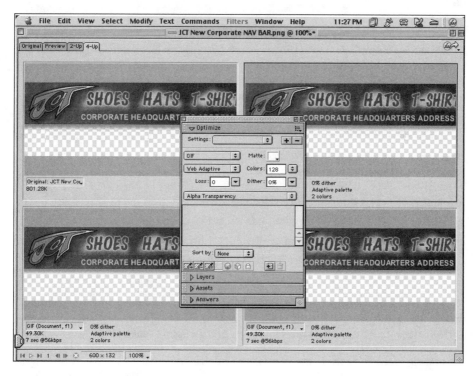

Figure 21.15   The 4-Up view allows Chris to tinker with the settings and then export the one that meets his quality and download time criteria.

Click one of the Preview panes. (You can tell which one you clicked by the thick border around the image.) In this case, I was interested in the second image selected in my 4-Up display.

This selection gave me the following important information:

- It is a .gif document.
- Its current size is 49.30KB.
- It will take seven seconds to load on a 56K modem.
- It has 0% dither on an Adaptive palette.

I always wonder if I can do better than that, so for the other two panels, I used different optimization settings and then compared the results against the previous settings. There is a lot of trial and error involved, but the time spent here is invaluable.

With each choice I make in the Optimize panel, I pay very careful attention to the detail in the image and the speed of the download.

Exporting from a 2-Up or 4-Up Preview Panel

Having settled on my best four settings, I carefully study each panel looking for the optimization setting that offers me the best balance between quality and speed, and I click that selection.

After I decide upon the setting, I click the Preview tab in the Document window to get a full screen view of my choice. Again, I carefully study the image to ensure my choice is the one that meets my quality and speed objectives.

Having made my final decision, I select File, Export Preview to open the Export Preview dialog box. The great thing about this dialog box is that it gives me the capability to further tweak the image before export. I can crop the image, apply a transparent background, and even reduce the number of colors. More often than not, I simply ignore these options, and click the Export button to open the Export dialog box.

Summary

Chris Flick neatly summarized this chapter in his discussion when he wrote:

"Ultimately, it comes down to the experience of the web designer. We are in the awkward position of having to make subjective choices when it comes to optimization. The choices inevitably involve a trade-off between the quality of the image and the speed of the download."

Optimization is the art of compromise, as we showed you by optimizing images in FreeHand and Fireworks MX.

In FreeHand, file reduction results from moving the image from the CMYK to RGB color space by replacing CMYK colors with RGB colors. We also showed you how to make FreeHand images more efficient by removing unnecessary and stray points. Another technique we demonstrated was how to edit a Fireworks MX document placed into FreeHand without leaving FreeHand. We finished the FreeHand section by showing you how to export FreeHand images as either a .gif or .png, and how to launch Fireworks MX immediately upon export of the FreeHand document.

The .gif file format is one of your two choices when it comes to images on the web. We showed you how to use the Optimize panel and the 4-Up previews in the Document window to apply various optimization settings to the preview panes on the canvas. By using these techniques, you obtain the best balance between download time and image quality. We also showed you how to compare images between the Mac and PC platforms by using the other platform's gamma settings on the image.

From there, we reviewed the creation of a .jpg image, and how to use the preview panes to compare image quality and download times using the .jpg quality slider in the Optimize panel. We also showed you why you should never apply .jpg compression to a .jpg image.

Chris Flick concluded the chapter by walking you through how he sliced and optimized the JCT navigation bar. He also showed you how to create slices using guides, the Slice tool, the Pen tool, and hotspots. He concluded his discussion by showing how to export the content in one of the preview panes on the Fireworks MX canvas.

Having learned how to optimize the visual elements on a web page, you should also understand how to optimize the non-visual elements. In the next chapter, we discuss a variety of techniques for optimizing the code that drives a web page.

MX

fireworks flash freehand coldfusion dreamweaver fireworks
amweaver fireworks flash freehand coldfusion dreamweave
oldfusion dreamweaver fireworks flash freehand coldfusio
eehand coldfusion dreamweaver fireworks flash freehand
orks flash freehand coldfusion dreamweaver fireworks
aver fireworks flash freehand coldfusion dreamweave

Site and Code Optimization

One of the most common complaints from

hard-core web developers is that Fireworks

MX and Dreamweaver MX produce *ugly*

code. What they mean by this rather deri-

sive statement is that the code is a bit com-

plex and too long.

A great example of this would be the code from another Macromedia application, Macromedia Director. Director has its own language to control interactivity called Lingo. When you want the playback head to go to a particular frame of the movie, you would write the following code:

```
On exitFrame me
Go to frame 2
End
```

The code is simple, direct, and succinct. For people new to the Director application, they can use Lingo by attaching prewritten code to the frame. Here is the prewritten code for a frame loop in Director:

```
-- DESCRIPTION --

on getBehaviorDescription me
  return \
    "GO TO FRAME X" & RETURN & RETURN & \
    "Moves the playback head to the chosen frame when the user clicks on
    ➥the sprite" & RETURN & RETURN & \
    "PERMITTED MEMBER TYPES:" & RETURN & \
    "Graphic members" & RETURN & RETURN & \
    "PARAMETERS:" & RETURN & \
    "* Go to which frame on mouseUp?"
end getBehaviorDescription


on getBehaviorTooltip me
  return \
    "Use with graphic members. " & \
    "Moves the playback head to the specified frame on mouseUp."
    ➥end getBehaviorTooltip
```

And so on for another 22 lines. The actual code that makes it happen:

```
on mouseUp me
  go myTargetFrame
end mouseUp
```

is buried in the middle of the script.

On the surface, this could be regarded as bloated code. In this case, it isn't. The author had to ask a simple question: "How would someone not familiar with the language easily create a command that goes to a specified frame?" The code would then be written to anticipate all of the potential scenarios.

Instead of looking at code as being bloated, ask a different question: "Did the command do what I wanted it to do?"

In almost all cases, the answer is yes. It works, and in many instances the client couldn't care less whether or not the code is bloated. The client will ask the same question, "Does it work?" Rarely will you be asked, "How does it work?"

The other aspect of the process involves the objects being driven by the code. This includes such specific interface items as buttons and links, and general items, such as the overall design of the page. The common question behind these items, again, is "Do they do what they are supposed to do?"

When it comes to optimizing how a site functions, there are various levels of optimization to consider. Three common optimization levels are the following:

- **Static**—The site is a collection of HTML pages using HTML, JavaScript, and other languages to make them functional.

- **Dynamic**—The site is a collection of templates into which the information is fed through middleware, such as ColdFusion. These sites are typically complex, and any optimization would require the services of an experienced coder.

- **Cosmetic** and **functional**—This is the easiest area of the process to address yet, strangely, it is one of the more overlooked areas when it comes to site optimization. People need to be able to use the web site with minimal guesswork. There is nothing worse than a really cool site that needs an owner's manual. Buttons should look like buttons. Links should be evident and obvious. Keep common page designs in a template, and common elements of a page can be stored as Library items, if necessary.

Still, there are a number of ways to optimize the functionality of a site as well as the code driving it.

The Cascading Style Sheet Solution in Dreamweaver MX

Cascading Style Sheets (CSS) are wonderful tools. A very simple definition of CSS is that they are style formats that can define the look and feel for a page as well as entire sites. CSS is being used more and more in place of HTML formatting tags because CSS style definitions need to be defined only once and the definition can affect the entire site. The uses of CSS vary enough to warrant their own book. Recommended reading is the New Riders book *Eric Meyer on CSS: Mastering the Language of Web Design*. The sheets that affect an entire site should be saved as an external style sheet; otherwise, you are setting yourself up for a maintenance nightmare.

To create an external Cascading Style Sheet, follow these steps:

1. Launch Dreamweaver MX and then open the JCT dynamic site you have been working on to this point in the book.

2. Select File, New to open the New Document dialog box. Select Basic Page in the Category section of the dialog box, and select CSS in the Basic Page section. Click Create when done. A new CSS document appears.

3. Immediately save the file so that it can be linked to the template. Name the file **jct.css**, and close the file when you are done. Now you can set up the style sheet through the template.

4. Open the Files panel by choosing Window, Assets and click the Templates icon. The templates appear in the Files panel. There should be one template in the site named main.dwt.cfm. Double-click the template file to open it. Alternately, you can open the templates folder in the Site view and then double-click the file.

5. To view the CSS styles, open the CSS Styles panel by selecting Window, CSS Styles. You can also access the CSS Styles panel by clicking the CSS Styles tab in the Design panel.

6. Click the Attach Style Sheet button at the bottom of the CSS Styles panel. The Link External Style Sheet dialog box appears.

7. Click the Browse button to open the Select Style Sheet File dialog box, or enter the name directly in the text box. In this case, it is probably best to use the file selector because of the addressing involved with using a template. Locate the jct.css file in the File Selector box, and click OK. Make sure the Link radio button is selected in the Link External Style Sheet dialog box. Click OK.

8. Click the Edit Styles button at the top of the CSS Styles panel to reveal a list of style sheets attached to the document. In this case, there is only one—td. Select the style.

9. Open the panel options and then select Duplicate from the pop-down list to open the Duplicate CSS Style dialog box, as shown in Figure 22.1.

10. Select the Redefine HTML Tag option, and select jct.css from the list in the Define In pop-down list. Click OK. The tag appears under the jct.css style sheet in the CSS Styles panel.

11. Select the item under the main.dwt.cfm in the CSS Styles panel. Click the trash-can. The style is removed from the template while being kept in the external style sheet.

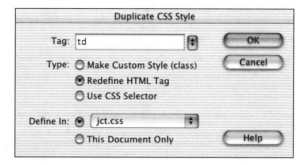

Figure 22.1 Style sheets are duplicated using the Duplicate command of the CSS Styles panel options.

You can add other styles, as desired, to the external style. Any page that links to the external style sheet now has a predefined set of styles.

12. Save the template. If any changes are made to the template, the Update Template Files dialog box, shown in Figure 22.2, appears. You can use this dialog box to update the pages on the site that use the template.

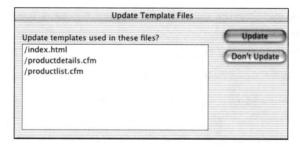

Figure 22.2 If you update one CSS sheet, the change ripples through the entire site.

13. Click the Update button. The Update Pages dialog box appears, as shown in Figure 22.3. A log of the pages that were updated displays.

As you have seen, grouping common elements, such as styles, together offers the developer some rather serious benefits. A major benefit is faster loading times for the pages. Grouped elements, such as style sheets, are cached so that they don't need to be reloaded twice from the same server. Another benefit is easier site maintenance. If a style needs to be changed, the change can be made quickly because the code is in one place, rather than being spread out among the various pages of the site.

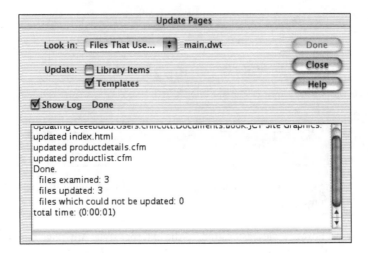

Figure 22.3   When a CSS sheet is changed, a log of the change is also created.

Taking Advantage of the Fireworks MX/Dreamweaver MX Connection

Studio allows a user one-click access from Dreamweaver MX to Fireworks MX to edit images, and back again to view the reflected changes in your web page. This is often referred to by Macromedia as *round-trip editing*. In this example, it is decided to add a slogan under the navigation bar. Because the navigation bar was designed and created in Fireworks MX, it makes sense to make the change in Fireworks MX.

Clicking the Edit button in the Dreamweaver MX's Property inspector enables you to jump between Dreamweaver MX and Fireworks MX. Any edits made in Fireworks MX are subsequently reflected in the Dreamweaver MX page.

To add a slogan to the navigation bar, follow these steps:

1. Open up the Dreamweaver MX template called **main** and then click one of the slices in the navigation menu.

2. Click the Edit button in Dreamweaver MX's Property inspector. Fireworks MX launches, and the navigation bar graphics open. If you are using the files from the exercise folder, Fireworks may ask you to locate the source .png file the first time around. After you indicate the location, Fireworks refers to that file from then on.

3. Select the Text tool from the Tools palette. Click in the empty space in the document.

4. Type in the slogan **We got yer back**.

5. Using the Fireworks MX Property inspector, adjust the font, size, and color to your taste. If available, use the MarkerFelt font (or any other font that will create a style more suited to your tastes) and set the text to a size of 38 points. Fill the text with a linear gradient fill and add an airbrush stroke and select Center in the Property inspector. Select the Fill Over Stroke check box so that the letters appear over the stroke. Type in the JCT slogan—**We got yer back!**

6. Create a new slice by selecting the Slice tool from Tools palette and drawing the slice as shown in Figure 22.4.

Figure 22.4   The words are added to the image. They are formatted, and a slice is added.

7. With the slice added, click the Done button at the top of the document window.

    The table is re-sliced and re-optimized by Fireworks MX. Fireworks MX also closes because you are done with it. All changes made automatically appear in the Dreamweaver MX template.

8. Save the template. An alert box appears asking if you want to update the rest of the site. Click Update.

Working with JavaScript Behaviors and HTML

Both Dreamweaver MX and Fireworks MX use JavaScript to code their rollovers and other effects driven by the behaviors in the applications. Knowing which JavaScript behavior works best in a given situation is intuitive, but all too often they have been used improperly.

Simple rollovers are good for simple rollovers. They are designed to swap one image with another, and nothing else. Don't use them for rolling over multiple slices.

The same advice stands for using the Swap Image Restore behavior. This behavior only remembers the last image that was rolled over using the Swap Image behavior. If you roll over two images, only the last one is restored back to normal. Your best bet is to use multiple Swap Image behaviors.

If you are creating navigation bars, take advantage of the Fireworks MX Set Nav Bar Image behavior. It is more functional than the others mentioned because you can have more than two states.

Don't concern yourself with combining behaviors. The code is tight and tested. In many instances, developers focus more on tight code than asking the question, "Does it work?"

Finally, don't alter the behaviors by hand. Fireworks MX and Dreamweaver MX will overwrite your changes. Both applications concern themselves with the content of the page, including code, and they simply revert anything that affects a behavior on the page.

When it comes to optimizing HTML, the use of Cascading Style Sheets reduces the number of optimization issues you may encounter. As you have seen in this chapter as well as in Chapter 19, "Building Dynamic Pages in Dreamweaver MX", we make extensive use of CSS. The reason is quite simple: People, not just browsers, are reading the page. You have also seen the distinct advantage Cascading Style Sheets offer the developer. One simple change, such as changing the body text from 10-point to 12-point type, applies to the entire site.

Another aspect of the coding issue is to look for extraneous tags. Open the main template. Show the head tags by selecting View, Head Content.

On the template, notice a Style Sheet tag that was left over when you removed the TD style tag. This tag is no longer needed because you are now linked to an external style sheet. You can select it and delete it.

You can also have Dreamweaver MX sweep through the pages and do the optimization automatically for you. This is accomplished through the use of the Clean Up HTML command.

To clean up your HTML page using Dreamweaver MX, follow these steps:

1. Select Commands, Clean Up HTML to open the Clean Up HTML/XHTML dialog box, shown in Figure 22.5.

2. To delete tags with no code between them, select the Empty Container Tags check box in the Remove section of the dialog box.

3. To eliminate tags that repeat the same code in the code block, select Redundant Nested Tags in the Remove section of the dialog box.

4. To remove any comments not created by Dreamweaver MX for items such as Library or template items, select Non-Dreamweaver HTML Comments in the Remove section of the dialog box.

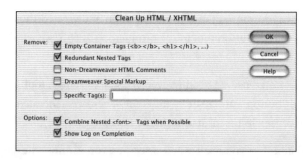

Figure 22.5   Use the Clean Up HTML/XHTML dialog box to reduce the page's file size, and to make the HTML code more efficient.

To specify which tags should be removed, select Specific Tag(s) in the Remove section of the dialog box and then enter the tag into the text box.

Note

A great candidate for this would be those annoying after-Christmas sites with the blinking letters. Remove the blink tag, and those obnoxious lights are turned off.

6. To consolidate two or more font tags when they control the same range of text, select Combine Nested <font> Tags when Possible in the Options section of the dialog box.

7. To be notified of the changes, select Show Log on Completion in the Options section of the dialog box.

8. Click OK when done, and save the template.

Note

It is always best to manually check your pages. Although the Clean Up HTML feature does an efficient job, it is not guaranteed to catch everything.

Fixing Flash Buttons

Flash is a great tool that is easily abused. Use the wrong Flash asset in the wrong place at the wrong time, and you can tie up a lot of memory as well as affect performance and sap bandwidth.

If we had decided to add more than one Flash button and created those buttons using Dreamweaver MX's Flash Button tool in the productdetails.cfm, we would have to carefully consider this decision.

Each Flash button, created using Dreamweaver MX's Flash Button tool, consumes bandwidth because each button you create is different. They are generated separately by a miniature version of Generator located inside of Dreamweaver MX.

Also remember that unless you use Flash 5 or earlier, you cannot edit the Flash Button templates because Generator is discontinued thanks to the release of Flash MX. It is included solely for the purposes of backward compatibility.

You can use two ways to optimize these Flash buttons:

- **Better method**—Create a dynamic Flash button (similar to the dynamic Flash text box created in Chapter 20, "Connecting with ColdFusion MX") and feed the URL through the query string as well as the text. This allows you one instance of the Flash button, thereby saving bandwidth. Performance may be affected, however, because of multiple instances of the Flash player.

- **Best method**—Use multiple Flash buttons in one Flash movie. Turn the button into a symbol and then use it more than once in a movie. Overhead is only one button, no matter how many times it is used. Fewer computing and bandwidth resources are consumed by the Flash player because the button is used only once.

Dealing with Ugly Code from Dreamweaver MX and Fireworks MX

The reason developers regard the code generated by Fireworks MX and Dreamweaver MX as ugly is because the code is generic to accommodate any number of possibilities that a user may throw at it. Because of this, there is more code to deal with these possibilities.

An example would be this bloated code, which is written for a simple rollover.

```
function MM_findObj(n, d) { //v4.01
  var p,i,x;  if(!d) d=document;
if((p=n.indexOf("?"))>0&&parent.frames.length) {
    d=parent.frames[n.substring(p+1)].document; n=n.substring(0,p);}
  if(!(x=d[n])&&d.all)  x=d.all[n];  for  (i=0;!x&&i<d.forms.length;i++)
  ➥x=d.forms[i][n];
  for(i=0;!x&&d.layers&&i<d.layers.length;i++)
  ➥x=MM_findObj(n,d.layers[i].document);
  if(!x && d.getElementById) x=d.getElementById(n);  return x;
}
```

```
function MM_swapImage() { //v3.0
    var   i,j=0,x,a=MM_swapImage.arguments;    document.MM_sr=new    Array;
    ➥for(i=0;i<(a.length-2);i+=3)
    if ((x=MM_findObj(a[i]))!=null){document.MM_sr[j++]=x;  if(!x.oSrc)
    ➥x.oSrc=x.src; x.src=a[i+2];}
}
```

In simple terms, the MM_swapImage() function gets a list of arguments containing data sets in the form of graphic name, blank, or URL. For example, the data to be searched for on a simple mouse over event would read as follows:

```
onMouseOver="MM_swapImage('shoes','','images/shoes_f2.gif','hats','','im
➥ages/hats_f2.gif',1)")
```

The problem is the function doesn't use the last argument, which is the `if` statement. Instead, it loops through all of the data sets and searches through the entire document to find the object.

It then stores the old graphic URL in case the swapImageRestore() function is used, and changes the graphic URL to point to the rollover.

In short, it is a lot like using an atom bomb to light the barbeque. The barbeque lights, but a ton of energy is wasted in the process.

In this case, the code is not only bloated, but it can also add in a few extra CPU cycles because finding the object is a recursive function—that is, it is a tree-like function that keeps calling itself at every branch until it has either found the object or has exhausted all of its branches.

Rollovers could be as simple as one line, such as:

```
onMouseOver="this.src='images/shoes_f2.gif'"
```

`this` is the current object that contains the `onMouseOver`. In this case, it is our image. When the mouse rolls over the object, that one line of code simply points the `src` property (the same as the SRC attribute in an IMG tag) to the new image.

Another example of ugly code is when Dreamweaver MX inserts unnecessary tags in the page. Here is an example of this one:

```
<td><font face="Arial, Helvetica, sans-serif"><img
src="navbar_images/jct_corner_logo.gif" width="111"
height="52"></font></td>
```

What's wrong here is there is no text; only an image. Although not technically an error, it bloats the page and increases load time.

A more advanced ugly code example would be the following server-side (ColdFusion) code taken from an Insert Record server behavior:

```
<cfif IsDefined("FORM.MM_InsertRecord") AND FORM.MM_InsertRecord EQ
➥"form1">
  <cfquery datasource="jct">
  INSERT INTO ProductType (ProductType, GraphicURL, ProductDescription)
  ➥VALUES
  (
  <cfif IsDefined("FORM.productType") AND #FORM.productType# NEQ "">
    '#FORM.productType#'
    <cfelse>
    NULL
  </cfif>
  ,
  <cfif IsDefined("FORM.graphicURL") AND #FORM.graphicURL# NEQ "">
    '#FORM.graphicURL#'
    <cfelse>
    NULL
  </cfif>
  ,
  <cfif IsDefined("FORM.productDescription") AND
  ➥#FORM.productDescription# NEQ "">
    '#FORM.productDescription#'
    <cfelse>
    NULL
  </cfif>
  )
  </cfquery>
  <cflocation url="test2.cfm">
</cfif>
```

The code is looking to see if a parameter named MM_InsertRecord was passed from the form, and to see if it was named form1. If it is named form1, the code creates an insert query and conditionally checks for each form element that you have passed to see if it not only exists, but is also not a blank string.

If both of the preceding conditions are met, the form value is used in the query; otherwise, a NULL value is used.

The page then redirects itself to the new page.

Why is this ugly? The form is its own response page. Not a good program flow.

A slightly more efficient routine would be better coded on the response page, and coded as such:

```
<cfparam name="productType" default="">
<cfparam name="productDescription " default="">
<cfparam name="graphicURL " default="">
<cfquery datasource="jct">
  INSERT INTO ProductType (ProductType, GraphicURL, ProductDescription)
  ➥VALUES
  ( #productType#, #productDescription#, #graphicURL#)
</cfquery>
```

cfparam tags are handy ways of defining default values in case the form elements don't exist. In this case, they check to see if an element exists; if not, the tag creates the element and supplies a default value. If the default attribute wasn't supplied, the page would error out, similar to failing an assert check to see if a certain condition is met within a piece of code.

The cfquery tag then inserts the values into the database from either the supplied form elements or the default values.

If there is one common thread running through these examples, it is that optimizing code is best left to the pros.

Using an External Code Editor with Dreamweaver MX

Dreamweaver MX allows you to launch an external HTML or text editor from within the application. The advantage is the ability to write the code and then switch back to Dreamweaver MX to work on the page in a graphical manner. When you return to Dreamweaver MX, it checks the code entered for any changes. If they are found, you are prompted to reload the document.

There are two types of editor you can use. You can use an integrated editor, such as HomeSite Plus (PC only) or BBEdit (Mac only). The other editor is a text editor, such as Notepad (PC), or SimpleText and TextEdit (Mac).

Using HomeSite Plus

When you install the HomeSite Plus application, it is automatically integrated with Dreamweaver MX upon installation.

To use HomeSite Plus, follow these steps:

1. Select Edit, Edit with HomeSite to open HomeSite.

2. Enter the code, or make your changes. When you are finished, save the changes.

3. To return to Dreamweaver MX, click Dreamweaver/UltraDev in the Editor toolbar.

Using BBEdit

There are a number of versions of this venerable Macintosh HTML editor.

To use BBEdit, follow these steps:

1. Select Edit, Edit with BBEdit to open the editor.

2. Make your changes, additions, or deletions to the code.

3. When finished, click the Dreamweaver button on the BBEdit Tools palette to return to Dreamweaver MX.

Using External Editors

Though you can use external editors with Dreamweaver MX, keep in mind the changes you make will not be synched with Dreamweaver MX. If changes are found, Dreamweaver MX prompts you to reload the affected document.

To choose an external editor, follow these steps:

1. Select Edit, Preferences to open the Preferences dialog box. Select File Types/Editors from the Category column dialog box.

2. If you are working on a Macintosh, deselect Enable BBEdit Integration.

3. Click the Browse button to open the Select External Editor dialog box, and navigate to your text editor's location on your computer. Select it, and click Open to return to the Preferences dialog box.

4. Select how you want Dreamweaver to notify you of your changes by selecting an option from the Reload Modified Files pop-down menu.

5. To let Dreamweaver know what to do when you launch the editor, select one of the three options in the Save On launch pop-down menu.

6. Click OK to close the Preferences dialog box.

7. To launch the chosen editor, select Edit, Edit With. The name of the editor that you chose is added to the end of Edit With. For example, if you had chosen CodeWarrior as your external editor, the menu item would read Edit with CodeWarrior.

Summary

There was a lot covered in this rather short chapter. We started off by talking about the fact that optimization applies both to the site and to code.

Though many developers tend to regard the code generated by Dreamweaver MX and Fireworks MX as bloated, we pointed out that in many cases the code is generic for a reason: to accommodate the user. We also pointed out there are three types of optimization that can take place—static, dynamic, and cosmetic and functional.

From there, we demonstrated a technique for managing changes throughout a site. By creating an external Cascading Style Sheet, you can deal with the coding optimization for cosmetic and functional optimization in one place only.

We showed how Dreamweaver MX and Fireworks MX combine to deal with cosmetic and functional optimization through the use of the Edit button in Dreamweaver MX. This button launches Fireworks MX, enabling you to make your changes. When you return to Dreamweaver, the changes are reflected in the Dreamweaver page.

We also talked about the use and abuse of the JavaScript behaviors in Fireworks MX and Dreamweaver MX. The bottom line here is the theme that has been running through this book: Use the right tool for the job at hand.

We also demonstrated how to use the Dreamweaver MX Clean Up HTML command and the head Content command from the View menu. The head Content command allows you to find any orphan tags that aren't being used. The Clean Up HTML command is a powerful tool for optimizing the HTML code generated by Dreamweaver MX, and we thoroughly reviewed the various areas of this deceptively simple dialog box.

We also discussed the use of the Flash button feature of Dreamweaver MX, and presented two techniques for optimizing a Flash button.

You can't talk about optimizing code without confronting the ugly code issue. We presented three examples of ugly code and offered potential fixes. The bottom line here is this job is solidly in the realm of the coder on your team.

We finished the chapter by demonstrating how to add and use an external HTML editor.

In the next chapter, "Working Out the Bugs and Going Live," we deal with many of the testing issues you will encounter prior to going live with the site.

Chapter 23

MX

Working Out the Bugs and Going Live

The site is complete. The big question facing the team now is: "Does it work?" The answer to this question is not as obvious as it may first appear. You may have been testing the pages as they were built using the Preview in Browser features of Fireworks MX and Dreamweaver MX, but these tests aren't the same as actually testing the site.

In many respects, the process moves back into looking at the forest rather than the trees. All of your efforts to this point focused on the bits and pieces of the site. There was very little concern regarding how it fits into the global picture. Now you have to test the entire site—not just a page, template, or animation—and make sure everything, and we mean **everything**, does what it is supposed to do.

Testing is a time-consuming process. You have to allot the time necessary to track down and fix mistakes such as spelling errors, links that go nowhere or go to the wrong page, images and animations that are in the wrong places, and so on. That's the easy part. The hard part is finding bugs and fixing them. This includes broken tables, functional errors such as the wrong font in a CSS style sheet, images that don't load, browser crashes because the page uses features that don't work in earlier browsers, and anything else that doesn't do what it is supposed to do.

After you make all of these repairs, you start the process over again to make sure everything works to the specifications prior to going live. The time spent here is invaluable, and your production budget should include a healthy chunk of time—about 10 percent of the time allotment—for quality assurance and testing.

The initial reaction to the 10 percent time allotment is, "That's easy for you to say." It is, and it is even harder to convince the client who wants the site posted yesterday how important this phase of the production process is. If you bow to the client's pressure and problems crop up, the blame for the problem and the expense to fix it lands squarely in your lap. It is understandable that time for this phase is at a premium. No project completely follows the initial plan, and all too often production deadlines have to be extended to accommodate late content or technical problems that cropped up. This time has to come from somewhere, and inevitably it is the testing phase that loses.

Understanding the Testing Process

The testing process can be as formal or informal as you like. It can be done in-house by a few of the team members, or you can retain an outside company to undertake the process for you. No matter what form it takes, do it.

The most important first step is ensuring the pages can be viewed in a browser.

Mention browser targeting to a web developer, and chances are they will recoil from you as though you were evil incarnate. Each browser release offers a variety of newer, more exciting features, and raises yet another unique set of compatibility issues.

In today's web development environment, you have to cope with the following:

- Browsers that are version 5.0 and higher, though they meet the W3C standards, implement those standards in their own way.

- Browsers from the same company that interpret code differently, depending on whether you are using the Macintosh or the PC version of the browser.

- A host of second-tier browsers ranging from I-cab to Opera.

- Version 3.0 and 2.0 browsers that are still in use, usually due to unwillingness on the part of the user to upgrade.

- Various iterations of AOL, which range from the proprietary to the iterative. For example, the 4.0 version of AOL was based on the Internet Explorer 4.0 browser but was not exactly the same as IE 4.0.

Dealing with Older Browsers

Older browsers still exist. Deal with it. The reason is despite the fact browsers are free, people just can't be bothered (or don't know how) to upgrade to the most current version.

It is infuriating to know that how a web site is presented onscreen depends entirely upon the browser engine making that happen. Unlike a word processing application where the interface looks and works (functionality) the same on all makes and models, browser functionality is limited to that built into the browser. This has made for some rather interesting decisions when it came to designing web sites. Do you build in a feature that works on the latest version of the browser? If you do, what about those who don't have it?

The issue around older browsers is they are not W3C (World Wide Web Consortium) standards compliant. For example, they can only use older HTML code (the current version is 4), which limits the use of Cascading Style Sheets in your designs.

Before there were standards, the major browser developers wrote proprietary tags for the HTML that were read in their particular browser. This was a never-ending source of friction between the development community and the browser manufacturers, such as Microsoft and Netscape. The developers had a valid complaint in that they wanted one set of tags that could be used by all of the browsers regardless of manufacture. Thus were born the W3C standards that are in place today.

Note

What is ironic about the W3C standards is that the most standard compliant browser on the market—Netscape 6.x—is the least used browser on the market today. This, however, may be a temporary situation until AOL adopts Netscape as their standard browser. One last bit of irony: AOL owns Netscape, and is currently using Internet Explorer as its standard.

JavaScript is another area of contention. Before there were standards, there was Microsoft's version—Jscript—and the version Netscape used. Developers discovered JavaScript was unreliable because the script that worked in Netscape didn't work in Explorer, and vice-versa. Again, developers started complaining, and the resolution occurred in 1997 with all of the interested parties agreeing to a standard for the language.

The standards body is located in Switzerland, and is called the European Computer Manufacturers Association (ECMA). Of course, the parties couldn't agree to the licensing of the name JavaScript, so a new name was introduced: ECMAScript. Flash MX's scripting language, Actionscript, is a derivative of ECMAScript.

Converting Pages in Dreamweaver MX

If you use layers and Cascading Style Sheets, you have a potential problem. What about those visitors who are using 3.0 browsers that can't understand layers and CSS? Though Dreamweaver MX is a marvelous tool, don't expect it to work its magic on the capabilities of the 3.0 browsers. What Dreamweaver MX can do to make it easier is to create the content that can be read by these browsers.

What Dreamweaver MX does not do is to take all of the features able to be read by 4.0 browsers and above and make them 3.0 compliant. Instead, Dreamweaver MX creates a 3.0 page based on your 4.0 page. After the page is completed, you can use the Check Browser behavior to scoot people using 3.0 browsers to the appropriate pages based on their browser version.

Note

Jordan Chilcott, one of the authors has the following advice to any developer encountering a client who wants an ecommerce site to be version 3.0 compliant. "Warmly welcome them into the new millennium, and quickly point them toward a newer, or more compatible, browser." The reason being is that all of the security certificates in version 3.0 browsers expired January 1, 2000. Version 3.0 browsers can no longer connect to a secure socket layer (SSL) of a server, making all transmissions unsecure. Y2K wasn't all bad.

Making Pages 3.0 Compatible

When the page is converted, layers are converted to nested tables and CSS styles are converted to inline character styles. Both are choices that Dreamweaver MX presents to you. Still, there are some conditions you have to meet prior to the conversion:

- The content must be in layers and absolutely positioned on the page.

- Layers must not overlap. If they do, you will be warned during the conversion. A quick way of avoiding overlapping layers is to select Modify, Arrange, Prevent Layer Overlaps

- Don't nest layers. They can't be converted.

Converting a Page

After prepping the page for conversion, you have only three choices to make—convert layers, convert CSS styles, or convert both layers and CSS styles.

To convert a page, follow these steps:

1. With a page open in Dreamweaver MX, select File, Convert, 3.0 Browser to open the Convert to 3.O Browser Compatible dialog box shown in Figure 23.1.

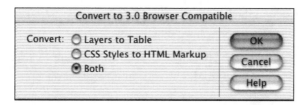

Figure 23.1   You have only three choices to make when converting a document to the 3.0 standard.

2. Make your choice and then click OK.

Dreamweaver MX starts converting the file. If there is a problem, Dreamweaver MX notifies you through a dialog box. Your only choice is to fix the problem and redo the conversion.

Note

When converting CSS to HTML, any CSS-specific feature, such as line spacing, that is not a part of regular HTML will be disregarded. As well, point sizes over 36 points will be set to the largest HTML size, which is 7.

Browser Sniffing

Because there are so many browsers and browser versions in use, it has become a common practice among web developers to create web pages geared to each browser and then use a JavaScript to direct the user to the appropriate page. This script is affectionately referred to as a *sniffer*, though the more formal term is *gateway script*.

If you use this technique, first create three pages: One for 4.0 and higher browsers, one for 3.0 browsers, and a blank page that serves as the home page for the sniffer. The sniffer is a Check Browser behavior that executes on the onLoad event of the blank page, which means the user never sees the blank page.

To create a sniffer using the Check Browser behavior, follow these steps:

1. Design the 4.0 page that uses layers and CSS.

2. Select File, Convert, 3.0 Browser Compatible. Save the new file with the same name, but add a prefix or suffix to the name. For example, if the 4.0 page is named 3LostSouls, the converted page would be named 3LostSouls30.

3. Create a new HTML page by selecting File, New. When the page opens, select Window, Behaviors or press Shift-F3 to open the Behaviors panel. Alternately, you can click the Behaviors tab in the Design panel.

4. Click the + sign in the Behavior inspector, and choose Check Browser from the list of behaviors in the pop-down menu.

5. The Check Browser dialog box opens, as shown in Figure 23.2. The keys to this dialog box are the URL and Alt URL text input areas at the bottom of the dialog box.

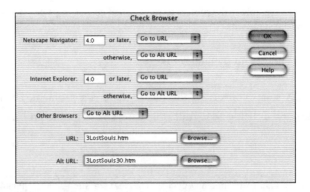

Figure 23.2   The Check Browser dialog box allows you to check for the user's browser version, and redirect the user to the page that is compatible with the detected browser.

6. Enter the URL for your 4.0 page from step 2 in the URL text entry area; then enter the URL for your 3.0 page from step 2 in the Alt URL text entry area.

7. Click OK. The script redirecting the user to the appropriate page is written.

8. If this blank page is to be the sniffer page, save it as index.htm, or whatever name your server uses as the default.

With the sniffer now in place, this is a good time to become paranoid. It is nice to have a sniffer, but this is the web and users can enter the site from any page in the site. This tends to defeat the purpose of the gateway.

To deal with this issue, follow these steps:

1. Open the 4.0 page, open the Behaviors panel and insert a Check Browser behavior.

2. When the Check Browser dialog box opens, enter the URL for the 3.0 page in the Alt URL input area.

3. In the browser area at the top of the dialog box, select Stay on This Page from the pop-down list. Do this for both browsers. Click OK and then save the file.

4. Open the 3.0 page and then add the Check Browser behavior. In this instance, the page for the 4.0 page is the Alt URL destination. You would also select Stay on This Page for both browsers.

5. Close the page when finished.

Testing the Page with Browser Targeting

Every page must be tested, and you should use as many browsers and systems as humanly possible. One of the most basic tests, code testing, can be conducted right in Dreamweaver MX. Browsers, depending on how you look at it, have either the good habit or bad habit of ignoring tags and attributes they don't understand. For example, Internet Explorer understands the object tag when a .swf file is placed on a page. Netscape doesn't. Netscape uses an Embed tag. This is why both tags are used when Flash MX generates the code for the .swf.

Dreamweaver MX's Browser Targeting feature enables you to check a page against a number of browser profiles. The profiles contained in Dreamweaver MX are

Internet Explorer 2.0

Internet Explorer 3.0

Internet Explorer 4.0

Internet Explorer 5.0

Internet Explorer 5.5

Internet Explorer 6.0

Netscape Navigator 2.0

Netscape Navigator 3.0

Netscape Navigator 4.0

Netscape Navigator 6.0

Opera 2.1

Opera 3.0

Opera 3.5

Opera 4.0

Opera 5.0

Opera 6.0

The interesting aspect of this Dreamweaver MX feature is that you can choose a profile that matches one particular browser, or you can choose a profile that matches all browsers.

Tip

Though the list is extensive, the key word is *profile*. Nothing can replace using the real browser. Here's a link to a browser graveyard that is one of the more comprehensive sites we have encountered: `http://browsers.evolt.org/`.

To test browser compatibility with a web page, follow these steps:

1. With the page open, select File, Check Page, Check Target Browsers to open the Check Target Browsers dialog box, shown in Figure 23.3.

Figure 23.3   The index page of the dynamic version of the JCT site is checked against a number of browser profiles.

2. Select the browser or browsers against which the page is to be checked.

3. Click the Check button.

4. After the check is completed, the results of the check appear in the Target Browser Check area of the Results panel as shown in Figure 23.4. You are told which line of the code has a problem, and notified of the specifics regarding the problem.

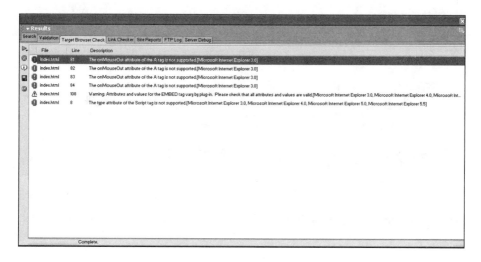

Figure 23.4   The check is complete, and there are some problems as shown in the Results panel.

The Target Browser Report panel is quite a piece of work, and a significant improvement over its previous iterations in Dreamweaver MX. The keys to working with this panel are the icons down the right side of the panel, as shown in Figure 23.4. They are, from top to bottom:

- **Green Arrow**—Check the page or the site in a targeted browser.

- **More Info**—Click this text bubble and a window opens presenting you with essentially the same text in the Description area of the Report panel.

- **Save Report**—Click the little disk and the Save as dialog box opens. You can then choose to save the report as an XML or text file.

- **Browse Report**—Click the globe and the report opens in a browser, as shown in Figure 23.5. You can then choose to print the report.

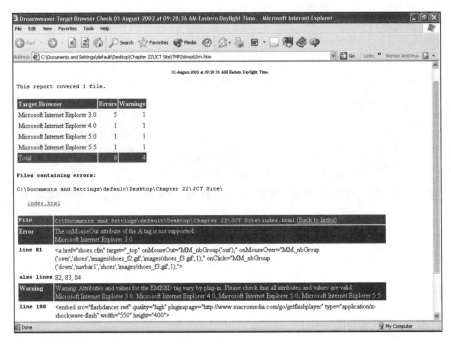

Figure 23.5   The ability to view the report in a browser and print out a copy from the browser makes your life easier.

Tip

The options in the Report panel are also available through the Report panel's Options pop-down menu. Be aware that after you close the Results panel, the report is deleted.

Browser Testing an Entire Site

It is just as easy to check an entire site in Dreamweaver MX as it is to test a single page. When you test the site, Dreamweaver MX checks all of the files in the root folder, including those that may not necessarily be used in the site.

To check an entire site, follow these steps:

1. With the Check Target Report panel open, select Check Target Browsers for Entire Site from the panel options pop-down menu. You can also click the Target Browsers button (the green arrow) in the Report and select Check Target Browsers for Entire Site. The Check Target Browsers dialog box appears.

2. Select your targeted browsers from the list and then click Check. Dreamweaver MX searches through all of the pages in the folder and displays any problems in the Target Browser Report window.

Finding Broken Links

Finding and fixing broken links is a time-consuming and tedious task. The reason is because sites are complex and can range from dozens to hundreds of pages linked to internal and external pages in the site. Orphan files (files that still exist in the site but to which there are no links in the site) can also be a problem because they take up server space and are a potential source of confusion to the team.

Dreamweaver MX contains a feature that identifies broken links and orphaned files.

To check a page and a site for broken links and orphan files, follow these steps:

1. Open a saved page and then select File, Check Page, Check Links. The Link Checker panel opens in the Report panel.

2. Select a report from the Show pop-down list in the Link Checker panel. Your choices are Broken Links, External Files, and Orphaned Files. Select your report, and a list of any broken links appears in the report.

Tip

Don't select Orphaned Files. This report is available only when you check the links site wide.

3. Having checked a page and reviewed the broken links, you can also use the Report panel to check the links throughout the site. Select Check Links Sitewide from the panel options, or click the green arrow and select Check Links Sitewide from the pop-down list.

4. Another method for checking the links in a site is to use the Site panel. Select the site you want to check from the Site List pop-down menu in the Site panel.

5. In the Site panel, select Site, Check Links Sitewide as shown in Figure 23.6.

6. Select your report from the Show pop-down menu in the Link Checker panel. You can then save the report, or open it in a browser and print it.

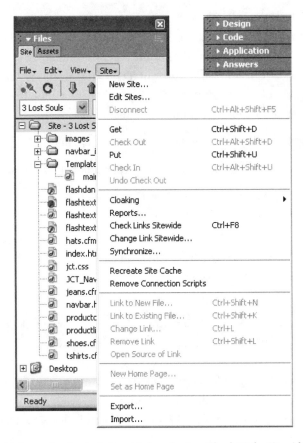

Figure 23.6   Links can be checked site wide by selecting Check Links Sitewide from the Site menu of the Site panel.

Fixing Broken Links

Having identified the broken links and orphaned files, they will have to be fixed.

To fix broken links in Dreamweaver MX, follow these steps:

1. In the Link Checker panel double-click one of the items in the list. Dreamweaver MX opens the page with the bad link, selects the link, and highlights the path and the filename in the Property inspector.

2. Change the link or the path in the Property inspector.

Tip

If the link is a reference to an image and the new image has the incorrect size, change the highlighted H and W Properties in the Property inspector, or click the Refresh button in the Property inspector.

Checking the Download Time and Size of a Page

Both Fireworks MX and Flash MX allow you to optimize images or animations to a pre-selected bandwidth. Dreamweaver MX offers you the same feature.

To select a page size and download time, follow these steps:

1. Select Edit, Preferences (Mac users using Dreamweaver MX under OS X should select Dreamweaver MX, Preferences) to open the Preferences dialog box.

2. Select Status Bar from the Category column on the left side of the dialog box. The Status Bar preferences, as shown in Figure 23.7, appears.

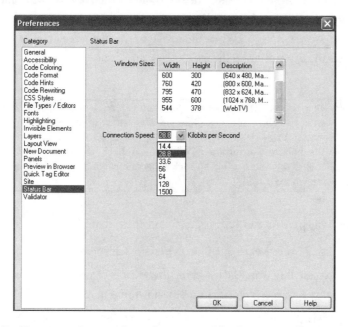

Figure 23.7   You can set the page size and target speed for the pages in the Dreamweaver MX Preferences dialog box.

3. Choose your page size from the Window Sizes list and then choose a connection speed from the Connection Speed pop-down menu. The most common speed is still 28.8. If the site is being developed for an intranet, select 1500.

4. When finished, click OK.

Accessibility in Dreamweaver MX

If you are developing government web sites, the big issue is accessibility. Pages need to read using various forms of readers, including browsers, screen readers, and so on. Accessibility has become a huge factor in web development, and Macromedia has built a number of accessibility features into Dreamweaver MX.

Macromedia designed Dreamweaver MX to accommodate people with disabilities. The application also lets you design pages that are accessible.

A common tool, used by the sight impaired, is a screen reader. Assume an individual with a visual disability visits the JCT site. The site is quite visual and colorful, and if it were accessible, the big red shoe image would have a description associated with it, such as "Boy's red shoes sizes 7 to 13." When the image opens, the screen reader picks up that text and reads the description so the user knows what is onscreen.

Note

> You should see accessibility technologies, such as screen readers, in action before you design sites with accessibility features. One of the authors visited a sight-impaired friend who was connected to the Internet. The first thing that caught the author's attention was the fact the monitor was turned off. When the author's friend started surfing with a screen reader, all of the text was played back so fast he had a hard time following it. His friend turned down the speed.

To add accessibility features to your pages, follow these steps:

1. Select Edit, Preferences to open the Preferences dialog box.

2. Select Accessibility from the list in the Preferences category, and select the applicable page accessibility features as shown in Figure 23.8. Click OK.

3. For each element selected, you are prompted on the Dreamweaver MX page to enter the tags and attributes when that element is inserted into a document.

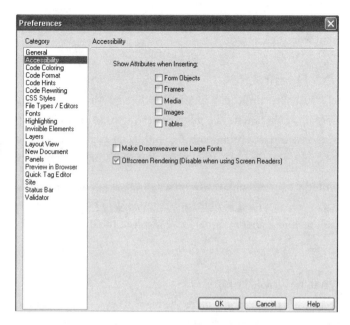

Figure 23.8   Making the site accessible to individuals with disabilities is accomplished through the Accessibility Preferences dialog box.

Testing the Site for Accessibility

The best way to ensure your site is accessible to all users is to design the site to the Section 508 Guidelines of the U.S. 1998 Rehabilitation Act. Information regarding this important aspect of the web design process can be found at `http://www.w3.org/WAI/` or `http://www.section508.gov`.

To prepare an accessibility report on a page, follow these steps:

1. Open the document to be checked.
2. Select Commands, Accessibility. The report appears in the Site reports panel.

Alpha Testing

Having stomped out the bugs, made sure the site works in a variety of browsers, and reviewed site accessibility, the time has arrived to really start testing the site. Think of an alpha test in terms of cleaning up a construction site. There are a lot of odds and ends that need to be picked up, you want to be sure the plumbing and electricity works, and make certain that there are no structural defects.

An alpha test does just that. It looks at the site on a global basis, and examines its structure and internal workings.

Deciding Who Does the Test

An alpha test is usually conducted internally when production is completed. Never involve the client in an alpha test. The purpose here is to ensure everything contained in the site works, and we can assure you, through bitter experience, not everything works. If you involve the client, you may be setting yourself up for some uncomfortable questions.

The designers on the team should be checking each page against the original design document, making sure everything is where it is supposed to be. The coders test the functionality of the site, and if there is a database involved the database team optimizes the database.

Knowing What to Look For

In many respects, what to look for is up to the team. They can take a quick pass through the site (not a good idea) or pore through each item on the site from images to code looking for problems to repair (a much better idea). Rather than get specific, here is a general list of elements to watch for:

- Look for potential bugs on a deeper level than a client would. Do links go where they're supposed to? Are rollovers showing the right image?

- Ensure the pages look uniform in modern-day browsers. They should look almost identical in the latest versions of Netscape and Internet Explorer.

- Pages should degrade gracefully on older browsers. In other words, features not available on a 3.0 browser should not cause errors, or be drastically evident that they may be missing. When a page degrades gracefully in a 3.0 browser, it means the developer took the time to do some browser testing.

- Use behaviors in the manner for which they were designed. Why do you need an Over While Down state on a button if it is not connected to a pop-down menu, for example?

- Ensure the design is not too tightly constrained. What looks great on your 21" display may not work on the 17" display in the next workstation.

- Ensure the database is optimized. If there are items in the database that aren't used, remove them.

- Ensure the dynamic code is functioning as expected. For example, does the product description text flow into the dynamic Flash text box on the page?

- Use efficient SQL statements. For example, don't just select everything in a table. It slows down the process.

- Are you using JavaScript in a spot where it would be more optimal to use back-end code? Too many people use mailto: URLs as Form actions. The problem is that not everyone is capable of using forms in this manner. Consider using a CFMAIL tag in ColdFusion.

Beta Testing

The beta test is the final check before the site goes live. By the time you have reached the beta stage, many of the usability, functionality, and design issues have been identified and resolved.

This test is usually conducted on your client staging server, or in a subdirectory of the server where the site will eventually reside.

Deciding Who Does the Beta Test

At this stage of the game, the team steps back and the client becomes heavily involved. The client's job is to make sure the site functions, with an emphasis on usability.

The team's job is to listen to the client and then start fixing the bugs identified.

When the client reports back, they will not be technical in their explanations of problems they encountered. They will tell you that when this button is clicked, such and such happens, but "I wanted something else to happen." You might even hear them say, "I can't search on anything." Instead of launching into a technical discussion to answer the questions, try to listen to the question and interpret what the client is saying. As well, repeat the question back to the client so that they may offer further information. Sometimes what they are asking you to fix is not always what you think they are asking for.

In the case of, "I can't search anything," the client doesn't care what your database looks like. They just care that they can search for one of their products and find it.

Finally, discern between what a fix is, and what a feature is. At this stage, no new code should be introduced unless required to fix a bug.

Fixing Bugs

The beta testers, if they do their jobs properly, will start sending you lists of items, ranging from the obvious to the obscure, that don't work. Obviously, you can't deal with these bugs as they come in. It is the prudent developer who puts into place a system that prioritizes the bugs.

The big ones are obvious. For example, clicking a button crashes Internet Explorer every time the button is clicked. There will also be the bugs that just can't be fixed because they are only occurring with that one user. A classic example would be links that are not underlined because they had the feature deselected in the preferences. If it can't be recreated, note this fact and then carry on.

After you complete your list and deal with each item on the list, test your fixes. Don't become discouraged if you wind up fixing the same thing several times.

Knowing What to Look For

Again, the rigorousness of the check is dependent upon the company and the scope of the project. Here are five items to look for after the client and the beta team have finished their tasks:

- Does the design work as planed? Have the designers go through the site one more time, looking for things such as HTML text that might be in the wrong spot, or an image treatment that does look quite right. Do it this on Macs and PCs.

- Does the HTML do what it is supposed to do? Look for things such as tables that don't line up properly, links that aren't identified, and so on. Again, use Macs and PCs for this check.

- Does the site work? Does all of the functionality built into the site meet the technical specifications set out at the beginning of the production process? If you are working on a dynamic site, use the site on the server where it will eventually reside.

- Is all the content in place? Make sure, for example, headlines look like headlines and that the text on the page is both readable and legible.

- Has everybody responsible for the project on the client's side of the fence signed off on the project? Every web designer we know has one story that involves launching a huge site and having to pull it down because the V.P. of Marketing hasn't approved it yet. The thing is that no one knew the V.P. of Marketing had the final approval.

Going Live

Having completed the beta testing, fixed all the bugs, and finally obtained all of the necessary approvals, the time has arrived to go live with the site and post it on the web.

This occurs by sending the files, using a File Transfer Protocol (FTP) transfer, to the live server. This should only occur after the site is debugged on the testing server; however, debugging is never really finished until the launch of the site. This is because all functional tests that occurred on the testing server must also be done on the live server.

One of the first tasks is to check and make sure that your ColdFusion MX datasource connection is set up and working. You should also ensure the database is secure. The best place to test this is out of the web server's site; however, if you are unable to do that, test the database's security within a secure area of the web site using an area that is being properly referred to by a domain server.

The Dreamweaver MX FTP Utilities

Posting a site to a server uses a File Transfer Protocol to move the files from a server to a local computer, or vice versa. Most developers are comfortable using tools such as WS_FTP, Fetch, or Vicomsoft FTP Client for this purpose. The weakness here is these applications are marvelous for moving files from one location to another, but are completely lacking in their capability to accommodate work groups, versioning, and file updates.

Dreamweaver MX's Site window is a wonderful management tool that takes full advantage of the features built into Dreamweaver MX, such as:

- Check In/Check Out
- Drag and drop from the remote to the local host
- The ability to check the links on an entire site
- The site map that allows the developer to see the site and rearrange the pieces, if necessary

The Get Files and Put Files buttons are two arrows that sit at the top of the Site window. One points down—the Get Files button—and one points up—the Put Files button. In many respects, these are the two most important buttons in the window. The Get Files button retrieves the selected files and folders from the testing or live server, and the Put Files button moves the files from the computer to the testing or live server. The advantage to you, the developer, is that any changes can be made and tested well before you go live with the site.

There are number of ways to move files from the local directory to the testing or live server, or from a server to the local directory. These methods include

- Selecting the files to be moved in the Site window and dragging them from the Local Files pane to the Remote Files pane, or vice versa.

- Selecting the files to be moved and then selecting Site, Get or Put, or press Ctrl-Shift-U (PC) or Command-Shift–U (Mac). If there are dependent files, you are prompted to include them with the move.

- Selecting the files to be moved and then clicking the Get Files or the Put Files button in the Site panel.

Still, these utilities are not exactly perfect, and the ftp capabilities of Dreamweaver MX are an eternal source of complaints among developers. For example:

- Don't be too terribly surprised if you encounter the eternal beach ball or watch because an ftp server decides to take a nap.

- You are not able to set permissions on a server. These are needed when sending up PERL/CGI scripts to a server.

- Sometimes the ftp server has difficulty distinguishing text and binary uploading. This can cause errors when it comes to uploading CGI scripts because servers expect only text.

It is the wise developer who has a separate ftp program, such as those mentioned earlier, in his back pocket. There are a variety of free, shareware, and commercial ftp applications out there. The best recommendation as to which one to chose will come from your ISP. They know, from bitter experience, which ftp applications work best with their server.

Knowing Your Host Provider's Capabilities

The time to find out that your file structure doesn't work isn't just before you go live. Your host provider should have been researched and decided upon long before beginning your design

Some providers disable certain CF tags because of security. These would include items such as file, ftp, and other security-compromising tags. If you know about these restrictions before you start, you won't have to carefully sift through the code, removing and replacing them at the end of the process. That can get expensive. Here are some brief tips to keep in mind when working with a host provider's server:

- It is very easy to upload a file that can take over the system. One way to overcome something like this is not to let the end user know where the file is going to be stored. Another way is to provide an Application.cfm in a page that redirects a user to the proper web site area, or simply store the files out of reach of the web server itself.

- Almost any type of file can be stored on a web server.

- When creating filenames, be aware of your server's limitations. For example, don't use spaces in a filename. Also, don't use special characters, such as a colon, exclamation mark, forward slash, or backslash. Various servers may interpret them as reserved keywords.

- Know which revision of middleware your server is using. For example, don't use functions specific to ColdFusion MX when the server is running ColdFusion 5.

- Almost all of the Dreamweaver MX server behaviors are backward compatible. They should not cause any problems.

Summary

This chapter has dealt with the testing process. We started off by explaining why it is so important to test the site, and suggested a time allotment of 10 percent of the time spent on the project be used for this all-important final phase of the process.

One of the biggest stumbling blocks on the web today is the proliferation of browsers in use. We explained how many of the features so common on the web—CSS and layers—simply can't be rendered by a version 3.0 browser.

We presented many of the tools in Dreamweaver that enable you to perform this important test ranging from converting pages to make them 3.0 compliant to creating a sniffer that detects the user's browser version and then redirects the user to the appropriate gateway page into the site.

There are some other testing tools available. Links can get broken, and you can have pages that go nowhere. We showed you how to use Dreamweaver MX's link checker feature to locate and repair broken links and orphan pages.

Accessibility to the web for people with physical disabilities is also an important issue. We showed you how to check your site for accessibility, and how to create an accessibility report in Dreamweaver MX.

There was also an overview of the alpha and the beta tests that should be done, and who should be doing these tests.

We finished the chapter by reviewing some of the tools in Dreamweaver MX that can be used to upload the files to the host server prior to going live, and some of the steps you should take to make the upload process as smooth as possible.

We finish the book in much the same manner that we started. We hope you have learned something, and that you have had fun building a web site with the Macromedia MX Studio. Remember, the amount of fun we have in this business should be illegal. May we all be arrested!

Index

Symbols

C

N

X-Y-Z

VOICES THAT MATTER

VISIT OUR WEB SITE

WWW.NEWRIDERS.COM

On our web site, you'll find information about our other books, authors, tables of contents, and book errata. You will also find information about book registration and how to purchase our books, both domestically and internationally.

EMAIL US

Contact us at: **nrfeedback@newriders.com**

- If you have comments or questions about this book
- To report errors that you have found in this book
- If you have a book proposal to submit or are interested in writing for New Riders
- If you are an expert in a computer topic or technology and are interested in being a technical editor who reviews manuscripts for technical accuracy

Contact us at: **nreducation@newriders.com**

- If you are an instructor from an educational institution who wants to preview New Riders books for classroom use. Email should include your name, title, school, department, address, phone number, office days/hours, text in use, and enrollment, along with your request for desk/examination copies and/or additional information.

Contact us at: **nrmedia@newriders.com**

- If you are a member of the media who is interested in reviewing copies of New Riders books. Send your name, mailing address, and email address, along with the name of the publication or web site you work for.

BULK PURCHASES/CORPORATE SALES

The publisher offers discounts on this book when ordered in quantity for bulk purchases and special sales. For sales within the U.S., please contact: Corporate and Government Sales (800) 382-3419 or **corpsales@pearsontechgroup.com**. Outside of the U.S., please contact: International Sales (317) 581-3793 or **international@pearsontechgroup.com**.

WRITE TO US

New Riders Publishing
201 W. 103rd St.
Indianapolis, IN 46290-1097

CALL/FAX US

Toll-free (800) 571-5840
If outside U.S. (317) 581-3500
Ask for New Riders
FAX: (317) 581-4663

New Riders

www.informit.com

YOUR GUIDE TO IT REFERENCE

New Riders has partnered with **InformIT.com** to bring technical information to your desktop. Drawing from New Riders authors and reviewers to provide additional information on topics of interest to you, **InformIT.com** provides free, in-depth information you won't find anywhere else.

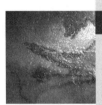

Articles

Keep your edge with thousands of free articles, in-depth features, interviews, and IT reference recommendations—all written by experts you know and trust.

Online Books

Answers in an instant from **InformIT Online Books'** 600+ fully searchable online books.

POWERED BY

Catalog

Review online sample chapters, author biographies and customer rankings and choose exactly the right book from a selection of over 5,000 titles.

www.newriders.com

Publishing the Voices that Matter

OUR AUTHORS

PRESS ROOM

| web development | design | photoshop | new media | 3-D | server technologies |

EDUCATORS

ABOUT US

CONTACT US

You already know that New Riders brings you the **Voices That Matter**.

But what does that mean? It means that New Riders brings you the

Voices that challenge your assumptions, take your talents to the next

level, or simply help you better understand the complex technical world

we're all navigating.

Visit **www.newriders.com** to find:

- ▸ 10% Discount and free shipping on book purchases
- ▸ Never before published chapters
- ▸ Sample chapters and excerpts
- ▸ Author bios and interviews
- ▸ Contests and enter-to-wins
- ▸ Up-to-date industry event information
- ▸ Book reviews
- ▸ Special offers from our friends and partners
- ▸ Info on how to join our User Group program
- ▸ Ways to have your Voice heard

New Riders

WWW.NEWRIDERS.COM

STUDIO MX

Fireworks MX Fundamentals
0735711534
Abigail Rudner
US$45.00

Inside Dreamweaver MX
073571181X
Laura Gutman,
Patty Ayers,
Donald S. Booth
US$45.00

Dreamweaver MX Magic
0735711798
Brad Halstead,
Josh Cavalier, et al.
US$39.99

Inside Flash MX
0735712549
Jody Keating,
Fig Leaf Software
US$49.99

ColdFusion MX From Static to Dynamic in 10 Steps
0735712964
Barry Moore
US$35.00

Flash MX Magic
0735711607
Matthew David, et al.
US$45.00

Fireworks MX Magic
0735711402
Lisa Lopuck
US$39.99

Inside ColdFusion MX
0735713049
John Cummings, Neil Ross,
Robi Sen
US$49.99

VOICES
THAT MATTER™